SOLIDWORKS Simulation 2026
A Power Guide for Beginners and Intermediate Users

CADArtifex

A premium provider of learning products and solutions
www.cadartifex.com

SOLIDWORKS Simulation 2026: A Power Guide for Beginners and Intermediate Users

Author: Sandeep Dogra
Email: info@cadartifex.com

Published by
CADArtifex
www.cadartifex.com

ISBN: 978-9394074439

NOTICE TO THE READER

The publisher and the author make no representations or warranties with respect to the accuracy or completeness of the contents of this work and specifically disclaim all warranties, including without limitation warranties of fitness for a particular purpose. Publisher does not guarantee any of the products described in the text nor perform any independent analysis in connection with any of the product information contained in the text. No warranty may be created or extended by sales or promotional materials. This work is sold with the understanding that the publisher is not engaged in rendering legal, accounting, or other professional services. Neither the publisher nor the author shall be liable for damages arising herefrom. Further, readers should be aware that Internet Websites listed in this work may have changed or disappeared between when this work was written and when it is read.

Examination Copies

Textbooks received as examination copies in any form such as paperback and eBook are for review only and may not be made available for the use of the student. These files may not be transferred to any other party. Resale of examination copies is prohibited.

Electronic Files

The electronic file/eBook in any form of this textbook is licensed to the original user only and may not be transferred to any other party.

Disclaimer

The author has made sincere efforts to ensure the accuracy of the material described herein, however the author makes no warranty, expressed or implied, with respect to the quality, correctness, accuracy, or freedom from error of this document or the products it describes.

www.cadartifex.com

Dedication

First and foremost, I would like to thank my parents for being a great support throughout my career and while writing this book.

Heartfelt gratitude goes to my wife and my sisters for their patience and endurance in supporting me to take up and successfully accomplish this challenge.

I would also like to acknowledge the efforts of the employees at CADArtifex for their dedication in editing the content of this book.

Video Courses by CADArtifex

CADArtifex offers a range of video courses designed to support students, educators, and professionals in developing practical CAD skills through structured, project-based learning. Available video courses include:

- SOLIDWORKS Mastery Pack – 11 Courses in 1 | Complete Beginner to Industry Training
- Fusion 360 Mastery Pack: Design, Sculpt & Build Real Projects (6-in-1 Course Combo)
- SOLIDWORKS for Beginners and Intermediate Users
- Learn SOLIDWORKS Sheet Metal: From Concept to Creation
- SOLIDWORKS Mechanical Design & Assemblies Masterclass
- Complete Fusion 360 All-in-One Course for Beginners
- Fusion 360 Surface Design & T-Spline Sculpting
- Complete FreeCAD for Beginners – No Experience Needed
- Complete Onshape for Beginners: Project-Based Approach
- Master Autodesk Inventor: From Basics to Advanced
- Mastering AutoCAD 2D & 3D for Beginners

For full course details and access, visit: ***cadartifex.com***

Contents at a Glance

Table of Contents

Preface

SOLIDWORKS Simulation, a product of Dassault Systemes SOLIDWORKS Corp., is one of the biggest technology providers to engineering software solutions that lets you create, simulate, publish, and manage the data. By providing advanced analysis techniques, SOLIDWORKS Simulation helps engineers to optimize performance of products and allows them to cut prototyping cost, create better and safer products, and save time as well as the development costs.

SOLIDWORKS Simulation is a Finite Element Analysis tool which enables critical engineering decisions to be made earlier in the design process. With this software, engineers have the tools to easily study the initial design and predict the performance of the complete digital prototype. The automatic meshing tools of this software generate mesh with high-quality elements on the first pass. SOLIDWORKS Simulation makes it possible to quickly validate design concepts before resources are invested in significant design changes or new products.

SOLIDWORKS Simulation 2026: A Power Guide for Beginners and Intermediate Users is a comprehensive textbook for instructor-led training and self-paced learning. It is an excellent resource for engineers and designers looking to master **Finite Element Analysis (FEA)** using **SOLIDWORKS Simulation**. It is ideal for new users and is a valuable teaching aid in classroom training. With 10 chapters spanning 398 pages, this guide covers a wide range of FEA techniques, including **Linear Static Analysis, Buckling Analysis, Fatigue Analysis, Frequency Analysis, Drop Test Analysis**, and **Non-linear Static Analysis**.

It explores key FEA concepts and methodologies, including Geometry Preparation, Boundary Conditions (loads and fixtures), Element Types, Interactions, Connectors, Meshing, Mesh Controls, Mesh Checks (Aspect Ratio and Jacobian checks), Adaptive Meshing (H-Adaptive and P-Adaptive), Iterative Methods (Newton-Raphson and Modified Newton-Raphson Schemes), Incremental Methods (Force, Displacement, or Arc Length), among others.

This textbook not only focuses on using the tools of SOLIDWORKS Simulation but also on the fundamentals of Finite Element Analysis (FEA) through various real-world case studies. The case studies used in this textbook allow users to solve various real-world engineering problems by using SOLIDWORKS Simulation step-by-step. Also, the Hands-on test drives given at the end of chapters allow users to experience the ease of use and immense capacities of SOLIDWORKS Simulation.

Who Should Read This Textbook

This textbook is written with a wide range of SOLIDWORKS Simulation users in mind, varying from beginners to advanced users and SOLIDWORKS Simulation instructors. The easy-to-follow chapters of this textbook allow you to easily understand concepts of Finite Element Analysis (FEA), SOLIDWORKS Simulation tools, and various types of analysis through case studies.

What Is Covered in This Textbook

SOLIDWORKS Simulation 2026: A Power Guide for Beginners and Intermediate Users textbook is designed to help you learn everything you need to know to start using SOLIDWORKS Simulation 2026 with straightforward, step-by-step case studies. This textbook covers the following topics:

*Chapter 1, "**Introduction to FEA and SOLIDWORKS Simulation**,"* introduces SOLIDWORKS Simulation, various types of analysis, introduction to Finite Element Analysis (FEA), and different phases of Finite Element Analysis (FEA): Pre-processing, Solution, and Post-processing. It also explains various terms and definitions used in Finite Element Analysis (FEA) in addition to different types of elements, the application areas of FEA, system requirements for installing SOLIDWORKS Simulation, and SOLIDWORKS interface. Besides, this chapter discusses how to invoke different SOLIDWORKS documents and how to start with SOLIDWORKS Simulation.

*Chapter 2, "**Introduction to Analysis Tools and Static Analysis**,"* introduces various assumptions for considering the linear static analysis problem and how to start with it in SOLIDWORKS Simulation. This chapter also explains how to define the analysis unit and material properties for geometry, adding a new material and customizing the material properties. Besides, it introduces boundary conditions (fixtures and loads), meshing geometry, and identifying poor quality mesh elements.

*Chapter 3, "**Case Studies of Static Analysis**,"* discusses various case studies of linear static analysis: Static Analysis of a Rectangular Plate, Static Analysis of a Bracket with Mesh Control, Static Analysis of a Symmetrical Model, Static Analysis of a Torispherical Head with Shell Elements, and Static Analysis of a Weldment Frame with Beam Elements.

*Chapter 4, "**Interactions and Connectors**,"* discusses various interactions and connectors available in SOLIDWORKS Simulation. It explains how to perform the static analysis of various case studies having interaction problems: Static Analysis of a Hook Assembly with Interactions, Static Analysis of a Flange Assembly with Bolt Connectors, and Static Analysis of an Assembly with Edge Weld Connectors.

*Chapter 5, "**Adaptive Mesh Methods**,"* discusses different Adaptive meshing methods (H-Adaptive and P-Adaptive) and how to setup an analysis with them.

*Chapter 6, "**Buckling Analysis**,"* introduces the concept of the buckling analysis and how to perform the buckling analysis of different case studies: Buckling Analysis of a Pipe Support, Buckling Analysis of a Beam.

*Chapter 7, "**Fatigue Analysis**,"* discusses about the failure of a design due to fatigue when the design undergoes cyclic loads. It also explains how to perform the fatigue analysis.

*Chapter 8, "**Frequency Analysis**,"* introduces how to perform the frequency analysis to calculate the natural/resonant frequencies, the mode shapes associated to each natural frequency, and the mass participations in X, Y, and Z directions.

*Chapter 9, "**Drop Test Analysis**,"* introduces how to perform the drop test analysis to calculate the impact of a part or an assembly with a rigid or flexible floor.

*Chapter 10, "**Non-Linear Static Analysis**,"* introduces various assumptions for considering the non-linear static analysis problems. It discusses different iterative methods (Newton-Raphson (NR) scheme and Modified Newton-Raphson (MNR) scheme) and incremental methods (Force, Displacement, and Arc Length) to find the equilibrium solutions for the non-linear analysis. The chapter also discusses different types of non-linearities (material non-linearities, geometric non-linearities, and contact non-linearities) and how to perform the non-linear analysis of various case studies: Non-Linear Static Analysis of a Shackle, Non-Linear Static Analysis of a Handrail Clamp Assembly, and Non-Linear Static Analysis of a Cantilever Beam.

Some of the Icons/Terms used in this Textbook

The following icons and terms are used in this textbook:

Note

Note: Notes highlight information requiring special attention.

Tip

Tip: Tips provide additional advice, which increases the efficiency of the users.

Flyout

A Flyout is a list in which a set of tools are grouped together, see Figure 1.

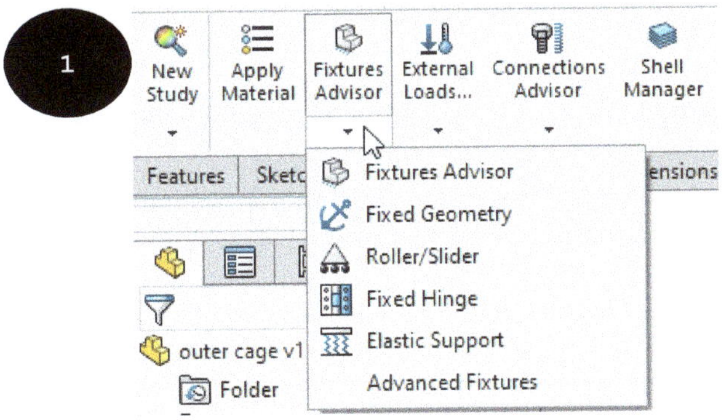

Drop-down List

A drop-down list is a list in which a set of options are grouped together, see Figure 2.

Rollout

A rollout is an area in which drop-down list, fields, buttons, check boxes are available to specify various parameters, see Figure 2. A rollout can either be in an expanded or in a collapsed form. You can expand or collapse a rollout by clicking on the arrow available on the right side of its title bar, see Figure 2.

Field
A Field allows you to select entities from the graphics area, see Figure 2. Also, it allows you to enter a new value or modify an existing/default value.

Check box
A Check box allows you to turn on or off the uses of a particular option, see Figure 2.

2

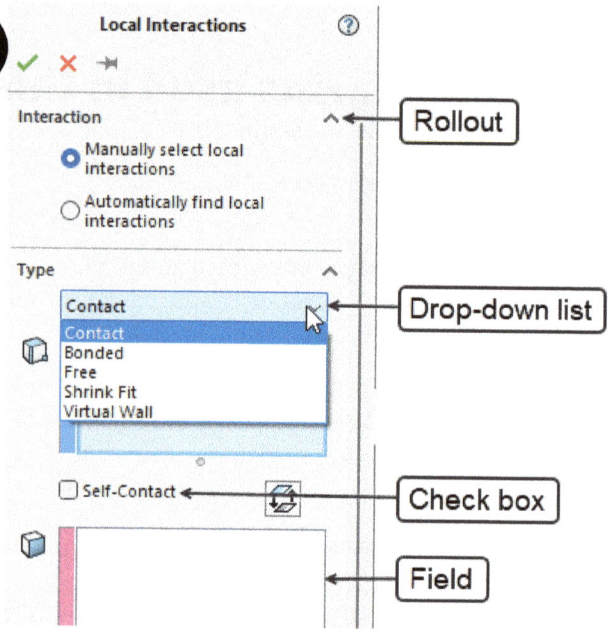

How to Download Online Resources
Students and faculty members can **download parts/models** used in the illustrations, Case Studies, and Hands-on Test Drives (exercises) of the textbook. In addition, faculty can also download PowerPoint Presentations (PPTs) of each chapter of the textbook.

To download the free online teaching and learning resources of the textbook, log in to our website (***cadartifex.com/login***) and navigate to the respective textbook page to access and download its resources. If you are a new user, you need to first sign up (***cadartifex.com/register***) for downloading the online resources of the textbook.

How to Contact the Author
We truly value your feedback and suggestions. Please feel free to reach out to us at ***info@cadartifex***.com or visit ***www.cadartifex.com*** to share your feedback and download additional learning resources.

We would like to express our sincere gratitude to you for purchasing the **SOLIDWORKS Simulation 2026: A Power Guide for Beginners and Intermediate Users** textbook, we hope that the information and concepts introduced in this textbook help you to accomplish your professional goals.

CHAPTER

1

Introduction to FEA and SOLIDWORKS Simulation

In this chapter, the following topics will be discussed:

- Introduction to SOLIDWORKS Simulation
- Introduction to Finite Element Analysis (FEA)
- Working with Different Phases of FEA
- Important Terms and Definitions used in FEA
- Different Areas of Application of FEA
- Installing SOLIDWORKS Simulation
- Getting Started with SOLIDWORKS Simulation
- Identifying SOLIDWORKS Documents
- Adding CommandManager Tabs
- Invoking SOLIDWORKS Simulation

Welcome to the world of Computer Aided Engineering (CAE) with SOLIDWORKS Simulation. SOLIDWORKS Simulation is a product of Dassault Systemes SOLIDWORKS Corp., one of the biggest technology providers of engineering software solutions that let you create, simulate, publish, and manage data. By providing advanced analysis techniques, SOLIDWORKS Simulation helps engineers optimize the performance of products and allows them to cut prototyping costs, create better and safer products, and save time as well as development costs.

Introduction to SOLIDWORKS Simulation

SOLIDWORKS Simulation is a Finite Element Analysis software that enables us to arrive at critical engineering decisions early on in the design process. With the tools of this analysis software, engineers are enabled to easily study the initial design and predict the performance of the complete digital prototype. The automatic meshing tools of this software generate a mesh with high-quality elements on the first pass. It also enables engineers to directly edit the mesh for accurate placement of loads and constraints and simplifies geometry by using its powerful modeling capabilities. SOLIDWORKS Simulation makes it possible to quickly validate the design concepts before resources are invested in significant design changes or new products.

SOLIDWORKS Simulation provides a wide range of linear and non-linear materials for a better understanding of the real-world behavior of products; in addition, it provides engineers with the knowledge of how a product will perform in the real-world environment.

SOLIDWORKS Simulation is fully integrated with SOLIDWORKS and supports efficient workflow in today's multi-CAD environments by providing direct exchange of geometry with other CAD applications such as Creo Parametric, CATIA V5, NX (Unigraphic), Solid Edge, Autodesk Inventor and so on. This feature of SOLIDWORKS Simulation helps you make iterative design changes without redefining material, loads, constraints, or other simulation data when working with the native CAD format. You can also import the geometry of universal file formats such as ACIS®, IGES, STEP, and STL for solid models as well as import the CDL, DXF™, and IGES for wireframe models.

SOLIDWORKS Simulation provides a broad range of simulation tools to perform various types of analysis, which helps engineers integrate product performance knowledge in the early stages of the design cycle.

The various types of analysis that can be carried out using SOLIDWORKS Simulation are discussed below.

Linear Static Analysis

Linear static analysis is used to calculate displacement, strain, stress, and reaction forces of an object under the impact of applied load. In linear static analysis, the material properties of an object are assumed to behave linearly under the impact of applied load and the object returns to its original configuration once the load has been removed. Also, the load is assumed to be constant and does not vary with respect to time. In this analysis, the displacement is assumed to be smaller due to the applied load.

Frequency Analysis

Frequency analysis is used to calculate the natural or resonant frequencies and the associated mode shapes of a structure. Natural or resonant frequency is the frequency of an object at which it vibrates when disturbed from its resting position. By knowing the natural frequencies of an object, you can ensure that the actual operating frequency of the object does not coincide with any of its natural frequencies to avoid the failure of the object due to resonance.

Buckling Analysis

Buckling analysis is used to calculate the buckling load, which is also known as a critical load when the model can start buckling, even if the maximum stress developed in the model is within the yield strength of the material. Buckling refers to the occurrence of a larger deformation due to axial loads exerting on structures such as long slender columns and thin sheet components.

Thermal Analysis

Thermal analysis is used to calculate the temperature distribution in an object as a result of conduction, convection, and radiation. It helps to avoid overheating and melting conditions. Apart from the calculation of temperature distribution, this analysis also determines the related thermal quantities such as thermal distribution, amount of heat loss and gain, thermal gradients, and thermal fluxes.

Drop Test Analysis

Drop test analysis is used to calculate the response of an object when it is dropped on a rigid or flexible floor.

Fatigue Analysis

Fatigue analysis is used to calculate the stress at which an object fails when it undergoes repeated loading and unloading conditions which weakens the object after some time and causes failure of the object even at a stress value within the allowable stress limit. Using this analysis, you can also predict the whole life span and total damage of the object due to repeated loading and unloading conditions.

Non-linear Analysis

Non-linear analysis is used to calculate displacement, stress, strain, and reaction forces of the non-linear mechanical problems, which include large deformation, plasticity, creep, and so on. In this analysis, the material properties of an object are assumed to exceed its elastic region under the impact of applied load and experience plastic deformation. This means the object will not return to its original configuration even after removing the applied load. Non-linear analysis can undergo static analysis (applied load or field conditions do not vary with respect to time) and dynamic analysis (applied load or field conditions vary with respect to time).

Linear Dynamic Analysis

Linear dynamic analysis is used to calculate the response of an object in a dynamic loading environment. In this analysis, the load or boundary conditions vary with time due to the exertion of sudden load on an object. Also, the material of the object is assumed to behave linearly under the impact of the applied load and the object will return to its original shape once the load has been removed from the object. This analysis includes oscillating loads, impacts, collisions, and random loads. The linear dynamic analysis is classified into four main categories, which are discussed below.

Modal time history

The modal time history analysis is used to analyze the response to load as the function of time.

Harmonic

The harmonic analysis is used to analyze the response of an object to harmonically time-varying loads.

Random vibration

The random vibration analysis is used to calculate maximum stresses caused due to vibration, which occurs in response to non-deterministic loads including the loads generated on the wheel of a car while running on a rough road, base accelerations generated by earthquakes, pressure generated by air turbulence, and other similar types of load. In random vibration analysis, the input entered into the system is in the form of 'Power Spectral Density (PSD)', which is represented as vibration frequencies.

Response Spectrum

The Response spectrum analysis is used to calculate the response of a structure that undergoes sudden forces or shocks due to earthquakes, wind loads, ocean wave loads, and so on. It is also assumed that the shocks or forces occur in a fixed area.

Pressure Vessel Design Analysis

The pressure vessel design analysis is used to analyze pressure vessels. In this analysis, you can combine the results of static analysis with a different set of loads such as dead loads, live loads, thermal loads, seismic loads, and so on.

Introduction to Finite Element Analysis (FEA)

Finite Element Analysis (FEA) uses a numerical technique that is known as Finite Element Method (FEM) to solve engineering problems. The Finite Element Method (FEM) is the most widely used and accepted method to solve engineering problems such as stress analysis, deflections, reactions, vibrations, fluid flow, heat transfer, electrical, magnetic fields, and so on because of its suitability, numerical efficiency, and generality for computer application.

The whole concept of FEM can be explained with a small example of measuring the area of an unknown geometry of a plate, see Figure 1.1. There are many ways to measure the area of an unknown geometry, however, the best way to measure the area of the geometry is by dividing the entire geometry into different known geometries whose areas can be easily calculated, see Figure 1.2. After measuring the area of each known geometry, you can assemble them to get the total area of the geometry.

1.1

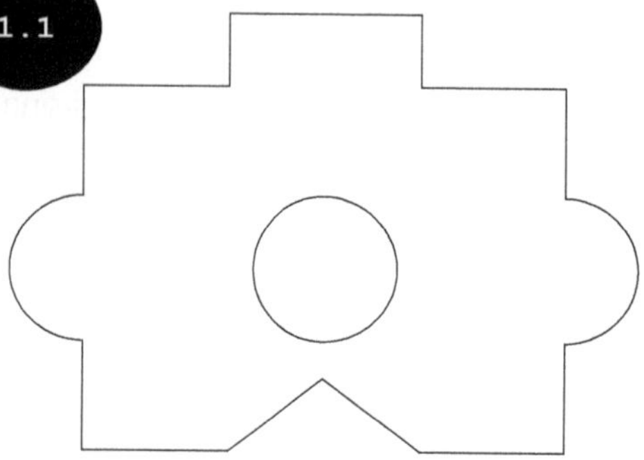

1.2

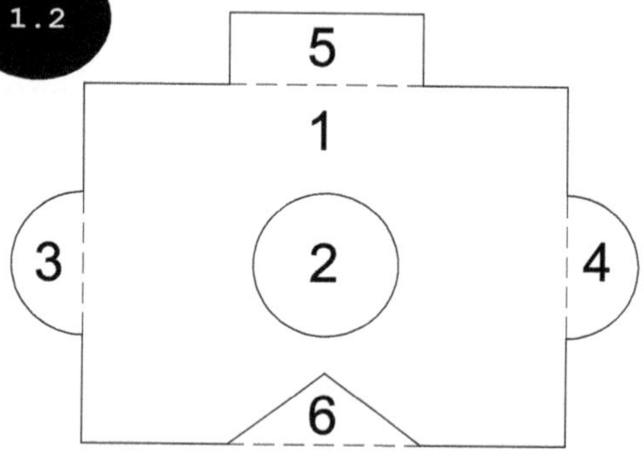

The same concept is used in FEM to calculate stresses, displacements, strains, reaction forces, temperature, frequency, vibrations, and so on of a complex structure. FEM divides the entire complex structure into a finite number of pieces of simple geometric shapes called elements, see Figure 1.3. It replaces a complex engineering problem with multiple simple problems that can be solved easily.

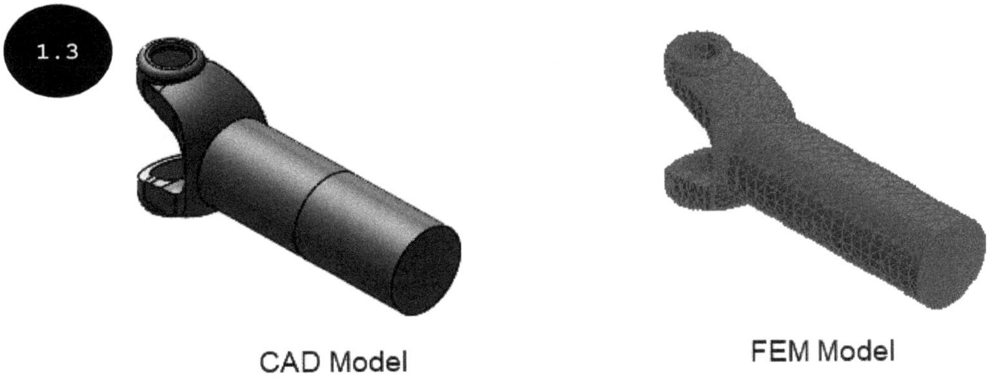

It is clear from the above figure that a FEM model consists of several finite elements that collectively represent the entire structure. Note that the geometries of the real-world mechanical structures are complex and to accurately represent their shapes, more finite elements are required due to which the computational time to calculate the response of all elements gets increased. Therefore in Finite Element Analysis (FEA), a proper balance needs to be maintained between the accuracy of results and the computational time. This makes the Finite Element Analysis (FEA) a suitable method for finding approximate solutions to engineering problems.

Working with Different Phases of FEA

Before you start performing an analysis, it is important to understand the different phases of Finite Element Analysis (FEA). As discussed, SOLIDWORKS Simulation is a Finite Element Analysis (FEA) tool which uses a numerical technique known as Finite Element Method (FEM) to solve engineering problems. In Finite Element Analysis (FEA), the entire process of analyzing an engineering design is divided into three phases: Pre-processing, Solution, and Post-processing. The phases are discussed below.

Pre-processing

The Pre-processing phase involves creating/importing CAD models, simplifying geometry, selecting analysis type, assigning material properties, defining boundary conditions (external loads and supports), and meshing the model, see Figure 1.4.

Solution

The Solution phase is completely automatic in SOLIDWORKS Simulation. In this phase, the system generates matrices for individual finite elements, which are then assembled to generate a global matrix equation for the structure. Further, it solves the global matrix equation to compute displacement, which is then used to compute stress, strain, and reaction forces. Note that in this phase the computed results are stored in numerical form.

Post-processing

In the Post-processing phase, the results generated in the Solution phase appear in graphical form for checking or analyzing them, see Figure 1.4. You can also animate the structure response based on the results obtained from the Solution phase. The graphical representation of results is very useful in understanding the correct behavior of the structure.

1.4

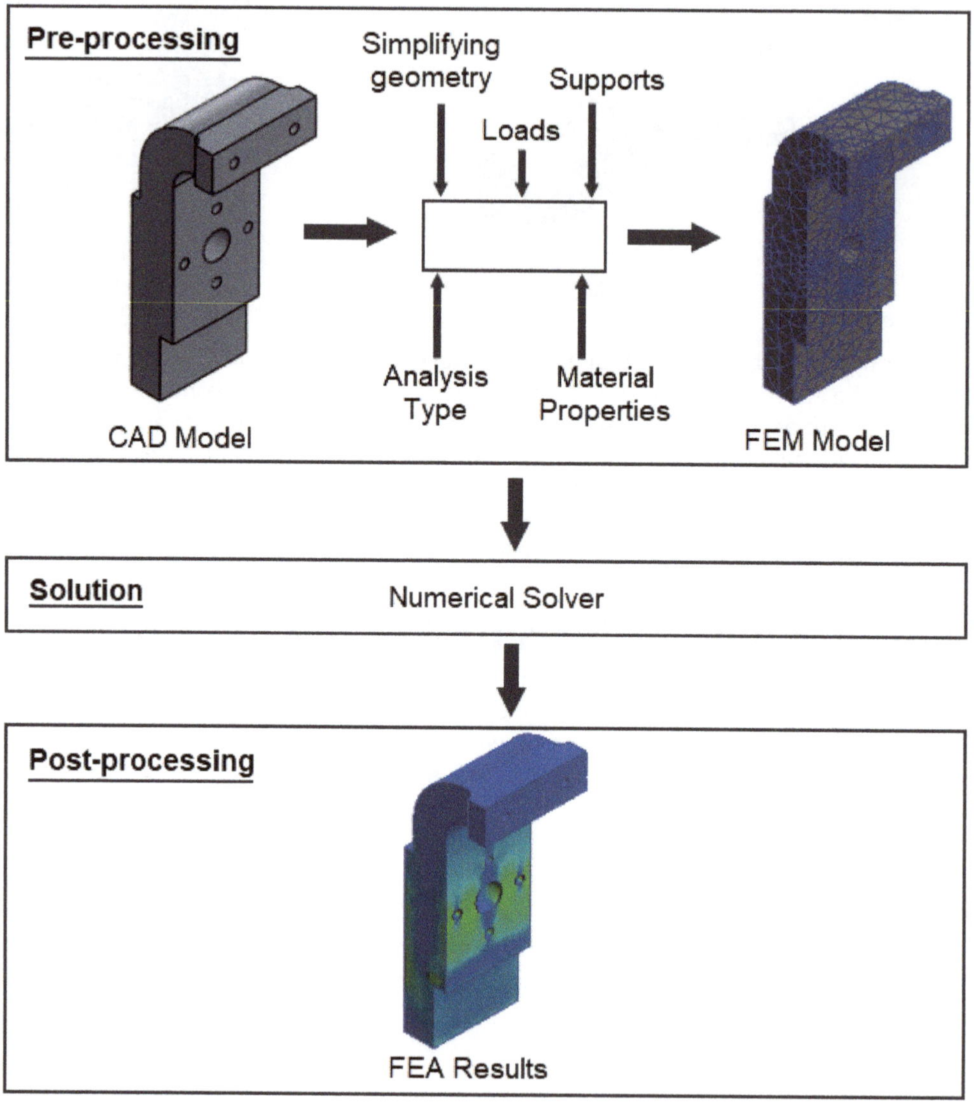

Important Terms and Definitions used in FEA

Some of the important terms and definitions used in Finite Element Analysis (FEA) are discussed below.

Stress

Stress is defined as the force per unit area. When an object is subjected to an external force, the internal resistance offered by the object is known as stress.

$$\sigma = F/A$$

Where,

σ = Stress
F = External force acting on the object
A = Cross-sectional area of the object

Stress has various forms, however, they are mainly categorized into three types: Tensile Stress, Compressive Stress, and Shear Stress, all of which are discussed below.

Tensile Stress

When an object is subjected to tensile forces, the internal resistance applied by the object against the increase in its length is known as tensile stress, see Figure 1.5.

1.5

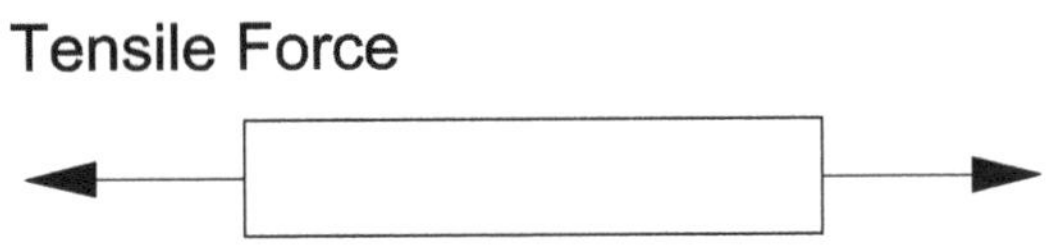

Compressive Stress

When an object is subjected to compressive forces, the internal resistance applied by the object against the decrease in its length is known as compressive stress, see Figure 1.6.

1.6

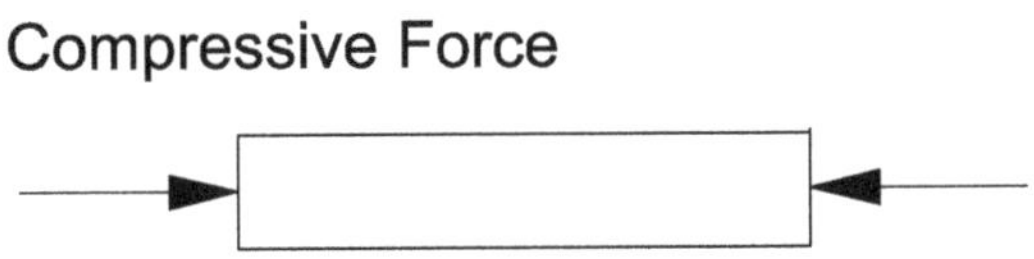

Shear Stress

Shear stress occurs when two objects tend to slide over one another due to the application of external forces, which are parallel to the plane of shear, see Figure 1.7.

1.7

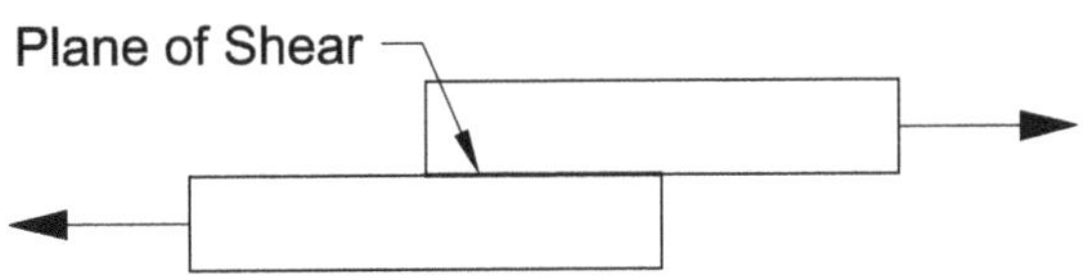

Strain

Strain is defined as the ratio of change in length to the original length of the object when it undergoes deformation due to the application of an external force, see Figure 1.8.

1.8

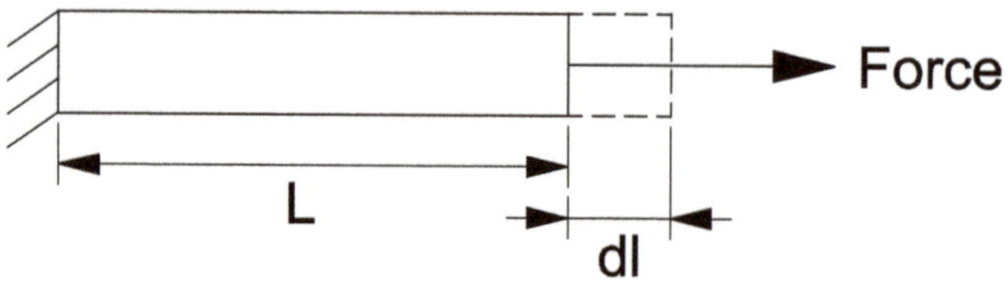

$\varepsilon = dl/L$

Where,

ε = Strain
dl = Change in length of the object
L = Original length of the object

Load

Load is defined as the external force acting on an object.

Displacement

Displacement is defined as the change in length or position of an object.

Hooke's Law

According to Hooke's Law, the ratio of stress to strain is constant. It states that stress is directly proportional to strain within the elastic region of the stress-strain curve of a material when the material is subjected to an external load, see Figure 1.9.

Constant = Stress (σ) /Strain (ε) [within the elastic region]

1.9

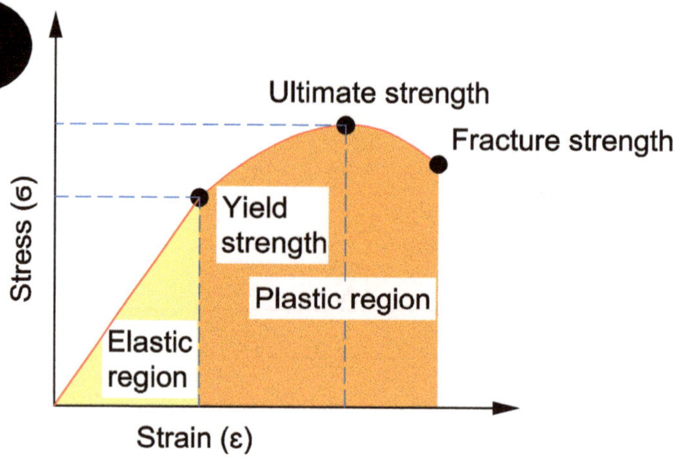

Yield Strength

Yield strength is defined as the maximum stress (yield stress) up to which a material deforms elastically under the impact of an applied load and returns to its original configuration once the load is removed. It is also defined as the stress under which a material begins to deform plastically.

Ultimate Strength

Ultimate strength is defined as the maximum stress that a material can withstand when it is subjected to an external load. It is also defined as the stress beyond which a material begins to fail or weaken.

Fracture Strength

Fracture strength is defined as the breaking stress under which a material fails due to fracture or breakage.

Young's Modulus

Young's modulus is also known as the modulus of elasticity or the elastic modulus. It defines the relationship between stress and strain of a material as per Hooke's law. It measures the stiffness of a material.

$$E = Stress\ (\sigma) / Strain\ (\varepsilon)$$
$$E = F*L / A*dl$$
$$F = E*A*dl / L$$
$$F = (E*A / L) * dl$$
$$F = K * X$$

Where,

*K = Stiffness (E*A / L)*
E = Young's modulus
A = Cross-section area
L = Original length
X = Change in length (dl)
F = Applied force

Stiffness

Stiffness is defined as the property of a material that offers resistance against its deformation when it is subjected to an external force.

$$K = F / dl$$

Where,

K = Stiffness
F = Applied external force
dl = Displacement (change in length)

Poisson's Ratio

Poisson's ratio is defined as the ratio of lateral strain to the axial or longitudinal strain of a material in the direction of the applied load, see Figure 1.10. The Poisson's ratio of a material within the elastic limit is constant. This implies that the ratio of lateral strain to the axial or longitudinal strain of a material within the elastic limit is constant.

$$\mu = \varepsilon_{lateral} / \varepsilon_{axial}$$

Where,

μ = *Poisson's ratio*
$\varepsilon_{lateral}$ = *Lateral strain*
ε_{axial} = *Axial or longitudinal strain*

1.10

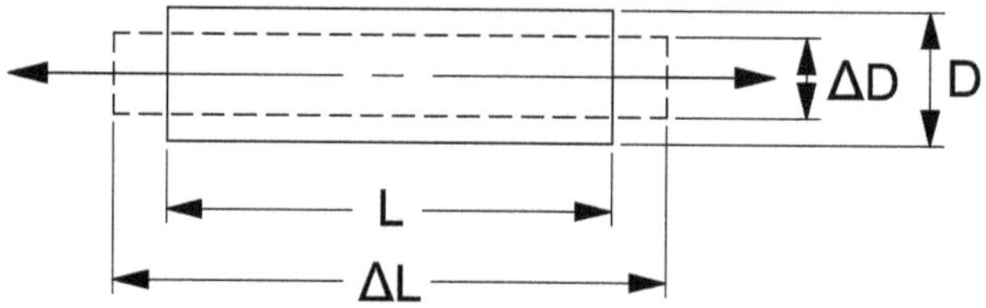

Axial or Longitudinal strain $(\varepsilon_{axial}) = \Delta L - L / L = dl_a / L$

Where,

L = *Initial/Original length*
ΔL = *Final length*
dl_a = *Change in length in axial direction*

Lateral strain $(\varepsilon_{lateral}) = \Delta D - D / D = dl_l / D$

Where,

D = *Initial/Original width*
ΔD = *Final width*
dl_l = *Change in width in lateral direction*

Creep

Creep is defined as the tendency of a material to deform slowly or gradually. It increases with time under the impact of stress which is below the yield strength of the material, see Figure 1.11. It is a material property, which depends on both stress and temperature.

1.11

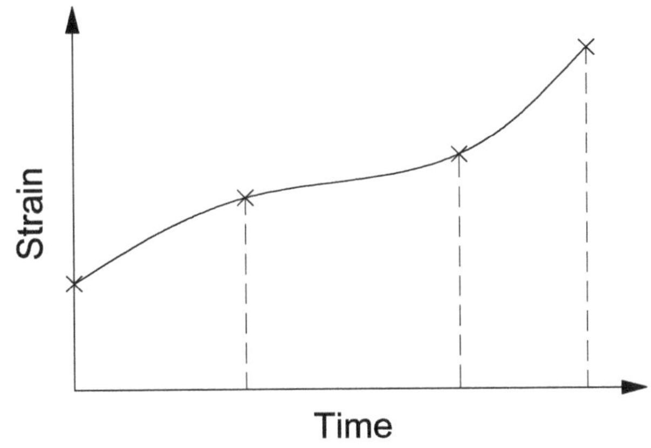

Meshing

Meshing is defined as the process of dividing an object into a finite number of pieces with simple geometric shapes called elements, see Figure 1.12.

1.12

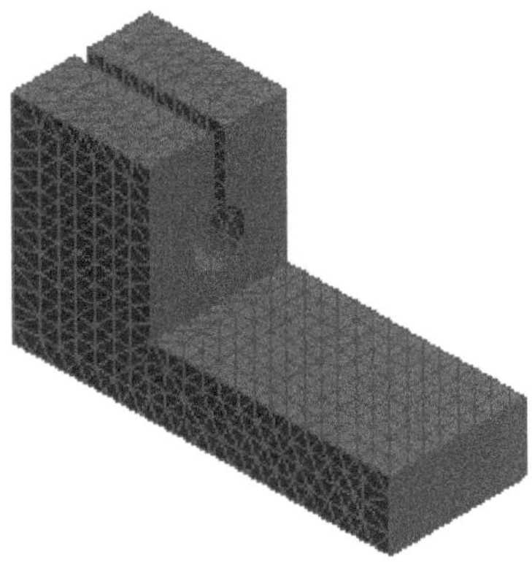

Elements

Elements are small pieces of simple geometric shapes into which an object is divided while meshing. Elements are mainly categorized into three types: 1D elements, 2D elements, and 3D elements, see the table given below:

Element Type	Element Shape
1D Element	

2D Element	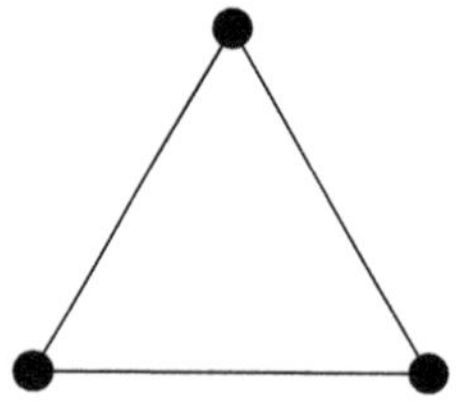 First Order Triangular element	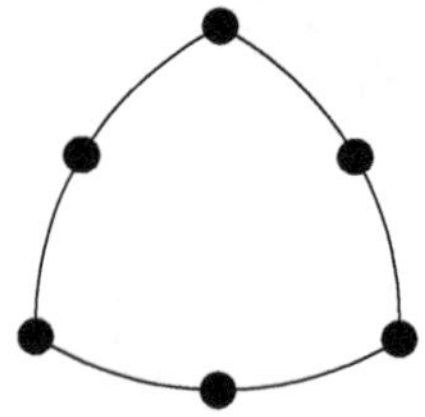 Second Order Triangular element
	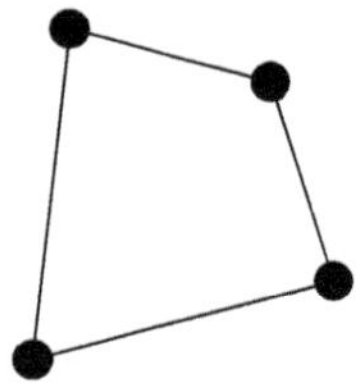 First Order Quadrilateral element	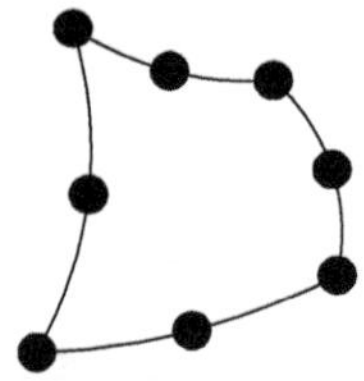 Second Order Quadrilateral element
3D Element	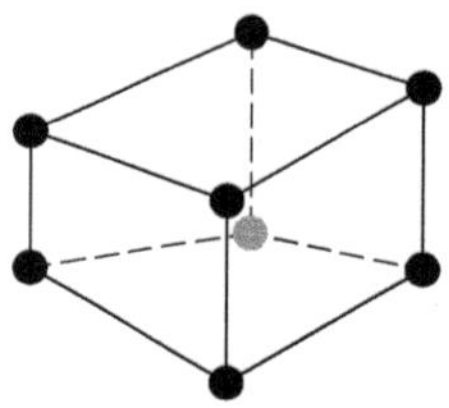 First Order Hexahedral element	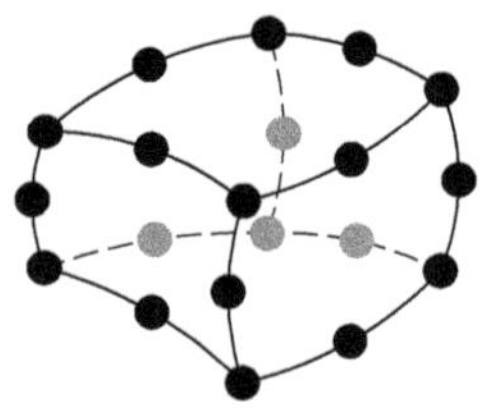 Second Order Hexahedral element
	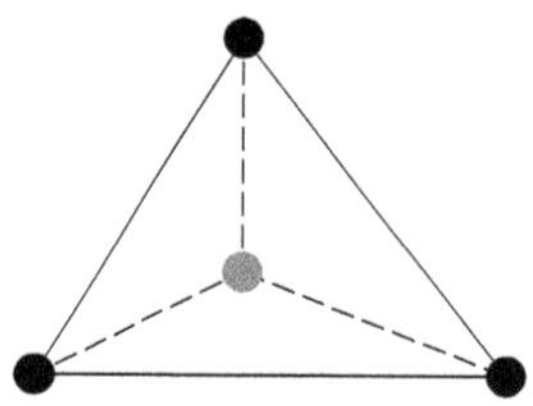 First Order Tetrahedral element	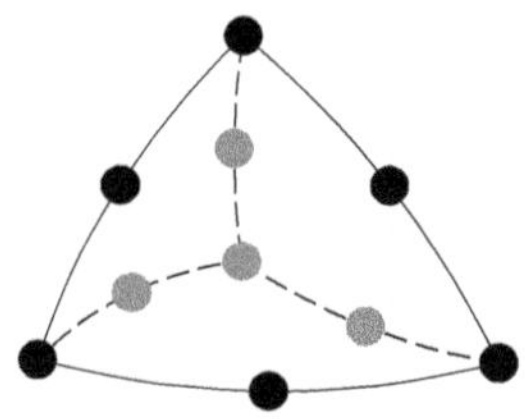 Second Order Tetrahedral element

Nodes
Elements are connected at common points called nodes, see Figures 1.13 and 1.14. The nodes define the shape of elements. If you move a node of an element, the shape of the element will change depending on the new position of the node.

1.13

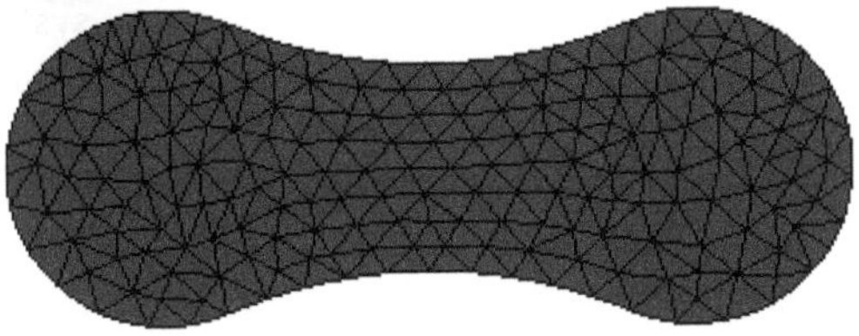

1.14

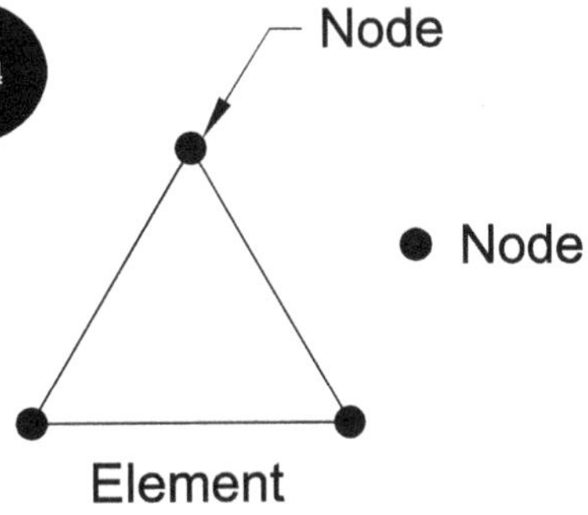

Different Areas of Application of FEA
The Finite Element Analysis (FEA) was developed for the nuclear research and aerospace industries. However, with the advent of modern technologies, it is now widely used as the accepted method in all engineering disciplines (mechanical, civil, electrical, automobile, etc.). The areas of applications of FEA include:

1. Structure analysis
2. Thermal analysis
3. Buckling analysis
4. Fluid flow analysis
5. Frequency analysis
6. Mould flow analysis
7. Drop test
8. Pressure vessel design
9. Fatigue analysis
10. Vibrations
11. Electromagnetic analysis
12. Biomechanics, and many more

Installing SOLIDWORKS Simulation
SOLIDWORKS Simulation is fully integrated with SOLIDWORKS. To install SOLIDWORKS Simulation, you must have SOLIDWORKS installed on your system. If these softwares are not installed on your system, you first need to install them. However, before installing the software, you need to evaluate the system requirements and ensure that your system is capable of running SOLIDWORKS and SOLIDWORKS Simulation adequately. The system requirements for installing the same are listed below:

1. Operating Systems: Windows 10 - 64-bit, Windows 11 - 64-bit
2. RAM: 8 GB or more (16 GB or more recommended)
3. Disk Space: 10 GB or more

4. Processor: x86_64 (Intel 64 or AMD64)
5. Graphics Card: SOLIDWORKS certified graphics cards and drivers

For more information about the system requirements for SOLIDWORKS, visit: *solidworks.com/sw/support/SystemRequirements.html*

Getting Started with SOLIDWORKS Simulation

Once SOLIDWORKS 2026 and SOLIDWORKS Simulation 2026 have been installed on your system, start by double-clicking on the SOLIDWORKS 2026 icon on your desktop screen. Then the system prepares for starting SOLIDWORKS and SOLIDWORKS Simulation by loading all the required files. Once all the required files have been loaded, the initial screen of SOLIDWORKS 2026 appears along with a **Welcome** dialog box, see Figure 1.15. If you are starting SOLIDWORKS for the first time after installing the software, the **SOLIDWORKS License Agreement** window appears. Click on the **Accept** button in the **SOLIDWORKS License Agreement** window to accept the license agreement and start SOLIDWORKS.

1.15

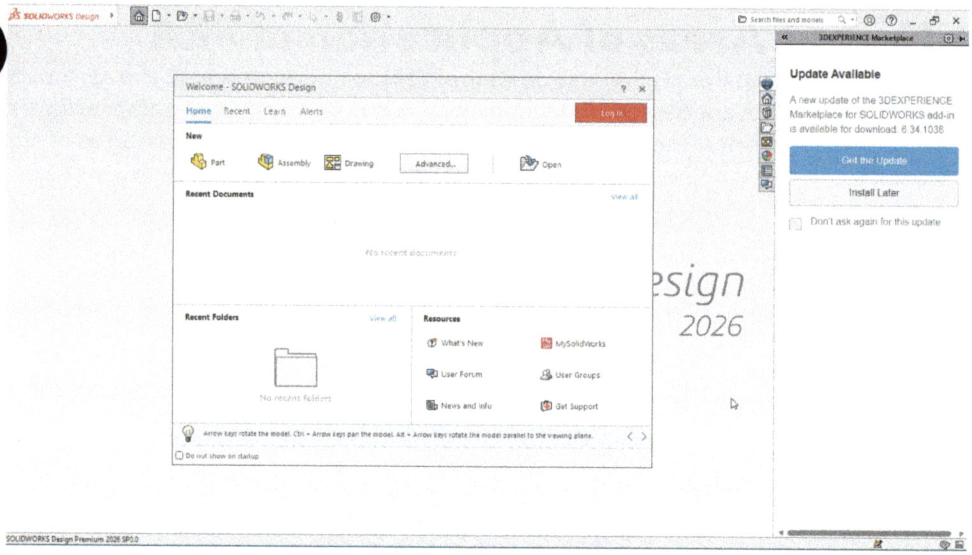

In SOLIDWORKS 2026, the **Welcome** dialog box appears every time you start SOLIDWORKS and is a convenient way to invoke new SOLIDWORKS documents or environments, open existing documents, view recent documents and folders, access SOLIDWORKS resources, and stay updated on SOLIDWORKS news.

The **Welcome** dialog box has four tabs: **Home**, **Recent**, **Learn**, and **Alerts**. The options in the **Home** tab are used to invoke new SOLIDWORKS documents, open existing documents, view recent documents and folders, and access SOLIDWORKS resources. The **Recent** tab displays a longer list of recent documents and folders. The **Learn** tab is used to access instructional resources such as tutorials, sample models, access to 3D Content Center, certification program, and many more, to help you learn more about SOLIDWORKS. The **Alerts** tab keeps you updated with SOLIDWORKS news and provides different types of alerts in different sections including **Troubleshooting** and **Technical Alerts**.

Tip: If the **Welcome** dialog box does not appear on the screen then you can invoke it by clicking on the **Welcome to SOLIDWORKS** tool in the **Standard** toolbar. Alternatively, you can click on **Help > Welcome to SOLIDWORKS** in the SOLIDWORKS Design Menus or the **Welcome to SOLIDWORKS** option in the **SOLIDWORKS Resources Task Pane** to invoke the **Welcome** dialog box. You will learn more about **Standard** toolbar, SOLIDWORKS Design Menus, and Task Pane later in this chapter.

Note that SOLIDWORKS Simulation can be invoked within the Part modeling and Assembly environments of SOLIDWORKS, therefore, it is important to get familiar with different environments of SOLIDWORKS. The methods for invoking different environments of SOLIDWORKS are discussed below.

Invoking the Part Modeling Environment

The Part Modeling environment in SOLIDWORKS is used to create 3D solid models, surface models, and sheet metal components. This environment provides powerful parametric tools that allow users to design, modify, and optimize parts efficiently.

Additionally, it enables access to SOLIDWORKS Simulation, where users can perform Finite Element Analysis (FEA) to evaluate the structural behavior, stress distribution, and performance of a part or component under real-world loading conditions.

To invoke the Part modeling environment, click on the **Part** button in the **Welcome** dialog box. The Part modeling environment gets invoked and the initial screen of the Part modeling environment appears, as shown in Figure 1.16. Alternatively, to invoke the Part modeling environment, click on the **New** tool in the **Standard** toolbar; the **New SOLIDWORKS Document** dialog box appears, see Figure 1.17. In this dialog box, ensure that the **Part** button is activated and then click on the **OK** button to invoke the Part modeling environment. You will learn how to invoke SOLIDWORKS Simulation within the Part modeling environment later in this chapter.

1.16

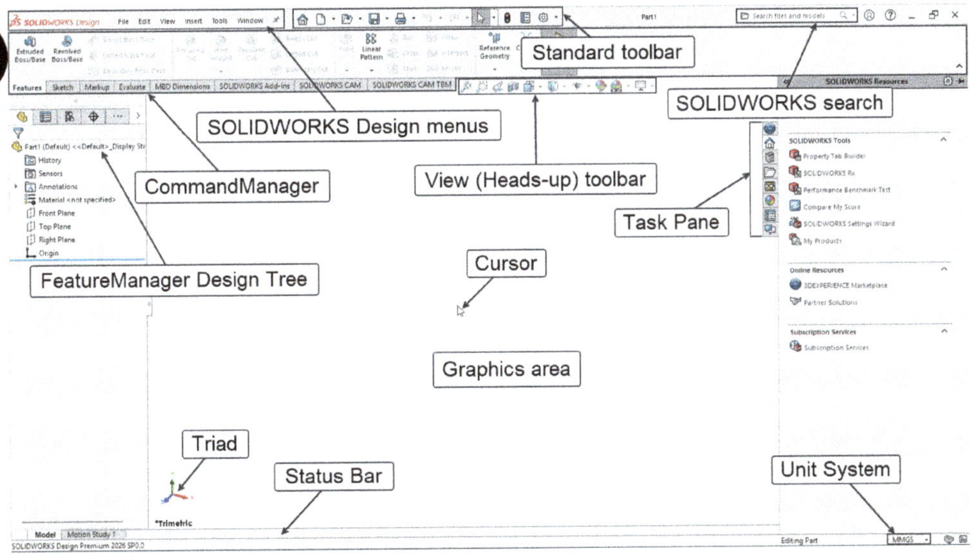

1.17

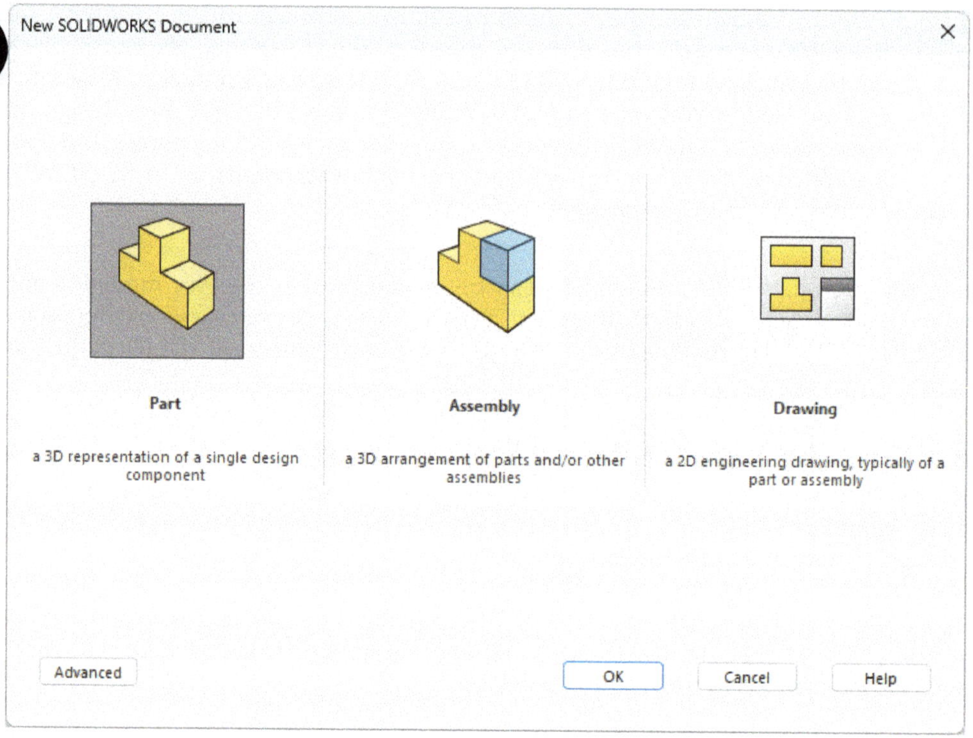

Note: If you are invoking the Part modeling environment for the first time after installing the software, the **Units and Dimension Standard** dialog box will appear, see Figure 1.18. In this dialog box, you can specify the unit system as the default unit system for SOLIDWORKS.

1.18

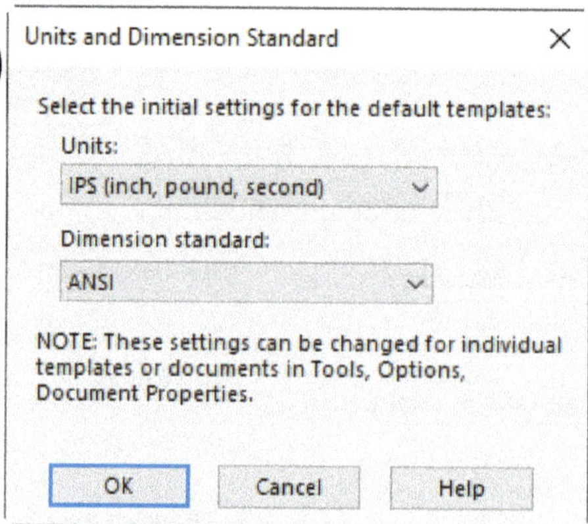

It is evident from the initial screen of the Part modeling environment that SOLIDWORKS is very user-friendly and easy to operate. Some of the components of the initial screen are discussed next.

Standard Toolbar

The **Standard** toolbar contains a set of the most frequently used tools such as **New**, **Open**, and **Save**, see Figure 1.19.

1.19

SOLIDWORKS Design Menus

The SOLIDWORKS Design Menus contain different menus such as **File**, **View**, and **Tools** for using different tools of SOLIDWORKS, see Figure 1.20.

1.20

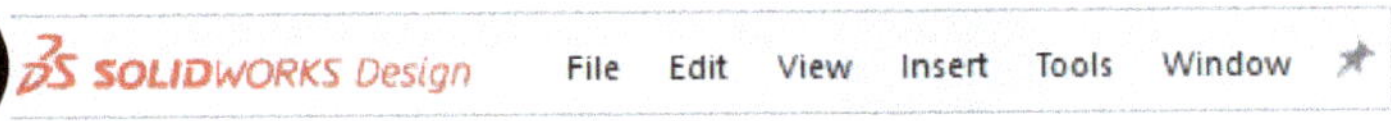

Note that the SOLIDWORKS Design Menus appear when you move the cursor over SOLIDWORKS Design, which is available at the top left corner of the screen. You can keep the SOLIDWORKS Design Menus visible all the time by clicking on the push-pin button available at the end of the SOLIDWORKS Design Menus. Note that the availability of the tools in different menus depends upon the type of environment invoked.

SOLIDWORKS Search

The SOLIDWORKS Search is a search tool, which is used to search for commands, tools, knowledge databases (help topics), community forums, files, models, and so on, see Figure 1.21.

1.21

CommandManager

CommandManager is available at the top of the graphics area. It provides access to different SOLIDWORKS tools. There are various CommandManagers such as **Features CommandManager**, **Sketch CommandManager**, **Evaluate CommandManager**, and so on which are available in the Part modeling environment. When the **Features** tab is activated in the CommandManager, the **Features CommandManager** appears, which provides access to different tools for creating 3D solid models, see Figure 1.22. On clicking on the **Sketch** tab, the **Sketch CommandManager** appears, which provides access to different tools for creating sketches.

1.22

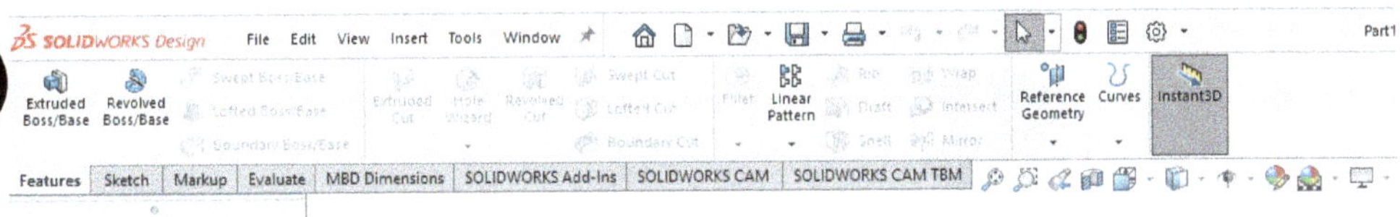

Note that the tabs of some of the CommandManagers such as **Surfaces CommandManager** and **Sheet Metal CommandManager** are not displayed in the CommandManager by default. You will learn about adding these tabs later in this chapter.

Note: Different environments (Part, Assembly, and Drawing) of SOLIDWORKS are provided with different sets of CommandManagers.

FeatureManager Design Tree

FeatureManager Design Tree appears on the left side of the graphics area, it keeps a record of all the operations or features used for creating a model, see Figure 1.23. Note that the first feature appears at the top and the subsequently created features appear one after the other in the FeatureManager Design Tree. Also, in the FeatureManager Design Tree, three default planes and an origin appear by default, see Figure 1.23.

1.23

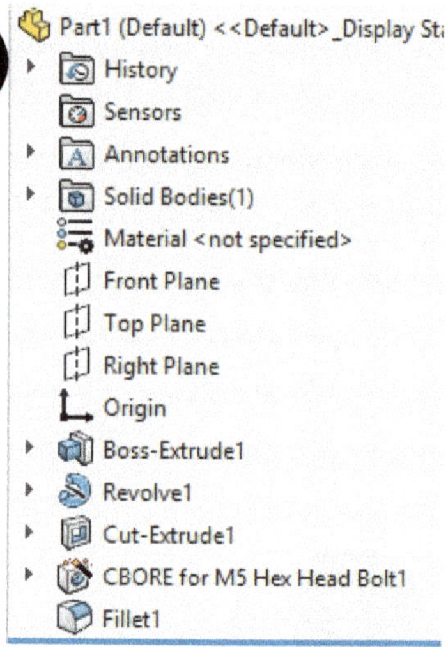

Tip: Features are logically performed operations for creating a component. In other words, a component can be designed by creating a number of features such as extrude, sweep, hole, fillet, draft, and so on.

View (Heads-Up) Toolbar

The **View (Heads-Up)** toolbar is available at the top center of the graphics area, see Figure 1.24. It is provided with different sets of tools, which are used to manipulate the view and display of a model available in the graphics area.

1.24

Status Bar

The Status Bar is available at the bottom of the graphics area, and it provides information about the action to be performed based on the currently active tool. Also, it displays the current state of a sketch being created, the coordinate system, and so on.

Task Pane

Task Pane appears on the right side of the screen with various tabs such as **SOLIDWORKS Resources**, **Design Library**, **File Explorer**, **View Palette**, **Appearances, Scenes, and Decals**, **Custom Properties**, and **3DEXPERIENCE Marketplace** for accessing various online resources of SOLIDWORKS, several applications, subscription services, library and so on, see Figure 1.25.

1.25

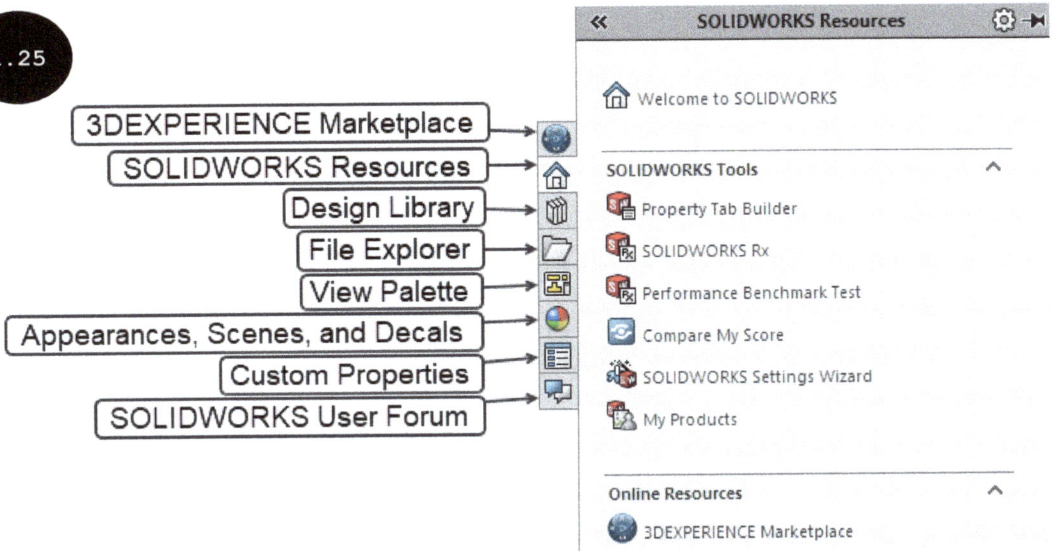

Invoking the Assembly Environment

The Assembly environment is used for assembling different components of an assembly concerning each other by applying the required mates, see Figure 1.26. You can also access SOLIDWORKS Simulation within the Assembly environment to perform Finite Element Analysis (FEA) on an assembly or assembly components. To invoke the Assembly environment, click on the **Assembly** button in the **Welcome** dialog box. Then the Assembly environment is invoked with the **Open** dialog box along with the **Begin Assembly PropertyManager**, see Figure 1.27. You will learn how to invoke SOLIDWORKS Simulation within the Assembly environment later in this chapter.

1.26

1.27

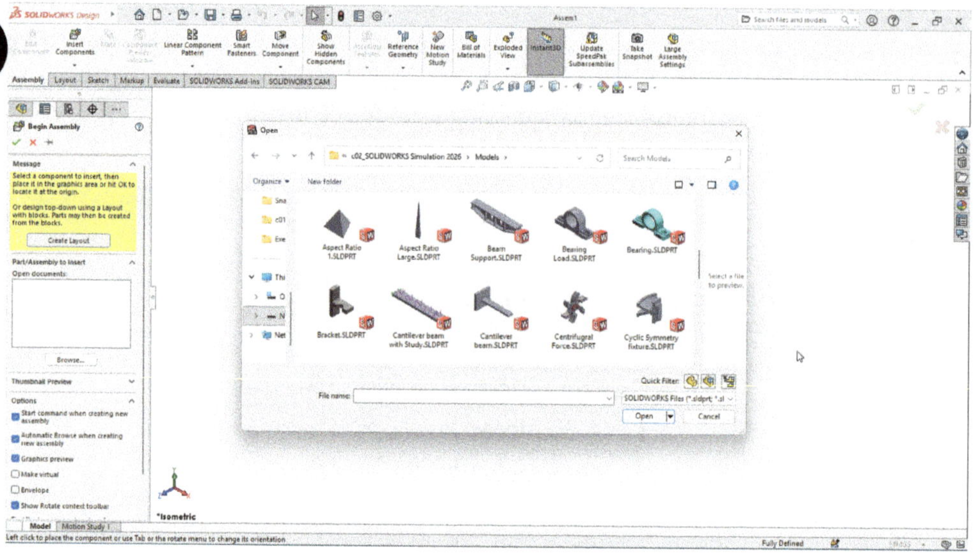

Alternatively, to invoke the Assembly environment, click on the **New** tool in the **Standard** toolbar. A **New SOLIDWORKS Document** dialog box appears. In this dialog box, click on the **Assembly** button and then click on the **OK** button.

Invoking the Drawing Environment

The Drawing environment of SOLIDWORKS is used to create 2D drawings of parts or assemblies, see Figure 1.28. To invoke the Drawing environment, click on the **New** tool in the **Standard** toolbar. The **New SOLIDWORKS Document** dialog box appears. In this dialog box, click on the **Drawing** button and then click on the **OK** button. Then the **Sheet Format/Size** dialog box appears. After the dialog box has appeared, you can use the options in this dialog box to select the sheet size/format to be used for creating drawings. You can also invoke the **Sheet Format/Size** dialog box by clicking on the **Drawing** button in the **Welcome** dialog box. Once you have defined the sheet size and format in the **Sheet Format/Size** dialog box, click on the **OK** button. The initial screen of the Drawing environment appears with the **Model View PropertyManager** on the left of the drawing sheet, see Figure 1.29. The **Model View PropertyManager** is used to insert a component or an assembly into the Drawing environment for creating its drawing views.

1.28

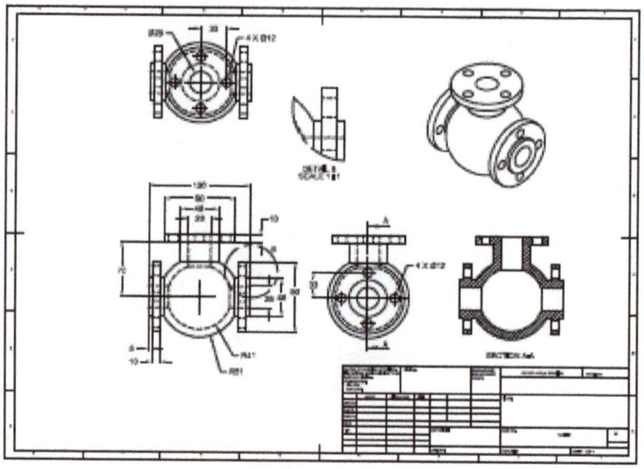

1.29

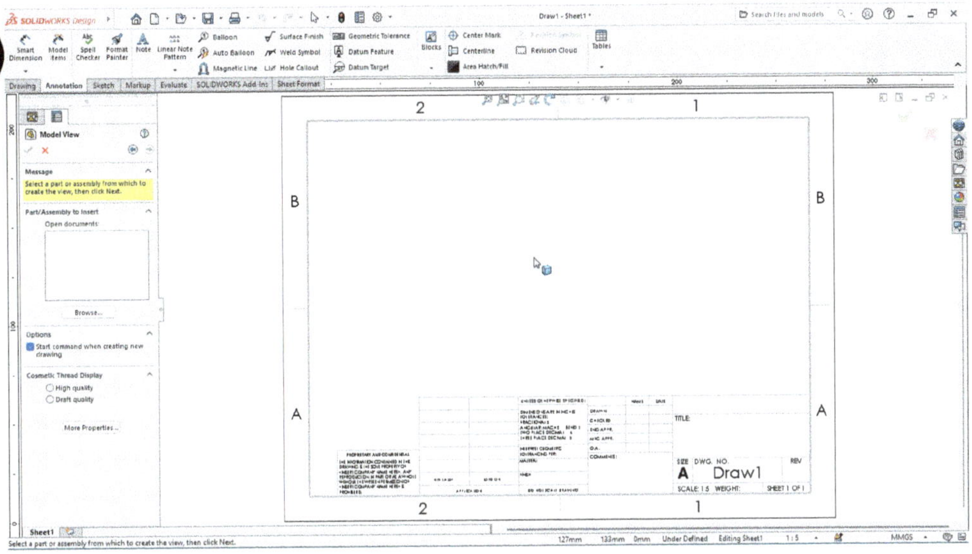

Identifying SOLIDWORKS Documents

The documents created in different environments (Part, Assembly, and Drawing) of SOLIDWORKS have different file extensions, see the table given below:

Environments	File Extension
Part Modeling Environment	*.sldprt
Assembly Modeling Environment	*.sldasm
Drawing Modeling Environment	*.slddrw

Adding CommandManager Tabs

In addition to the default CommandManagers, such as the Features CommandManager and the Sketch CommandManager, you can customize the interface by adding additional CommandManagers as required. This flexibility allows users to organize tools based on their workflow and access frequently used commands more efficiently.

To add a CommandManager, right-click on any of the available CommandManager tabs. A shortcut menu appears. In this menu, move the cursor over the **Tabs** option. A cascading menu appears, see Figure 1.30. This cascading menu displays a list of CommandManagers. A tick mark in front of the CommandManager indicates that the respective CommandManager has already been added. Click on the required CommandManager in the cascading menu, the respective CommandManager tab is added to the CommandManager.

1.30

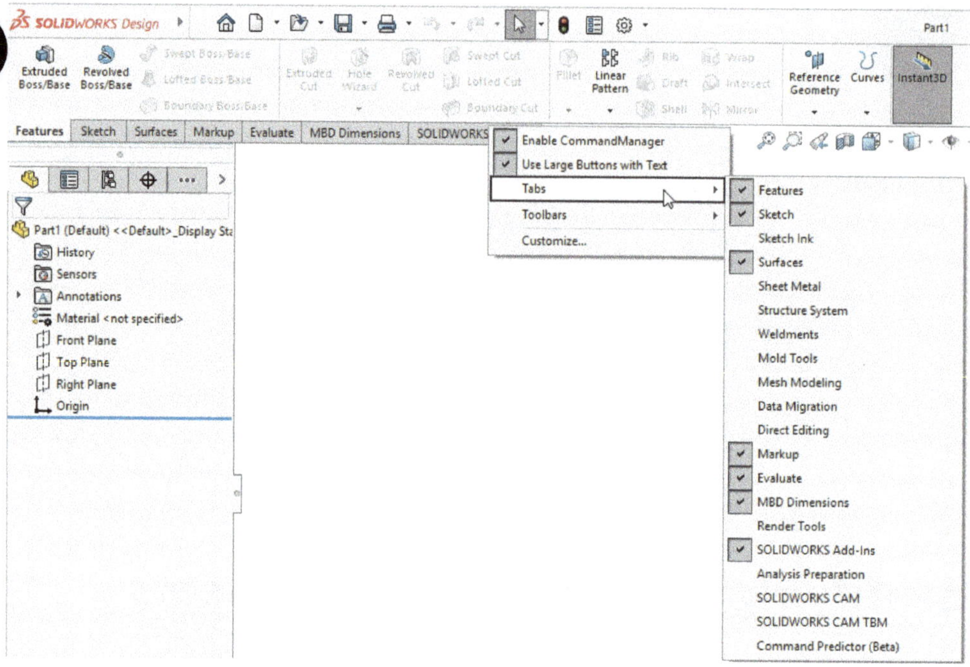

Invoking SOLIDWORKS Simulation

SOLIDWORKS Simulation can be invoked within the Part modeling and Assembly environments of SOLIDWORKS to perform various types of Finite Element Analysis (FEA). To start SOLIDWORKS Simulation, click on **Tools > Add-Ins** in the SOLIDWORKS Design Menus, see Figure 1.31. The **Add-Ins** dialog box appears, see Figure 1.32.

1.31

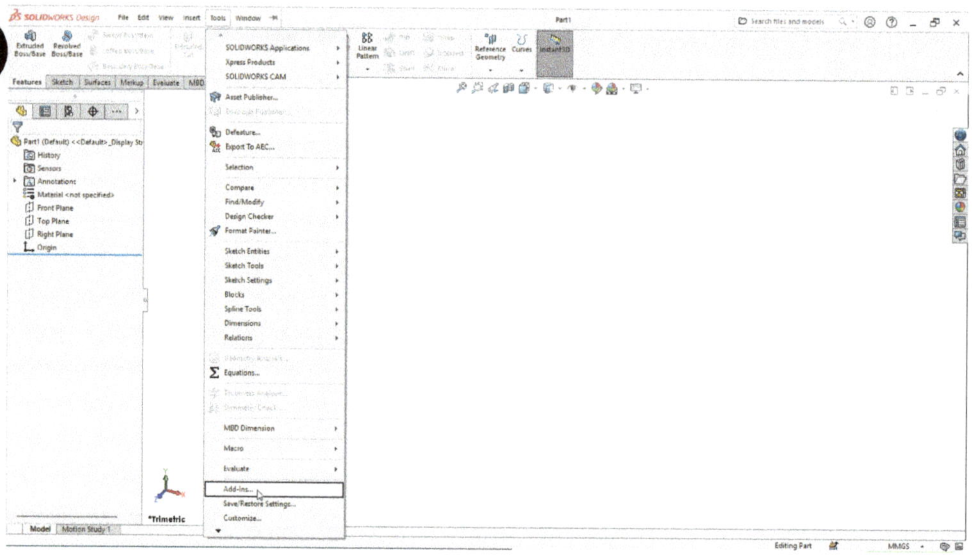

Note: You may need to expand the **Tools** menu of the SOLIDWORKS Design Menus by clicking on the arrow at its bottom to display the **Add-Ins** tool, as shown in Figure 1.31.

1.32

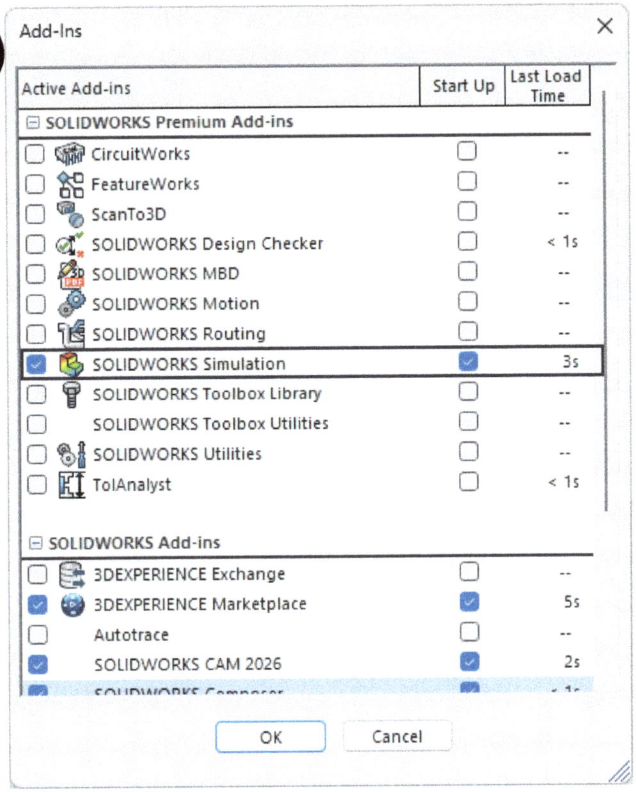

In the **Add-Ins** dialog box, select the check boxes available on both the left and right of the **SOLIDWORKS Simulation** option, see Figure 1.32. After selecting the required options, click the **OK** button.

Once activated, SOLIDWORKS Simulation is loaded, and the **Simulation** menu is added to the SOLIDWORKS Design Menus, see Figure 1.33. Additionally, the **Simulation** tab appears in the CommandManager, see Figure 1.33.

The **Simulation** menu and the **Simulation** tab provide different sets of tools that allow you to perform various types of Finite Element Analysis (FEA), including structural, thermal, and other engineering studies.

1.33

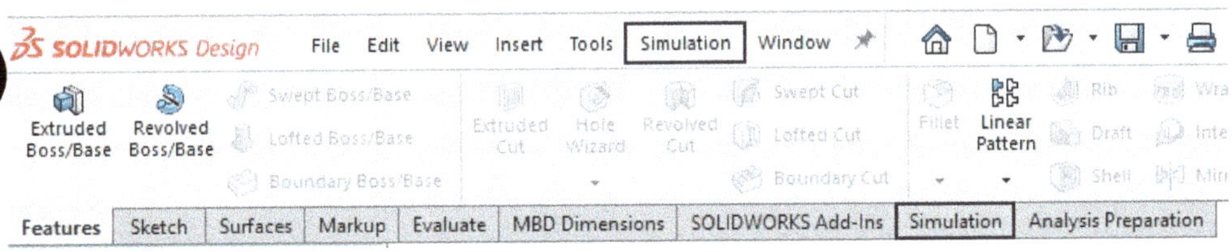

If the **Simulation** tab is not displayed in the CommandManager of SOLIDWORKS by default, you can add it manually. To do this, right-click on any existing tab in the CommandManager. A shortcut menu appears. In this menu, move the cursor over the **Tabs** option and then select **Simulation** from the cascading menu.

Alternatively, click the **SOLIDWORKS Add-Ins** tab in the CommandManager to display the tools of the **SOLIDWORKS Add-Ins CommandManager**, see Figure 1.34. Then, click the **SOLIDWORKS Simulation** tool to activate and display the Simulation tools.

1.34

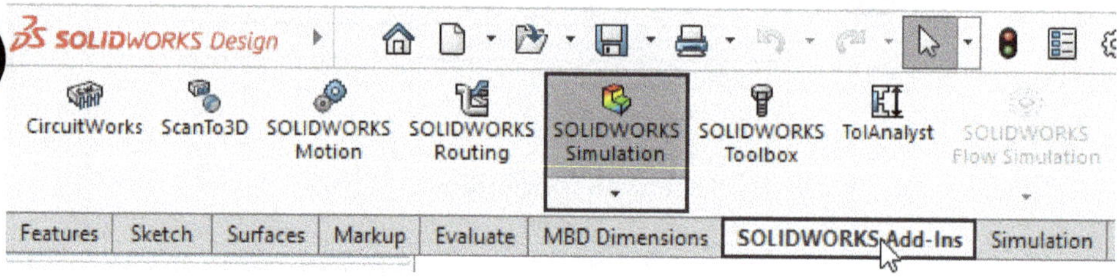

Note: As mentioned earlier, in the **Add-Ins** dialog box, two check boxes are available for the **SOLIDWORKS Simulation** option. If you select the check box on the right, SOLIDWORKS Simulation will be loaded automatically every time SOLIDWORKS is started. If you select the check box on the left, SOLIDWORKS Simulation will be loaded only for the current session. To ensure that SOLIDWORKS Simulation is loaded for both the current session and automatically for all future sessions, you must select both check boxes in the **Add-Ins** dialog box.

If the **SOLIDWORKS Simulation** option is not available in the **Add-Ins** dialog box then you first need to install SOLIDWORKS Simulation on your system.

After invoking SOLIDWORKS Simulation in SOLIDWORKS, click the **Simulation** tab in the CommandManager. The **Simulation CommandManager** appears, see Figure 1.35. This CommandManager contains tools required to perform various types of Finite Element Analysis (FEA).

Note that initially, most tools in the **Simulation CommandManager** are disabled. These tools become available only after you define the type of analysis to be performed. The analysis type can be specified using the **New Study** tool available in the **Simulation CommandManager**.

1.35

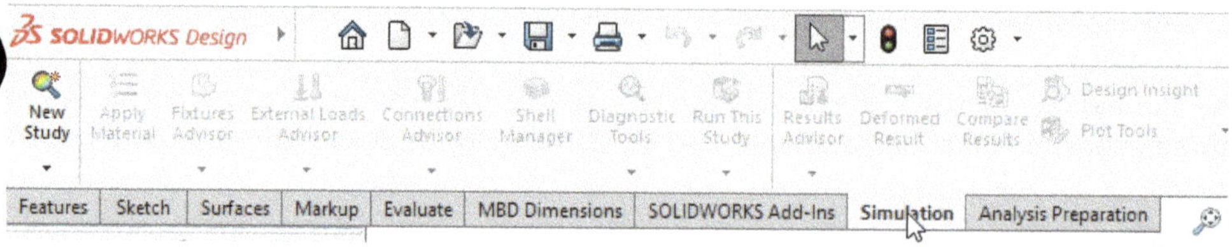

Note that before defining the type of analysis using the **New Study** tool, you must first create or import the required geometry in SOLIDWORKS, as the analysis is performed on an existing model. You will learn about performing different types of analyses in detail in the later chapters of this textbook.

Summary

This chapter introduced SOLIDWORKS Simulation, covering various types of analysis and the fundamentals of Finite Element Analysis (FEA). It explored different phases of FEA, including pre-processing, solution, and post-processing, while explaining key terms and definitions. Additionally, the chapter discussed element types, application areas of FEA, system requirements for installing SOLIDWORKS Simulation, the SOLIDWORKS interface, how to invoke different SOLIDWORKS documents, and how to get started with SOLIDWORKS Simulation.

Questions

Complete the following sentences:

- In the linear static analysis, the material properties of an object are assumed to behave _________ under the impact of applied load.
- The _________ analysis is used to calculate the natural or resonant frequencies and the associated mode shapes of a structure.
- The _________ analysis is used to calculate the stress at which an object fails when it undergoes repeated loading and unloading processes.
- The Finite Element Analysis (FEA) uses a numerical technique known as _________ to solve engineering problems.
- In the Finite Element Analysis (FEA), the entire process of analyzing the engineering design is divided into three phases _________, _________, and _________.
- _________ is defined as the process of dividing an object into a finite number of pieces with simple geometric shapes called elements.
- Elements are mainly categorized into _________, _________, and _________.
- The _________ strength is defined as the maximum stress that a material can withstand when subjected to an external load.

- _________ is defined as the ratio of change in length to the original length of the object when it undergoes deformation due to the application of external load.
- The _________ strength is defined as the maximum stress up to which a material deforms elastically under the impact of applied load and returns to its original configuration once the load is removed.
- _________ is defined as the property of a material which offers resistance against the deformation of a material when it is subjected to an external force.

CHAPTER
2

Introduction to Analysis Tools and Static Analysis

In this chapter, the following topics will be discussed:

- Making Assumptions for Linear Static Analysis
- Working with Linear Static Analysis
- Defining Analysis Units
- Assigning Material Properties
- Creating New Material Library, Category, and Material
- Editing Properties of a Standard Material
- Deleting Material Library, Category, and Material
- Defining Boundary Conditions
- Applying Fixtures/Restraints
- Applying Loads
- Meshing a Geometry
- Identifying Poor Quality Mesh Elements

In SOLIDWORKS Simulation, you need to have a model available in the graphics area for performing an analysis. Since SOLIDWORKS Simulation is fully integrated within the SOLIDWORKS software, you can design any real-world mechanical 3D model in SOLIDWORKS and then easily perform the necessary analysis using SOLIDWORKS Simulation. It helps engineers to take advantage of 3D CAD data such as materials, assembly mates, and configurations which are stored within the model. SOLIDWORKS being a parametric 3D modeling software allows you to create or edit any real-world mechanical design, as required. To learn about creating real-world 3D mechanical models using SOLIDWORKS, refer to ***SOLIDWORKS 2026: A Power Guide for Beginners and Intermediate Users*** textbook published by CADArtifex.

In addition to creating a model in SOLIDWORKS, you can also import a model created in another CAD software and perform the required analysis on it. SOLIDWORKS Simulation supports a wide range of CAD formats: *CATIA V5 (*.catpart;*.catproduct)*, *ProE/Creo (*.prt;*.asm)*, *Inventor (*.ipt;*.iam)*, *Solid Edge (*.par;*.asm)*, and so on. Moreover, you can also import models saved in neutral file formats such as **.SAT*, **.STP*, **.IGES*, and **.STEP* to perform analysis using the SOLIDWORKS Simulation.

Note: When you import a model created in another CAD software or saved in a neutral file format such as **.STP*, **.IGES*, and **.STEP*, the SOLIDWORKS message window appears. This message window confirms whether you wish to run import diagnostics on the model. The import diagnostics is used for repairing broken faces and removing gaps between the faces of the model to make it a valid solid model for analysis. Note that while importing a model created in another CAD software or saved in a neutral file, you may find some topological issues in the geometry. These problems need to be resolved by using the **Import Diagnostics** feature of SOLIDWORKS before you can carry out any analysis. Click on the **Yes** button in the **SOLIDWORKS** message window to run the import diagnostics on the model. If the **SOLIDWORKS** message does not invoke automatically, click on the imported model in the **FeatureManager Design Tree** and then right-click. A shortcut menu appears. In this shortcut menu, click on the **Import Diagnostics** option to invoke the **Import Diagnostics PropertyManager**.

After creating or importing a CAD model in SOLIDWORKS, the crucial next step is choosing the most suitable type of analysis. The selection depends on the specific engineering problem being addressed. In Finite Element Analysis (FEA), certain engineering assumptions must be made to understand the problem better. Based on these assumptions, the appropriate analysis type can be determined. Below are key engineering assumptions that justify selecting a Linear Static analysis.

Making Assumptions for Linear Static Analysis

Linear static analysis is used to calculate displacements, strains, stresses, and reaction forces in a geometry subjected to applied loads. This analysis can be performed if the following assumptions hold true for the given engineering problem.

1. The applied load on the structure remains constant over time.
2. The load is gradually and uniformly applied to the structure until it reaches its full magnitude, after which it remains constant.
3. The displacement resulting from the applied load is assumed to be small.
4. The change in stiffness is considered negligible due to minimal displacement, applied load, and related factors.
5. The material is assumed to exhibit linear behavior, adhering to Hooke's Law, where stress is proportional to strain. Under this assumption, the structure is expected to return to its original configuration once the load is removed, see Figure 2.1.
6. The change in material properties is considered negligible due to the minimal displacement and the material's linear behavior.
7. The material is assumed to remain within the elastic region of the stress-strain curve under the application of applied load, as shown in Figure 2.2.
8. Boundary conditions do not vary due to the application of load.

2.1

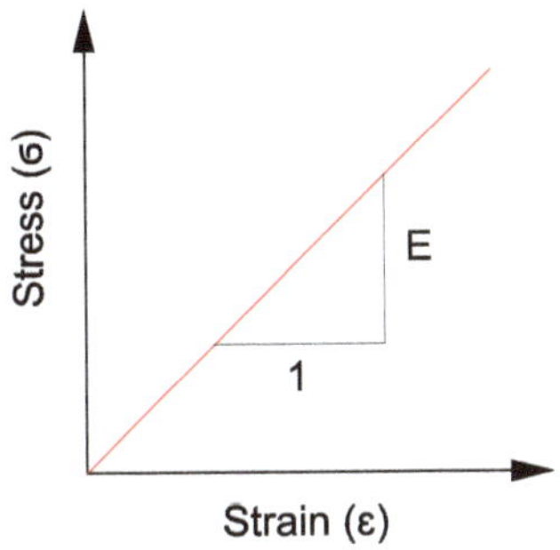

2.2

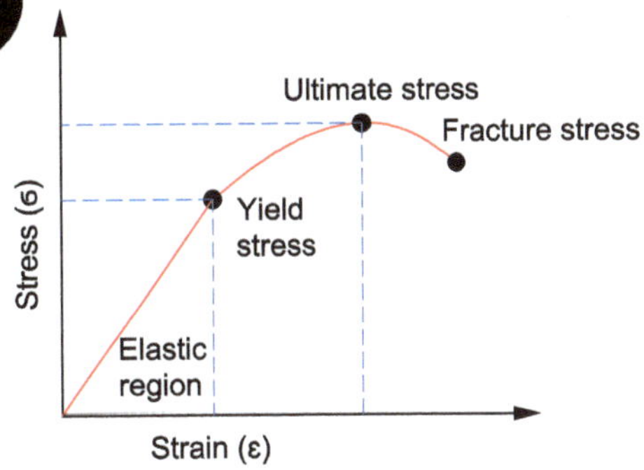

If the aforementioned assumptions hold true for the problem at hand, you can proceed with performing the linear static analysis. In this analysis, the linear finite element equilibrium equation to be solved is as follows:

$$[F] = [K][X]$$

Where,

F = Applied load
K = System stiffness (*stiffness is constant*)
X = Displacement

Note: In linear static analysis, if the force doubles, the displacement is assumed to be doubled, see Figure 2.3.

2.3

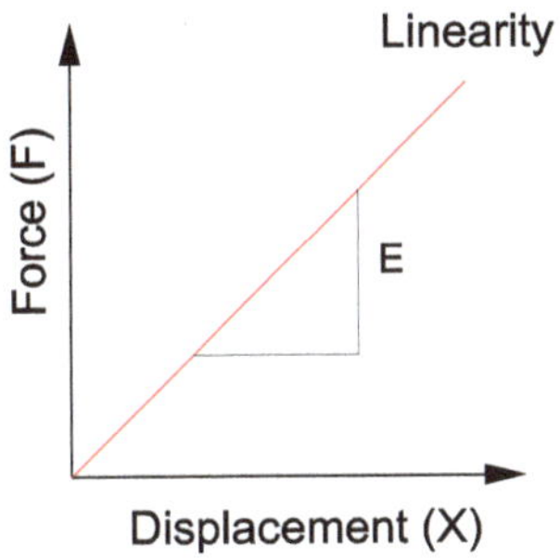

Working with Linear Static Analysis

To start with linear static analysis, first create or import a 3D model in SOLIDWORKS and then click on the **Simulation** tab in the CommandManager. The tools of the **Simulation CommandManager** appear, see Figure 2.4.

2.4

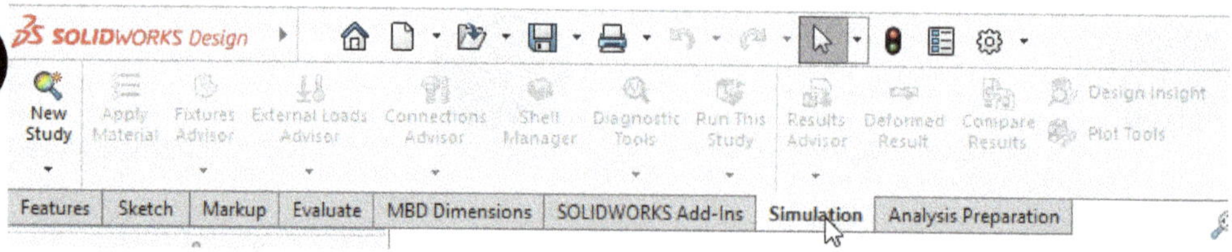

If the **Simulation** tab is not available in the CommandManager, click on the **SOLIDWORKS Add-Ins** tab in the CommandManager. The tools in the **SOLIDWORKS Add-Ins CommandManager** appear. Next, click on the **SOLIDWORKS Simulation** tool, see Figure 2.5. The **Simulation** tab gets added to the CommandManager. Alternatively, click on **Tools > Add-Ins** in the SOLIDWORKS Design Menus to invoke the **Add-Ins** dialog box and then select the check boxes on the left and right of the **SOLIDWORKS Simulation** option in the dialog box. Next, click **OK**.

2.5

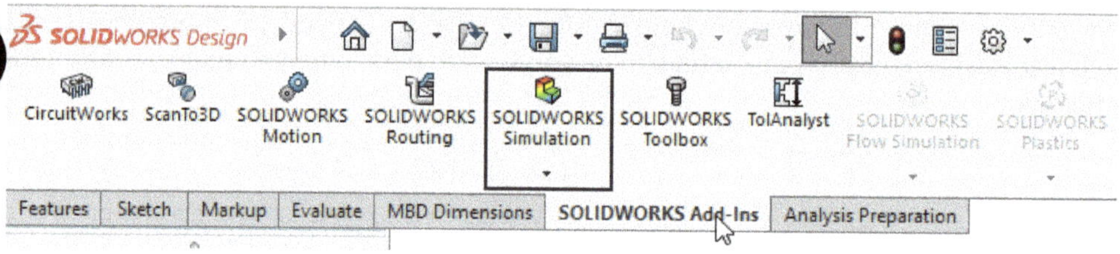

Initially, most of the tools in the **Simulation CommandManager** are not enabled, refer to Figure 2.4. All these tools will get enabled only after defining the type of analysis to be performed. To define the type of analysis, click on the **New Study** tool in the **Simulation CommandManager**, see Figure 2.6. The **Study PropertyManager** appears on the left of the graphics area, see Figure 2.7.

2.6

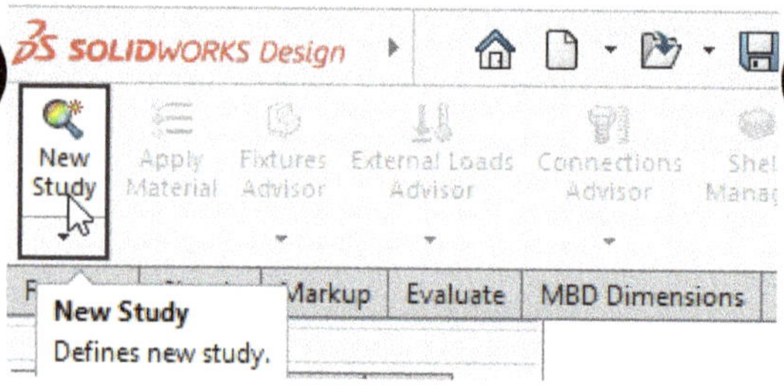

2.7

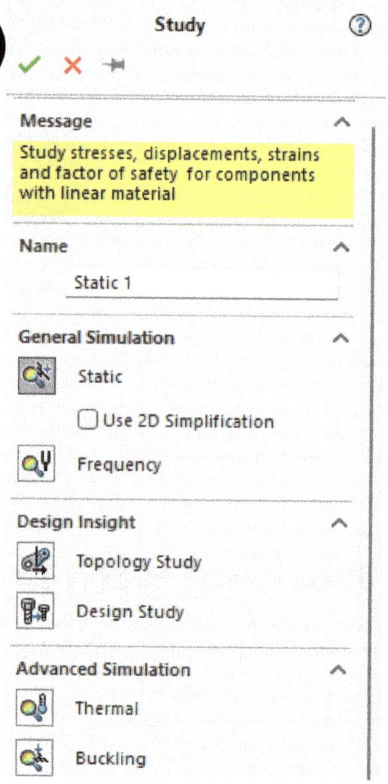

Note: Before you start any analysis in SOLIDWORKS Simulation, you need to ensure that the geometry to be analyzed is available in the graphics area. If the geometry is not available then on clicking the **New Study** tool, the **Simulation** window appears which informs you that there is no geometry for simulation to analyze, see Figure 2.8. Click on the **OK** button in this window and then create or import a geometry to be analyzed.

2.8

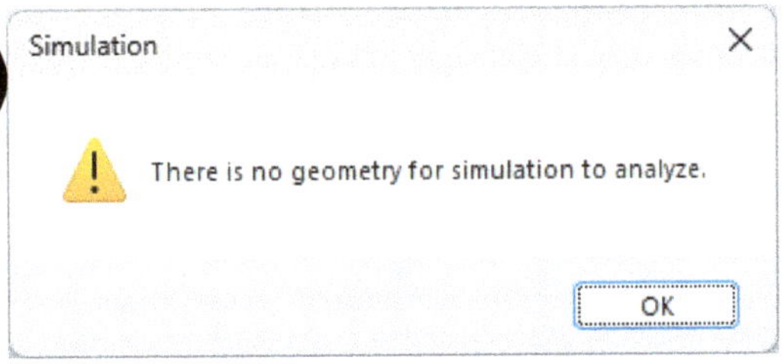

In the **Study PropertyManager**, you can select the type of analysis to be performed. By default, the **Static** button is activated in the **General Simulation** rollout of the PropertyManager, refer to Figure 2.7. This button is used to perform the linear static analysis. By using this PropertyManager, you can choose the required type of the analysis to be performed. In this chapter, you will learn about linear static analysis. Therefore, ensure that the **Static** button is activated in the PropertyManager. Next, specify the name of the analysis in the **Name** field of the PropertyManager and then click on the green tick-mark ✓ button. The initial screen of SOLIDWORKS Simulation appears on starting the linear static analysis, see Figure 2.9.

2.9

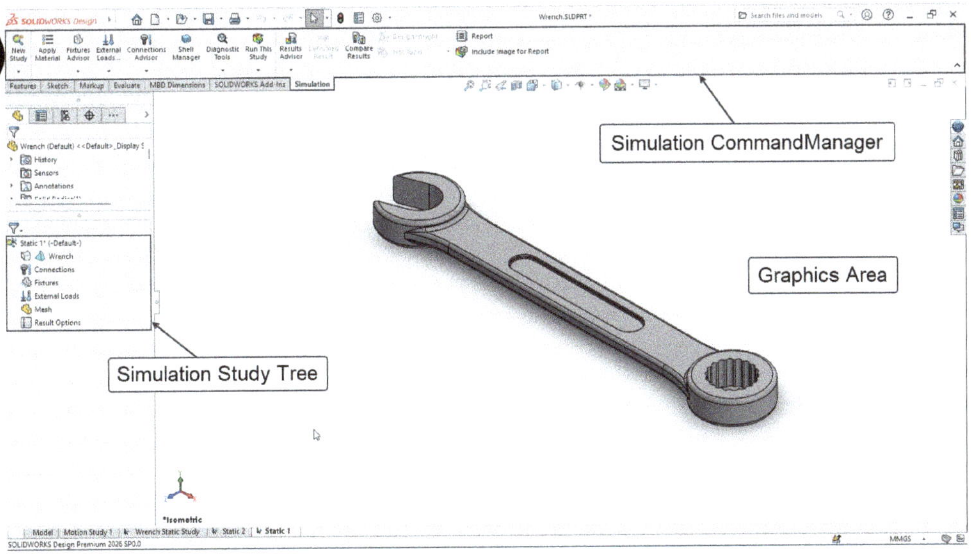

It is evident from the above figure that after selecting the type of analysis, all the tools of the **Simulation CommandManager** are enabled. Also, the Simulation Study Tree appears on the left of the graphics area, see Figure 2.9. The Simulation Study Tree keeps a record of the analysis data used and displays the results.

Now that the analysis type has been defined, the next step is to set up the analysis units in SOLIDWORKS Simulation. This is essential before proceeding with defining material properties, applying boundary conditions (fixtures and loads), and generating the mesh to ensure all inputs are in the correct units, preventing errors and ensuring reliable simulation results.

Defining Analysis Units

SOLIDWORKS Simulation allows you to define analysis units as per your requirement. To do this, click on **Simulation > Options** in the SOLIDWORKS Design Menus, see Figure 2.10. The **System Options** dialog box appears.

2.10

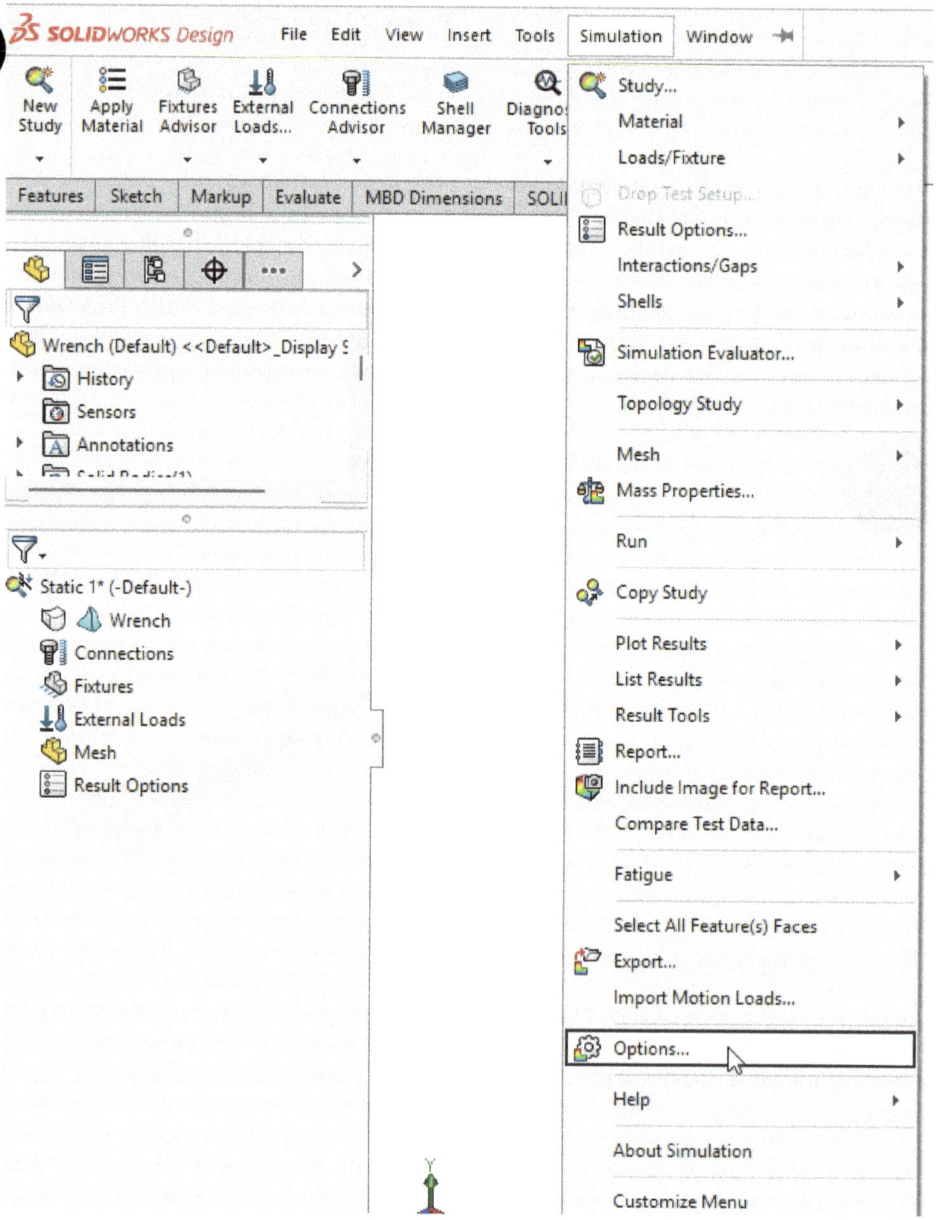

In the **System Options** dialog box, click on the **Default Options** tab. The name of the dialog box changes to **Default Options**, see Figure 2.11. Next, click on the **Units** option in the **Default Options** dialog box. The options related to defining units appear on the right side of the dialog box, see Figure 2.11. Now, you can select the required predefined standard unit system: **SI (MKS)**, **English (IPS)**, or **Metric (G)** in the **Unit system** area of the dialog box. For example, to set the metric unit system, click on the **Metric (G)** radio button. By default, in the metric unit system, the length is measured in centimeters, temperature is measured in celsius, angular velocity is measured in hertz, and pressure/stress is calculated in kgf/cm^2.

2.11

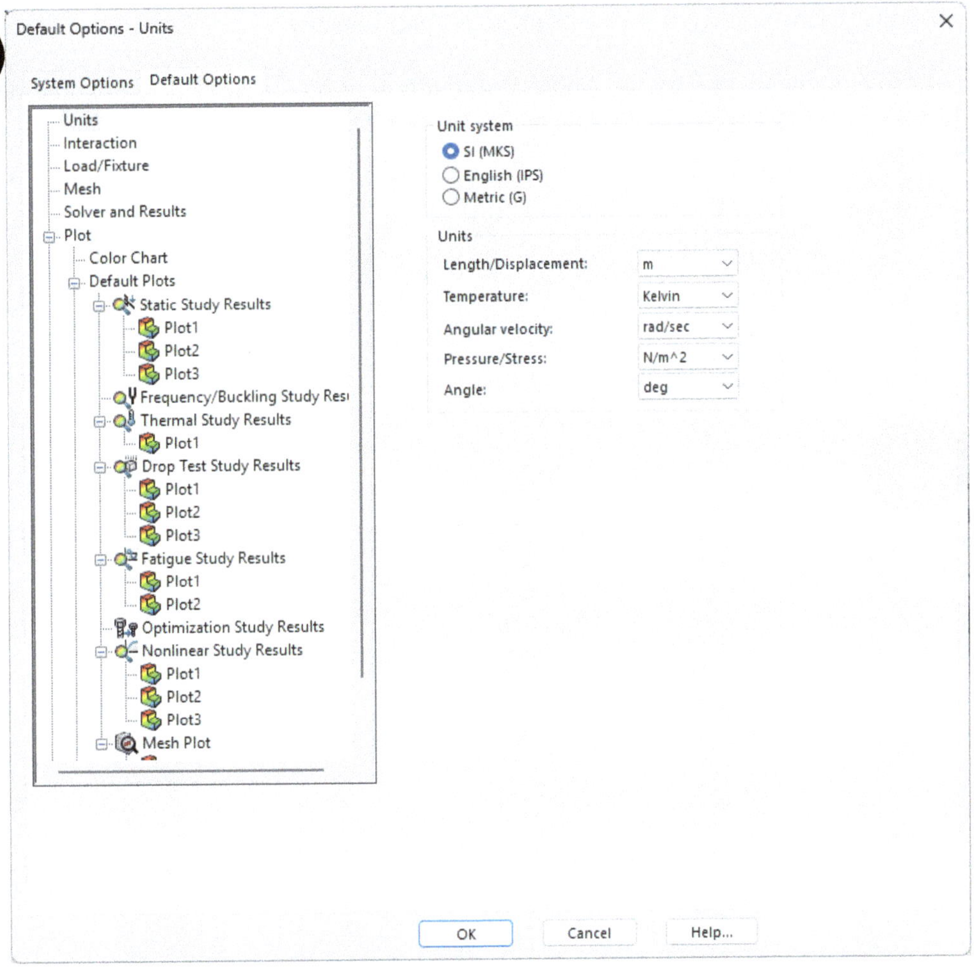

You can also customize the units of the predefined unit systems by using the drop-down lists available in the **Units** area of the dialog box. After defining the analysis units in the dialog box, click on the **OK** button.

Assigning Material Properties

SOLIDWORKS Simulation is provided with the **SOLIDWORKS Materials** library which contains various types of standard materials. In the library, the different sets of materials are arranged in different categories. For example, the various types of steel materials are available in the Steel category and the various types of iron materials are available in the Iron category. You can assign a required standard material to the model by using the **SOLIDWORKS Materials** library. On assigning a material to a model, all its material properties such as elastic modulus, density, tensile strength, and yield strength get assigned to the model and define its physical characteristics.

To assign a material, click on the **Apply Material** tool of the **Simulation CommandManager**, see Figure 2.12. The **Material** dialog box appears, see Figure 2.13.

2.12

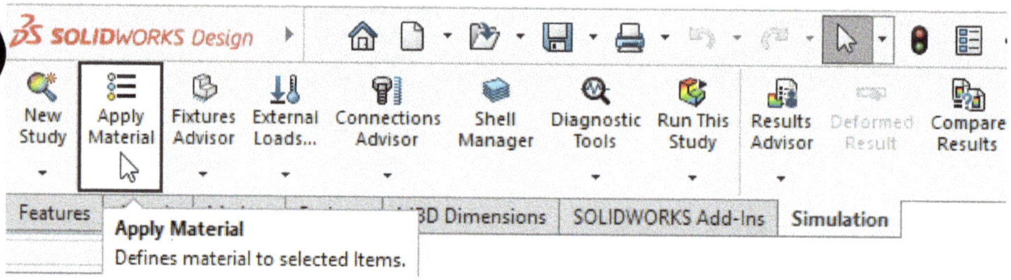

2.13

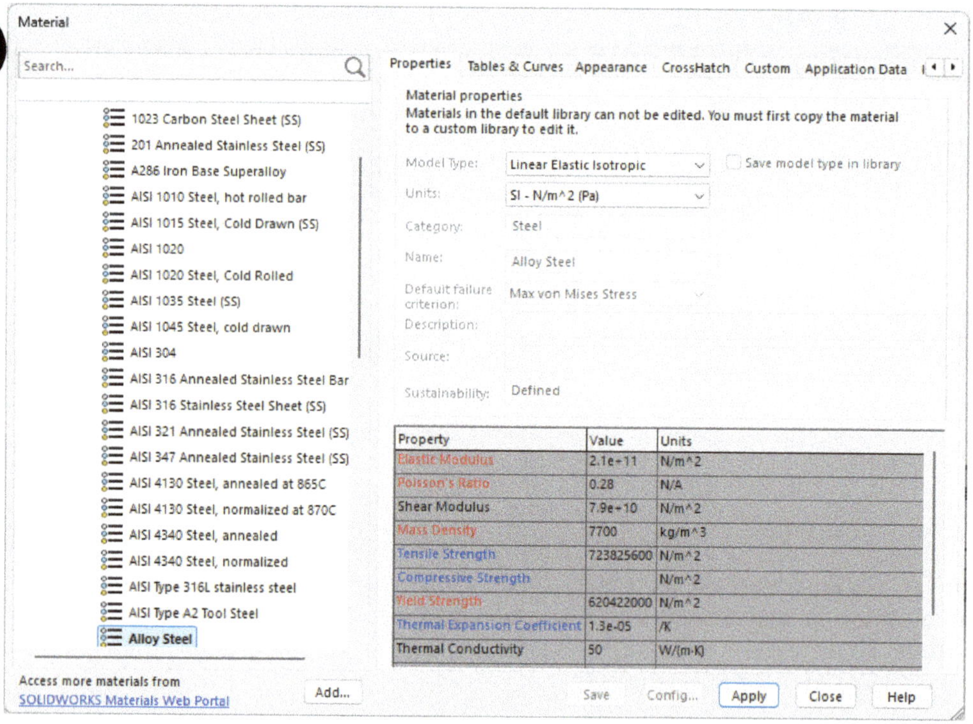

Alternatively, to invoke the **Material** dialog box, right-click on the *name of the model* in the Simulation Study Tree. A shortcut menu appears, see Figure 2.14. In this shortcut menu, click on the **Apply/Edit Material** tool.

2.14

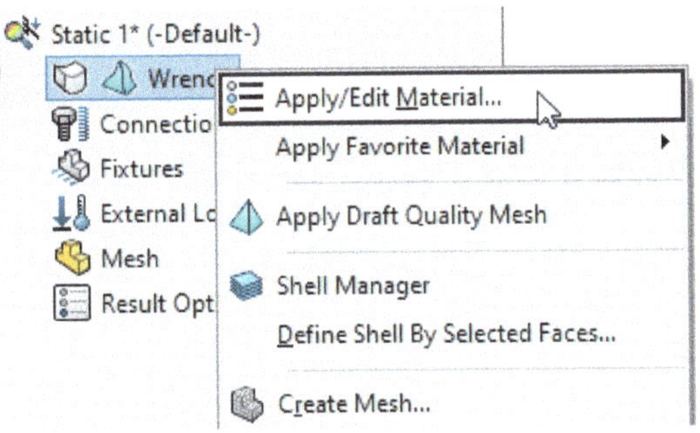

In the **Material** dialog box, the **SOLIDWORKS Materials** library appears on the left. Expand it by clicking on the > sign available in front of it, if not expanded by default. On expanding the **SOLIDWORKS Materials** library, all the available material categories such as Steel, Iron, and Aluminum Alloys appear. Next, expand the required material category by clicking on the > sign available in front of it to display the list of materials available in it. Figure 2.15 shows the expanded view of Steel material category.

2.15

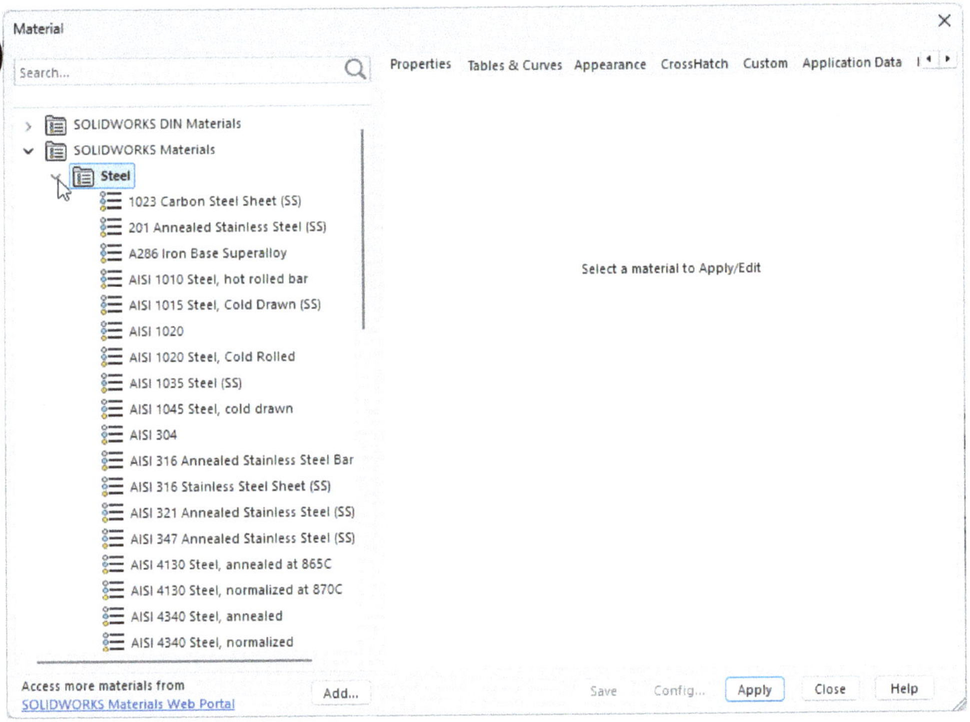

In the expanded material category, click on the required material to assign it to the model. The material properties of the selected material appear on the right panel of the dialog box, see Figure 2.16. Note that the material properties are read-only. As a result, you can not edit them. After selecting the required material, click on the **Apply** button and then the **Close** button to close the dialog box. The material properties of the selected material get assigned to the model and the material name appears next to the model name in the Simulation Study Tree, see Figure 2.17.

Tip: You can also search the material to be assigned by entering its name in the **Search** box that is available at the top left corner of the **Material** dialog box.

2.16

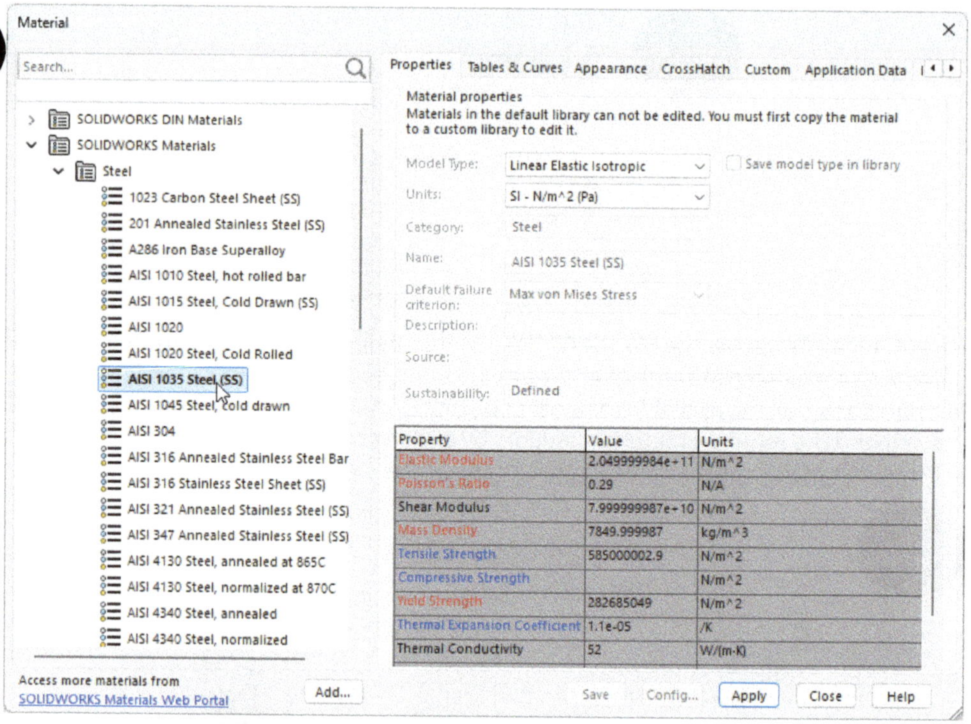

2.17

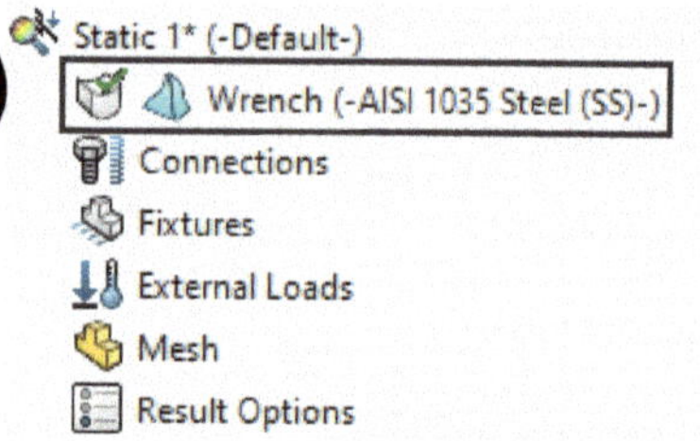

As discussed, the materials available in the **SOLIDWORKS Materials** library are read only and you cannot edit or modify their material properties. However, by using the **Custom Materials** library of the **Material** dialog box, you can create custom materials and edit the properties of the existing materials. In the **Custom Materials** library, you can create a new material category and then create new custom materials in it. In addition to the default material libraries such as **SOLIDWORKS Materials** and **Custom Materials**, you can also create new material libraries and store customized materials in it. The methods for creating a new material library, a new material category, and a custom material are discussed next.

Creating New Material Library, Category, and Material

To create a new material library in the **Material** dialog box, click on an existing material library and then right-click. A shortcut menu appears, see Figure 2.18. In the shortcut menu, click on the **New Library** option. The **Save As** dialog box appears. In this dialog box, enter the name of the material database for the material library in the **File name** field and then click on the **Save** button. The material database of the specified name is saved and the material library gets added to the **Material** dialog box, see Figure 2.19. In this figure, the **CADArtifex_Materials** library is added to the **Material** dialog box. After adding a material library, you can add material categories and customized materials. The methods for adding material categories and customized materials are discussed next.

2.18

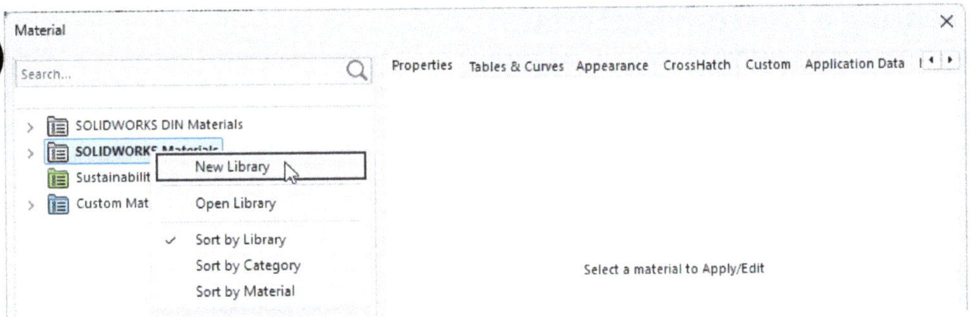

2.19

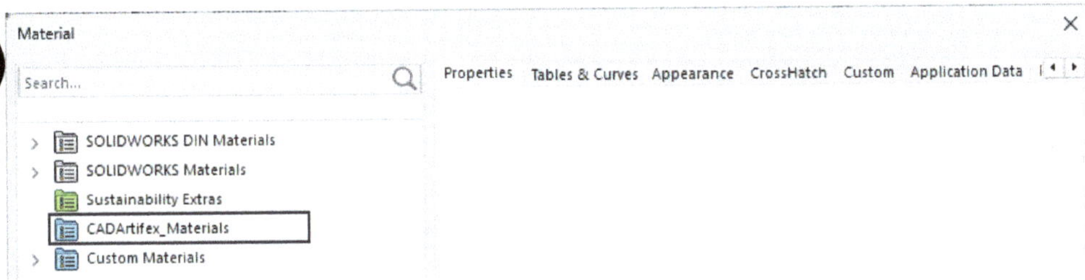

Creating a New Material Category

In SOLIDWORKS Simulation, you can create a material category in a user-defined material library or the **Custom Materials** library. To create a material category, right-click on a material library (user-defined or **Custom Materials**). A shortcut menu appears, see Figure 2.20. In this shortcut menu, click on the **New Category** option. A new category is created in the selected material library and its default name *New Category* appears in an edit field. You can edit or change the default name of the newly created material category and then click anywhere in the dialog box. Figure 2.21 shows the **Material** dialog box with the **Steel MFG** material category created in the **CADArtifex_Materials** library. Similarly, you can create multiple material categories. After creating a material category, you can create custom materials in it. The method for creating custom materials is discussed next.

2.20

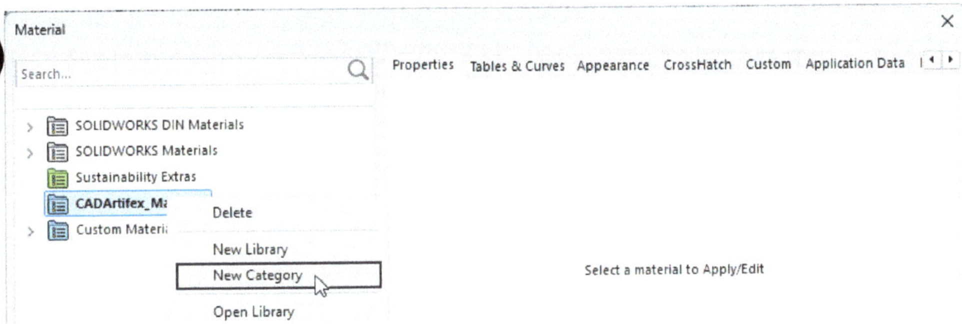

2.21

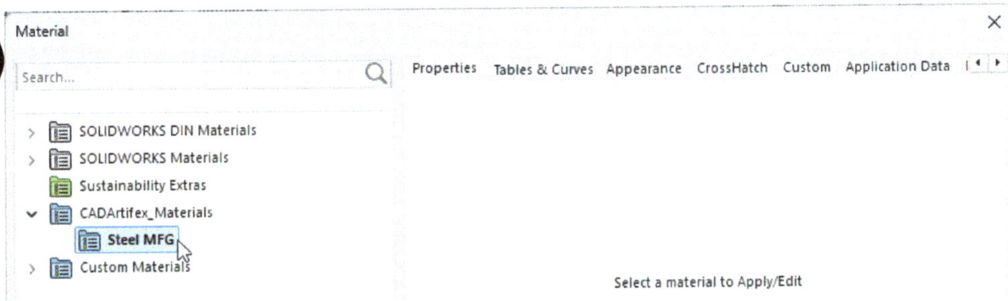

Creating a Custom Material

To create a new custom material, right-click on a material category. A shortcut menu appears, see Figure 2.22. In this shortcut menu, click on the **New Material** option. The new material is added in the selected material category and its default name *Default* appears in an edit field. You can edit or change the default name of the newly added material and then click anywhere in the dialog box. The default material properties of the newly added material appear on the lower right panel of the dialog box in the **Properties** tab, see Figure 2.23.

2.22

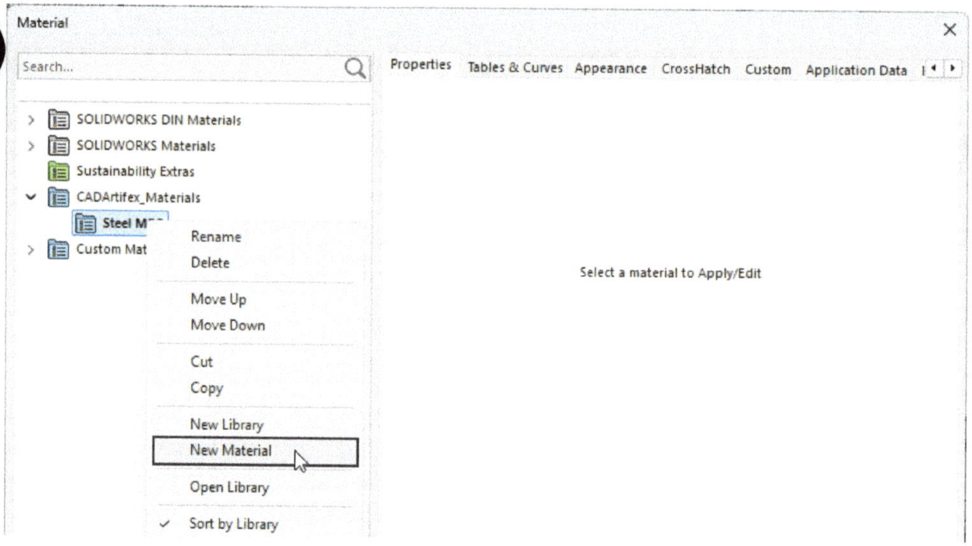

2.23

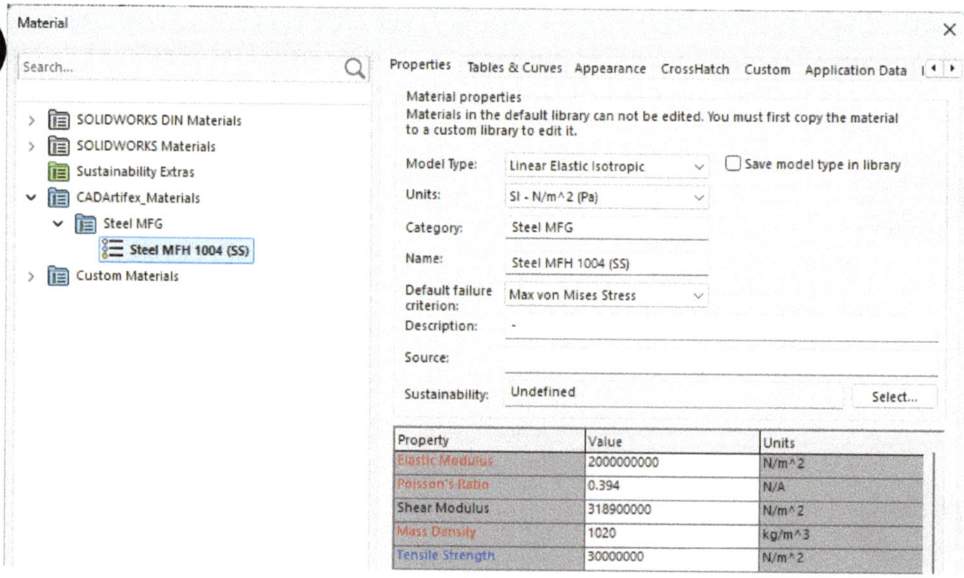

Note: Material properties highlighted in red indicate mandatory inputs that must be specified, while those highlighted in blue are optional. The necessity of these properties depends on the currently active analysis study and the selected material type.

By using the options in the right panel of the dialog box, you can specify material properties of the selected material such as elastic modulus, Poisson's ratio, density, and yield strength, as required. In addition to specifying material properties, you can also define other properties such as type of model, units for material properties, and creep effect by using the options available on the upper right panel of the dialog box, see Figure 2.23. The options available in the **Properties** tab of the **Material** dialog box are discussed later in this chapter. After specifying the required material properties for the newly added material, click on the **Apply** button. The material with specified material properties is created in the selected material category. Similarly, you can create multiple materials in a material category.

Editing Properties of a Standard Material

As discussed, the standard materials available in the **SOLIDWORKS Materials** library are read-only materials and you cannot edit their material properties. However, you can copy a standard material from the **SOLIDWORKS Materials** library and paste it in a custom material library to make the necessary changes in its material properties.

To do this, select a standard material in the **SOLIDWORKS Materials** library and then right-click to display the shortcut menu. Next, click on the **Copy** option in the shortcut menu. The selected material is copied. Now, expand a custom material library and then select a category to paste the copied material. Next, right-click to display the shortcut menu and then click on the **Paste** option. The copied material is added in the selected material category of the custom material library. Now, you can edit its material properties such as elastic modulus, Poisson's ratio, density, and yield strength using the options in the right panel of the **Properties** tab in the dialog box. Some of the options of the **Properties** tab in the **Material** dialog box are discussed next.

Model Type

The **Model Type** drop-down list of the **Properties** tab is used to select the type of material such as linear elastic isotropic, linear elastic orthotropic, non-linear elastic, or plasticity - von mises.

Note that the availability of material types in this drop-down list depends upon the type of analysis being performed. Figure 2.24 shows the **Model Type** drop-down list for the linear static analysis and Figure 2.25 shows the **Model Type** drop-down list for the non-linear static analysis.

2.24

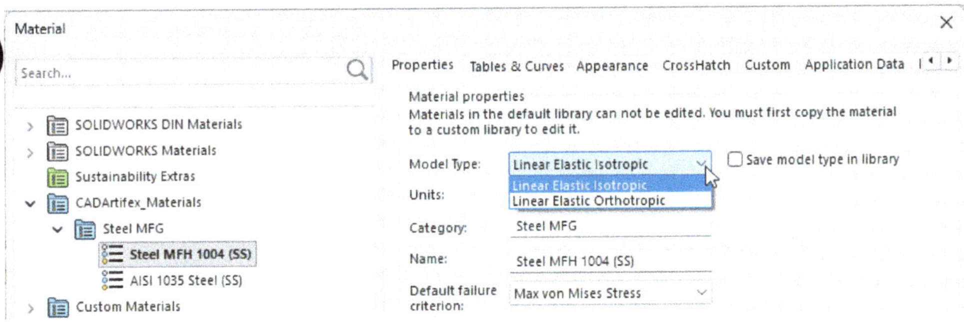

2.25

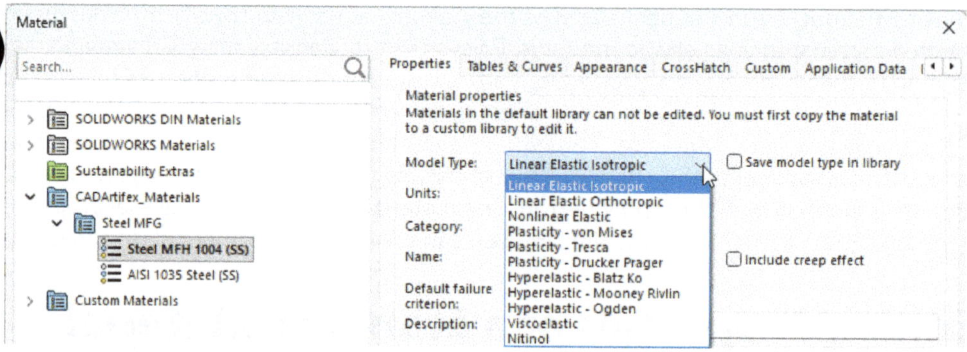

Save model type in library

On selecting the **Save model type in library** check box in the dialog box, the type of material selected in the **Model Type** drop-down list for the custom material will be saved in the material database such that the next time you apply this custom material to a different study, the same model type will be selected by default in the **Model Type** drop-down list of the dialog box.

Units

The **Units** drop-down list is used for selecting a unit system such as **SI - N/m^2 (Pa)**, **English (IPS)**, or **Metric (MKS)** for defining the values of the material properties, see Figure 2.26.

2.26

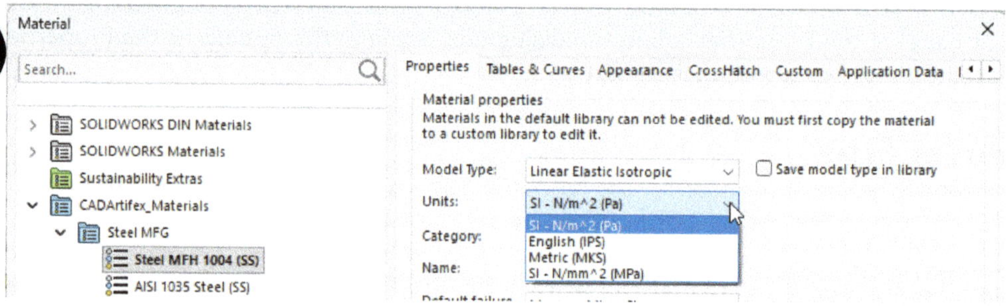

Include Creep Effect

Creep is the plastic deformation of a material when the material is subjected to stress which is below the yield strength of the material. In SOLIDWORKS Simulation, you can include the effect of creep in the material by selecting the **Include creep effect** check box, refer to Figure 2.25. Note that this check box is available while performing the non-linear analysis for Linear Elastic Isotropic, Non-linear Elastic, Plasticity - von Mises, Plasticity - Tresca, Plasticity - Drucker Prager, Hyperelastic - Blatz Ko, Hyperelastic - Mooney Rivlin, or Hyperelastic - Orgden material types. You will learn about performing non-linear analysis in later chapters.

Reference Geometry

The **Reference Geometry** field is available only when the **Linear Elastic Orthotropic** material type is selected in the **Model Type** drop-down list. This field is used for defining orthogonal directions of the orthotropic material by selecting a reference geometry. Note that the properties of an orthotropic material are not constant and vary in the orthogonal directions. As a result, you need to select a reference geometry to define the orthogonal directions. You can select a plane, an axis, or a coordinate system as the reference geometry to define the orthogonal directions of an orthotropic material.

Category

The **Category** field displays the name of the category of the selected material. You can update or rename the category name by entering a new name in this field. Note that the new name of the category entered in this field will be applied when you click on the **Apply** button in the **Material** dialog box.

Name

The **Name** field displays the name of the selected material. You can enter a new name for the material in this field.

Default failure criterion

The **Default failure criterion** drop-down list is used to set the default failure criterion factor for computing the factor of safety. Note that the selected failure criterion factor is used for computing the factor of safety only when you compute the factor of safety by using the **Automatic** option. You will learn more about the computing factor of safety in later chapters.

Description

The **Description** field is used to add description or comment about the material. You can enter a description or comment containing upto 256 characters in this field.

Source

The **Source** field is used to specify the source of reference of the custom material.

Properties table

The **Properties** table of the **Material** dialog box is used to specify the properties of the material such as elastic modulus, Poisson ratio, density, and yield strength. You can specify the physical properties of the material in the respective fields of the **Properties** table, see Figure 2.27.

2.27

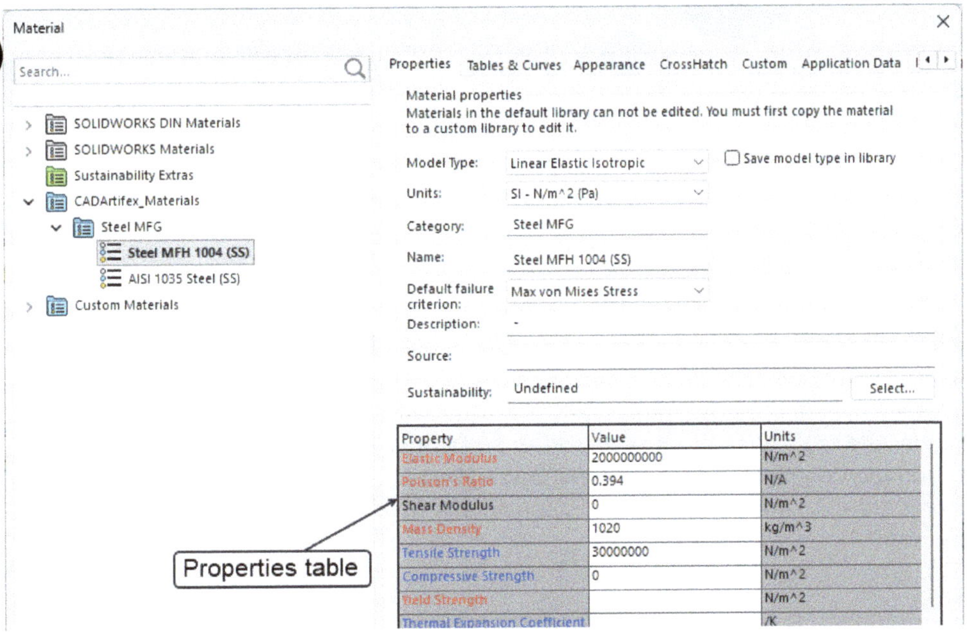

Note that the material properties highlighted in red indicate that they are mandatory to be specified and the material properties in blue are optional based on the currently active analysis study and the material type.

Deleting Material Library, Category, and Material

You can delete a custom material library, a material category, or a material using the **Material** dialog box. To delete a custom material library, select the material library in the **Material** dialog box and then right-click. A shortcut menu appears, see Figure 2.28. In this shortcut menu, click on the **Delete** option. The **SOLIDWORKS** message window appears, which informs that you are about to delete *'name of the material library'* and its contents, see Figure 2.29. Click on the **Yes** button in the **SOLIDWORKS** message window to confirm the action of deleting the selected material library, after which it is no longer available in the dialog box.

2.28

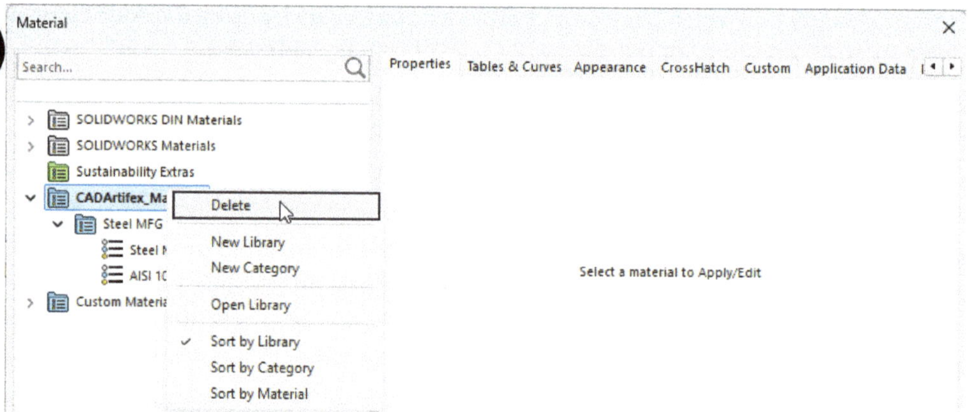

2.29

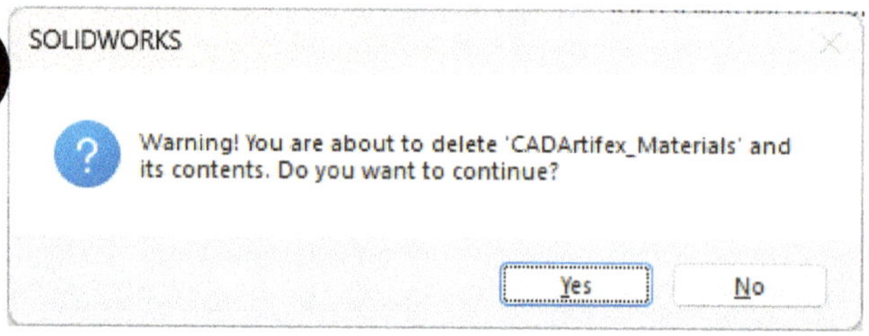

Similarly, you can delete a custom material category and a material. Note that you cannot delete the SOLIDWORKS **Materials** library or its categories and materials.

Defining Boundary Conditions

Defining boundary conditions is one of the most important steps in the pre-processing phase of an analysis. Boundary conditions represent the effect of surrounding environment on the model which includes the application of external load and restraints. In SOLIDWORKS Simulation, you can define the boundary conditions by applying fixtures and external load such as force, torque, and pressure. The fixtures are also known as restraints or constraints which are used to remove the degrees of freedom of a model.

Depending upon the application of the model in real-world conditions, you need to apply fixtures and load to it. For example, in the case of the cantilever beam, one end is fixed with the wall while the other end is free and an external force of 100 N is acting on its top face in the real conditions, see Figure 2.30. In such a case, you need to apply a fix restraint to the fixed end and a 100 N force on the top face of the cantilever beam in SOLIDWORKS Simulation, see Figure 2.31.

2.30

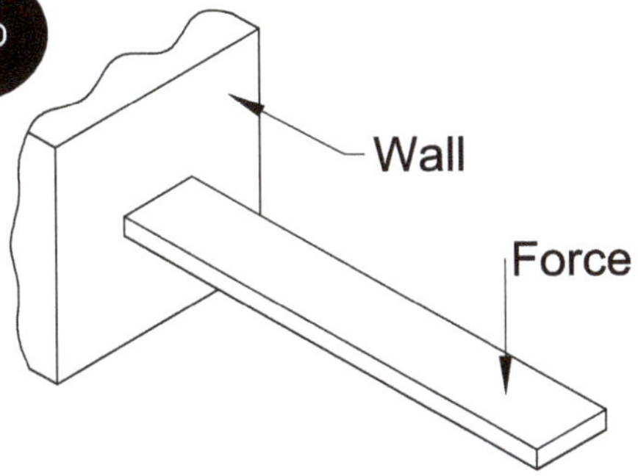

2.31

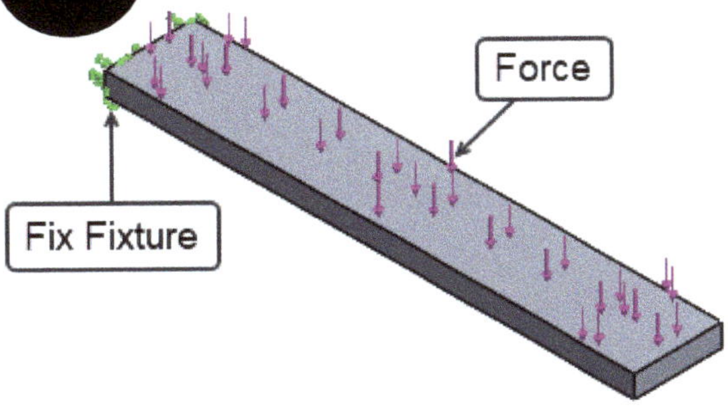

SOLIDWORKS Simulation provides you with various types of fixtures and external load in order to satisfy the real-world conditions of a model.

Applying Fixtures/Restraints

Fixtures are also known as restraints and constraints, and act as rigid support. By applying fixtures, you can remove the required degrees of freedom of the model. SOLIDWORKS Simulation provides you with two type of fixtures: **Standard** and **Advanced**. Both these types of fixtures are discussed next.

Applying Standard Fixtures

Standard fixtures include Fixed Geometry, Roller/Slider, Fixed Hinge, and Immovable (No translation) fixtures. Standard fixtures are available in the **Fixtures** flyout of the **Simulation CommandManager**, see Figure 2.32. Alternatively, to access the Standard fixtures, right-click on the **Fixtures** option in the Simulation Study Tree and then click on the required Standard fixture in the shortcut menu that appears, see Figure 2.33. The Standard fixtures are discussed next.

2.32

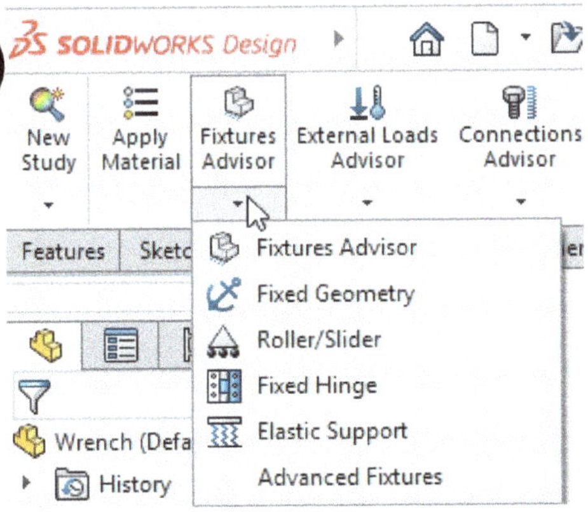

2.33

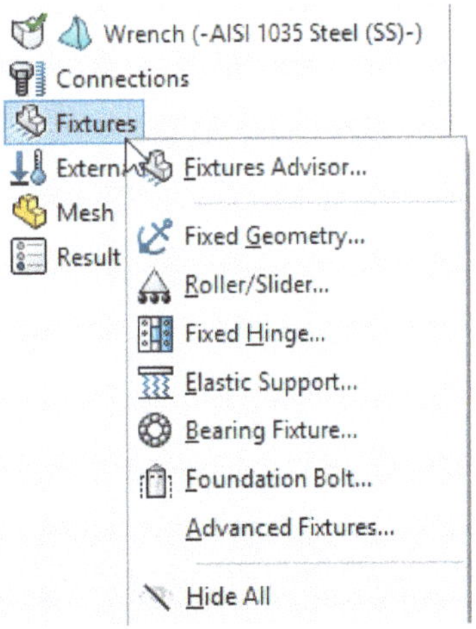

Fixed Geometry Fixture

The Fixed Geometry fixture is used to fix or remove all translational and rotational degrees of freedom of a solid model, see Figure 2.34. You can apply the Fixed Geometry fixture to vertices, edges, and faces of a model.

2.34

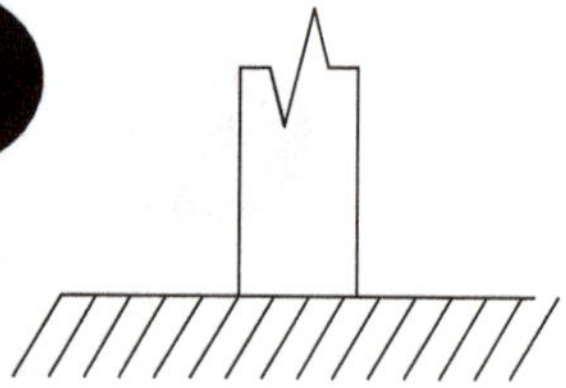

Fixed Support
(No translational or rotational movements)

Note that the effect of the Fixed Geometry fixture depends on the type of geometry selected. It is important to understand it to make a stable model for analysis. For example, if the Fixed Geometry fixture is applied to a vertex, the model can still rotate about that fixed vertex, meaning not all degrees of freedom are fully constrained. Similarly, fixing an edge of a 3D model allows the model to rotate around that edge. However, when a face is fixed, all degrees of freedom are completely constrained, preventing both rotation and translation in any direction.

To apply the Fixed Geometry fixture, invoke the **Fixture** flyout by clicking on the arrow at the bottom of the **Fixtures Advisor** tool in the **Simulation CommandManager** and then click on the **Fixed Geometry** tool, see Figure 2.35. The **Fixture PropertyManager** appears, see Figure 2.36.

2.35

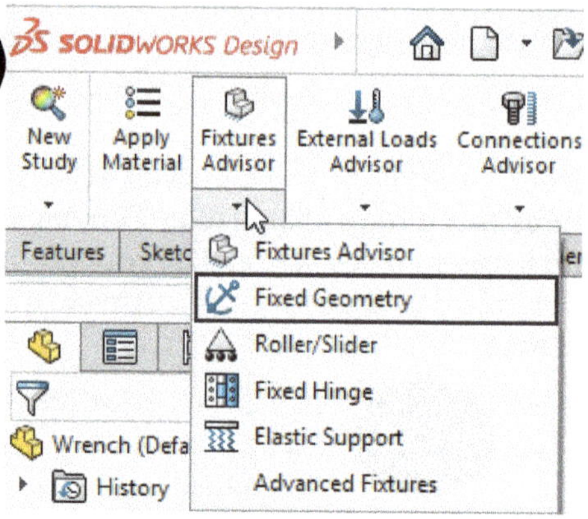

2.36

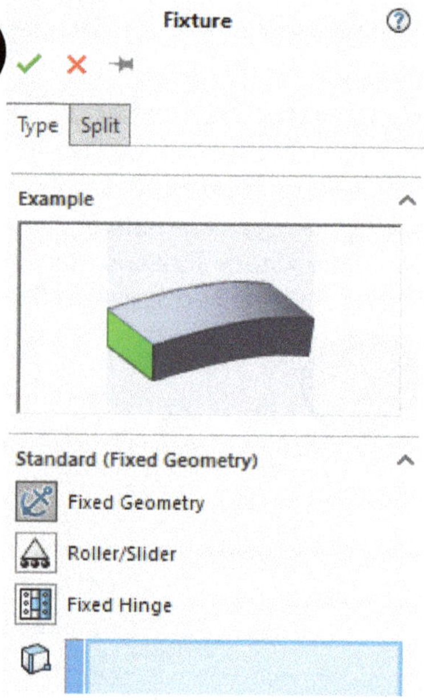

Select the required geometry of the model such as a face, an edge, or a vertex to apply the Fixed Geometry fixture. You can select a single or multiple geometries to apply the fixture. The symbol of the Fixed Geometry fixture appears on the selected geometry in the graphics area, see Figure 2.37. Also, the name of the selected geometry appears in the **Faces, Edges, Vertices for Fixture** field of the **Fixture PropertyManager**. Next, click on the green tick-mark button in the PropertyManager. The Fixed Geometry fixture is applied to the selected geometry of the model.

2.37

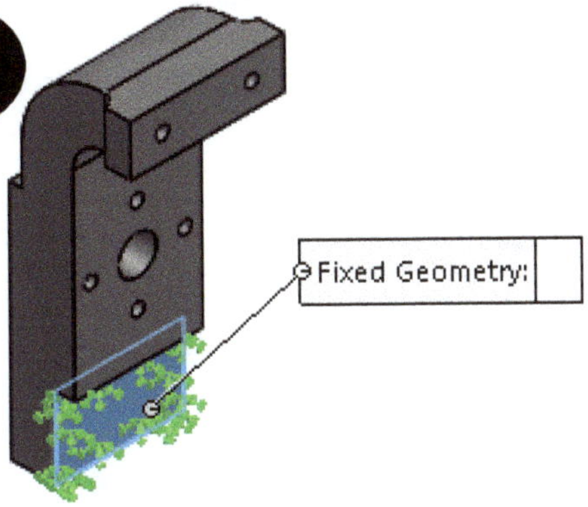

Roller/Slider Fixture

The Roller/Slider fixture is used to apply a restraint to a planar face such that its movement in the direction normal to the planar face gets restricted and it allows movement within the plane of the face, see Figure 2.38.

To apply the Roller/Slider fixture, invoke the **Fixture** flyout in the **Simulation CommandManager** and then click on the **Roller/Slider** tool. The **Fixture PropertyManager** appears, see Figure 2.39.

2.38

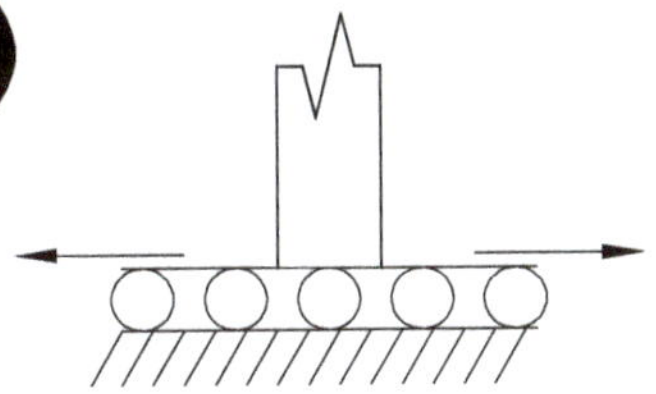

Roller/Slider Fixture

(Moves freely within the plane of face and No movements in the direction normal to the planar face)

2.39

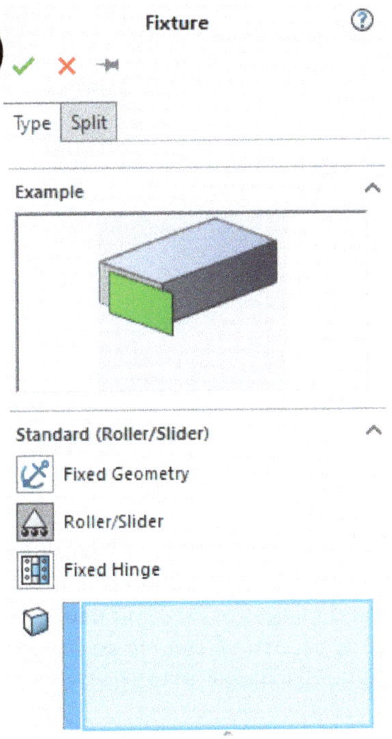

Select a planar face of the model to apply the **Roller/Slider** fixture. You can also select multiple planar faces to apply this fixture. After selecting a face, the symbol of Roller/Slider fixture appears on the selected face in the graphics area, see Figure 2.40. Also, the name of the selected face appears in the **Faces for Fixture** field of the PropertyManager. Next, click on the green tick-mark button in the PropertyManager. The Roller/Slider fixture is applied. The selected planar face can move freely within its plane of face and its movement along the direction normal to the planar face gets restricted.

2.40

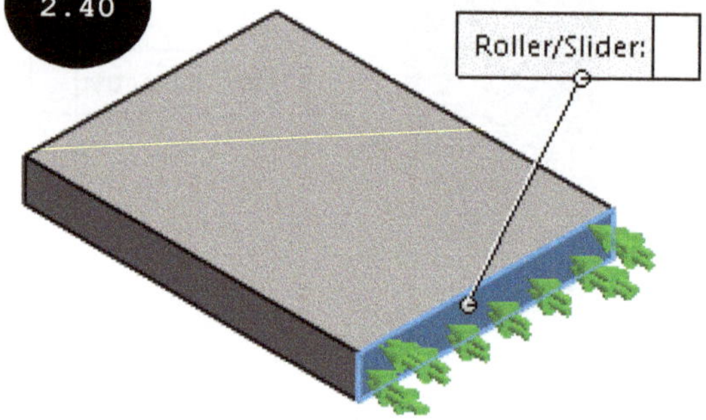

Fixed Hinge Fixture

The Fixed Hinge fixture is used to apply restraints to a cylindrical face such that it can only rotate about its axis of rotation. In other words, on applying the Fixed Hinge fixture to a cylindrical face, all degrees of freedom of the component get fixed except its rotational degree of freedom about the axis of the selected cylindrical face, see Figure 2.41.

2.41

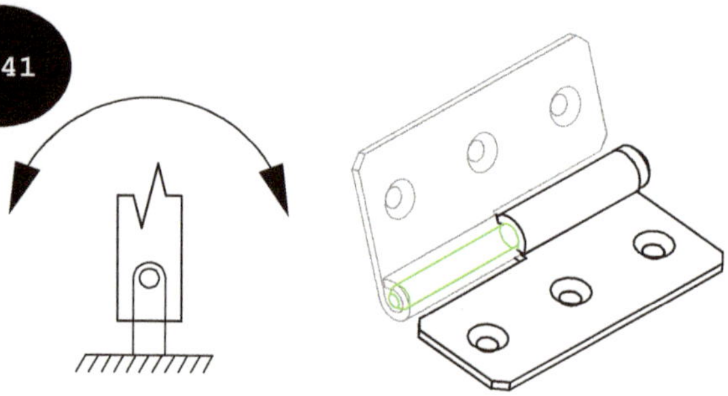

To apply the Fixed Hinge fixture, invoke the **Fixture** flyout and then click on the **Fixed Hinge** tool. The **Fixture PropertyManager** appears, see Figure 2.42. Select a cylindrical face of the model to apply the Fixed Hinge fixture. You can also select multiple cylindrical faces. After selecting a cylindrical face, a symbol of the Fixed Hinge fixture appears on it in the graphics area, see Figure 2.43. Next, click on the green tick-mark button in the PropertyManager. The Fixed Hinge fixture is applied.

2.42

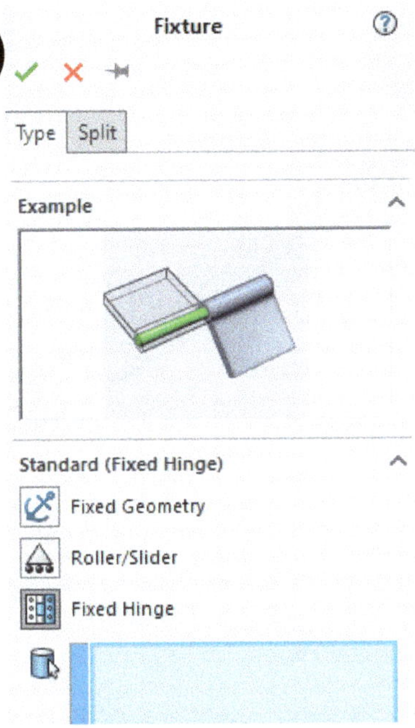

2.43

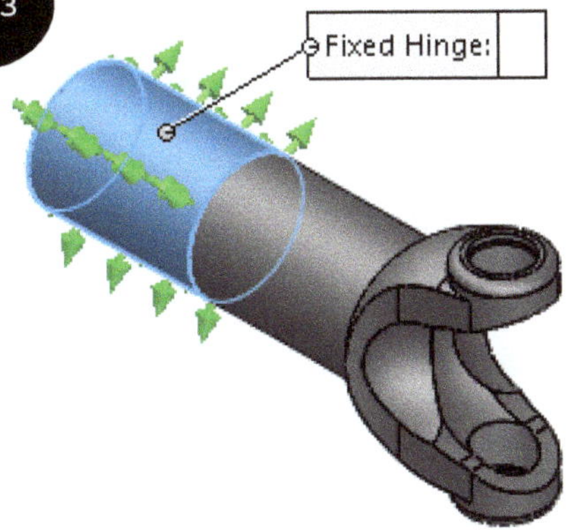

Immovable (No translation) Fixture

The Immovable (No translation) fixture is used to fix or remove all the translational degrees of freedom of a shell, beam, or truss geometry. You can apply the Immovable (No translation) fixture to vertices, edges, faces, and beam joints of a geometry. Note that this fixture is not applicable to 3D solid models.

To apply the Immovable (No translation) fixture, invoke the **Fixture** flyout in the **Simulation CommandManager** and then click on the **Fixed Geometry** tool. The **Fixture PropertyManager** appears.

In this PropertyManager, click on the **Immovable (No translation)** button, see Figure 2.44. Note that the **Immovable (No translation)** button is only available for a shell, beam, or truss geometry. Next, select faces, edges, vertices, or joints to apply the Immovable (No translation) fixture. A symbol of the Immovable (No translation) fixture appears on the selected geometry in the graphics area, see Figures 2.45 and 2.46. In Figure 2.45, the Immovable (No translation) fixture is applied on the edges of a shell geometry, and in Figure 2.46, the Immovable (No translation) fixture is applied on the joints of a beam geometry. You will learn more about shell, beam, and truss geometries later in this chapter. Next, click on the green tick-mark ✓ button in the PropertyManager. The **Immovable (No translation)** fixture is applied.

2.44

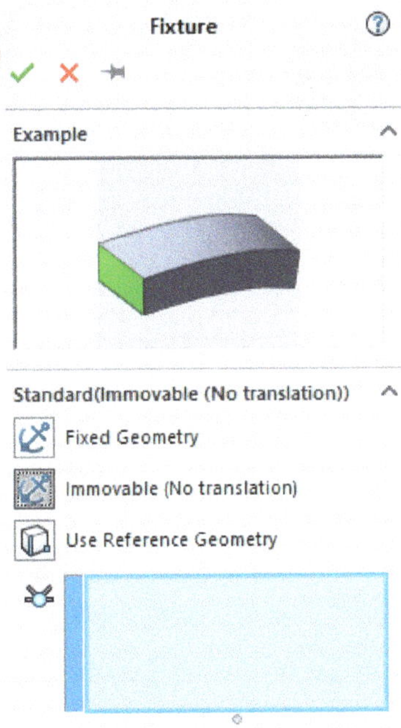

2.45

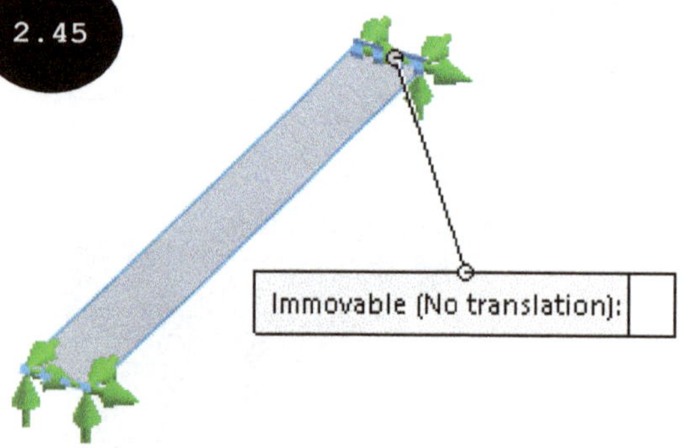

2.46

Applying Advanced Fixtures

In addition to the Standard fixtures such as **Fixed Geometry**, **Roller/Slider**, and **Fixed Hinge**, SOLIDWORKS Simulation also provides Advanced fixtures: Symmetry, Cyclic Symmetry, Use Reference Geometry, On Flat Faces, On Cylindrical Faces, and On Spherical Faces.

To access these advanced fixtures, invoke the **Fixtures** flyout in the **Simulation CommandManager** and then click on the **Advanced Fixtures** tool, see Figure 2.47. The **Fixture PropertyManager** appears with the expanded **Advanced** rollout, see Figure 2.48. Note that the name of the **Advanced** rollout depends upon the type of advanced fixture selected. For example, by default, the **Use Reference Geometry** button is selected in this rollout. As a result, the name of the **Advanced** rollout appears as **Advanced (Use Reference Geometry)**.

2.47

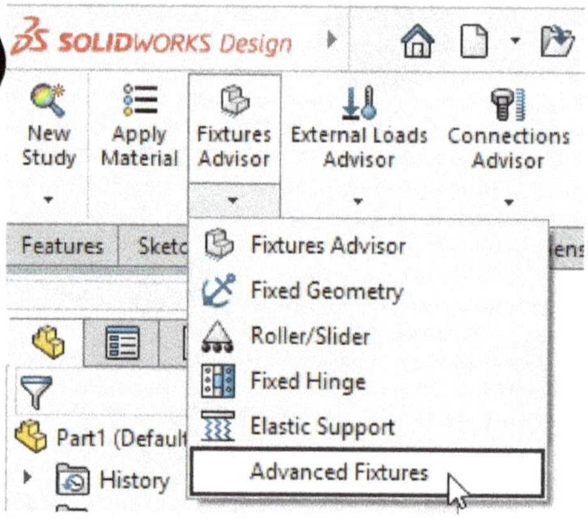

2.48

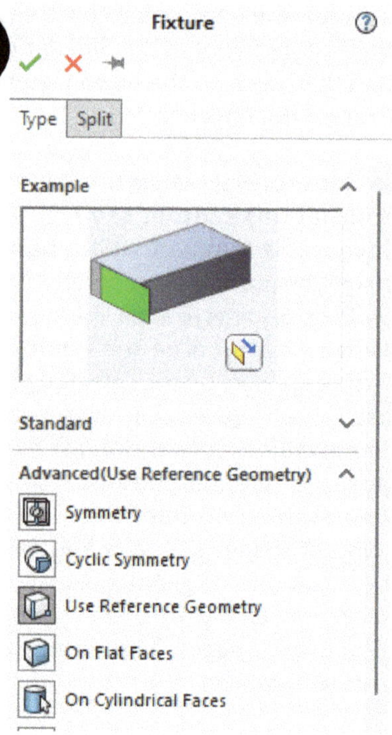

Alternatively, to access the Advanced fixtures, right-click on the **Fixtures** option in the Simulation Study Tree and then click on the **Advanced Fixtures** tool in the shortcut menu that appears. The advanced fixtures are discussed next.

Symmetry Fixture

The Symmetry fixture is used to analyze one half of the model which is symmetric about a symmetric plane and the results can be obtained for the complete model. Figure 2.49 shows a complete model and Figure 2.50 shows one half of the model that can be analyzed to obtain the results of the complete model. Note that because of the symmetry, you can analyze one half of the model instead of analyzing the complete model to reduce the computational time of the analysis and to obtain accurate results for the complete model. On applying the Symmetry fixture, the symmetric face of the model cannot move in its normal direction.

2.49

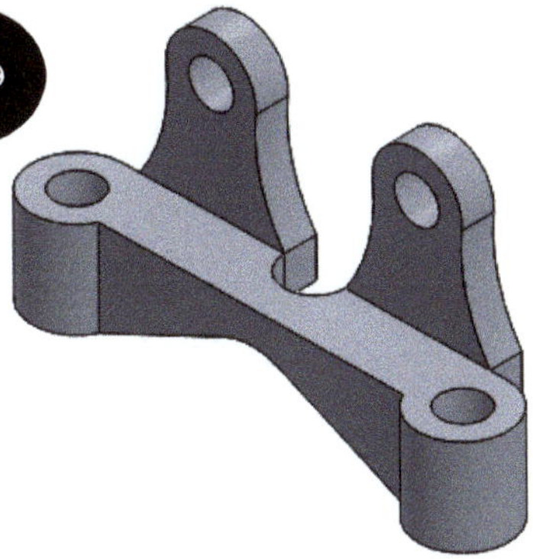

2.50

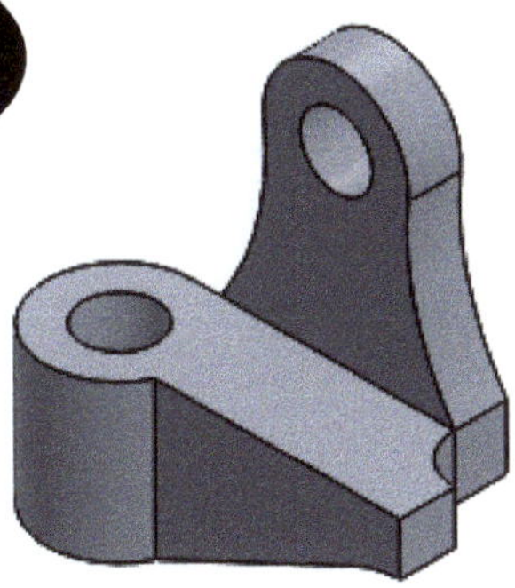

To apply the Symmetric fixture, click on the **Symmetry** button in the **Advanced** rollout of the **Fixture PropertyManager**. The **Planar Faces for Fixture** field becomes available in the PropertyManager, see Figure 2.51. This field is used for selecting symmetric faces of the model. Select a symmetric face of the model in the graphics area. A preview of the other symmetric half of the model appears in the graphics area and a symbol of the Symmetric fixture appears on the selected face, see Figure 2.52. Next, click on the green tick-mark button in the PropertyManager. The Symmetry fixture is applied.

2.51

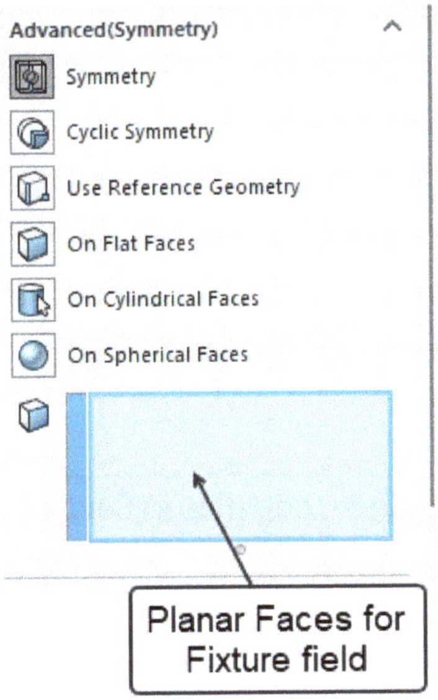

2.52

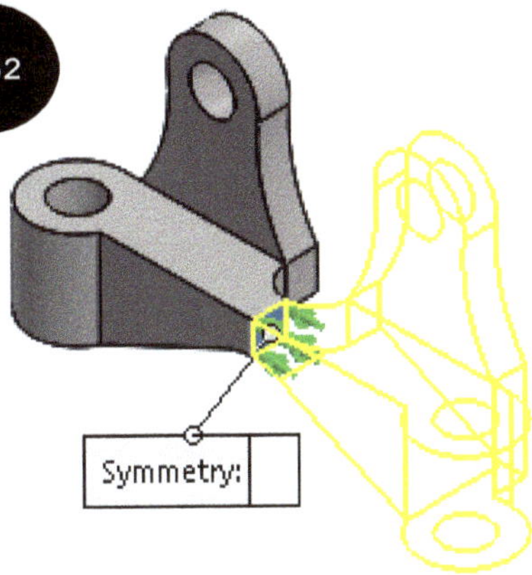

Cyclic Symmetry Fixture

The Cyclic Symmetry fixture is used to analyze a portion of a circular model having a 360-degrees angle and the results are obtained for the complete circular model. In the Cyclic Symmetry fixture, a portion of the circular model is considered to be repeated or patterned about the axis of revolution of the symmetry to form the complete model.

Figure 2.53 shows a circular model and Figure 2.54 shows a portion of the model that can be analyzed to obtain the results for the complete model. To analyze a portion of a circular model using the Cyclic Symmetry fixture, you need to select its cutting faces and the axis of revolution. Note that on applying the Cyclic Symmetry fixture, the cutting faces of the model cannot move in their normal direction.

2.53

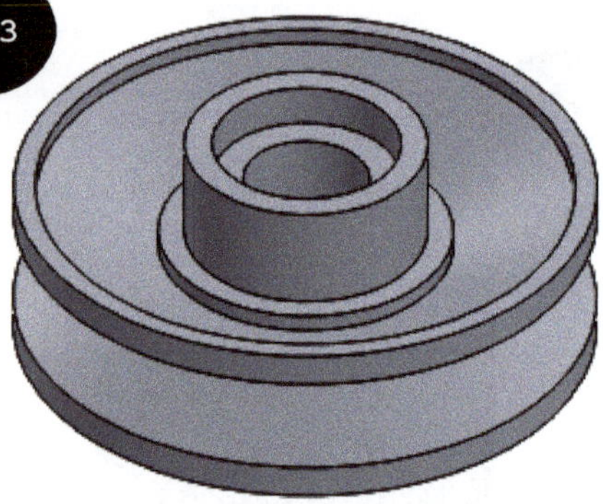

2.54

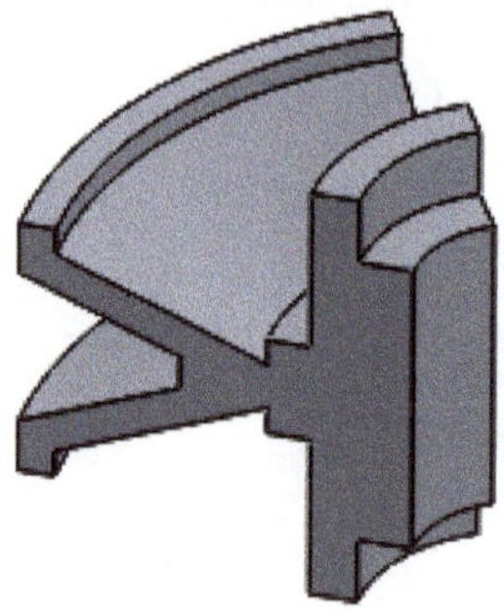

To apply the Cyclic Symmetry fixture, click on the **Cyclic Symmetry** button in the **Advanced** rollout of the **Fixture PropertyManager**. The **Selection (Face)** and **Axis** fields become available in the rollout, see Figure 2.55.

2.55

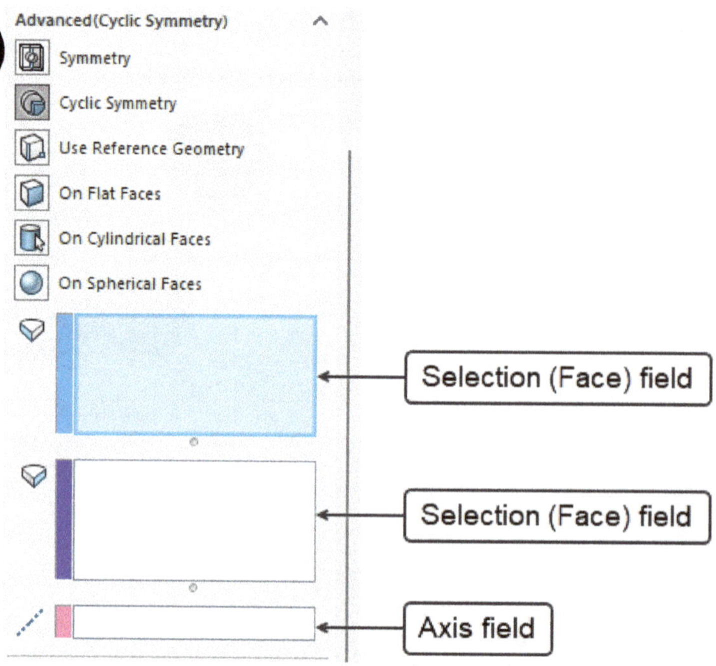

The **Selection (Face)** fields of the PropertyManager are used for selecting cutting faces of the circular model and the **Axis** field is used for selecting the axis of revolution of the model. By default, the first **Selection (Face)** field is activated in the PropertyManager. As a result, you are prompted to select the first cutting face. Select the first cutting face, see Figure 2.56. Next, click on the second **Selection (Face)** field in the **Advanced** rollout to activate it and then select the second cutting face, see Figure 2.56. Next, click on the **Axis** field in the **Advanced** rollout and then select the axis of revolution. A preview of the complete model appears by patterning the portion of the model around the axis of revolution, see Figure 2.57. Note that the axis of revolution must lie at the intersection of two selected cutting faces so that the portion of the model can be patterned around it to represent the complete model. Next, click on the green tick-mark button in the PropertyManager. The Cyclic Symmetry fixture is applied.

2.56

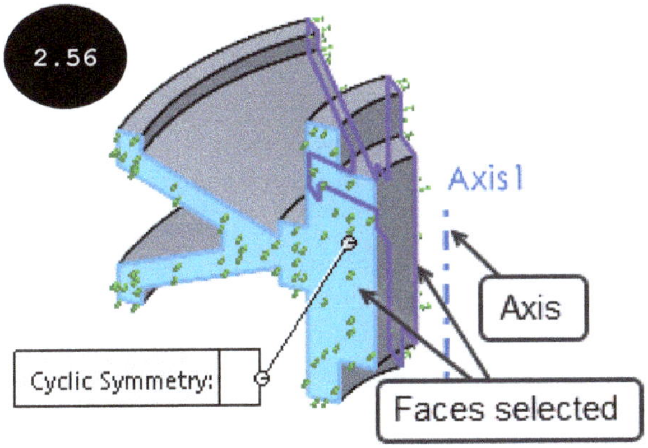

2.57

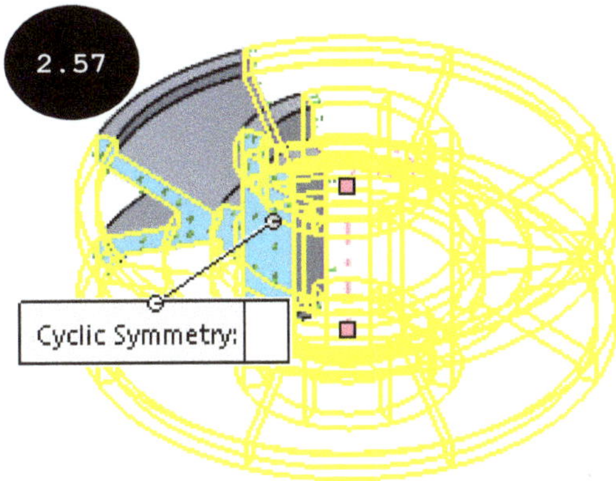

Use Reference Geometry Fixture

The Use Reference Geometry fixture is used for restricting degrees of freedom of faces (planar or curved), edges, and vertices of a solid model with respect to a reference geometry. You can select a plane, an axis, an edge, or a planar face as the reference geometry to restrict degrees of freedom of faces, edges, and vertices of a solid model.

Note that the number of degrees of freedom that can be restricted depends on the reference geometry selected. For example, if you select a plane or a planar face as the reference geometry then the translational degrees of freedom of faces, edges, or vertices of a model will be restricted in the X axis, Y axis, and in the direction normal to the plane or planar face selected as reference geometry.

If you select an edge as the reference geometry then the translational degrees of freedom in the direction of the selected edge will be restricted. Similarly, if you select an axis then the translational degrees of freedom in the radial, circumferential, and axial directions will be restricted.

Note that in case of the beam and shell, you can also restrict the rotational degrees of freedom using the Use Reference Geometry fixture. You will learn more about shell, beam, and truss geometries later in this chapter.

To apply the Use Reference Geometry fixture, click the **Use Reference Geometry** button in the **Advanced** rollout of the PropertyManager. This enables the **Faces, Edges, Vertices for Fixture** and **Face, Edge, Plane, Axis for Direction** fields in the **Advanced** rollout, see Figure 2.58. By default, the **Faces, Edges, Vertices for Fixture** field is activated, prompting you to select faces, edges, or vertices of the model.

2.58

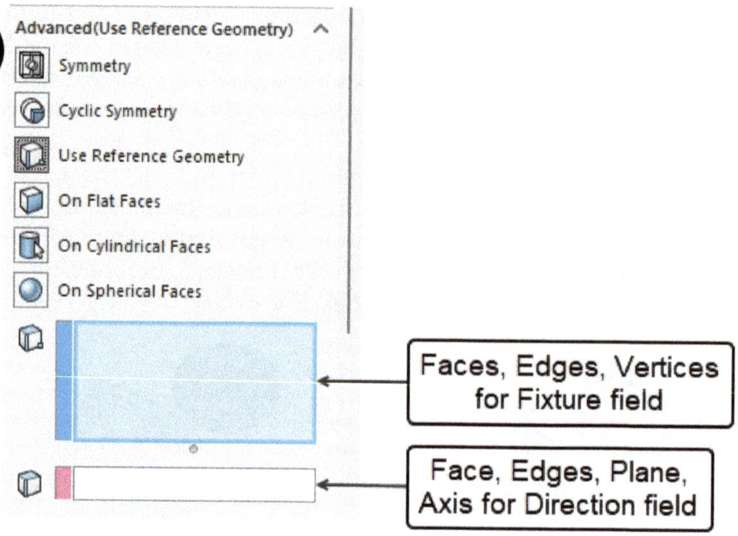

Select the desired faces, edges, or vertices to apply the Use Reference Geometry fixture, see Figure 2.59. In this figure, a planar face is selected to restrict its translational movements.

Next, click on the **Face, Edge, Plane, Axis for Direction** field in the PropertyManager and choose a reference geometry, such as a plane, planar face, edge, or axis, see Figure 2.59. In this example, the Top plane is selected as the reference geometry.

2.59

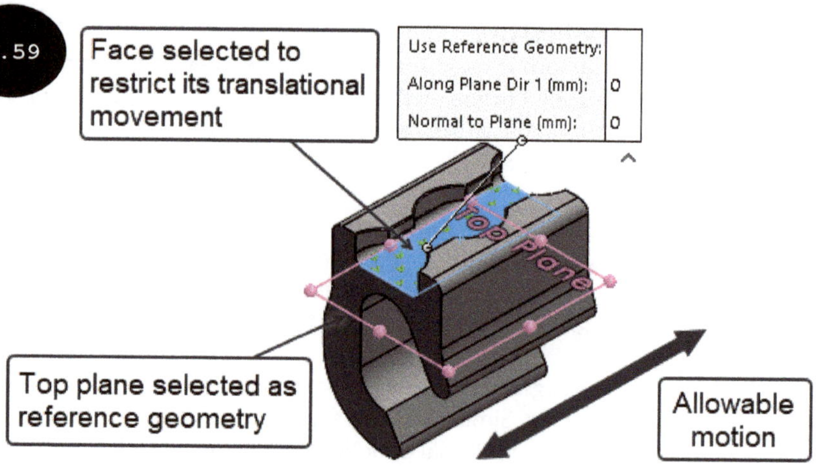

Finally, use the **Translations** rollout in the PropertyManager to define the specific directions in which you want to restrict the translational movement of the selected face relative to the reference geometry, see Figure 2.60.

2.60

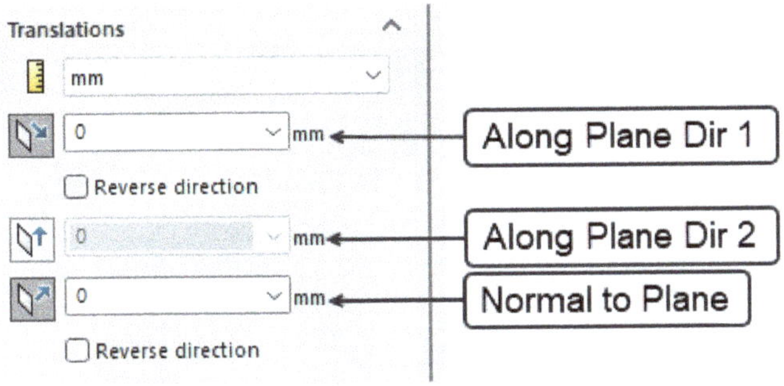

In the **Translations** rollout of the PropertyManager, click on a required button: **Along Plane Dir 1**, **Along Plane Dir 2**, or **Normal to Plane** to activate it, see Figure 2.60. In this figure, the **Along Plane Dir 1** and **Normal to Plane** buttons are activated.

Note that as soon as you click on one of these buttons, an edit field is enabled with **0** (zero) value entered in it, see Figure 2.60. The **0** (zero) value means that the translational motion for the selected faces, edges, or vertices is restricted along the respective direction. You can also enter any value other than **0** (zero) in the edit fields to allow permissible motion for the selected faces, edges, or vertices in the respective directions.

If you do not activate any of the mentioned buttons, and leave it unspecified in the **Translations** rollout then the selected faces, edges, or vertices are allowed to translate freely along the respective direction. Next, click on the green tick-mark button in the PropertyManager. The Use Reference Geometry fixture is applied to the selected faces, edges, or vertices.

Note: In case of the shell, beam and truss, you can also restrict or allow permissible rotational motions for faces, edges, vertices, or joints of the model by using the **Rotation** rollouts of the **Fixture PropertyManager**. This rollout is only available for shells, beams, and trusses. You will learn more about shell, beam, and truss geometries later in this chapter.

On Flat Faces Fixture

The On Flat Faces fixture is same as the Use Reference Geometry fixture with the only difference that the On Flat Faces fixture can only be applied to the planar faces.

It is used for restricting or allowing permissible motions to the selected faces relative to their directions (Direction 1, Direction 2, and Normal), see Figure 2.61. In this figure, the translational movements along the Direction 1 and in the direction normal to the selected face are restricted by specifying **0** (zero) in the **Along Face Dir 1** and **Normal to Face** fields of the **Translation** rollout in the PropertyManager, respectively.

2.61

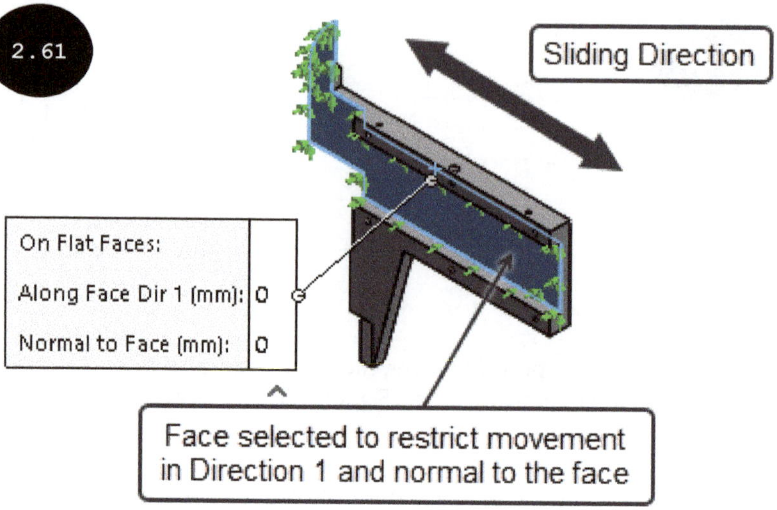

On Cylindrical Faces Fixture

The On Cylindrical Faces fixture is used to restrict cylindrical faces of a model to translate in its radial, circumferential, and axial directions, see Figure 2.62. In this figure, the On Cylindrical Faces fixture is applied to a cylindrical face of the model such that its movements in the radial and circumferential directions are restricted.

2.62

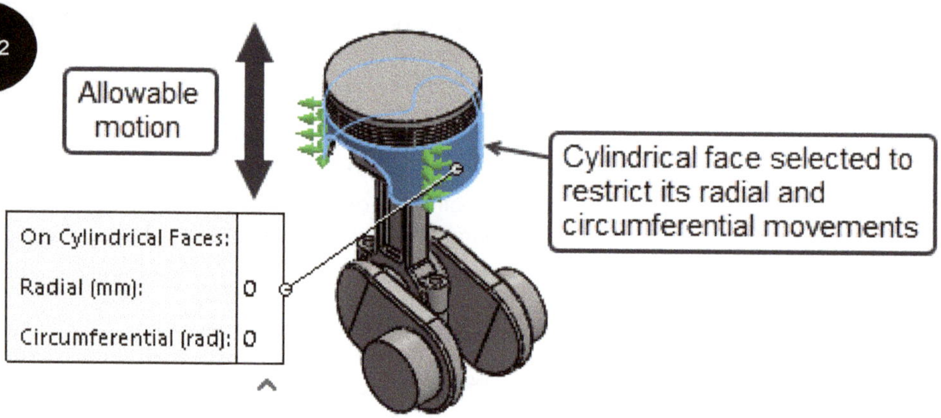

To apply the On Cylindrical Faces fixture, click on the **On Cylindrical Faces** button in the **Advanced** rollout of the PropertyManager and then select one or more cylindrical faces of the model to apply this fixture. Next, select the required direction button (**Radial**, **Circumferential**, or **Axial**) in the **Translations** rollout and then specify the translation value in the enabled edit field. Note that on entering **0** (zero) translation value, the translational motion gets restricted along the respective direction. Also, the direction left unspecified will be free for movements. Next, click on the green tick-mark button in the PropertyManager. The On Cylindrical Faces fixture is applied.

On Spherical Faces Fixture

The On Spherical Faces fixture is used to restrict the spherical faces of a model to translate in its radial, longitudinal, and latitudinal directions, see Figure 2.63. In this figure, the On Spherical Faces fixture is applied to a spherical face of the model such that its movement in the radial direction is restricted and the model is free to move in its longitudinal and latitudinal directions around the center point of the selected spherical face.

2.63

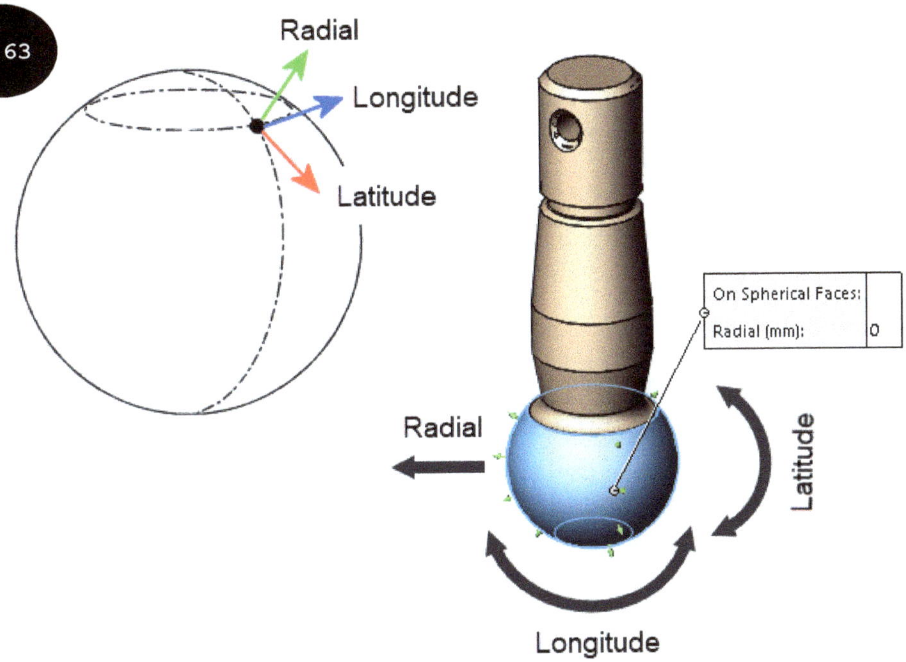

To apply the On Spherical Faces fixture, click on the **On Spherical Faces** button in the **Advanced** rollout of the PropertyManager and then select one or more spherical faces to apply this fixture. Next, select the required direction button (**Radial**, **Longitude**, or **Latitude**) in the **Translations** rollout and then specify the translation value in the edit field enabled. Note that on entering **0** (zero) translation value, the translational motion gets restricted along the respective direction. Also, the direction left unspecified will be free for movements. Next, click on the green tick-mark button of the PropertyManager. The On Spherical Faces fixture is applied.

Applying Loads

The internal and external forces such as force, pressure, and temperature, acting on an object are known as loads. Defining loads is a very important step in FEA to evaluate the response of an object under the given loading condition. In SOLIDWORKS Simulation, the tools used for applying different types of loads are available in the **External Loads** flyout, see Figure 2.64. You can invoke this flyout by clicking on the arrow available at the bottom of the **External Loads Advisor** tool in the **Simulation CommandManager**.

Alternatively, to access the different types of loads, right-click on the **External Loads** option in the Simulation Study Tree and then click on the required load in the shortcut menu that appears, see Figure 2.65. The different types of loads are discussed next.

2.64

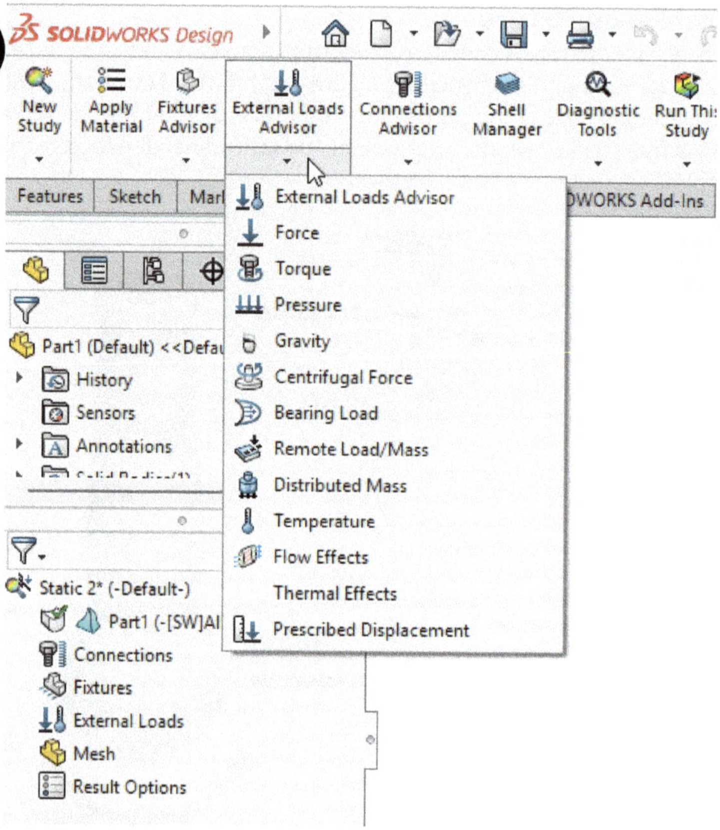
SOLIDWORKS Design
New Study
Apply Material
Fixtures Advisor
External Loads Advisor
Connections Advisor
Shell Manager
Diagnostic Tools
Run This Study
Features
Sketch
WORKS Add-Ins
External Loads Advisor
Force
Torque
Pressure
Gravity
Centrifugal Force
Bearing Load
Remote Load/Mass
Distributed Mass
Temperature
Flow Effects
Thermal Effects
Prescribed Displacement
Part1 (Default) <<Defau
History
Sensors
Annotations
Static 2* (-Default-)
Part1 (-[SW]Al
Connections
Fixtures
External Loads
Mesh
Result Options

2.65

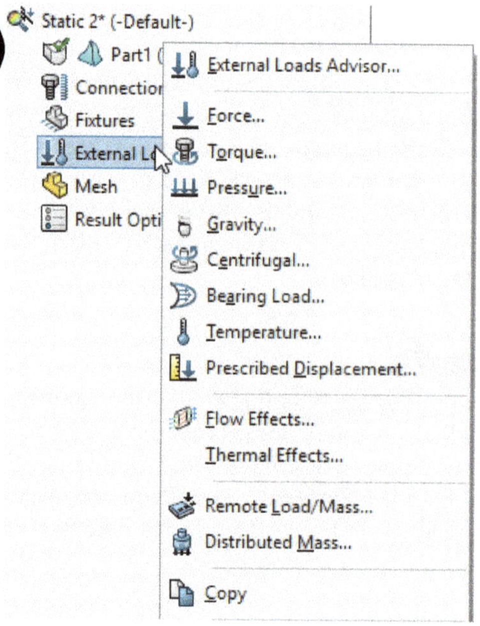
Static 2* (-Default-)
Part1
Connectior
Fixtures
External Lo
Mesh
Result Opti
External Loads Advisor...
Force...
Torque...
Pressure...
Gravity...
Centrifugal...
Bearing Load...
Temperature...
Prescribed Displacement...
Flow Effects...
Thermal Effects...
Remote Load/Mass...
Distributed Mass...
Copy

Applying the Force

In SOLIDWORKS Simulation, you can apply a uniformly or non-uniformly distributed external force on faces, edges, reference points, vertices, beams, and beam joints by using the **Force** tool.

To apply an external force, invoke the **External Loads** flyout, (refer to Figure 2.64) and then click on the **Force** tool. The **Force/Torque PropertyManager** appears, see Figure 2.66. Alternatively, right-click on the **External Loads** option in the Simulation Study Tree and then click on the **Force** tool in the shortcut menu that appears, refer to Figure 2.65. The options of the **Force/Torque PropertyManager** are discussed next.

2.66

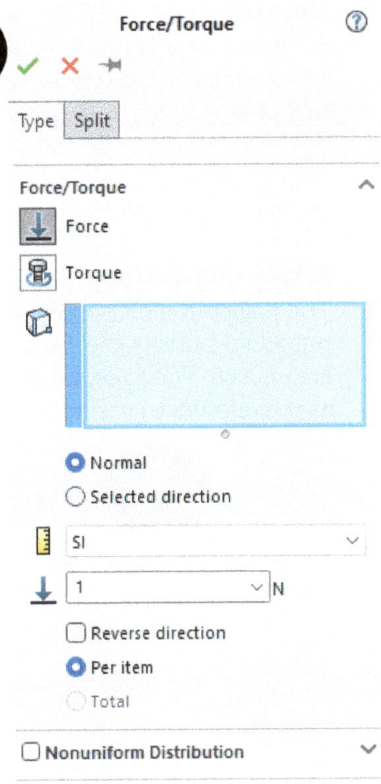

Force/Torque Rollout

The options in the **Force/Torque** rollout of the PropertyManager are used for specifying parameters for defining the uniformly distributed force or torque. By default, the **Force** button is activated in this rollout, see Figure 2.66. As a result, the options available in this rollout are used for defining the uniformly distributed force. The options are discussed next.

Note: On activating the **Torque** button in the **Force/Torque** rollout, you can apply the torque to the faces of the model. You will learn more about applying torque later in this chapter.

Faces and Shell Edges for Normal Force

By default, the **Faces and Shell Edges for Normal Force** field is activated in the **Force/Torque** rollout. As a result, you can select faces, edges, vertices, and reference points of the model to apply the force, see Figure 2.67. In this figure, a face of the model is selected to apply the force. Note that in the case of a beam structure, you can select beams, joints, and vertices for applying the force.

2.67

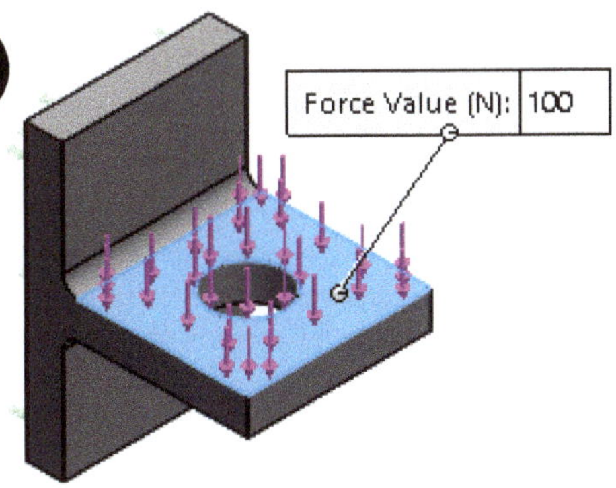

Normal

By default, the **Normal** radio button is selected in this rollout. As a result, on selecting a face of the model, the force is applied in the direction normal to the selected face, automatically, refer to Figure 2.67. You can also define the direction of force other than the normal direction by using the **Selected direction** radio button. Note that if you have selected an edge, a reference point, or a vertex for applying the force, then the direction of force will not be defined automatically and you need to define it by using the **Selected direction** radio button, which is discussed below.

Selected direction

The **Selected direction** radio button is used for defining the direction of the force. On selecting this radio button, the **Face, Edge, Plane for Direction** field, and the **Force** rollout appear, see Figure 2.68. The **Face, Edge, Plane for Direction** field is used to select a face, an edge, or a plane, as the reference geometry for defining the direction of force.

2.68

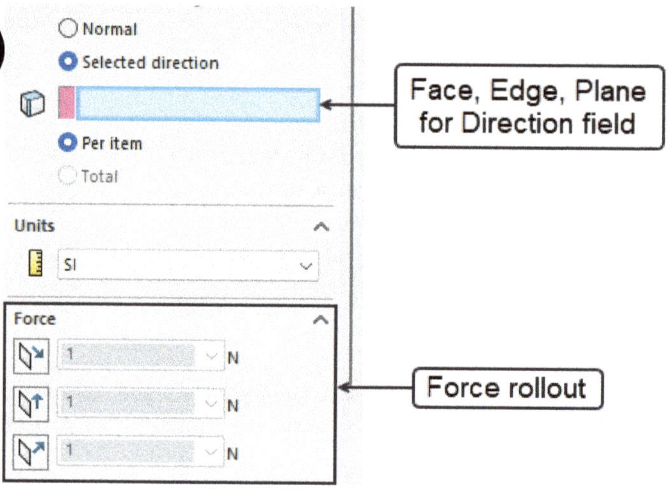

After selecting a reference geometry, click on the required button: **Along Plane Dir 1, Along Plane Dir 2**, or **Normal to Plane** in the **Force** rollout to define the direction of force with respect to the reference geometry selected. After selecting a direction button (**Along Plane Dir 1, Along Plane Dir 2**, or **Normal to Plane**), the respective field is enabled in front of it, where you can enter the magnitude of the force.

Unit

The **Unit** drop-down list is used for selecting the unit for the magnitude of the force. You can select the **SI**, **English (IPS)**, or **Metric (G)** unit by using this drop-down list, see Figure 2.69.

2.69

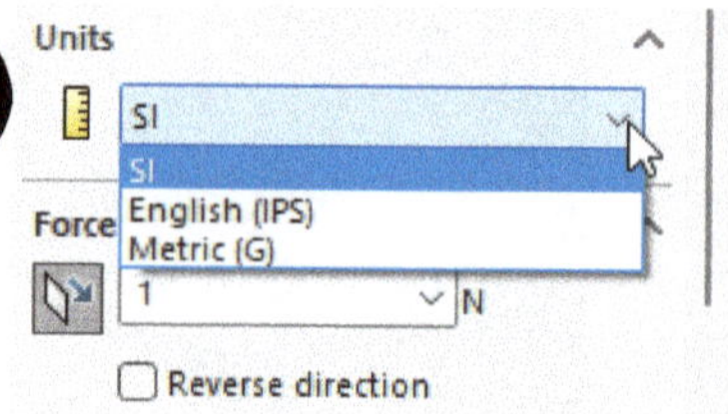

Force Value
The **Force Value** field is used for entering the magnitude of the force. Note that this field is available only when the **Normal** radio button is selected.

Per item
On selecting the **Per item** radio button, the specified magnitude of the force is applied to all the selected geometries. For example, if you have specified 100 N as the magnitude of the force on two vertices of the model, then on selecting this radio button, a magnitude of 100 N is applied on each of the selected vertices (100 + 100 = 200 N). So, the total magnitude acting on the complete body becomes 200 N.

Total
On selecting the **Total** radio button, the specified magnitude of the force is distributed among all the selected geometries, equally. For example, if you have specified 100 N as the total magnitude of the force on two vertices of the model, then on selecting this radio button, a magnitude of 50 N is applied on each of the selected vertices (50 + 50 = 100 N). So, the total magnitude acting on the body remains the same that is 100 N.

Reverse direction
The **Reverse direction** check box is used for reversing the direction of the force applied.

Nonuniform Distribution Rollout

The **Nonuniform Distribution** rollout of the PropertyManager is used for applying a non-uniformly distributed load. By default, this rollout is collapsed. To expand this rollout, click on the check box available in its title bar, see Figure 2.70. The options in this rollout are discussed below:

2.70

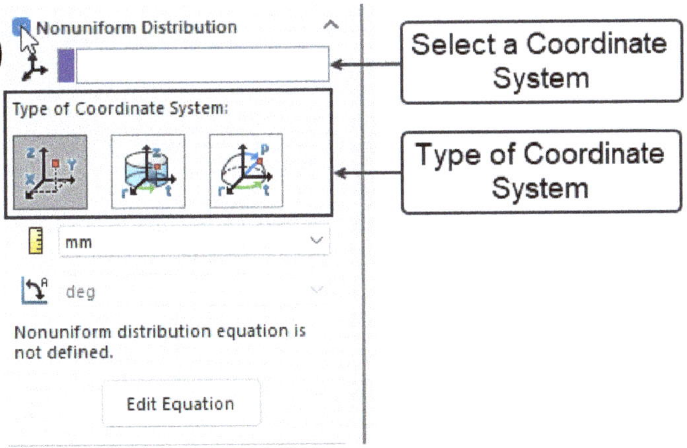

Select a Coordinate System
The **Select a Coordinate System** field of the **Nonuniform Distribution** rollout is used for selecting a coordinate system to measure a non-uniform load. After selecting a coordinate system, you need to define the non-uniform distribution equations of the load. You will learn about non-uniform distribution equation later in this chapter.

Tip: To create a coordinate system, first exit the PropertyManager and then click on the **Features** tab in the CommandManager. Next, click on **Reference Geometry > Coordinate System** in the **Features CommandManager**, see Figure 2.71. The **Coordinate System PropertyManager** appears, see Figure 2.72. Select a vertex or a point of the model as the origin of the coordinate system. You can also define the origin by specifying coordinates of the desired point. The preview of the coordinate system appears in the graphics area. Select an edge or a linear entity to define the X axis direction of the coordinate system. You can flip the direction of the X axis by using the **Reverse X Axis Direction** button available in front of the **X axis** field. Next, select an edge or a linear entity to define the Y axis direction of the coordinate system. Next, click on the green tick-mark button in the PropertyManager. The coordinate system is created.

2.71

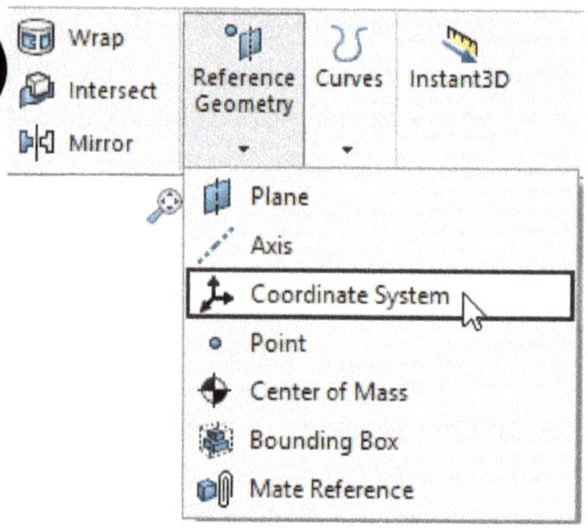

2.72

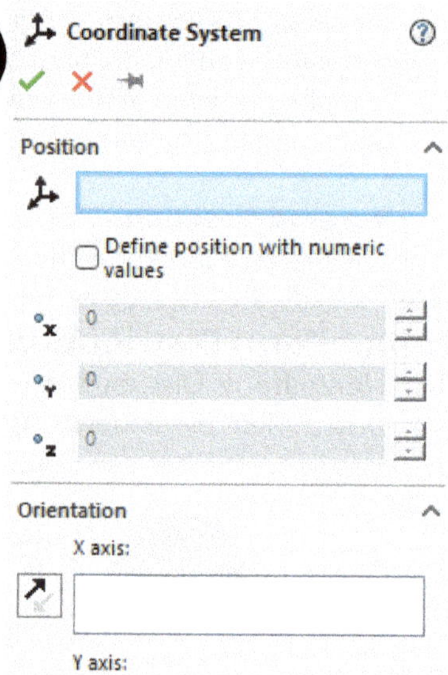

Type of Coordinate System

The **Type of Coordinate System** area of the **Nonuniform Distribution** rollout is used for selecting the type of coordinate system, refer to Figure 2.70. You can select the Cartesian (X, Y, Z), Cylindrical (radial "r", circumferential "t", axial "z"), or Spherical (radial "r", longitude "t", latitude "p") type coordinate system by clicking on the respective button in this area. Note that depending upon the type of coordinate system selected [Cartesian (X, Y, Z), Cylindrical (r, t, z), or Spherical (r, t, p)], you can define the equation for the non-uniform distribution of force by using the **Edit Equation** button, which is discussed below.

Edit Equation

The **Edit Equation** button is used for displaying the **Edit Equation** dialog box for defining the equation of the non-uniformly distributed force. Click on the **Edit Equation** button. The **Edit Equation** dialog box appears, see Figure 2.73.

2.73

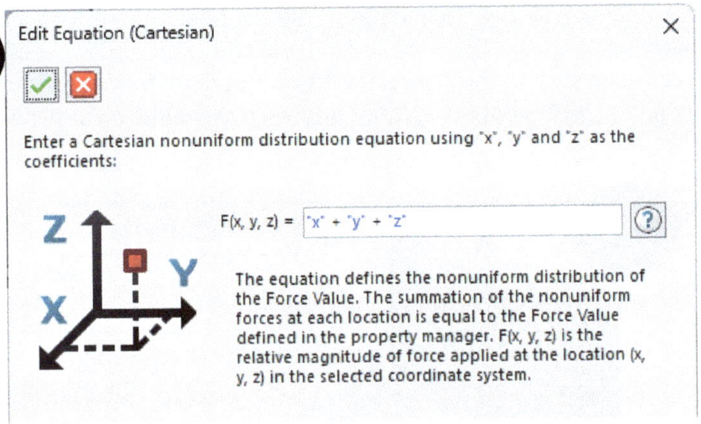

In the **Edit Equation** dialog box, you can define the equation for the non-uniform distribution of force. Note that for the Cartesian coordinate system, you can enter an equation by using x, y, and z as coefficients. Similarly, for the Cylindrical coordinate system, you can enter an equation by using r, t, and z as coefficients and for the Spherical coordinate system, you can enter an equation by using r, t, and p as coefficients. Examples of non-uniform distribution equations based on different coordinates are given below:

Non-uniform distribution equations based on Cartesian coordinate system (x, y, z)	F (x, y, z) = 2 * "x" + 1 * "y" + 1 * "z"
Non-uniform distribution equation based on Cylindrical coordinate system (r, t, z)	F (r, t, z) = 1 * "r" + 3* "t" + 1 * "z"
Non-uniform distribution equation based on Spherical coordinate system (r, t, p)	F (r, t, p) = 3 * "r" + 1 * "t" + 1 * "p"

Note: While entering the equation, a drop-down list appears, see Figure 2.74. In this drop-down list, you can select the mathematical functions and coefficients. You need to enter coefficients inside quotation marks. For example, F = 1 * "x" + 2 * "y" + 1 * "z", where, F is the relative magnitude of the force at an integration point along the force varying direction.

2.74

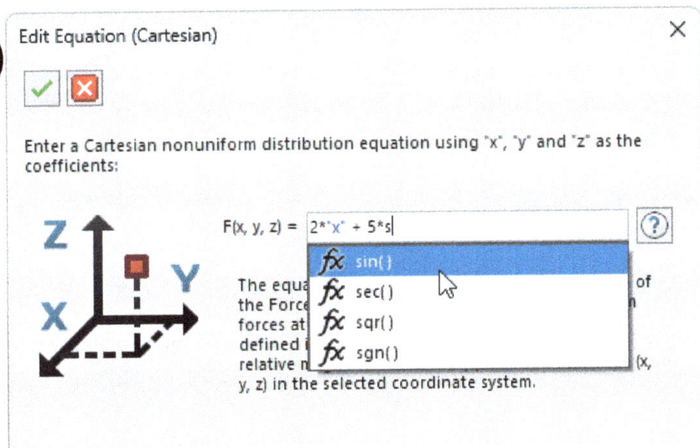

After entering the equation for the non-uniformly distributed force, click on the green tick-mark button in the **Edit Equation** dialog box. The non-uniformly distributed force is applied on the selected face of the model, see Figure 2.75. In this figure, the force is non-uniformly distributed along the X-axis of the coordinate system. Note that you cannot apply a non-uniformly distributed force on an edge or a vertex of the model.

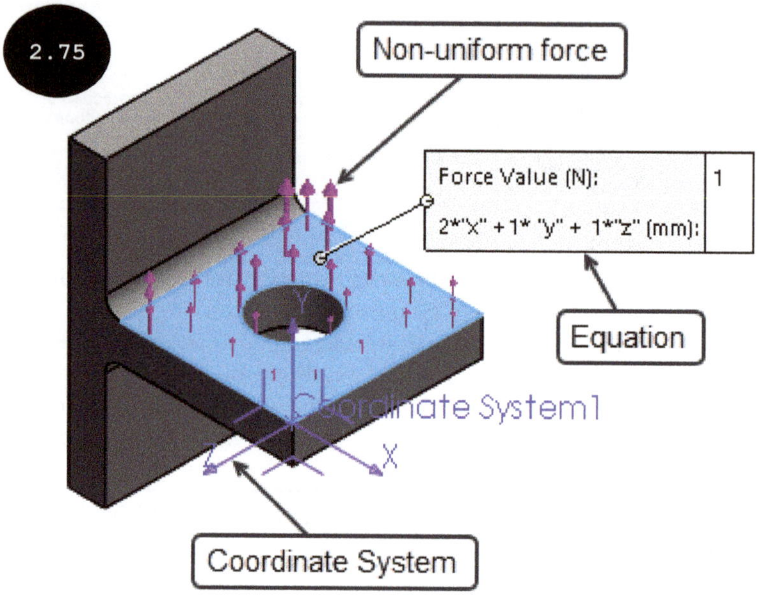

Symbol Settings Rollout

The **Symbol Settings** rollout is used for specifying the color and size of the force symbols that appear in the graphics area. By default, this rollout is collapsed. To expand this rollout, click on the arrow in its title bar, see Figure 2.76.

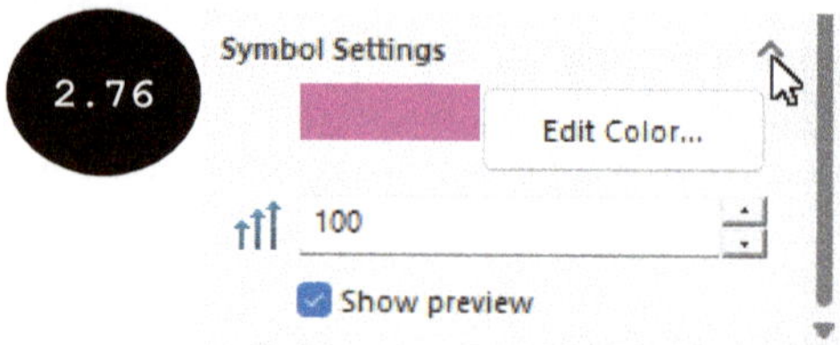

After specifying the required parameters for defining the force in the **Force/Torque PropertyManager**, click on the green tick-mark button in the PropertyManager. The force of the specified parameters is applied on the selected geometry of the model.

Applying the Torque

You can apply a uniformly or non-uniformly distributed torque on the faces of a model by using the **Torque** tool. The torque is a rotational force which causes an object to rotate about an axis.

To apply the torque, invoke the **External Loads** flyout, (see Figure 2.77), and then click on the **Torque** tool. The **Force/Torque PropertyManager** appears with the **Torque** button activated in it, see

Figure 2.78. Alternatively, right-click on the **External Loads** option in the Simulation Study Tree and then click on the **Torque** tool in the shortcut menu that appears. The options in the PropertyManager are discussed next.

2.77

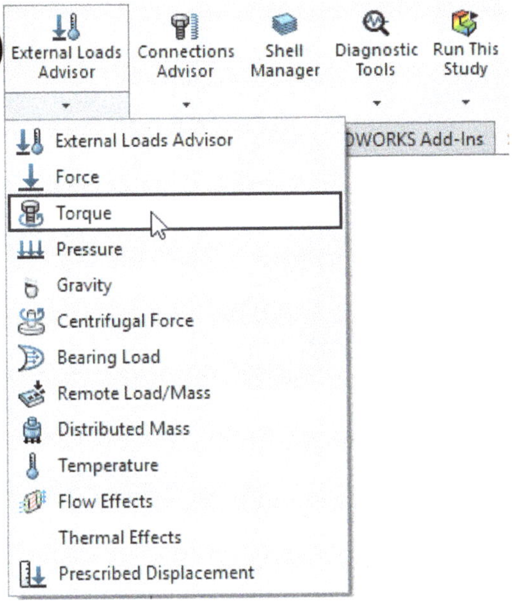

2.78

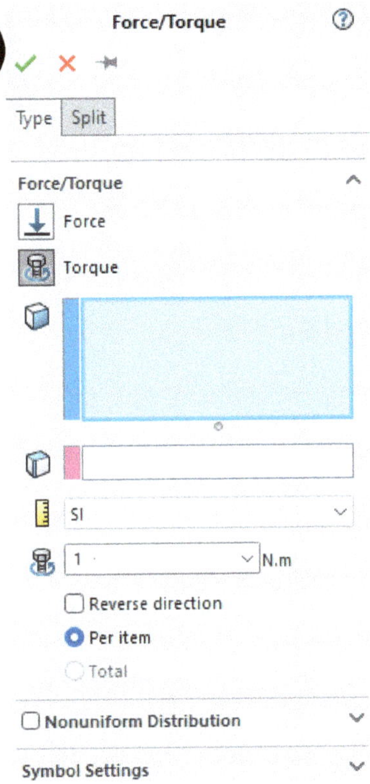

Force/Torque Rollout

In the **Force/Torque** rollout of the PropertyManager, the **Torque** button is activated, see Figure 2.78. As a result, the options available in this rollout are used for defining the uniformly distributed torque. The options are discussed below.

Note: You can apply a force or torque by activating the **Force** or **Torque** button in the **Force/Torque** rollout of the PropertyManager, respectively.

Faces for Torque

The **Faces for Torque** field of the rollout is activated, by default. As a result, you can select one or more cylindrical faces of the model to apply the torque, see Figure 2.79.

Axis, Cylindrical Face for Direction

The **Axis, Cylindrical Face for Direction** field is used for selecting an axis, an edge, or a cylindrical face to define the axis of torque, see Figure 2.79.

2.79

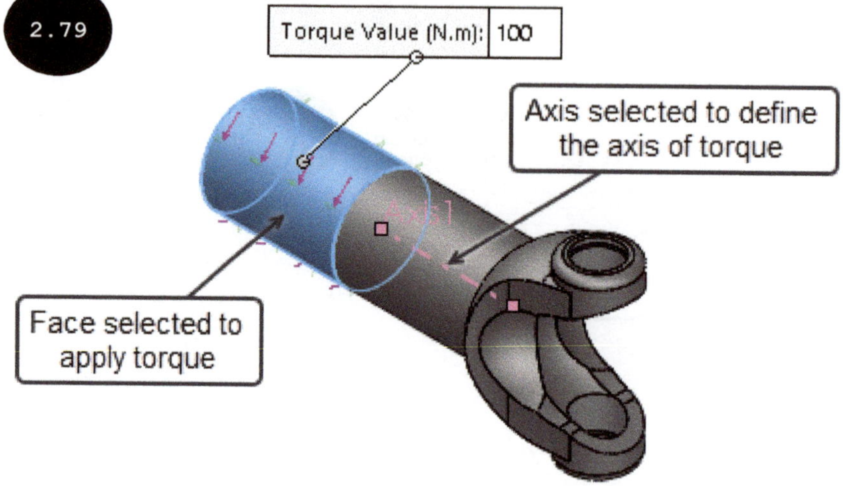

Unit

The **Unit** drop-down list is used for selecting a unit for measuring the torque magnitude. You can select **SI**, **English (IPS)**, or **Metric (G)** unit by using this drop-down list.

Torque Value

The **Torque Value** field is used for specifying the magnitude of the torque.

The remaining options in this rollout are the same as discussed earlier.

Nonuniform Distribution Rollout

The options in the **Nonuniform Distribution** rollout of the PropertyManager are used for defining the equation for non-uniformly distributed torque. The options in this rollout are same as discussed earlier.

After specifying the required parameters for defining the uniform or non-uniform torque in the **Force/Torque PropertyManager**, click on the green tick-mark button. A torque with specified parameters is applied on the selected cylindrical face or cylindrical faces of the model.

Applying the Pressure

You can apply the uniformly or non-uniformly distributed pressure on faces of a model by using the **Pressure** tool. The pressure is an exertion of the force applied on a face per unit area.

To apply the pressure on faces of a model, invoke the **External Loads** flyout, see Figure 2.80 and then click on the **Pressure** tool. The **Pressure PropertyManager** appears, see Figure 2.81. Alternatively, right-click on the **External Loads** option in the Simulation Study Tree and then click on the **Pressure** tool in the shortcut menu that appears to invoke the **Pressure PropertyManager**. The options in the PropertyManager are discussed below.

2.80

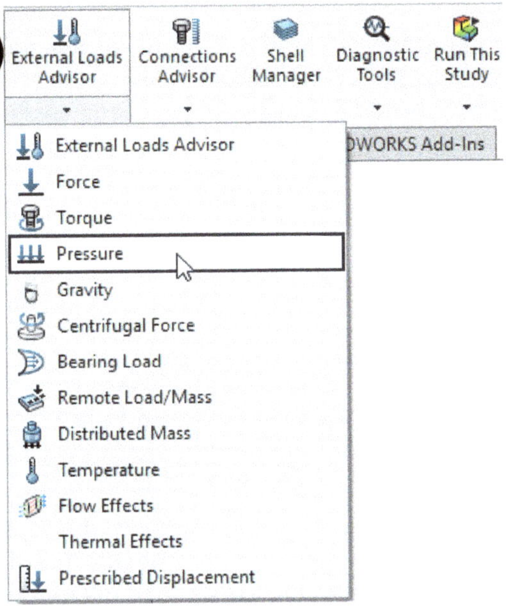

2.81

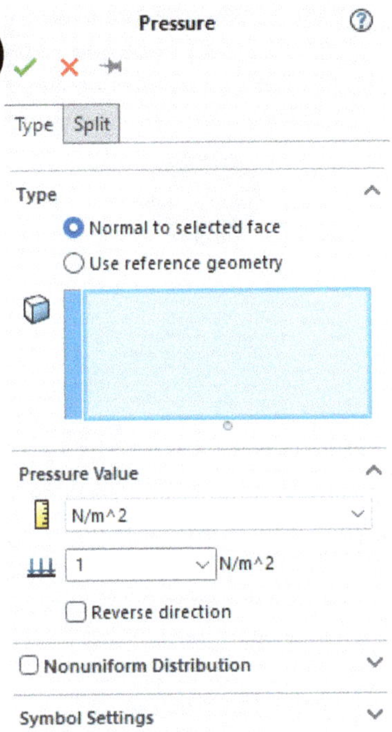

Type

The options in the **Type** rollout of the PropertyManager are used for selecting faces of the model to apply pressure and to define the direction of pressure applied. The options are discussed below.

Faces for Pressure

By default, the **Faces for Pressure** field is activated in the **Type** rollout of the PropertyManager. As a result, you can select one or more faces of the model to apply the pressure.

Normal to selected face

By default, the **Normal to selected face** radio button is selected in the rollout. As a result, the pressure is applied in a direction normal to the selected face or faces of the model, see Figure 2.82.

2.82

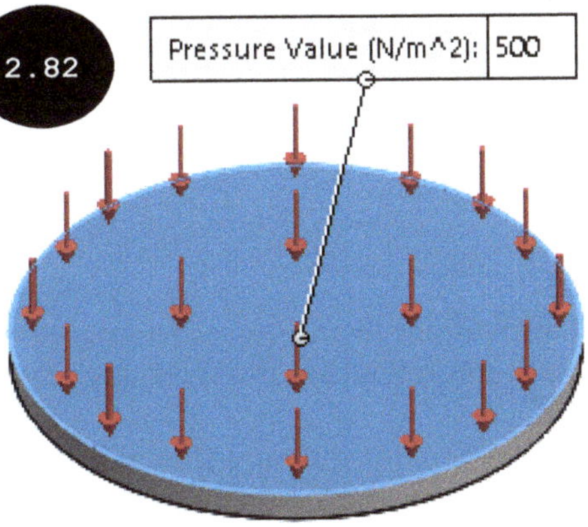

Use reference geometry

The **Use reference geometry** radio button is used for applying the pressure in a direction, which is defined by a reference geometry. When you select this radio button, the **Face, Edge, Plane, Axis for Direction** field and **Direction** drop-down list become available in the rollout, see Figure 2.83.

2.83

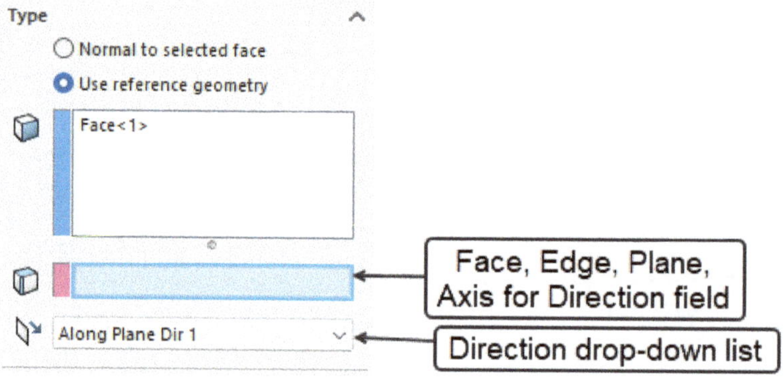

The **Face, Edge, Plane, Axis for Direction** field is used for selecting a face, an edge, a plane, or an axis as the reference geometry for defining the direction of the pressure. The **Direction** drop-down list is used for defining the direction of pressure with respect to the selected reference geometry.

Note that the availability of options in the **Direction** drop-down list depends on the type of reference geometry selected. For example, if you select a planar face or a plane as the reference geometry, then you can select the **Along Plane Dir 1**, **Along Plane Dir 2**, or **Normal to Plane** option in the **Direction** drop-down list to define the direction of the pressure. If you select a cylindrical face or an axis as the reference geometry, then you can select the **Radial**, **Circumferential**, or **Axial** option to define the direction of the pressure. If you select an edge as the reference geometry, then the **Direction** drop-down list will not be enabled and you can define the direction of the pressure along the selected edge.

Pressure Value

The **Unit** drop-down list of the **Pressure Value** rollout is used for selecting the unit for pressure, see Figure 2.84. The **Pressure Value** field of the rollout is used for defining the value of pressure. The **Reverse direction** check box is used for reversing the direction of pressure.

2.84

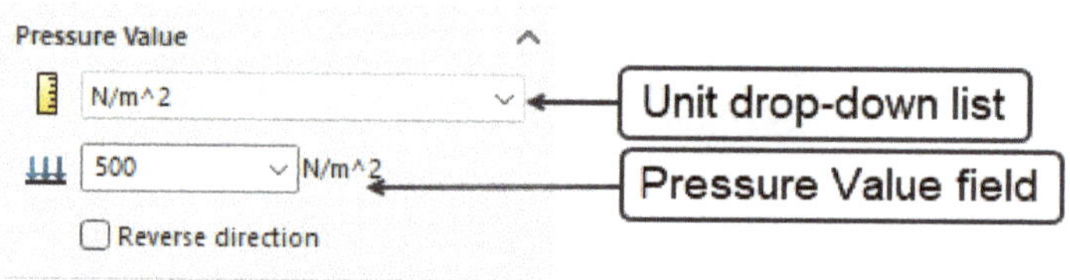

Nonuniform Distribution

The options in the **Nonuniform Distribution** rollout are used to define the equation for the non-uniformly distributed pressure. The options in this rollout are the same as discussed earlier.

After specifying the required parameters for defining the uniform or non-uniform pressure in the PropertyManager, click on the green tick-mark button in the PropertyManager. A pressure with specified parameters is applied on the selected face or faces of the model.

Applying the Gravity

Gravity is defined as the gravitational force, which is acting on all objects in the universe and causes objects to fall toward the earth. You can apply the gravitational force on a model by using the **Gravity** tool.

To apply gravity on a model, invoke the **External Loads** flyout in the **Simulation CommandManager** and then click on the **Gravity** tool. The **Gravity PropertyManager** appears, see Figure 2.85. The options are discussed below.

Selected Reference

The **Face, Edge, Plane for Direction** field of the **Selected Reference** rollout is used for selecting a planar face, a plane, or an edge to define the direction of the gravitational force. By default, the **Top Plane** is selected in this field to define the direction of the gravitational force. Note that the gravitational force is applied normal to the selected planar face or the plane, see Figure 2.86. However, if you have selected an edge, then the gravitational force is applied along the selected edge.

2.85

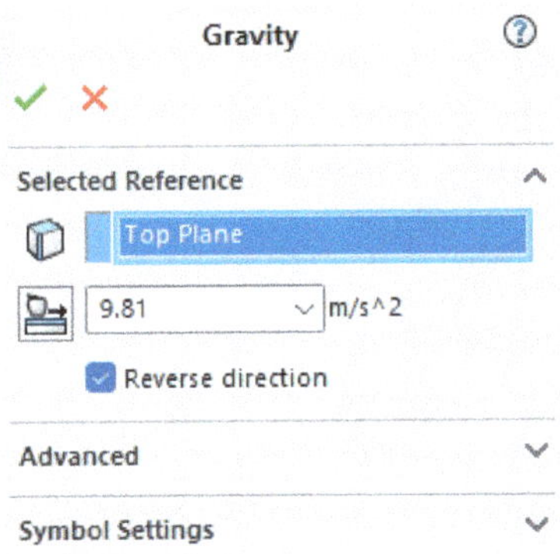

2.86

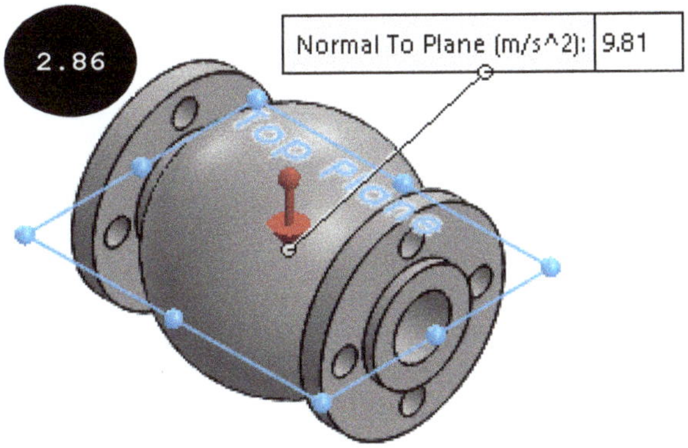

The **Apply Earth's gravity** field is used for specifying the value of gravity of the earth. By default, the gravity of earth is 9.81 m/s^2. The **Reverse direction** check box is used to reverse the direction of the gravitational force applied.

Advanced

In addition to applying a gravitational force normal to the selected planar face or the plane, you can also apply it in other directions of the selected planar face or plane by using the **Along Plane Dir 1** and **Along Plane Dir 2** fields of the **Advanced** rollout. By default, this rollout is in collapsed form. To expand this rollout, click on the arrow available in its title bar, see Figure 2.87.

2.87

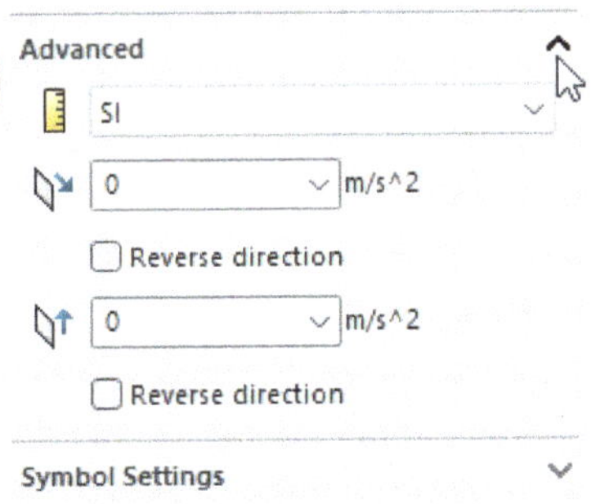

After specifying the required parameters for defining the gravity in the PropertyManager, click on the green tick-mark button. The gravity with specified parameters is applied on the object.

Applying the Centrifugal Force

The Centrifugal force is defined as the force, which is acting on a rotating object in the outward direction from its axis of rotation. You can apply the centrifugal force by using the **Centrifugal Force** tool.

To apply the centrifugal force on a rotating object, invoke the **External Loads** flyout in the **Simulation CommandManager** and then click on the **Centrifugal Force** tool. The **Centrifugal PropertyManager** appears, see Figure 2.88. Alternatively, right-click on the **External Loads** option in the Simulation Study Tree and then click on the **Centrifugal** tool in the shortcut menu that appears. The options in the PropertyManager are discussed below.

Selected Reference

The **Axis, Edge, Cylindrical Face for Direction** field of the **Selected Reference** rollout is used for selecting an axis, an edge, or a cylindrical face to define the axis of rotation of the object, see Figure 2.89. In this figure, the cylindrical face of the model is selected to define the axis of rotation.

2.88

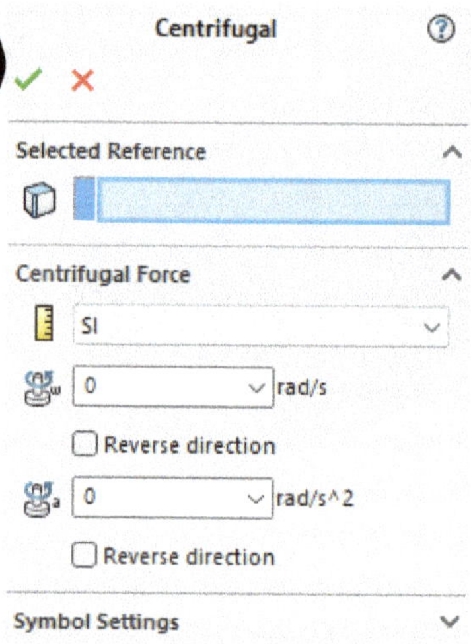

2.89

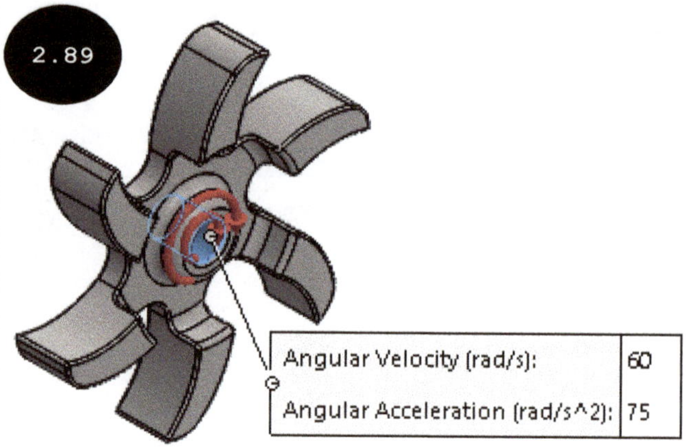

Centrifugal Force

The options in the **Centrifugal Force** rollout are used to specify the angular velocity and acceleration of the object. The options are discussed below.

Unit

This drop-down list is used to select the units for defining the angular velocity and acceleration values.

Angular Velocity

This field is used to specify the value of the angular velocity.

Angular Acceleration

This field is used to specify the value of the angular acceleration.

Reverse direction

You can reverse the direction of angular velocity and angular acceleration using the respective **Reverse direction** check box of the rollout.

After specifying the angular velocity and angular acceleration, click on the green tick-mark button in the PropertyManager. The centrifugal force of specified angular velocity and angular acceleration is applied on the object.

Applying the Bearing Load

Bearing load is defined as the load that occurs in the cylindrical faces having contact with each other. For example, the contact between shafts and bearings/bushings. In SOLIDWORKS Simulation, you can apply the bearing load by using the **Bearing Load** tool.

2.90

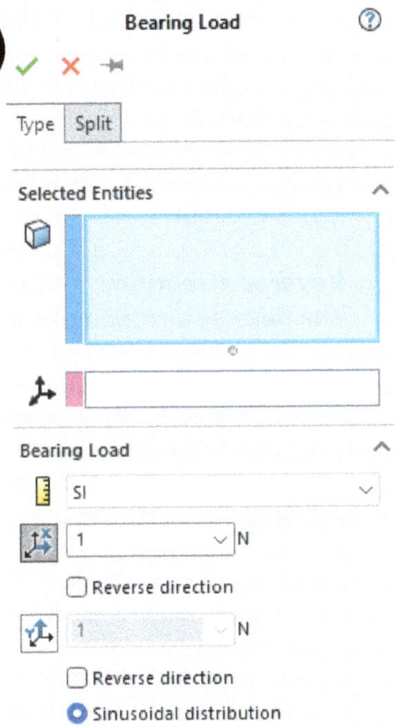

To apply the bearing load, invoke the **External Loads** flyout in the **Simulation CommandManager** and then click on the **Bearing Load** tool. The **Bearing Load PropertyManager** appears, see Figure 2.90. Alternatively, right-click on the **External Loads** option in the Simulation Study Tree and then click on the **Bearing Load** tool in the shortcut menu that appears. The options in the PropertyManager are discussed below.

Selected Entities

The options in the **Selected Entities** rollout of the PropertyManager are used to select the cylindrical faces to apply the bearing load. The options are discussed below.

Cylindrical Faces or Shell Circular Edges for Bearing Load

The **Cylindrical Faces or Shell Circular Edges for Bearing Load** field of the **Selected Entities** rollout is used to select one or more cylindrical faces of same radius to apply the bearing load. Note that the cylindrical faces do not need to be full 360-degrees. You can split the faces by using the **Split** tool of the **Features CommandManager**.

Select a Coordinate System

The **Select a Coordinate System** field is used to select the coordinate system, which defines the direction of bearing load. Note that the z-axis of the coordinate system must be aligned with the axis of cylindrical face selected, see Figure 2.91.

2.91

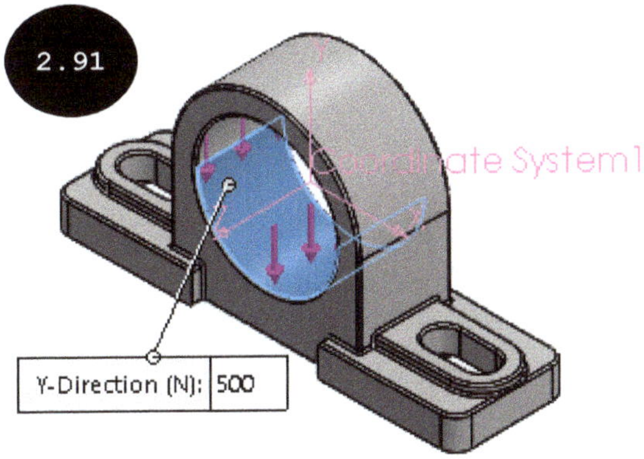

Bearing Load

The options in the **Bearing Load** rollout are used for specifying the bearing load along the X-axis or Y-axis of the coordinate system. The options are discussed below.

Unit
The **Unit** drop-down list is used to select the unit for defining the bearing load.

X-Direction
The **X-Direction** field is used to specify the bearing load value along the X-axis of the coordinate system.

Y-Direction
The **Y-Direction** field is used to specify the bearing load value along the Y-axis of the coordinate system. To activate the **Y-Direction** field, click on the **Y-Direction** button available in front of it in the rollout.

Reverse direction
The **Reverse direction** check box is used to reverse the direction of the bearing load.

Sinusoidal distribution
On selecting the **Sinusoidal distribution** radio button, the applied bearing load follows the sinusoidal load distribution on the selected cylindrical face.

Parabolic distribution
On selecting the **Parabolic distribution** radio button, the applied bearing load follows the parabolic load distribution on the selected cylindrical face.

After specifying the bearing load on one or more cylindrical faces, click on the green tick-mark button in the PropertyManager. The bearing load is applied on the object.

Applying the Remote Loads/Mass
The Remote Loads/Mass is defined as the load which originates at a remote location in the space and its effects are transferred to the model geometry, see Figure 2.92. To define the remote location in the space, you can specify the X, Y, and Z coordinates with respect to the global coordinate system or a user-defined coordinate system.

2.92

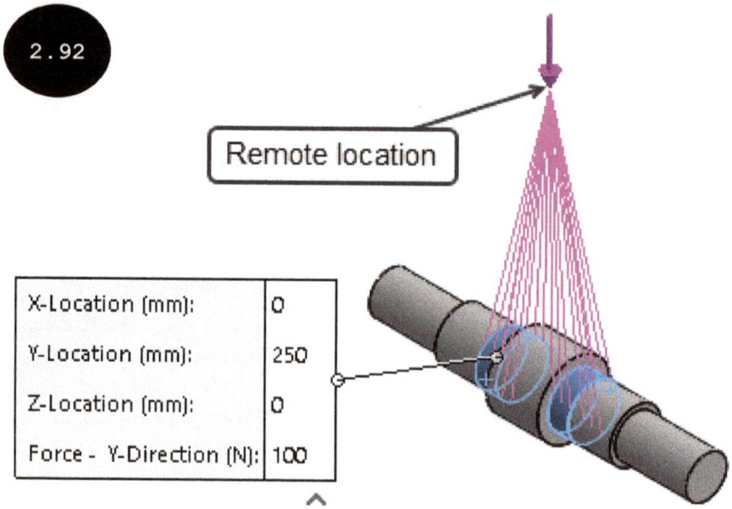

To apply the remote load, invoke the **External Loads** flyout in the **Simulation CommandManager** and then click on the **Remote Loads/Mass** tool. The **Remote Loads/Mass PropertyManager** appears, see Figure 2.93. Alternatively, right-click on the **External Loads** option in the Simulation Study Tree and then click on the **Remote Loads/Mass** tool in the shortcut menu that appears. The options in the PropertyManager are discussed below.

2.93

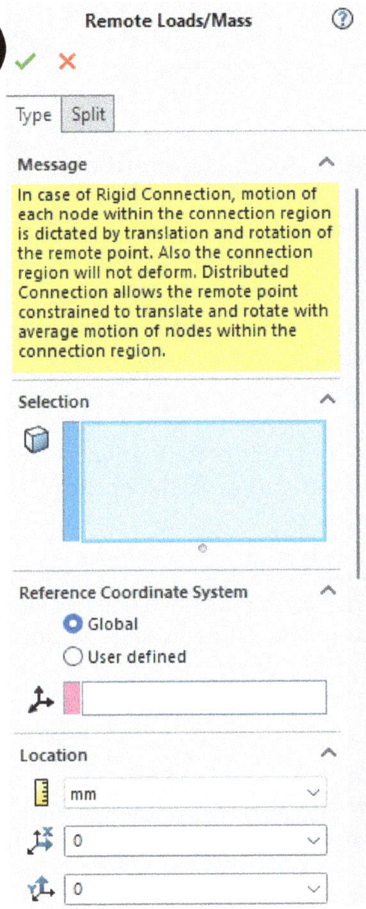

Faces for Remote Load

The **Faces for Remote Load** field of the **Selection** rollout is used to select the faces of the model to apply the remote load.

Reference Coordinate System

The options in the **Reference Coordinate System** rollout are used to select a coordinate system to define the location and direction of the remote load. By default, the **Global** radio button is selected in this rollout. As a result, you can define the location and direction of the remote load with respect to the global coordinate system. To define the location and direction of remote load with respect to a user defined coordinate system, select the **User defined** radio button. On doing so, the **Select a Coordinate System** field gets enabled in the rollout which is used for selecting a coordinate system from the graphics area.

Location

The options in the **Location** rollout are used for specifying the X, Y, and Z coordinates of the remote location with respect to the coordinate system selected (global or user-defined).

Translational Components

The options in the **Translational Components** rollout are used for specifying the remote forces or translation values along X, Y, and Z axes by activating the respective direction buttons such as **X-Direction**, **Y-Direction**, and **Z-Direction**.

Note that on activating a direction button (**X-Direction**, **Y-Direction**, or **Z-Direction**), the **Force** and **Translation** buttons become enabled in front of it for specifying the force or translation value in the respective direction, see Figure 2.94. Of these two buttons, the **Force** button is activated by default. As a result, you can specify the force value in the field that appears in front of the activated direction button. To specify the translation value, you need to activate the **Translation** button.

2.94

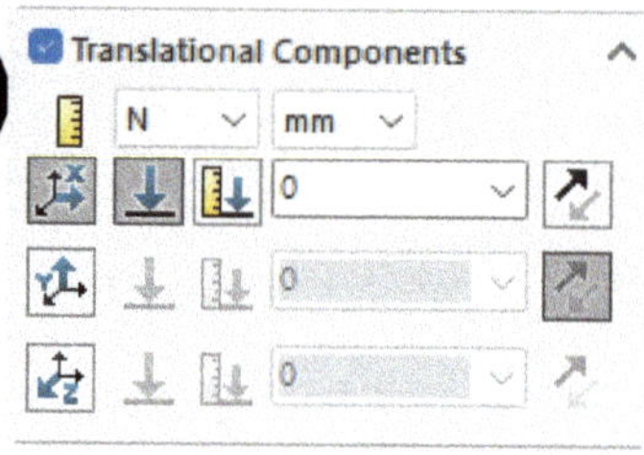

You can also reverse the direction of force or translation by clicking on the **Reverse direction** button. Note that defining the force or translation value depends upon whether the load or displacement is to be applied at the remote location.

Tip: You can define the units for force and translation values by using the **Force Unit** and **Translation Unit** drop-down lists in the **Translation Components** rollout of the PropertyManager, respectively.

Rotational Components

By default, the **Rotational Components** rollout is collapsed. To expand this rollout, select the check box that is available in its title bar. After expanding the **Rotational Components** rollout, you can specify the remote moment or rotation values about X, Y, and Z axes by activating the respective direction buttons such as **X-Direction**, **Y-Direction**, and **Z-Direction**.

Note that when you activate a direction button (**X-Direction**, **Y-Direction**, or **Z-Direction**), the **Moment** and **Rotation** buttons become enabled in front of it for specifying the moment or rotation value in the respective direction, see Figure 2.95. Of these two buttons, the **Moment** button is activated by default. As a result, you can specify the moment in the field that appears in front of the activated direction button.

2.95

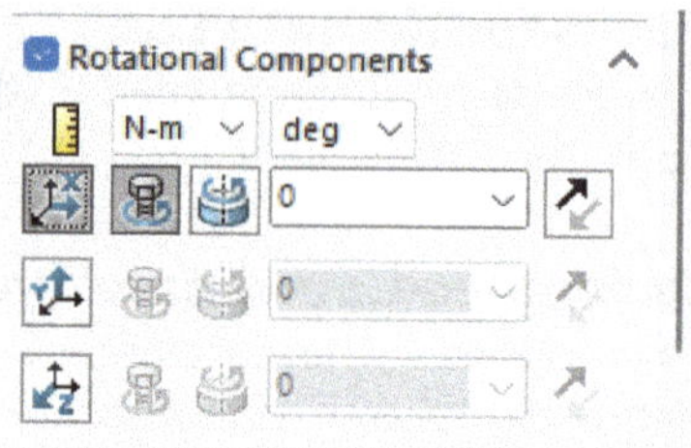

To specify the rotation value, you need to activate the **Rotation** button. You can also reverse the direction of moment or rotation by clicking on the **Reverse direction** button.

Note: Defining the moment or rotation value depends upon whether the load or displacement is to be applied at the remote location.

Connection Type

The **Connection Type** rollout is used to define the type of connection between the remote load/displacement location and the faces of the model. The options in this rollout are discussed below.

Distributed

On selecting the **Distributed** radio button in this rollout, you can define the connection between the remote location and the faces of the model as **Default (constant)**, **Linear**, **Quadratic**, or **Cubic** by selecting the respective option in the **Weighting Factor** drop-down list. Note that this drop-down list is enabled in the **Connection Type** rollout only when the **Distributed** radio button is selected. The options in this drop-down list are discussed below.

Default (constant): On selecting the **Default (constant)** option, the weight factors of the applied remote load is assumed to be uniformly distributed on the faces of the model and the connection between the remote location and the faces of the model is considered to be adequately flexible. SOLIDWORKS Simulation calculates equivalent forces (shear force and moment) and applies them on the faces of the model based on the applied remote load and the distance between the remote load location and the faces of the model, see Figure 2.96.

2.96

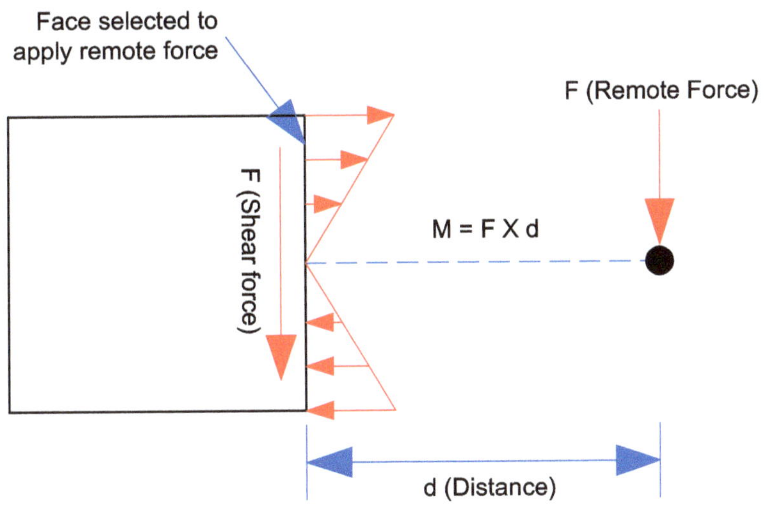

Linear: On selecting the **Linear** option, the weight factors of the applied load are assumed to be linearly decreasing with distance from the remote location.

Quadratic: On selecting the **Quadratic** option, the weight factors of the applied load are assumed to be decreasing with distance from the remote location following a quadratic polynomial formulation.

Cubic: On selecting the **Cubic** option, the weight factors of the applied load are assumed to be decreasing with distance from the remote location following a cubic polynomial formulation.

Rigid

On selecting the **Rigid** radio button in the **Connection Type** rollout, you can define the connection between the remote location and the faces of the model as rigid. In this connection type, the applied remote load/moment/mass is transferred to the faces of the model by considering that the remote load location and the faces of the model are connected with rigid bars, see Figure 2.97. It develops high stress near the selected faces of the model.

2.97

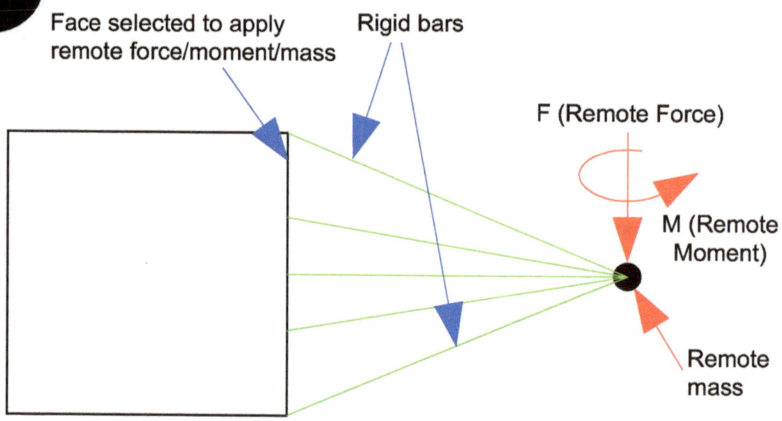

Mass

By default, this rollout is in collapsed form. To expand this rollout, click on the check box available in its title bar. The **Remote Mass** field of this rollout is used to specify the value of the remote mass and the remaining fields are used for specifying the mass moment of inertia in the respective directions. The **Unit** drop-down list of this rollout is used to specify the unit for the mass values.

After specifying the required parameters for the remote load, click on the green tick-mark button in the PropertyManager. The remote load is applied.

Meshing a Geometry

Meshing is a very important process of analysis in which a given geometry is divided into a number of discrete finite elements which are connected at common points called nodes, see Figure 2.98.

In SOLIDWORKS Simulation, the type of elements used for dividing the geometry depends on the type of geometry being meshed. For example, to mesh a 3D solid geometry, tetrahedral solid elements are used. To mesh a surface or sheet metal geometry (2D planar geometry), triangular shell elements are used. Similarly, to mesh a weldment/structure geometry (1D line geometry), beam/truss elements are used.

SOLIDWORKS Simulation uses an automatic mesher for meshing a geometry. As a result, it is limited to tetrahedral solid elements for 3D solid geometries and triangular shell elements for 2D planar geometries (surface and sheet metal). In automatic meshers, these element types are most reliable for meshing geometries.

2.98

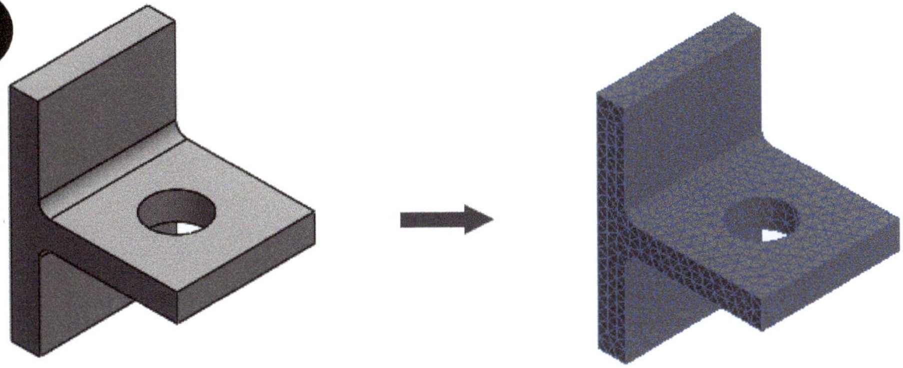

After Meshing

SOLIDWORKS Simulation uses five types of elements for meshing a geometry: First Order Solid Tetrahedral elements, Second Order Solid Tetrahedral Elements, First Order Triangular Shell elements, Second Order Triangular Shell elements, and Two Node elements. These elements are discussed below:

Different Types of Elements

Element Type	Description
First Order Solid Tetrahedral Elements	The First Order Solid Tetrahedral elements are also known as Draft elements. Each First Order Solid Tetrahedral element is defined by four corner nodes which are connected by six straight edges, see Figure 2.99. Each node has three degrees of freedom (translations). Due to the straight edges of draft elements, they do not map properly on curved boundaries, see Figure 2.100. Also, draft elements do not provide accurate results. However, due to less number of nodes and degrees of freedom, the draft elements require less computational time and are generally used for quick evaluation of a model. 2.99 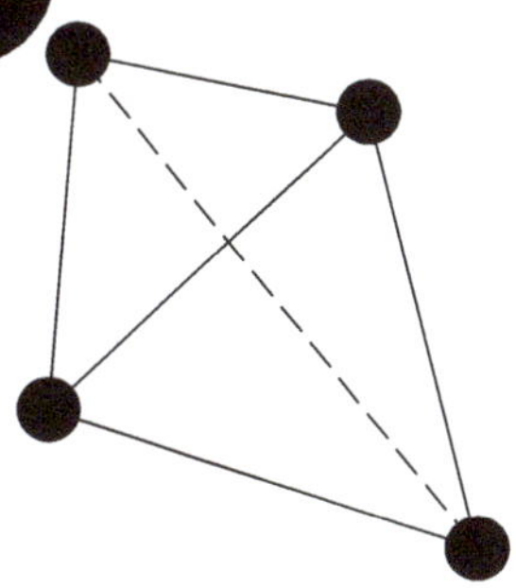 2.100 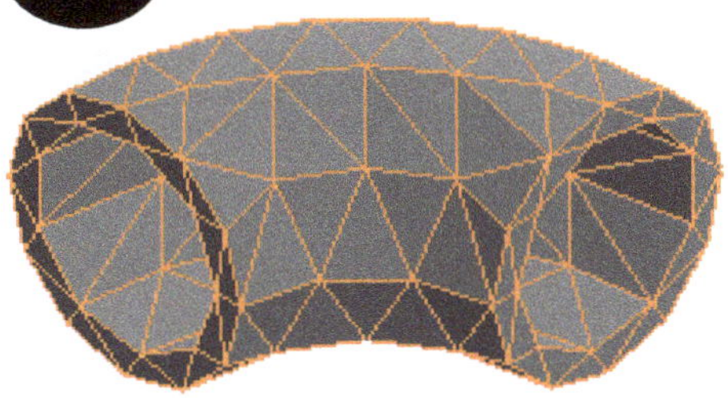

Second Order Solid Tetrahedral Elements	The Second Order Solid Tetrahedral elements are also known as High quality elements. Each Second Order Tetrahedral element is defined by four corner nodes and six mid-side nodes which are connected by six curvilinear edges, see Figure 2.101. Due to the curvilinear edges of high quality elements, they map properly on curved boundaries, see Figure 2.102. Also, high quality elements provide better results than draft elements. However, due to higher number of nodes and degrees of freedom, the high quality elements require greater computational time and are mostly recommended for final evaluation of a model. 2.101 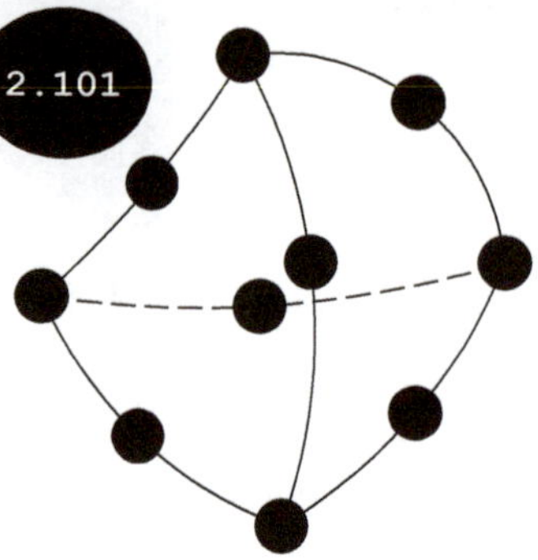 2.102 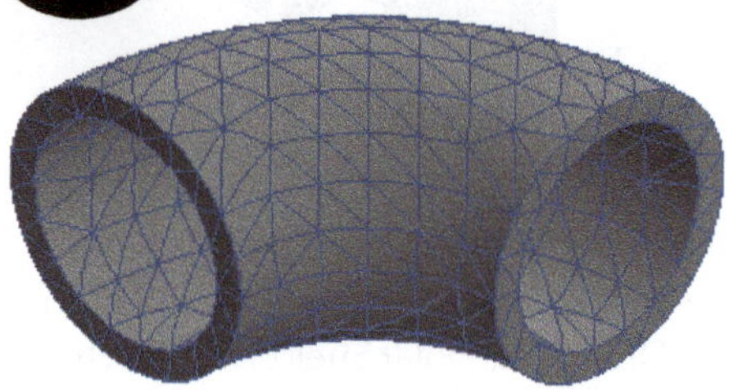
First Order Triangular Shell Elements	Similar to the First Order Solid Tetrahedral elements, the First Order Triangular Shell elements are also known as Draft elements with the only difference that the First Order Triangular Shell elements are defined by three corner nodes which are connected by three straight edges, see Figure 2.103. Each node has six degrees of freedom (three translations and three rotations). Due to the straight edges, the draft elements do not map properly on curved boundaries, (see Figure 2.104) and the results are not accurate. However, the draft elements require less computational time and are used for quick evaluation. The Triangular Shell elements are 2D elements and are used for meshing surface and sheet metal geometries, see Figure 2.104. This figure shows a surface geometry meshed with the First Order Triangular Shell elements (Draft elements). 2.103 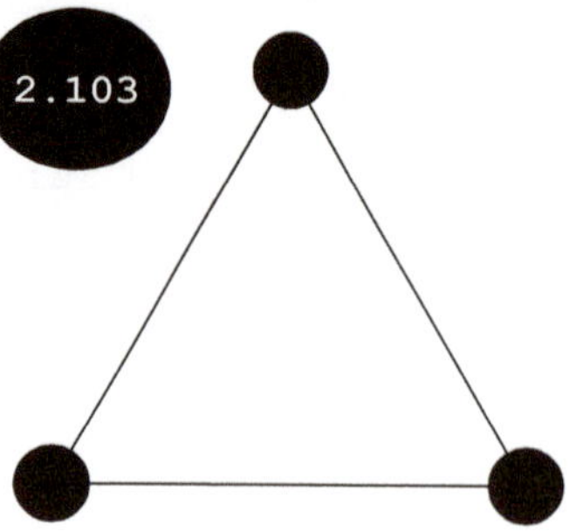 2.104 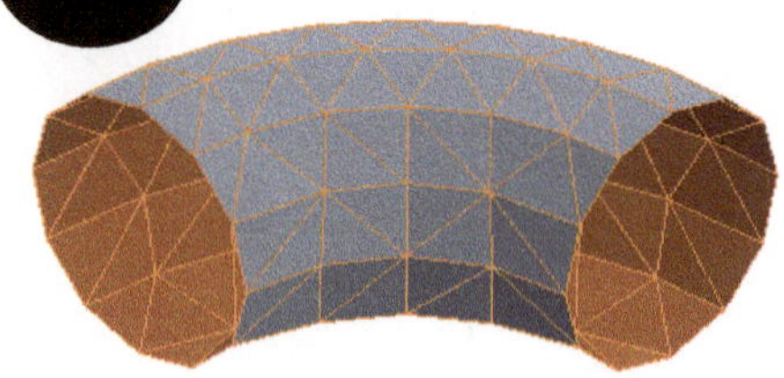

<table>
<tr>
<td>Second Order Triangular Shell Elements</td>
<td>The Second Order Triangular Shell elements are High quality elements having three corner nodes and three mid-side nodes which are connected by three curvilinear edges, see Figure 2.105. Due to the curvilinear edges of high quality elements, they map properly on curved boundaries and provide better results than draft elements. However, the high quality elements require greater computational time and are recommended for final evaluation.
2.105
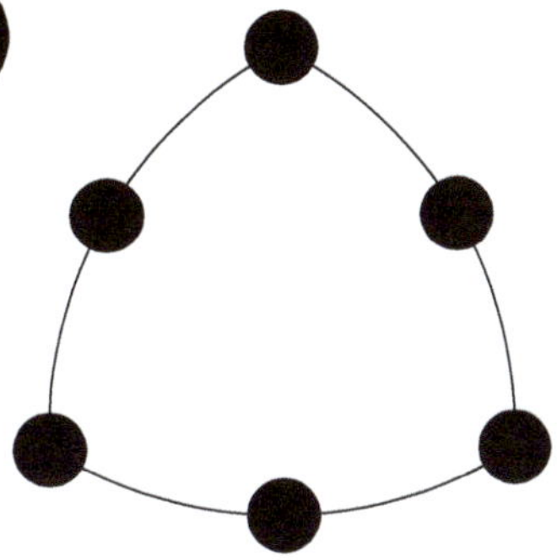
The Triangular Shell elements are 2D elements and are used for meshing surface and sheet metal geometries, see Figure 2.106. This figure shows a sheet metal geometry meshed with the Second Order Triangular Shell elements (High quality elements). Note that in case of a sheet metal geometry, the thickness of the shell elements is automatically extracted from the geometry. However, in case of a surface geometry, you need to define the thickness of the shell elements.
2.106
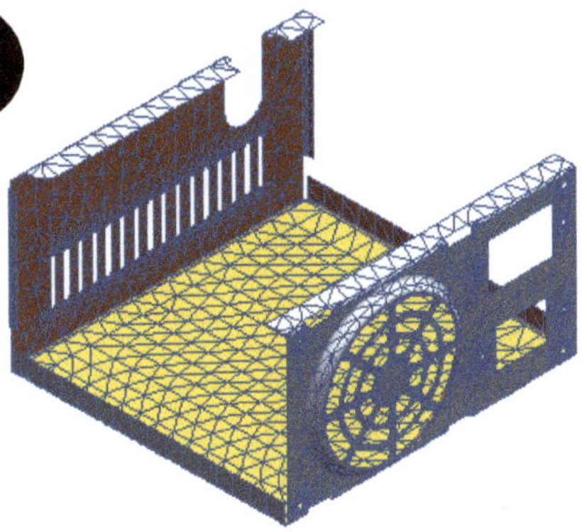</td>
</tr>
</table>

Two Node Beam Elements	The Two Node Beam elements are also known as Line elements. As the name suggests, each beam element is connected end-to-end with two nodes, see Figure 2.107. Each node has six degrees of freedom (three translations and three rotations). The Two Node Beam elements are 1D elements and are used for meshing weldment/structure geometries. When you mesh a weldment geometry, the beam elements are represented by hollow cylinders similar to the one shown in Figure 2.108. The beam elements can resist axial, bending, torsional, and shear loads. In SOLIDWORKS Simulation, you can also mesh a weldment/structure geometry with the truss elements. The truss elements are a special type of beam elements which resist axial loads only. 2.107  2.108 

Creating Mesh on a Geometry

SOLIDWORKS Simulation uses an automatic mesher for meshing a geometry based on mesh parameters such as global element size and tolerance. To mesh a geometry, click on the down arrow at the bottom of the **Run This Study** tool in the **Simulation CommandManager**, see Figure 2.109. A flyout appears. In this flyout, click on the **Create Mesh** tool. The **Mesh PropertyManager** appears, see Figure 2.110. Alternatively, right-click on the **Mesh** option in the **Simulation Study Tree** and then click on the **Create Mesh** tool in the shortcut menu that appears to invoke the **Mesh PropertyManager**.

2.109

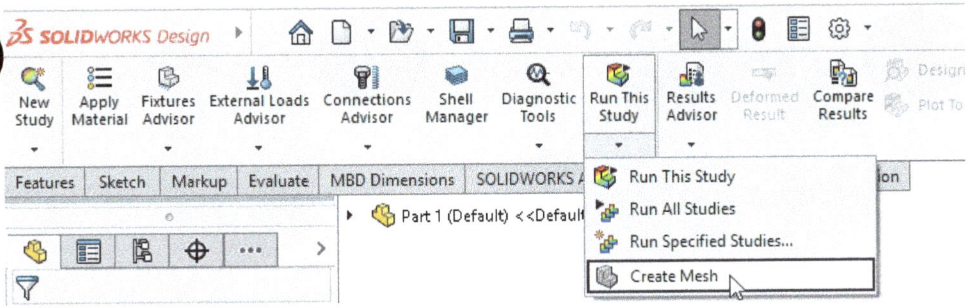

2.110

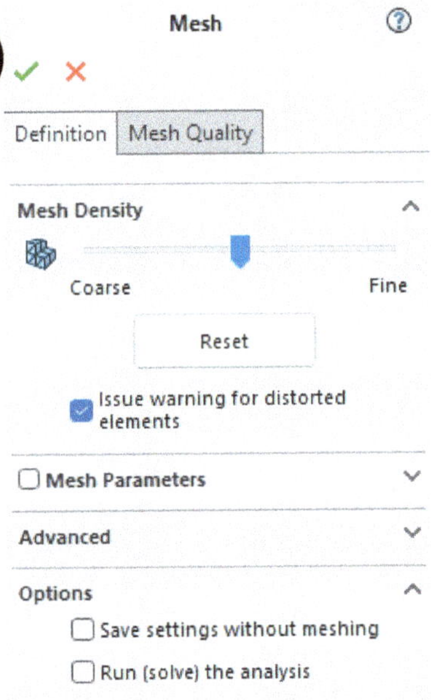

The options in the **Mesh PropertyManager** are used for defining the mesh parameters and are discussed below.

Mesh Density

The Slider in the **Mesh Density** rollout is used to set the global mesh element size and tolerance by dragging it. By default, SOLIDWORKS Simulation calculates the default global element size for a geometry based on its volume, surface area, and other geometric details. You can drag the Slider toward the right to set the fine global mesh element size and toward the left to set the coarse mesh element size. Figure 2.111 shows a geometry with fine mesh and Figure 2.112 shows the geometry with coarse mesh. The **Reset** button in this rollout is used for resetting the global mesh element size to the default settings.

2.111

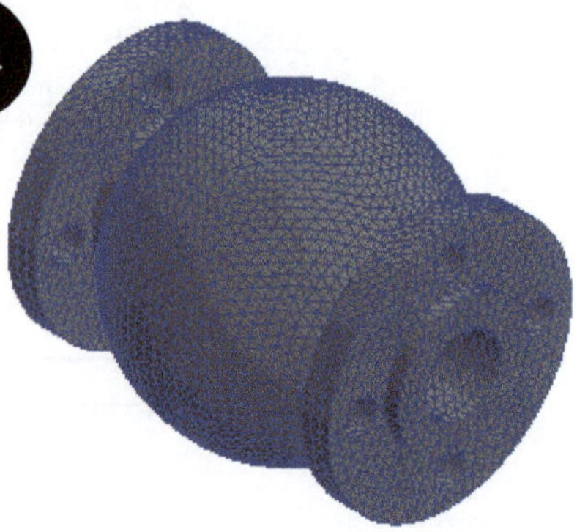

2.112

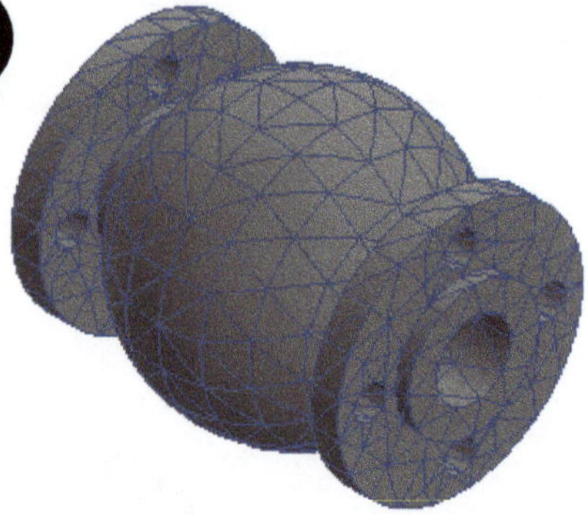

Note: The mesh size directly affects the accuracy of results. The smaller (finer) the element size, more accurate are the results you get. However, the computational time to generate the results gets increased. On the other hand, the larger (coarser) the element size, less accurate are the results you get. However, the computational time gets decreased.

Issue warning for distorted elements

On selecting this check box, SOLIDWORKS issues a warning when distorted elements are detected in a mesh. Distorted elements are the elements having negative Jacobian ratio. The concept of Jacobian Ratio is discussed later in this chapter.

Note: The **Issue Warning for distorted elements** check box is available only for high quality mesh. You can choose draft or high quality mesh of a body by using the options available in the **Mesh Quality** tab of the PropertyManager, which are discussed later in this chapter.

Mesh Parameters

The options in the **Mesh Parameters** rollout is used for defining the mesh parameters. By default, this rollout is in collapsed form. To expand this rollout, click on the check box in its title bar, see Figure 2.113. The options of this rollout are discussed below.

2.113

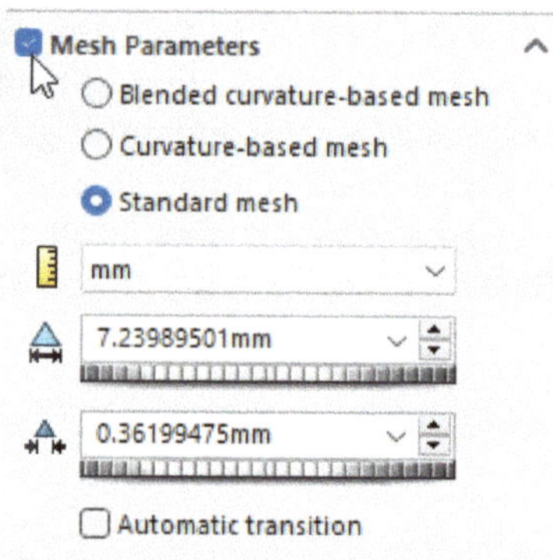

Standard mesh

By default, the **Standard mesh** radio button is selected in the **Mesh Parameters** rollout. As a result, you can specify the global element size and tolerance value in the **Global Size** and **Tolerance** fields of the rollout, respectively.

Note that the standard mesh keeps the mesh element size uniform throughout the geometry as per the global element size and tolerance value specified. It does not refine the mesh in the curvature areas or small features of the geometry which may have high stress, see Figure 2.114. It can affect the accuracy of results. The **Automatic transition** check box is used to apply mesh controls automatically to high curvature areas or small features of the geometry to generate a fine mesh in such areas, see Figure 2.115. Figure 2.114 shows a mesh geometry with the **Automatic transition** check box cleared and Figure 2.115 shows the mesh geometry with the **Automatic transition** check box selected.

2.114

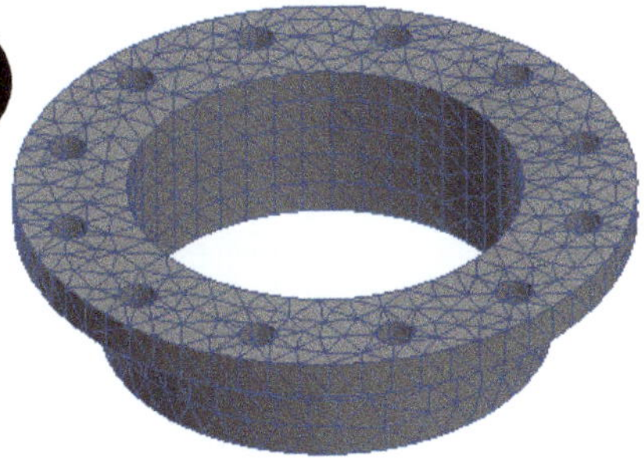

2.115

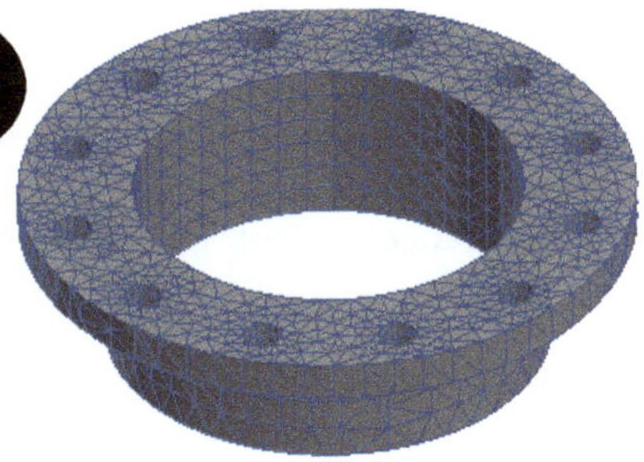

Curvature-based mesh

On selecting the **Curvature-based mesh** radio button, you can specify the maximum element size, minimum element size, minimum number of elements in a circle, and element size growth ratio in the respective fields of the rollout. Note that the curvature-based mesh automatically refines the mesh based on the specified parameters such that it creates more number of small elements in the curvature areas or small features of the geometry to get more accurate results, see Figure 2.116. It is used to create a mesh with variable element size, varying between the maximum and minimum element sizes specified in the respective fields of the rollout.

2.116

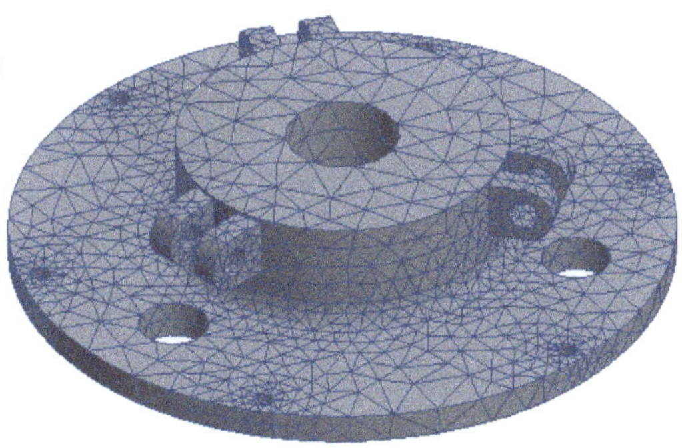

Blended curvature-based mesh

The **Blended curvature-based mesh** radio button is used to create a blended curvature-based mesh for a geometry which fails to mesh with the standard mesh or curvature-based mesh. It is used to create a mesh with high quality elements having low Aspect Ratio.

On selecting this radio button, you can specify the maximum element size, minimum element size, minimum number of elements in a circle, and element size growth ratio in the respective fields of the rollout for creating the blended curvature-based mesh. Note that the blended curvature-based mesh runs on a single central processor unit (CPU). As a result, the meshing process becomes slow.

Note: In SOLIDWORKS Simulation, you can define any mesher type as the default mesher. To do this, click on **Simulation** > **Options** in the SOLIDWORKS Design Menus and then click on the **Default Options** tab in the dialog box that appears. Next, click on the **Mesh** option on the left panel of the dialog box and then select the required radio button (**Standard**, **Curvature-based**, or **Blended curvature-based**) in the **Mesher type** area of the dialog box as the default mesher type for meshing a geometry.

Advanced

The options in the **Advanced** rollout are used for defining the quality of mesh in a geometry. Figure 2.117 shows the expanded **Advanced** rollout. The options are discussed below.

2.117

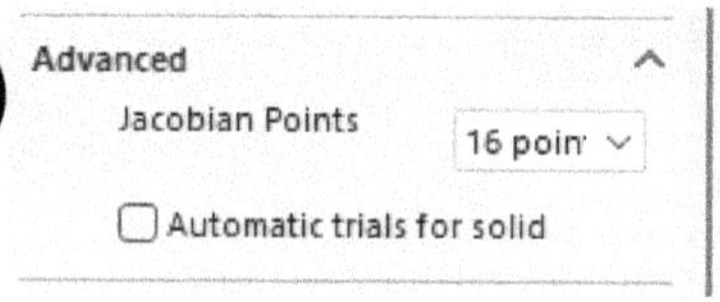

Jacobian points

The **Jacobian points** drop-down list is used to set the number of integration points (**4**, **16**, **29** gaussian points or **At nodes**) located within each element of a mesh to check its quality. The quality of mesh is important to ensure the accuracy of results.

SOLIDWORKS Simulation uses Aspect Ratio and Jacobian Points to check the quality of a mesh. By default, the Aspect Ratio check is used by SOLIDWORKS Simulation to check the quality of a mesh. The Aspect Ratio of an element is calculated as the ratio of the longest edge length to the shortest edge length of the element. By default, a perfect tetrahedral element has an Aspect Ratio equal to 1.0, see Figure 2.118. However, meshing a geometry with the elements having perfect Aspect Ratio is not possible due to its curved edges or small features. Figure 2.119 shows a tetrahedral element with a large Aspect Ratio. When the difference between the edges of an element becomes large, the accuracy of the results deteriorates.

2.118

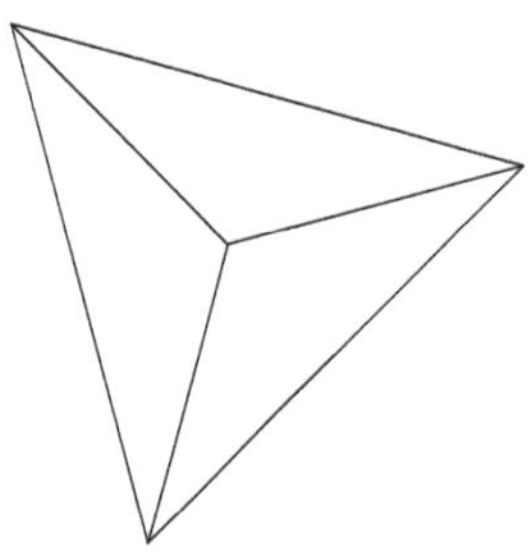

2.119

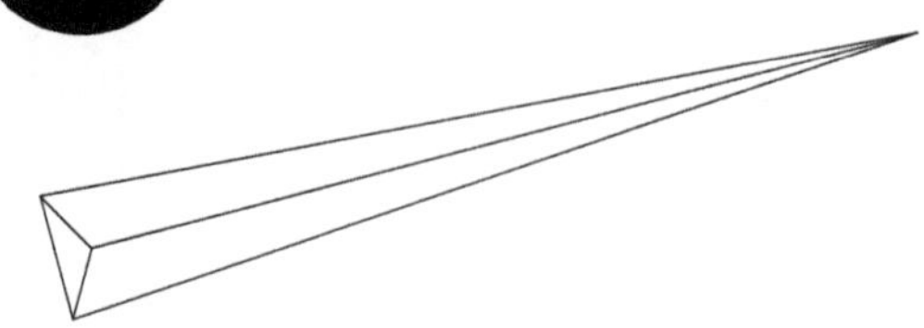

Similar to the Aspect Ratio check, the Jacobian check is also used to check the quality of a mesh as per the Jacobian Ratio. The Jacobian Ratio of an element is calculated based on the locations of the mid-side nodes on the edges of the element. A perfect tetrahedral element has all its mid-side nodes placed exactly at the middle of the edges. The Jacobian ratio of a perfect tetrahedral element is 1.0 and it increases as the curvatures of the boundaries increase. The Jacobian check is available for second order elements (high quality) since the mid-side nodes of the second order elements are placed on the curved boundaries to map the geometry accurately. Based on stochastic studies, a Jacobian ratio less than 30 is acceptable. However, a good-quality mesh has a Jacobian ratio between 1 and 10. SOLIDWORKS Simulation automatically adjusts the placement of mid-side nodes of an element to ensure it passes the Jacobian check.

Automatic trials for solid

The **Automatic trials for solid** check box is available when the **Standard Mesh** radio button is selected in the **Mesh Parameters** rollout to create standard mesh on a geometry. On selecting the **Automatic trials for solid** check box, the program automatically performs the next iteration and re-meshes the geometry with a smaller global element size, everytime the meshing fails. You can define the maximum number of mesh trials in the **Number of trials** field that appears below the **Automatic trials for solid** check box. Also, the ratio by which the global element size reduces in every iteration is 0.8.

Options

The **Save settings without meshing** check box of the **Options** rollout is used to save the parameters specified in the PropertyManager without meshing the geometry. The **Run (solve) the analysis** check box is used to run the analysis immediately after meshing the geometry. By default, both these check boxes are cleared.

Note: SOLIDWORKS Simulation automatically defines the type of elements to be used to mesh the geometry depending on its type. For a 3D solid geometry, it uses tetrahedral solid elements and for a surface/sheet metal geometry, it uses triangular shell elements. Also, for a weldment/structure geometry, it uses beam elements.

Besides using tetrahedral solid elements for a 3D solid geometry, you can also use triangular shell elements and beam elements for meshing a 3D solid geometry. For example, if the 3D solid geometry is having uniform thickness then you can treat it as a 2D geometry and use the shell elements for meshing it to reduce the computational time. The method for meshing a 3D solid geometry by using the shell and beam elements is discussed in later chapters.

Mesh Quality

In SOLIDWORKS Simulation, you can create a hybrid mesh by choosing both draft and high quality mesh for different bodies in a single mesh definition. To do this, activate the **Mesh Quality** tab in the **Mesh PropertyManager**, see Figure 2.120. By default, the high quality mesh is specified for all the bodies or parts of an assembly. You can choose to apply draft quality mesh for selected or all bodies by choosing the **Apply draft mesh quality** ⌄ or **Apply draft mesh quality to all** ⌄⌄ button, respectively in the **Specify** rollout in the **Mesh Quality** tab in the **Mesh PropertyManager**. In Figure 2.120, the high quality mesh is specified to Piston Head, Piston Pin, and Shaft and the draft quality mesh is specified to Piston Rod and Piston Rod Cap.

2.120

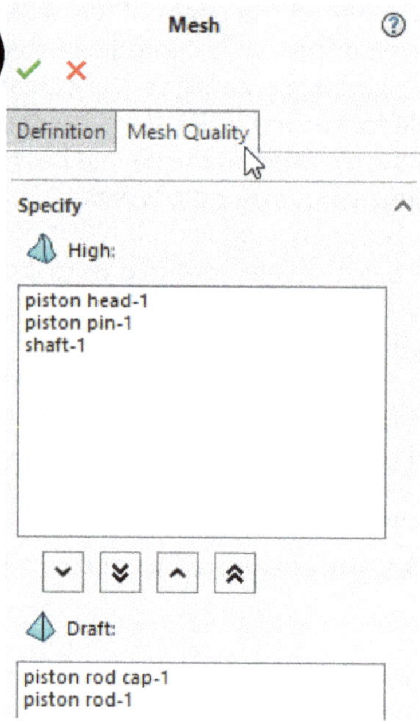

Note: The hybrid mesh that has both draft and high quality mesh elements, is available only for linear static studies with solid bodies.

After specifying all the required mesh parameters, click on the green tick-mark button in the PropertyManager. The **Mesh Progress** window appears which displays the progress of meshing the geometry, see Figure 2.121. After the geometry is meshed, the **Mesh Progress** window is closed automatically and the meshed geometry appears in the graphics area, see Figure 2.122. Also, a folder named "**Mesh Quality Plot**" with the mesh quality result gets added under the **Mesh** node in the Simulation Study Tree, see Figure 2.123.

2.121

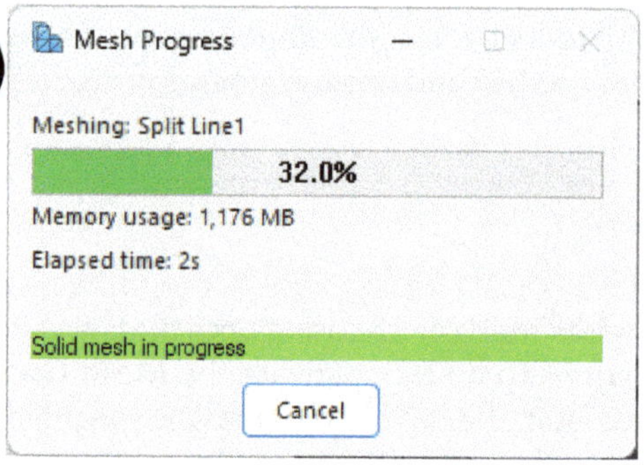

2.122

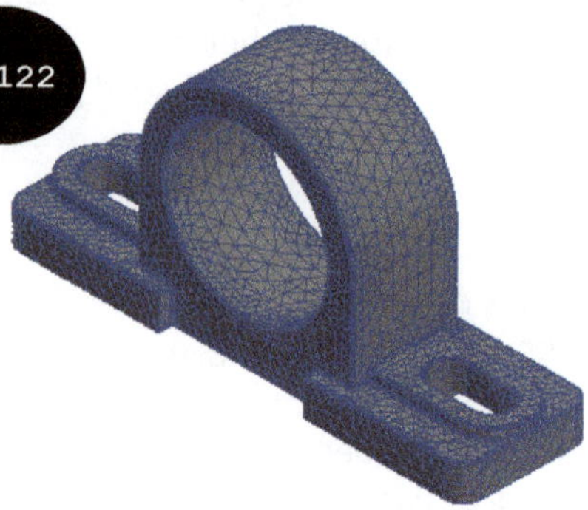

2.123

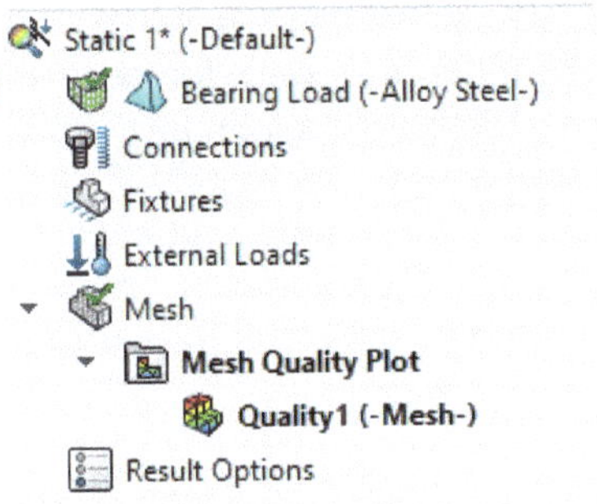

Tip: To mesh a surface geometry, you first need to define the thickness of the shell elements. Similarly, to mesh a weldment geometry, first you need to define the number of joints. You will learn more about meshing a surface, a sheet metal, and a weldment geometry in later chapters.

Identifying Poor Quality Mesh Elements

After generating the mesh on a geometry, you can identify its poor quality mesh elements based on the defined failure criterion by using the **Mesh Quality Diagnostics PropertyManager**. To do this, right-click on the **Mesh** node in the Simulation Study Tree and then click on the **Mesh Quality Diagnostics** option in the shortcut menu that appears, see Figure 2.124. The **Mesh Quality Diagnostics PropertyManager** appears, see Figure 2.125. Next, select the required method for measuring the quality of mesh elements in the **Mesh element quality criterion** drop-down list of the **Display** rollout.

2.124

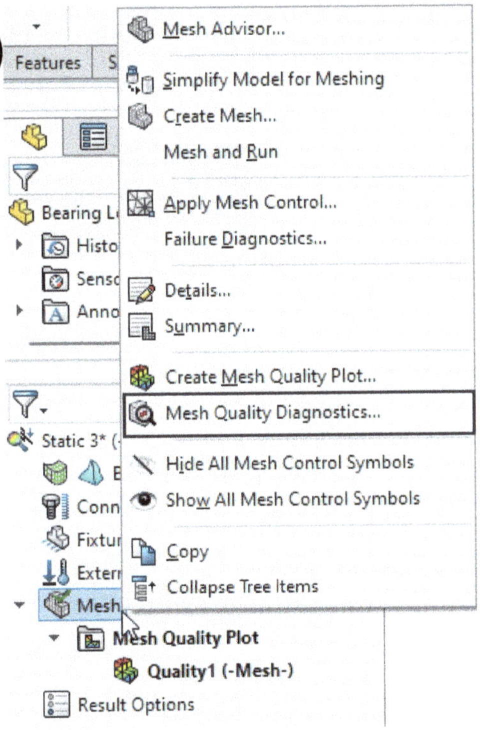

2.125

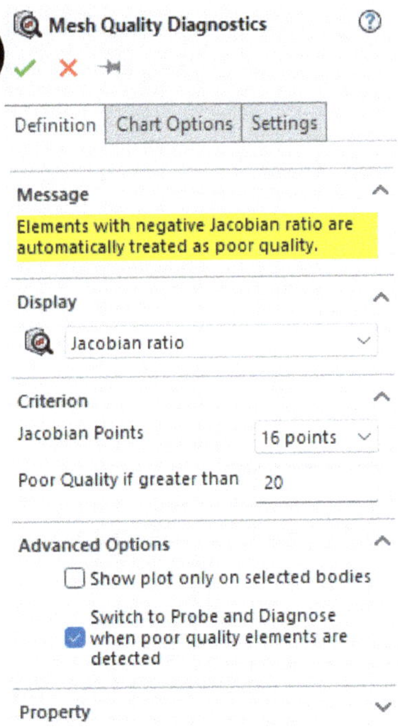

Depending upon the method selected for defining the quality of mesh elements, specify the criterion parameters in the **Criterion** rollout of the PropertyManager. In the **Poor Quality if greater than** field of the PropertyManager, you need to define the minimum threshold for the selected method to determine the quality of the mesh elements. For example, by default, the value **20** is entered in this field. As result, the mesh elements with a jacobian ratio or aspect ratio greater than 20 will be treated as poor-quality elements. Next, click on the green tick-mark button. The **Mesh Quality Diagnostic** plot with defined failure criterion appears in the graphics area, refer to Figure 2.126. Also, it is added in the **Mesh Quality Plot** folder of the Simulation Study Tree.

Note that if poor quality mesh elements get detected based on the defined failure criterion as shown in Figure 2.126, then the **Mesh Quality Diagnostic** plot appears along with the **Probe and Diagnose PropertyManager**, see Figure 2.127, since the **Switch to Probe and Diagnose when poor quality elements are detected** check box is selected in the **Advanced Options** rollout of the **Mesh Quality Diagnostics PropertyManager**, by default, refer to Figure 2.125.

2.126

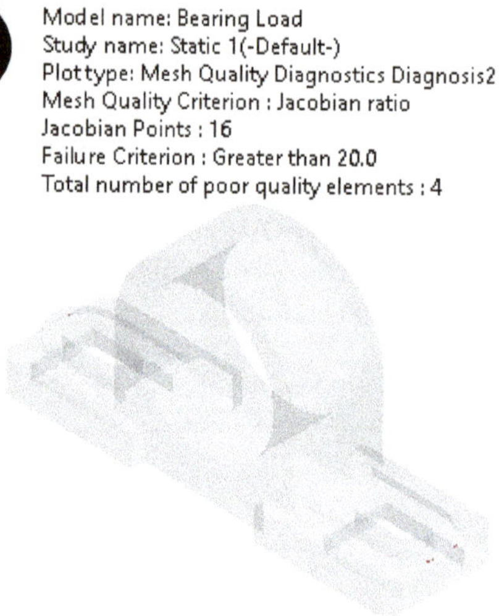

2.127

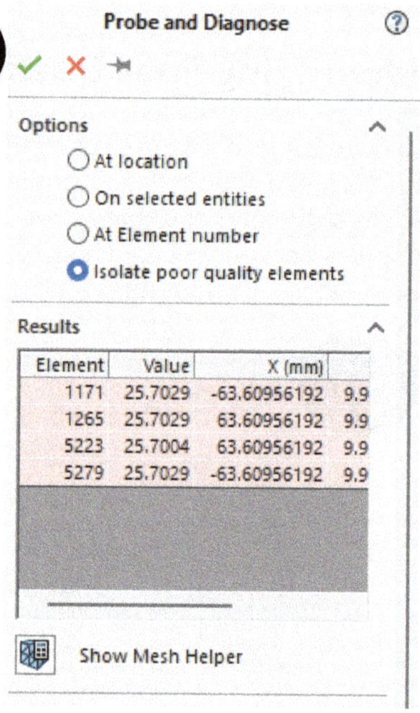

The options in the **Probe and Diagnose PropertyManager** are used for probing poor quality mesh elements in the graphics area and for taking appropriate action for improving them. By default, the **Isolate poor quality elements** radio button is selected in the **Options** rollout of the PropertyManager. As a result, all the poor quality elements get isolated or probed in the graphics area and their respective results get displayed in the **Results** rollout of the PropertyManager.

You can select the required option in the **Options** rollout to probe the poor quality elements in the graphics area and display their results in the **Results** rollout. The **Show Mesh Helper** button in the

Results rollout is used to display the **Mesh Helper** rollout to take appropriate actions for improving the mesh quality. The **Summary** rollout is used to display a summary of poor quality elements, which includes total number of poor quality elements, mesh quality criterion, and failure criterion. Also, the options in the **Report Options** rollout are used to generate a report and save the results data as *.csv* file, capture image, and copy result to clipboard.

After reviewing the poor quality mesh elements or taking the appropriate actions to improve them, exit the PropertyManager.

In SOLIDWORKS Simulation, after defining the material properties, boundary conditions (loads and fixtures), and generating the mesh on a geometry, you can run the analysis to get the results. You will learn about performing different types of analysis in later chapters. The various step-by-step case studies on the linear static analysis are discussed in the next chapter.

Summary

In this chapter, you have learned about the fundamental assumptions of linear static analysis and how to set it up in SOLIDWORKS Simulation. You explored how to define analysis units, assign standard material properties, and create a custom material library, including adding new material categories and user-defined materials.

Additionally, you learned how to edit standard material properties, manage custom materials, and delete material libraries and categories. The chapter also covered defining boundary conditions, applying fixtures/restraints and loads, meshing a geometry, and identifying poor-quality mesh elements to ensure accurate and reliable simulation results.

These skills will help you confidently set up and conduct linear static analysis in SOLIDWORKS Simulation, allowing you to evaluate structural performance, optimize designs, and make informed engineering decisions.

Questions

Complete the following sentences:

- To perform linear static analysis, the material is assumed to be within the ________ region of the stress-strain curve due to the applied load.
- The materials available in the ______ library are read only materials.
- SOLIDWORKS Simulation provides two type of fixtures: ______ and ______ .
- Standard fixtures include ______ , ______ , ______ , and ______ .
- The ______ fixture is used for applying restraints to a cylindrical face such that it can only rotate about its axis of rotation.

- The ______ fixture is used for analyzing one half of the model which is symmetric about a symmetric plane and the results are obtained for the complete model.
- By default, the gravity of the earth is ______ m/s^2.
- The ______ is defined as the load which originates at a remote location in the space and its effect transfers to the model geometry.
- The ______ process is used for dividing a geometry into a number of discrete finite elements.
- By default, the ______ elements are used for meshing a 3D solid geometry.
- The First Order Solid Tetrahedral elements are also known as ______ elements.
- In SOLIDWORKS Simulation, the ______ and ______ checks are used for checking the quality of a mesh.
- SOLIDWORKS Simulation automatically defines the type of elements to be used for ______ the geometry.
- In a ______ geometry, the thickness of the shell elements is automatically extracted from the geometry.

CHAPTER

3

Case Studies of Static Analysis

In this chapter, the following topics will be discussed:

- Static Analysis of a Rectangular Plate
- Static Analysis of a Bracket with Mesh Control
- Static Analysis of a Symmetrical Model
- Static Analysis of a Torispherical Head with Shell Elements
- Static Analysis of a Weldment Frame with Beam Elements
- Static Analysis of a Beam Support
- Static Analysis of a Bearing House

In the previous chapter, you learned about the key assumptions of linear static analysis and explored various options for assigning material properties, applying boundary conditions (fixtures and loads), meshing a geometry, and more.

In this chapter, you will apply these concepts by conducting various case studies in linear static analysis, gaining practical experience in setting up simulations and interpreting results.

Case Study 1: Static Analysis of a Rectangular Plate

In this case study, you will perform the linear static analysis of a rectangular plate shown in Figure 3.1 and determine stress under a tensile load.

3.1

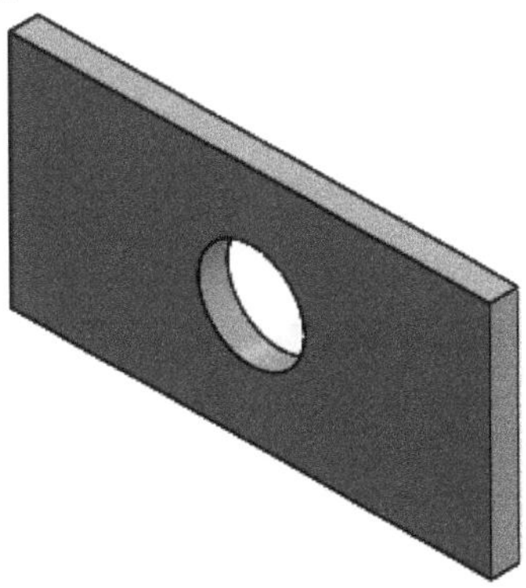

Project Description

The rectangular plate is fixed at one end (see Figure 3.2) and the 5000 N load is uniformly distributed along the other (opposite) end face of the plate, see Figure 3.2. The plate is made up of **AISI 1020** steel material.

3.2

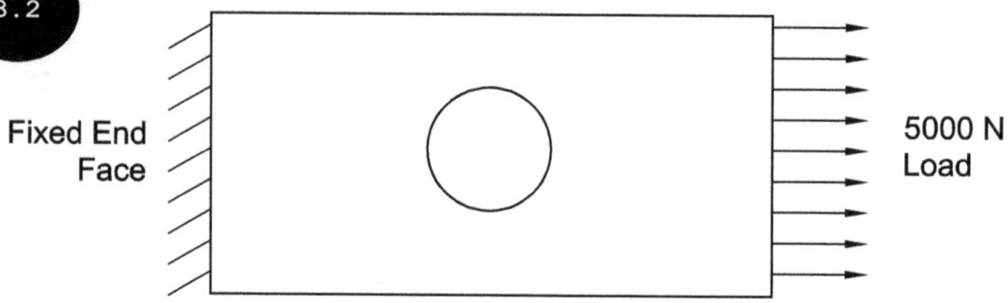

Project Summary

In this case study, you will run two static studies. In the first study, you will generate a high-quality standard mesh with a global element size of 6 mm and tolerance value of 0.3 mm as the mesh parameters, and in the second study, you will generate a curvature-based mesh with a maximum element size of 1.5 mm and minimum element size of 1 mm as the mesh parameters to compare the difference in the results. Specify the unit system as SI (MKS) with displacement in mm and stress in N/mm^2 (MPa) units.

The following sequence summarizes the case study outline:

1. Downloading Files of Chapter 3
2. Starting SOLIDWORKS and SOLIDWORKS Simulation
3. Starting the First Static Study
4. Defining Units and Results Settings
5. Assigning the Material
6. Applying the Fixture
7. Applying the Load
8. Generating the Mesh
9. Running the Analysis
10. Displaying Stress, Displacement, and Strain Results
11. Annotating Maximum and Minimum Stresses
12. Displaying the 1st Principal Stress Plot
13. Displaying the von Mises Stress in the True Scale
14. Saving Results
15. Running the Second Static Study
16. Comparing Results of two Static Studies
17. Saving Results

Section 1: Downloading Files of Chapter 3

1. Log on to the CADArtifex website (***cadartifex.com/login/***) using the Email OTP that will be sent to your registered email ID. If you are a new user, you must first sign up on the CADArtifex website as a **Learner** (***cadartifex.com/register***).

2. After logging in to your account, navigate to the textbook titled "**SOLIDWORKS Simulation 2026: A Power Guide for Beginners and Intermediate Users: Colored**" using the **Browse Resources** option available in the left menu to download its resources. Alternatively, you can enter the name of the textbook in the **Search** box to locate it quickly.

Note: All resource files for the textbook are available under the **Online Resources** tab on the respective textbook page.

---

3. In the **Online Resources** tab, expand the **Case Studies** rollout and click the **Download** button corresponding to **C03 Case Studies**. In the confirmation window that appears, click the **Confirm** button. The download of the C03 Case Studies file will begin. After the download is complete, unzip the file. It is recommended that you create a folder named "**SOLIDWORKS Simulation**" on your local drive and then create a subfolder inside it named "**Case Studies**".

4. Save the extracted **C03 Case Studies** folder in the **Case Studies** subfolder created inside the **SOLIDWORKS Simulation** folder.

Section 2: Starting SOLIDWORKS and SOLIDWORKS Simulation

1. Double-click on the SOLIDWORKS icon on your desktop to start SOLIDWORKS.

2. Click on the **Open** button in the **Welcome** dialog box. The **Open** dialog box appears. Alternatively, click on the **Open** tool in the **Standard** toolbar to invoke the **Open** dialog box.

3. In the **Open** dialog box, browse to the location > ***SOLIDWORKS Simulation > Case Studies > C03 Case Studies > Case Study 1*** in the local drive of your system. Next, select the **Rectangular Plate** model and then click on the **Open** button in the dialog box. The Rectangular Plate model is opened in SOLIDWORKS, see Figure 3.3.

3.3

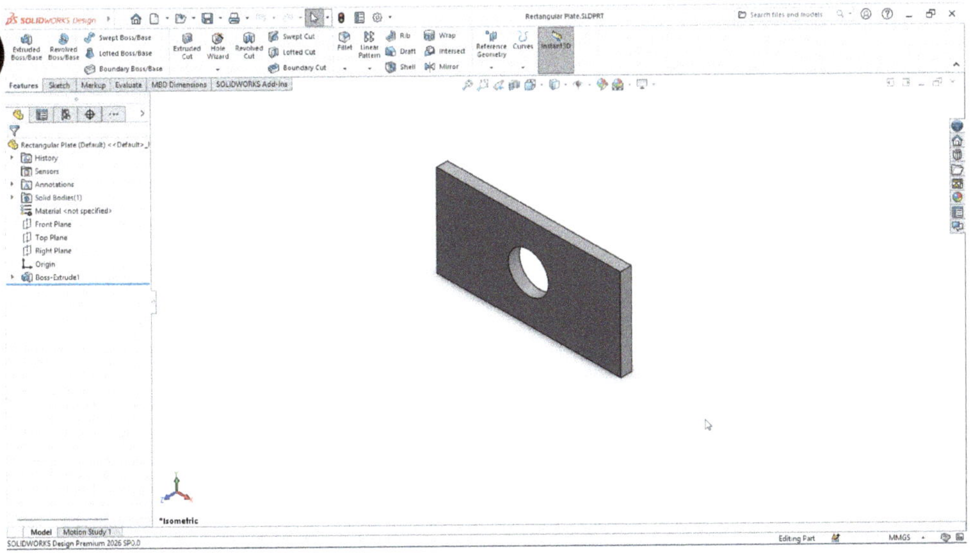

Now, you need to invoke SOLIDWORKS Simulation.

4. Click on the **Tools > Add-Ins** in the SOLIDWORKS Design Menus, see Figure 3.4. The **Add-Ins** dialog box appears, see Figure 3.5.

3.4

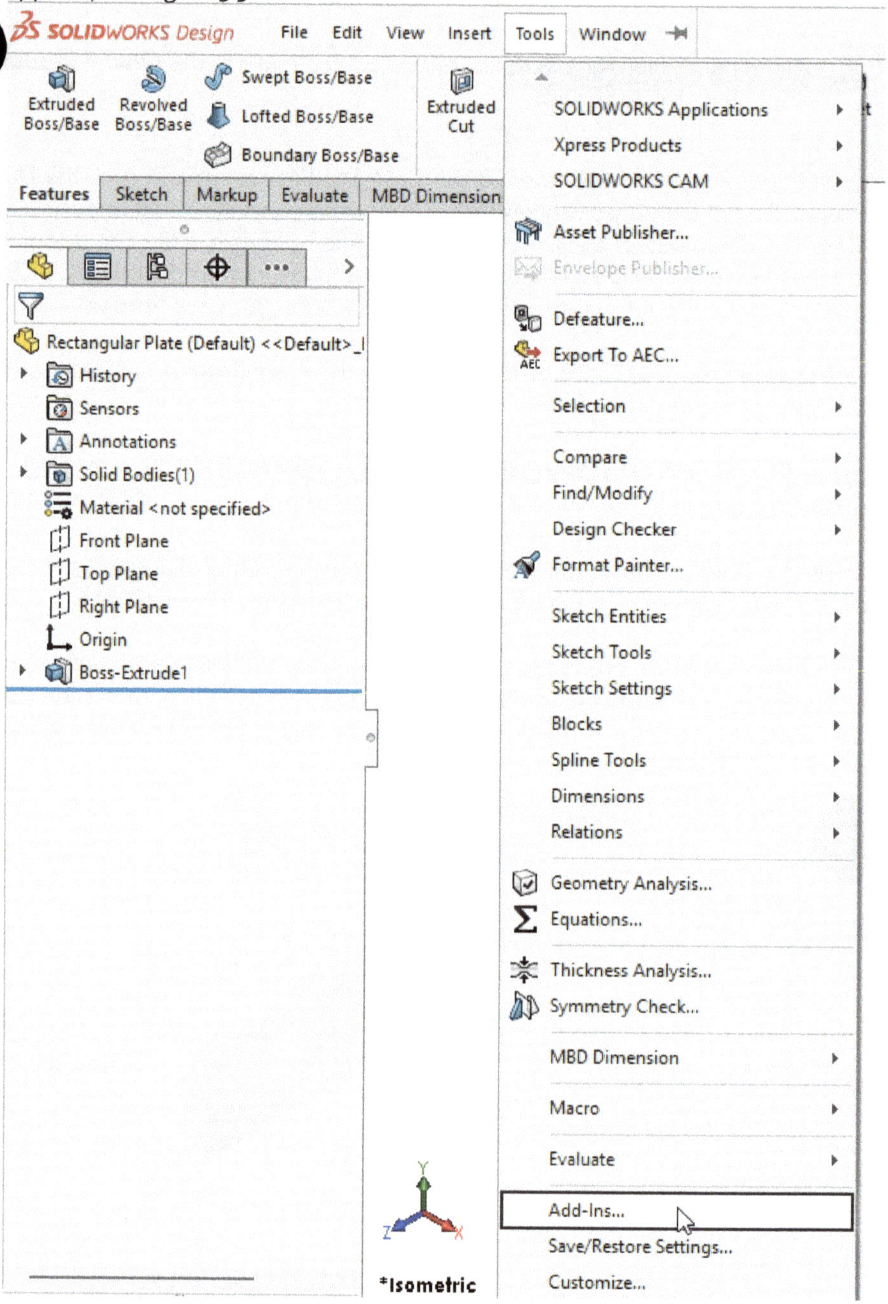

5. Select the check boxes available on the left and right of the **SOLIDWORKS Simulation** option in the **Add-Ins** dialog box, see Figure 3.5.

6. Click on the **OK** button in the dialog box. The **Simulation** and **Analysis Preparation** tabs are added to the CommandManager.

Note: If the **Simulation** tab is already added in the CommandManager then you can skip the steps 4, 5, and 6.

3.5

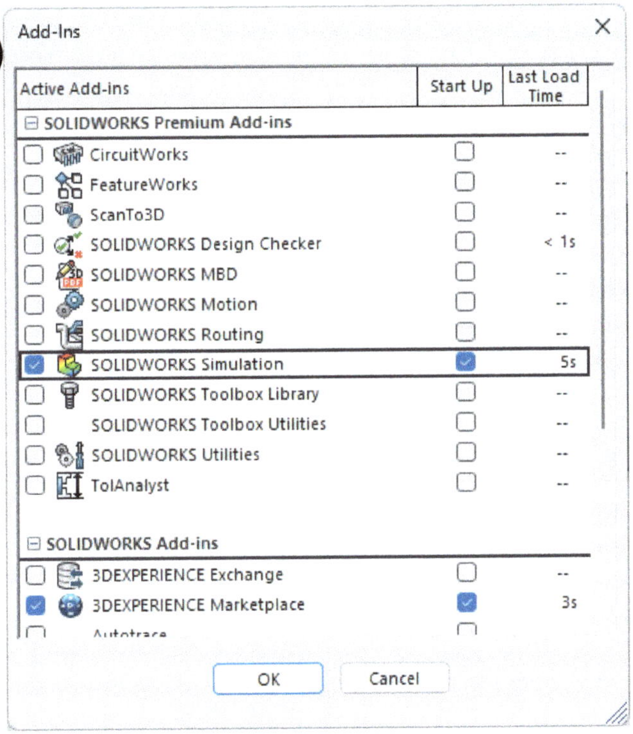

Section 3: Starting the First Static Study

1. Click on the **Simulation** tab in the **CommandManager**. The tools of the **Simulation CommandManager** appear, see Figure 3.6.

3.6

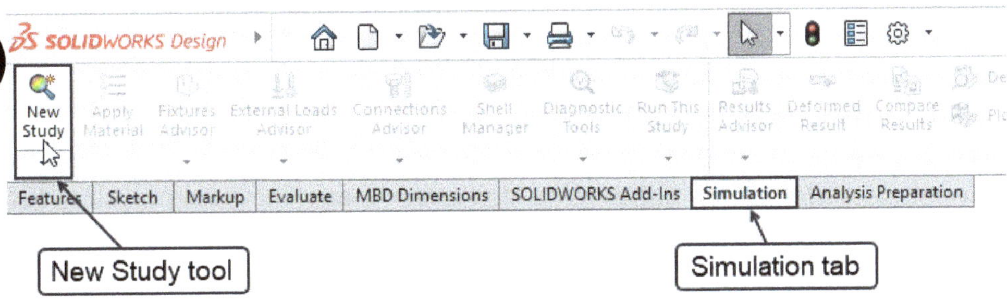

2. Click on the **New Study** tool in the **Simulation CommandManager**, see Figure 3.6. The **Study PropertyManager** appears, see Figure 3.7.

3. Ensure that the **Static** button is activated in the **General Simulation** rollout of the **Study PropertyManager** to perform the linear static analysis on the model.

4. Enter **Standard Mesh Study** as the name of the study in the **Study name** field of the **Name** rollout in the PropertyManager.

5. Click on the green tick-mark button in the **Study PropertyManager**. The various tools for performing the static analysis are enabled in the **Simulation CommandManager**.

3.7

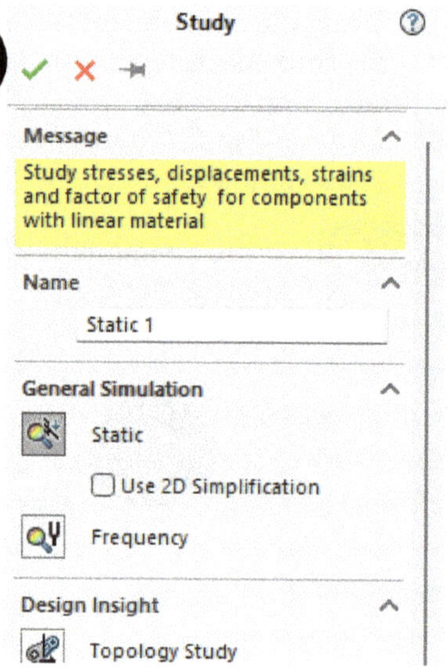

Section 4: Defining Units and Results Settings

Before you start with the analysis process, it is important to set the units and results settings for SOLIDWORKS Simulation.

1. Click on the **Simulation > Options** in the SOLIDWORKS Design Menus. The **System Options** dialog box appears.

2. In this dialog box, click on the **Default Options** tab. The name of the dialog box changes to the **Default Options**, see Figure 3.8.

3.8

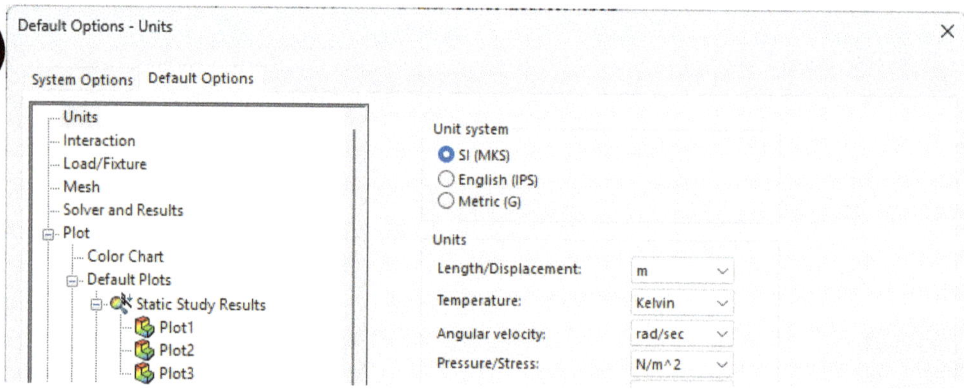

3. Ensure that the **Units** option is selected in the left panel of the dialog box.

4. Select the **SI (MKS)** radio button in the **Unit system** area of the dialog box. Next, ensure that the **mm** unit is selected in the **Length/Displacement** drop-down list and the **N/mm^2 (MPa)** unit is selected in the **Pressure/Stress** drop-down list of the **Units** area, see Figure 3.9.

3.9

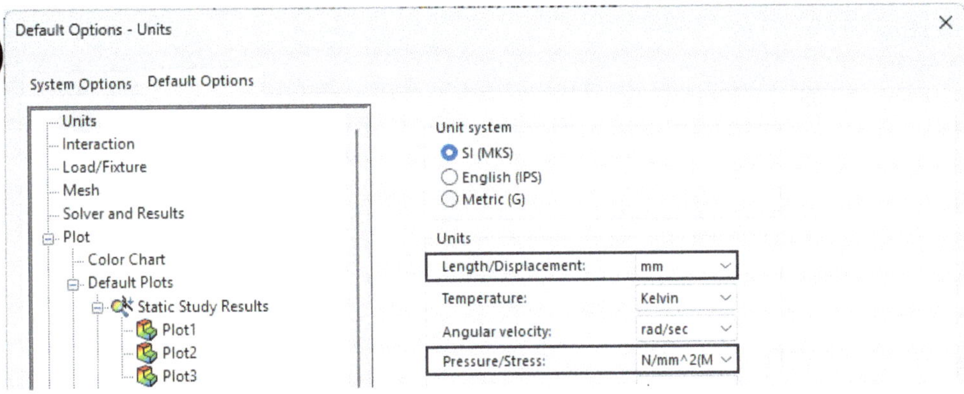

Now, you need to set the results settings.

5. Click on the **Solver and Results** option in the dialog box and then select the **Automatic** radio button in the **Default solver** area of the dialog box, see Figure 3.10.

3.10

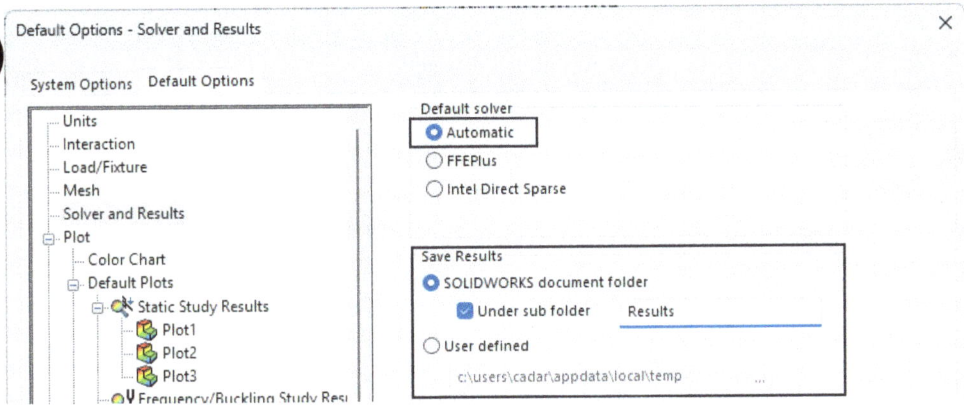

6. Select the **Under sub folder** check box in the **Save Results** area of the dialog box and then enter **Results** in the field enabled in front of it, see Figure 3.10. By doing so, the **Results** sub-folder will be created automatically in the same directory where the model is saved to save the results of the analysis.

   Note that by default, the **Under sub folder** check box is cleared. As a result, the analysis results are saved in the same folder where the model is saved. You can also specify a folder in the user-defined location to save the analysis results by using the **User-defined** radio button of the **Save Results** area in the dialog box.

7. After specifying the units and result settings, click on the **OK** button to accept the changes and exit the dialog box.

Note: By default, for every static analysis, SOLIDWORKS Simulation creates plots for the stress, displacement, and strain results. This happens because in the **Static Study Results** node of the dialog box, the three plots (**Plot1**, **Plot2**, and **Plot3**) for stress, displacement, and strain are added by default, see Figure 3.10. You can change the plot settings of a plot as required by clicking on it and then selecting the required result type. You can also add more result plots for the analysis. To do this, right-click on the **Static Study Results** node of the dialog box and then click on the **Add New Plot** tool in the shortcut menu that appears. Next, set the required result type for the newly added plot.

Section 5: Assigning the Material

1. Click on the **Apply Material** tool in the **Simulation CommandManager**. The **Material** dialog box appears, see Figure 3.11. Alternatively, right-click on the name of the model (**Rectangular Plate**) in the Simulation Study Tree and then click on the **Apply/Edit material** tool in the shortcut menu that appears.

2. Expand the **Steel** category of the **SOLIDWORKS Materials** library in the **Material** dialog box and then select the **AISI 1020** steel material, see Figure 3.11. The material properties of the selected material appear on the right panel of the dialog box.

3.11

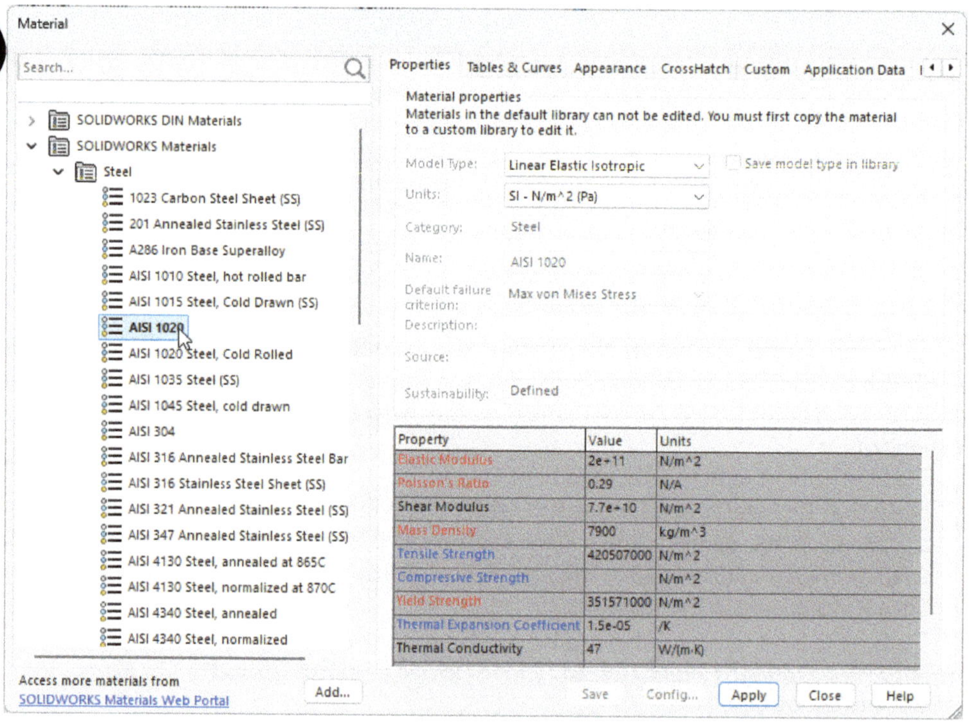

3. Click on the **Apply** button and then the **Close** button in the dialog box. The material is assigned to the model.

Section 6: Applying the Fixture

1. Invoke the **Fixture** flyout by clicking on the arrow at the bottom of the **Fixtures Advisor** tool in the **Simulation CommandManager** and then click on the **Fixed Geometry** tool, see Figure 3.12. The **Fixture PropertyManager** appears, see Figure 3.13. Alternatively, right-click on the **Fixtures** option in the Simulation Study Tree and then click on the **Fixed Geometry** tool in the shortcut menu that appears to invoke the **Fixture PropertyManager**.

3.12

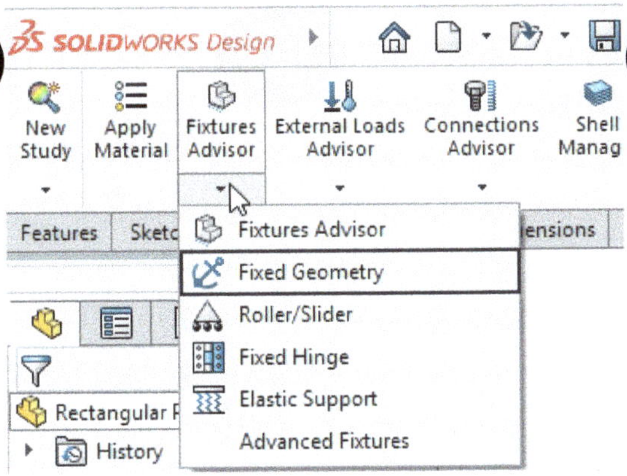

3.13

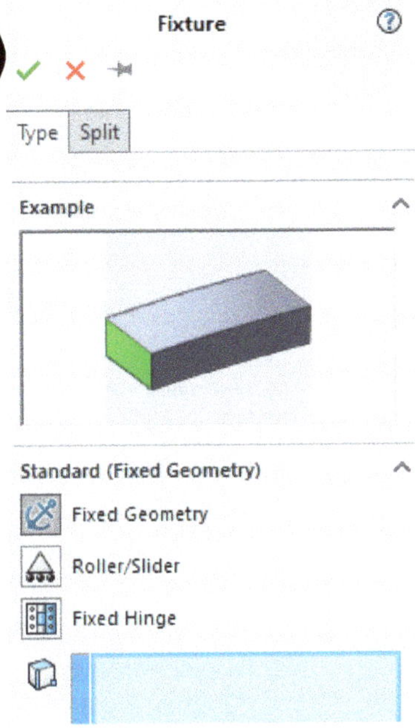

2. Rotate the model such that the left end face of the model can be viewed and then select it to apply the Fixed Geometry fixture. The symbol of the Fixed Geometry fixture appears on the selected face, see Figure 3.14.

3.14

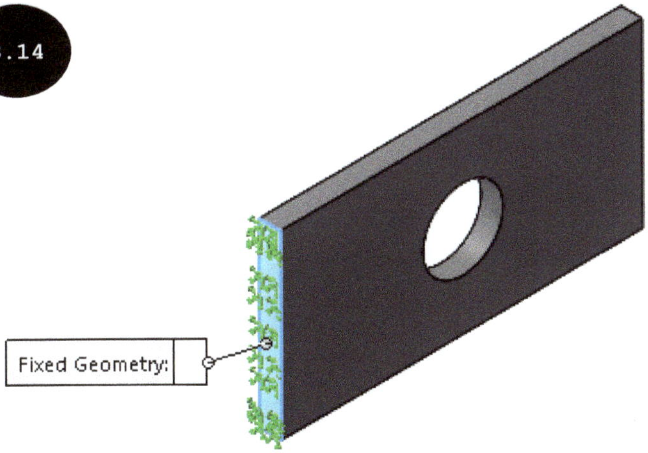

3. Click on the green tick-mark button in the PropertyManager. The Fixed Geometry fixture is applied to the selected face of the model.

Section 7: Applying the Load

1. Invoke the **External Loads** flyout by clicking on the arrow at the bottom of the **External Loads Advisor** tool in the **Simulation CommandManager** and then click on the **Force** tool, see Figure 3.15. The **Force/Torque PropertyManager** appears, see Figure 3.16. Alternatively, right-click on the **External Loads** option in the Simulation Study Tree and then click on the **Force** tool in the shortcut menu that appears to invoke the **Force/Torque PropertyManager**.

3.15

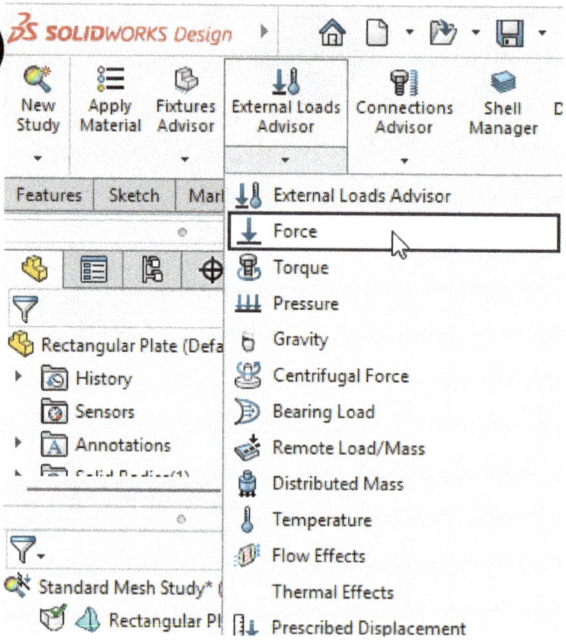

3.16

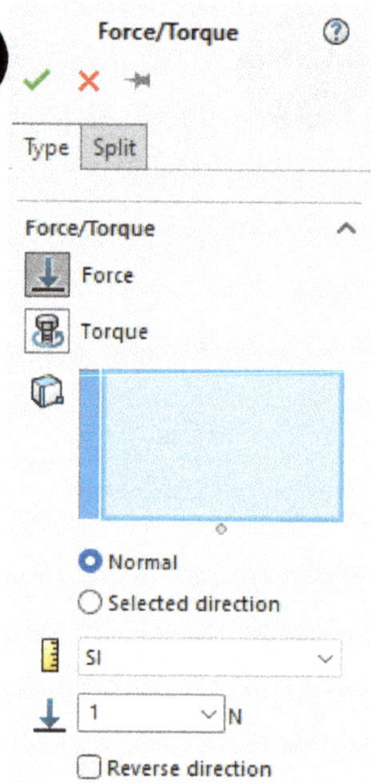

2. Change the orientation of the model to isometric and then select the right end face of the model to apply the load. The symbol of the load appears on the selected face, see Figure 3.17.

3. Ensure that the **Normal** radio button is selected.

4. Enter **5000** in the **Force Value** field of the PropertyManager.

5. Select the **Reverse direction** button to reverse the direction of force like the one shown in Figure 3.17.

3.17

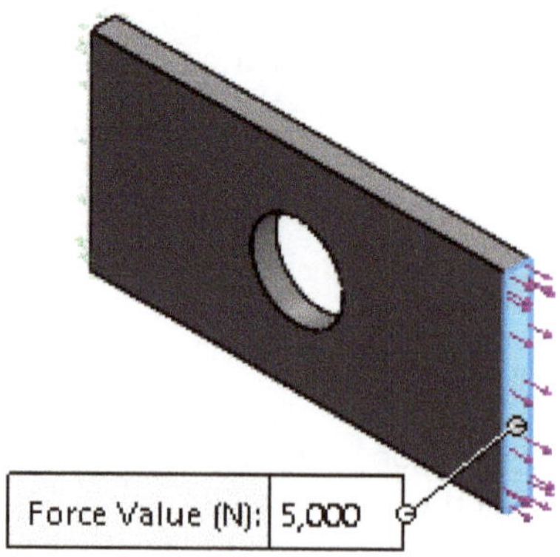

6. Click on the green tick-mark button in the PropertyManager. The 5000 N load is applied on the selected face of the model.

Section 8: Generating the Mesh

After defining the material properties and boundary conditions (fixtures and loads), you need to generate the mesh on the model. In this case study, you will first generate the standard mesh and then generate the curvature-based mesh to compare the difference in the results.

1. Click on the down arrow at the bottom of the **Run This Study** tool in the **Simulation CommandManager**. A flyout appears, see Figure 3.18. Next, click on the **Create Mesh** tool. The **Mesh PropertyManager** appears, see Figure 3.19. Alternatively, right-click on the **Mesh** option in the Simulation Study Tree and then click on the **Create Mesh** tool in the shortcut menu that appears to invoke the **Mesh PropertyManager**.

3.18

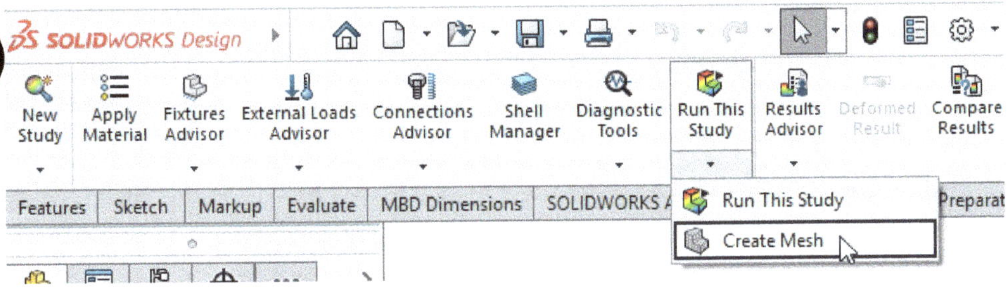

3.19

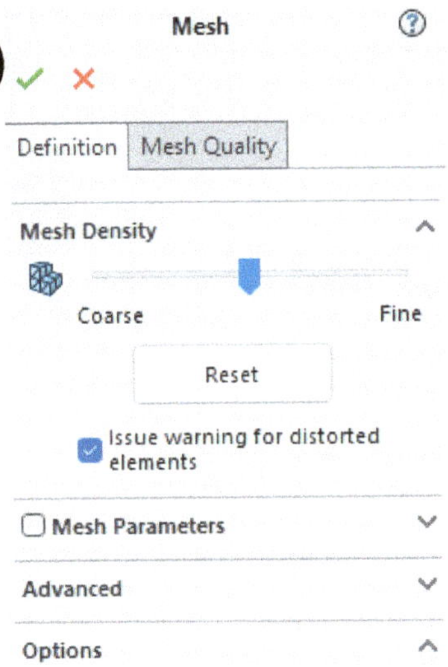

2. Expand the **Mesh Parameters** rollout of the PropertyManager by clicking on the check box in its title bar, see Figure 3.20.

3. Ensure that the **Standard mesh** radio button is selected in the expanded **Mesh Parameters** rollout. The **Global Size** and **Tolerance** fields of the rollout display the default global mesh size and tolerance values, respectively. SOLIDWORKS Simulation automatically calculates the default mesh parameters based on the volume, surface area, and other details of the model.

4. Enter 6 mm as the global element size in the **Global Size** field of the **Mesh Parameters** rollout. Also, ensure that the tolerance value is specified as 0.3 mm in the **Tolerance field** of the rollout, see Figure 3.20.

5. Click on the **Mesh Quality** tab in the PropertyManager, see Figure 3.21.

3.20

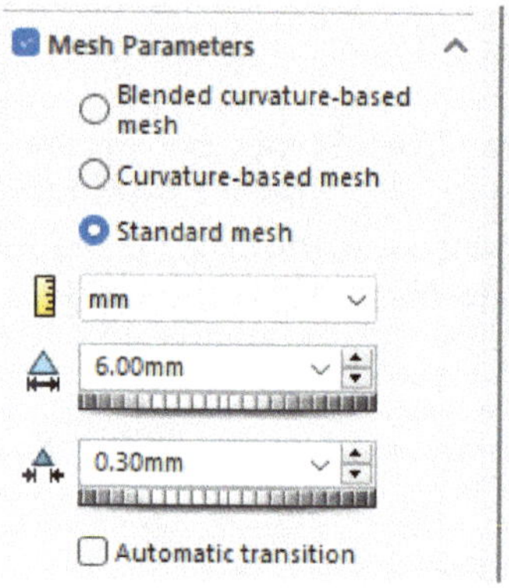

3.21

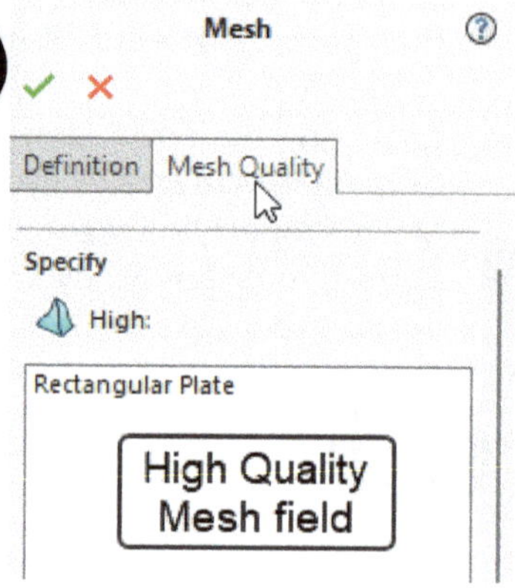

6. Ensure that the name of the model (Rectangular Plate) appears in the **High Quality Mesh** field for generating a mesh with high-quality tetrahedral solid elements, see Figure 3.21.

7. After defining all the mesh parameters, click on the green tick-mark button ✓ in the PropertyManager. The **Mesh Progress** window appears which displays the progress of generating the mesh in the model, see Figure 3.22. After the process of meshing the model is complete, the meshed model appears in the graphics area, see Figure 3.23.

3.22

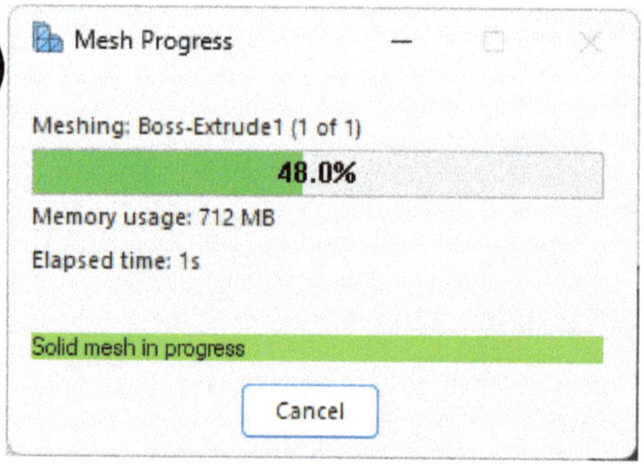

3.23

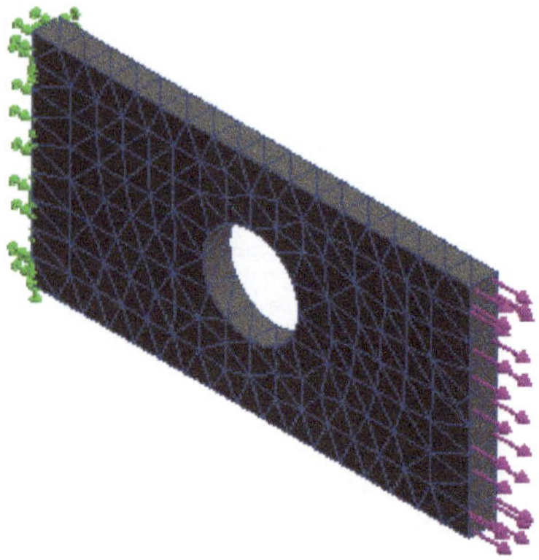

Section 9: Running the Analysis

After defining the material properties, boundary conditions (fixtures and loads), and generating the mesh, you can run the analysis.

1. Click on the **Run This Study** tool in the **Simulation CommandManager**, see Figure 3.24. The **Standard Mesh Study** (*name of the study*) window appears which displays the progress of the analysis, see Figure 3.25.

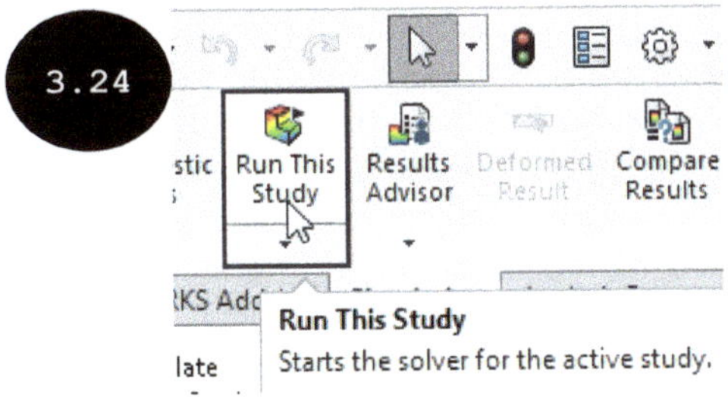

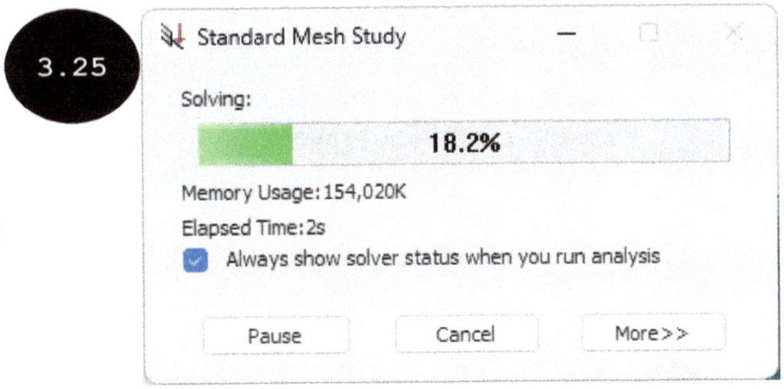

Note that the computational time to complete the analysis depends on the number of elements, nodes, and degrees of freedom to be solved by the solver. After the process of running the analysis is complete, the **Results** folder is added to the Simulation Study Tree with the stress, displacement, and strain results, see Figure 3.26. By default, the **Stress** result is activated in the **Results** folder. Consequently, the stress distribution on the model and the von Mises stress plot appear in the graphics area, see Figure 3.27.

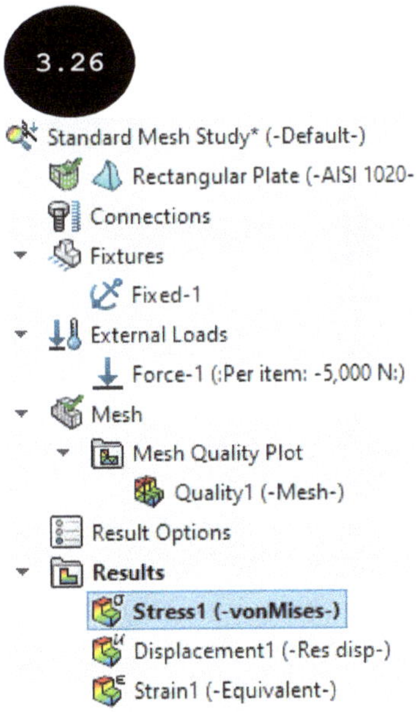

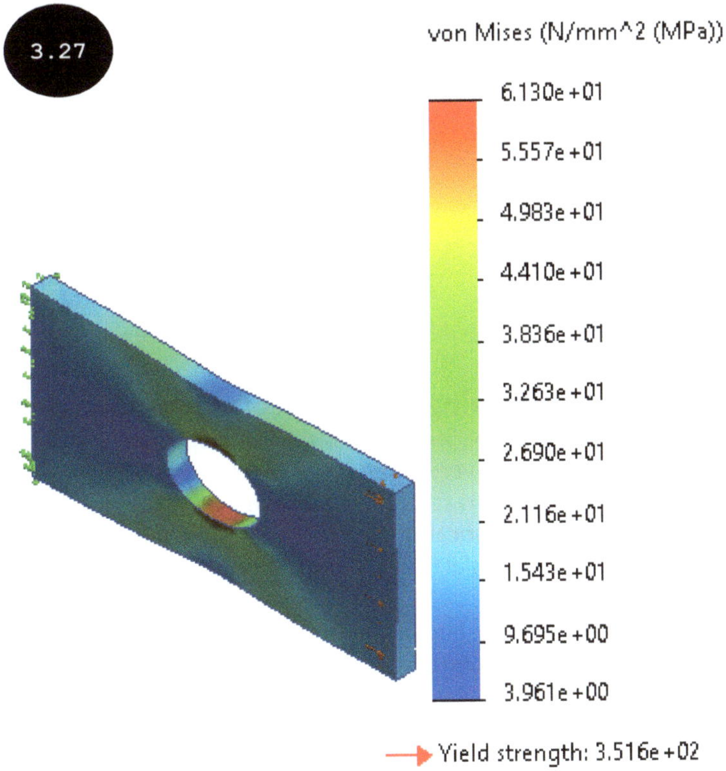

Note: You can set the Number Format for the stress result values to floating as shown in Figure 3.28. To do this, double-click on the von Mises stress plot in the graphics area. The **Stress plot PropertyManager** appears on the left of the graphics area. In this PropertyManager, click on the **Chart Options** tab and then select the **floating** option in the **Number Format** drop-down list of the **Position/Format** rollout in the PropertyManager. Next, click on the green tick-mark button in the PropertyManager.

3.28

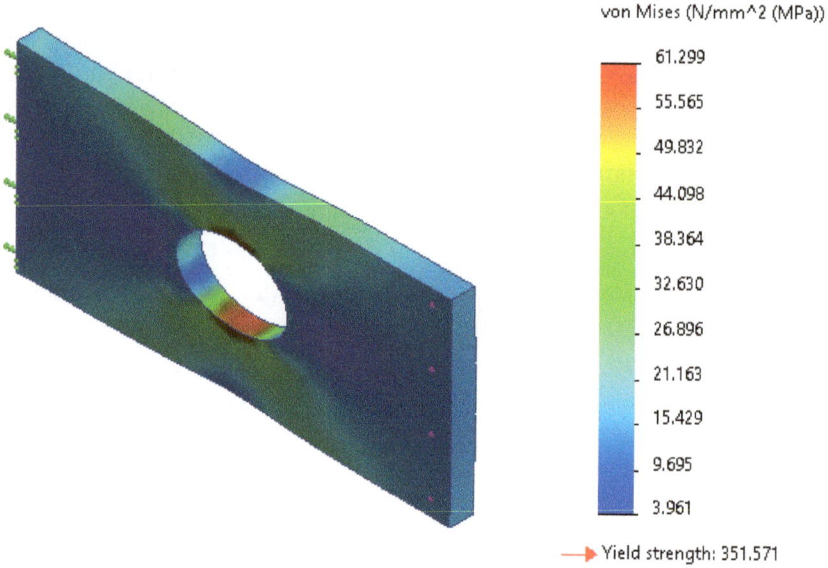

Section 10: Displaying Stress, Displacement, and Strain Results

1. Double-click on the **Stress1 (-vonMises-)** option in the **Results** folder of the Simulation Study Tree to display the von Mises stress results, if not displayed by default, refer to Figure 3.27. The maximum von Mises stress in the model under the applied load is **6.130e+01** (61.299) N/mm^2 (MPa) which is significantly within the yield strength of the material that is 351.571 N/mm^2 (MPa). The area of the model having the maximum von Mises stress is marked in red, see Figure 3.29.

   Note that you may find a slight difference in the result values depending on the service pack installed on your system.

3.29

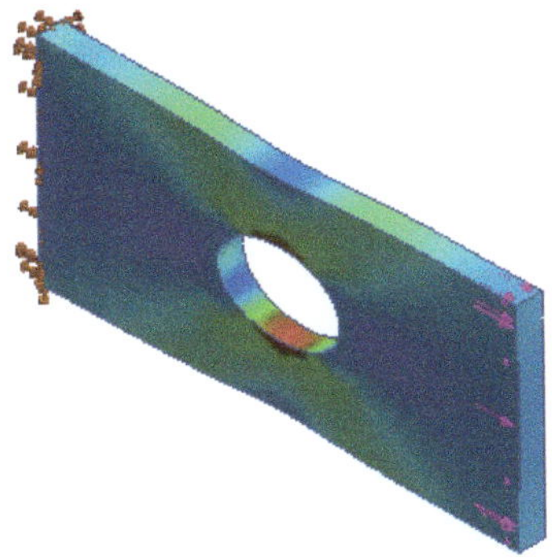

2. To display the displacement result and the resultant displacement (URES) plot, double-click on the **Displacement1 (-Res disp-)** option in the **Results** folder of the Simulation Study Tree. Figure 3.30 shows the displacement distribution on the model and the resultant displacement (URES) plot. The maximum resultant displacement of the model under the applied load is **1.084e-02** mm (0.01084 mm) which is a considerably small displacement. Also, the area of the model having the maximum resultant displacement is marked in red, see Figure 3.30.

3.30

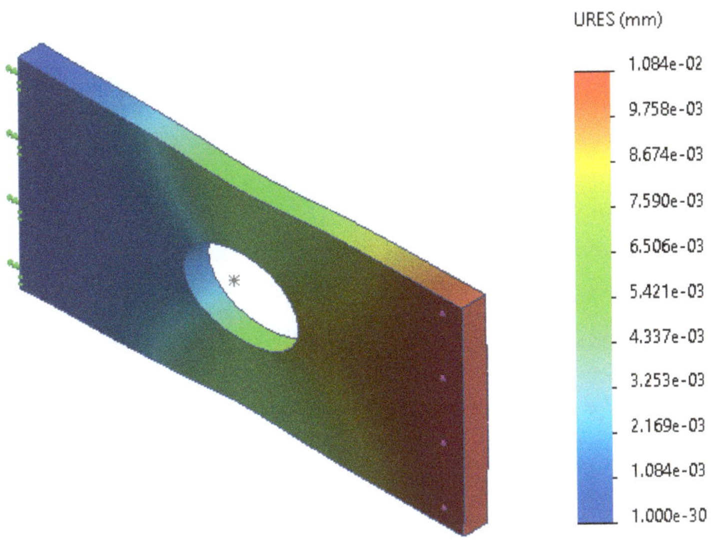

3. Similarly, to display the strain result and the equivalent strain (ESTRN) plot, double-click on the **Strain1 (-Equivalent-)** option in the **Results** folder of the Simulation Study Tree. Figure 3.31 shows the strain distribution on the model and the equivalent strain (ESTRN) plot. It is evident from the equivalent strain (ESTRN) plot shown in Figure 3.31, that the maximum equivalent strain on the model under the applied load is **2.110e-04** (0.000211) . Note that the strain results are unitless.

3.31

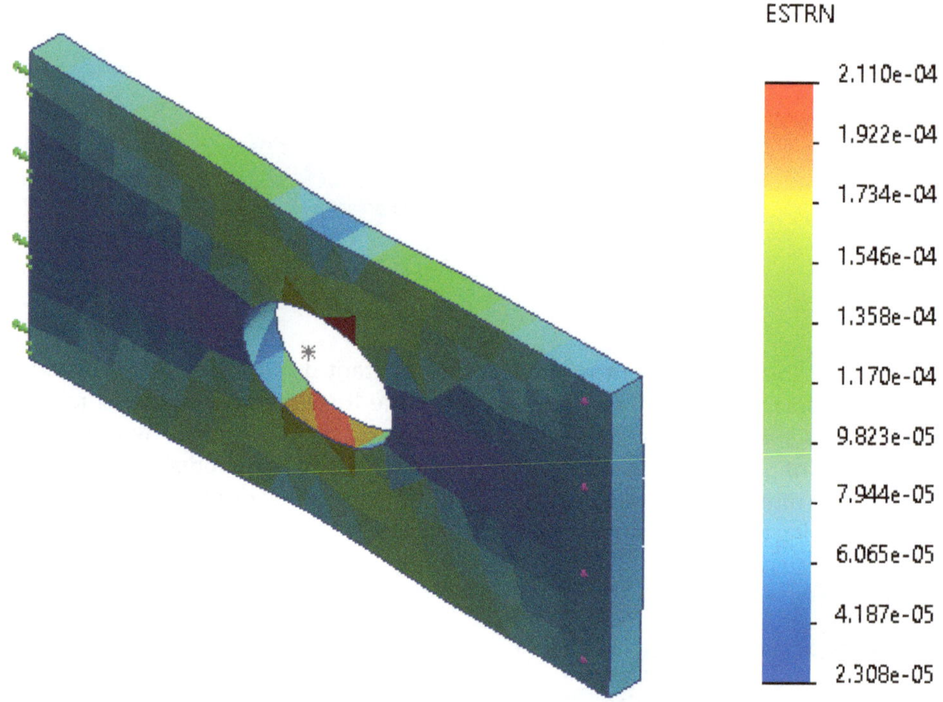

Note: You may observe slight variations in the result values depending on the service pack version of SOLIDWORKS installed on your system. These minor differences occur due to updates and improvements made in different service packs.

Section 11: Annotating Maximum and Minimum Stresses

In SOLIDWORKS Simulation, you can annotate the maximum and minimum stresses in the model by editing the stress plot settings.

1. Double-click on the **Stess1 (-vonMises-)** option in the **Results** folder of the Simulation Study Tree to display the stress results.

2. Right-click on the **Stess1 (-vonMises-)** option in the **Results** folder of the Simulation Study Tree. A shortcut menu appears, see Figure 3.32.

3. Click on the **Edit Definition** tool in the shortcut menu, see Figure 3.32. The **Stress plot PropertyManager** appears, see Figure 3.33. Alternatively, double-click on the von Mises stress plot that appears in the graphics area to display the **Stress plot PropertyManager**.

4. Click on the **Chart Options** tab in the PropertyManager, see Figure 3.33.

3.32

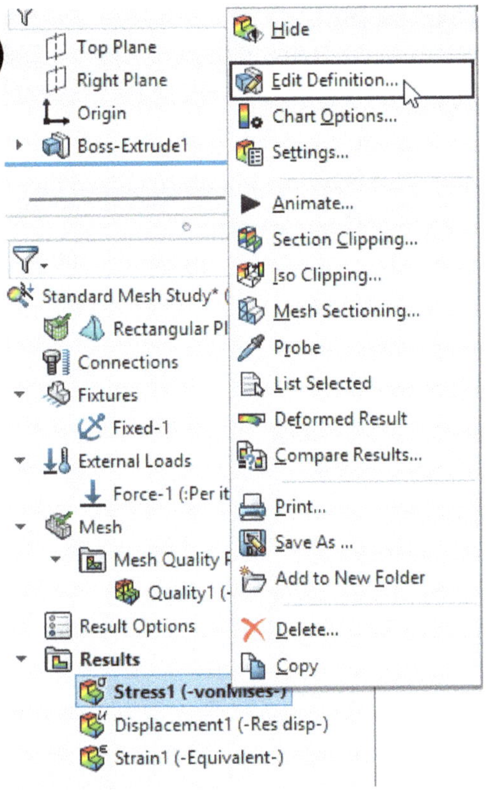

3.33

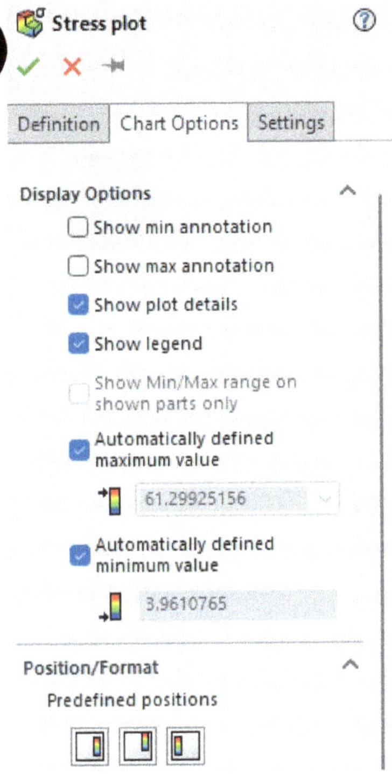

5. Select the **Show min annotation** and **Show max annotation** check boxes in the **Display Options** rollout of the PropertyManager.

6. Click on the green tick-mark button ✓ in the PropertyManager. The minimum and maximum stresses are annotated in the model, see Figure 3.34.

3.34

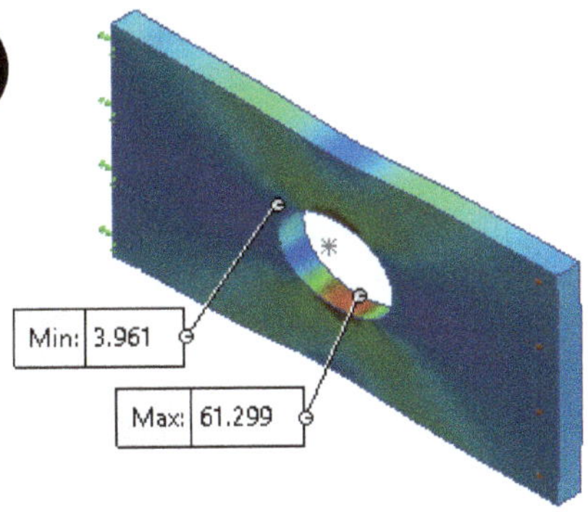

Note: Similar to annotating maximum and minimum stresses in the model, you can also annotate the maximum and minimum displacement and strain in the model.

Section 12: Displaying the 1st Principal Stress Plot

1. Right-click on the **Results** folder in the Simulation Study Tree and then click on the **Define Stress Plot** tool in the shortcut menu that appears, see Figure 3.35. The **Stress plot PropertyManager** appears.

3.35

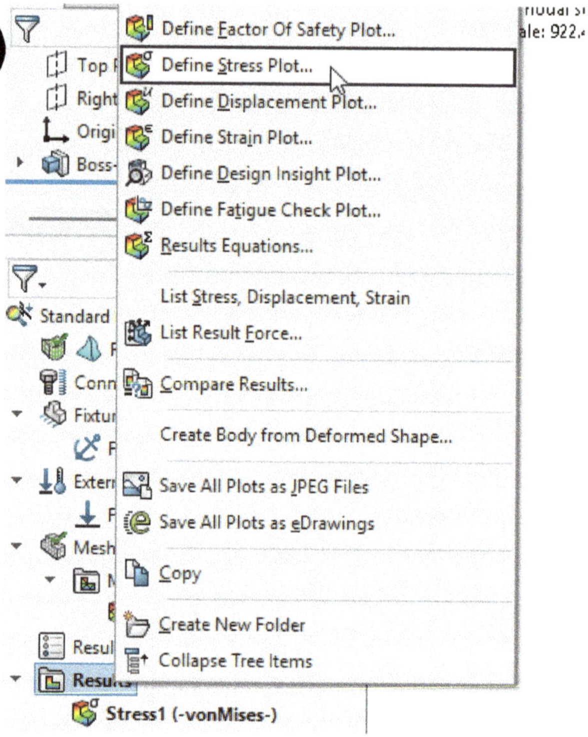

2. Click on the **Definition** tab in the **Stress plot PropertyManager**. The options of the **Definition** tab of the PropertyManager appear.

3. In the **Display** rollout of the PropertyManager, invoke the **Component** drop-down list (see Figure 3.36) and then select the **P1: 1st Principal Stress** option.

Note: The options in the **Component** drop-down list of the **Display** rollout are used for selecting a stress component to display its corresponding stress result. You can also change the unit of the stress measurement by using the **Units** drop-down list of the **Display** rollout. The options of the **Advanced Options** and **Deformed shape** rollouts are discussed later in this chapter.

4. Click on the green tick-mark button in the PropertyManager. The 1st Principal Stress plot appears in the graphics area, see Figure 3.37. Also, it is added in the **Results** folder of the Simulation Study Tree with the name **Stress2 (-1st principal-)**.

3.36

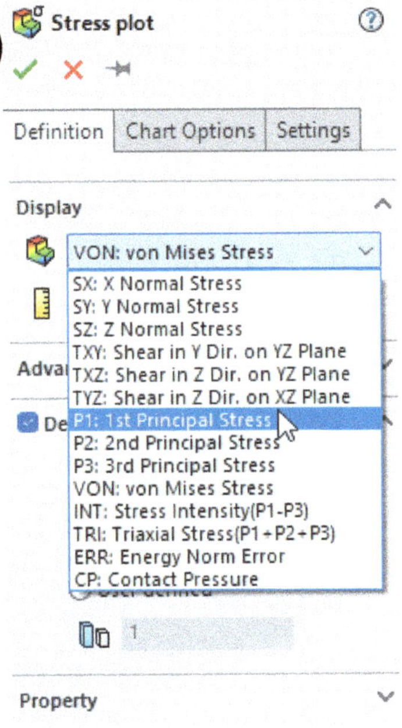

3.37

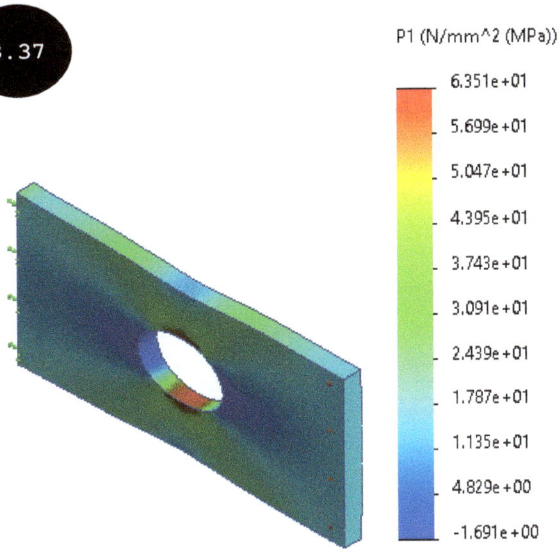

It is evident from Figure 3.37 that the maximum 1st principal stress is 6.351e+01 (63.511917) N/mm^2 (MPa) which is close to the maximum von Mises stress value of 6.130e+01 (61.299252) N/mm^2 (MPa). This is because the uniformly distributed tensile load mainly results in tensile stress along the longitudinal direction of the model.

Tip: You can also edit an existing stress plot for displaying the 1st principal stress results on the model. To do this, right-click on the name of the stress plot to be edited in the **Results** folder of the Simulation Study Tree and then click on the **Edit Definition** tool in the shortcut menu that appears. Next, select the **P1: 1st Principal Stress** option in the **Component** drop-down list of the **Display** rollout in the PropertyManager. Next, click on the green tick-mark button.

Section 13: Displaying the von Mises Stress in the True Scale

By default, the deformed shape of the model appears in Automatic scale in the graphics area. In this section, you will display the deformed shape in True scale for von Mises stress result.

1. Double-click on the **Stress1 (-von Mises-)** option in the **Results** folder of the Simulation Study Tree to display the von Mises stress plot in the graphics area. Next, double-click on the von Mises stress plot. The **Stress plot PropertyManager** appears.

2. Click on the **Definition** tab in the **Stress plot PropertyManager**. The options of the **Definition** tab of the PropertyManager appear, see Figure 3.38.

3. Select the **True scale** radio button in the **Deformed shape** rollout, see Figure 3.38.

Tip: You can also display the deformed shape of the model as per the user defined scale by selecting the **User defined** radio button and then entering the scale value in the **Scale Factor** field enabled below this radio button in the rollout.

4. Click on the green tick-mark button in the PropertyManager. The deformed shape of the model in the True scale appears in the graphics area, see Figure 3.39.

3.38

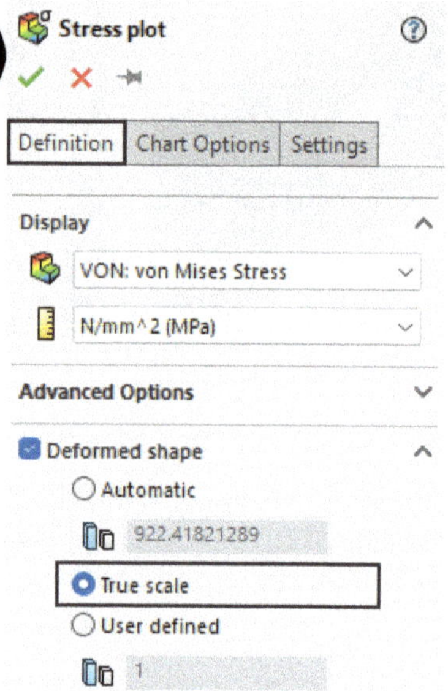

3.39

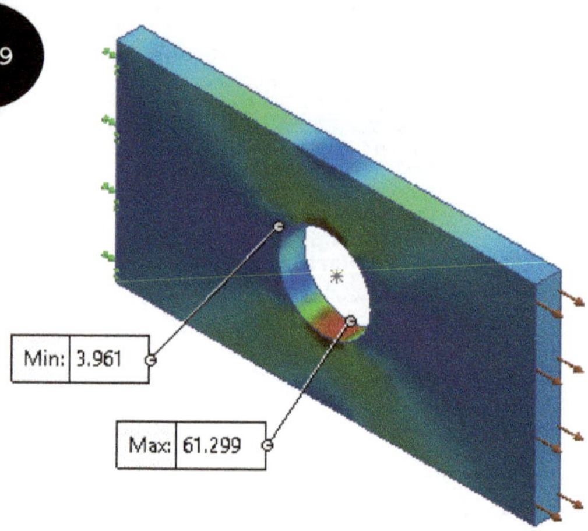

Similarly, you can display the deformed shape of the model in the True scale for the displacement and strain results.

Section 14: Saving Results

1. Click on the **Save** tool in the **Standard** toolbar. The model and its results are saved in the location > *SOLIDWORKS Simulation* > *Case Studies* > *C03 Case Studies* > *Case Study 1* of the local drive of your system. The results are saved in the *Results* sub-folder, which is created automatically inside the *Case Study 1* folder.

Section 15: Running the Second Static Study

After completing the static study with standard mesh, you need to run the new static study with the curvature-based mesh as mentioned in this Case Study description to compare the difference in results.

1. Right-click on the **Standard Mesh Study** tab (*name of the study*) in the lower-left corner of the graphics area, see Figure 3.40. A shortcut menu appears.

3.40

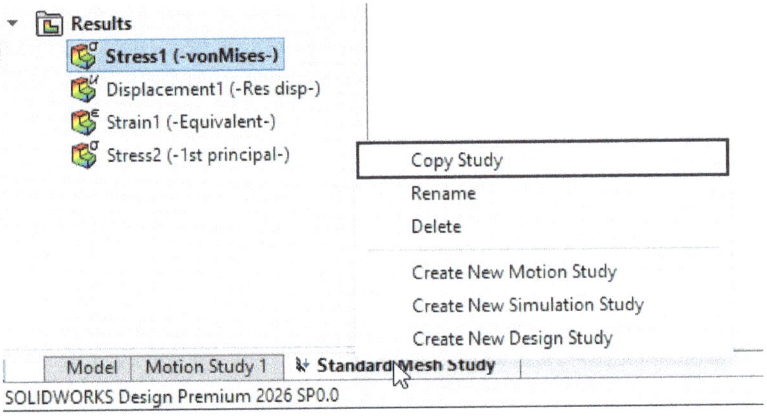

2. Click on the **Copy Study** tool in this shortcut menu to create a duplicate copy of the existing study. The **Copy Study PropertyManager** appears, see Figure 3.41.

3.41

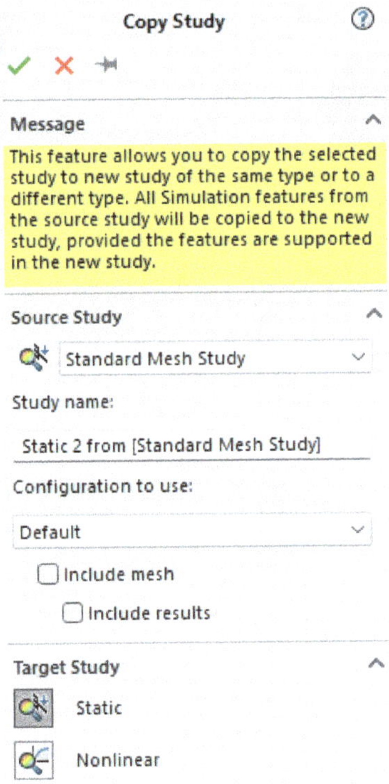

3. Ensure that the **Include mesh** and **Include results** check boxes are cleared in the **Source Study** rollout of the PropertyManager to exclude the existing mesh parameters and results in the new duplicate copy of the study being created.

4. Enter **Curvature-based Mesh Study** in the **Study name** field of the PropertyManager and then click on the green tick-mark ✓ button. A new static study is created with the same parameters as that of the existing static study and a new tab "**Curvature-based Mesh Study**" is added next to the tab of the existing study (**Standard Mesh Study**) in the lower-left corner of the graphics area.

Note: The newly created study is activated by default. You can switch between the studies by clicking on the respective tabs available at the lower left corner of the graphics area.

Tip: You can also create a new study from scratch and then drag the required parameters such as material, fixtures, and loads from the Simulation Study Tree of the existing study to the tab of the new study.

Now, you need to run the analysis with a curvature-based mesh. Note that all other parameters such as material, fixtures, and loads are the same as that of the existing study.

5. Right-click on the **Mesh** option in the Simulation Study Tree of the newly created study (**Curvature-based Mesh Study**). A shortcut menu appears, see Figure 3.42.

6. Click on the **Create Mesh** tool in the shortcut menu. The **Mesh PropertyManager** appears.

3.42

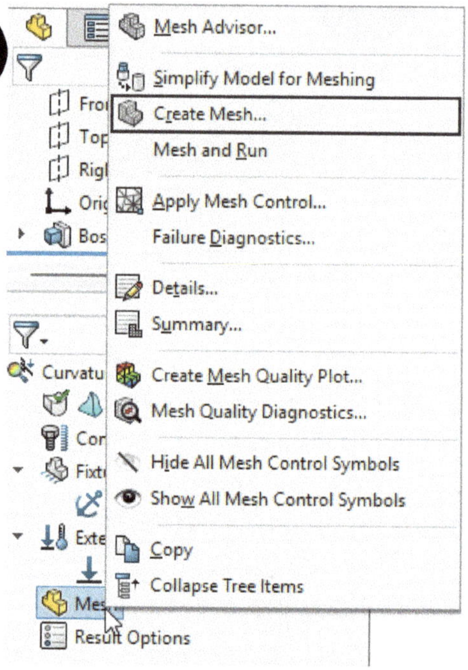

7. Expand the **Mesh Parameters** rollout of the PropertyManager by selecting the check box in its title bar, see Figure 3.43.

8. Select the **Curvature-based mesh** radio button in the expanded **Mesh Parameters** rollout, see Figure 3.43. The **Maximum element size, Minimum element size, Min number of elements in a circle**, and **Element size growth ratio** fields appear with default parameters in the rollout.

9. Enter **1.5 mm** as the maximum element size in the **Maximum element size** field and **1 mm** as the minimum element size in the **Minimum element size** field of the PropertyManager, see Figure 3.43. Also, accept the default values entered in the **Min number of elements in a circle** and **Element size growth ratio** fields, refer to Figure 3.43.

10. Click on the green tick-mark button in the PropertyManager. The **Mesh Progress** window appears which displays the progress of generating the mesh in the model. After the process of meshing the model is complete, the meshed model appears in the graphics area, see Figure 3.44.

3.43

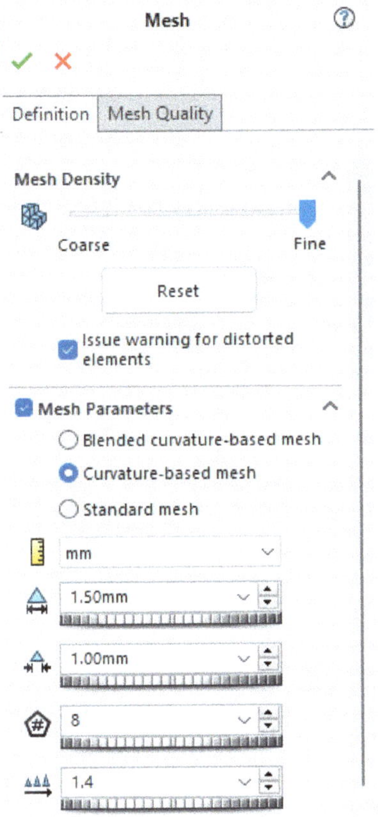

3.44

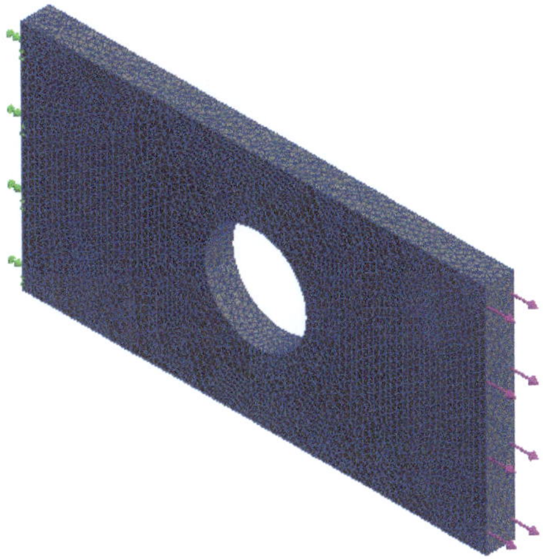

Note: As discussed in earlier chapters, SOLIDWORKS Simulation generates mesh with tetrahedral solid elements automatically for solid geometry.

11. Click on the **Run This Study** tool in the **Simulation CommandManager**. The **Curvature-based Mesh Study** (*name of the study*) window appears which displays the progress of the analysis.

    After the process of running the analysis is completed, the **Results** folder of the Simulation Study Tree is updated as per the new mesh parameters. Also, the stress distribution on the model and the von Mises stress plot appear in the graphics area, see Figure 3.45.

3.45

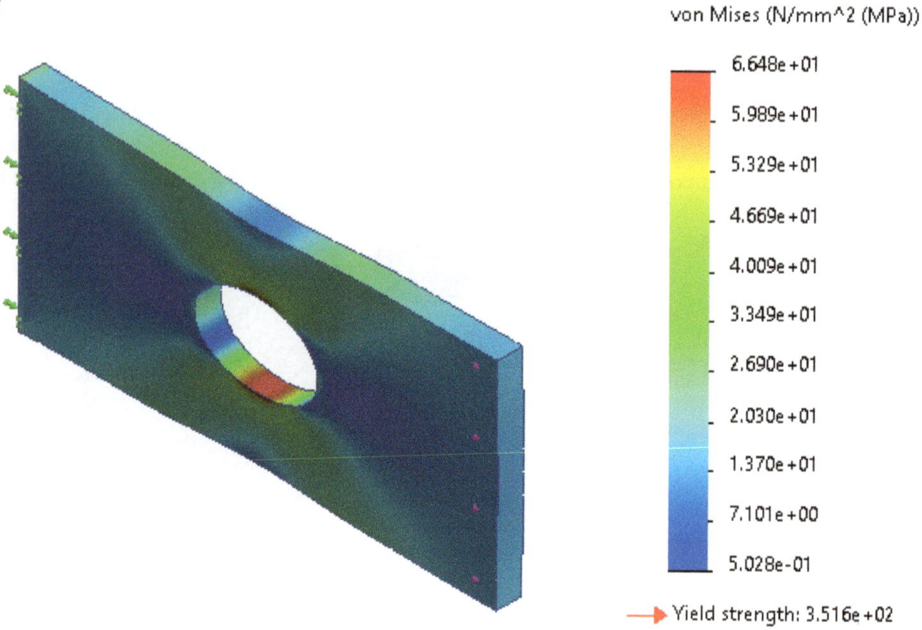

It is evident from Figure 3.45 that in the curvature-based mesh study, the maximum von Mises stress in the model under the applied load is 6.648e +01 (**66.484**) N/mm^2 (MPa).

12. To display the displacement and strain results, click on the **Displacement (-Res disp-)** and **Strain1 (-Equivalent-)** options in the Simulation Study Tree, respectively.

Section 16: Comparing Results of two Static Studies

After performing two studies with different mesh parameters, you can compare the results. In this case study, you will compare the stress and displacement results of both studies.

1. Right-click on the **Results** folder in the Simulation Study Tree. A shortcut menu appears, see Figure 3.46.

2. Click on the **Compare Results** tool in the shortcut menu. The **Compare Results PropertyManager** appears, see Figure 3.47.

3. Select the **All studies in this configuration** radio button and then select four results to be compared by selecting the **Stress1 (-vonMises-)** and **Displacement1 (-Res disp-)** check boxes of the **Standard Mesh Study** and **Curvature-based Mesh Study** studies in the PropertyManager, see Figure 3.47.

4. Click on the green tick-mark button ✓ in the PropertyManager. The graphics screen of the SOLIDWORKS Simulation gets divided and displays the stress and displacement results of both studies, see Figure 3.48.

3.46

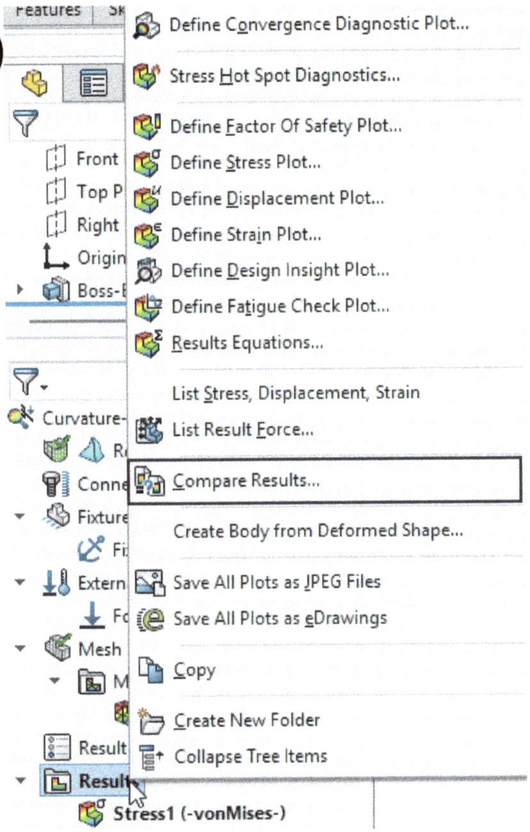
Features
Define Convergence Diagnostic Plot...
Stress Hot Spot Diagnostics...
Define Factor Of Safety Plot...
Define Stress Plot...
Define Displacement Plot...
Define Strain Plot...
Define Design Insight Plot...
Define Fatigue Check Plot...
Results Equations...
List Stress, Displacement, Strain
List Result Force...
Compare Results...
Create Body from Deformed Shape...
Save All Plots as JPEG Files
Save All Plots as eDrawings
Copy
Create New Folder
Collapse Tree Items
Front
Top P
Right
Origin
Boss-
Curvature-
Conne
Fixture
Extern
Mesh
Result
Results
Stress1 (-vonMises-)

3.47

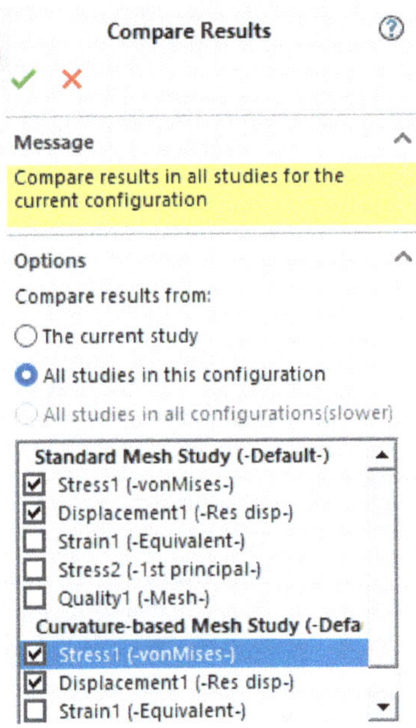
Compare Results
Message
Compare results in all studies for the current configuration
Options
Compare results from:
The current study
All studies in this configuration
All studies in all configurations(slower)
Standard Mesh Study (-Default-)
Stress1 (-vonMises-)
Displacement1 (-Res disp-)
Strain1 (-Equivalent-)
Stress2 (-1st principal-)
Quality1 (-Mesh-)
Curvature-based Mesh Study (-Defa
Stress1 (-vonMises-)
Displacement1 (-Res disp-)
Strain1 (-Equivalent-)

3.48

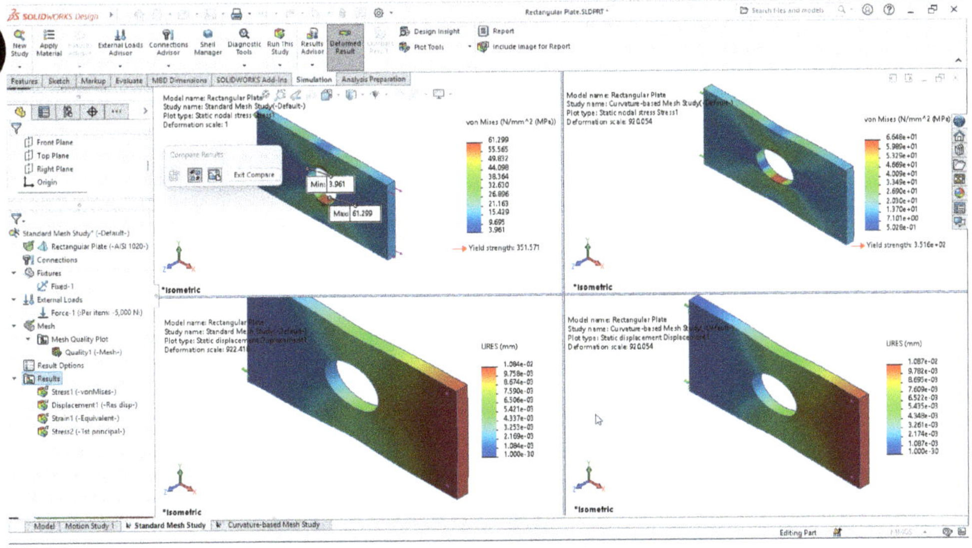
Exit Compare
*Isometric
*Isometric
*Isometric
*Isometric

Now, you can compare the stress and displacement results of both studies. The table given below summarizes the results of both the studies.

Study	Mesh Type	Max. Stress [N/mm^2 (MPa)]	Max. Displacement [mm]	Max. Strain
Standard Mesh Study	Standard Mesh	61.299	0.01084	0.000211
Curvature-based Mesh Study	Curvature-based Mesh	66.484	0.01087	0.000269

Note: In both the studies, all the properties such as materials and boundary conditions (fixtures and loads) are same except the type of mesh due to which there is a small difference in the results, since the mesh parameters affect the results. The difference in results can be large, if the geometry is complex. Note that finer the mesh density, more accurate the results are but the computational time will increase due to increase in number of elements, nodes, and degrees of freedom in the fine mesh.

5. After comparing the results, click on the **Exit Compare** button in the **Compare Results** window which appears in the graphics area.

Section 17: Saving Results

1. Click on the **Save** tool in the **Standard** toolbar. The model and its results are saved in the location > *SOLIDWORKS Simulation > Case Studies > C03 Case Studies > Case Study 1* of the local drive of your system. The results are saved in the *Results* sub-folder, which is created automatically inside the *Case Study 1* folder.

Case Study 2: Static Analysis of a Bracket with Mesh Control

In this case study, you will perform the linear static analysis of a Bracket shown in Figure 3.49 and determine the stress under a uniformly distributed load.

3.49

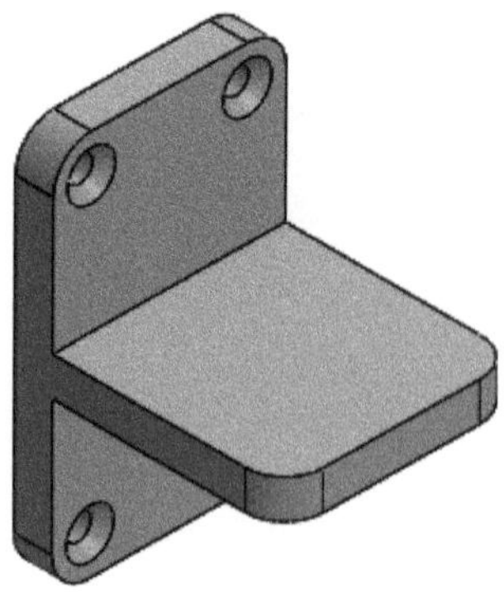

Project Description
The Bracket is fixed at its four holes and a 1200 N load is uniformly distributed along its top face, see Figure 3.50. The Bracket is made up of **AISI 304** steel material.

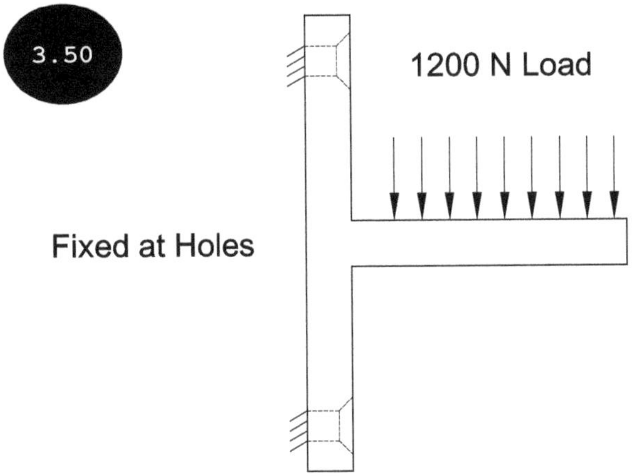

Project Summary
In this case study, you will first generate a high-quality curvature-based mesh with default parameters and then refine the mesh at the upper corner of the Bracket where the high stresses are located, by applying mesh control. Specify the unit system as SI (MKS) with displacement in mm and stress in N/mm^2 (MPa) units.

The following sequence summarizes the case study outline:

1. Downloading Files of Chapter 3
2. Opening the Bracket Model
3. Starting the Static Study
4. Defining Units
5. Assigning the Material
6. Applying the Fixture
7. Applying the Load
8. Generating the Mesh
9. Running the Analysis
10. Displaying Stress, Displacement, and Strain Results
11. Annotating Maximum and Minimum Stresses
12. Applying the Mesh Control and Running the Analysis
13. Comparing Stress Results Before and After Mesh Control
14. Creating the Iso Plot
15. Saving Results

Section 1: Downloading Files of Chapter 3

1. Log on to the CADArtifex website (*cadartifex.com/login/*) using the Email OTP to download the files of this chapter. If you are a new user, you must first **sign up** on the website as a Learner (*cadartifex.com/register*).

Note: If you have already downloaded the **C03 Case Studies** file in **Case Study 1** and saved it in the location **SOLIDWORKS Simulation > Case Studies**, you can skip the steps in this session.

2. After logging in, navigate to the textbook titled "**SOLIDWORKS Simulation 2026: A Power Guide for Beginners and Intermediate Users: Colored**" using the **Browse Resources** option available in the left menu to download its resources. Alternatively, you can enter the name of the textbook in the **Search** box to locate it quickly.

3. In the **Online Resources** tab, expand the **Case Studies** rollout and click the **Download** button corresponding to **C03 Case Studies**. In the confirmation window that appears, click the **Confirm** button. The download of the **C03 Case Studies** file will begin. After the download is complete, unzip the file. It is recommended that you create a folder named "**SOLIDWORKS Simulation**" on your local drive and then create a subfolder inside it named "**Case Studies**".

4. Save the extracted **C03 Case Studies** folder in the **Case Studies** subfolder created inside the **SOLIDWORKS Simulation** folder.

Section 2: Opening the Bracket Model

1. Double-click on the SOLIDWORKS icon on your desktop to start SOLIDWORKS, if not already started.

2. Click on the **Open** button in the Welcome dialog box. The **Open** dialog box appears. Alternatively, click on the **Open** tool in the **Standard** toolbar to invoke the **Open** dialog box.

3. Browse to the location > ***SOLIDWORKS Simulation > Case Studies > C03 Case Studies > Case Study 2*** of the local drive of your system. Next, select the **Bracket** model and then click on the **Open** button in the dialog box. The Bracket model is opened in SOLIDWORKS, see Figure 3.51.

3.51

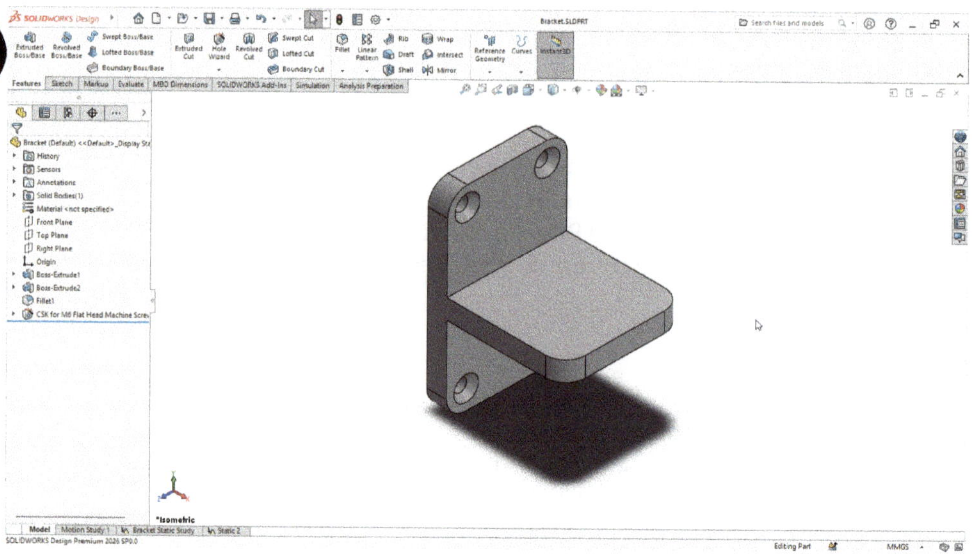

Section 3: Starting the Static Study

1. Click on the **Simulation** tab in the **CommandManager**. The tools of the **Simulation CommandManager** appear, see Figure 3.52.

3.52

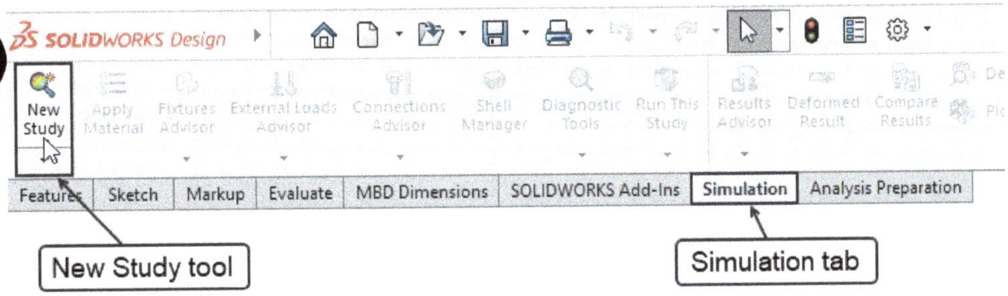

Note: If the **Simulation** tab is not added in the CommandManager then you need to customize it as discussed earlier.

2. Click on the **New Study** tool in the **Simulation CommandManager**. The **Study PropertyManager** appears, see Figure 3.53.

3. Ensure that the **Static** button is activated in the **Study PropertyManager** to perform the linear static analysis on the Bracket model.

4. Enter in the **Study name** field of the PropertyManager.

5. Click on the green tick-mark button in the **Study PropertyManager**. The various tools for performing the static analysis are enabled in the **Simulation CommandManager**. Also, the static study with the name **Bracket Static Study** is added to the Simulation Study Tree, see Figure 3.54.

3.53

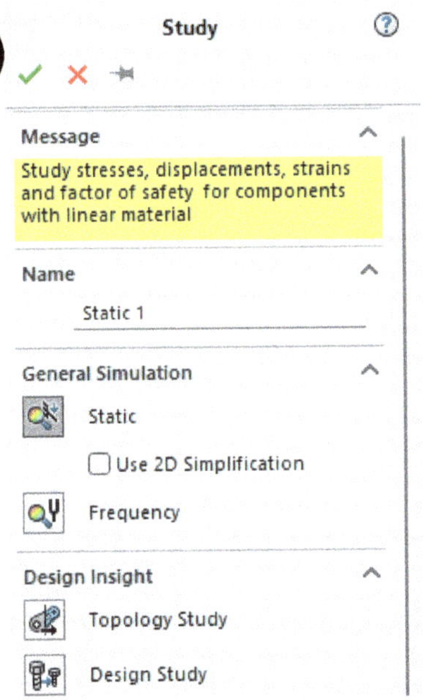

3.54

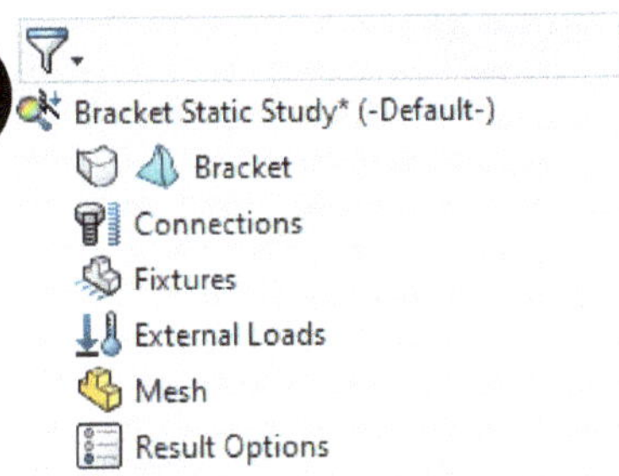

Section 4: Defining Units

Before you start with the analysis process, it is important to set the units.

1. Click on the **Simulation** > **Options** in the SOLIDWORKS Design Menus. The **System Options** dialog box appears.

2. In this dialog box, click on the **Default Options** tab. The name of the dialog box changes to the **Default Options**, see Figure 3.55.

3. Ensure that the **Units** option is selected in the dialog box and the options for specifying the units appear on the right panel of the dialog box, see Figure 3.55.

3.55

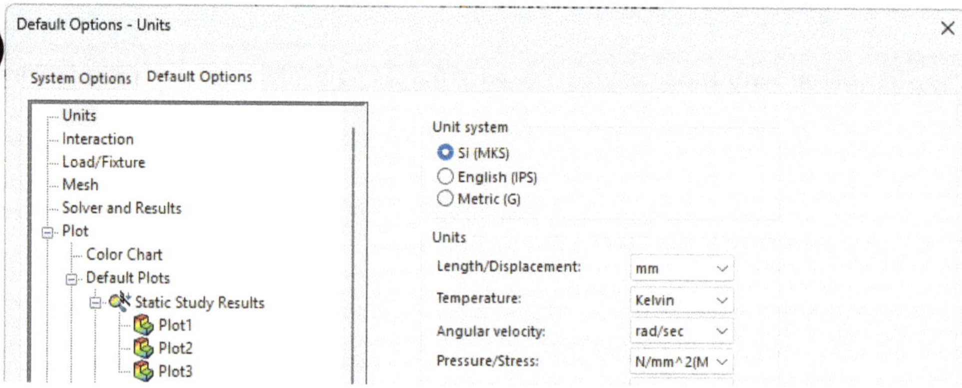

4. Select the **SI (MKS)** radio button in the **Unit system** area of the dialog box. Next, ensure that the **mm** unit is selected in the **Length/Displacement** drop-down list and the **N/mm^2 (MPa)** unit is selected in the **Pressure/Stress** drop-down list of the **Units** area, see Figure 3.56.

3.56

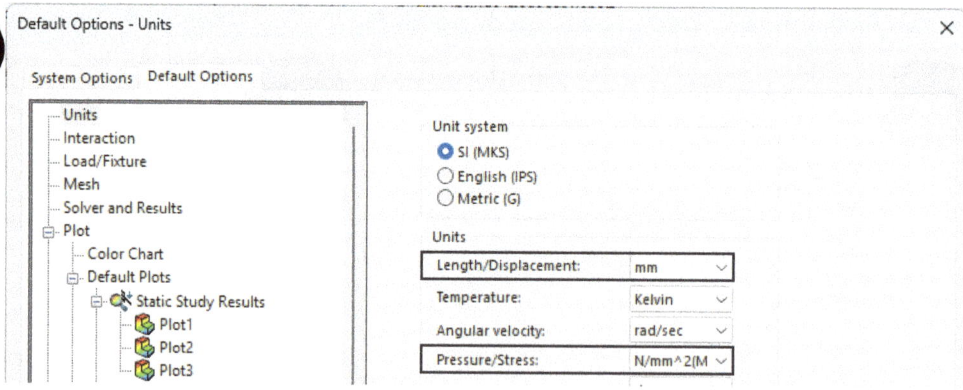

5. After specifying the units, click on the **OK** button to accept the change and exit the dialog box.

Section 5: Assigning the Material

1. Click on the **Apply Material** tool in the **Simulation CommandManager**. The **Material** dialog box appears, see Figure 3.57. Alternatively, right-click on the name of the model (**Bracket**) in the Simulation Study Tree and then click on the **Apply/Edit material** tool in the shortcut menu that appears.

2. Expand the **Steel** category of the **SOLIDWORKS Materials** library in the **Material** dialog box and then select the **AISI 304** steel material, see Figure 3.57. The material properties of the selected material appear on the right panel of the dialog box.

3.57

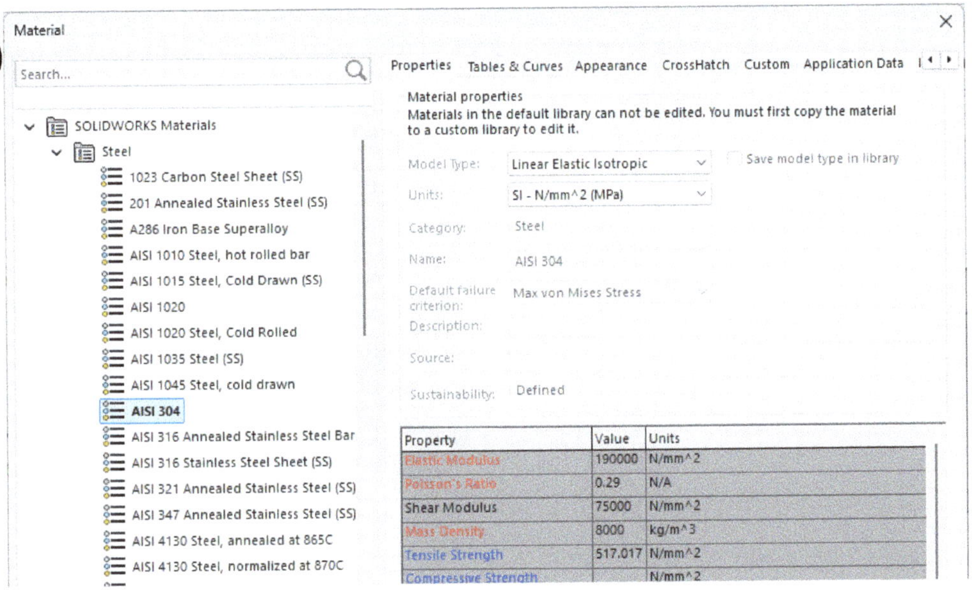

3. Click on the **Apply** button and then the **Close** button in the dialog box. The material is assigned to the model.

Section 6: Applying the Fixture

1. Right-click on the **Fixtures** option in the Simulation Study Tree. A shortcut menu appears, see Figure 3.58. In this shortcut menu, click on the **Fixed Geometry** tool. The **Fixture PropertyManager** appears, see Figure 3.59.

3.58

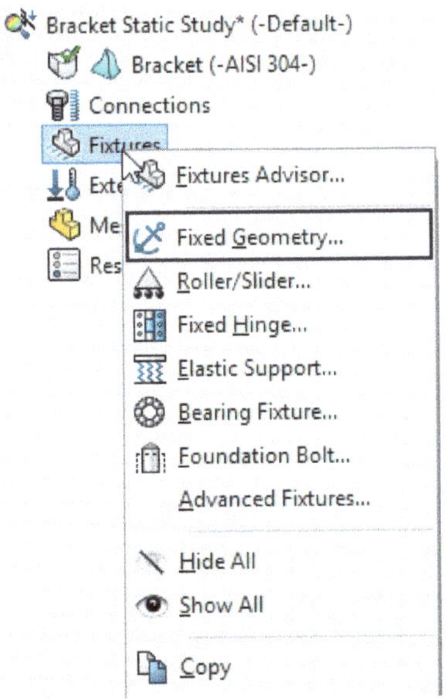

3.59

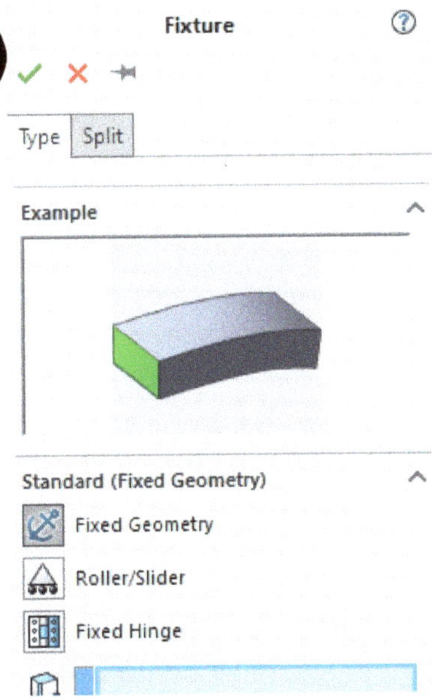

Alternatively, invoke the **Fixture** flyout by clicking on the arrow at the bottom of the **Fixtures Advisor** tool in the **Simulation CommandManager** and then click on the **Fixed Geometry** tool.

2. Select the inner circular face of all the holes of the model one by one to apply the Fixed Geometry fixture. The symbol of the Fixed Geometry fixture appears on the selected faces, see Figure 3.60.

3.60

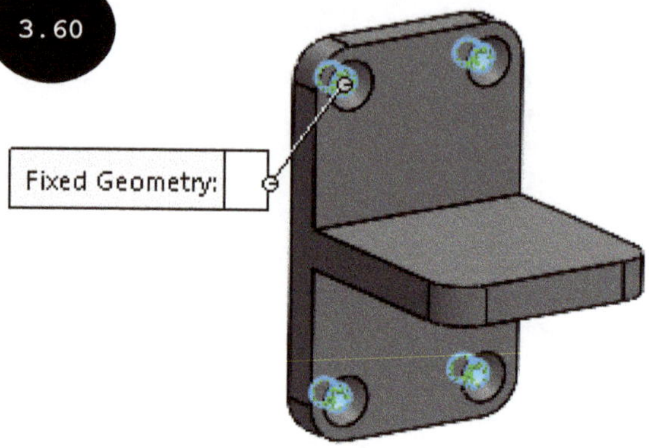

3. Click on the green tick-mark button in the PropertyManager. The Fixed Geometry fixture is applied to the holes of the model. Also, the Fixed Geometry fixture (**Fixed-1**) is added under the **Fixtures** options in the Simulation Study Tree, see Figure 3.61.

3.61

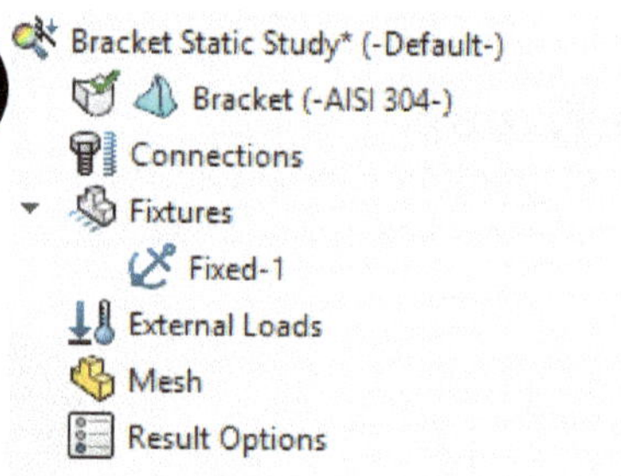

Tip: To edit an applied fixture, right-click on the name of the fixture listed under the **Fixtures** option in the Simulation Study Tree and then click on the **Edit Definition** tool in the shortcut menu that appears. The **Fixture PropertyManager** appears. By using this PropertyManager, you can edit the selected fixture and then click on its green tick-mark button to accept the change and close the PropertyManager.

Section 7: Applying the Load

1. Right-click on the **External Loads** option in the Simulation Study Tree. A shortcut menu appears, see Figure 3.62. In this shortcut menu, click on the **Force** tool. The **Force/Torque PropertyManager** appears, see Figure 3.63. Alternatively, invoke the **External Loads** flyout by clicking on the arrow at the bottom of the **External Loads Advisor** tool in the **Simulation CommandManager** and then click on the **Force** tool.

3.62

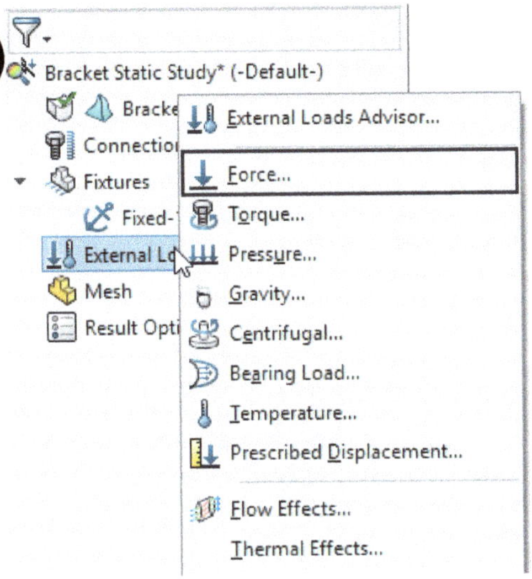

3.63

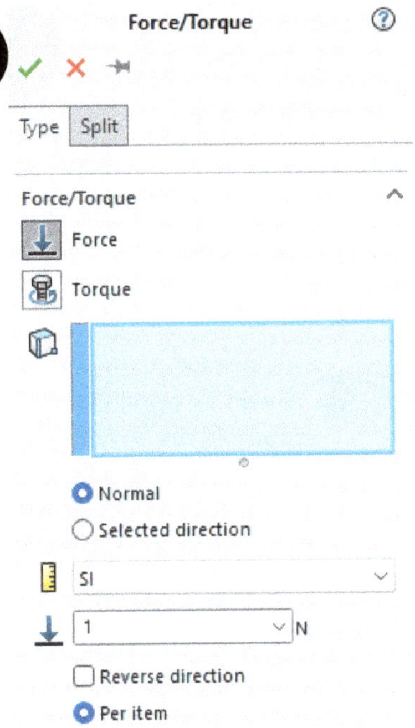

2. Select the top face of the model to apply the load, see Figure 3.64. The symbol of the load appears on the selected face.

3.64

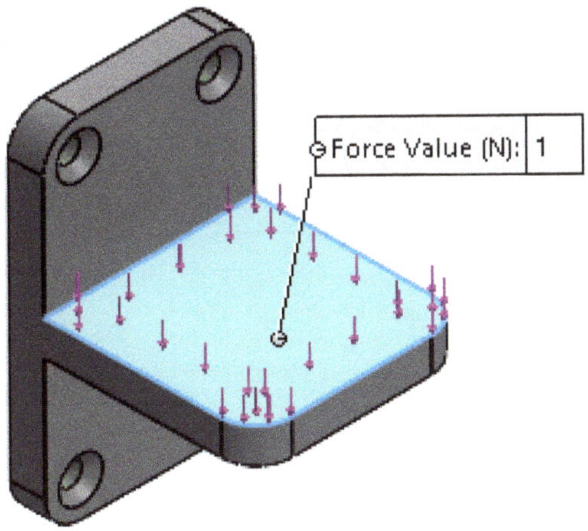

3. Ensure that the **Normal** radio button is selected to apply the load normal to the face.

4. Enter **1200** in the **Force Value** field of the PropertyManager.

5. Click on the green tick-mark button ✓ in the PropertyManager. The 1200 N load is applied on the selected face of the model. Also, the default name [**Force-1 (: Per item: 1,200 N:)**] of the applied load is added under the **External Loads** option in the Simulation Study Tree, see Figure 3.65.

3.65

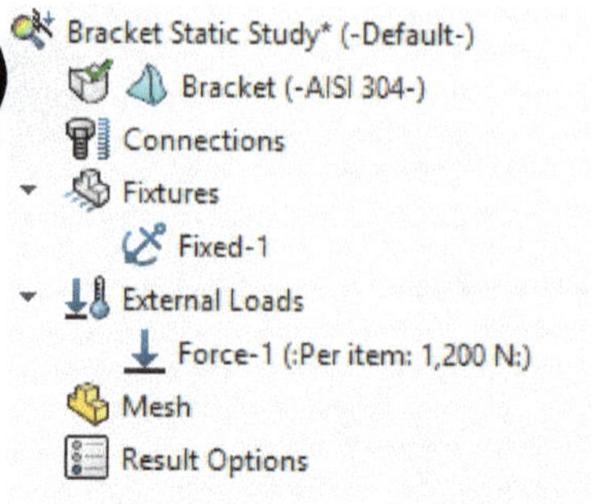

Tip: To edit an applied load, right-click on the name of the load listed under the **External Loads** option in the Simulation Study Tree and then click on the **Edit Definition** tool in the shortcut menu that appears. The **Force/Torque PropertyManager** appears. By using this PropertyManager, you can edit the load parameters and then click on the green tick-mark button to accept the change and close the PropertyManager.

Section 8: Generating the Mesh

After defining the material properties and boundary conditions (fixtures and loads), you need to generate a mesh on the model. In this case study, you will first generate a curvature-based mesh with default parameters and then apply the mesh control at the upper corner of the Bracket, where the high stresses are located.

1. Right-click on the **Mesh** option in the Simulation Study Tree and then click on the **Create Mesh** tool in the shortcut menu that appears, see Figure 3.66. The **Mesh PropertyManager** appears, see Figure 3.67. Alternatively, click on the arrow at the bottom of the **Run This Study** tool in the **Simulation CommandManager** and then click on the **Create Mesh** tool in the flyout that appears.

3.66

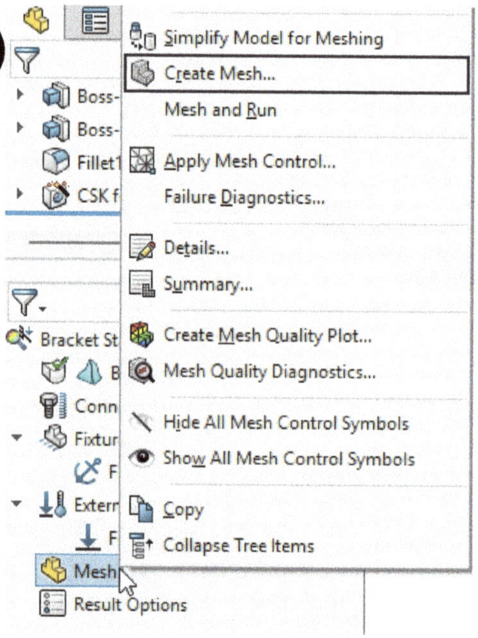

3.67

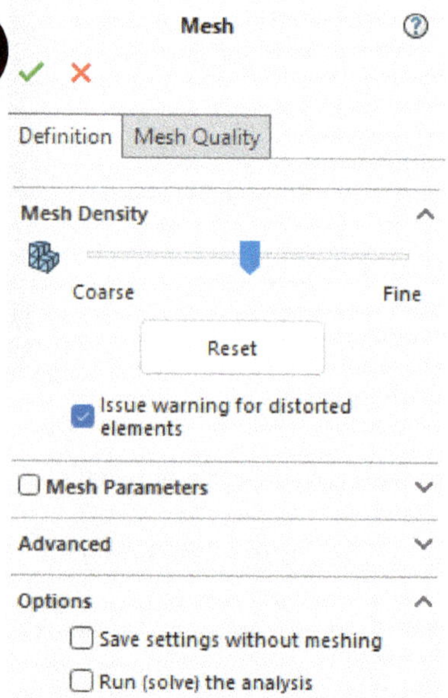

2. Expand the **Mesh Parameters** rollout of the PropertyManager by clicking on the check box in its title bar, see Figure 3.68.

3.68

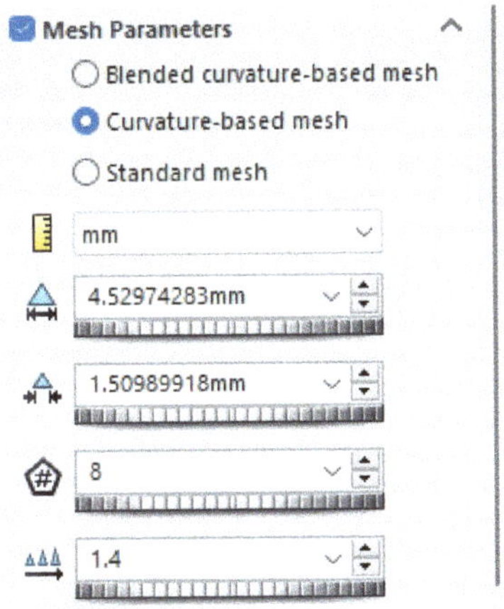

3. Select the **Curvature-based mesh** radio button in the expanded **Mesh Parameters** rollout, see Figure 3.68. The **Maximum element size, Minimum element size, Min number of elements in a circle**, and **Element size growth ratio** fields appear in the rollout with the default parameters, see Figure 3.68. SOLIDWORKS Simulation automatically calculates the mesh parameters based on the volume, surface area, and other details of the model and sets the default mesh with the medium mesh density.

4. Accept the default mesh parameters in the respective fields of the **Mesh Parameters** rollout.

5. Click on the **Mesh Quality** tab in the PropertyManager, see Figure 3.69.

6. Ensure that the name of the model (Bracket) appears in the **High Quality Mesh** field to mesh the model with high-quality (second order) tetrahedral solid elements, see Figure 3.69.

7. After defining all the mesh parameters, click on the green tick-mark button in the PropertyManager. The **Mesh Progress** window appears which displays the progress of meshing the model. After the process of meshing the model is complete, the meshed model appears in the graphics area, see Figure 3.70.

3.69

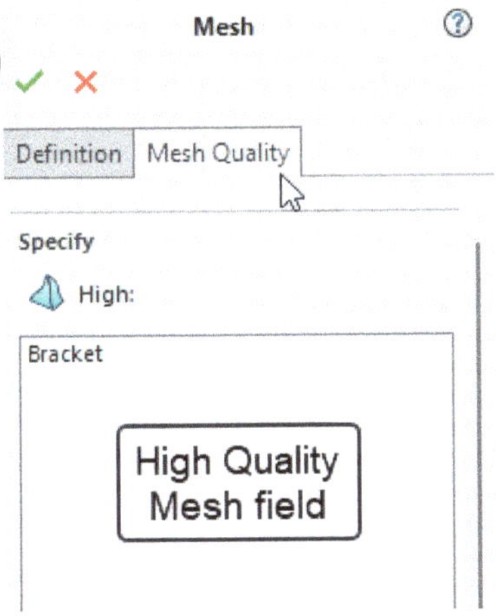

3.70

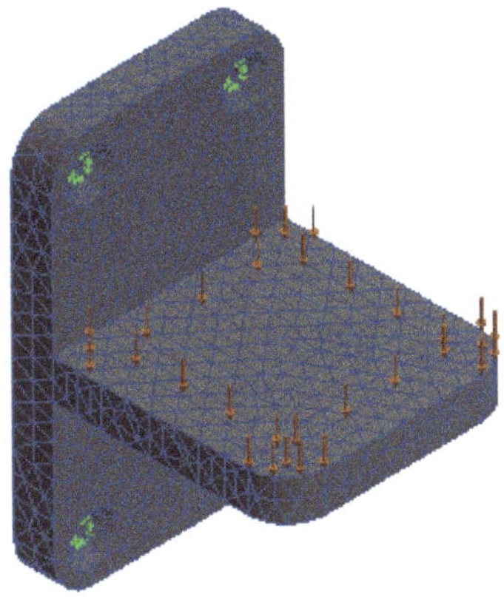

Note: As discussed in the previous chapter, SOLIDWORKS Simulation automatically generates mesh with tetrahedral solid elements for solid geometry.

Section 9: Running the Analysis

After defining the material properties, boundary conditions (fixtures and loads), and generating the mesh, you can run the analysis.

1. Click on the **Run This Study** tool in the **Simulation CommandManager**. The **Bracket Static Study** (*name of the study*) window appears which displays the progress of analysis, see Figure 3.71.

3.71

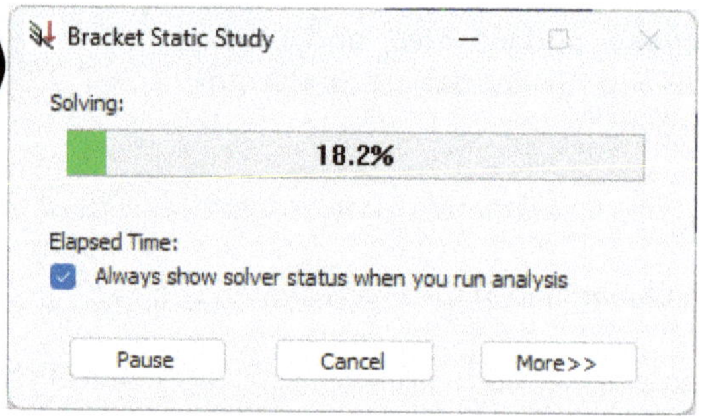

Note: The computational time to complete the analysis depends on the number of elements, nodes, and degrees of freedom to be solved by the solver.

2. After the process of running the analysis is completed, the **Results** folder is added to the Simulation Study Tree with the stress, displacement, and strain results, see Figure 3.72. By default, the **Stress** result is activated in the **Results** folder. Consequently, the stress distribution on the model and the von Mises stress plot appear in the graphics area, see Figure 3.73.

3.72

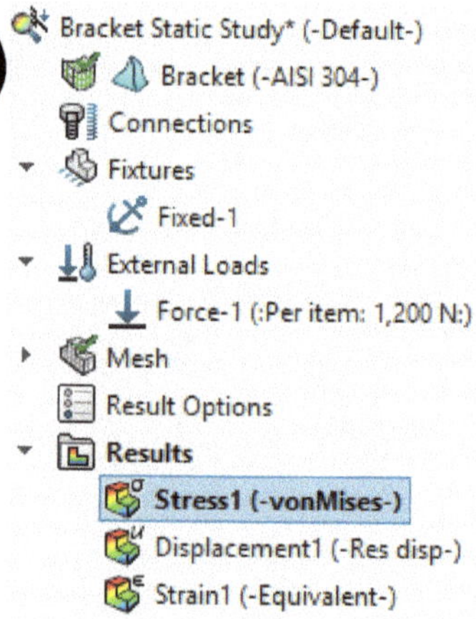

3.73

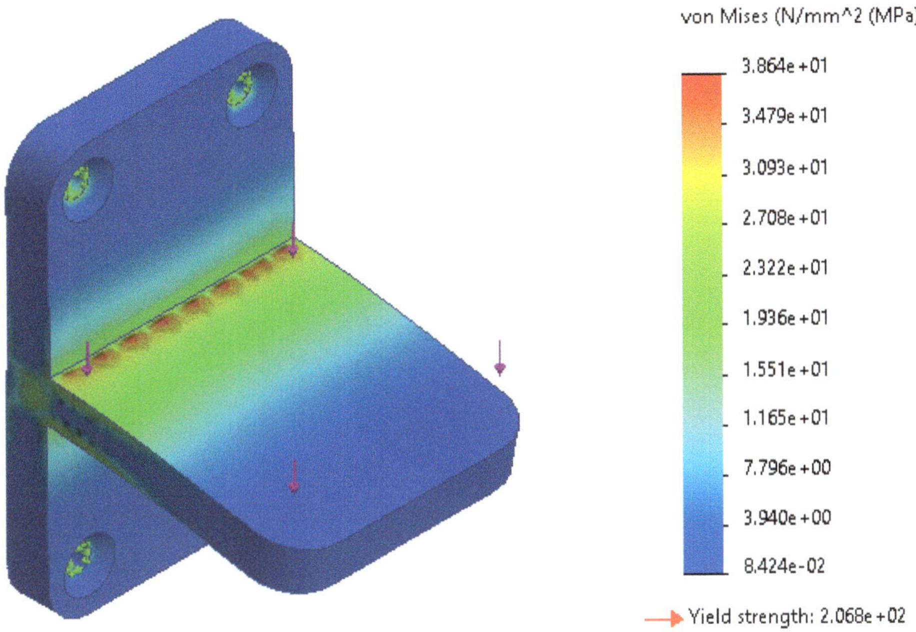

Section 10: Displaying Stress, Displacement, and Strain Results

1. Double-click on the **Stress1 (-vonMises-)** option in the **Results** folder of the Simulation Study Tree to display the von Mises stress results, if not displayed by default, refer to Figure 3.73. It is evident from Figure 3.73 that the maximum von Mises stress in the model under the applied load is **3.864e+01** (38.643) N/mm^2 (MPa) which is significantly within the yield stress of the material that is **2.068e+02** (206.807) N/mm^2 (MPa). The area of the model having the maximum von Mises stress is marked in red. Note that you may find a slight difference in the result values depending on the service pack installed on your system.

2. To display the displacement result and the resultant displacement (URES) plot, double-click on the **Displacement1 (-Res disp-)** option in the **Results** folder of the Simulation Study Tree. Figure 3.74 shows the displacement distribution on the model and the resultant displacement (URES) plot. It is evident from the resultant displacement (URES) plot that the maximum resultant displacement of the model under the applied load is **5.210e-02** (0.052) mm which is a considerably small displacement. Also, the area of the model having the maximum resultant displacement is marked in red.

3. Similarly, to display the strain result and the equivalent strain (ESTRN) plot, double-click on the **Strain1 (-Equivalent-)** option in the **Results** folder of the Simulation Study Tree. Figure 3.75 shows the strain distribution on the model and the equivalent strain (ESTRN) plot. It is evident from the equivalent strain (ESTRN) plot that the maximum equivalent strain on the model is **1.388e-04** (0.000139). Note that the strain results are unitless.

3.74

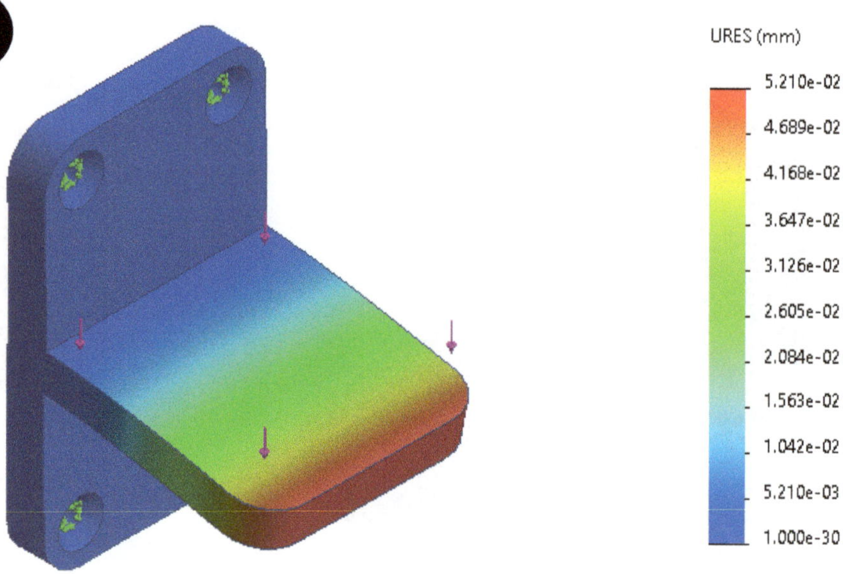
URES (mm)
5.210e-02
4.689e-02
4.168e-02
3.647e-02
3.126e-02
2.605e-02
2.084e-02
1.563e-02
1.042e-02
5.210e-03
1.000e-30

3.75

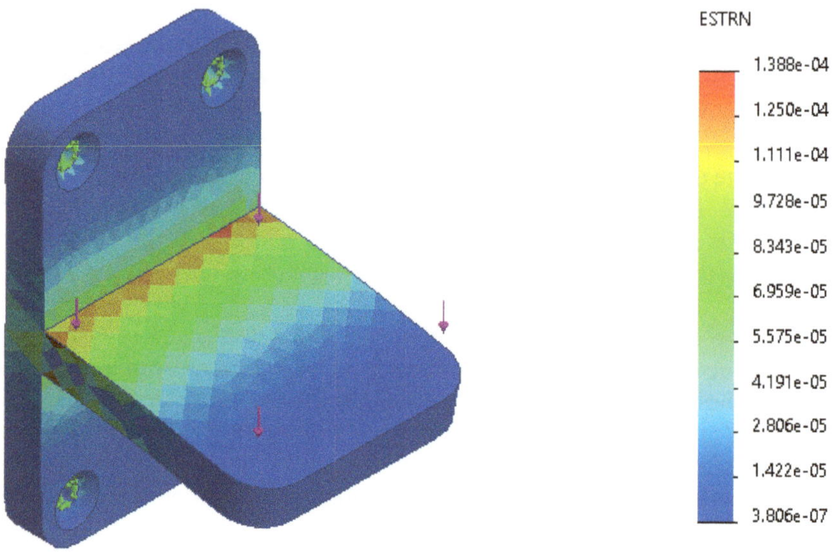
ESTRN
1.388e-04
1.250e-04
1.111e-04
9.728e-05
8.343e-05
6.959e-05
5.575e-05
4.191e-05
2.806e-05
1.422e-05
3.806e-07

Section 11: Annotating Maximum and Minimum Stresses

In SOLIDWORKS Simulation, you can annotate the maximum and minimum stresses in the model by editing the stress plot settings.

1. Double-click on the **Stess1 (-vonMises-)** option in the **Results** folder of the Simulation Study Tree to display the stress results.

2. Right-click on the **Stess1 (-vonMises-)** option in the **Results** folder of the Simulation Study Tree. A shortcut menu appears, see Figure 3.76.

3. Click on the **Edit Definition** tool in the shortcut menu. The **Stress plot PropertyManager** appears, see Figure 3.77. Alternatively, double-click on the von Mises stress plot that appears in the graphics area to display the **Stress plot PropertyManager**.

4. In the **Stress plot PropertyManager**, click on the **Chart Options** tab to display the options available in this tab, see Figure 3.77.

3.76

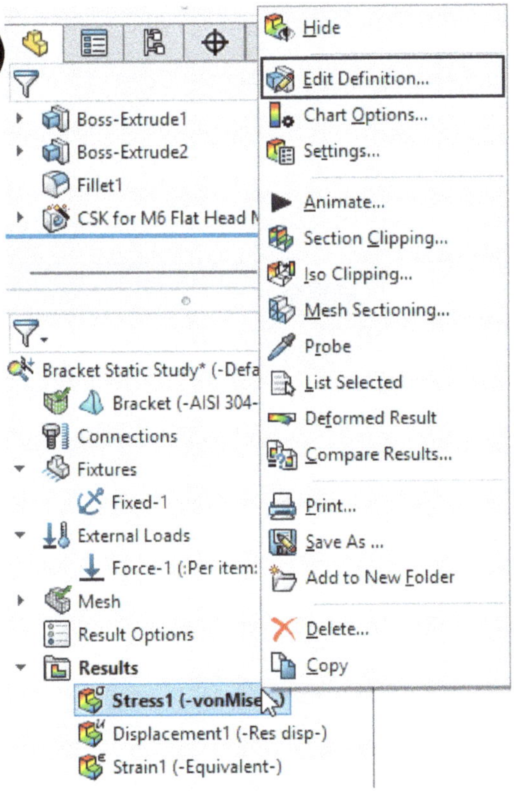

3.77

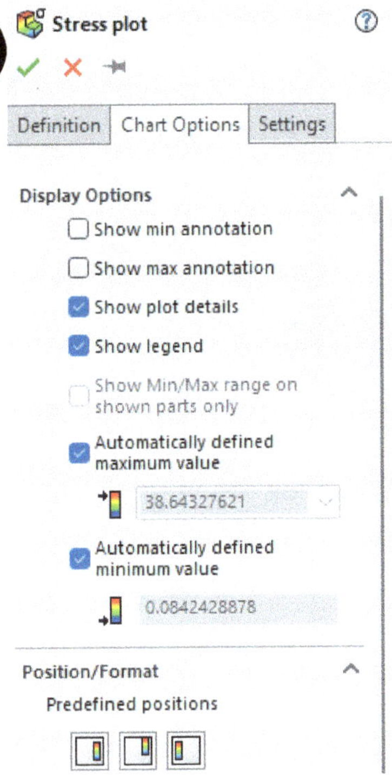

5. Select the **Show min annotation** and **Show max annotation** checkboxes in the **Display Options** rollout of the PropertyManager.

6. Click on the green tick-mark button ✓ in the PropertyManager. The minimum and maximum stresses are annotated in the model, see Figure 3.78.

3.78

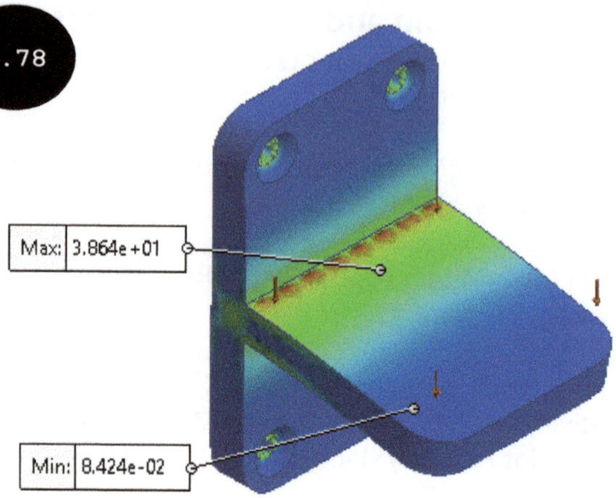

It is evident from Figure 3.78 that the maximum von Mises stress is located near the upper corner of the Bracket. Therefore, we need to refine the mesh to get accurate results at the corner where the maximum stresses are located.

Section 12: Applying the Mesh Control and Running the Analysis

1. Right-click on the **Mesh** option in the Simulation Study Tree. A shortcut menu appears, see Figure 3.79.

2. Click on the **Apply Mesh Control** tool in the shortcut menu, see Figure 3.79. The **Mesh Control PropertyManager** appears, see Figure 3.80.

3.79

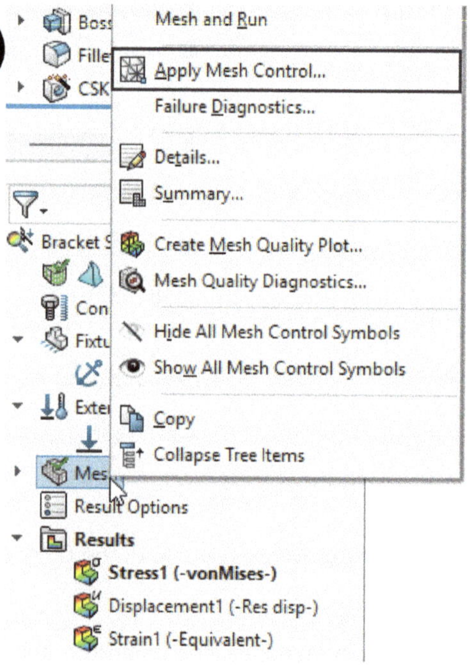

3.80

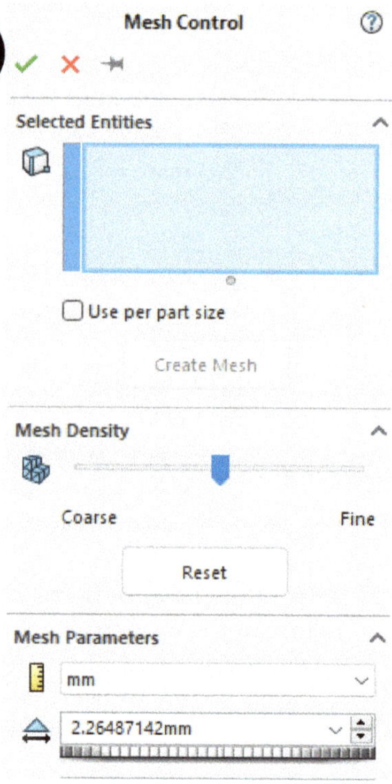

3. Select the upper intersecting edge of the model to apply the mesh control, see Figure 3.81. The name of the selected edge appears in the **Faces, Edges, Vertices, Reference Points, and Components for Mesh Control** field of the **Selected Entities** rollout in the PropertyManager. Also, a callout gets attached to the selected edge in the graphics area, see Figure 3.81.

4. Drag the Slider toward the extreme right in the **Mesh Density** rollout of the PropertyManager to create a fine mesh on the selected edge of the model, see Figure 3.82. Note that as you drag the Slider, the element size in the **Element Size** field of the **Mesh Parameters** gets reduced.

3.81

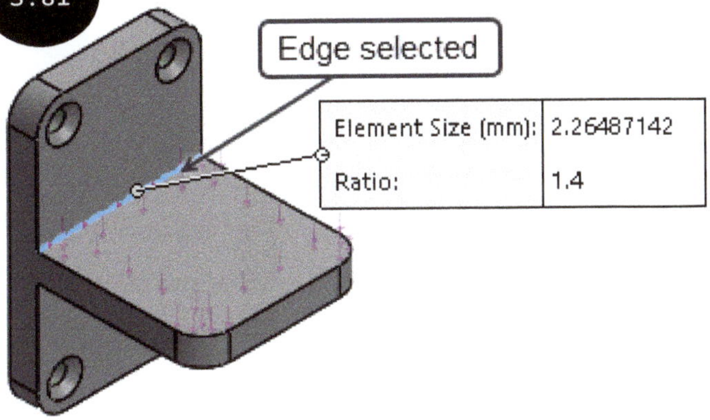

3.82

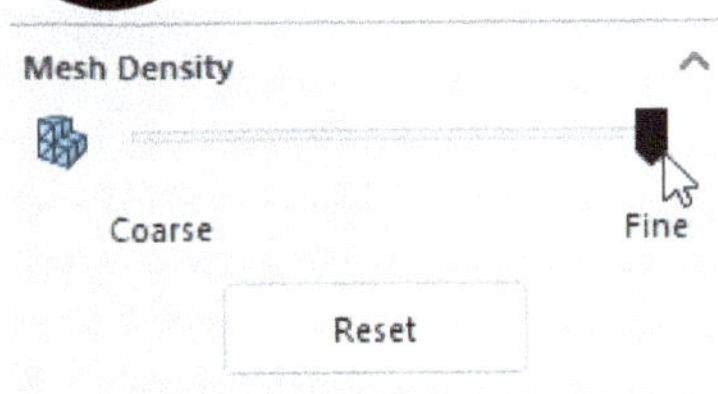

5. Click on the **Create Mesh** button in the **Selected Entities** rollout of the PropertyManager. The **Simulation** message window appears. In this window, click on the **Yes** button to continue meshing the selected entity. The **Mesh Progress** window appears which displays the progress of meshing the model. After the process of meshing the model is completed, the meshed model appears in the graphics area, see Figure 3.83. Note that smaller elements (fine mesh) are created along the selected edge.

3.83

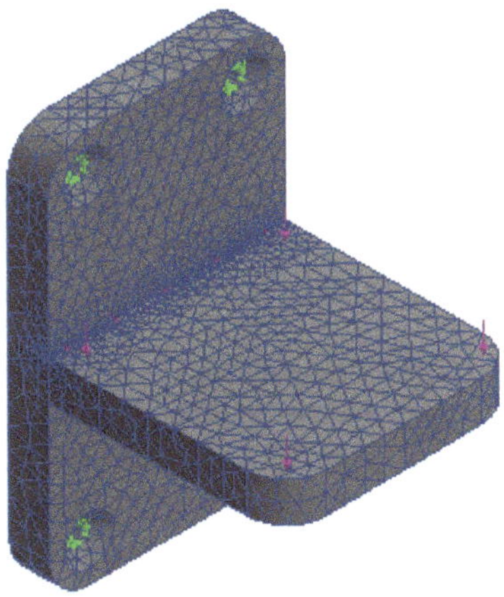

Now, you need to run the analysis again to get the results after applying mesh control.

6. Click on the **Run This Study** tool in the **Simulation CommandManager**. The **Bracket Static Study** (*name of the study*) window appears which displays the progress of the analysis. After the process of running the analysis is complete, the **Results** folder gets updated in the Simulation Study Tree with updated stress, displacement, and strain results. Also, the stress distribution on the model and the von Mises stress plot appear in the graphics area, see Figure 3.84.

3.84

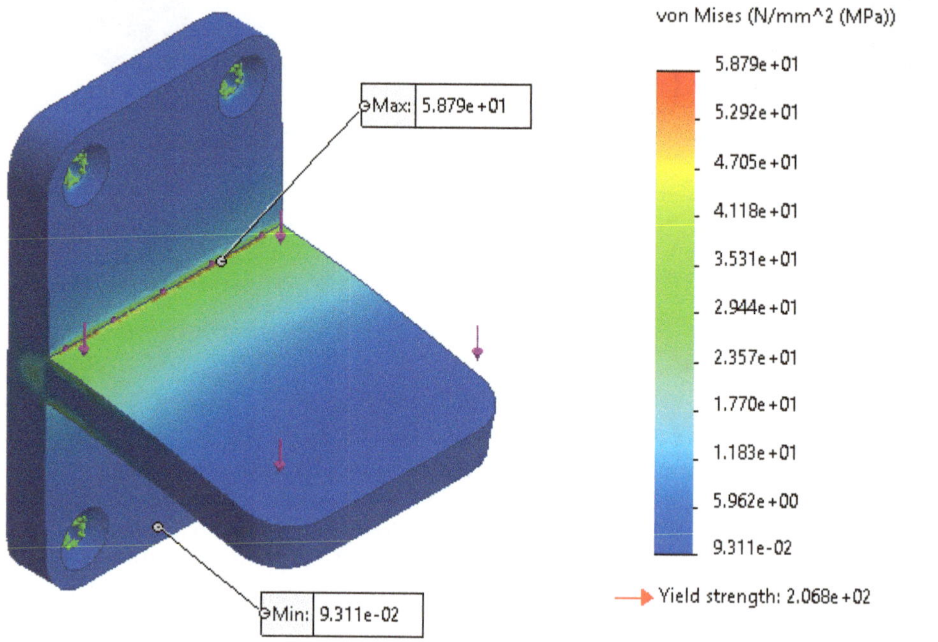

Section 13: Comparing Stress Results Before and After Mesh Control

1. Ensure that the von Mises stress result is displayed in the graphics area, refer to Figure 3.84. If it is not displayed, then you need to double-click on the **Stress1 (-vonMises-)** option in the **Results** folder of the Simulation Study Tree to display the von Mises stress results. It is evident from the above figure that the maximum von Mises stress in the model after applying the mesh control is **5.879e+01** (58.786) N/mm^2 (MPa).

   Notice the difference between the maximum von Mises stress in the model before and after applying the mesh control. Before applying the mesh control, the maximum von Mises stress was **3.864e+01** (38.643) N/mm^2 (MPa) whereas, after applying the mesh control, the maximum von Mises stress is **5.879e+01** (58.786) N/mm^2 (MPa). This is because a fine mesh is created along the edge of the model having high stress. The fine mesh generates a higher number of small elements which gives more accurate results but the computational time increases due to a higher number of elements, nodes, and degrees of freedom.

Section 14: Creating the Iso Plot

Now, you need to create the Iso plot to display the von Mises stresses between the **30 N/mm^2 (MPa)** and **5.879e+01 N/mm^2 (MPa)** range in the model.

Note: The Iso plot is used for displaying the user-defined range of results in portions of the model.

1. Click on the **Plot Tools** in the **Simulation CommandManager**. The **Plot Tools** flyout appears, see Figure 3.85. In this flyout, click on the **Iso Clipping** tool. The **Iso Clipping PropertyManager** appears, see Figure 3.86. Alternatively, click on the **Stress1 (-vonMises-)** option in the **Results** folder of the Simulation Study Tree and then click on the **Iso Clipping** tool.

3.85

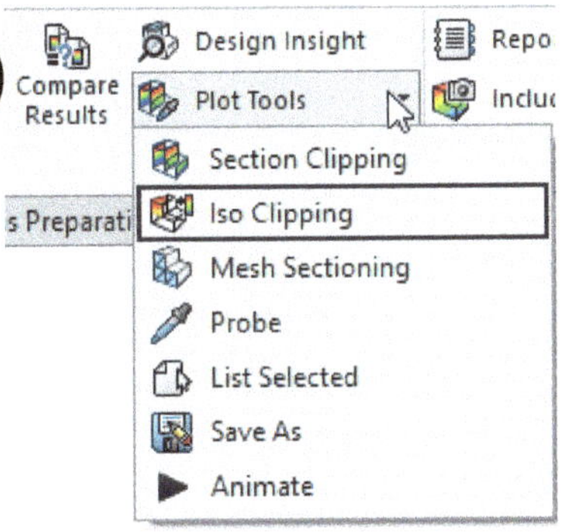

3.86

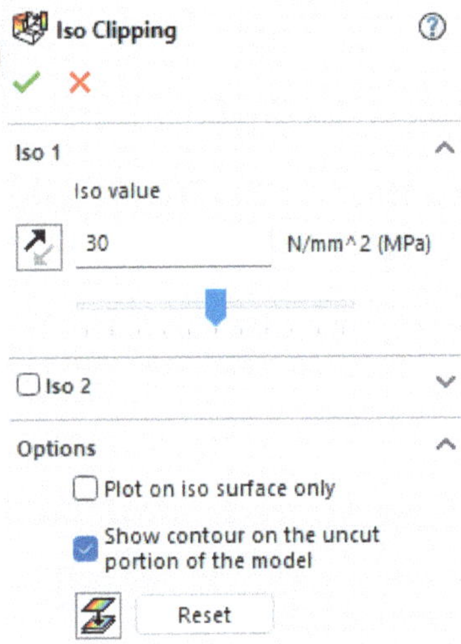

2. Enter **30** in the **Iso value** field of the **Iso 1** rollout in the PropertyManager, refer to Figure 3.86.

3. Expand the **Iso 2** rollout of the PropertyManager by selecting the check box in its title bar, (see Figure 3.87) and then drag the Slider toward the extreme right to display the maximum von Mises value in the **Iso value** field of the rollout, see Figure 3.87. Notice that the portions of the model where the von Mises stress is between the specified range are displayed in the graphics area, see Figure 3.88.

3.87

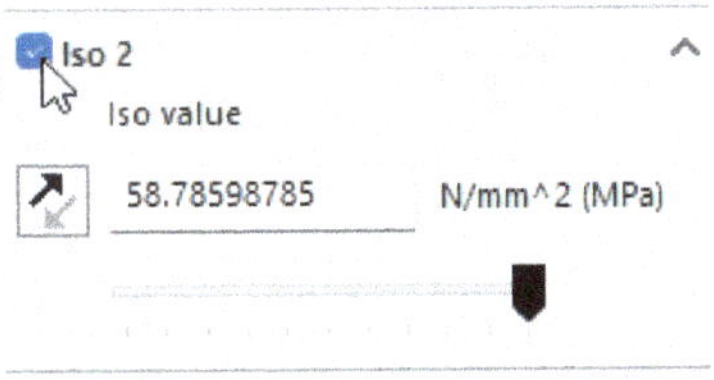

3.88

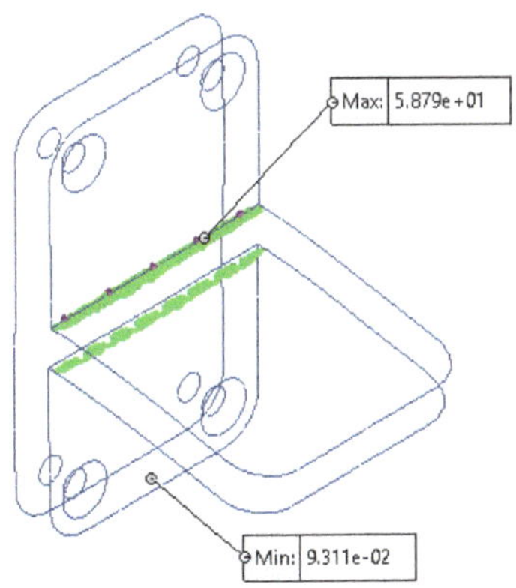

Note: In Figure 3.88, the symbols of fixtures and loads are hidden for clarity of image. To hide the fixture symbols, right-click on the fixture name listed under the **Fixtures** option in the Simulation Study Tree and then click on the **Hide** tool in the shortcut menu that appears. Similarly, to hide the load symbols, right-click on the load name listed under the **External Loads** option in the Simulation Study Tree and then click on the **Hide** tool in the shortcut menu that appears.

4. After creating the Iso plot and reviewing the portions of the model where the von Mises stress is between the **30 N/mm^2 (MPa)** and **6.151e+01 N/mm^2 (MPa)**, click on the **Clipping on/off** button in the **Options** rollout of the **Iso Clipping PropertyManager** to turn off the display of the Iso plot. This button is used for turning on and off the display of Iso plot in the graphics area.

5. Click on the green tick-mark button in the PropertyManager.

Section 15: Saving Results

Now, you need to save the results.

1. Click on the **Save** tool in the **Standard** toolbar. The model and its results are saved in the location > *SOLIDWORKS Simulation > Case Studies > C03 Case Studies > Case Study 2.*

Case Study 3: Static Analysis of a Symmetrical Model

In this case study, you will perform the linear static analysis of a symmetrical model shown in Figure 3.89 and determine the stress under a uniformly distributed load.

3.89

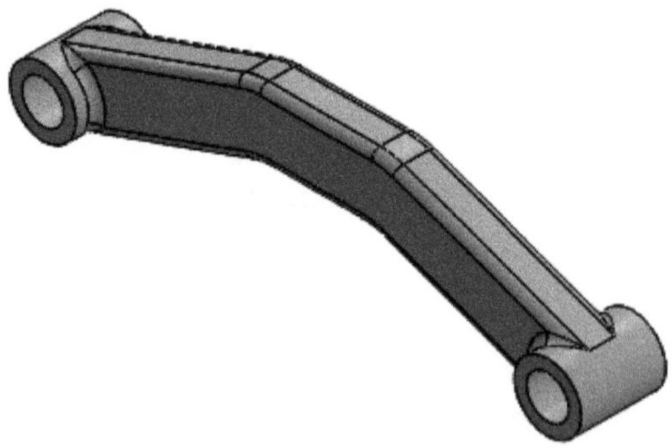

Project Description

The model is fixed at two holes and a 65200 N load is applied on its top face, see Figure 3.90. The model is made up of **AISI 1035 Steel (SS)** material.

3.90

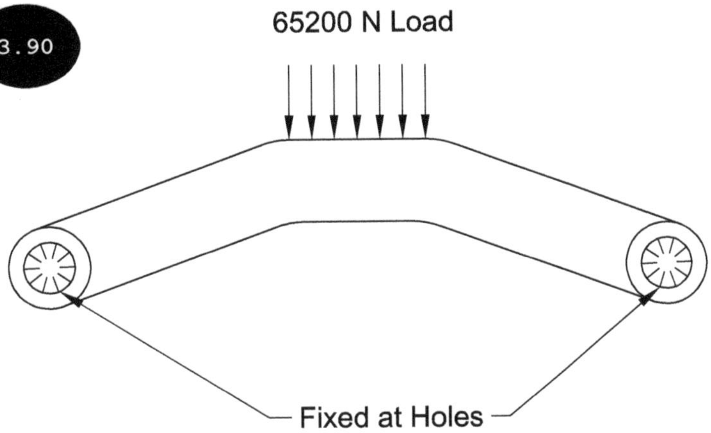

Project Summary

In this case study, you will run a static study on half of the model and obtain the results for the complete model. In the study, you will generate a high-quality curvature-based mesh with a maximum element size of 3 mm and minimum element size of 0.5 mm. You will determine the stress, displacement, strain, and factor of safety of the model under the applied load. You will also animate the stress distribution on the model. Specify the unit system as SI (MKS) with displacement in mm and stress in N/mm^2 (MPa) units.

The following sequence summarizes the case study outline:

1. Downloading Files of Chapter 3
2. Opening the Model
3. Starting the Static Study
4. Defining Units
5. Assigning the Material
6. Splitting the Model
7. Applying the Fixture
8. Applying the Load
9. Generating the Mesh
10. Running the Analysis
11. Displaying Stress, Displacement, and Strain Results
12. Animating the Stress Distribution on the Model
13. Defining the Factor of Safety
14. Saving Results

Section 1: Downloading Files of Chapter 3

1. Log on to the CADArtifex website (*cadartifex.com/login/*) using the Email OTP sent to your registered email ID. After logging in, download the file for this chapter (**C03 Case Studies**) if it has not already been downloaded in an earlier case study.

   If you are a new user, you must first sign up on the website as a **Learner** (*cadartifex.com/register*) to access and download the online resources.

2. Save the extracted **C03 Case Studies** folder in the location ***SOLIDWORKS Simulation > Case Studies*** on the local drive of your system. If these folders have not been created earlier, create them in the local drive before saving the extracted folder.

Section 2: Opening the Model

1. Double-click on the SOLIDWORKS icon on your desktop to start SOLIDWORKS, if not already started.

2. Click on the **Open** button in the **Welcome** dialog box or click on the **Open** tool in the **Standard** toolbar. The **Open** dialog box appears.

3. Browse to the location > ***SOLIDWORKS Simulation > Case Studies > C03 Case Studies > Case Study 3*** on the local drive of your system. Next, select the **Symmetrical Model** and then click on the **Open** button in the dialog box. The Symmetrical Model is opened in SOLIDWORKS, see Figure 3.91.

3.91

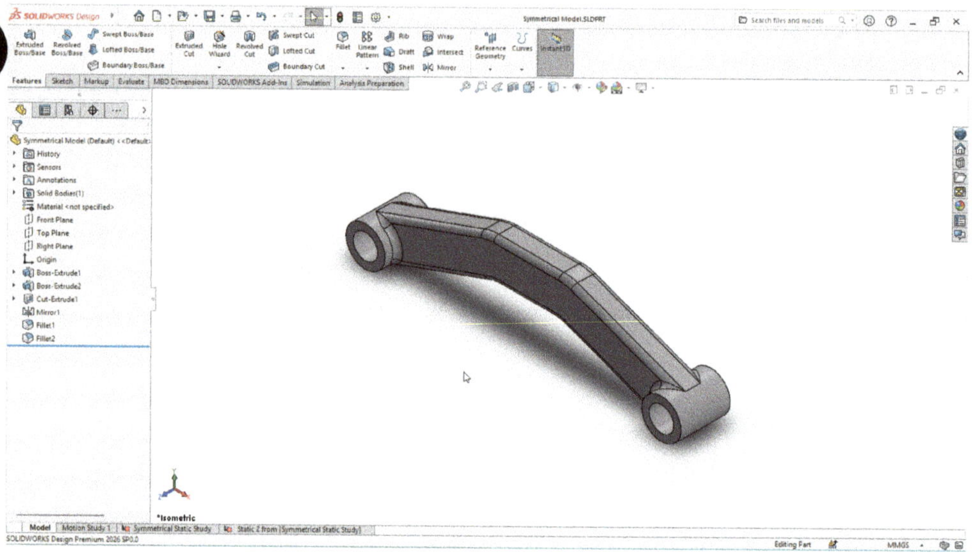

Section 3: Starting the Static Study

1. Click on the **Simulation** tab in the **CommandManager**. The tools of the **Simulation CommandManager** appear, see Figure 3.92.

3.92

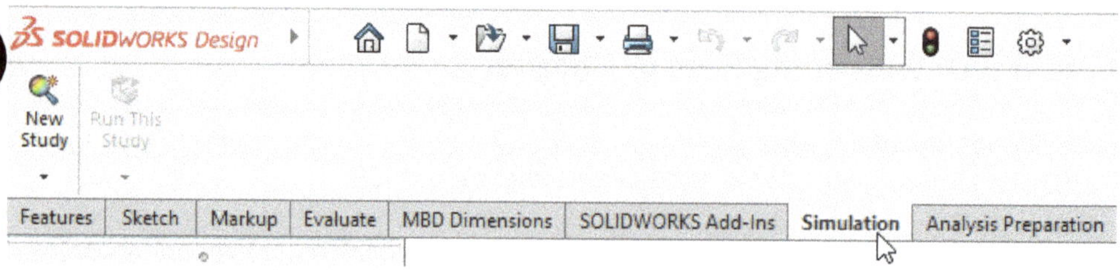

Note: If the **Simulation** tab is not added in the CommandManager then you need to add it as discussed earlier.

2. Click on the **New Study** tool in the **Simulation CommandManager**. The **Study PropertyManager** appears to the left of the graphics area.

3. Ensure that the **Static** button is activated in the **Study PropertyManager** to perform the linear static analysis on the model.

4. Enter **Symmetrical Static Study** in the **Study name** field of the **Name** rollout in the PropertyManager.

5. Click on the green tick-mark button in the PropertyManager. The various tools for performing the static analysis are enabled in the **Simulation CommandManager**. Also, the **Symmetrical Static Study** is added to the Simulation Study Tree, see Figure 3.93.

3.93

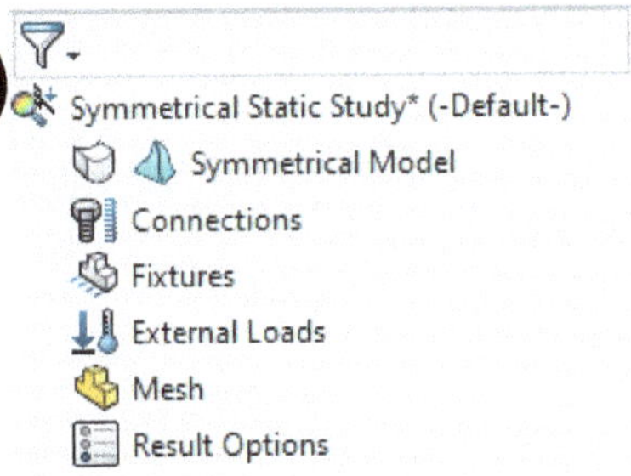

Section 4: Defining Units

Before you start with the analysis process, it is important to set the units.

1. Click on the **Simulation** > **Options** in the SOLIDWORKS Design Menus. The **System Options** dialog box appears.

2. Click on the **Default Options** tab in this dialog box. The name of the dialog box changes to the **Default Options**, see Figure 3.94.

3. Ensure that the **Units** option is selected in the dialog box and the options for specifying the units appear on the right panel of the dialog box, see Figure 3.94.

4. Select the **SI (MKS)** radio button in the **Unit system** area of the dialog box. Next, ensure that the **mm** unit is selected in the **Length/Displacement** drop-down list and the **N/mm^2 (MPa)** unit is selected in the **Pressure/Stress** drop-down list of the **Units** area, see Figure 3.94.

3.94

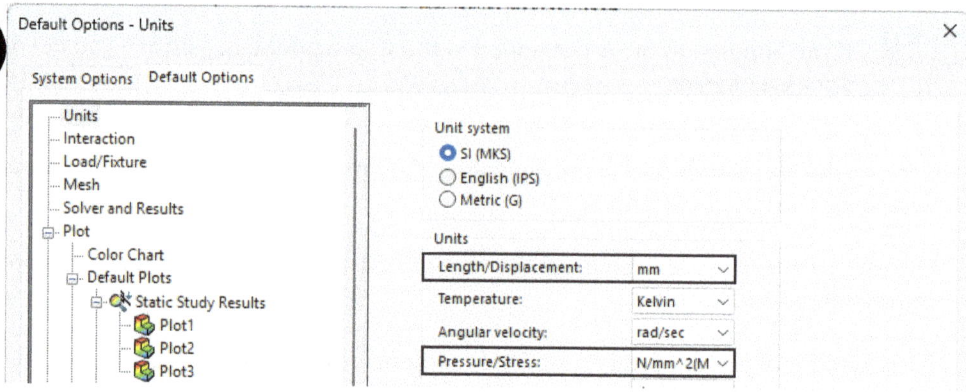

5. After specifying the units, click on the **OK** button to accept the changes and exit the dialog box.

Section 5: Assigning the Material

1. Click on the **Apply Material** tool in the **Simulation CommandManager**. The **Material** dialog box appears.

2. Expand the **Steel** category of the **SOLIDWORKS Materials** library in the **Material** dialog box and then select the **AISI 1035 Steel (SS)** material, see Figure 3.95. The properties of the selected material appear on the right panel of the dialog box.

3.95

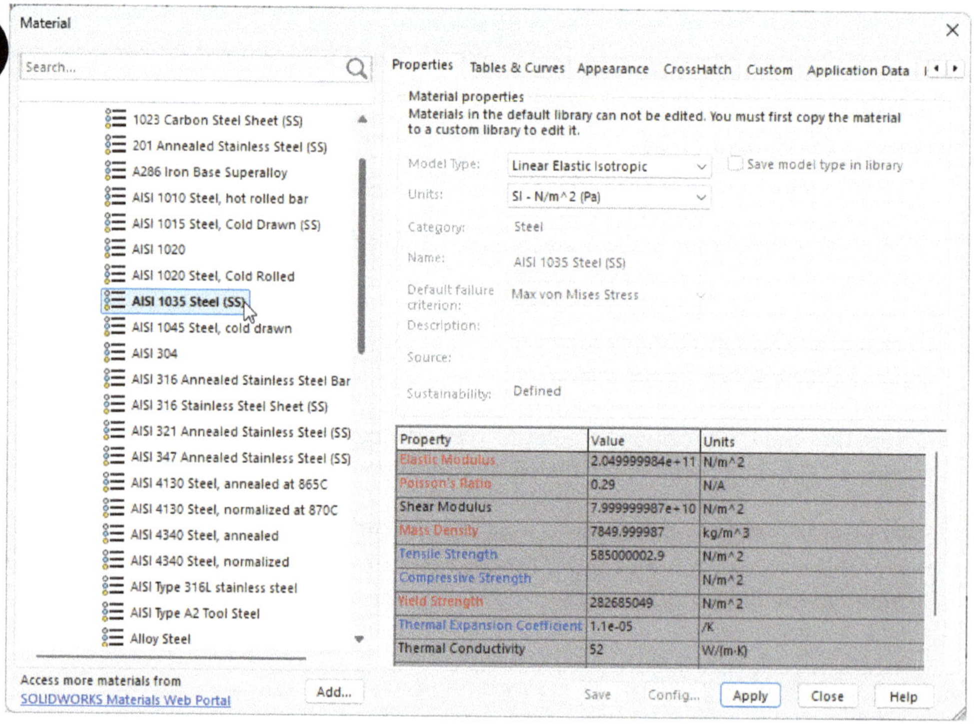

3. Click on the **Apply** button and then the **Close** button in the dialog box. The material is assigned to the model.

Section 6: Splitting the Model

As the model geometry and boundary conditions (fixtures and loads) are symmetric about its mid -plane, you can split the model to perform the analysis on one of its halves and obtain the results for the complete model. Performing analysis on one-half of the symmetrical model reduces the computation time.

1. Click on the **Analysis Preparation** tab in the CommandManager and then click on the **Split** tool, see Figure 3.96. The **Split PropertyManager** appears, see Figure 3.97.

3.96

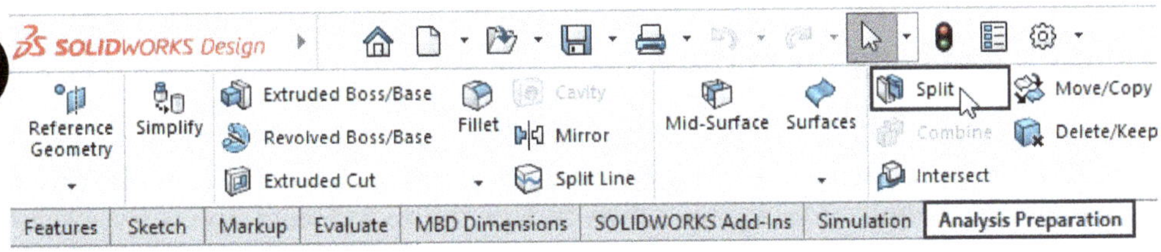

2. Expand the FeatureManager Design Tree, which is now at the upper left corner of the graphics area, and then click on the **Right Plane** as the plane to split the model, see Figure 3.98.

3.97

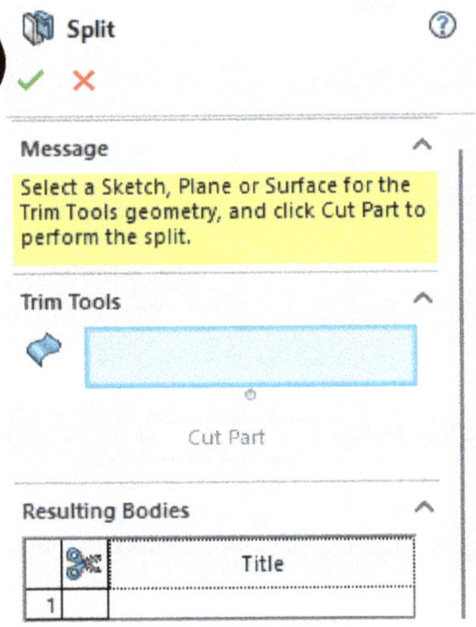

3.98

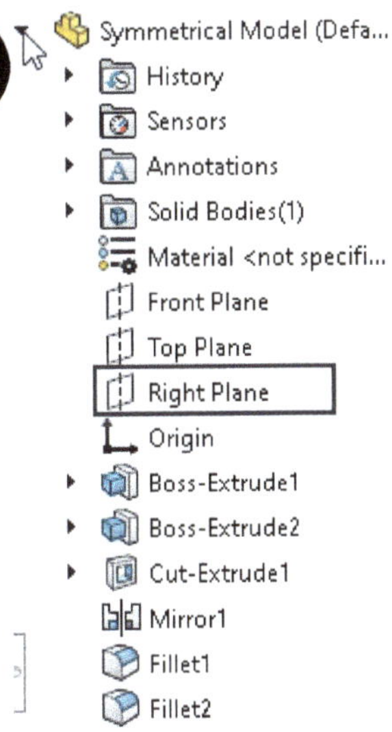

3. Click on the **Cut Part** button in the **Trim Tools** rollout of the **Split PropertyManager**. The model is divided into two bodies, which are listed in the **Resulting Bodies** rollout of the PropertyManager, see Figure 3.99.

4. Select the check box corresponding to the first body in the **Resulting Bodies** rollout of the PropertyManager, see Figure 3.99.

3.99

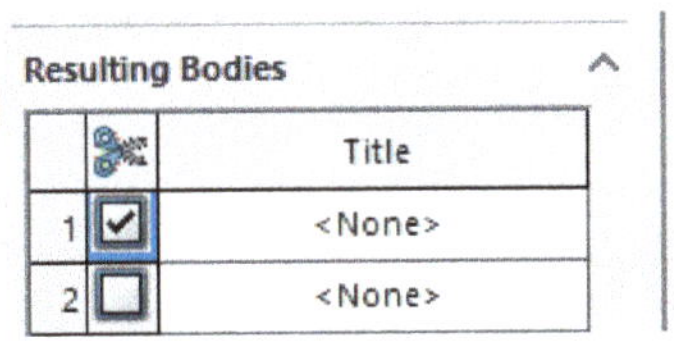

5. Select the **Consume cut bodies** check box in the **Resulting Bodies** rollout of the PropertyManager.

6. Click on the green tick-mark button ✓ in the PropertyManager. The selected body of the model gets deleted and the model appears similar to the one shown in Figure 3.100.

3.100

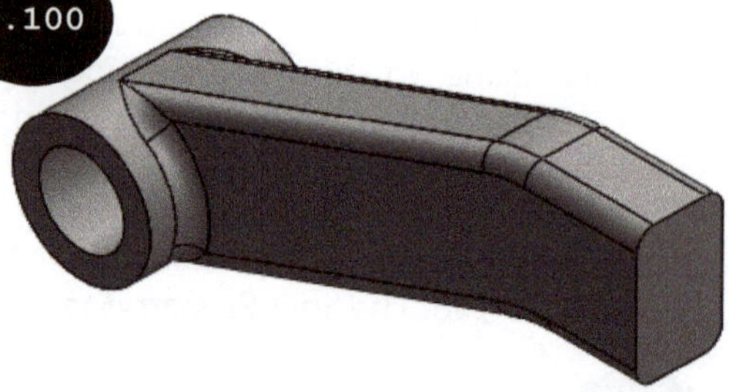

Section 7: Applying the Fixture

Now, you need to apply the Fixed and Symmetry fixtures to the model.

1. Invoke the **Fixture** flyout by clicking on the arrow at the bottom of the **Fixtures Advisor** tool in the **Simulation CommandManager** and then click on the **Fixed Geometry** tool, see Figure 3.101. The **Fixture PropertyManager** appears, see Figure 3.102.

3.101

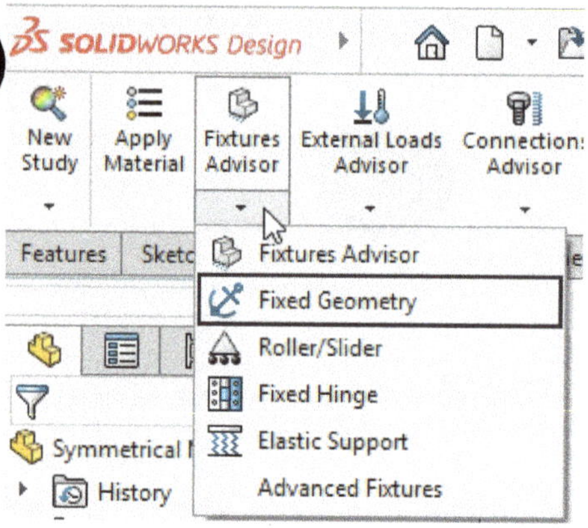

3.102

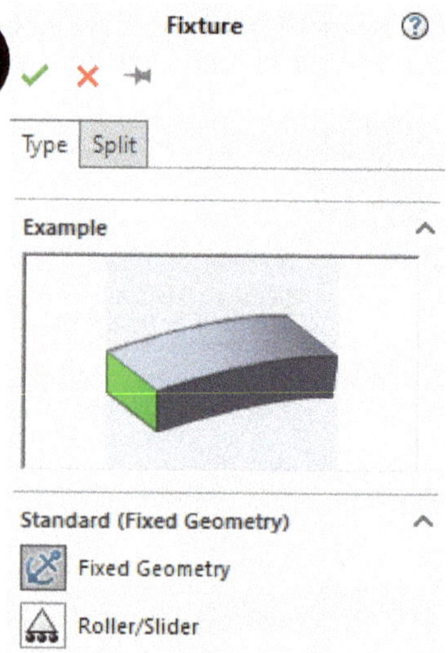

2. Select the circular face of the hole to apply the Fixed Geometry fixture. The symbol of the Fixed Geometry fixture appears on the selected face, see Figure 3.103. Next, click on the green tick-mark button ✓ in the PropertyManager to apply the Fixed Geometry fixture.

3.103

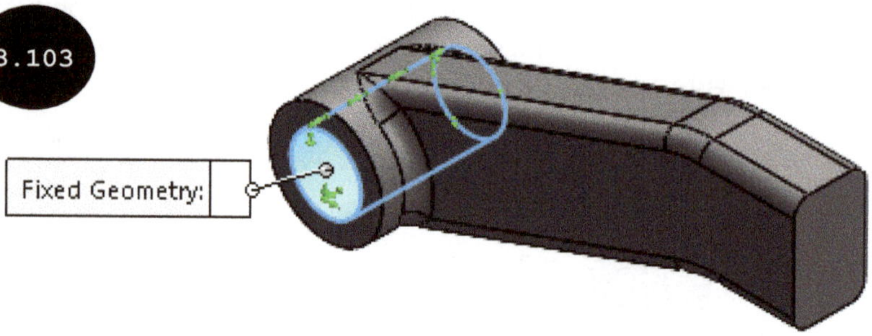

Now, you need to apply the Symmetry fixture on the cutting face of the model.

3. Invoke the **Fixture** flyout by clicking on the arrow at the bottom of the **Fixtures Advisor** tool in the **Simulation CommandManager** and then click on the **Advanced Fixtures** tool, see Figure 3.104. The **Fixture PropertyManager** appears with the expanded **Advanced** rollout.

4. Click on the **Symmetry** button in the **Advanced** rollout of the PropertyManager and then select the cutting face as the symmetric face of the model in the graphics area. A preview of the other symmetric half of the model appears in the graphics area and the symbol of the Symmetry fixture appears on the selected face, see Figure 3.105.

3.104

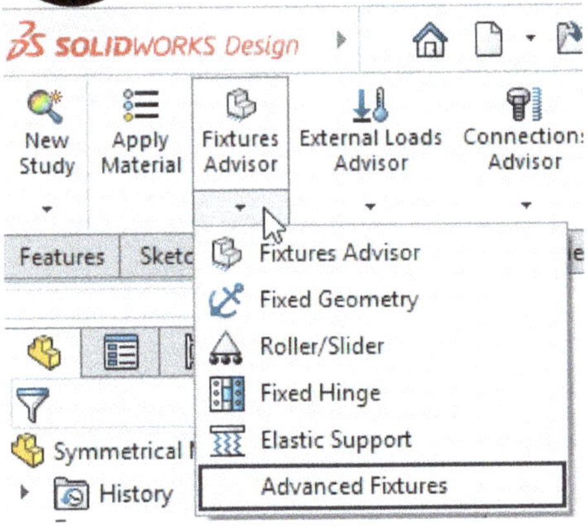

3.105

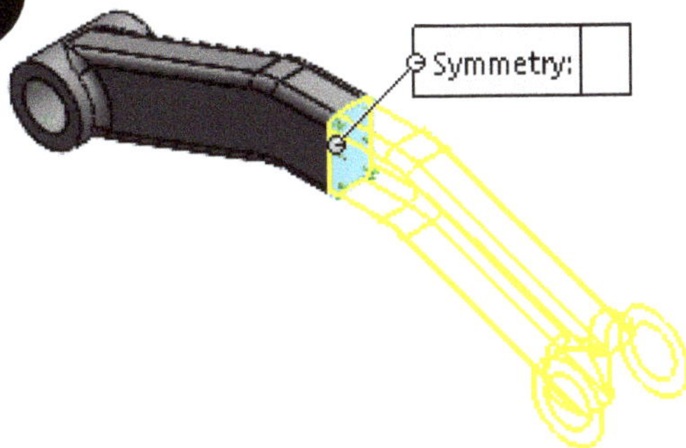

5. Click on the green tick-mark button in the PropertyManager. The Symmetry fixture is applied on the selected face of the model.

Section 8: Applying the Load

Now, you need to apply the load.

1. Invoke the **External Loads** flyout in the **Simulation CommandManager** (see Figure 3.106) and then click on the **Force** tool. The **Force/Torque PropertyManager** appears.

3.106

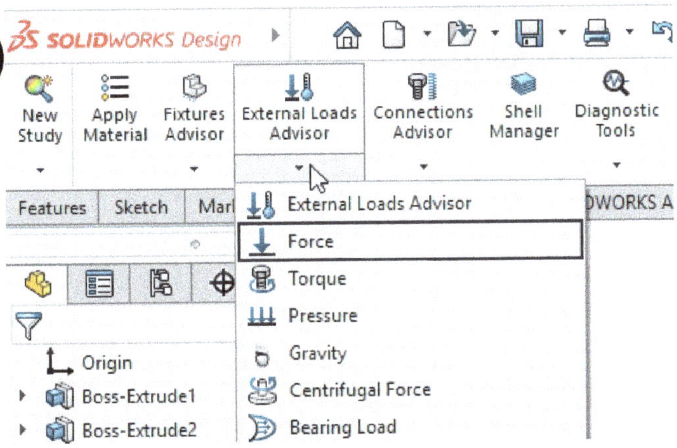

2. Select the top horizontal face of the model to apply the load, see Figure 3.107. The symbol of the load appears on the selected face.

3.107

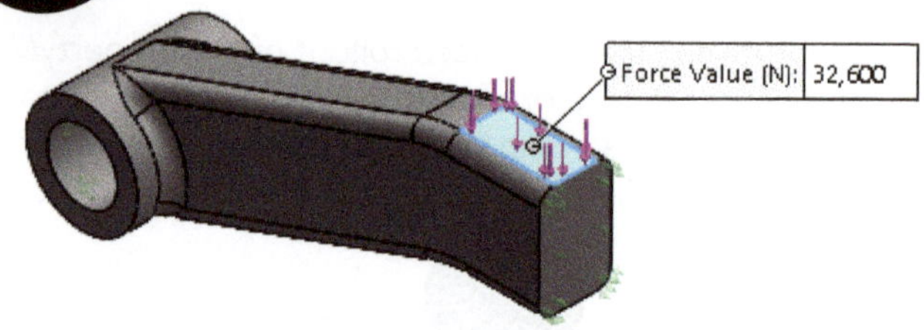

3. Ensure that the **Normal** radio button is selected to apply the load normal to the face.

4. Enter **32600** (65200/2 = 32600) in the **Force** field of the PropertyManager.

5. Click on the green tick-mark button in the PropertyManager. The 32600 N load is applied on the selected face of the model.

Section 9: Generating the Mesh

As mentioned in the project summary, you need to generate a curvature-based mesh with a maximum element size of 3 mm and a minimum element size of 0.5 mm.

1. Right-click on the **Mesh** option in the Simulation Study Tree and then click on the **Create Mesh** tool in the shortcut menu that appears to invoke the **Mesh PropertyManager**.

2. Expand the **Mesh Parameters** rollout of the PropertyManager by clicking on the check box in its title bar.

3. Select the **Curvature-based mesh** radio button in the expanded **Mesh Parameters** rollout and then enter 3 mm as the maximum element size and 0.5 mm as the minimum element size in the respective fields of the PropertyManager, see Figure 3.108.

3.108

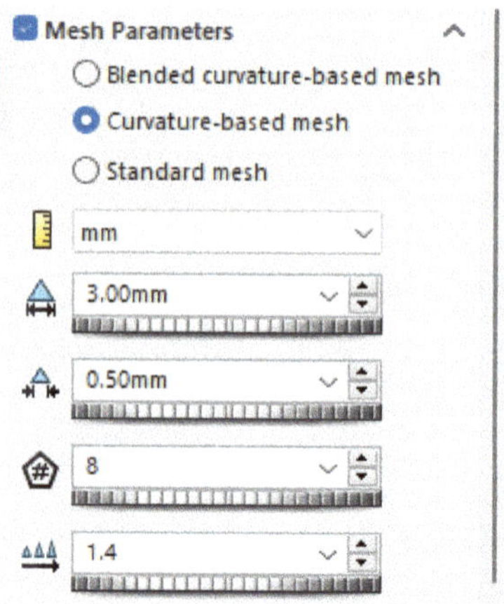

4. Accept the other default mesh parameters and then click on the green tick-mark button ✓. The **Mesh Progress** window appears which displays the progress of meshing in the model. After the meshing is complete, the meshed model appears, see Figure 3.109. Note that SOLIDWORKS Simulation generates mesh with tetrahedral solid elements for solid geometry.

3.109

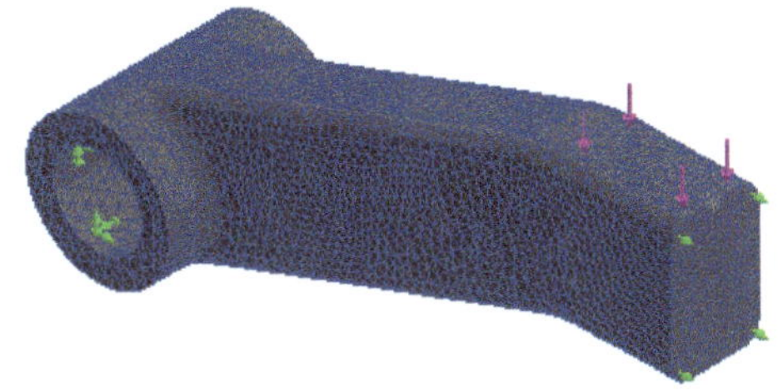

Section 10: Running the Analysis

Now, you need to run the analysis.

1. Click on the **Run This Study** tool in the **Simulation CommandManager**. The **Symmetrical Static Study** (*name of the study*) window appears which displays the progress of the analysis.

2. After the process of running the analysis is complete, the **Results** folder is added to the Simulation Study Tree with the stress, displacement, and strain results. By default, the **Stress** result is activated in the **Results** folder. As a result, the stress distribution on the model and the von Mises stress plot appear in the graphics area, see Figure 3.110.

3.110

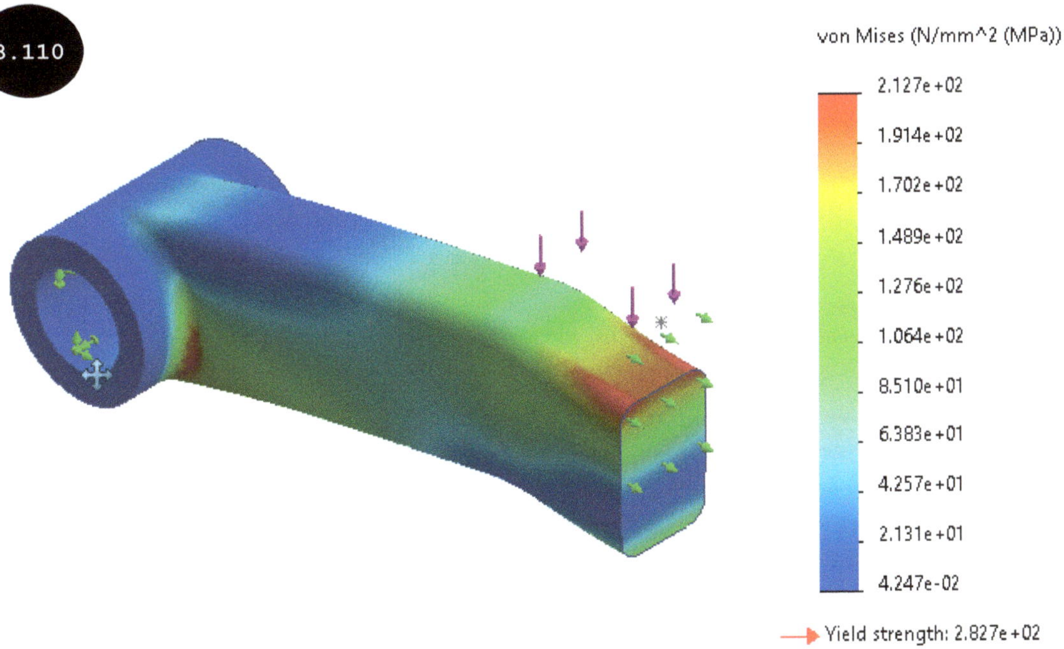

Section 11: Displaying Stress, Displacement, and Strain Results

1. Display the von Mises stress results if not displayed by default, refer to Figure 3.107. Notice that the maximum von Mises stress in the model under the applied load is **2.127e+02** (212.681) N/mm^2 (MPa) which is within the yield strength of the material that is **2.827e+02** (282.685) N/mm^2 (MPa). Note that you may find a slight difference in the result values depending on the service pack installed on your system.

Note: If the maximum von Mises stress of the model exceeds the yield strength of the material, your design is likely to fail under the applied load. You may need to optimize the design and validate the boundary conditions (fixtures/loads), or material properties to make it a valid design to withstand the applied load.

Now, you need to display the stress distribution on the complete model.

2. Right-click on the **Stress1 (-vonMises-)** option in the **Results** folder of the Simulation Study Tree and then click on the **Edit Definition** tool in the shortcut menu that appears. The **Stress plot PropertyManager** appears, see Figure 3.111.

3. Ensure that the **Definition** tab is activated in the PropertyManager. Next, expand its **Advanced Options** rollout by clicking on the arrow in its title bar, see Figure 3.112.

4. Select the **Display symmetric results** check box in the **Advanced Options** rollout, see Figure 3.112.

3.111

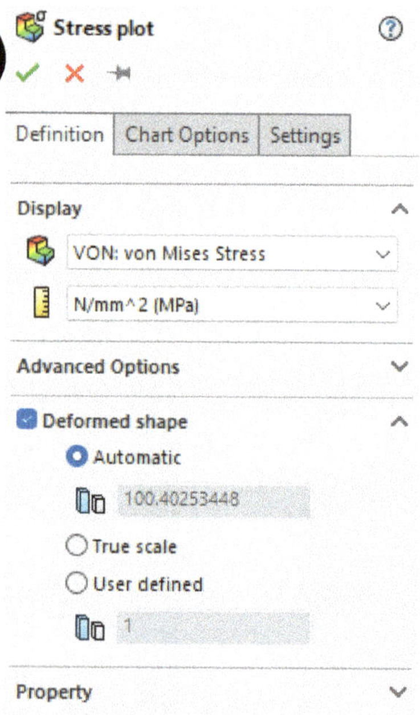

3.112

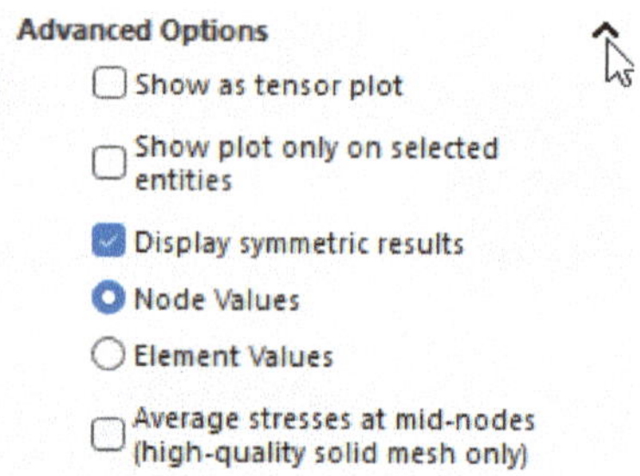

5. Click on the green tick-mark button in the PropertyManager. The stress distribution on the complete model appears in the graphics area, see Figure 3.113.

3.113

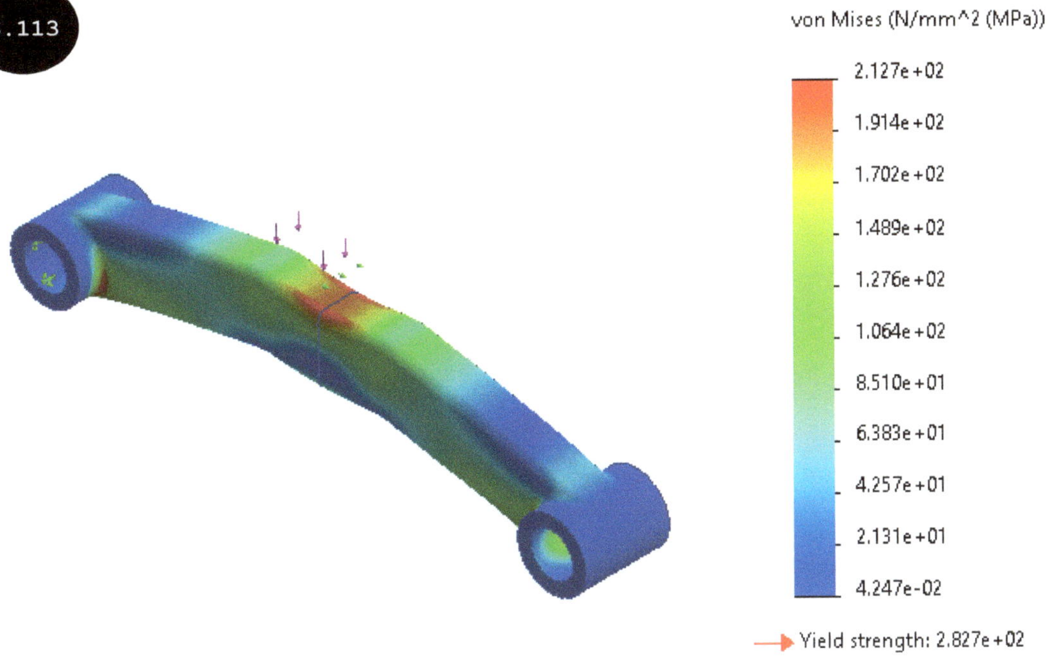

6. Similarly, display the displacement and strain results by double-clicking on the respective option in the **Results** folder of the Simulation Study Tree. The maximum resultant displacement of the model under the applied load is **1.693e-01** (0.169) mm and the maximum equivalent strain on the model is **8.527e-04** (0.001).

Section 12: Animating the Stress Distribution on the Model

Now, you will animate the stress distribution and review the deformed shape of the model.

1. Display the von Mises stress results, if not displayed in the graphics area, and then right-click on the **Stress1 (-vonMises-)** option in the **Results** folder of the Simulation Study Tree. A shortcut menu appears. In this shortcut menu, click on the **Animate** tool. The **Animation PropertyManager** appears, see Figure 3.114. Also, the animated effects of the deformed shape of the model start in the graphics area with default settings. You can change the animation settings by using the PropertyManager.

2. To save the animation as an AVI file, select the **Save as AVI file** check box in the PropertyManager. Next, specify the path to save the file.

3.114

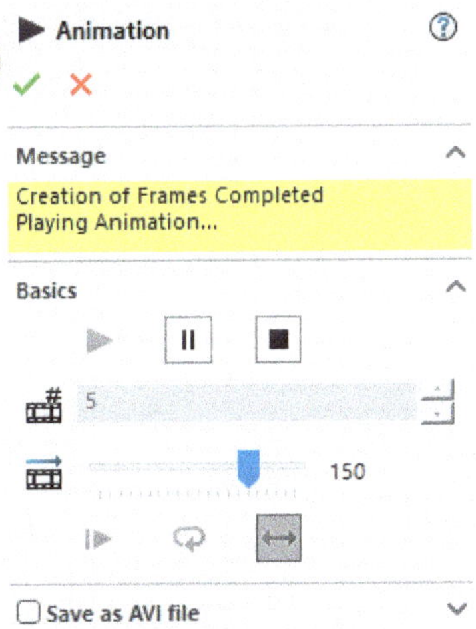

3. After reviewing the animated effects of the deformed shape, click on the green tick-mark button in the PropertyManager to exit the PropertyManager and save the AVI file in the specified location.

Note: By default, the deformed shape of the model does not appear in the true scale. To display the deformed shape of the model in true scale, you need to edit the plot and select the **True scale** radio button in the **Deformed shape** rollout of the PropertyManager.

Section 13: Defining the Factor of Safety

Now, you need to define the Factor of Safety of the design.

1. Right-click on the **Results** folder in the Simulation Study Tree. A shortcut menu appears, see Figure 3.115.

2. Click on the **Define Factor Of Safety Plot** tool in the shortcut menu. The **Factor of Safety PropertyManager** appears, see Figure 3.116.

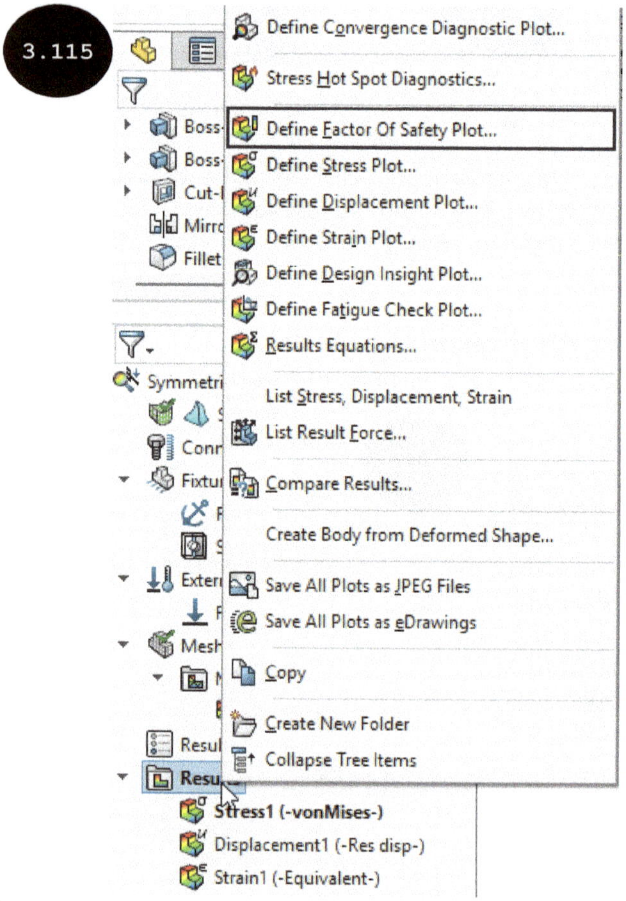

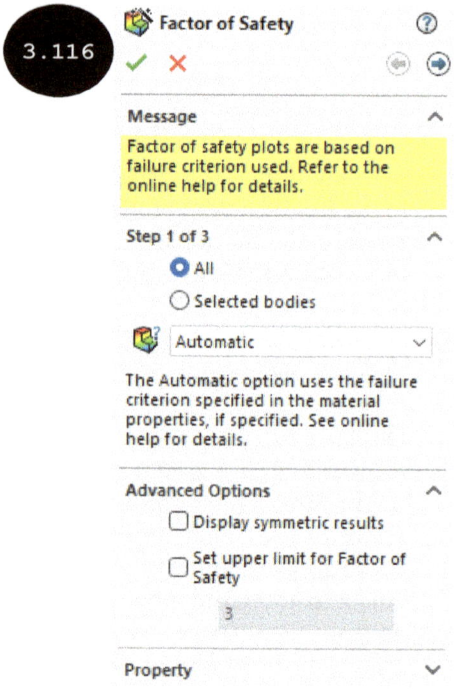

3. Select the **Display symmetric results** check box in the **Advanced Options** rollout of the PropertyManager to display the results for the complete model.

4. Accept the other default parameters and then click on the green tick-mark button in the PropertyManager. The **Factor of Safety1 (-FOS-)** plot is added in the **Results** folder of the Simulation Study Tree. Also, the Factor of Safety distribution on the model and its plot appear in the graphics area, see Figure 3.117.

   Notice that the minimum Factor of Safety of the model is **1.329e+00** (1.330), which indicates that the model is safe and can withstand the applied load. The Factor of Safety is the ratio of the allowable stress to the actual stress.

Note: If the Factor of Safety equals to 1, it indicates that the stress is exactly at the allowable limit and the model can withstand only the design load. A Factor of Safety less than 1 indicates that the failure of the model is likely under the design load, whereas, a Factor of Safety greater than 1 indicates that the stress is within the allowable limit. Greater the Factor of Safety, stronger is the design. However, a higher Factor of Safety sometimes leads to over designing of the product.

3.117

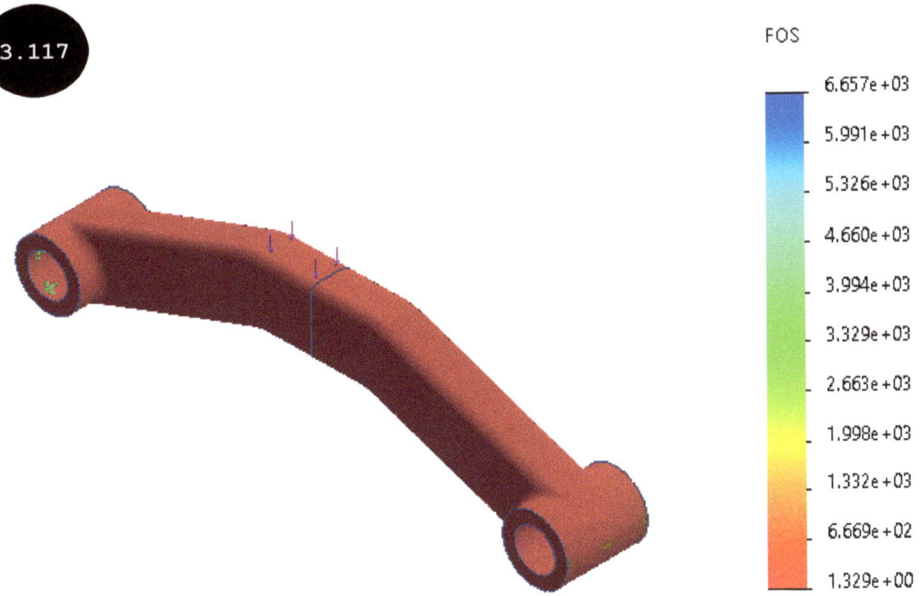

Section 14: Saving Results

Now, you need to save the results.

1. Click on the **Save** tool in the **Standard** toolbar. The model and its results are saved in the location > *SOLIDWORKS Simulation > Case Studies > C03 Case Studies > Case Study 3*.

Case Study 4: Static Analysis of a Torispherical Head with Shell Elements

In this case study, you will perform the linear static analysis of a Torispherical Head with shell elements shown in Figure 3.118 and determine the stress under a uniformly distributed pressure.

3.118

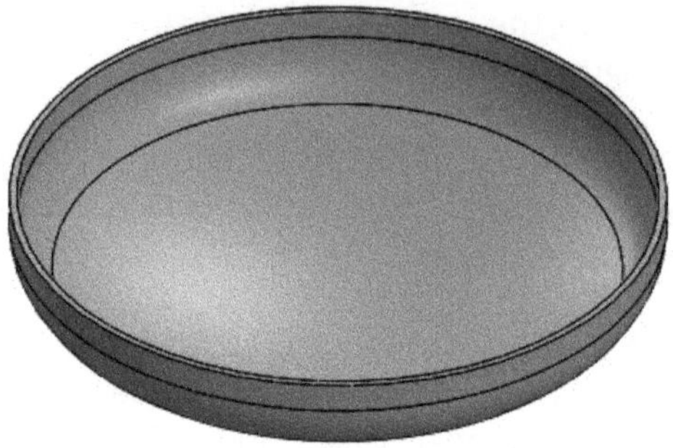

Project Description

The torispherical head is fixed at its top face and a 500 psi pressure is uniformly distributed along its inner faces, see Figure 3.119. The model is made up of **Alloy Steel (SS)** material.

3.119

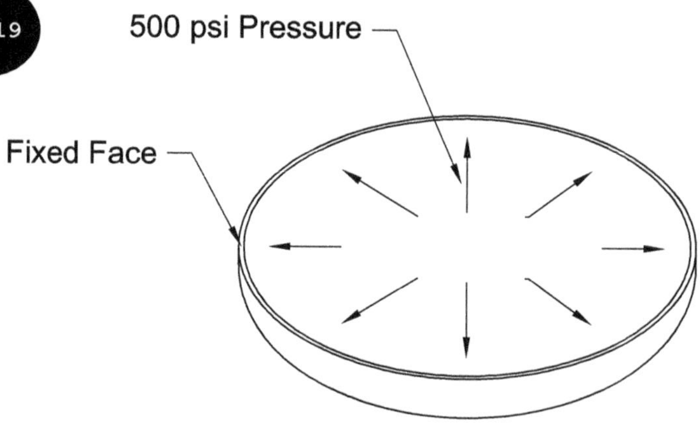

Project Summary

In this case study, you will run a static study on the torispherical head having a uniform thickness of 18 mm. As the torispherical head has uniform thickness, you need to mesh the model with shell elements which helps reduce the computational time without compromising on the quality of results. You need to generate a high-quality curvature-based mesh with a maximum element size of 50 mm and a minimum element size of 1 mm. Also, you need to determine the stress, displacement, strain, and factor of safety of the model under the applied pressure. Specify the unit system as SI (MKS) with displacement in mm and stress in PSI units.

The following sequence summarizes the case study outline:

1. Starting the Static Study
2. Defining Shell Elements for 3D Solid Geometry
3. Defining the Fixture, Pressure, and Material

4. Generating the Mesh with Shell Elements
5. Displaying Mesh Details
6. Running the Analysis
7. Displaying Stress, Displacement, and Strain Results
8. Defining the Factor of Safety
9. Saving Results

Section 1: Starting the Static Study

1. Start SOLIDWORKS and then open the Torispherical Head model from the location *SOLIDWORKS Simulation > Case Studies > C03 Case Studies > Case Study 4*.

Note: You need to download the **C03 Case Studies** file by logging on to the CADArtifex website (*cadartifex.com/login*), if it has not been downloaded earlier.

If you are a new user, you must first register on the CADArtifex website as a Learner to access and download the files.

2. When the Torispherical Head model is open in SOLIDWORKS, click on the **Simulation** tab in the **CommandManager**. The tools of the **Simulation CommandManager** appear, see Figure 3.120.

3.120

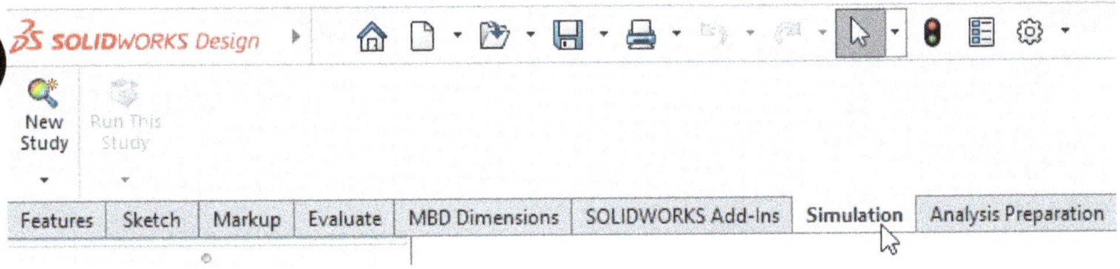

Note: If the **Simulation** tab is not added in the CommandManager then you need to add it as discussed earlier.

3. Click on the **New Study** tool in the **Simulation CommandManager**. The **Study PropertyManager** appears to the left of the graphics area.

4. Ensure that the **Static** button is activated in the **Study PropertyManager** to perform the linear static analysis on the model.

5. Enter **Torispherical Head Study** in the **Study name** field of the **Name** rollout in the PropertyManager.

6. Click on the green tick-mark button in the PropertyManager. The various tools for performing the static analysis are enabled in the **Simulation CommandManager**. Also, the **Torispherical Head Study** is added to the Simulation Study Tree.

Section 2: Defining Shell Elements for 3D Solid Geometry

As mentioned in the project summary, the torispherical head has uniform thickness and you need to define shell elements for meshing it.

Note: When you perform analysis on a model, SOLIDWORKS Simulation automatically identifies the type of geometry (3D solid, 2D, or 1D line) and generates mesh elements accordingly. For example, it generates tetrahedral solid elements for 3D solid geometry, triangular shell elements for 2D geometry, and beam elements for 1D line geometry. However, you can change the type of geometry. For example, if a 3D model is having uniform thickness, you can change its geometry type from 3D solid to 2D geometry for meshing it with triangular shell elements. It helps in reducing the computational time without affecting the results.

1. Right-click on the **Torispherical Head** (*name of the model*) in the Simulation Study Tree. A shortcut menu appears, see Figure 3.121.

2. Click on the **Define Shell By Selected Faces** tool in the shortcut menu, see Figure 3.121. The **Shell Definition PropertyManager** appears, see Figure 3.122.

3.121

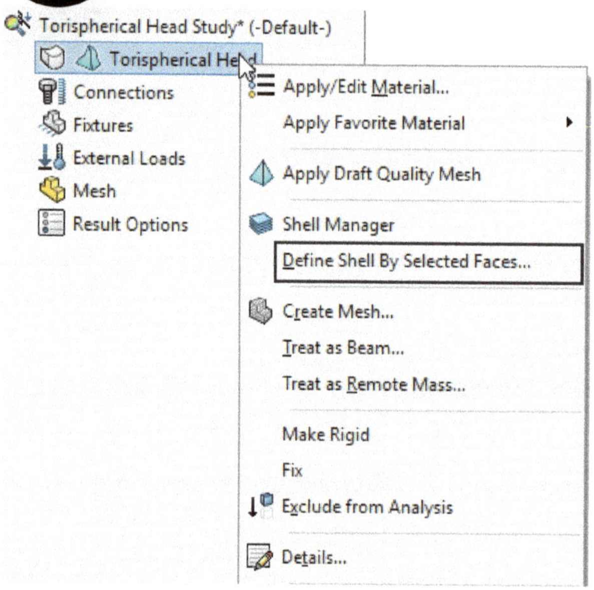

3.122

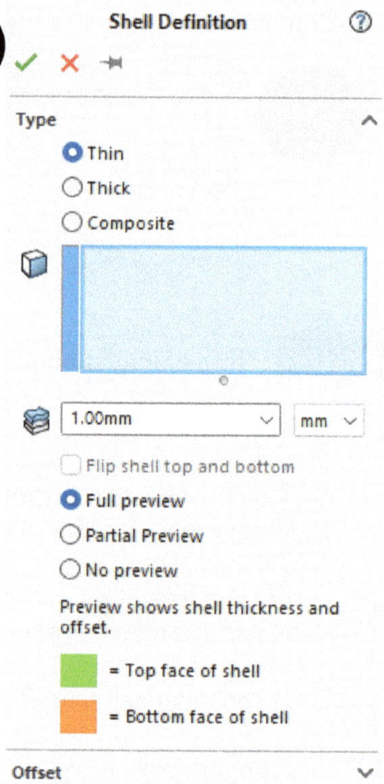

Tip: The options in the **Type** rollout of the **Shell Definition PropertyManager** are used for defining the type of 2D geometry (thin, thick, or composite) for representing the 3D model. The **Thin** radio button of this rollout is used for defining thin 2D geometry when the 3D model has a thickness-to-span ratio equal to or less than 0.05. The **Thick** radio button is used for defining thick 2D geometry when the 3D model has thickness-to-span ratio more than 0.05. The **Composite** radio button is used for defining composite 2D geometry having multiple layers of different materials. This radio button is used when the 3D model has multiple layers of different materials.

On selecting the **Composite** radio button, the **Composite Options** rollout appears in the PropertyManager, see Figure 3.123. The options in this rollout are used for defining the arrangement of different material layers as symmetric or as asymmetric to the mid plane of the geometry, or the sandwich type arrangement. You can also define the same material for all the material layers by selecting the **All Plies Same Material** check box in this rollout. The **Total Plies** field of this rollout is used for defining the number of layers of materials. The **Rotate 0° Reference** check box is used for setting the rotational angle of the layers to 0 degree. By default, it is set to 90 degrees. The **Thickness**, **Angle**, and **Material** columns of the Table in this rollout are used for specifying the thickness, angle, and material of a layer by double-clicking on the respective fields.

3.123

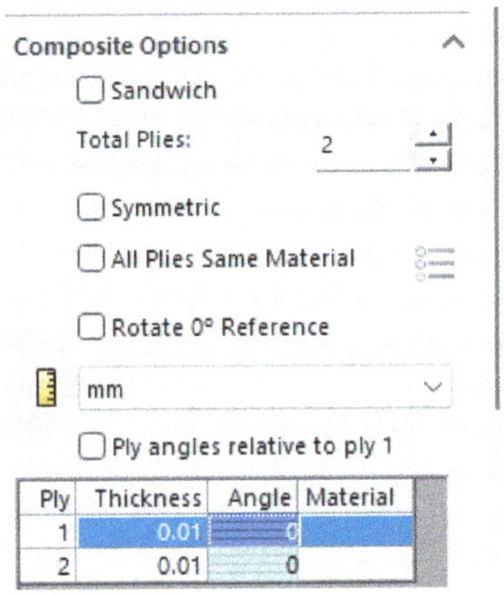

3. Ensure that the **Thin** radio button is selected in the **Type** rollout of the PropertyManager.

4. Ensure that the **Full preview** radio button is selected to display the preview of the geometry in the graphics area.

5. Select the inner faces (three faces) of the model. The color of the selected faces changes in the graphics area, see Figure 3.124.

6. Enter **18** in the **Shell thickness** field of the PropertyManager as the thickness of the geometry.

Tip: When you perform an analysis on a sheet metal component, SOLIDWORKS Simulation automatically identifies it as a 2D geometry and the thickness is automatically extracted from the sheet metal component. On the other hand, for surface component, SOLIDWORKS Simulation automatically identifies it as a 2D geometry, but you need to define the thickness manually, as discussed in the above steps.

7. Expand the **Offset** rollout of the PropertyManager by clicking on the arrow in its title bar, see Figure 3.125.

3.124

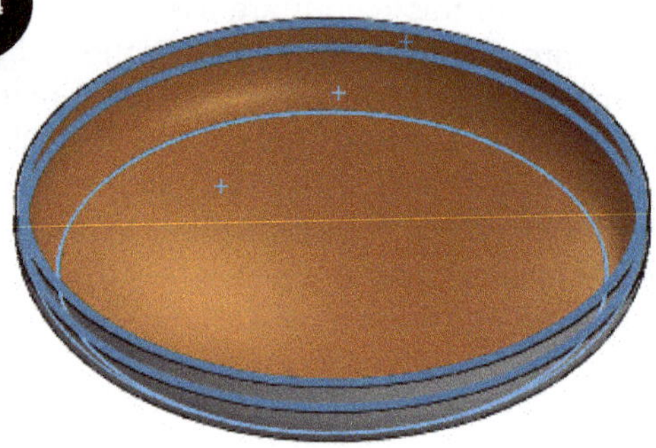

3.125

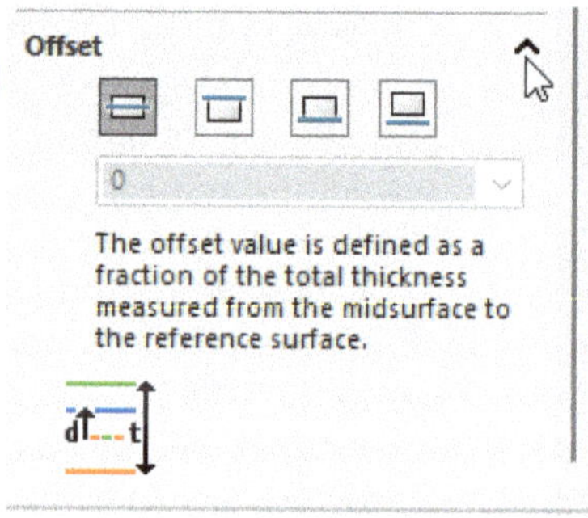

Tip: By default, the **Middle surface** button is activated in the **Offset** rollout. As a result, the selected faces of the model are used as middle faces of the model and the thickness is added symmetrically on both the sides.

8. Click on the **Bottom surface** button in this rollout to add thickness on the outer side of the selected faces of the model.

9. Click on the green tick-mark button in the PropertyManager. The 2D geometry (shell) is defined with a specified thickness and the geometry type is updated in the Simulation Study Tree, see Figure 3.126.

3.126

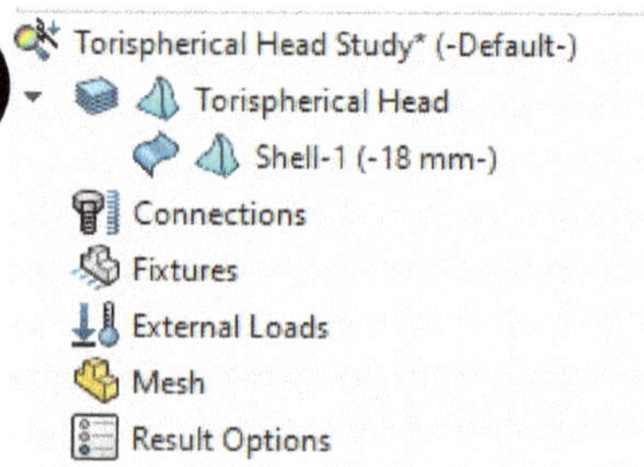

Section 3: Defining the Fixture, Pressure, and Material

Now, you need to apply the fixture and the pressure on the geometry.

1. Right-click on the **Fixtures** option in the Simulation Study Tree and then click on the **Fixed Geometry** tool in the shortcut menu that appears. The **Fixture PropertyManager** appears.

2. Select the inner circular edge of the model to apply the Fixed Geometry fixture, (see Figure 3.127) as you have defined the 2D geometry by selecting the inner faces of the model. Next, click on the green tick-mark ✓ button in the PropertyManager.

3.127

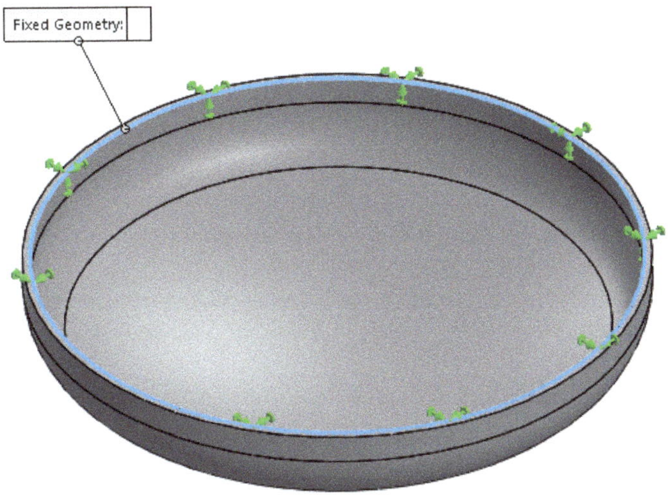

After applying the fixture, you need to apply the pressure.

3. Right-click on the **External Loads** option in the Simulation Study Tree and then click on the **Pressure** tool in the shortcut menu that appears. The **Pressure PropertyManager** appears.

4. Ensure that the **Normal to selected face** radio button is selected in the PropertyManager.

5. Select the **psi** option in the **Unit** drop-down list of the **Pressure Value** rollout in the PropertyManager as the unit of pressure.

6. Enter **500** in the **Pressure Value** field of the PropertyManager.

7. Select the inner faces (three faces) of the model to apply a uniformly distributed pressure of 500 psi, see Figure 3.128.

3.128

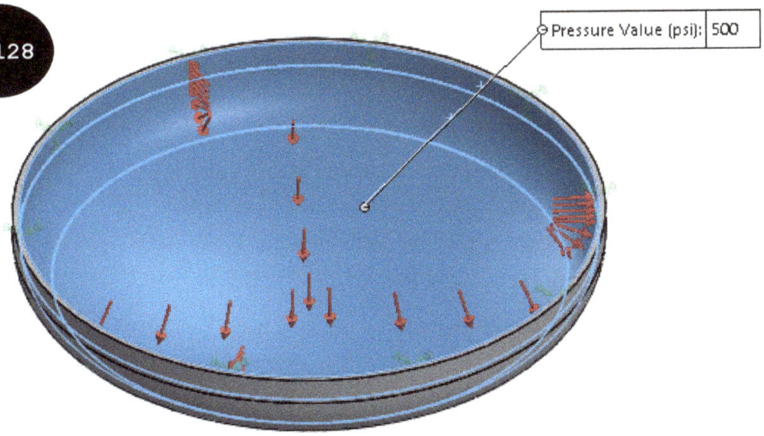

8. Click on the green tick-mark ✓ button in the PropertyManager. A uniformly distributed pressure of 500 psi is applied to the inner faces of the model.

   Now, you need to define the material of the geometry.

9. Invoke the **Material** dialog box by clicking on the **Apply Material** tool in the **Simulation CommandManager** and then apply the **Alloy Steel (SS)** material. Next, close the dialog box.

Section 4: Generating the Mesh with Shell Elements

As mentioned in the project summary, you need to generate a curvature-based mesh with a maximum element size of 50 mm and a minimum element size of 1 mm.

1. Right-click on the **Mesh** option in the Simulation Study Tree and then click on the **Create Mesh** tool in the shortcut menu that appears to invoke the **Mesh PropertyManager**.

2. Expand the **Mesh Parameters** rollout of the PropertyManager.

3. Select the **Curvature-based mesh** radio button in the expanded **Mesh Parameters** rollout and then enter **50 mm** as the maximum element size and **1 mm** as the minimum element size in the respective fields of the PropertyManager.

4. Select the **High** option in the **Mesh Quality** of the **Advanced** rollout.

5. Accept the other default mesh parameters and then click on the green tick-mark ✓ button . The **Mesh Progress** window appears. After the meshing is complete, the 2D meshed geometry with shell elements appears in the graphics area, see Figure 3.129.

3.129

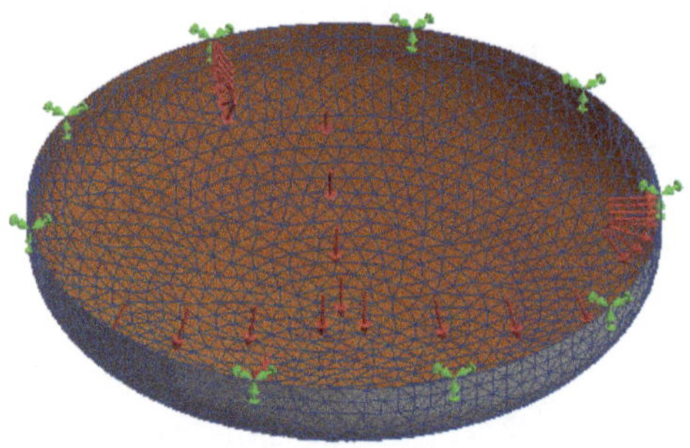

Note: As the geometry of the model is defined as 2D geometry, SOLIDWORKS Simulation automatically meshes the geometry with shell elements.

Section 5: Displaying Mesh Details

After generating the mesh, you can display the mesh details.

1. Right-click on the **Mesh** option in the Simulation Study Tree and then click on the **Details** tool in the shortcut menu that appears. The **Mesh Details** window appears, see Figure 3.130. This window

displays the mesh details such as mesh type, mesher used, maximum element size, minimum element size, mesh quality, total number of nodes, and the total number of elements.

3.130

Mesh Details

Study name	Torispherical Head Study* (-Default-)
DetailsMesh type	Shell Mesh Using Surfaces
Mesher Used	Curvature-based mesh
Jacobian check for shell	On
Max Element Size	50 mm
Min Element Size	1 mm
Mesh quality	High
Total nodes	5359
Total elements	2626
Time to complete mesh(hh:mm:ss)	00:00:02
Computer name	CADARTIFEX

Section 6: Running the Analysis

1. Click on the **Run This Study** tool in the **Simulation CommandManager**. The **Torispherical Head Study** (*name of the study*) window appears which displays the progress of the analysis. When it is complete, the **Results** folder is added to the Simulation Study Tree with the stress, displacement, and strain results. By default, the **Stress** result is activated. As a result, the stress distribution on the model and the von Mises stress plot appear, see Figure 3.131.

3.131

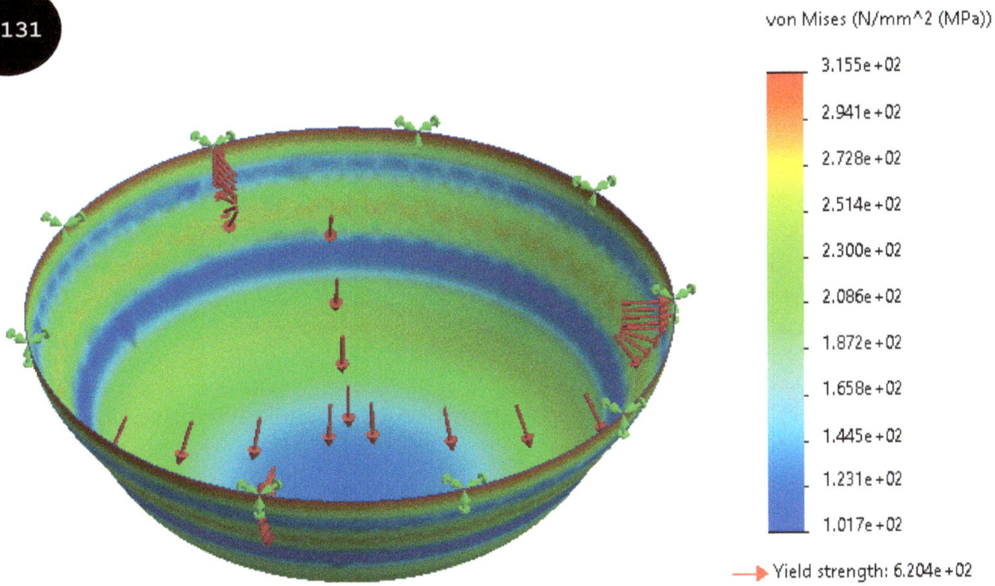

Note: By default, the deformed shape on the geometry does not appear in its actual shape. To display the actual deformed shape, right-click on a result (stress, displacement, and strain) in the Simulation Study Tree and then click on the **Edit Definition** tool in the shortcut menu that appears to invoke the respective PropertyManager. Next, select the **True scale** radio button in the **Deformed shape** rollout of the PropertyManager and then click on the green tick-mark button to close the PropertyManager. Figure 3.132 shows the deformed shape of the geometry with stress distribution in the true scale.

3.132

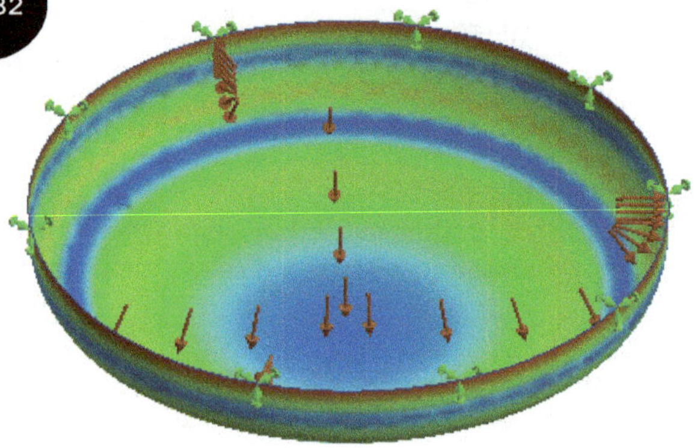

Section 7: Displaying Stress, Displacement, and Strain Results

1. Display the stress, displacement, and strain results of the model by double-clicking on the respective option in the **Results** folder of the Simulation Study Tree.

   Notice that the maximum von Mises stress in the model under the applied pressure is **3.155e+02** (315.515) N/mm^2 (MPa) which is considerably within the yield stress of the material that is **6.204e+02** (620.422) N/mm^2 (MPa). The maximum resultant displacement of the model under the applied pressure is **2.669e+00** (2.669) mm and the maximum equivalent strain on the model is **9.846e-04** (.001).

Note: You may find a slight difference in the result values depending on the service pack installed on your system.

Section 8: Defining the Factor of Safety

Now, you need to define the Factor of Safety of the design.

1. Right-click on the **Results** folder in the Simulation Study Tree. A shortcut menu appears, see Figure 3.133.
2. Click on the **Define Factor Of Safety Plot** tool in the shortcut menu. The **Factor of Safety PropertyManager** appears, see Figure 3.134.

3.133

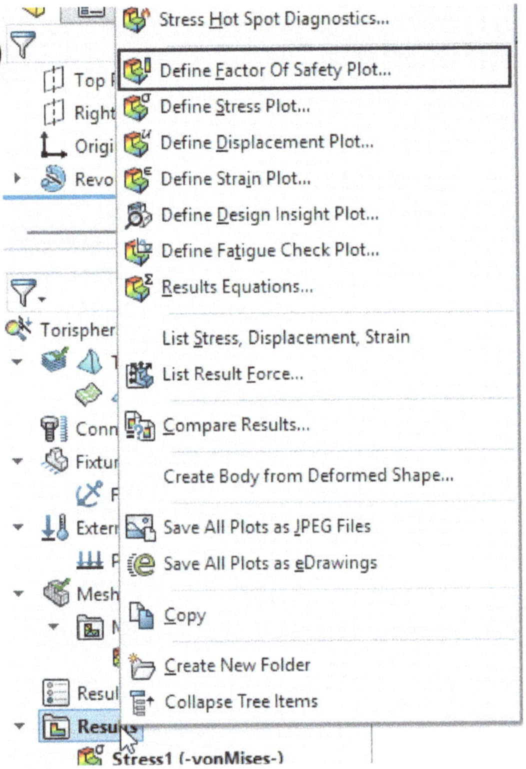

3.134

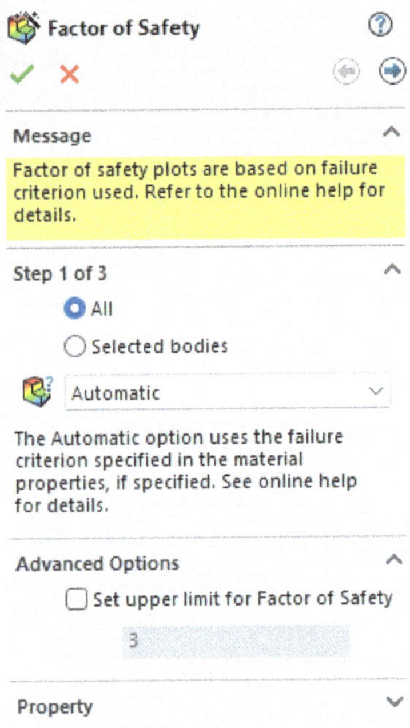

3. Accept the default parameters and then click on the green tick-mark button in the PropertyManager. The **Factor of Safety1 (-FOS-)** plot is added in the **Results** folder of the Simulation Study Tree. Also, the Factor of Safety distribution on the model and its plot appear in the graphics area, see Figure 3.135.

3.135

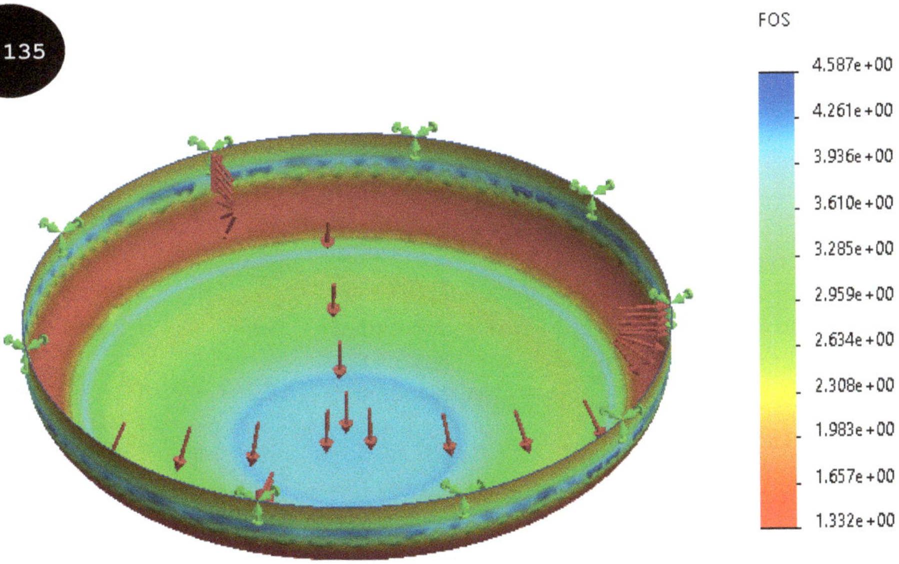

Notice that the minimum Factor of Safety of the model is **1.332e+00** (1.332), which indicates that the model is safe and can withstand the applied pressure. The Factor of Safety is the ratio of the allowable stress to the actual stress.

Note: If the Factor of Safety equals to 1, it indicates that the stress is exactly at the allowable limit and the model can withstand only the design load. A Factor of Safety less than 1 indicates that failure of the model is likely under the design load, whereas, a Factor of Safety greater than 1 indicates that the stress is within the allowable limit. Greater the Factor of Safety, stronger is the design. However, a higher Factor of Safety sometimes leads to over designing of the product.

Section 9: Saving Results

Now, you need to save the results.

1. Click on the **Save** tool in the **Standard** toolbar. The model and its results are saved in the location > *SOLIDWORKS Simulation > Case Studies > C03 Case Studies > Case Study 4*.

Case Study 5: Static Analysis of a Weldment Frame with Beam Elements

In this case study, you will perform the linear static analysis of a Weldment Frame with beam elements, (see Figure 3.136) and determine the stress under a uniformly distributed load.

3.136

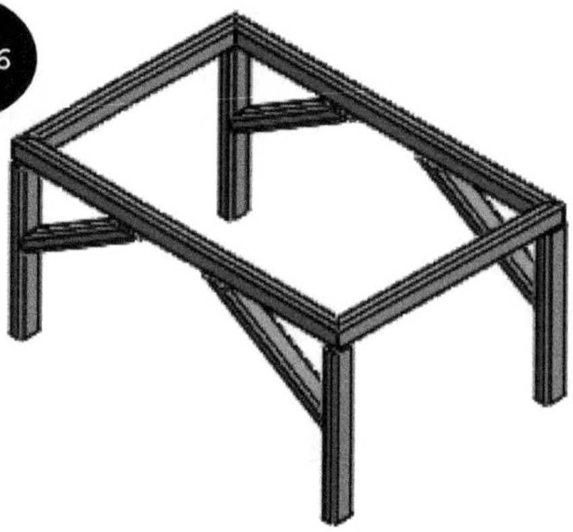

Project Description

All the legs of the Weldment Frame are fixed at its bottom and a 48000 N load is uniformly distributed along all the beams of the top frame, see Figure 3.137. The model is made up of **Plain Carbon Steel** material.

3.137

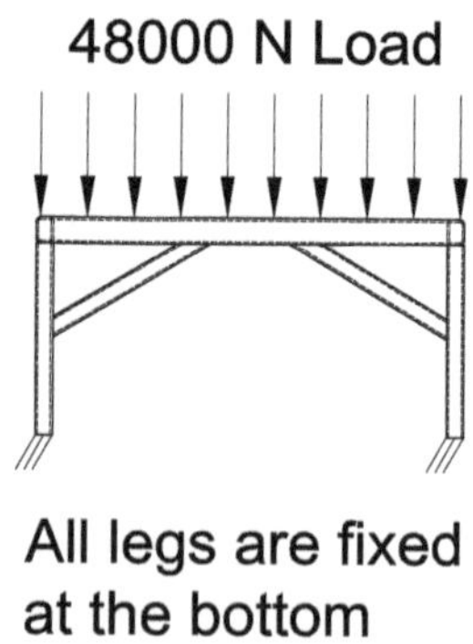

Project Summary

In this case study, you will run a static study on the Weldment Frame and determine the stress, displacement, and factor of safety of the model under the applied load. Also, you need to determine the axial stress, bending stress, and the bending moment diagram for an inclined member in the local directions 1 and 2.

The following sequence summarizes the case study outline:

1. Starting the Static Study
2. Defining Beam Joints
3. Defining the Material, Fixture, and Load
4. Generating the Mesh with Beam Elements
5. Running Analysis and Displaying Results
6. Displaying the Axial and Bending Stress Plots
7. Displaying the Bending Moment Diagram
8. Saving Results

Section 1: Starting the Static Study

1. Start SOLIDWORKS and then open the Weldment Frame model from the location > ***SOLIDWORKS Simulation > Case Studies > C03 Case Studies > Case Study 5***.

Note: You need to download the **C03 Case Studies** file by logging on to the CADArtifex website (***cadartifex.com/login***), if it has not already been downloaded.

2. After the Weldment Frame model is open in SOLIDWORKS, click on the **Simulation** tab in the **CommandManager**. The tools of the **Simulation CommandManager** appear.

3. Click on the **New Study** tool in the **Simulation CommandManager**. The **Study PropertyManager** appears to the left of the graphics area.

4. Ensure that the **Static** button is activated in the **Study PropertyManager**.

5. Enter **Weldment Frame Study** in the **Study name** field and then click on the green tick-mark button in the PropertyManager. The **Weldment Frame Study** is added to the Simulation Study Tree, see Figure 3.138. Also, the joints appear on the members of the frame in the graphics area, see Figure 3.139.

3.138

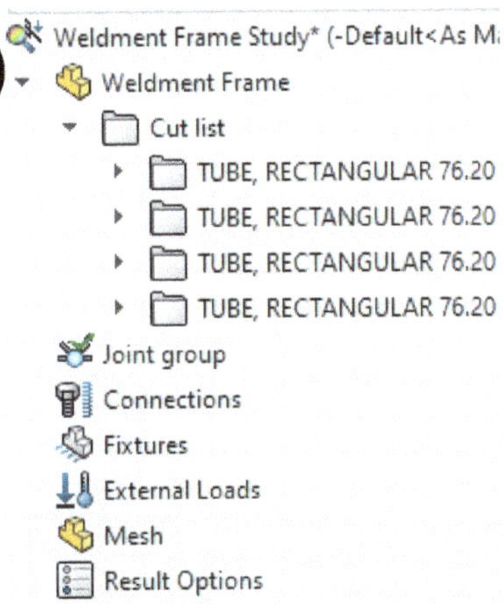

3.139

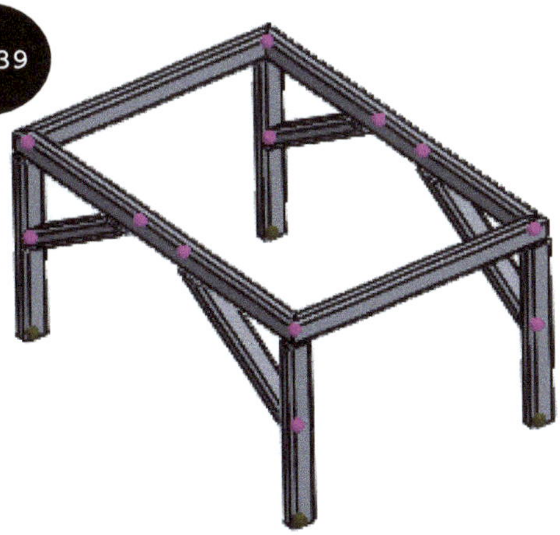

Notice that the joints appearing on the members in the graphics area are of two colors: magenta and yellow. A magenta joint is connected to two or more than two members, whereas a yellow joint is connected to a single member only and represents an open-end connection. You need to fix the yellow joints by applying fixtures or by connecting them with the other members manually to prepare the structure for analysis.

Tip: When you expand the **Weldment Frame > Cut list** folders in the Simulation Study Tree, you will notice that the members of the frame are represented by beam icons (refer to Figure 3.138) as SOLIDWORKS Simulation automatically identifies the members of the weldment structure as beam members (1D line) and calculates the number of joints in the structure. In SOLIDWORKS Simulation, beam members automatically mesh with beam elements. However, you can also treat a beam member of the structure as a solid body to mesh it with solid tetrahedral elements. To do this, right-click on the beam member in the respective sub-folders of the **Weldment Frame** folder in the Simulation Study Tree and then click on the **Treat as Solid** tool in the shortcut menu that appears. Similarly, you can treat a solid body as a beam member by selecting the **Treat as Beam** tool in the shortcut menu which appears on right-clicking on the solid body.

Section 2: Defining Beam Joints

SOLIDWORKS Simulation automatically calculates the joints between the end-to-end connected members of the structure. You can edit the calculated beam joints or recalculate them.

1. Right-click on the **Joint group** option in the Simulation Study Tree and then click on the **Edit** tool in the shortcut menu that appears, see Figure 3.140. The **Edit Joints PropertyManager** appears, see Figure 3.141.

3.140

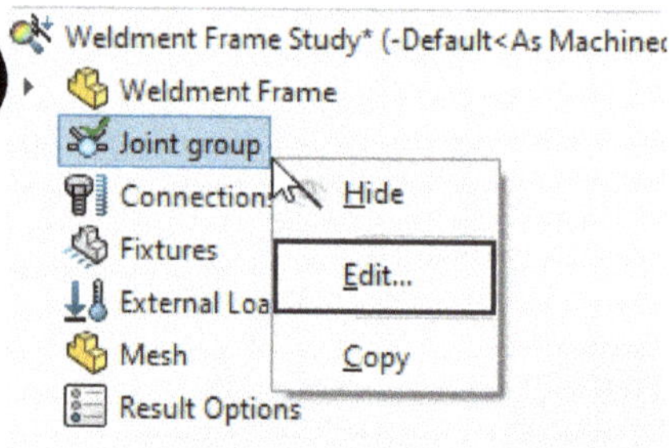

3.141

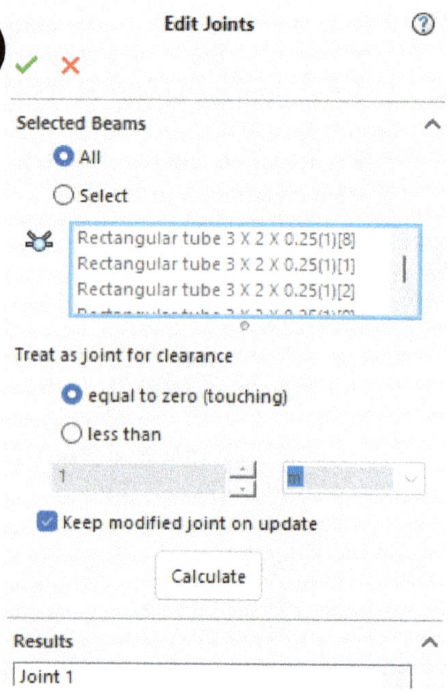

By default, the **All** radio button is selected in the **Selected Beams** rollout of the PropertyManager. As a result, the joints between all the end-to-end connected beam members of the structure are calculated. However, on selecting the **Select** radio button, you need to select the members of the structure between which you want to calculate the joints.

Note that in the **Treat as joint for clearance** area of the PropertyManager, the **equal to zero (touching)** radio button is selected by default. As a result, the joints are calculated between end-to-end touching members, by default. However, on selecting the **less than** radio button, you need to specify a clearance value in the field enabled below this radio button to create joints between the members that are within the specified clearance value.

2. Accept all the default parameters and then click on the **Calculate** button in the PropertyManager. The joints between the members are calculated and appear in the **Results** rollout of the PropertyManager.

3. Click on the green tick-mark button ✓ in the PropertyManager. The **Simulation** window appears, click on the **OK** button in this window.

Section 3: Defining the Material, Fixture, and Load

Now, you need to define the material, fixtures, and load on the structure.

1. Invoke the **Material** dialog box by clicking on the **Apply Material** tool in the **Simulation CommandManager** and then apply the **Plain Carbon Steel** material. Next, close the dialog box.

   Now, you need to define the fixtures.

2. Right-click on the **Fixtures** option in the Simulation Study Tree and then click on the **Fixed Geometry** tool in the shortcut menu that appears. The **Fixture PropertyManager** appears.

3. Select the yellow joints (four) that appear at the bottom of each leg (four legs) of the structure, see Figure 3.142. Next, click on the green tick-mark ✓ button in the PropertyManager. The Fixed Geometry fixtures are applied on the joints of the four legs of the structure, see Figure 3.142.

3.142

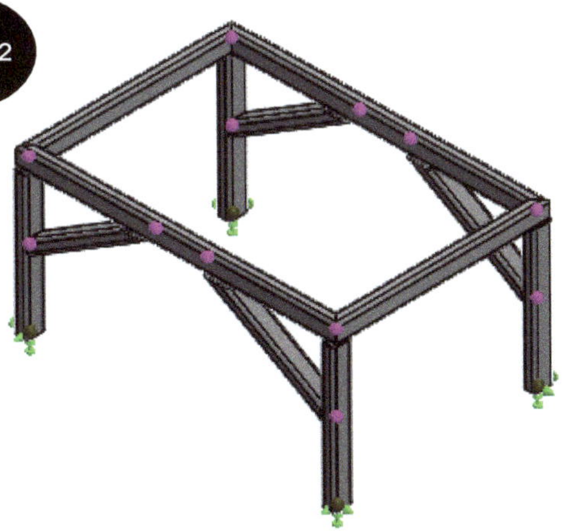

Now, you need to apply the load.

4. Right-click on the **External Loads** option in the Simulation Study Tree and then click on the **Force** tool in the shortcut menu that appears. The **Force/Torque PropertyManager** appears, see Figure 3.143.

3.143

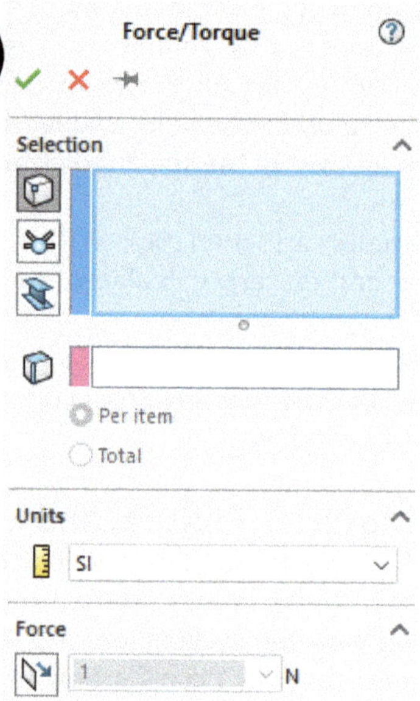

By default, the **Vertices, Points** button is activated in the **Selection** rollout of the PropertyManager. As a result, you can select vertices and points of the structure members to apply the load. On selecting the **Joints** button, you can select the beam joints to apply the load, whereas on selecting the **Beams** button, you can select the beams of the structure to apply the load.

5. Click on the **Beams** button in the **Selection** rollout of the PropertyManager.

6. Select the top horizontal beams (four beams) of the structure one by one. The names of the selected beams appear in the field of the **Selection** rollout in the PropertyManager, see Figure 3.144.

7. Click on the **Face, Edge, Plane for Direction** field of the **Selection** rollout in the PropertyManager, see Figure 3.144.

3.144

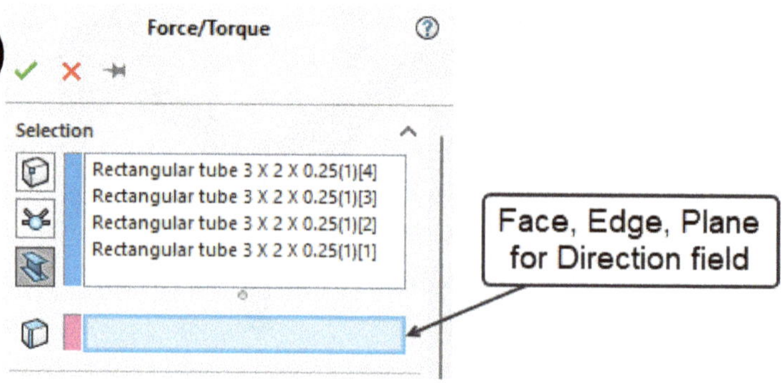

8. Expand the FeatureManager Design Tree which is now at the top left corner of the graphics area, see Figure 3.145 and then click on the **Top Plane** as the reference plane to define the direction of force.

9. Click on the **Normal to Plane** button in the **Force** rollout of the PropertyManager and then enter **48000** as the load magnitude, see Figure 3.146.

3.145

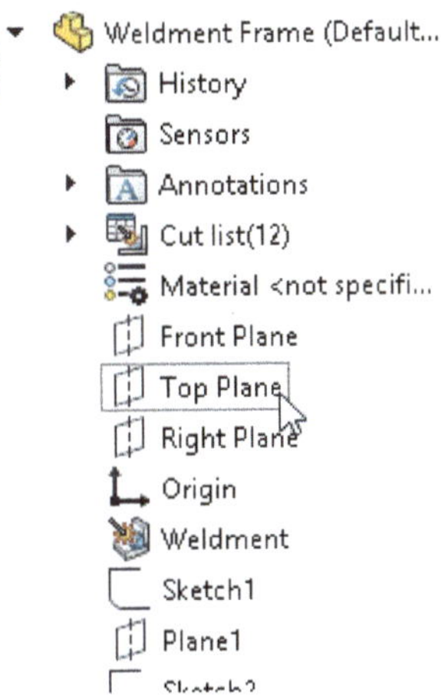

3.146

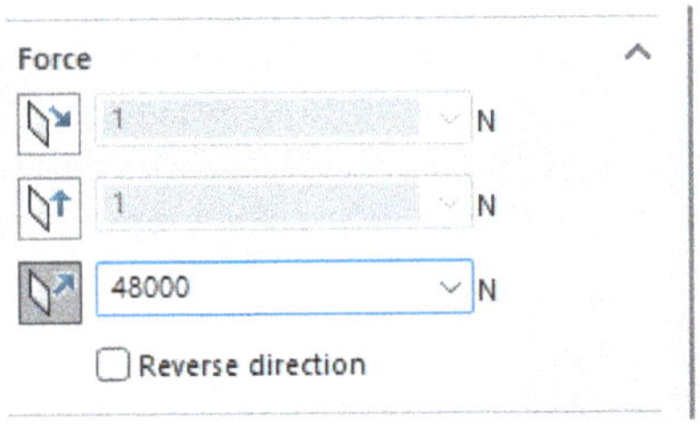

10. Select the **Reverse direction** check box in the **Force** rollout to reverse the direction of force to the downward direction.

11. Click on the green tick-mark button in the PropertyManager. The specified load is applied to the selected beams.

Section 4: Generating the Mesh with Beam Elements

1. Right-click on the **Mesh** option in the Simulation Study Tree and then click on the **Create Mesh** tool in the shortcut menu that appears. The **Mesh Progress** window appears and the process of meshing the structure starts. Once it is complete, the meshing is created with beam elements, which are represented by hollow cylinders in the graphics area, see Figure 3.147.

3.147

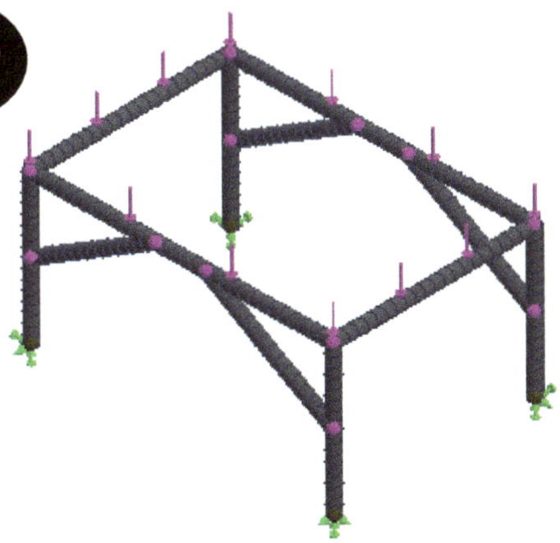

Note: SOLIDWORKS Simulation automatically meshes the weldment structure with beam elements.

Section 5: Running Analysis and Displaying Results

1. Click on the **Run This Study** tool in the **Simulation CommandManager**. The **Weldment Frame Study** (*name of the study*) window appears which displays the progress of the analysis. When it is complete, the **Results** folder is added to the Simulation Study Tree with the stress and displacement results. By default, the **Stress** result is activated. As a result, the stress distribution on the model and the Upper bound axial and bending plot appear, see Figure 3.148.

3.148

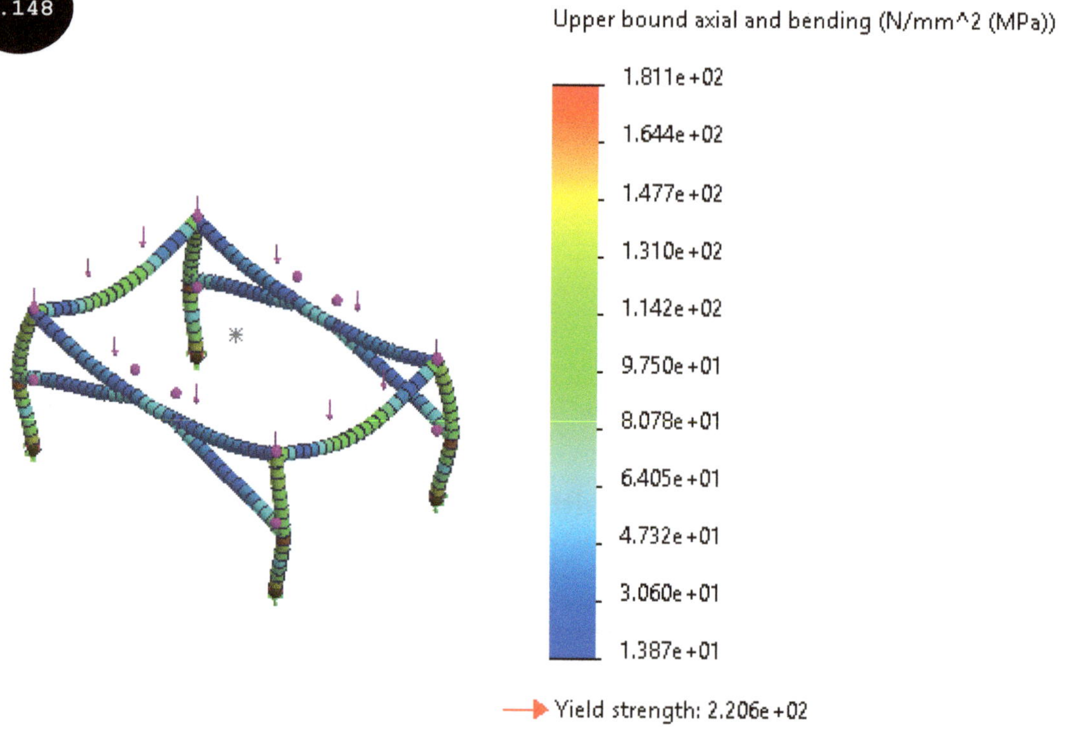

2. To display the resultant displacement, double-click on the **Displacement1 (-Res disp-)** option in the Simulation Study Tree.

Section 6: Displaying the Axial and Bending Stress Plots

1. Right-click on the **Results** folder in the Simulation Study Tree and then click on the **Define Stress Plot** tool in the shortcut menu that appears. The **Stress Plot PropertyManager** appears.

2. Select the **Axial** option in the **Beam stress** drop-down list of the **Definition** tab in the PropertyManager and then click on the green tick-mark button. The axial stress plot appears in the graphics area, see Figure 3.149. Notice that the maximum axial stress (tensile value) is **1.368e+00** (1.368) N/mm^2 (MPa) which is relatively low.

3.149

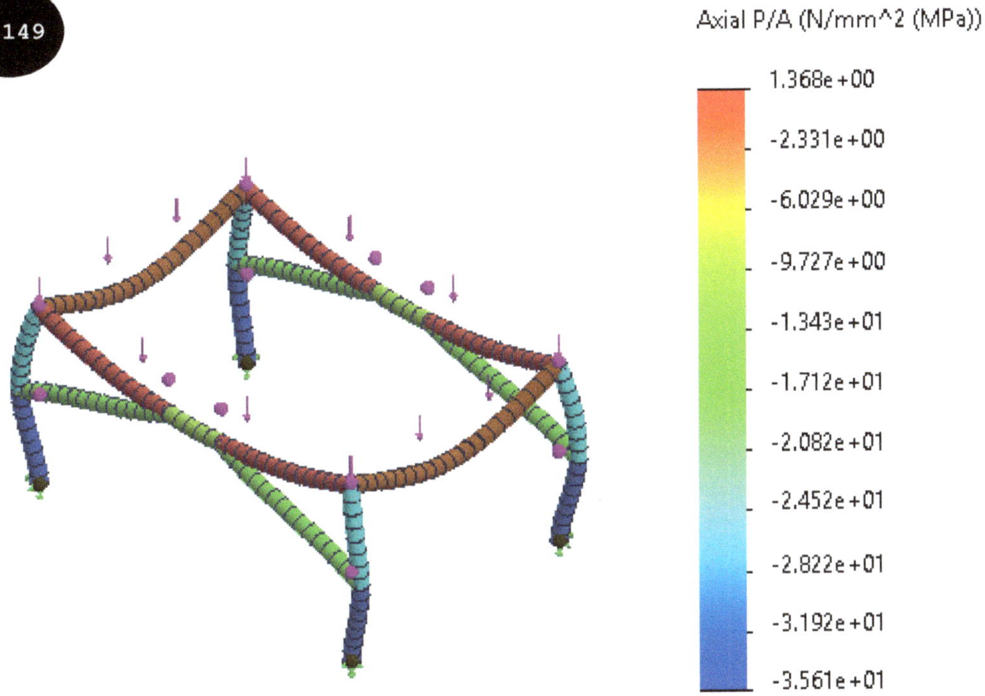

3. Similarly, you can display the bending stress in direction 1 and direction 2 by selecting the **Upper bound bending in DIR 1** and **Upper bound bending in DIR 2** options, respectively, in the **Beam stress** drop-down list of the **Definition** tab in the **Stress plot PropertyManager**.

Section 7: Displaying the Bending Moment Diagram

1. Right-click on the **Results** folder in the Simulation Study Tree and then click on the **Define Beam Diagrams** tool in the shortcut menu that appears. The **Beam Diagrams PropertyManager** appears.

2. Select the **Moment about Dir1** option in the **Component** drop-down list of the **Definition** tab in the PropertyManager, see Figure 3.150.

3.150

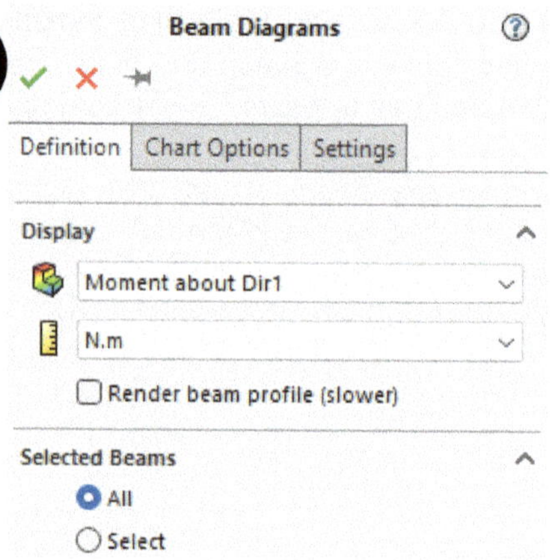

3. Select the **Select** radio button in the **Selected Beams** rollout of the PropertyManager and then select the front right inclined beam to display its bending moment diagram. Next, click on the green tick-mark button in the PropertyManager. The bending moment diagram of the selected beam in the local direction 1 appears in the graphics area, see Figure 3.151.

3.151

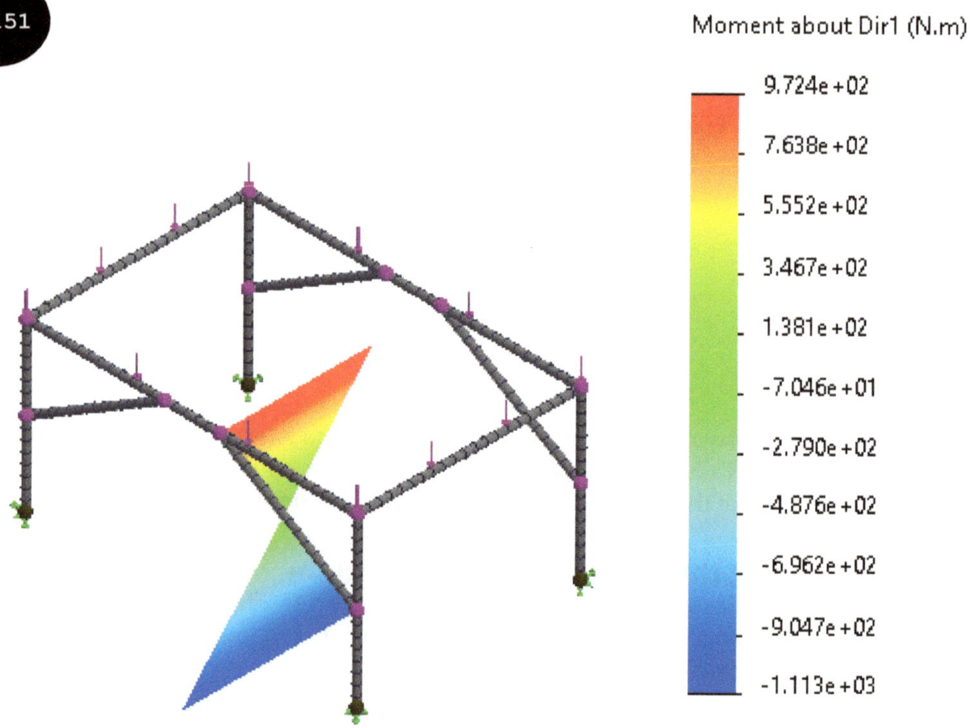

4. Similarly, you can display the bending moment diagram of a beam in the local direction 2.

Section 8: Saving Results

Now, you need to save the results.

1. Click on the **Save** tool in the **Standard** toolbar. The model and its results are saved in the location > *SOLIDWORKS Simulation > Case Studies > C03 Case Studies > Case Study 5*.

Hands-on Test Drive 1: Static Analysis of a Beam Support

Perform the linear static analysis of a Beam Support, (see Figure 3.152) and determine the stress, displacement, strain, and factor of safety under a uniformly distributed load.

3.152

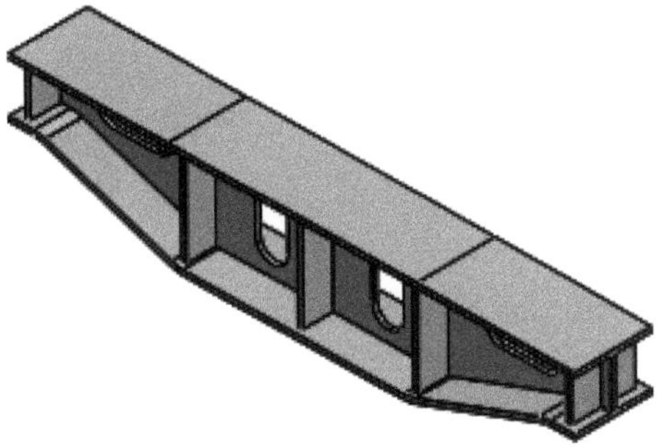

Project Description

The Beam Support is fixed at both its side bottom faces and a 12000 N load is uniformly distributed along its top middle face, see Figure 3.153. The model is made up of **Alloy Steel (SS)** material.

3.153

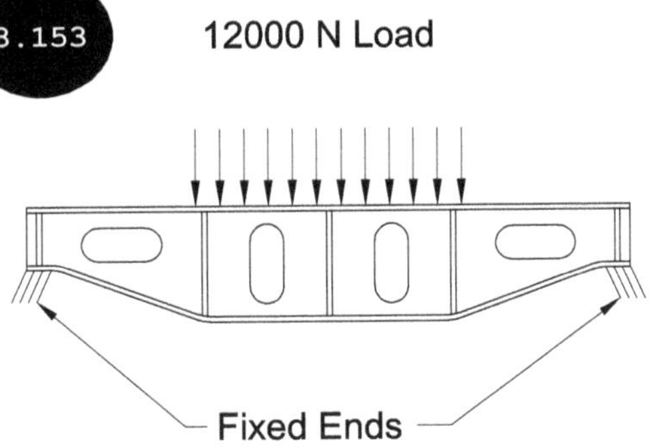

Project Summary

Run a static study on the Beam Support model. You need to generate a high-quality curvature-based mesh with a maximum element size of 5 mm and a minimum element size of 1 mm. Also, determine the stress, displacement, strain, and factor of safety of the model under the applied load, and animate the displacement distribution on the model in a true scale. Specify the unit system to SI (MKS) with displacement in mm and stress in N/mm^2 (MPa) units.

Hands-on Test Drive 2: Static Analysis of a Bearing House

Perform the linear static analysis of a Bearing House, (see Figure 3.154) and determine the stress, displacement, strain, and factor of safety under a sinusoidal distribution bearing load.

3.154

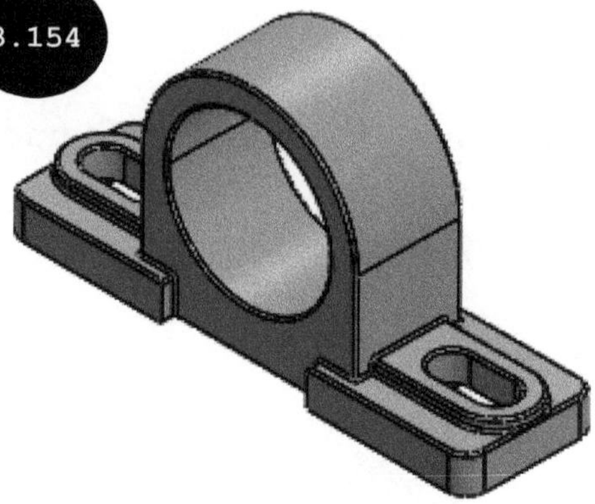

Project Description

The Bearing House is fixed at its bottom face and a 48500 N sinusoidally distributed load is applied along the lower half circular face of the model in the Y-direction, see Figure 3.155. The model is made up of **AISI 304** steel material.

3.155

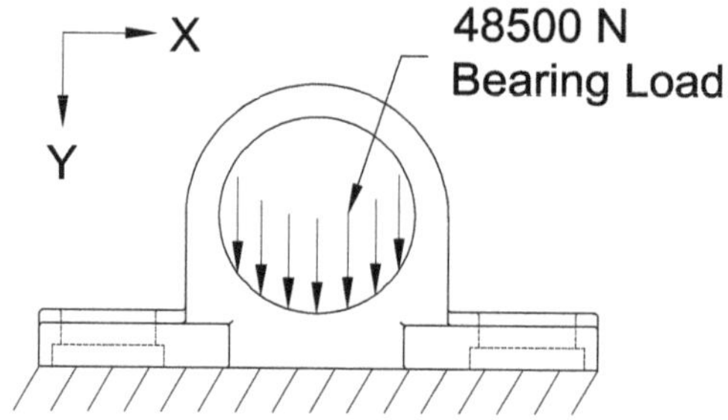

Project Summary

Run a static study on the Bearing House. You need to generate a high quality curvature-based mesh with default mesh parameters. Determine the stress, displacement, strain, and factor of safety of the model under the applied load. Also, animate the displacement distribution on the model in true scale. Specify the unit system to SI (MKS) with displacement in mm and stress in N/mm^2 (MPa) units.

Hint: *To apply the bearing load, you need to select a coordinate system that defines the direction of the load. Note that the Z-axis of the coordinate system must be aligned with the axis of the cylindrical face selected for applying the load.*

Summary

In this chapter, you explored various case studies to enhance your understanding of linear static analysis in SOLIDWORKS Simulation.

Case Study 1: Conducted multiple static studies with different mesh settings and compared results. You learned how to define units, result settings, material properties, fixtures, and loads, as well as analyze stress, displacement, strain, and principal stress.

Case Study 2: Applied mesh control to high-stress areas and compared results before and after refinement. You also created Iso plots to visualize stress distribution.

Case Study 3: Performed static analysis on a symmetrical model, analyzed stress, displacement, and strain, animated the deformed shape, and defined the factor of safety.

Case Study 4: Defined shell elements for a 3D solid geometry, generated a shell mesh, examined stress, displacement, strain, and evaluated the factor of safety under applied pressure.

Case Study 5: Analyzed a weldment structure using beam elements, defined beam joints, applied fixtures and loads, examined axial and bending stresses, and generated a bending moment diagram.

Through these case studies, you have developed practical skills in setting up simulations, refining mesh, analyzing results, and optimizing designs for structural performance. These learnings will help you perform more accurate and efficient simulations in future engineering applications.

Questions

Complete the following sentences:

- The _________ and _________ check boxes of the **Stress plot PropertyManager** are used for annotating the maximum and minimum stresses in the model.
- The _________ tool is used for applying mesh control where high stresses are located in the model.
- You can save the animation of a result in the _________ file format.
- A _________ less than 1 indicates that the failure of the model is likely under the design load.
- In SOLIDWORKS Simulation, the _________ elements are generated in meshing a 3D solid geometry.
- On performing an analysis on a _________ or a _________ component, SOLIDWORKS Simulation identifies it as a 2D geometry and generates mesh with shell elements.

- The _________ joints in beam members represent connection with two or more than two members and the _________ joints represent connection with single member only.
- The _________ tool is used for defining the bending moment diagram of a beam.
- The _________ tool is used for displaying the user-defined range of stresses in portions of the model.
- The **Shell Definition PropertyManager** is used for defining the 2D geometry as _________, _________, and _________.
- The _________ tool is used for comparing the results of multiple studies.
- The _________ tool is used for running the current analysis study.

CHAPTER

4

Interactions and Connectors

In this chapter, the following topics will be discussed:

- Working with Interactions
- Applying Interactions
- Working with Connectors
- Static Analysis of a Hook Assembly with Interactions
- Static Analysis of a Flange Assembly with Bolt Connectors
- Static Analysis of an Assembly with Edge Weld Connectors
- Static Analysis of a Leaf Spring Assembly
- Static Analysis of a Car Jack Assembly

In the previous chapter, you explored various case studies for linear static analysis of individual components. In this chapter, you will learn how to perform static analysis on assemblies consisting of multiple components.

Before beginning the analysis, it is crucial to understand interactions and connectors, as they define how the components within an assembly interact with each other. In SOLIDWORKS Simulation, you can specify different types of interactions, including Contact, Bonded, Free, and Virtual Wall, to accurately represent real-world conditions.

Additionally, you will explore how to define connections between components. For instance, if two components in an assembly are joined using bolts, instead of modeling the actual bolts, you can apply Bolt Connections to simplify the model and reduce computational time while maintaining accuracy.

This chapter will guide you through various types of interactions and connectors, helping you efficiently set up and analyze assembly simulations.

Working with Interactions

As discussed, before analyzing an assembly, it is essential to define how its components interact with each other. In SOLIDWORKS Simulation, you can specify different types of interactions to accurately represent real-world behavior. These include Contact, Bonded, Free, Shrink Fit, and Virtual Wall interactions. Each of these interaction types plays a crucial role in defining the mechanical behavior of the assembly during analysis. The following sections will explore these interaction types in detail.

Different Types of Interactions

<table>
<tr><th colspan="2">Types of Interactions</th></tr>
<tr><td>Contact</td><td>The Contact interaction is used to prevent interference between the selected components. On defining this interaction, the touching faces of the components can slide over each other or come apart, but cannot penetrate each other during simulation, see Figure 4.1.
4.1
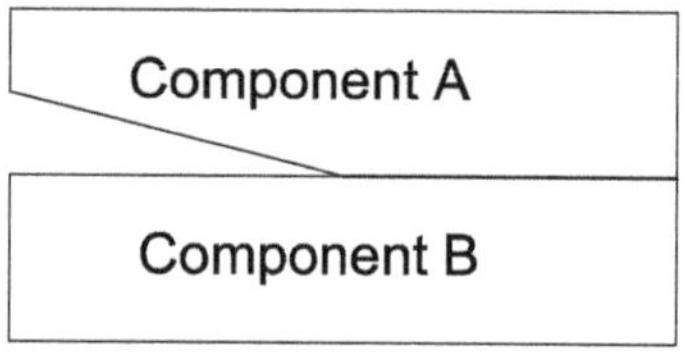
</td></tr>
<tr><td>Bonded</td><td>The Bonded interaction is used for applying a bonded connection between the touching faces of the components. On applying this interaction, the contacting components together act as a single component with the only difference that you can apply different material properties to the components, see Figure 4.2. By default, the Bonded interaction is applied between the components of an assembly.
4.2
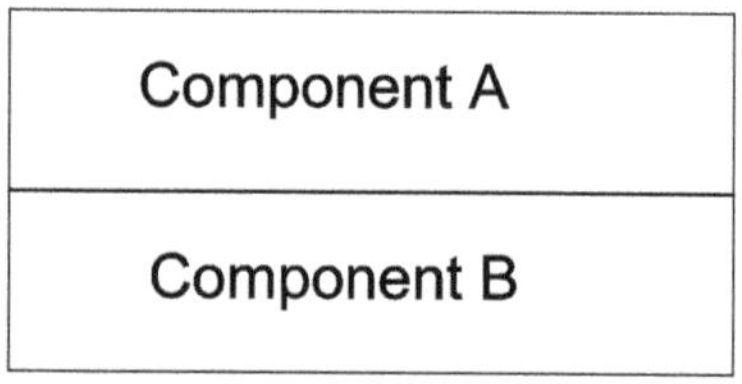
</td></tr>
<tr><td>Free</td><td>The Free interaction is used to allow interference between the selected components. On defining this interaction, the touching faces of the components can cause interference with each other during simulation, see Figure 4.3.
4.3
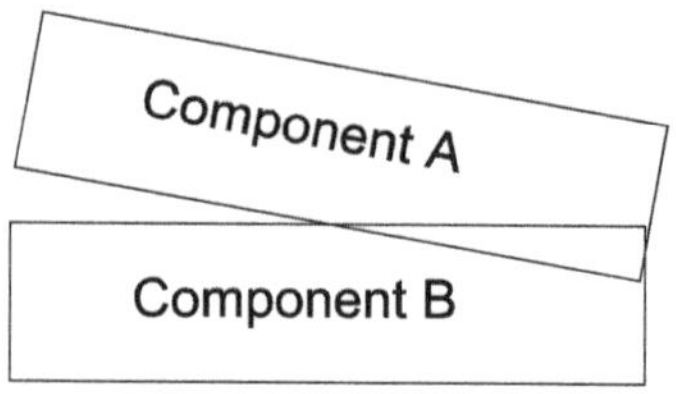
</td></tr>
</table>

Shrink Fit	The Shrink Fit interaction is used to determine the stresses between the components having interference with each other. For example, when you insert a shaft of 100 mm diameter into a hub of 99.95 mm diameter, then a 0.05 mm interference occurs between the components. To analyze such components, you need to apply the Shrink Fit interaction between the interference faces of the components, see Figure 4.4. 4.4 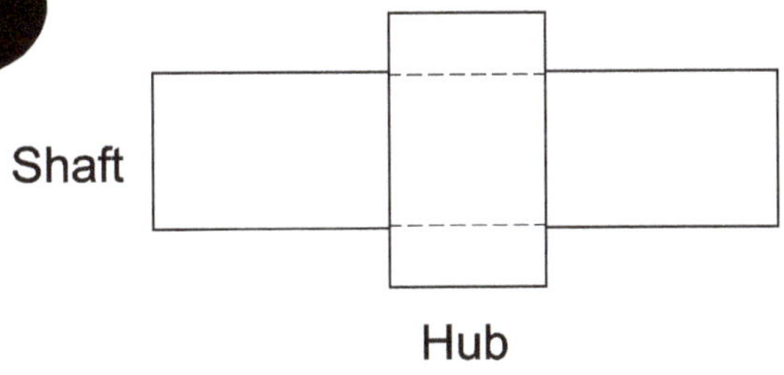
Virtual Wall	The Virtual Wall interaction is used to define an interaction between a component and a virtual wall which is represented by a reference plane. Note that a virtual wall can be rigid or flexible and you can define its coefficient of friction.

Applying Interactions

When analyzing an assembly in SOLIDWORKS Simulation, the **Connections** node is automatically added to the Simulation Study Tree. By default, a Bonded contact is applied as the global contact between all components, see Figure 4.5.

4.5

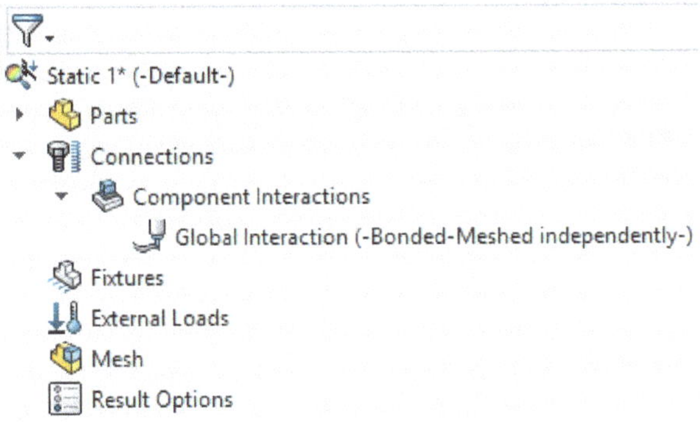

In SOLIDWORKS Simulation, interactions are categorized into two types:

Component Interaction: Includes Bonded, Contact, and Free interactions, which can be applied to an entire assembly or a set of components.

Local Interaction: Includes Contact, Bonded, Free, Shrink Fit, and Virtual Wall, which are applied only to touching faces or faces within a specified clearance range.

It is important to note that Local Interactions take precedence over Component Interactions, meaning they override the global interaction settings.

The following sections will discuss the methods for applying both Component and Local Interactions in detail.

Applying a Component Interaction

To apply a Component Interaction, click on the arrow at the bottom of the **Connections Advisor** tool in the **Simulation CommandManager**. The **Connections** flyout appears, see Figure 4.6. In this flyout, click on the **Component Interaction** tool. The **Component Interaction PropertyManager** appears, see Figure 4.7. Alternatively, right-click on the **Connections** node in the Simulation Study Tree and then click on the **Component Interaction** tool in the shortcut menu that appears to invoke the **Component Interaction PropertyManager**. The options in this PropertyManager are discussed next.

4.6

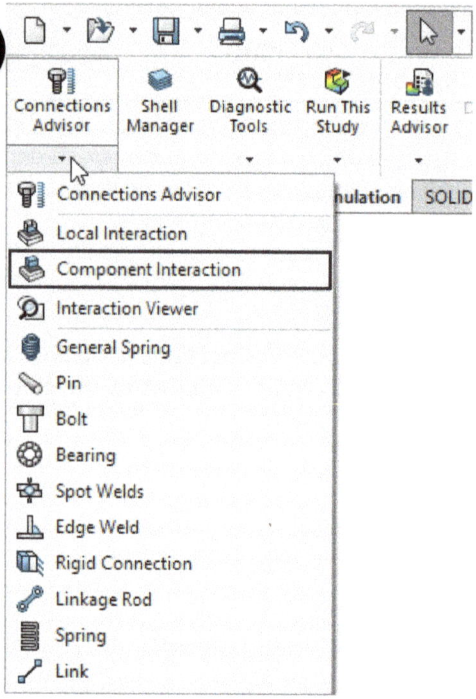

4.7

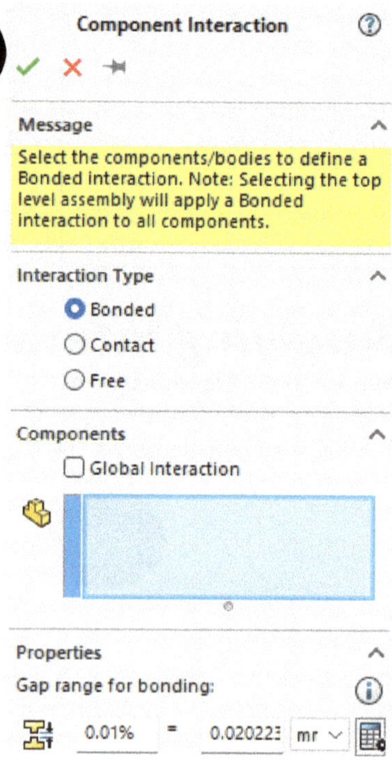

Interaction Type

The options in the **Interaction Type** rollout are used to select the type of component interaction to be applied between a set of components or the entire assembly. You can apply the Bonded, Contact, and Free component interactions by selecting the respective radio button in this rollout. The different types of interactions have already been discussed.

Note: By default, the Bonded component interaction is applied as the global interaction between all the components of the assembly. It can be overridden by applying the sets of component interactions and local interactions, manually. You will learn about local interactions later in this chapter.

Components

The **Select bodies that can come into interaction with one another** field in the **Components** rollout is used to select the set of components between which you want to apply the selected component interaction. You can select components either from the graphics area or the FeatureManager Design Tree. If you select the **Global Interaction** check box of this rollout, then the selected component interaction will be applied between all the components of the assembly as the global component interaction.

Properties

The **Properties** rollout of the PropertyManager is used to define the conditions for the selected interaction type. This rollout is not available for Free interaction type. The options in this rollout are discussed next.

Gap range for bonding

The **Gap range for bonding** area of the **Properties** rollout is available only when the **Bonded** radio button is selected in the **Interaction Type** rollout of the PropertyManager. The fields (**Maximum gap percent** and **Maximum gap**) in this area are used to specify the maximum allowable clearance value or gap between non-touching faces of the components for considering the bonded interaction. By default, the **0.01%** value is entered in the **Maximum gap percent** field of this area. As a result, if the clearance value between the non-touching faces of the components is less than or equal to 0.01% of the characteristic length of the model, then they are qualified for the bonded interaction. Note that the maximum allowable distance/gap value will automatically be calculated based on the specified percentage value in the **Maximum gap percent** field and the same gets displayed in the **Maximum gap** field of this area or vice-versa.

Calculate minimum gap

The **Calculate minimum gap** button in the **Properties** rollout is used to calculate the minimum distance between the non-touching faces of the selected components, see Figure 4.8. Note that this button is enabled only after selecting two or more components for applying the bonded interaction.

4.8

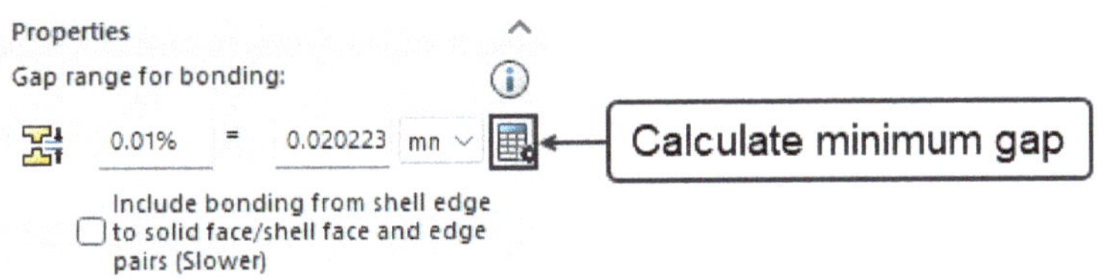

Gap range to consider contact

The **Gap range to consider contact** area in the **Properties** rollout is available only when the **Contact** radio button is selected in the **Interaction Type** rollout of the PropertyManager. The fields (**Maximum gap percent** and **Maximum gap**) in this area are used for specifying the maximum allowable clearance value or gap between non-touching faces of the components for considering the contact interaction. By default, a **10%** value is entered in the **Maximum gap percent** field of this area, see Figure 4.9. As a result, if the clearance value between the non-touching faces of the components is less than or equal to 10% of the characteristic length of the model, then they are qualified for the contact interaction. Note that the maximum allowable distance/gap value will automatically be calculated based on the specified percentage value in the **Maximum gap percent** field and the same gets displayed in the **Maximum gap** field of this area or vice-versa.

Stabilize the area if the gap is

The **Stabilize the area if the gap is** area is available in the **Properties** rollout when the **Contact** radio button is selected in the **Interaction Type** rollout. The fields (**Maximum gap percent** and **Maximum gap**) in this area are used for specifying the maximum allowable clearance value between non-touching faces of the components for applying the contact stabilization, see Figure 4.9. It helps the solver overcome instability issues and start the simulation by applying a small stiffness to the faces of the components that are within the specified clearance value.

Coefficient of friction

The **Coefficient of friction** check box is used to specify the coefficient of static friction between the faces of the selected components. You can specify the coefficient of static friction in the range from 0 to 1 in the **Coefficient of friction** field that gets enabled on selecting this check box in the rollout.

Advanced

The **Advanced** rollout of the PropertyManager is available only for the bonded interactions and is used to define the meshing in the connecting areas of the selected components, see Figure 4.10. The options in this rollout are discussed next.

4.9

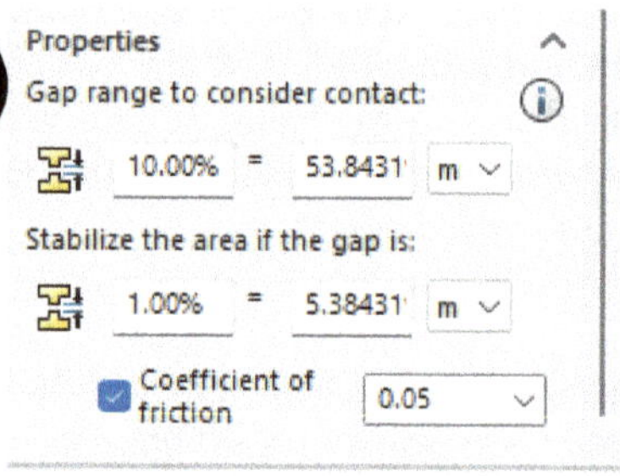

4.10

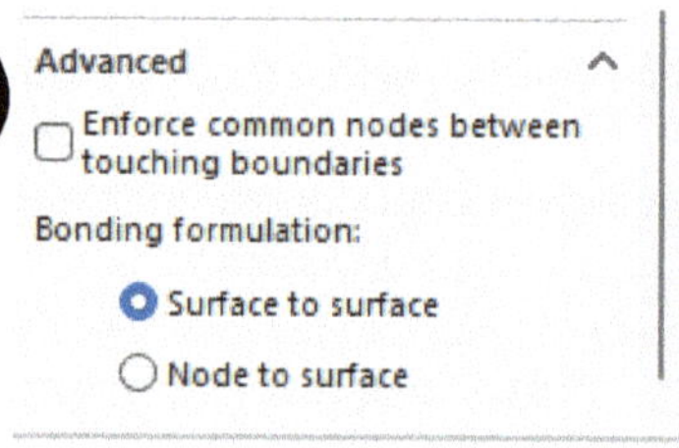

Enforce common nodes between touching boundaries

On selecting this check box, SOLIDWORKS Simulation creates a smooth mesh transition between the connecting areas of the selected components. It forms a node-to-node connection such that the nodes along the connecting areas merge with each other to ensure a perfect bonding between the components.

Tip: If the **Enforce common nodes between touching boundaries** check box is not selected, then SOLIDWORKS Simulation creates a mesh in each component of the assembly, independently, see Figure 4.11.

Bonding formulation

This area is used for specifying bonding formulations for meshing components, independently. The **Surface to surface** radio button is selected when the components have a large area of interaction during deformation, whereas, the **Node to surface** radio button is recommended when the area of interaction between the components during deformation reduces to a line or a point. Note that the **Surface to surface** method is slower but mostly gives more accurate results compared to the **Node to surface** method.

4.11

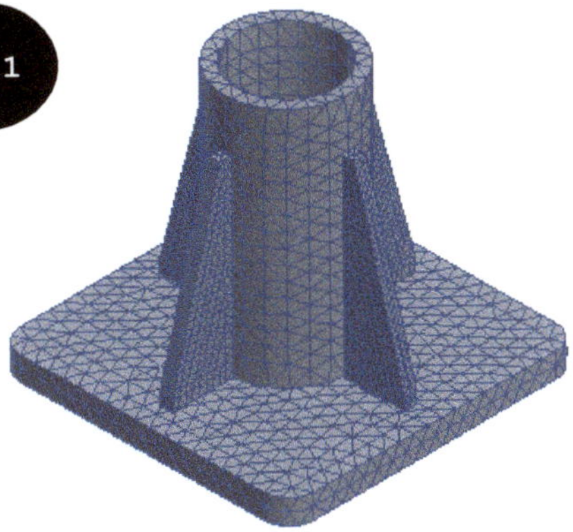

After defining the component interaction conditions in the PropertyManager, click on the green tick-mark button. The selected component interaction is applied between the selected components.

Applying a Local Interaction

To apply a Local Interaction between a set of touching faces of the components, click on the arrow at the bottom of the **Connections Advisor** tool in the **Simulation CommandManager**. The **Connections** flyout appears, see Figure 4.12. In this flyout, click on the **Local Interaction** tool. The **Local Interactions PropertyManager** appears, see Figure 4.13.

4.12

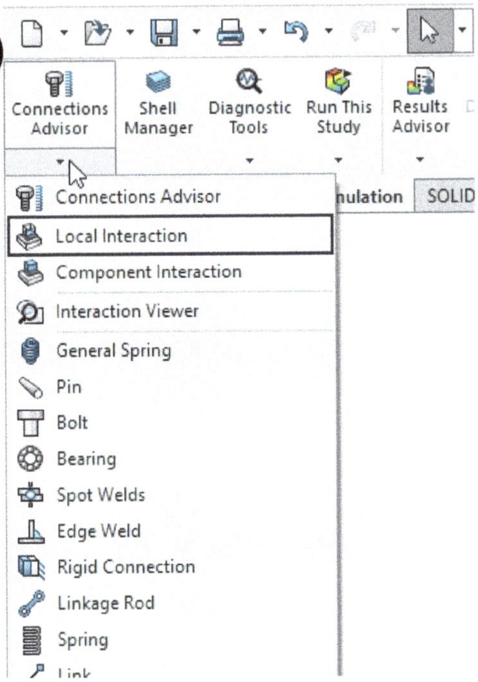

4.13

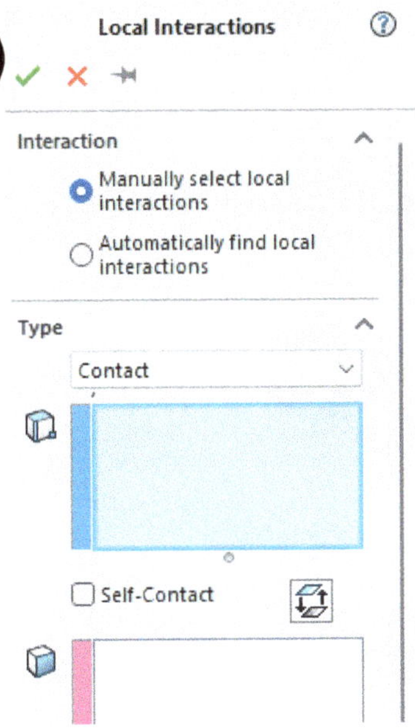

Alternatively, right-click on the **Connections** node in the Simulation Study Tree and then click on the **Local Interaction** tool in the shortcut menu that appears.

The options of the **Local Interactions PropertyManager** are used to apply local interactions by using two methods: Manual or Automatic. In the Manual method, you need to select a set of touching faces of the components for applying the local interaction, whereas in the Automatic method, you can select the components, and SOLIDWORKS Simulation automatically identifies different sets of touching faces of the selected components to apply local interactions between them. Both the methods are discussed next.

Applying a Local Interaction by using the Manual Method

1. After invoking the **Local Interactions PropertyManager**, select the **Manually select local interactions** radio button in the **Interaction** rollout of the PropertyManager, see Figure 4.13.

2. Select an interaction type: **Contact**, **Bonded**, **Free**, **Shrink Fit**, or **Virtual Wall** in the **Type** drop-down list, see Figure 4.14.

4.14

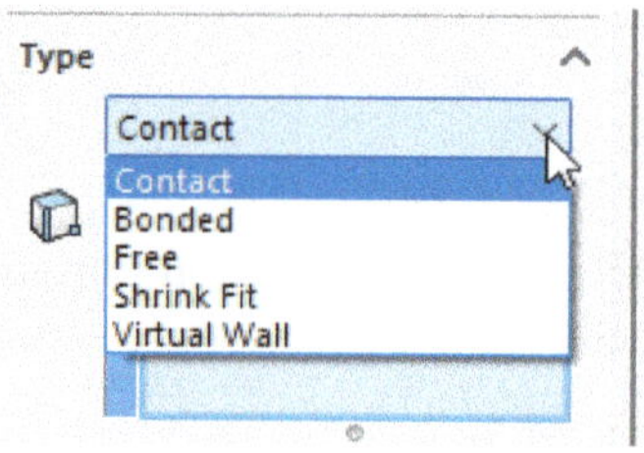

3. Select a face, an edge, or a vertex of a component as the first set of interaction entities from the graphics area, see Figure 4.15. The selected face/edge/vertex is highlighted in blue and its name appears in the **Faces, Edges, Vertices for Set 1** field of the **Type** rollout in the PropertyManager. Note that you can also select multiple faces/edges/vertices as the first set of interaction entities.

Tip: Sometimes it is difficult to select the faces of the touching components to apply an interaction between them. Therefore, it is recommended to explode the assembly view and then select the faces, see Figure 4.15. You can explode the assembly view by using the **Exploded view** tool of the **Assembly CommandManager**.

4. Click on the **Faces for Set 2** field in the **Type** rollout of the PropertyManager to activate it. Next, select a face of another component as the second set of interaction entities, see Figure 4.15. You can also select multiple faces as the second set of interaction entities.

4.15

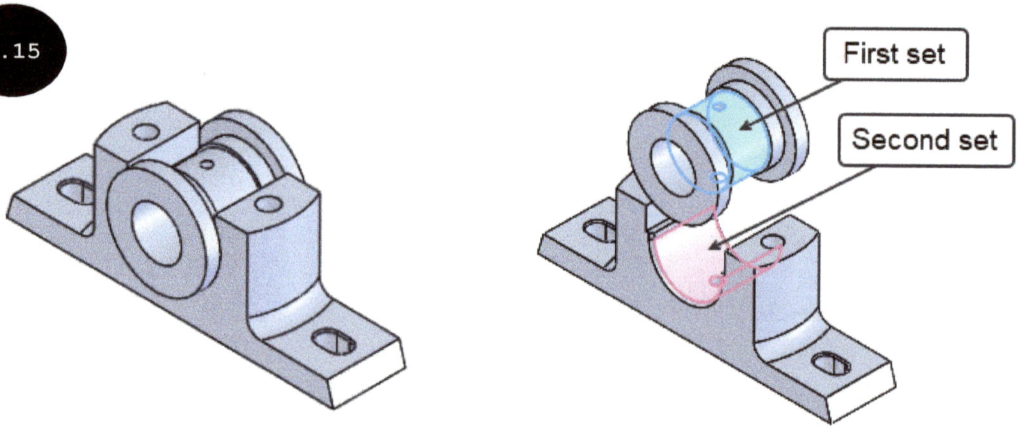

Collapsed view Exploded view

Swap interaction faces: The **Swap interaction faces** button of the **Type** rollout is used for interchanging the selections for the first and second sets of interaction entities.

Note: For the Contact and Virtual Wall interactions, you can also define the clearance settings between the components using the options in the **Properties** rollout of the PropertyManager. These options are same as discussed earlier except the **Contact offset** check box. When you select the **Contact offset** check box, the **If gap is less than** and **Unlimited gap distance** radio buttons get enabled in the **Properties** rollout, see Figure 4.16. The **If gap is less than** radio button is used to ignore the clearance which is within the clearance value specified in the field enabled below this radio button. The **Unlimited gap distance** radio button is used to ignore the clearance that exists between the selected set of faces and assuming that the faces are initially in contact with each other.

Also, for the Contact and Shrink Fit interactions, you can specify the friction coefficient between the faces of the components by selecting the **Coefficient of friction** check box of the **Properties** rollout. You can specify friction coefficient value up to 1.

5. After selecting the type of interaction and the set of entities, click on the green tick-mark button in the PropertyManager. The selected interaction type is applied between the selected entities.

Applying a Local Interaction by using the Automatic Method

1. Invoke the **Local Interactions PropertyManager** and then select the **Automatically find local interactions** radio button in the **Interaction** rollout of the PropertyManager, see Figure 4.17.

4.16

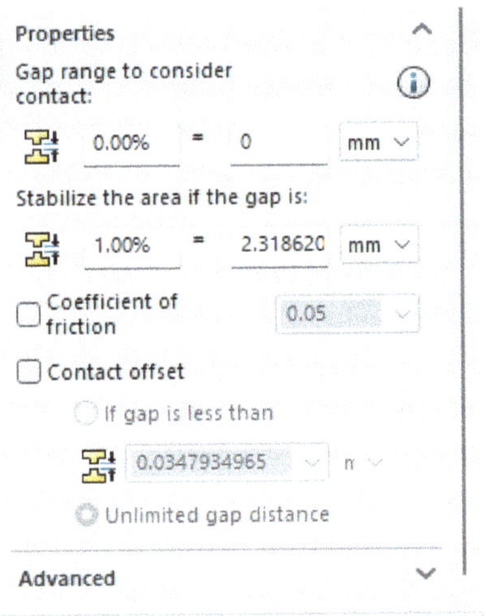

4.17

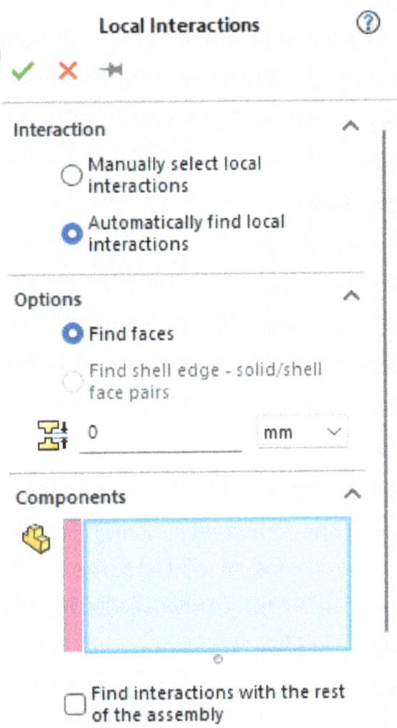

By default, the **Find faces** radio button is selected in the **Options** rollout of the PropertyManager, see Figure 4.17. As a result, the faces of the selected components meet the criteria specified in the **Maximum Clearance** field and get identified automatically for applying the local interactions.

2. Select the **Find faces** radio button in the **Options** rollout of the PropertyManager to identify the faces of the components that are within the allowable clearance value specified in the **Maximum Clearance** field of the **Options** rollout.

3. Enter the maximum allowable clearance value in the **Maximum Clearance** field of the **Options** rollout, as required.

4. Select the components from the graphics area or the FeatureManager Design Tree.

5. After selecting the components, click on the **Find local interactions** button in the **Components** rollout of the PropertyManager. All sets of faces that are within the specified clearance value between the selected components get identified and are listed in the **Results** rollout of the PropertyManager, see Figure 4.18.

4.18

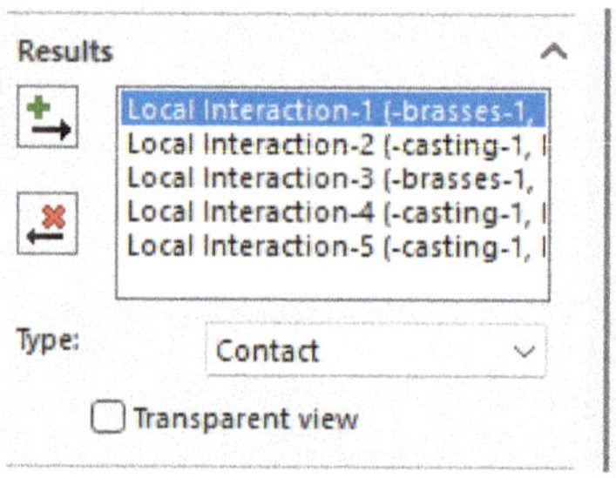

6. Select a set of faces in the **Results** rollout of the PropertyManager by clicking the left mouse button to apply an interaction between them. You can also select multiple sets of faces in the **Results** rollout by pressing the CTRL key. Note that, when you select a set of faces in the **Results** rollout, the respective faces of the components get highlighted in the graphics area.

Tip: On selecting the **Transparent view** check box in the **Results** rollout, the identified faces of the selected set get highlighted in the graphics area in the transparent view.

7. Select an interaction type: **Contact**, **Bonded**, or **Free** in the **Type** drop-down list of the **Results** rollout in the PropertyManager to apply it between one or more selected set of faces in the **Results** rollout.

8. Click on the **Create local interactions** button in the **Results** rollout of the PropertyManager. The selected interaction is applied between one or more selected set of faces. Also, the selected set or sets of faces get removed from the list in the **Results** rollout. Note that you can apply different interactions between the different sets of faces.

9. After applying the interactions between the required sets of faces of the components, click on the green tick-mark button in the PropertyManager.

Note: All the applied interactions (component interactions and local interactions) are listed in sub-nodes under the **Connections** node of the Simulation Study Tree, see Figure 4.19. In this figure, the Bonded component interaction is applied as the global interaction between all components of the assembly. Also, the Contact local interactions are applied between the five sets of faces. As discussed, local interactions have precedence over component interactions and the component interactions have precedence over global interaction.

4.19

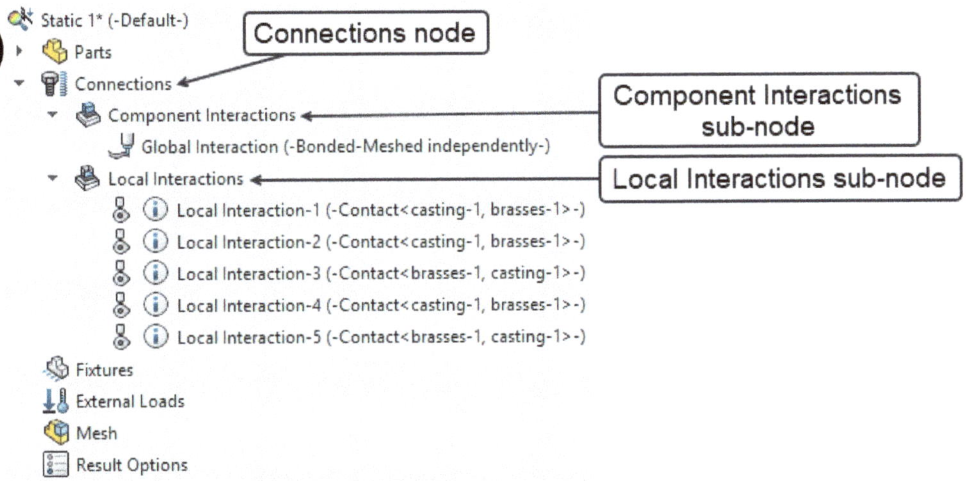

Working with Connectors

In SOLIDWORKS Simulation, you can also define the type of connection such as Pin, Bolt, Bearing, Spot/Edge Welds, and Spring between the components. On doing so, you do not need to create the actual geometry of the connectors. This helps in reducing the computational time and speed up the analysis process without compromising the accuracy of the results. The different types of connectors are discussed next.

Applying a Bolted connector

In SOLIDWORKS Simulation, you can apply a bolted connector between two or more components by using the **Bolt** tool. The method for applying a bolted connector is discussed below:

1. Click on the arrow at the bottom of the **Connections Advisor** tool in the **Simulation CommandManager**. The **Connections** flyout appears, see Figure 4.20. In this flyout, click on the **Bolt** tool. The **Connectors PropertyManager** appears, see Figure 4.21.

   In the **Type** rollout of the PropertyManager, you need to select the type of bolted connector to be applied between the components by clicking on the respective button: **Standard or Counterbore with Nut**, **Countersink with Nut**, **Standard or Counterbore Screw**, **Countersink Screw**, **Foundation Bolt**. By default, the **Standard or Counterbore with Nut** button is activated. As a result, the **Circular Edge of The Bolt Head Hole** and **Circular Edge of The Bolt Nut Hole** fields appear in the **Type** rollout of the PropertyManager.

4.20

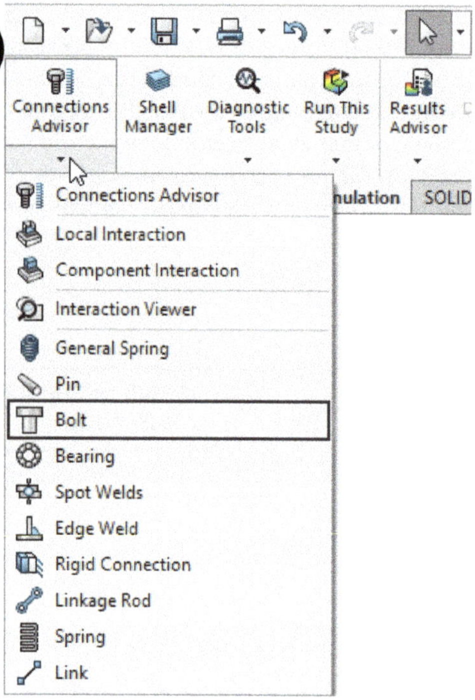

4.21

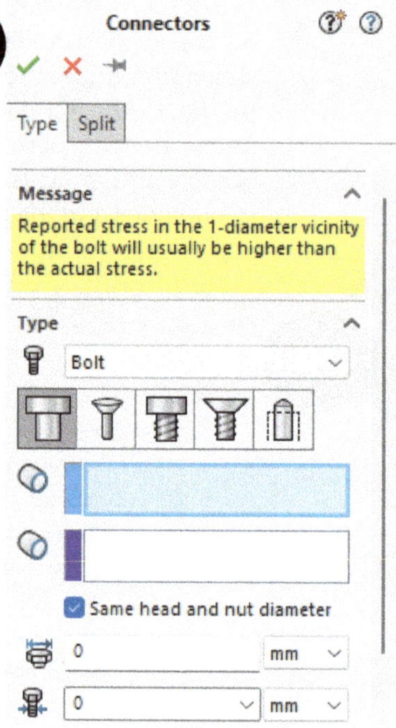

2. Ensure that the **Standard or Counterbore with Nut** button is activated in the **Type** rollout of the PropertyManager to apply the counterbore bolted connection.

Note: The **Standard or Counterbore with Nut** button is used for applying a counterbore bolted connection by selecting two circular edges which define the bolt head and bolt nut location. The **Countersink with Nut** button is used for applying a countersink bolted connection by selecting a conical face to define the bolt head and a circular edge to define the bolt nut location. The **Standard or Counterbore Screw** button is used for applying a counterbore screw connection by selecting a circular edge to define the bolt head and the hole faces to define the threads. The **Countersink Screw** button is used for applying a countersink screw connection by selecting a conical face to define the bolt head and the hole faces to define the threads. The **Foundation Bolt** button is used for applying a bolted connection between a component and a wall/ground by selecting a circular edge to define the bolt nut location and a target plane to define the virtual wall.

3. Select a circular edge to define the bolt head location, see Figure 4.22. A callout gets attached to the selected circular edge in the graphics area with default parameters (head diameter and nominal shank diameter) of the bolt, see Figure 4.22. Also, the name of the selected edge appears in the **Circular Edge of The Bolt Head Hole** field of the PropertyManager. Note that when you select a circular edge, the head diameter and nominal shank diameter of the bolt are automatically calculated by the program based on the diameter of the selected circular edge. You can edit these values by using the **Head Diameter** and **Nominal Shank Diameter** fields of the **Type** rollout in the PropertyManager.

4.22

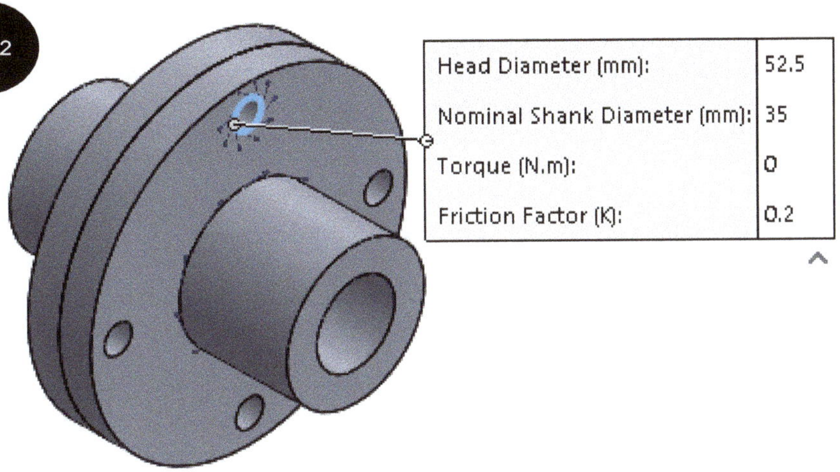

After defining the bolt head location, you need to define the bolt nut location.

4. Click on the **Circular Edge of The Bolt Nut Hole** field in the **Type** rollout and then select a circular edge to define the bolt nut location, see Figure 4.23. By default, the **Same head and nut diameter** check box is selected in the **Type** rollout of the PropertyManager. As a result, the nut diameter remains the same as the head diameter. To specify a different diameter for the nut, clear this check box and then specify the required nut diameter in the **Nut Diameter** field that appears in the **Type** rollout.

4.23

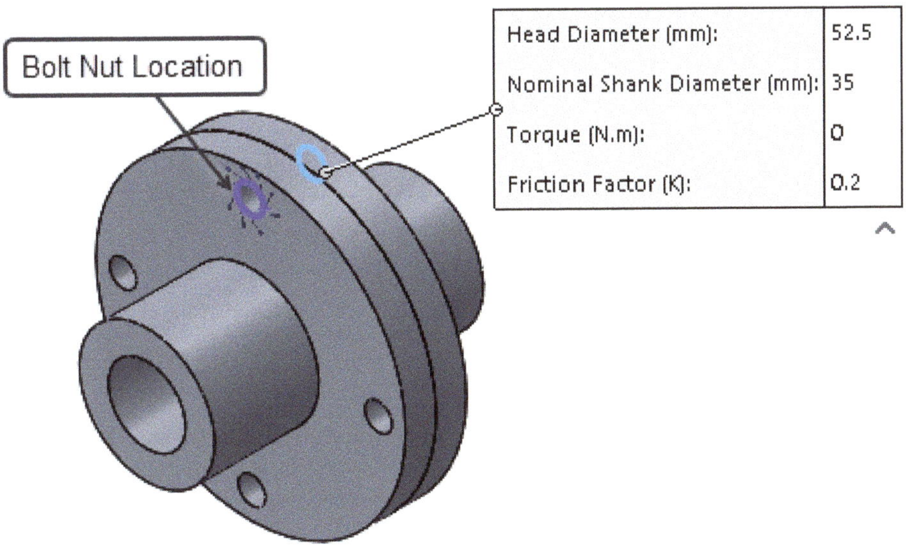

5. Select the Distributed or Rigid connection type by selecting the respective radio button in the **Connection Type** rollout.

Note: The Distributed connection type allows deformation of the faces attached, which delivers a more realistic representation of a connector's behavior as compared to the Rigid connection type, where the faces are rigidly connected. Note that the Distributed connection type is available for linear static studies only.

Now, you need to define the material properties of the bolt.

6. Ensure that the **Library** radio button is selected in the **Material** rollout of the PropertyManager to select a standard material from the SOLIDWORKS Material Library, see Figure 4.24.

7. Click on the **Select Material** button in the **Material** rollout of the PropertyManager. The **Material** dialog box appears. In this dialog box, select the required material. Next, click on the **Apply** button and then the **Close** button to apply the selected material to the bolted connection and close the dialog box, respectively.

Note: You can also apply the custom material properties to the bolted connection. To do this, select the **Custom** radio button in the **Material** rollout of the PropertyManager and then specify the custom material properties in the respective fields that get enabled in the rollout, see Figure 4.25.

4.24

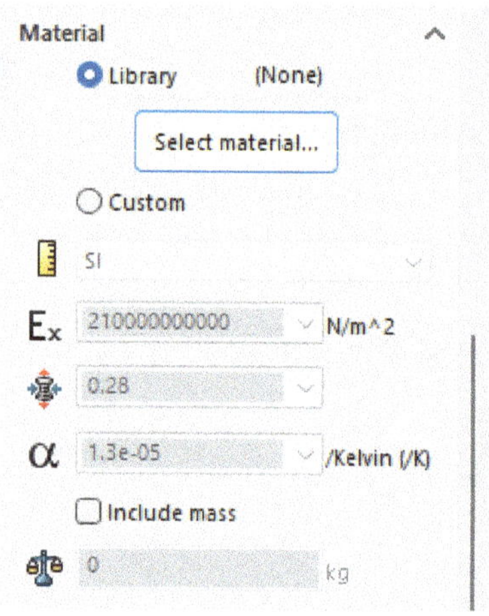

4.25

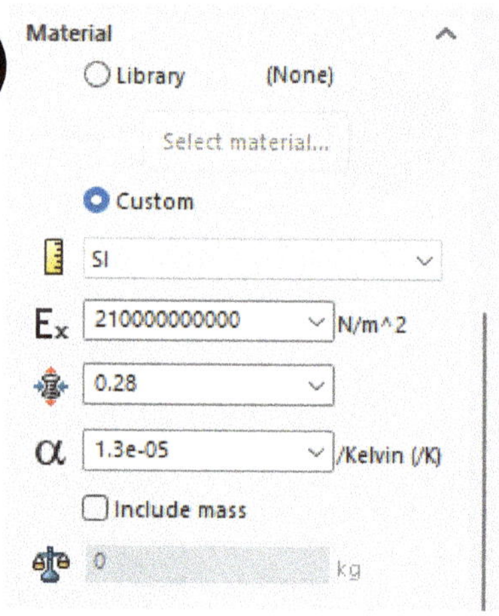

8. Specify the known axial or torque pre-load acting on the bolt by selecting the **Axial** or **Torque** radio button respectively, in the **Pre-load** rollout of the PropertyManager. The options in this rollout are used for specifying the known axial or torque pre-load acting on the bolt. By default, the axial or torque load is defined as 0 (zero). This implies that no axial or torque pre-load is acting on the bolt.

9. Accept the remaining default options in the PropertyManager and then click on the green tick-mark button. The bolt connection is applied between the components and its representation appears in the graphics area, see Figure 4.26. Also, the applied bolt connection is listed under the **Connectors** node in the Simulation Study Tree, see Figure 4.27.

4.26

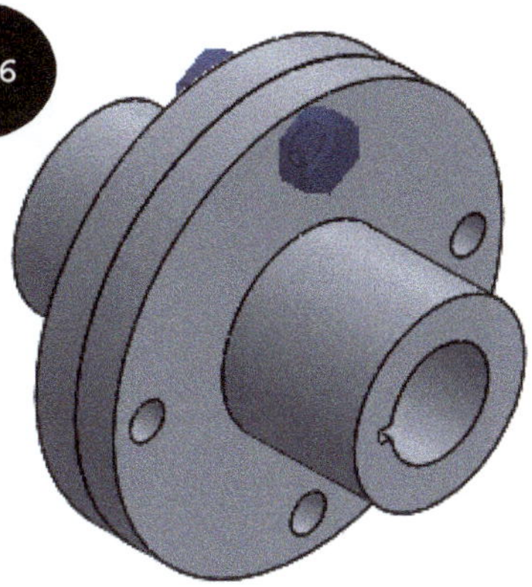

4.27

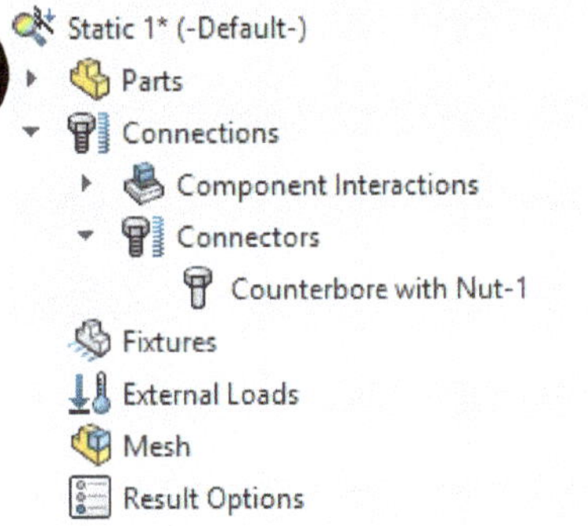

You can also apply a bolted connection between more than two components. To do this, follow the steps (1 through 8) mentioned above and then expand the **Advanced Options** rollout of the **Connectors PropertyManager**, see Figure 4.28. Next, select the **Bolt series** check box and then click on the **Allow faces for bolt series** field to activate it in the expanded **Advanced Options** rollout. Next, select the cylindrical hole faces of the middle components, see Figure 4.29.

4.28

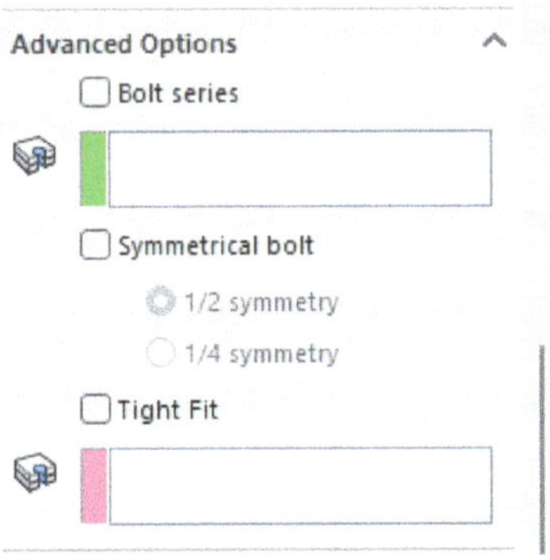

4.29

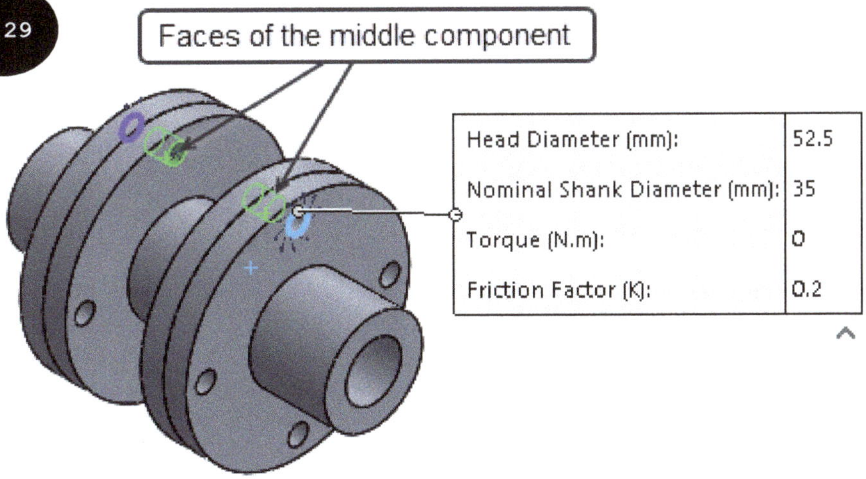

After selecting the cylindrical faces of the middle components, click on the green tick-mark button in the PropertyManager. Figure 4.30 shows a bolted connection applied between more than two components.

4.30

Note: The **Tight Fit** check box of the **Advanced Options** rollout is used to define the tight fit bolt connection when the diameter of the bolt shank is equal to the diameter of the hole faces. To do this, you need to select the **Tight Fit** check box and then activate the **Shank interaction faces** field by clicking on it. Next, you need to select the hole faces which are in contact with the bolt shank.

Similar to applying a counterbore with nut type bolt connector, you can apply a countersink with a nut, counterbore screw, countersink screw, and foundation bolt by using the **Connectors PropertyManager**.

Applying a Pin connector

In SOLIDWORKS Simulation, you can apply a pin connector between the cylindrical faces of the components that rotate against the pin by using the **Pin** tool. The method for applying a pin connector is discussed below:

1. Click on the arrow at the bottom of the **Connections Advisor** tool in the **Simulation CommandManager**. The **Connections** flyout appears, see Figure 4.31. In this flyout, click on the **Pin** tool. The **Connectors PropertyManager** appears, see Figure 4.32. Alternatively, right-click on the **Connections** node in the Simulation Study Tree and then click on the **Pin** tool in the shortcut menu that appears.

   By default, the **Cylindrical Faces/Edges** field is activated in the **Type** rollout of the PropertyManager. As a result, you can select the cylindrical faces of the components.

4.31

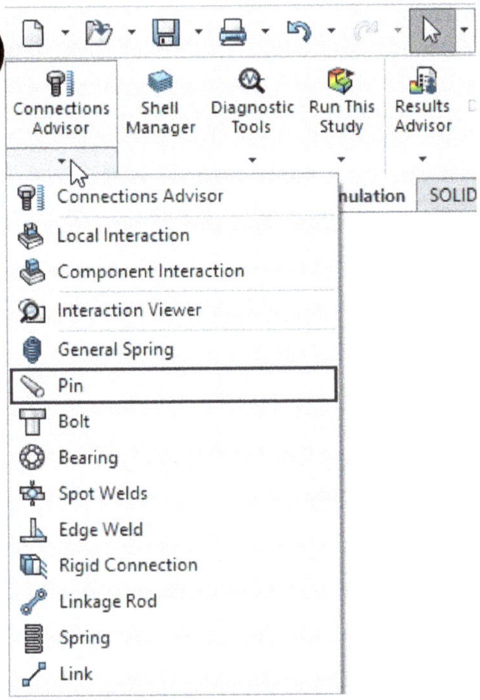

4.32

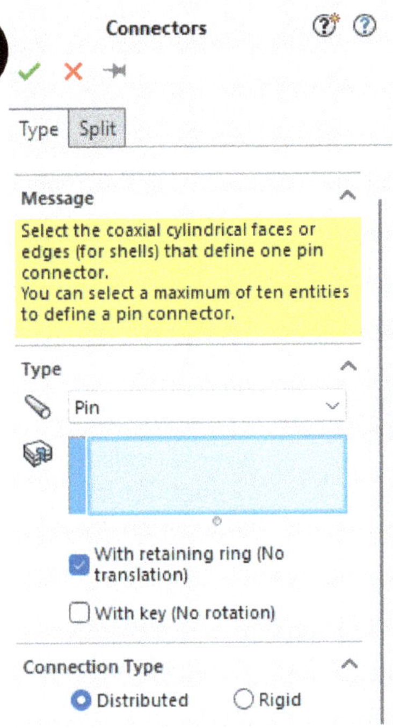

2. Select a cylindrical face of the first component, see Figure 4.33. You can select a single 360-degree cylindrical face or multiple cylindrical faces of smaller angles to apply the pin connector. The selected face is highlighted with a callout attached to it in the graphics area, see Figure 4.33. Also, the name of the selected face appears in the **Cylindrical Faces/Edges** field of the rollout. Note that for shell geometry, you can select a cylindrical edge.

3. After selecting a cylindrical face of the first component, select a cylindrical face of the second component, see Figure 4.34.

4.33

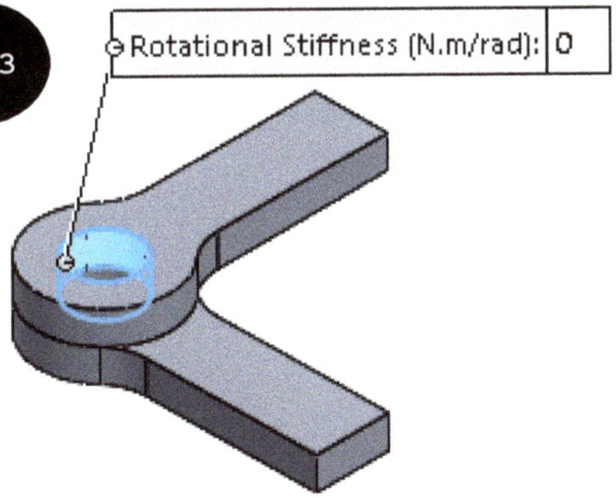

4.34

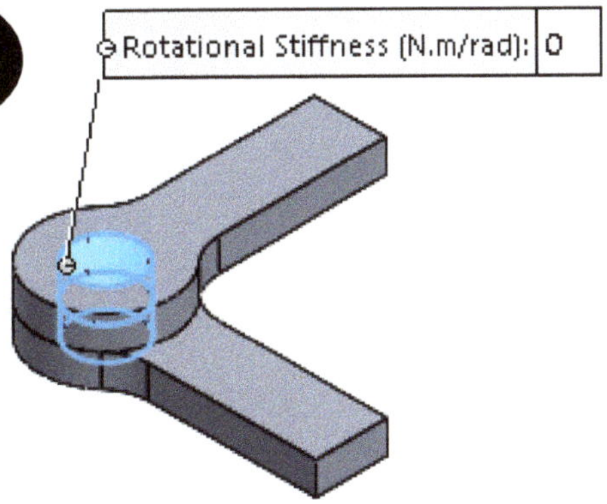

By default, the **With retaining ring (No translation)** check box is selected in the **Type** rollout of the PropertyManager. As a result, the relative axial translation between the selected faces of the components gets restricted. On selecting the **With key (No rotation)** check box, the relative rotation between the selected faces of the components gets restricted.

4. Ensure that the **With retaining ring (No translation)** check box is selected in the **Type** rollout of the PropertyManager to restrict the relative axial translation between the selected faces.

   You can specify the rotational stiffness in the **Rotational Stiffness** field of the **Option** rollout in the PropertyManager. Note that this field is not enabled when the **With key (No rotation)** check box is selected in the **Type** rollout. You can also specify the axial stiffness in the axial direction in the **Axial Stiffness** field of the **Option** rollout. This field is not enabled when the **With retaining ring (No translation)** check box is selected.

5. Select the Distributed or Rigid connection type by selecting the respective radio button in the **Connection Type** rollout.

Note: The Distributed connection type allows deformation of the faces attached, which delivers a more realistic representation of a connector's behavior as compared to the Rigid connection type, where the faces are rigidly connected. Note that the Distributed connection type is available for linear static studies only.

6. Expand the **Strength Data** rollout of the PropertyManager and then specify the yield strength of the pin material in the **Pin Strength** field of the rollout.

7. Specify the factor of safety ratio in the **Safety Factor** field of the rollout. Note that the pin fails when the combined load of the pin exceeds the ratio of the specified factor of safety.

   You can also specify the known tensile stress location/area of the pin in the **Tensile Stress Area** field of the **Strength Data** rollout.

8. Click on the green tick-mark button in the PropertyManager. The pin is applied between the selected cylindrical faces and its representation appears in the graphics area, see Figure 4.35. Also, the applied pin connection gets listed under the **Connectors** node in the Simulation Study Tree.

4.35

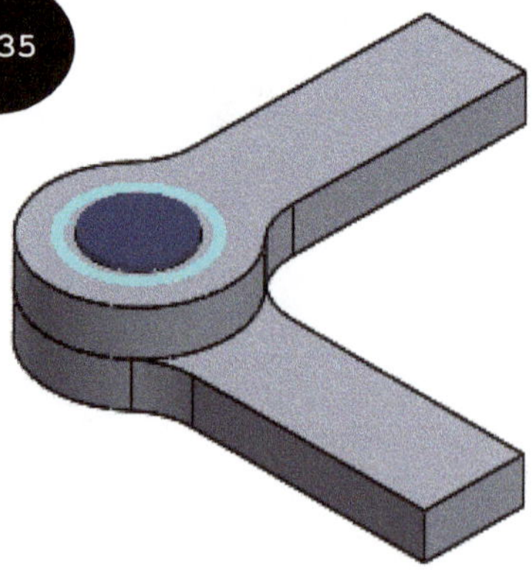

Applying a Link connector

In SOLIDWORKS Simulation, you can apply a link connector between two components that are connected by a rigid bar (link) with each other, see Figure 4.36. The method for applying a link connector is discussed below:

4.36

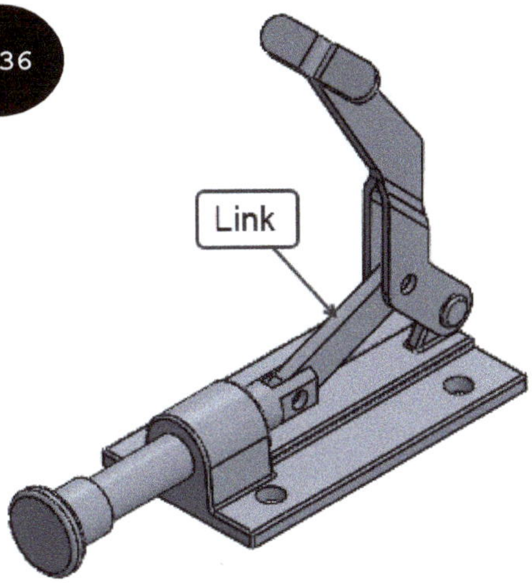

1. Right-click on the **Connections** node in the Simulation Study Tree. A shortcut menu appears, see Figure 4.37. In this shortcut menu, click on the **Link** tool. The **Connectors PropertyManager** appears, see Figure 4.38. Alternatively, click on the arrow at the bottom of the **Connections Advisor** tool in the **Simulation CommandManager** and then click on the **Link** tool in the **Connectors** flyout that appears.

4.37

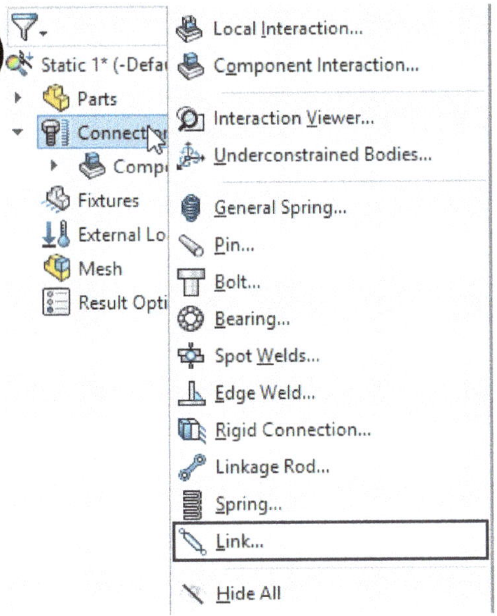

4.38

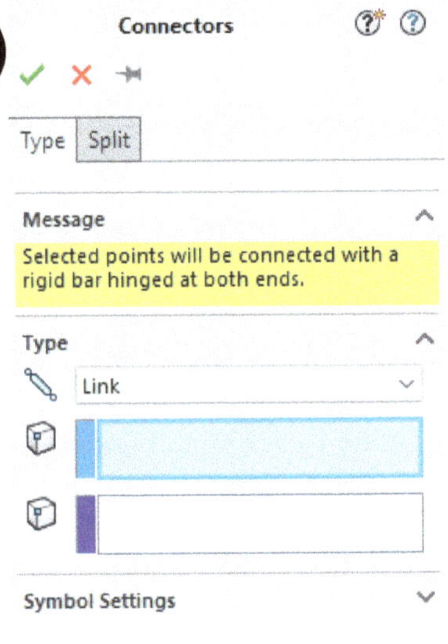

To apply a link connector between two components, you need to specify hinged end locations on both components. You can do so by selecting either vertices or reference points, refer to Figure 4.39. In this figure, two reference points (Point1 and Point2) are created on the hinged end locations of the components to define the end locations.

2. Select a vertex or a reference point to define the hinged end location of the first component, see Figure 4.39. In this figure, a reference point (Point1) is selected.

3. Click on the **Vertex or Point for Second location** field in the PropertyManager and then select a vertex or a reference point to define the hinged end location of the second component, see Figure 4.39. In this figure, a reference point (Point2) is selected.

4. Click on the green tick-mark button in the PropertyManager. The link connector is applied between the selected components, see Figure 4.40.

4.39

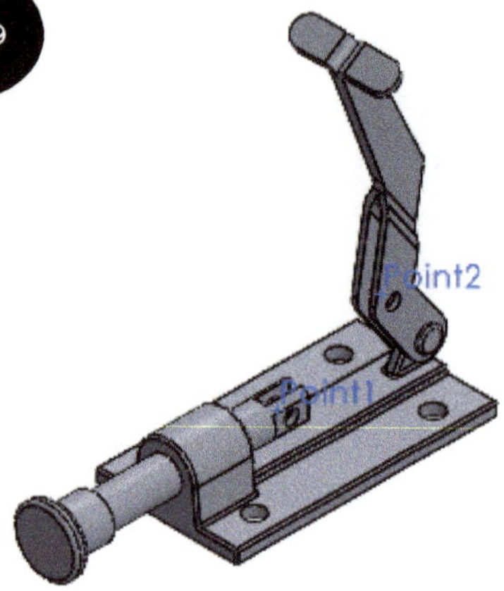

4.40

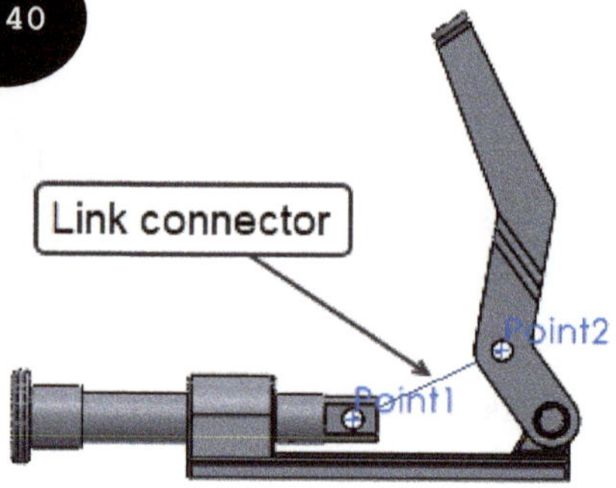

Note: The applied link connector acts as rigid bar between two components and the distance between the specified locations of the components remains same during the deformation.

Applying a Bearing connector

You can apply a bearing connector between components that represent shaft and housing mechanism, see Figure 4.41. The bearing connector is used when the shaft is more rigid than the housing. The method for applying a bearing connector is discussed below:

1. Right-click on the **Connections** node in the Simulation Study Tree and then click on the **Bearing** tool in the shortcut menu that appears. The **Connectors PropertyManager** appears. Alternatively, invoke the **Connectors** flyout in the **Simulation CommandManager** and then click on the **Bearing** tool.

   By default, the **For shaft: Cylindrical face** field is activated in the **Type** rollout of the PropertyManager. As a result, you can select a cylindrical face of the shaft. For shell geometry, you need to select a circular edge.

2. Select a circular face of the shaft where the bearing is connected between the shaft and the housing, see Figure 4.41.

Note: You need to split the shaft face by creating split lines using the **Split Line** tool to define the bearing connector on the portion of the shaft where the bearing is connected. In Figure 4.41, split lines are created on the shaft to ensure proper location of the bearing connector.

3. Click on the **For housing: Cylindrical face or circular edge of shell** field in the **Type** rollout of the PropertyManager. Next, select a cylindrical face of the housing where the bearing is resting on it, see Figure 4.42.

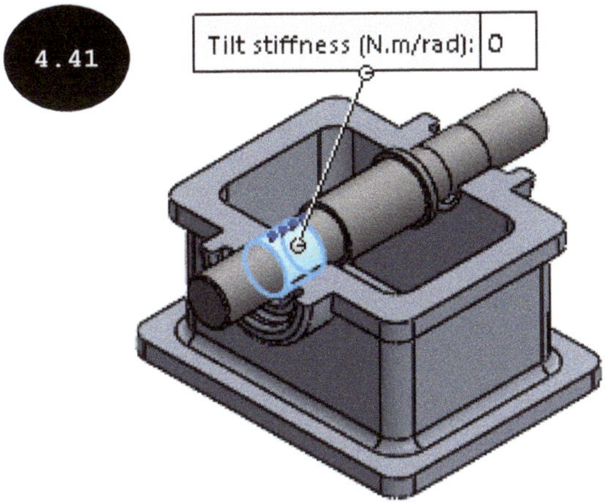

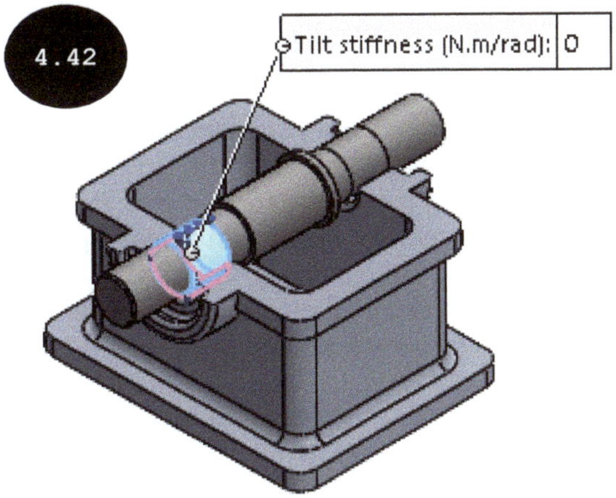

By default, the **Distributed** option is selected in the **Connection Type** rollout of the PropertyManager. As a result, the distributed coupling connection is applied between the selected geometries (shaft and housing) to allow relative movement between each other. You can also define the rigid or spring connection type between the selected geometries by selecting the respective option (**Rigid** or **Spring**) in the drop-down list of the **Connection Type** rollout, see Figure 4.43.

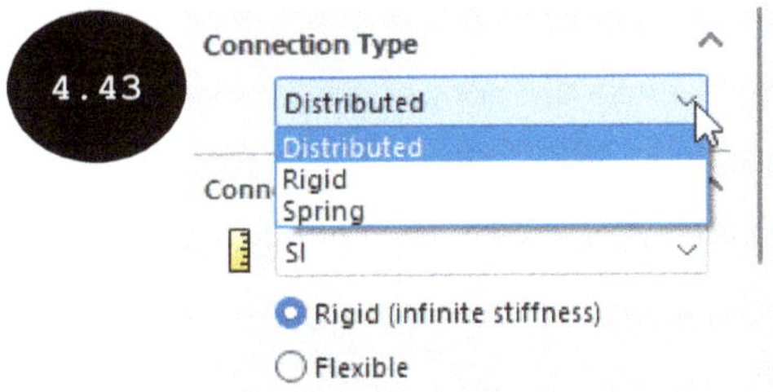

4. Ensure that the **Distributed** option is selected in the drop-down list of the **Connection Type** rollout of the PropertyManager.

5. Ensure that the **Rigid (infinite stiffness)** radio button is selected in the **Connector Stiffness** rollout of the **PropertyManager** to block any lateral or axial translation for the selected face of the shaft by applying a high stiffness value to the connector.

   On selecting the **Flexible** radio button, you can define the total lateral and axial stiffness values in the respective fields which are enabled below this radio button. The **Flexible** radio button is used when you want to allow the lateral or axial translation for the selected face of the shaft.

6. Ensure that the tilt stiffness value is set to **0** in the **Tilt stiffness** field of the **Connector Stiffness** rollout.

Note: By using the **Tilt stiffness** field, you can define the self-alignment parameter for the bearing connector, enabling the off-axis rotation of the shaft.

7. Click on the green tick-mark button in the PropertyManager. The bearing connector is applied between the shaft and the housing.

Applying a Spot Weld connector

4.44

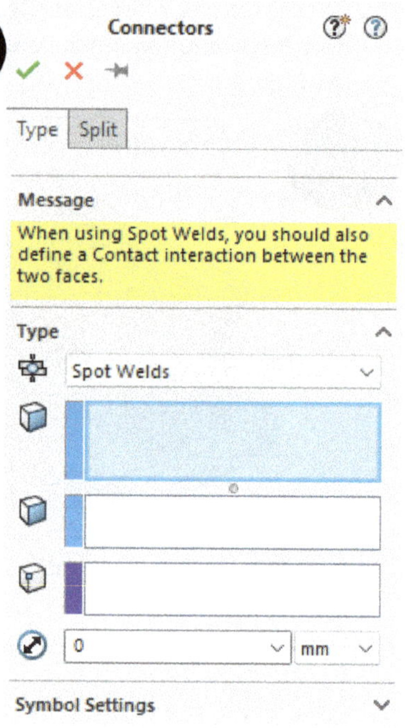

You can apply a spot weld connector between two thin components that are connected to each other with a spot weld. The method for applying a spot weld connector is discussed below:

1. Right-click on the **Connections** node in the Simulation Study Tree and then click on the **Spot Welds** tool in the shortcut menu that appears. The **Connectors PropertyManager** appears, see Figure 4.44. Alternatively, invoke the **Connectors** flyout in the **Simulation CommandManager** and then click on the **Spot Welds** tool.

   By default, the **Spot Weld First Face** field is activated in the **Type** rollout of the PropertyManager. As a result, you can select a connected face of the first component to apply the spot weld connector.

2. Select the connected face of the first component, see Figure 4.45. A callout is attached to the selected face and the name of the face appears in the **Spot Weld First Face** field of the PropertyManager.

3. Click on the **Spot Weld Second Face** field in the **Type** rollout and then select the connected face of the second component, see Figure 4.46. In Figures 4.45 and 4.46, the outer planar faces of the components are selected to apply the spot weld connector.

4.45

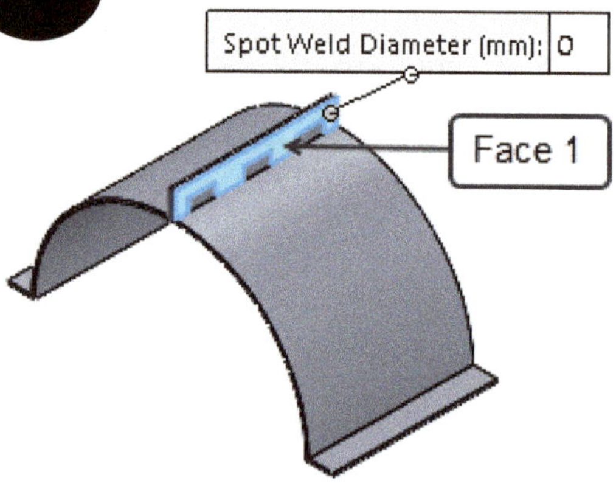

4.46

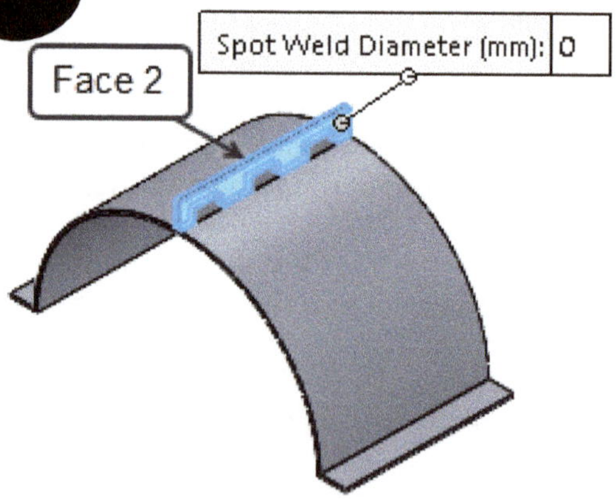

After selecting the faces of the components that are connected by the spot weld, you need to define the weld location on any one of the selected faces. Note that you can define the weld location by selecting the vertices or assembly reference points.

4. Click on the **Spot Weld Locations** field in the **Type** rollout and then select vertices or assembly reference points one by one to define the spot weld locations, see Figure 4.47. In this figure, six (6) vertices of the first selected face are selected to define the spot weld locations.

Note: You need to split a face by creating split lines using the **Split Line** tool so that you can select the vertices which are created by split lines. In Figure 4.47, the split lines are created on the first selected face and their vertices are selected to define the spot weld locations.

4.47

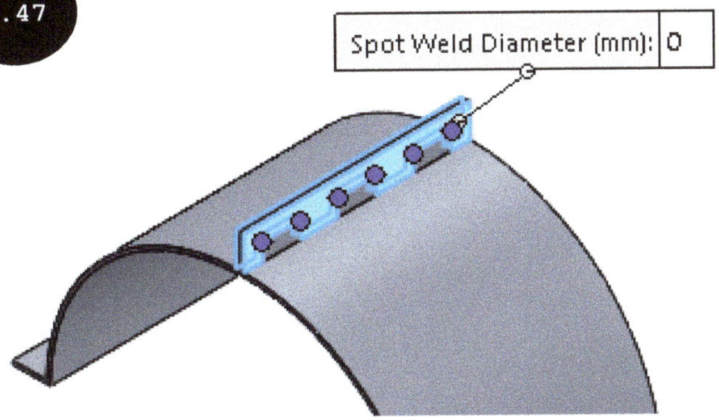

After defining the spot weld location, you need to define the spot weld diameter.

5. Enter a spot weld diameter value in the **Spot Weld Diameter** field of the PropertyManager. Note that the spot weld diameter should be less than 12.5 mm.

6. Click on the green tick-mark button in the PropertyManager. The spot weld connector is applied between the selected faces of the components.

4.48

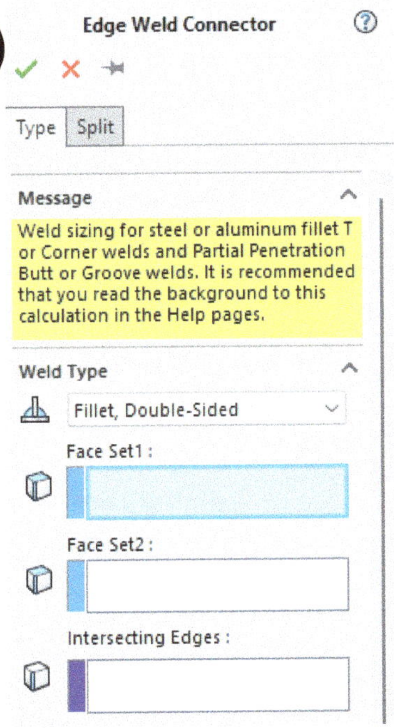

Applying an Edge Weld connector

You can apply an edge weld connector between two metal components. By applying an edge weld connector, you can determine the appropriate weld size required to connect components. The method for applying an edge weld connector is discussed below:

1. Right-click on the **Connections** node in the Simulation Study Tree and then click on the **Edge Weld** tool in the shortcut menu that appears. The **Edge Weld Connector PropertyManager** appears, see Figure 4.48. Alternatively, invoke the **Connectors** flyout in the **Simulation CommandManager** and then click on the **Edge Weld** tool.

2. Select a weld type in the **Type** drop-down list of the **Weld Type** rollout in the PropertyManager. You can apply a single-sided or a double-sided fillet weld or groove weld by selecting the appropriate weld type in the **Type** drop-down list, see Figure 4.49.

4.49

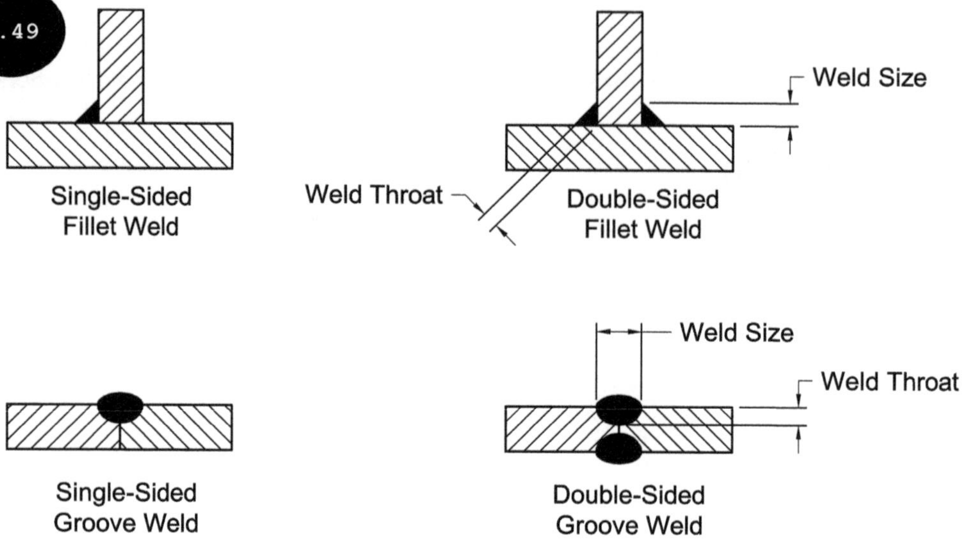

After selecting the type of weld, you need to select two faces and an intersecting edge of the selected faces to apply the weld. By default, the **Face Set1** field is activated in the **Weld Type** rollout of the PropertyManager. As a result, you can select the face of a shell or sheet metal component.

3. Select a face of a shell (surface/2D geometry) or a sheet metal component as the first face to apply the edge weld, see Figure 4.50. The face gets selected and its name appears in the **Face Set1** field of the PropertyManager.

Note: You can apply an edge weld connector between two shell/sheet metal components as well as between a shell/sheet metal component and a solid component. However, the first selected face should be of a shell/sheet metal component. In Figure 4.50, the vertical plate is a sheet metal component and the bottom horizontal plate is a 3D solid component.

4. Click on the **Face Set2** field in the **Weld Type** rollout of the PropertyManager and then select a face of another shell/sheet metal component or the solid component, see Figure 4.50.

Note: For applying a fillet weld, the selected faces of two components should be perpendicular to each other, whereas for applying a groove weld, the selected faces of two components should be parallel to each other.

The intersecting edge between the selected faces gets automatically selected for the fillet weld and the preview of the weld appears in the graphics area with the default estimated weld size, see Figure 4.50. You need to select a touching or non-touching edge of the selected faces as the intersecting edge, if not selected by default.

4.50

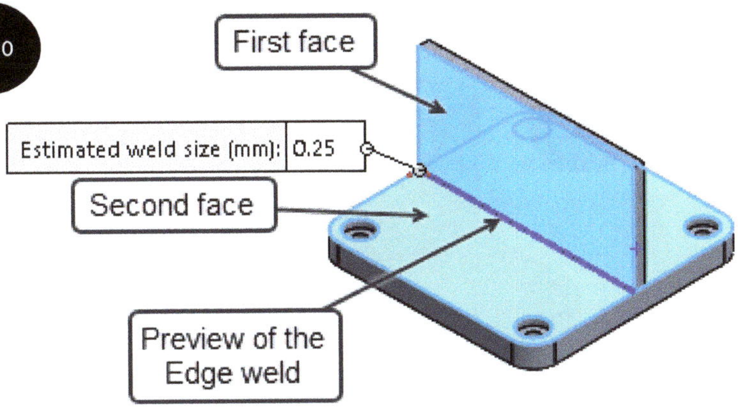

5. Select a welding standard; American Standard or European Standard, by selecting the respective radio button in the **Weld Sizing** rollout of the PropertyManager, see Figure 4.51. Next, specify the electrode material properties of the weld.

4.51

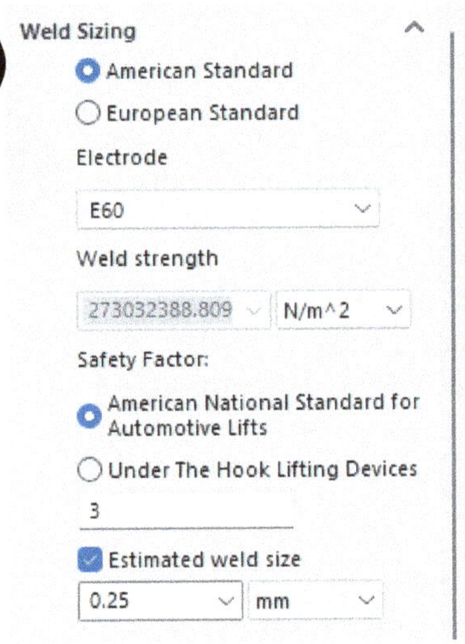

Note: For American Standard, you need to specify the electrode material. You can select the required standard electrode material in the **Electrode** drop-down list of the **Weld Sizing** rollout. In case of custom material, you can select the **Custom steel or Custom Aluminum** option in the drop-down list and enter the weld strength of the material in the **Weld strength** field of the rollout.

For European Standard, you need to specify the material ultimate tensile strength and correlation factor in the respective fields of the rollout.

6. Specify the estimated weld size value in the **Estimated weld size** field of the **Weld Sizing** rollout in the PropertyManager. Note that SOLIDWORKS Simulation automatically calculates the appropriate weld size required for the weld connector and compares it with the value specified in the **Estimated weld size** field.

7. Click on the green tick-mark button in the PropertyManager. The edge weld connector is applied between the selected faces of the components, see Figure 4.52.

4.52

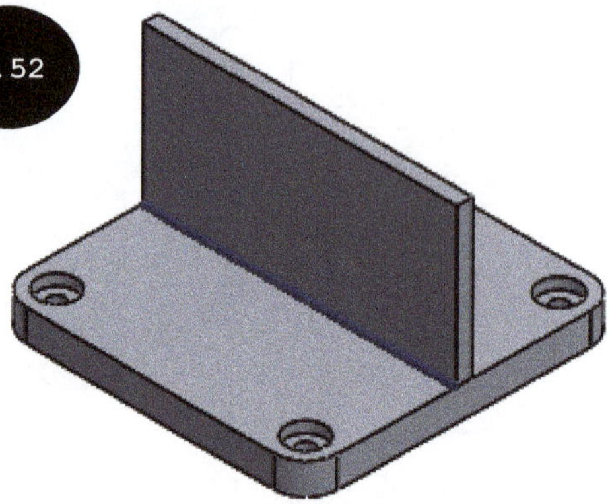

Applying a Linkage Rod connector

You can apply a linkage rod connector between two components that are connected to each other with a connecting rod. The method for applying a linkage rod connector is discussed below:

4.53

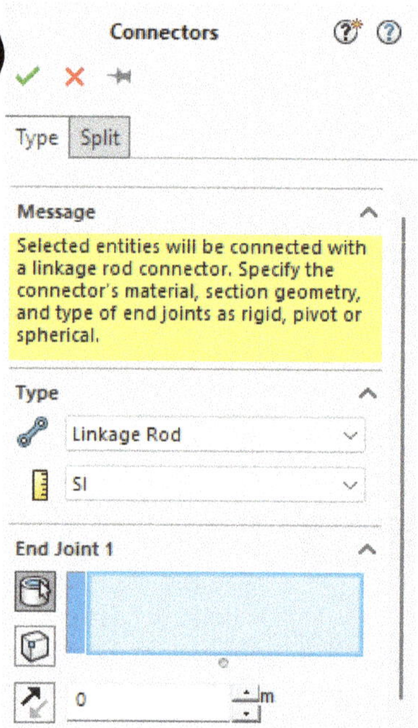

1. Right-click on the **Connections** node in the Simulation Study Tree and then click on the **Linkage Rod** tool in the shortcut menu that appears. The Connectors PropertyManager appears, see Figure 4.53. Alternatively, click on the arrow at the bottom of the **Connections Advisor** tool in the **Simulation CommandManager** and then click on **Linkage Rod** tool in the **Connectors** flyout that appears. Note that, this connector is not available for non-linear and thermal studies.

   To apply a linkage rod connector between two components, you need to specify the end locations on both the components.

2. Select concentric cylindrical faces of the first component for defining the end location where one end of the connecting rod is to be connected, refer to Figure 4.54.

Note: By default, the **Concentric cylindrical faces or edges (for shells)** button is activated in the **End Joint 1** rollout of the PropertyManager. As a result, you can select concentric cylindrical faces or cylindrical edges (for shells) of the first component where one end of the connecting rod is to be connected. To select vertices for defining the end location of the connecting rod, you need to activate the **Vertex** button in the **End Joint 1** rollout of the PropertyManager.

3. Specify the offset distance of the linkage rod connector from the specified cylindrical faces in the **Offset distance** field, if required. Note that, this field is optional and is not available if vertices are selected for defining the end location of the connecting rod.

4. Specify the type of joint (rigid, pivot, or spherical) for the linkage rod connector with the first component by selecting the respective button (**Rigid joint, Pivot joint**, or **Spherical joint**) in the **End Joint 1** rollout.

Note: Rigid joint restricts all relative motion between the linkage rod and the first component. Pivot joint allows rotational motion between the linkage rod and the first component about the axis that is normal to the axis of linkage rod. Spherical joint acts like a ball and socket joint between the linkage rod and the first component where the ball can rotate inside the socket.

5. Click on the **Concentric cylindrical faces or edges (for shells)** field in the **End Joint 2** rollout of the PropertyManager and then select concentric cylindrical faces of the second component for defining the end location where the other end of the connecting rod is to be connected, refer to Figure 4.54.

4.54

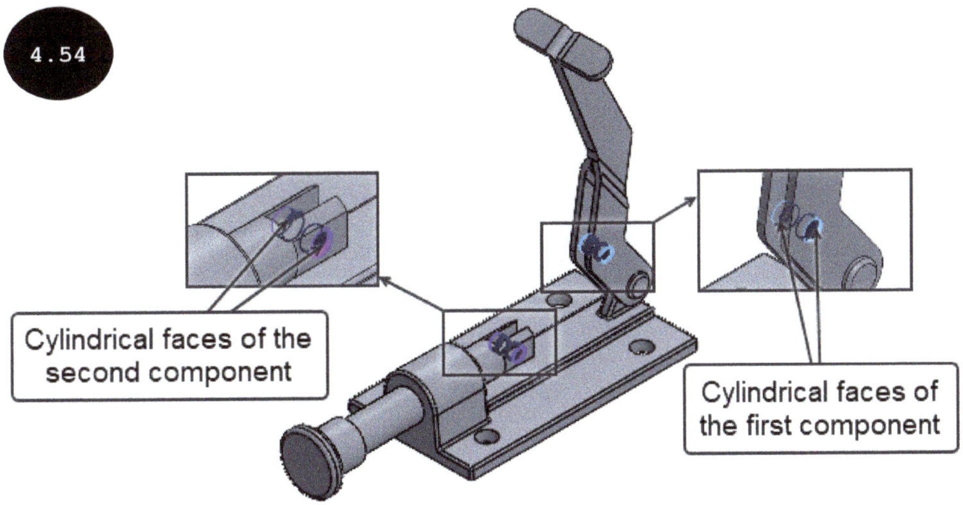

6. Specify the required type of joint (rigid, pivot, or spherical) for the linkage rod connector with the second component by selecting the respective button in the **End Joint 2** rollout of the PropertyManager.

7. Specify the required cross-section for the linkage rod by selecting the respective option (**Solid circular, Hollow circular, Solid rectangular**, or **Hollow rectangular**) in the **Type** drop-down list of the **Section Parameters** rollout.

8. Specify the required parameters or dimensions for the linkage rod cross-section in the respective fields that appear below the **Type** drop-down list of the **Section Parameters** rollout. A preview of the linkage rod connector appears, see Figure 4.55. In Figure 4.55, the solid circular cross-section of the linkage rod is shown.

9. Specify the material for the linkage rod connector in the **Material** rollout.

10. Click on the green tick-mark button in the PropertyManager. The linkage rod connector is applied between the selected components, see Figure 4.56.

4.55

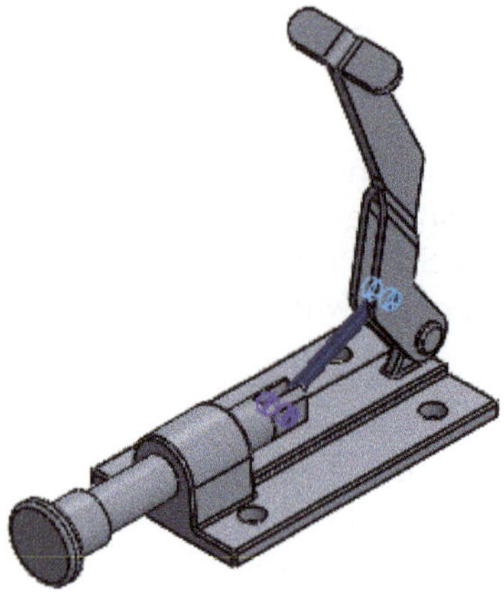

4.56

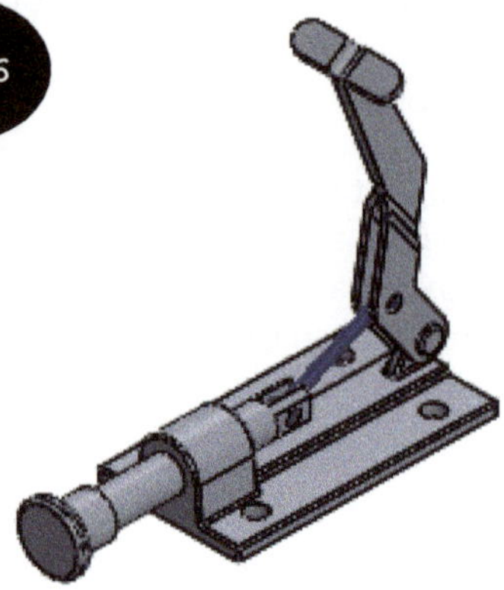

Case Study 1: Static Analysis of a Hook Assembly with Interactions

In this case study, you will perform the linear static analysis of a Hook assembly shown in Figure 4.57 and determine the stresses under the applied load.

4.57

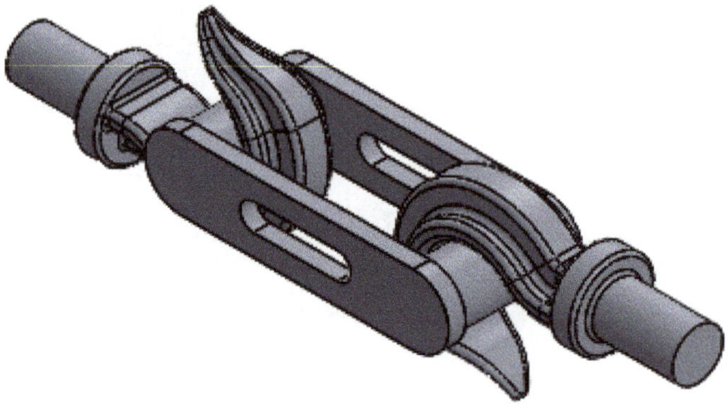

Project Description

The Hook assembly is fixed at one end and 17000 N load is applied along the other end, see Figure 4.58. All the components of the assembly are made up of **Alloy Steel** material.

4.58

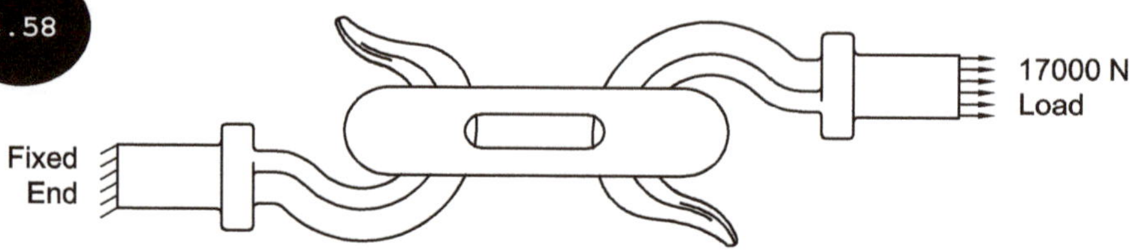

Project Summary
In this case study, you will generate a high-quality curvature-based mesh with maximum element size as 16 mm and minimum element size as 3.2 mm. Also, you need to define the Contact interaction between interacting sets of the assembly components. Specify the unit system to SI (MKS) with displacement in mm and stress in N/mm^2 (MPa) units.

The following sequence summarizes the case study outline:

1. Downloading Files of Chapter 4
2. Opening the Hook Assembly
3. Starting the Static Study
4. Defining Units
5. Assigning Materials
6. Applying Fixtures
7. Applying Interactions
8. Applying the Load
9. Generating the Mesh
10. Running Analysis and Displaying Results
11. Displaying Stress Results for one Assembly Component
12. Saving Results

Section 1: Downloading Files of Chapter 4

1. Log on to the CADArtifex website (*cadartifex.com/login/*) using the Email OTP that will be sent to your registered email ID. If you are a new user, you must first sign up on the CADArtifex website as a **Learner** (*cadartifex.com/register*).

2. After logging in to your account, navigate to the textbook titled "**SOLIDWORKS Simulation 2026: A Power Guide for Beginners and Intermediate Users: Colored**" using the **Browse Resources** option available in the left menu to download its resources. Alternatively, you can enter the name of the textbook in the **Search** box to locate it quickly.

3. In the **Online Resources** tab, expand the **Case Studies** rollout and click the **Download** button corresponding to **C04 Case Studies**. In the confirmation window that appears, click the **Confirm** button. The download of the **C04 Case Studies** file will begin. After the download is complete, unzip the file.

4. Save the extracted **C04 Case Studies** folder in the location *SOLIDWORKS Simulation > Case Studies*. You need to create these folders, if not created earlier.

Section 2: Opening the Hook Assembly

1. Start SOLIDWORKS, if not started already.

2. Click the **Open** button in the **Welcome** dialog box or select the **Open** tool from the **Standard** toolbar. The **Open** dialog box appears.

3. Browse to the location > *SOLIDWORKS Simulation > Case Studies > C04 Case Studies > Case Study 1* in the local drive of your system. Next, select the **Hook Assembly** and click on the **Open** button. The Hook Assembly is opened in SOLIDWORKS, see Figure 4.59.

4.59

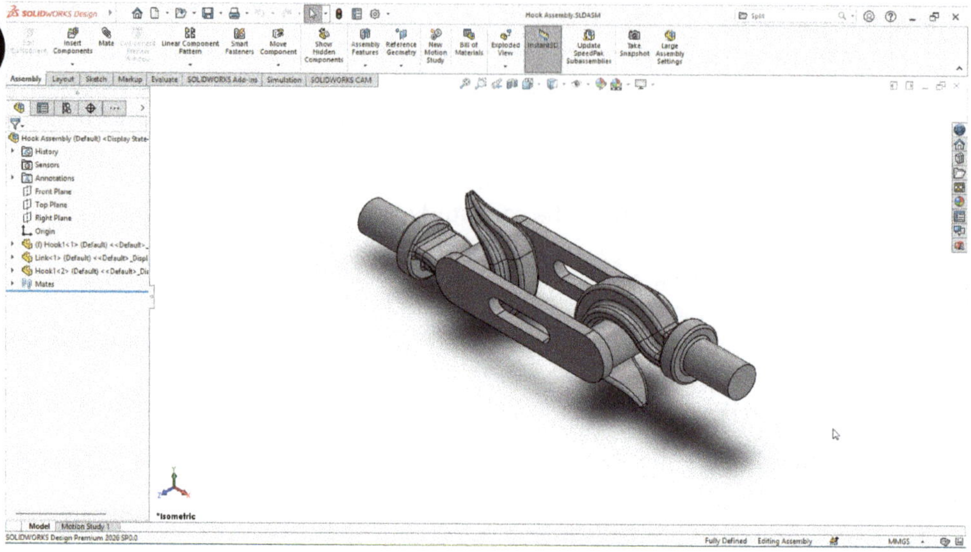

Section 3: Starting the Static Study

1. Click on the **Simulation** tab in the **CommandManager**. The tools of the **Simulation CommandManager** appear.

Note: If the **Simulation** tab is not added in the CommandManager then you need to add it as discussed earlier.

2. Click on the **New Study** tool in the **Simulation CommandManager**. The **Study PropertyManager** appears to the left of the graphics area.

3. Ensure that the **Static** button is activated in the **Study PropertyManager** to perform the linear static analysis on the model.

4. Enter **Hook Static Study** in the **Study name** field of the **Name** rollout in the PropertyManager.

5. Click on the green tick-mark button ✓ in the PropertyManager. The various tools to perform the static analysis are enabled in the **Simulation CommandManager**. Also, the **Hook Static Study** is added to the Simulation Study Tree, see Figure 4.60.

4.60

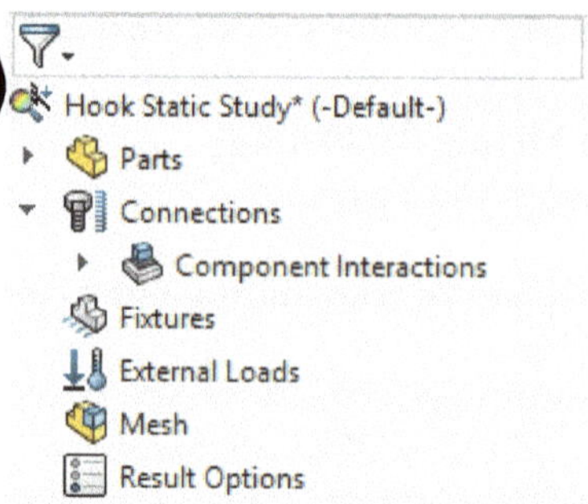

Section 4: Defining Units

Before you start performing the analysis, it is important to set the units.

1. Click on the **Simulation > Options** in the SOLIDWORKS Design Menus. The **System Options** dialog box appears.

2. In this dialog box, click on the **Default Options** tab. The name of the dialog box changes to **Default Options**. Next, ensure that the **Units** option is selected in the dialog box.

3. Select the **SI (MKS)** radio button in the **Unit system** area of the dialog box. Next, ensure that the **mm** unit is selected in the **Length/Displacement** drop-down list and the **N/mm^2 (MPa)** unit is selected in the **Pressure/Stress** drop-down list of the **Units** area.

4. After specifying the units, click on the **OK** button to accept the changes and exit the dialog box.

Section 5: Assigning Materials

As mentioned in the project description, all the components of the assembly are made up of Alloy Steel material. Therefore, you need to apply this material to all the components.

1. Right-click on the **Parts** node in the Simulation Study Tree and then click on the **Apply Material to All** tool in the shortcut menu that appears. The **Material** dialog box appears.

2. Expand the **Steel** category of the **SOLIDWORKS Materials** library of the dialog box and then click on the **Alloy Steel** material. The material properties of the selected material appear on the right panel of the dialog box.

3. Click on the **Apply** button and then click on the **Close** button. The Alloy Steel material is assigned to all the components of the assembly.

Tip: To apply material to each individual component of the assembly, expand the **Parts** node of the Simulation Study Tree. All the components of the assembly appear in the expanded **Parts** node, see Figure 4.61. Now, you can right-click on a component in the expanded **Parts** node and then click on the **Apply/Edit Material** tool in the shortcut menu that appears. On doing so, the **Material** dialog box appears. In this dialog box, select a material and then click on the **Apply** button. Next, click on the **Close** button. The material is assigned to the selected component. Similarly, you can assign a material to other components of the assembly.

4.61

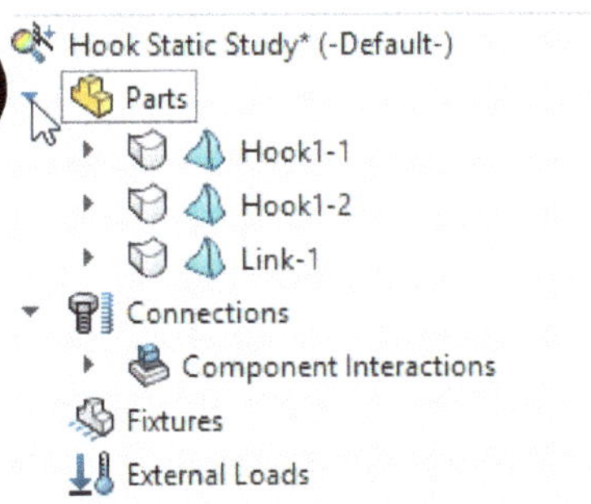

Section 6: Applying Fixtures

Now, you need to apply fixtures to make the assembly suitable for the analysis.

1. Right-click on the **Fixtures** option in the Simulation Study Tree and then click on the **Fixed Geometry** tool in the shortcut menu that appears. The **Fixture PropertyManager** appears to the left of the graphics area.

2. Rotate the model such that you can view the end face of the left Hook component of the assembly and then select it to apply the Fixed Geometry fixture, see Figure 4.62.

3. Click on the green tick-mark button in the PropertyManager. The Fixed Geometry fixture is applied to the selected face of the component.

   Now, you need to apply the On Flat Faces fixture to the Link component of the assembly.

4. Change the current orientation of the assembly to Isometric.

5. Right-click on the **Fixtures** option in the Simulation Study Tree and then click on the **Advanced Fixtures** tool in the shortcut menu that appears. The **Fixture PropertyManager** appears with the expanded **Advanced** rollout on the left of the graphics area, see Figure 4.63.

4.62

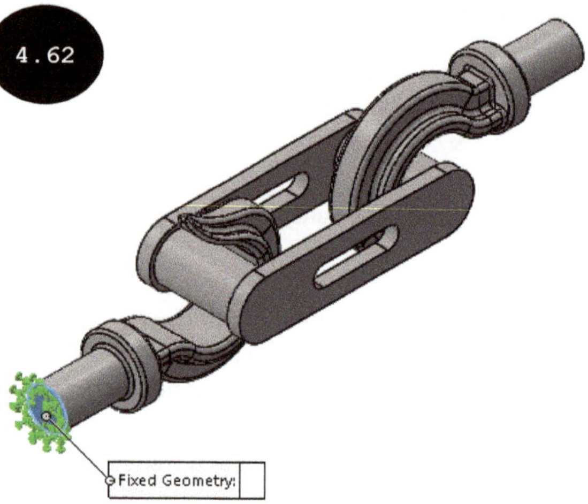

4.63

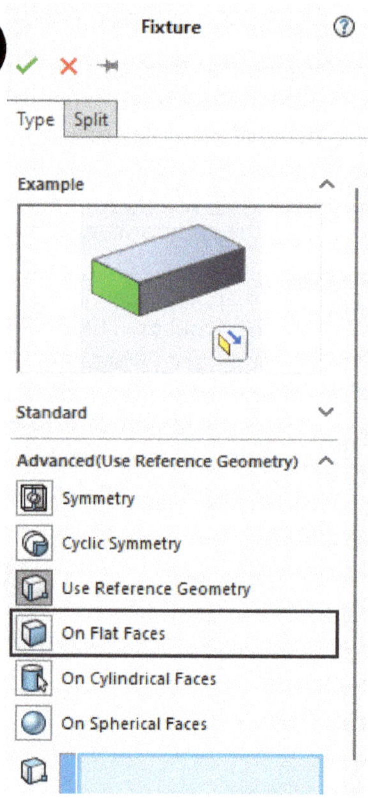

6. Click on the **On Flat Faces** button in the **Advanced** rollout of the PropertyManager.

7. Select the front planar face of the Link component of the assembly to apply the fixture, see Figure 4.64.

8. Scroll down in the PropertyManager and then click on the **Normal to Face** button and the **Along Face Dir 1** button in the **Translations** rollout of the PropertyManager, see Figure 4.65. By default, the **0** value is specified in the fields enabled in front of both buttons. This means that the translation movement is restricted along direction 1 and normal to the face selected. However, the component can move along the direction 2 of the selected face.

4.64

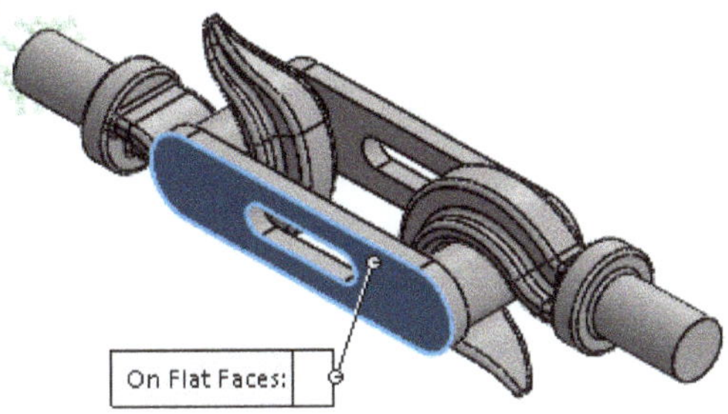

4.65

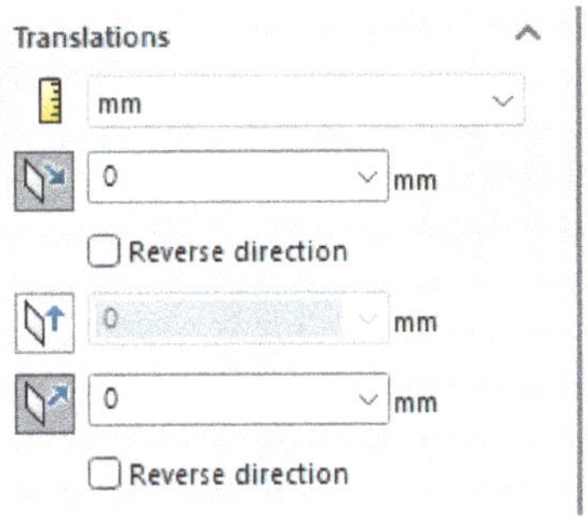

9. Click on the green tick-mark button in the PropertyManager. The On Flat Faces fixture is applied to the selected face of the component.

   Now, you need to apply the Use Reference Geometry fixture to the right Hook component of the assembly.

10. Right-click on the **Fixtures** option in the Simulation Study Tree and then click on the **Advanced Fixtures** tool in the shortcut menu that appears. The **Fixture PropertyManager** appears.

11. Ensure that the **Use Reference Geometry** button is activated in the **Advanced** rollout of the PropertyManager.

12. Select the cylindrical face of the right Hook component to apply the fixture, see Figure 4.66.

4.66

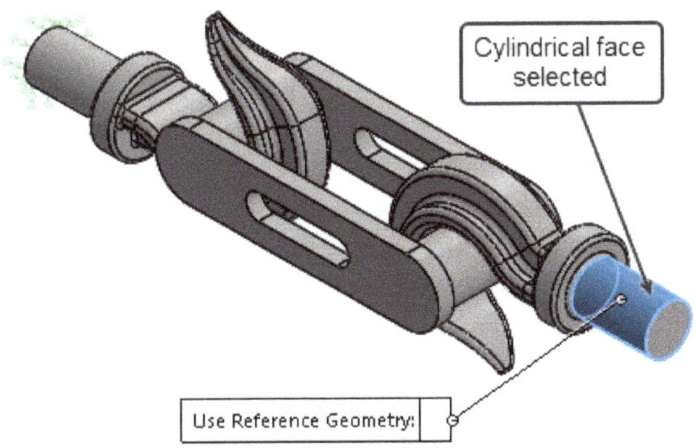

13. Click on the **Face, Edge, Plane, Axis for Direction** field in the **Advanced** rollout of the PropertyManager.

14. Expand the FeatureManager Design Tree, which is now at the top left corner of the graphics area, and then click on the **Top Plane** of the assembly to define the direction of the fixture, see Figure 4.67.

15. Scroll down in the PropertyManager and then click on the **Normal to Plane** and the **Along Plane Dir 2** buttons in the **Translations** rollout of the PropertyManager, see Figure 4.68. By default, the **0** value is specified in the fields enabled in front of both the buttons. This means that the translation movement is restricted along direction 2 and normal to the plane selected. However, the component can move along direction 1 of the selected plane.

4.67

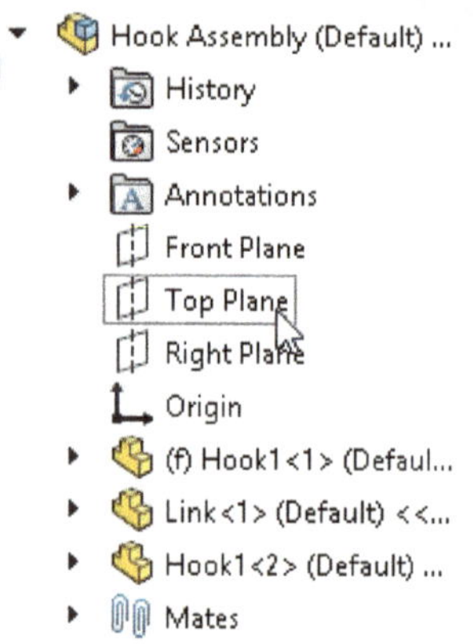

4.68

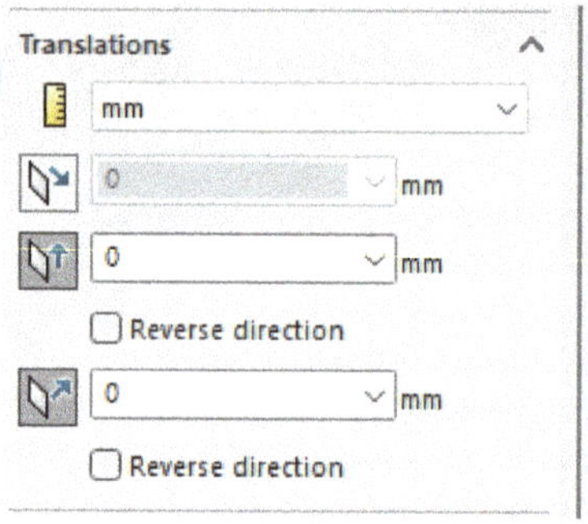

16. Click on the green tick-mark button in the PropertyManager. The Use Reference Geometry fixture is applied to the selected cylindrical face of the component.

Section 7: Applying Interactions

After applying the fixtures, you need to define the interaction conditions between the components of the assembly.

Tip: By default, the Bonded component interaction is applied as a global interaction between all the components of the assembly. You need to apply the Contact interaction between the components of the assembly.

1. Expand the **Component Interactions** sub-node in the **Connections** node of the Simulation Study Tree, see Figure 4.69.

2. Right-click on a **Global Interaction** option in the expanded **Component Interactions** sub-node and then click on the **Edit Definition** tool in the shortcut menu that appears, see Figure 4.69. The **Component Interaction PropertyManager** appears, see Figure 4.70.

4.69

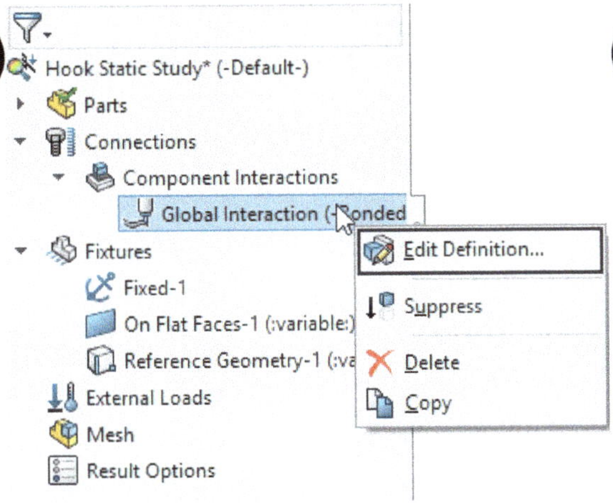

4.70

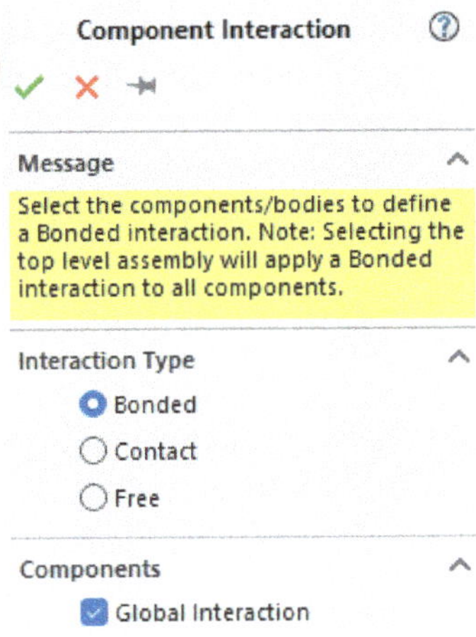

3. Select the **Contact** radio button in the **Interaction Type** rollout of the PropertyManager.

4. Click on the green tick-mark button in the PropertyManager.

Section 8: Applying the Load

Now, you need to apply the load on the end face of the right Hook component.

1. Right-click on the **External Loads** option in the Simulation Study Tree and then click on the **Force** tool in the shortcut menu that appears. The **Force/Torque PropertyManager** appears.

2. Select the end face of the right Hook component of the assembly to apply the load, see Figure 4.71. The symbol of the load appears on the selected face.

3. Ensure that the **Normal** radio button is selected to apply the load normal to the face.

4. Enter **17000** in the **Force Value** field of the PropertyManager.

5. Select the **Reverse direction** check box in the PropertyManager to reverse the direction of force toward the right, see Figure 4.71.

4.71

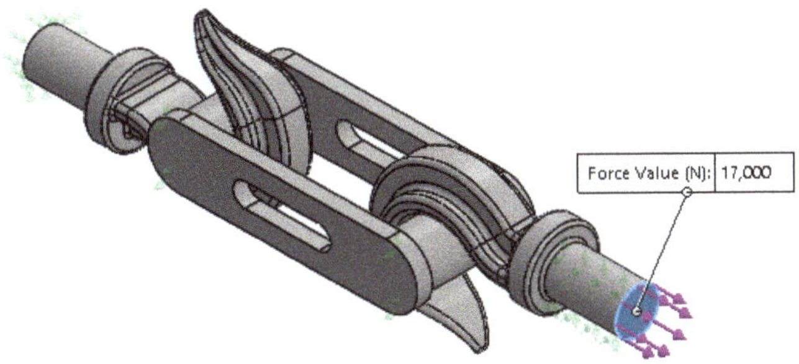

6. Click on the green tick-mark button in the PropertyManager. The **17000** N load is applied on the selected face of the right Hook component.

Section 9: Generating the Mesh

Now, you need to generate the curvature-based mesh with default parameters.

1. Right-click on the **Mesh** option in the Simulation Study Tree and then click on the **Create Mesh** tool in the shortcut menu that appears to invoke the **Mesh PropertyManager**.

2. Expand the **Mesh Parameters** rollout of the PropertyManager by clicking on the check box in its title bar.

3. Select the **Curvature-based mesh** radio button in the expanded **Mesh Parameters** rollout. Next, change the maximum element size to 16 mm and the minimum element size to 3.2 mm in their respective fields of the rollout, see Figure 4.72.

4.72

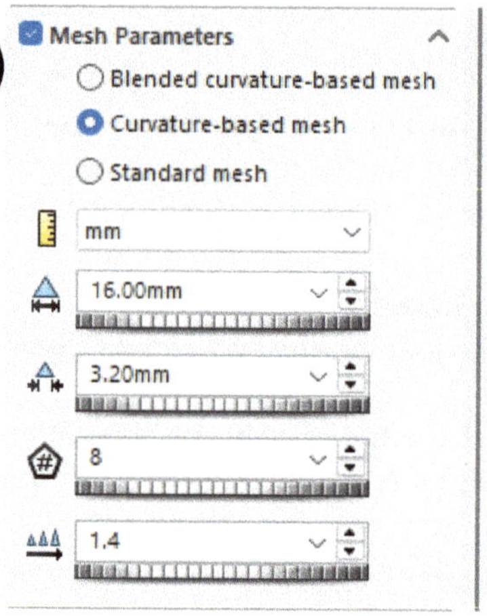

4. Accept the other default mesh parameters and then click on the green tick-mark button ✓. The **Mesh Progress** window appears which displays the progress of meshing in the model. After the meshing is complete, the meshed model appears, see Figure 4.73.

4.73

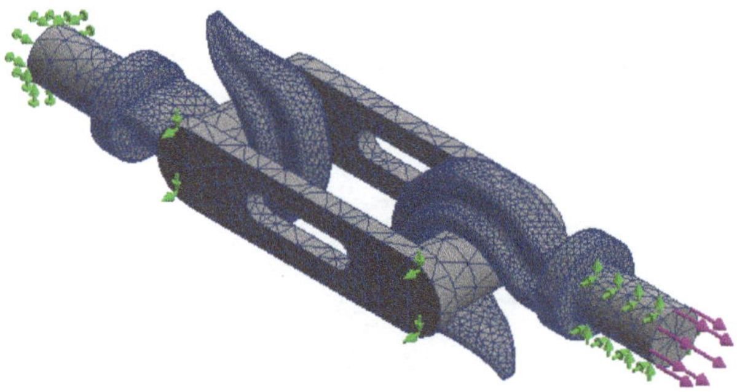

Section 10: Running Analysis and Displaying Results

Now, you need to run the analysis.

1. Click on the **Run This Study** tool in the **Simulation CommandManager**. The **Hook Static Study** (*name of the study*) window appears which displays the progress of the analysis.

2. After the process of running the analysis is completed, the **Results** folder is added to the Simulation Study Tree with the stress, displacement, and strain results. By default, the **Stress** result is activated in the **Results** folder. As a result, the stress distribution on the model and the von Mises stress plot appear in the graphics area, see Figure 4.74.

4.74

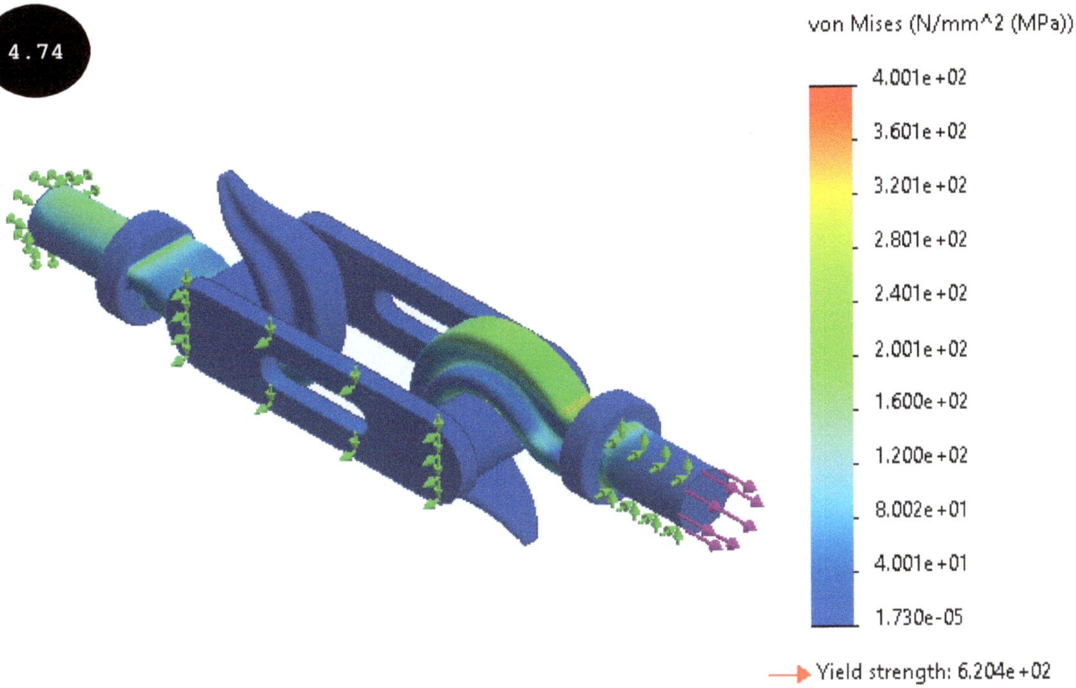

The maximum von Mises stress in the model under the applied load is **4.001e+02** (400.112) N/mm^2 (MPa) which is within the yield stress of the material that is **6.204e+02** (620.422) N/mm^2 (MPa). Note that you may find a slight difference in the result values depending on the service pack installed on your system.

You may observe slight variations in the result values depending on the service pack version of SOLIDWORKS installed on your system. These minor differences occur due to updates and improvements made in different service packs.

Note: If the maximum von Mises stress of the model exceeds the yield strength of the material, your design is likely to fail under the applied load. You may need to optimize the design and validate the boundary conditions (fixtures/loads) or material properties, to make it a valid design to withstand the applied load.

3. Double-click on the **Displacement1 (-Res disp-)** option in the **Results** folder of the Simulation Study Tree. The displacement distribution on the assembly and the resultant displacement (URES) plot appear in the graphics area, see Figure 4.75. The maximum resultant displacement on the assembly under the applied load is **9.677e-01** (0.968) mm.

4.75

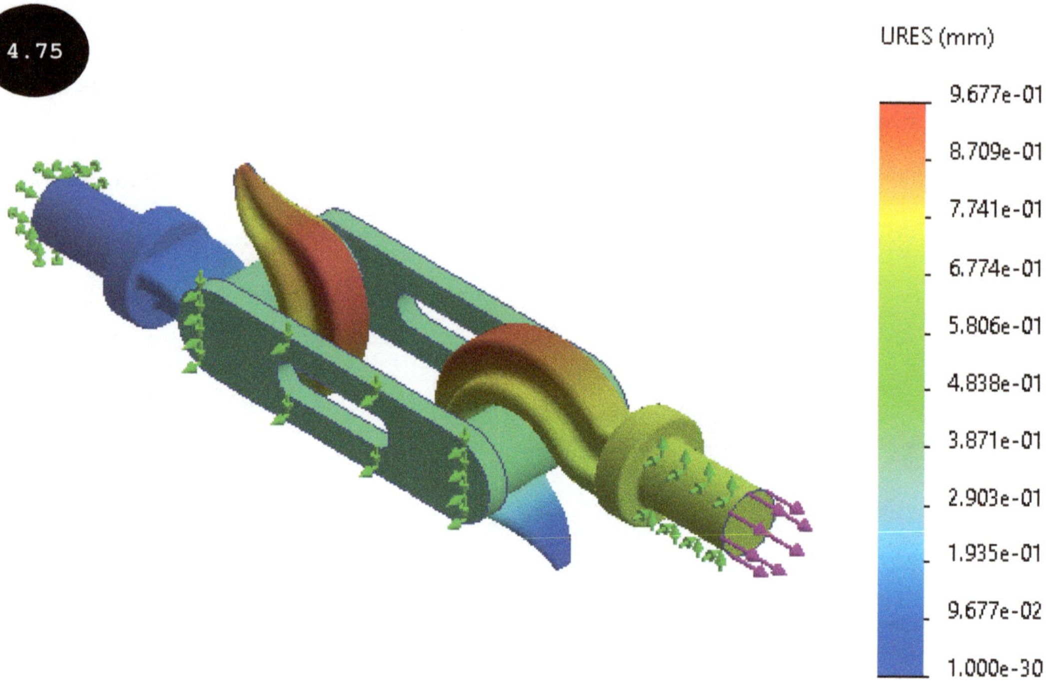

4. Similarly, review the strain results by clicking on the **Strain1 (-Equivalent-)** option in the Simulation Study Tree.

5. Animate the displacement distribution on the model to review the deformed shape of the components and the contact conditions by using the **Animate** tool. This tool is available in the shortcut menu, which appears by right-clicking on the **Displacement1 (-Res disp-)** option in the **Results** folder of the Simulation Study Tree.

Section 11: Displaying Stress Results for one Assembly Component

1. Right-click on the **Results** folder in the Simulation Study Tree and then click on the **Define Stress Plot** tool in the shortcut menu that appears. The **Stress plot PropertyManager** appears.

2. Expand the **Advanced Options** rollout of the **Stress plot PropertyManager**.

3. Select the **Show plot only on selected entities** check box in the expanded **Advanced Options** rollout. The selection field appears in the rollout, see Figure 4.76.

4. Click on the **Select bodies for the plot** button on the left of the selection field in the **Advanced Options** rollout to select a component of the assembly for displaying its stress plot.

4.76

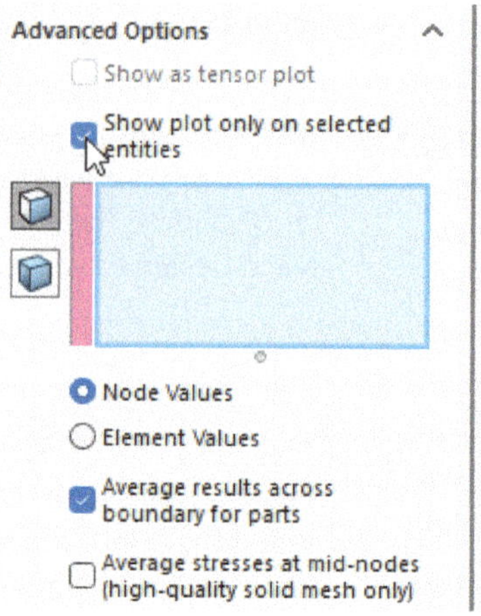

5. Select the right Hook component of the assembly to display its stress plot. Next, click on the green tick-mark button in the PropertyManager. All the components of the assembly are hidden except the selected component, see Figure 4.77.

4.77

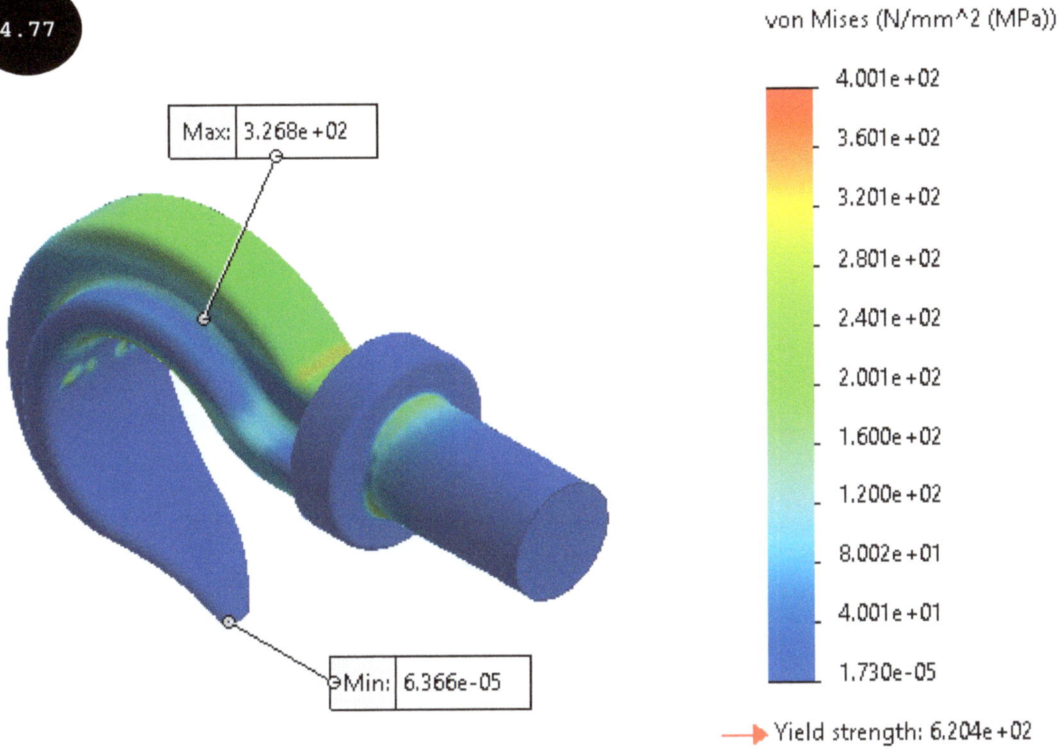

Note: In Figure 4.77, the display of fixtures and load symbols are hidden for the clarity of image. To hide a fixture, right-click on the fixture name listed under the **Fixtures** node in the Simulation Study Tree and then click on the **Hide** tool in the shortcut menu that appears. Similarly, to hide a load, right-click on the load name listed under the **External Loads** node in the Simulation Study Tree and then click on the **Hide** tool in the shortcut menu that appears.

Now, you can display the maximum and minimum stress areas in the right Hook component of the assembly.

6. Double-click on the von Mises stress plot that appears in the graphics area. The **Stress plot PropertyManager** appears to the left of the graphics area.

7. Ensure that the **Chart Options** tab is activated in the PropertyManager. Next, select the **Show max annotation** and **Show min annotation** checkboxes in the **Display Options** rollout of the PropertyManager, see Figure 4.78.

4.78

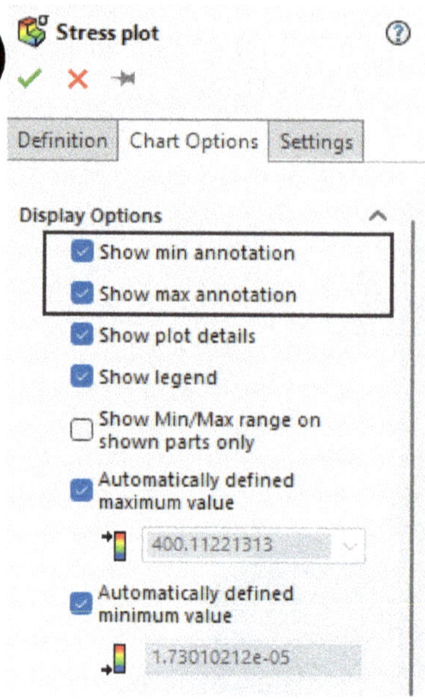

8. Click on the green tick-mark button ✓ in the PropertyManager. The minimum and maximum stresses are annotated on the right Hook component, see Figure 4.79.

9. Similarly, you can display the stress, strain, or displacement plot for other components of the assembly and annotate their maximum and minimum stress, strain, or displacement areas, respectively.

4.79

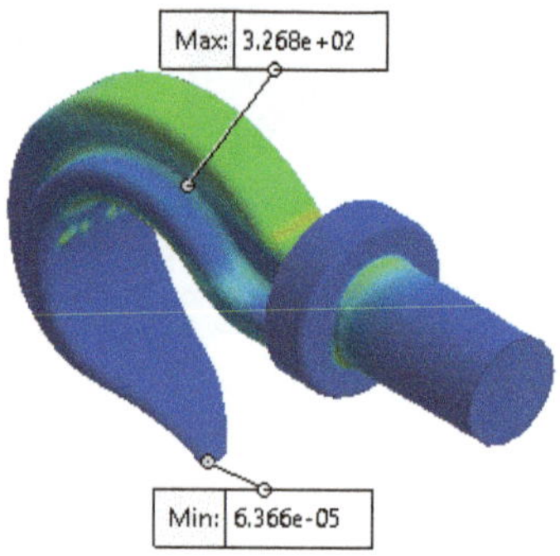

Section 12: Generating a Word Report

Now, you can generate the report for the current analysis study in a Word document.

1. Click on the **Report** tool in the **Simulation CommandManager**, see Figure 4.80. The **Report Options** dialog box appears, see Figure 4.81. The options in this dialog box are discussed next.

4.80

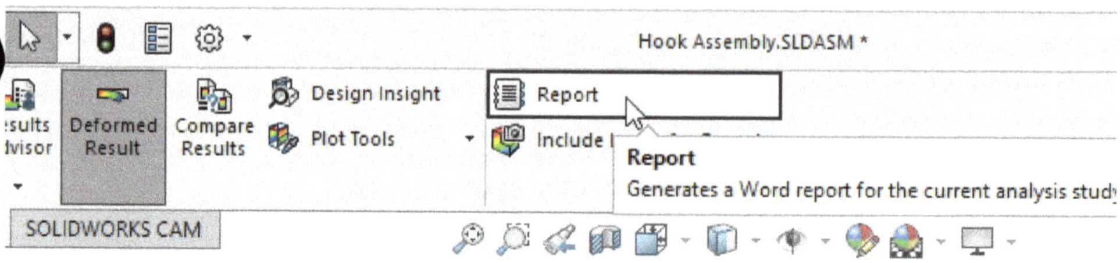

4.81

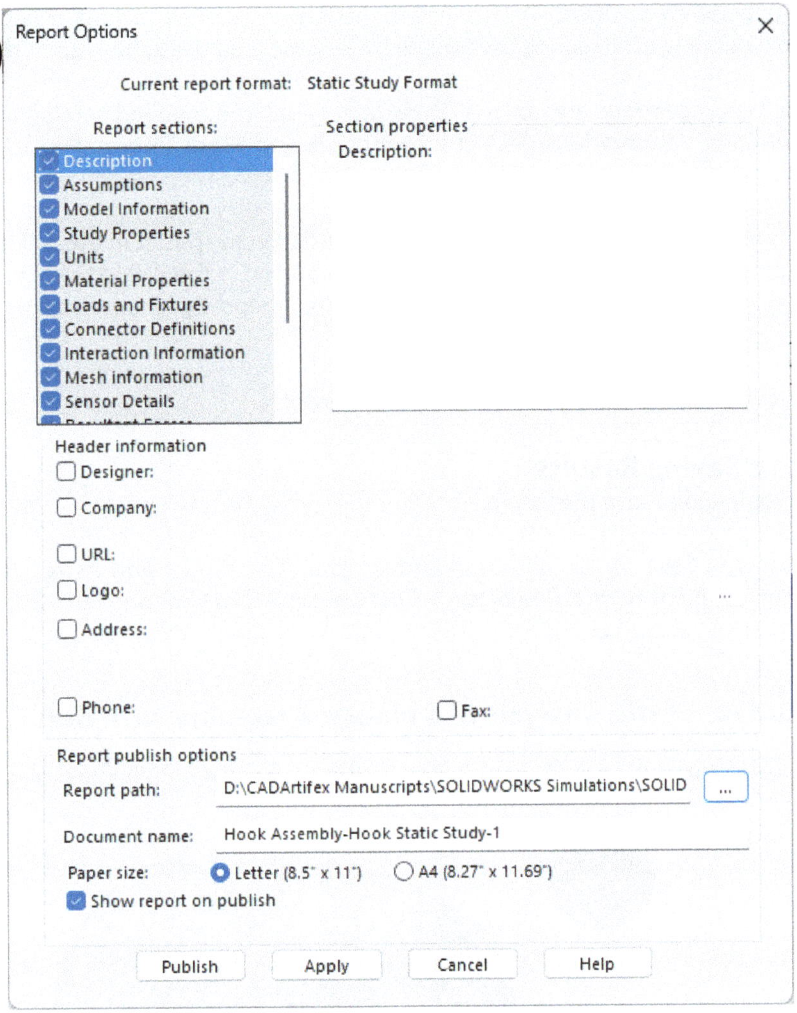

Report sections: The **Report sections** area of the dialog box is used for including or excluding the required sections such as Descriptions, Assumptions, Model Information, and Mesh Information in the report of the current analysis study by selecting or clearing the respective check boxes.

Section properties: The **Section properties** area of the dialog box allows you to customize the properties of the section selected in the **Report sections** area of the dialog box.

Header information: The **Header information** area is used for including information such as the designer's name, company's name, URL, logo, and address in the report by selecting the respective check boxes. For example, to include the name of the company in the report, select the **Company** check box and then enter the name of the company in the respective field that gets enabled in front of the check box.

Report publish options: The options in the **Report publish options** area of the dialog box are used for defining a location to save the file, file name, and the paper size of the report.

2. In the **Report sections area** of the dialog box, select the required section check boxes such as **Descriptions**, **Assumptions**, **Model Information**, and **Mesh Information** to be included in the report.

3. Specify all other required information to be included in the report in the dialog box. Next, click on the **Apply** button and then click on the **Publish** button in the dialog box. The process to publish the report gets started and once it is done, a Word report gets opened for the current analysis study.

4. After reviewing the report, you can save and close it.

Section 13: Saving Results

Now, you need to save the results.

1. Click on the **Save** tool in the **Standard** toolbar. The model and its results are saved in the location > *SOLIDWORKS Simulation* > *Case Studies* > *C04 Case Studies* > *Case Study 1*.

Case Study 2: Static Analysis of a Flange Assembly with Bolt Connectors

In this case study, you will perform the static analysis of a Flange assembly with Bolt connectors, see Figure 4.82.

4.82

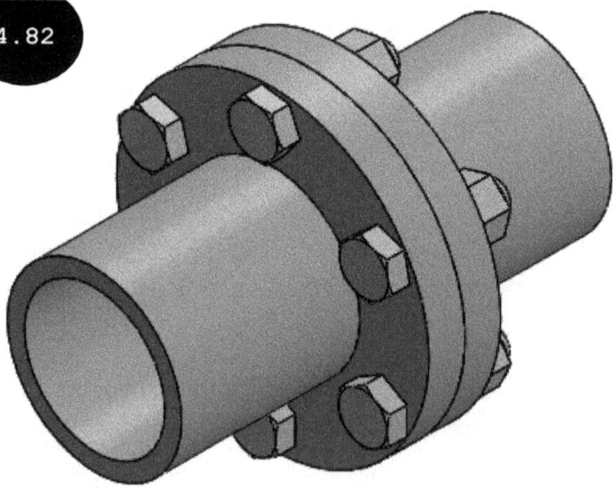

Project Description

The Flange assembly is fixed at one end and an 8000 N downward load is applied on its other end, see Figure 4.83. Both the flanges of the assembly are made up of **AISI 304** steel material and the bolts are made up of **Alloy Steel** material.

4.83

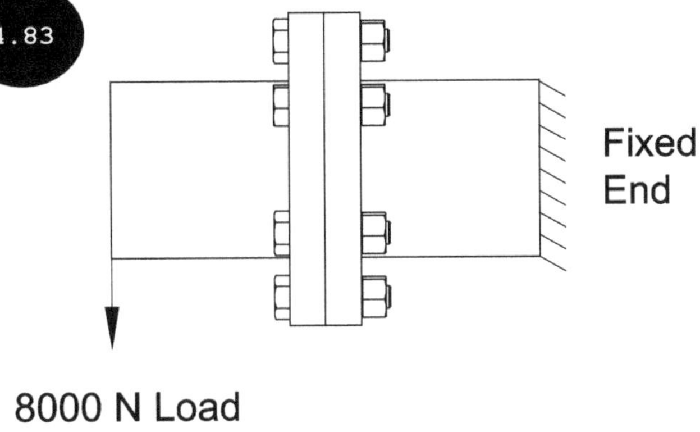

Project Summary

In this case study, you will run a static study of the Flange assembly shown in Figure 4.82. In this assembly, the bolts are added by using the SOLIDWORKS Toolbox. Therefore, you will convert these bolts into bolt connectors, automatically. Also, generate a high-quality curvature-based mesh with default parameters. Besides, define Contact interaction as the global component interaction between the components of the assembly. Specify the unit system to SI (MKS) with displacement in mm and stress in N/mm^2 (MPa) units.

The following sequence summarizes the case study outline:

1. Downloading Files of Chapter 4
2. Opening the Flange Assembly
3. Starting the Static Study and Defining Bolt Connectors
4. Reviewing Properties of Bolt Connectors
5. Assigning Materials
6. Applying Fixtures
7. Applying Interactions
8. Applying the Load
9. Generating the Mesh
10. Running Analysis and Displaying Results
11. Displaying Bolt Connectors Forces
12. Saving Results

Section 1: Downloading Files of Chapter 4

1. Log on to the CADArtifex website (*cadartifex.com/login/*) using the Email OTP sent to your registered email ID. After logging in, download the file for this chapter (**C04 Case Studies**) if it has not already been downloaded in an earlier case study.

2. Save the extracted **C04 Case Studies** folder in the location ***SOLIDWORKS Simulation > Case Studies*** on the local drive of your system. If these folders have not been created earlier, create them in the local drive before saving the extracted folder.

Section 2: Opening the Flange Assembly

1. Start SOLIDWORKS, if not already started.

2. Click on the **Open** button in the **Welcome** dialog box or click on the **Open** tool in the **Standard** toolbar. The **Open** dialog box appears.

3. Browse to the location > ***SOLIDWORKS Simulation* > *Case Studies* > *C04 Case Studies* > *Case Study 2*** of the local drive of your system. Next, select the **Flange Assembly** and then click on the **Open** button in the dialog box. The Flange Assembly opens in SOLIDWORKS.

Section 3: Starting the Static Study and Defining Bolt Connectors

1. Click on the **Simulation** tab in the **CommandManager**. The tools of the **Simulation CommandManager** appear.

2. Click on the **New Study** tool in the **Simulation CommandManager**. The **Study PropertyManager** appears to the left of the graphics area.

3. Ensure that the **Static** button is activated in the **Study PropertyManager**.

   In the Flange assembly, the bolts are added by using the SOLIDWORKS Toolbox. As a result, you can convert them directly into bolt connectors.

4. Select the **Convert Toolbox fasteners to bolt connectors (may take time)** check box in the PropertyManager, see Figure 4.84.

4.84

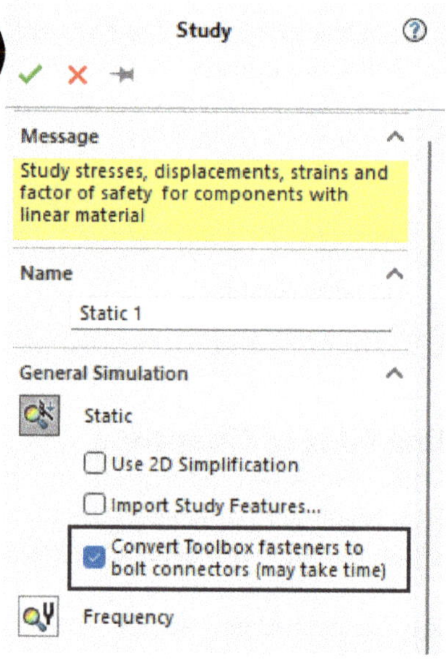

5. Enter **With Bolt Connectors Study** in the **Study name** field in the PropertyManager.

6. Click on the green tick-mark button in the PropertyManager. The **Simulation** window appears which informs that 6 bolt connectors have been created successfully, see Figure 4.85.

4.85

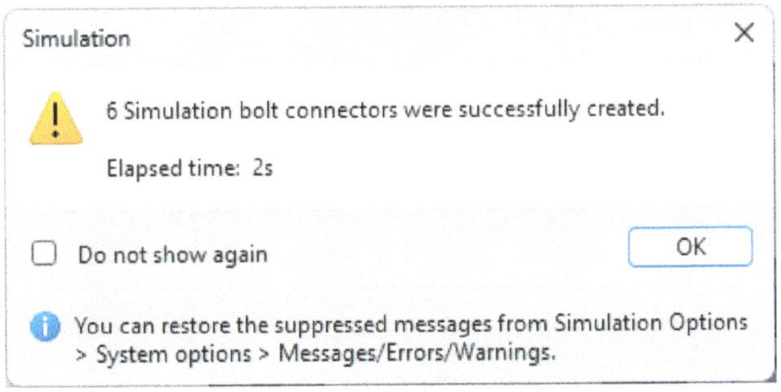

7. Click on the **OK** button in the **Simulation** window. All the bolts of the assembly are converted into bolt connectors and the assembly appears in the graphics area, as shown in Figure 4.86. Also, the six bolt connectors get added under the **Connectors** node in the Simulation Study Tree, see Figure 4.87. This figure shows the expanded view of the **Connectors** node.

4.86

4.87

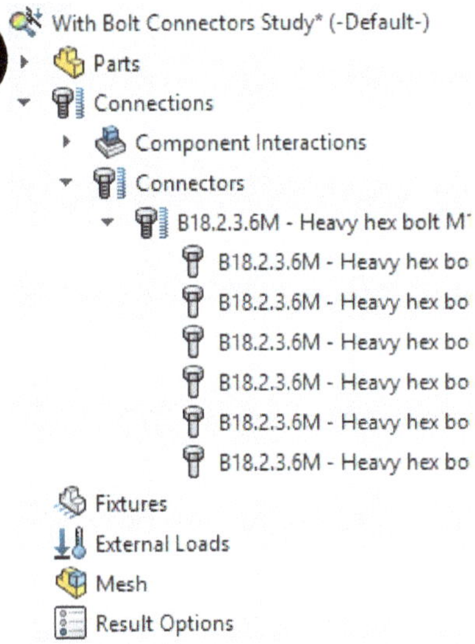

Section 4: Reviewing the Properties of Bolt Connectors

Now, you need to review the properties of bolt connectors.

1. Expand the sub-nodes of the **Connectors** node in the Simulation Study Tree, see Figure 4.87.

2. Right-click on a bolt connector in the expanded **Connectors** node and then click on the **Edit Definition** tool in the shortcut menu that appears, see Figure 4.88. The **Connectors PropertyManager** appears, see Figure 4.89.

4.88

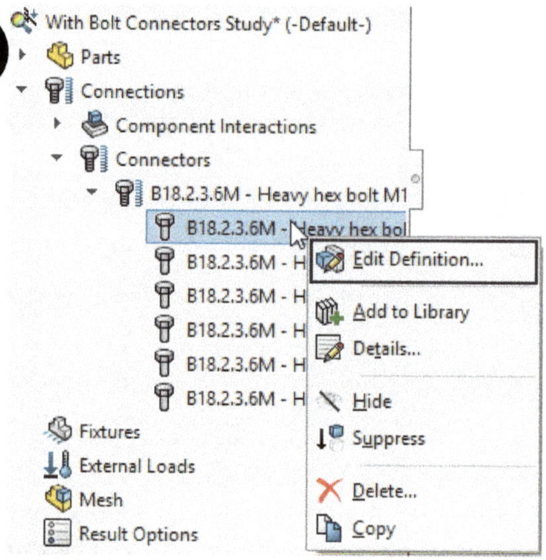

4.89

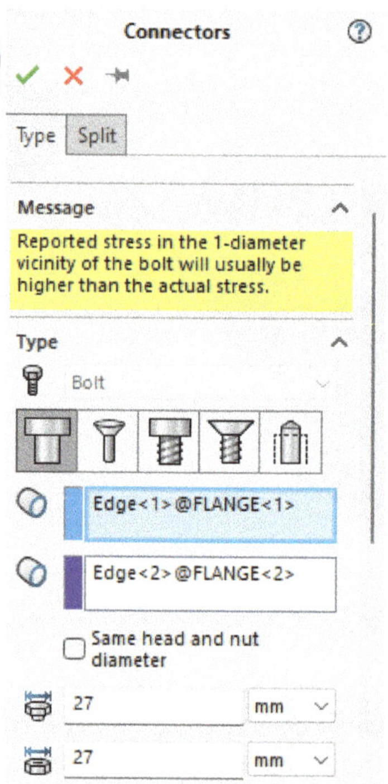

In the **Connectors PropertyManager**, the bolt parameters such as head diameter, nut diameter, nominal shank diameter, bolt strength data, and axial pre-load are automatically extracted from the original bolts, since the original bolts were added by using the SOLIDWORKS Toolbox.

3. Ensure that the Alloy Steel material is assigned to the bolt connector in the **Material** rollout of the PropertyManager.

4. Exit the **Connectors PropertyManager** by clicking on its green tick-mark button.

Note: If the bolts are not added in the original assembly then you need to add the bolt connectors manually by using the **Bolt** tool. To do this, right-click on the **Connections** node in the Simulation Study Tree and then click on the **Bolt** tool in the shortcut menu that appears. The **Connectors PropertyManager** appears. In this PropertyManager, you need to define bolt properties such as bolt head and nut locations, material, and pre-load.

Section 5: Assigning Materials

Now, you need to apply the **AISI 304** steel material to the flanges of the assembly.

1. Right-click on the **Parts** node in the Simulation Study Tree and then click on the **Apply Material to All** tool in the shortcut menu that appears. The **Material** dialog box appears.

2. In this dialog box, expand the **Steel** category of the **SOLIDWORKS Materials** library and then click on the **AISI 304** material.

3. Click on the **Apply** button and then click on the **Close** button. The AISI 304 steel material is assigned to the flanges of the assembly.

Tip: To apply material to each individual component of the assembly, expand the **Parts** node in the Simulation Study Tree and then right-click on a component to display the shortcut menu. Next, click on the **Apply/Edit Material** tool in the shortcut menu to display the **Material** dialog box for applying the material to the selected component.

Section 6: Applying Fixtures

Now, you need to apply the Fixed Geometry fixture to one end of the assembly.

1. Right-click on the **Fixtures** option in the Simulation Study Tree and then click on the **Fixed Geometry** tool in the shortcut menu that appears. The **Fixture PropertyManager** appears to the left of the graphics area.

2. Rotate the model such that you can view the end face of the right Flange component of the assembly and then select it to apply the Fixed Geometry fixture, see Figure 4.90.

3. Click on the green tick-mark button ✓ in the PropertyManager. The Fixed Geometry fixture is applied to the selected face of the component.

4.90

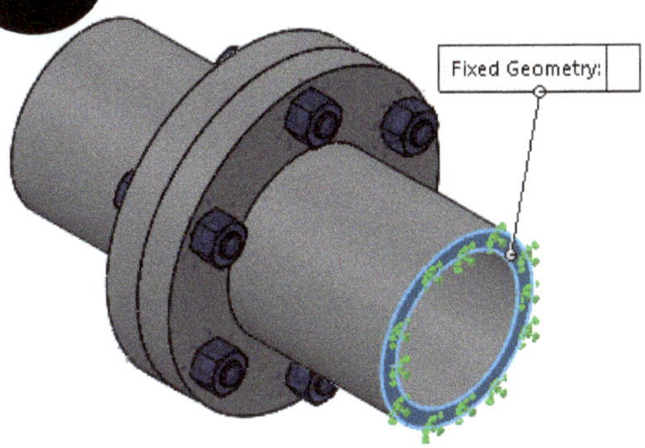

Section 7: Applying Interactions

By default, the Bonded component interaction is applied as the global interaction between all the components of the assembly. You need to edit it to apply the Contact component interaction as the global interaction between the components of the assembly.

1. Expand the **Component Interactions** sub-node of the **Connections** node in the Simulation Study Tree and then right-click on the **Global Interaction (-Bonded-Meshed independently-)** option to display a shortcut menu, see Figure 4.91.

4.91

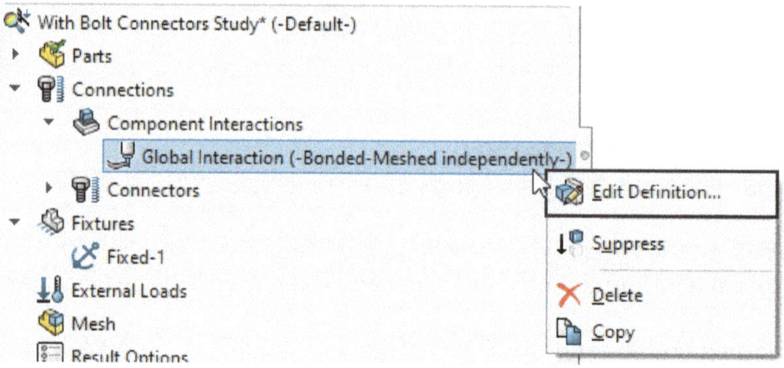

2. Click on the **Edit Definition** tool in the shortcut menu. The **Component Interaction PropertyManager** appears.

3. Select the **Contact** radio button in the **Interaction Type** rollout of the PropertyManager and then click on the green tick-mark button. The Contact component interaction is applied as the global interaction between the assembly components.

Section 8: Applying the Load

Now, you need to apply the downward load on the end face of the left Flange component.

1. Right-click on the **External Loads** option in the Simulation Study Tree and then click on the **Force** tool in the shortcut menu that appears. The **Force/Torque PropertyManager** appears.

2. Select the end face of the left Flange component of the assembly, see Figure 4.92. The symbol of load appears on the selected face.

4.92

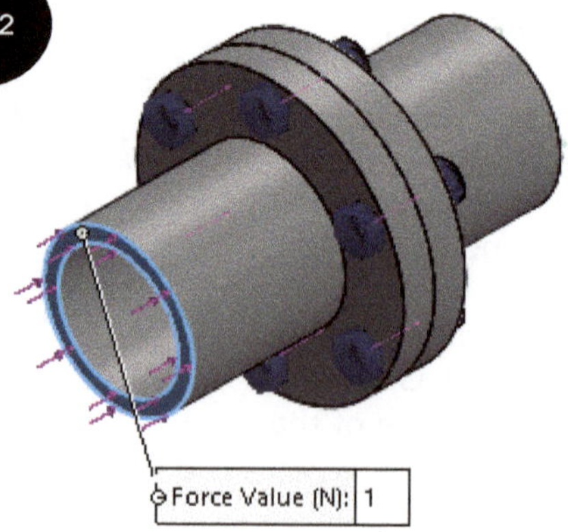

3. Select the **Selected direction** radio button in the **Force/Torque** rollout of the PropertyManager. The **Face, Edge, Plane for Direction** field appears in the rollout.

4. Expand the FeatureManager Design Tree, which is now at the top left corner of the graphics area and then click on the **Top Plane** of the assembly as the reference plane to define the direction of force, see Figure 4.93.

4.93

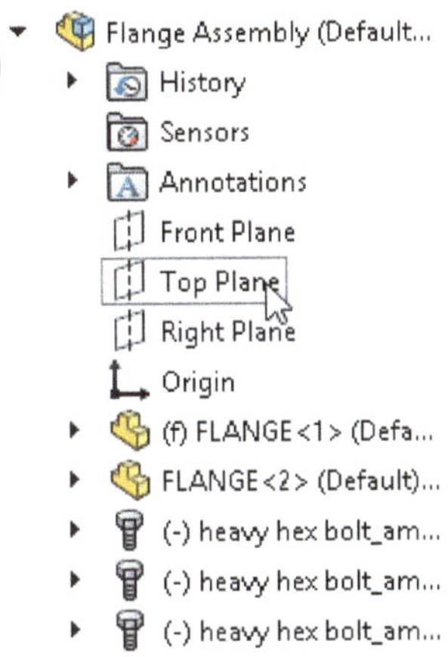

5. Scroll down in the PropertyManager and then click on the **Normal to Plane** button in the **Force** rollout, see Figure 4.94.

6. Enter **8000** in the field enabled in front of the **Normal to Plane** button, see Figure 4.94.

7. Select the **Reverse direction** check box in the PropertyManager to reverse the direction of force downward, see Figure 4.95.

4.94

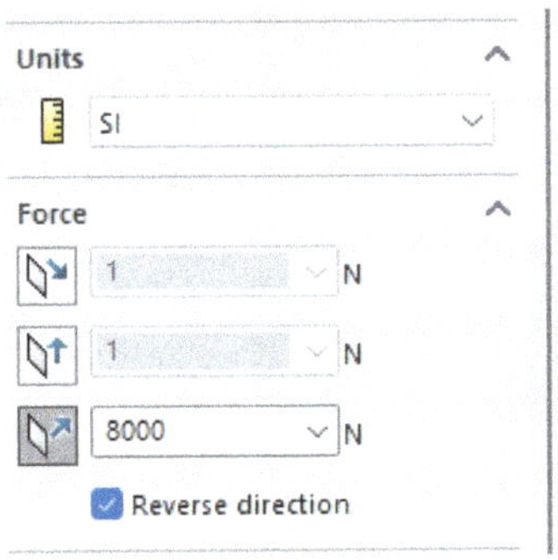

4.95

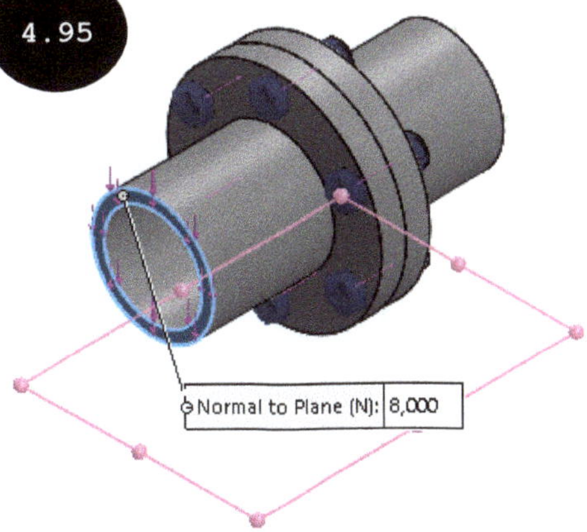

8. Click on the green tick-mark button in the PropertyManager. The 8000 N load is applied on the selected face of the left Flange component.

Section 9: Generating the Mesh

Now, you need to generate the curvature-based mesh with default parameters.

1. Right-click on the **Mesh** option in the Simulation Study Tree and then click on the **Create Mesh** tool in the shortcut menu that appears. The **Mesh PropertyManager** appears.

2. Expand the **Mesh Parameters** rollout of the PropertyManager.

3. Select the **Curvature-based mesh** radio button in the expanded **Mesh Parameters** rollout. Next, accept the other default mesh parameters and then click on the green tick-mark button ✓. The **Mesh Progress** window appears and once the meshing is complete, the meshed model appears, see Figure 4.96.

4.96

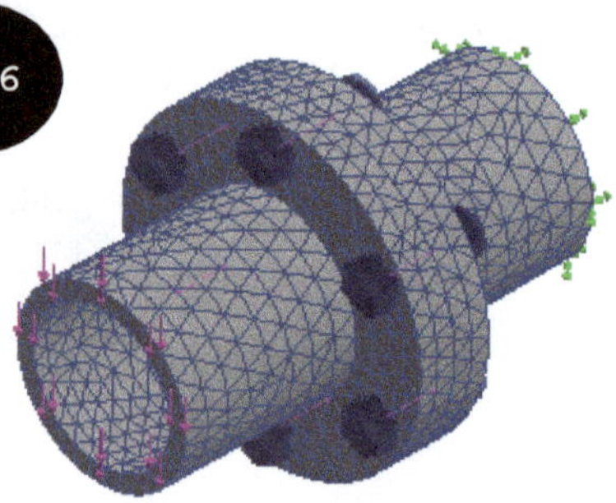

Section 10: Running Analysis and Displaying Results

Now, you need to run the analysis.

1. Click on the **Run This Study** tool in the **Simulation CommandManager**. The **With Bolt Connectors Study** (*name of the study*) window appears which displays the progress of the analysis.

2. After the process of running the analysis is completed, the **Results** folder is added to the Simulation Study Tree with the stress, displacement, and strain results. By default, the **Stress** result is activated in the **Results** folder. As a result, the stress distribution on the model and the von Mises stress plot appear in the graphics area, see Figure 4.97.

4.97

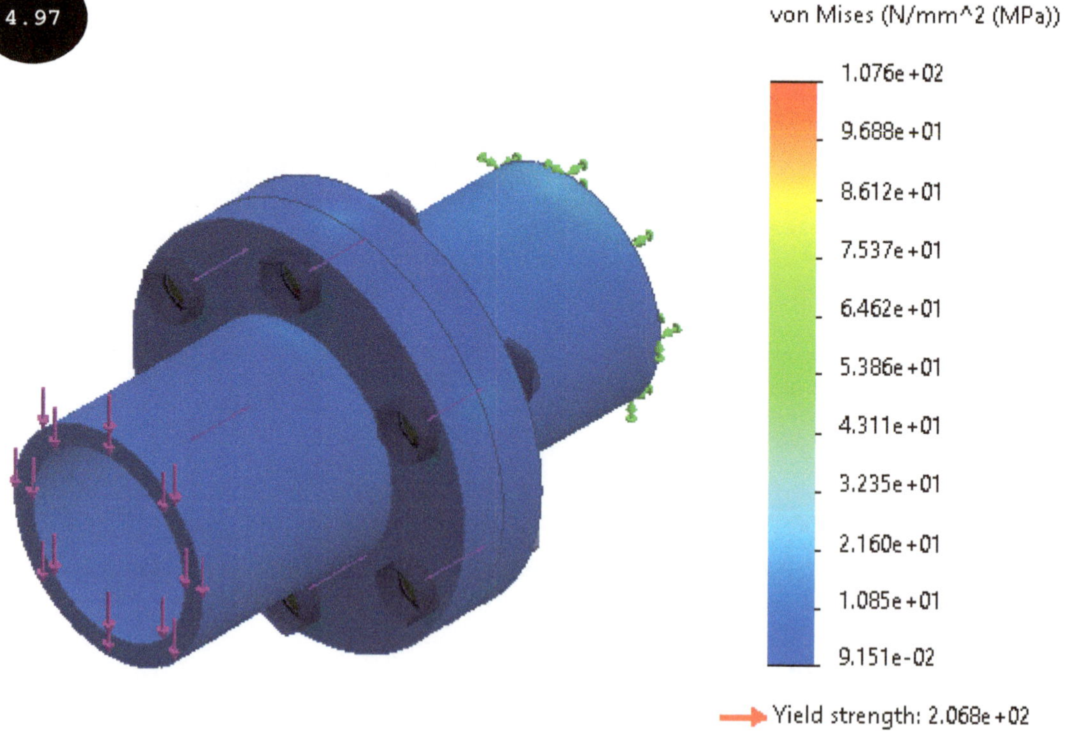

The maximum von Mises stress in the model under the applied load is **1.076e+02** (107.631) N/mm^2 (MPa) which is within the yield stress of the material that is **2.068e+02** (206.807) N/mm^2 (MPa).

3. Double-click on the **Displacement1 (-Res disp-)** option in the **Results** folder of the Simulation Study Tree to display the displacement distribution on the assembly and the resultant displacement (URES) plot. Similarly, display the strain results by clicking on the **Strain1 (-Equivalent-)** option.

4. Display the Factor of Safety plot by clicking on the **Define Factor Of Safety Plot** tool in the shortcut menu which appears by right-clicking on the **Results** folder in Simulation Study Tree.

5. Animate the stress distribution on the model to review the deformed shape of the components and the interaction conditions by using the **Animate** tool.

Section 11: Displaying Bolt Connectors Forces

1. Right-click on the **Results** folder in the Simulation Study Tree and then click on the **List Connector Force** tool in the shortcut menu that appears. The **Result Force PropertyManager** appears, see Figure 4.98.

2. Ensure that the **Connector force** radio button is selected in the **Options** rollout. All the forces such as shear, axial, bending, and torque of each connector appear in the **Connector Force** rollout of the PropertyManager, see Figure 4.98. You can expand the width of the PropertyManager by dragging it to display the results.

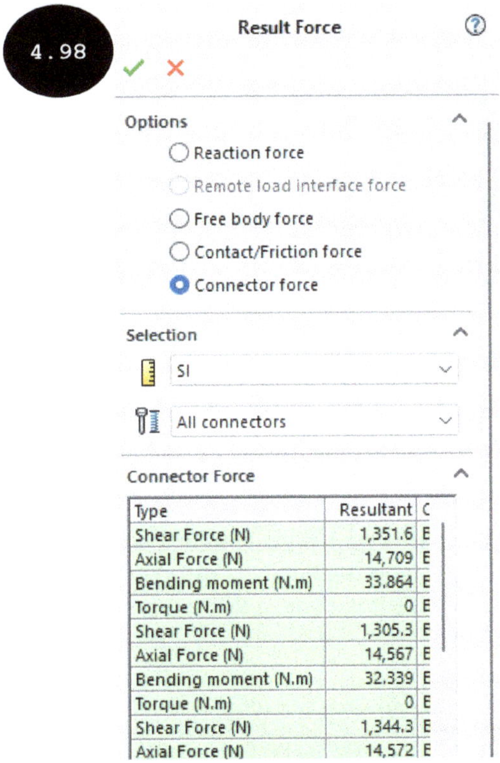

Tip: By default, the **All connectors** option is selected in the **Connector** drop-down list in the **Selection** rollout of the PropertyManager. As a result, the forces such as shear, axial, bending, and torque, developed in all bolt connectors of the assembly appear in the **Connector Force** rollout of the PropertyManager. You can select the required option in this drop-down list to display the forces of the selected connector type only.

3. After reviewing the forces of the bolt connectors, exit the PropertyManager by clicking on its green tick-mark button.

Section 12: Generating a Word Report

Now, you can generate the report for the current analysis study in a Word document.

1. Click on the **Report** tool in the **Simulation CommandManager**, see Figure 4.99. The **Report Options** dialog box appears, see Figure 4.100. The options in this dialog box are discussed earlier.

4.99

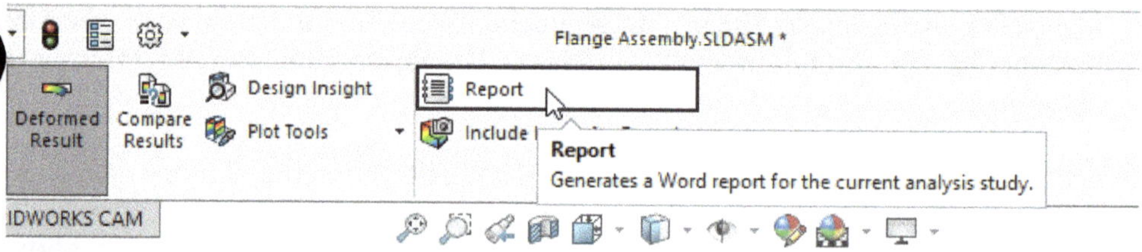

4.100

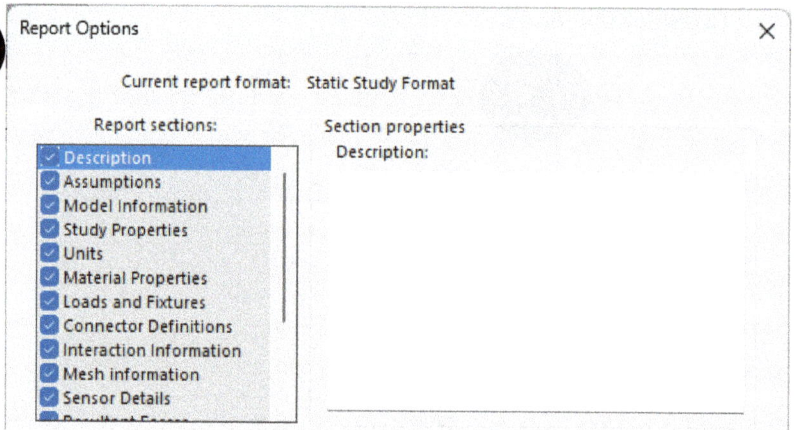

2. In the **Report sections area** of the dialog box, select the required section check boxes such as **Descriptions**, **Assumptions**, **Model Information**, and **Mesh Information** to be included in the report.

3. Specify other required information to be included in the report in the dialog box. Next, click on the **Apply** button and then click on the **Publish** button in the dialog box. The process to publish the report gets started, and once it is done, a Word report gets opened for the current analysis study.

4. After reviewing the report, you can save and close it.

Section 13: Saving Results

Now, you need to save the results.

1. Click on the **Save** tool in the **Standard** toolbar. The model and its results are saved in the location > *SOLIDWORKS Simulation > Case Studies > C04 Case Studies > Case Study 2*.

Case Study 3: Static Analysis of an Assembly with Edge Weld Connectors

In this case study, you will perform the static analysis of a Hanger Assembly with Edge Weld and bolt connectors, see Figure 4.101.

4.101

Project Description

The Hanger Assembly is fixed at one end and a 600 N downward load is applied on its other end, see Figure 4.102. All the components of the assembly are made up of **AISI 1035 Steel (SS)** material.

4.102

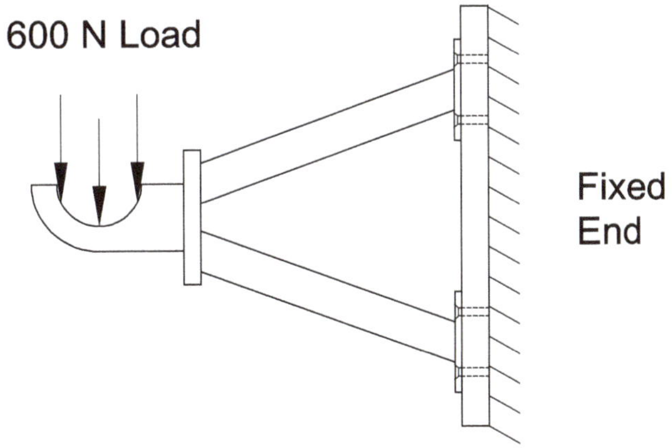

Project Summary

In this case study, you will run a static study of a Hanger assembly shown in Figure 4.101. The connecting rod components of the assembly are surface components and you need to mesh these components with shell elements having 1 mm thickness. Also, you need to apply the edge weld connectors to weld these components (connecting rods) with the other components of the assembly. You need to use the American standard weld with an E60 electrode and a 2 mm estimated weld size for welding the connecting rods. You need to apply the bolt connectors to connect the back plates of the assembly. The bolt connectors are of Alloy Steel material with 100 lbf axial pre-load. You need to generate a high-quality curvature-based mesh with default parameters. Since the assembly has a combination of 3D solid and 2D (surface) geometries, you will experience mixed meshing on the assembly.

The following sequence summarizes the case study outline:

1. Downloading Files of Chapter 4
2. Opening the Hanger Assembly
3. Starting the Static Study
4. Defining Thickness for the Surface (Shell) Geometries
5. Assigning Materials
6. Applying Fixtures
7. Applying Interactions
8. Applying Edge Weld Connectors
9. Applying Bolt Connectors
10. Applying the Load
11. Generating the Mesh
12. Running Analysis and Displaying Results
13. Displaying Weld Results
14. Saving Results

Section 1: Downloading Files of Chapter 4

1. Log on to the CADArtifex website (*cadartifex.com/login/*) using the Email OTP sent to your registered email ID. After logging in, download the file for this chapter (**C04 Case Studies**) if it has not already been downloaded in an earlier case study.

2. Save the extracted **C04 Case Studies** folder in the location ***SOLIDWORKS Simulation > Case Studies*** on the local drive of your system. If these folders have not been created earlier, create them in the local drive before saving the extracted folder.

Section 2: Opening the Hanger Assembly

1. Start SOLIDWORKS, if not already started.

2. Click on the **Open** button in the **Welcome** dialog box or the **Open** tool in the **Standard** toolbar. The **Open** dialog box appears.

3. Browse to the location > *SOLIDWORKS Simulation* > *Case Studies* > *C04 Case Studies* > *Case Study 3*. Next, select the **Hanger Assembly** and then click on the **Open** button in the dialog box. The Hanger Assembly is opened in SOLIDWORKS.

Section 3: Starting the Static Study

1. Click on the **Simulation** tab in the **CommandManager**. The tools of the **Simulation CommandManager** appear.

2. Click on the **New Study** tool in the **Simulation CommandManager**. The **Study PropertyManager** appears to the left of the graphics area.

3. Ensure that the **Static** button is activated in the **Study PropertyManager**.

4. Enter **Hanger ASM with Weld Study** in the **Study name** field of the PropertyManager.

5. Click on the green tick-mark button in the PropertyManager. The tools to perform the static analysis are enabled in the **Simulation CommandManager**. Also, the **Hanger ASM with Weld Study** is added to the Simulation Study Tree, see Figure 4.103.

4.103

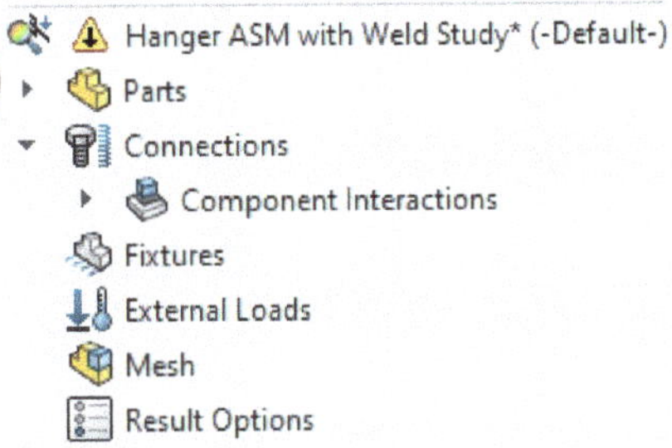

Notice a warning icon on the left of the study name in the Simulation Study Tree, since the assembly has surface components with undefined thickness. You need to define the thickness of the surface components.

Section 4: Defining Thickness for the Surface (Shell) Geometries

As mentioned in the project description, the connecting rod components of the assembly are surface components and you need to define the thickness for these components.

1. Expand the **Parts** node in the Simulation Study Tree. All the components of the assembly appear in the expanded **Parts** node, see Figure 4.104.

4.104

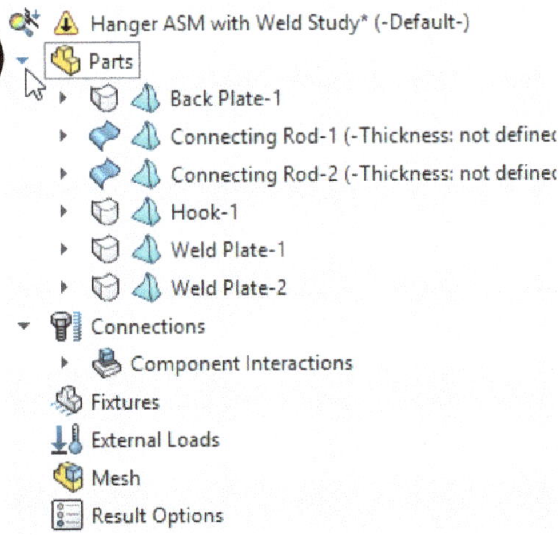

2. Right-click on the **Connecting Rod-1** surface component in the **Parts** node of the Simulation Study Tree and then click on the **Edit Definition** tool in the shortcut menu that appears, see Figure 4.105. The **Shell Definition PropertyManager** appears to the left of the graphics area.

4.105

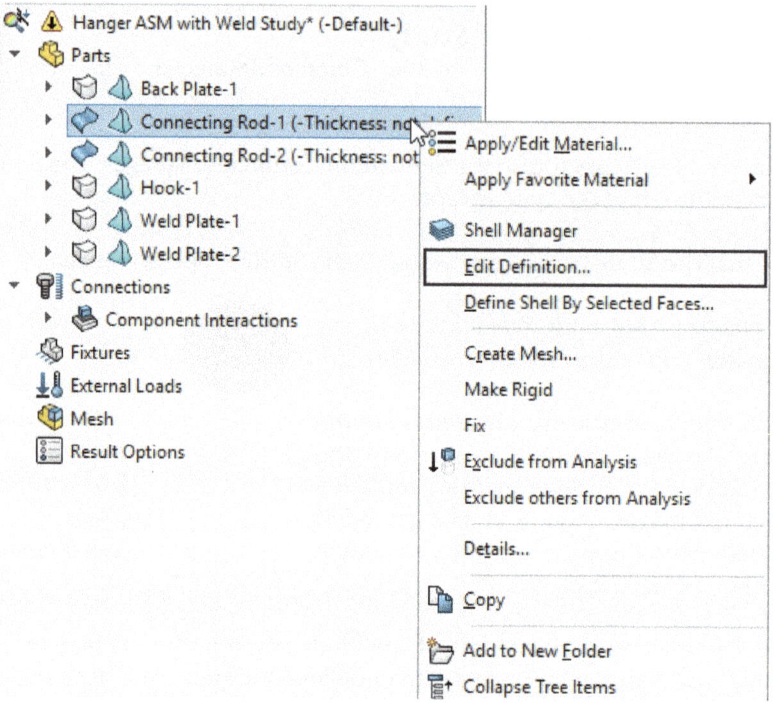

3. Enter 1 mm in the **Shell thickness** field of the PropertyManager and then click on the green tick-mark button. The thickness for the selected component is specified as 1 mm.

4. Similarly, specify the 1 mm thickness to the second connecting rod component (**Connecting Rod-2**) of the assembly.

Section 5: Assigning Materials

Now, you need to apply the **AISI 1035 Steel** material to all the components of the assembly.

1. Right-click on the **Parts** node in the Simulation Study Tree and then click on the **Apply Material to All** tool in the shortcut menu that appears. The **Material** dialog box appears.

2. Select the **AISI 1035 Steel (SS)** material in the **Steel** category of the **SOLIDWORKS Materials** library and then click on the **Apply** button in the dialog box. Next, click on the **Close** button to close the dialog box. The AISI 1035 Steel (SS) material is assigned to all the components of the assembly.

Tip: To apply a material to each individual component of the assembly, expand the **Parts** node of the Simulation Study Tree and then right-click on a component to display a shortcut menu. Next, click on the **Apply/Edit Material** tool in the shortcut menu to display the **Material** dialog box for applying the material to the selected component.

Section 6: Applying Fixtures

Now, you need to apply the Fixed Geometry fixture.

1. Invoke the **Fixture PropertyManager** and then apply the Fixed Geometry fixture on the back face of the Black Plate component, see Figure 4.106. Next, exit the PropertyManager.

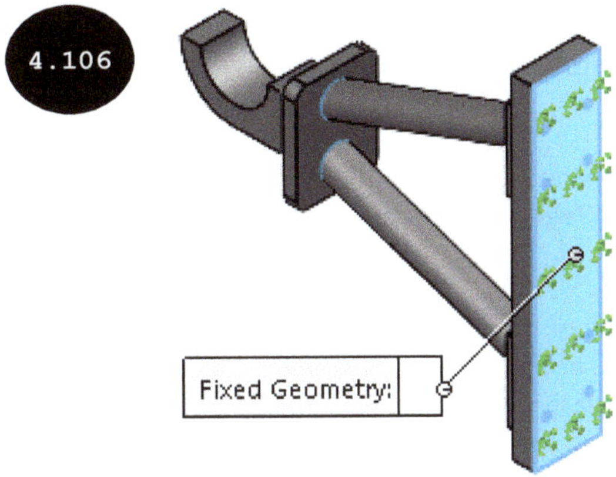

Section 7: Applying Interactions

You need to apply the Contact component interaction between the Back Plate and Weld Plate components of the assembly.

1. Right-click on the **Connections** node in the Simulation Study Tree and then select the **Component Interaction** option in the shortcut menu that appears. The **Component Interaction PropertyManager** appears.
2. Select the **Contact** radio button in the **Interaction Type** rollout of the PropertyManager.
3. Select the upper Weld Plate and the Back Plate in the graphics area, see Figure 4.107. The components get selected. Next, click on the green tick-mark button. The Contact component interaction gets applied between the selected components.
4. Similarly, apply the Contact component interaction between the lower Weld Plate and the Back Plate components, see Figure 4.108.

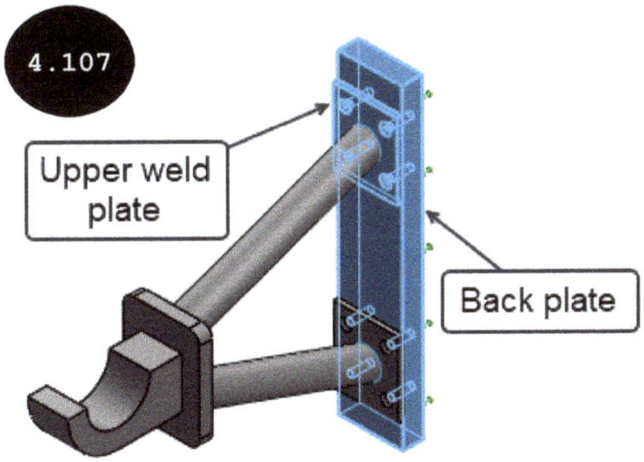

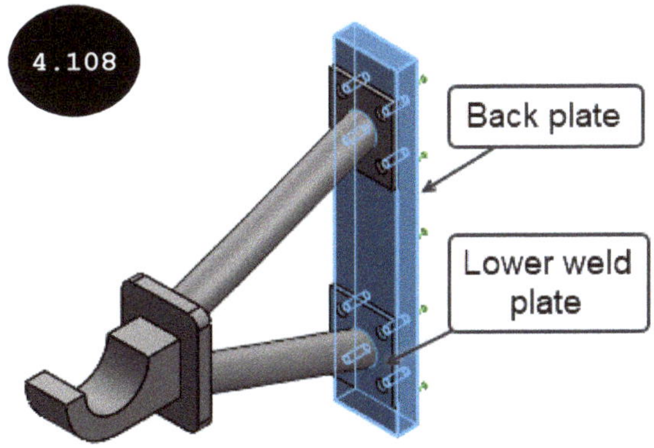

Section 8: Applying Edge Weld Connectors

Now, you need to apply the edge weld connectors to weld the connecting rod components of the assembly.

1. Right-click on the **Connections** node in the Simulation Study Tree and then click on the **Edge Weld** tool in the shortcut menu that appears. The **Edge Weld Connector PropertyManager** appears, see Figure 4.109.

4.109

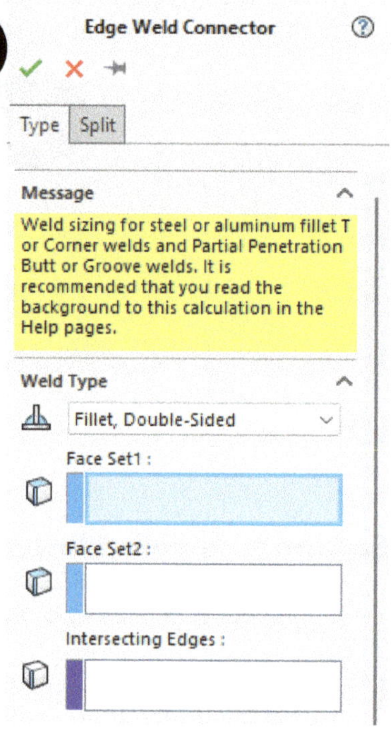

2. Select the **Fillet, Single-Sided** option in the **Type** drop-down list of the **Weld Type** rollout in the PropertyManager.
3. Select the cylindrical face of the upper connecting rod as the first weld face, see Figure 4.110. The name of the selected face appears in the **Face Set 1** field of the PropertyManager.
4. Click on the **Face Set 2** field in the PropertyManager and then select the front face of the upper weld plate as the second weld face, see Figure 4.111. The intersecting edge between the selected faces is defined automatically, and the preview of the weld appears with the default estimated weld size at the intersecting edge.

4.110

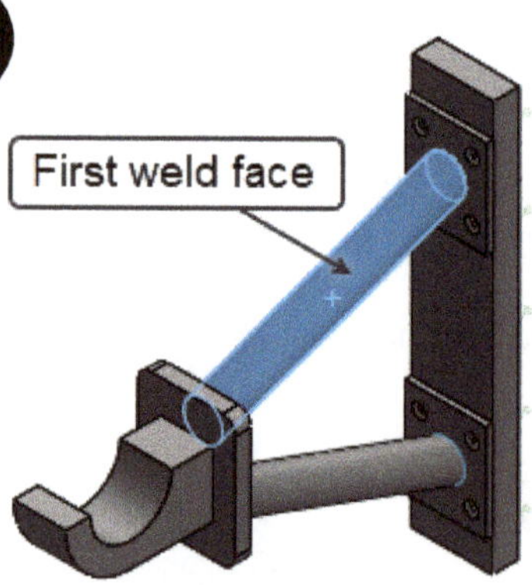

4.111

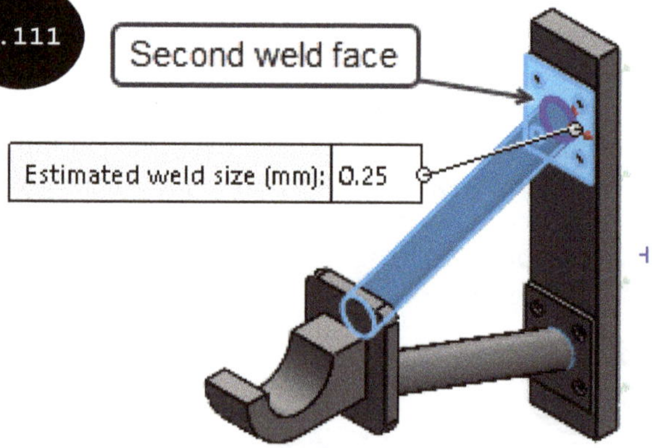

5. Select the **American Standard** radio button in the **Weld Sizing** rollout of the PropertyManager.
6. Select the **E60** option in the **Electrode** drop-down list and then enter **2** mm in the **Estimated weld size** field of the **Weld Sizing** rollout.
7. Accept the remaining default options and then click on the green tick-mark button in the PropertyManager. The single-sided edge weld is applied, see Figure 4.112.

8. Similarly, add three more edge welds (Weld 2, Weld 3, and Weld 4) on the intersecting edges of the connecting rod components, see Figure 4.113.

4.112

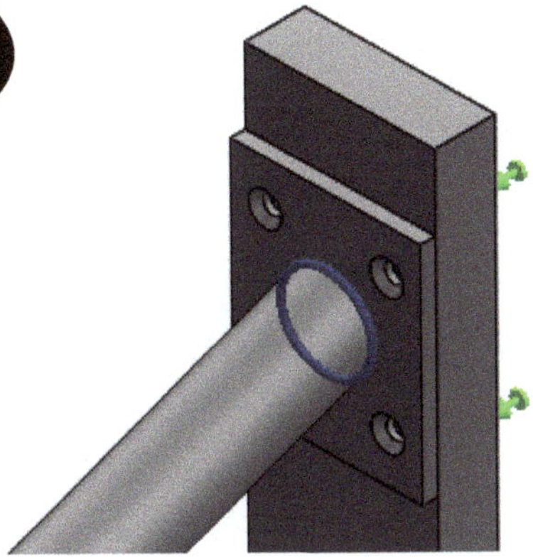

4.113

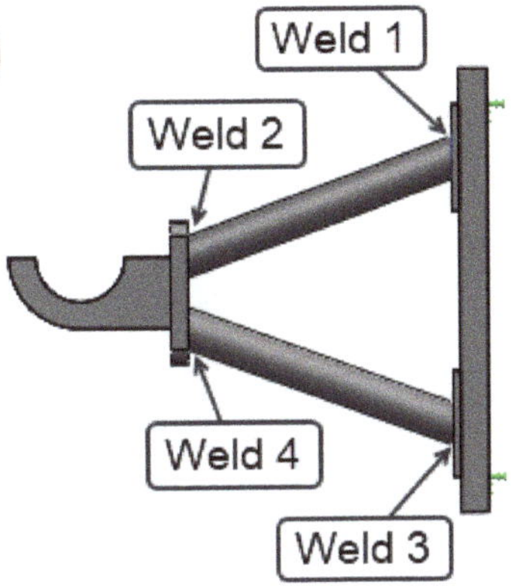

Section 9: Applying Bolt Connectors

Now, you need to apply the bolt connectors.

1. Right-click on the **Connections** node in the Simulation Study Tree and then click on the **Bolt** tool in the shortcut menu that appears. The **Connectors PropertyManager** appears, see Figure 4.114.

2. Click on the **Countersink with Nut** button  in the **Type** rollout of the PropertyManager.

4.114

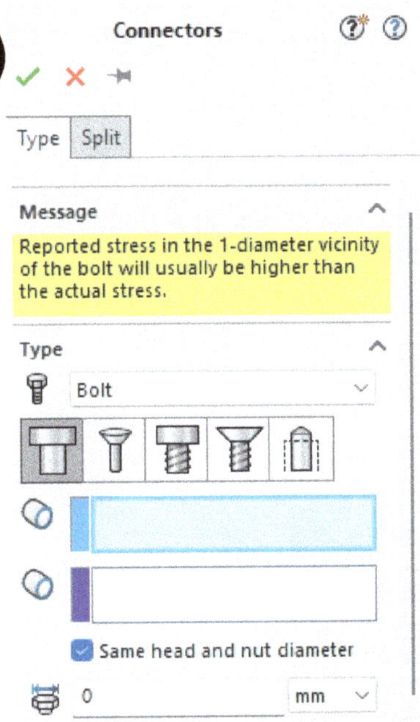

3. Click on the **Conical Face** field in the **Type** rollout of the PropertyManager and then select the conical face of the upper right countersink hole, see Figure 4.115.

4. Click on the **Circular Edge of The Bolt Nut Hole** field in the **Type** rollout and then select the circular edge of the back plate to define the nut location, see Figure 4.116. Note that you need to rotate the assembly to select the circular edge of the back plate.

4.115

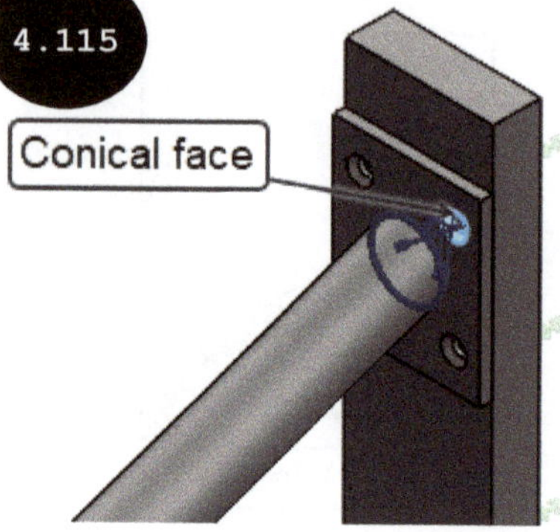

4.116

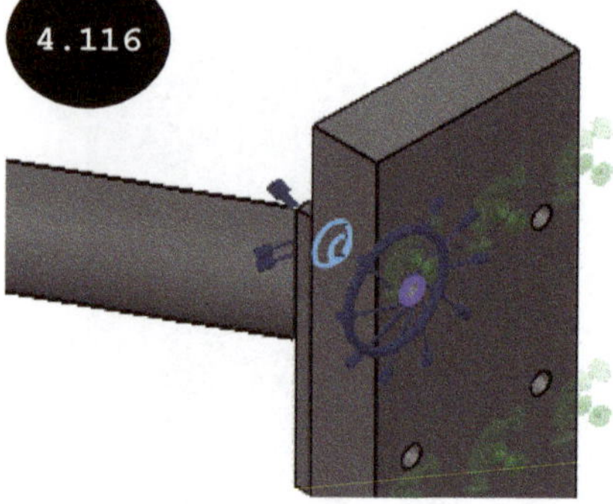

In the **Nut Diameter** and **Nominal Shank Diameter** fields of the **Type** rollout, the nut diameter and nominal shank diameter of the bolt are defined automatically based on the conical face selected.

5. Ensure that the Alloy Steel material is selected as the material of the bolt connector in the **Material** rollout of the PropertyManager.

6. Select the **English (IPS)** option in the **Unit** drop-down list of the **Pre-load** rollout in the PropertyManager as the unit to define the pre-load of the bolt connector.

7. Select the **Axial** radio button and then enter **100** lbf in the **Axial load** field of the **Pre-load** rollout in the PropertyManager.

8. Accept the remaining default options and then click on the green tick-mark button in the PropertyManager. The countersink bolt connector is added, see Figure 4.117.

9. Similarly, add the remaining seven countersink bolt connectors with the same parameters. Figure 4.118 shows the assembly after adding all the bolt connectors.

4.117

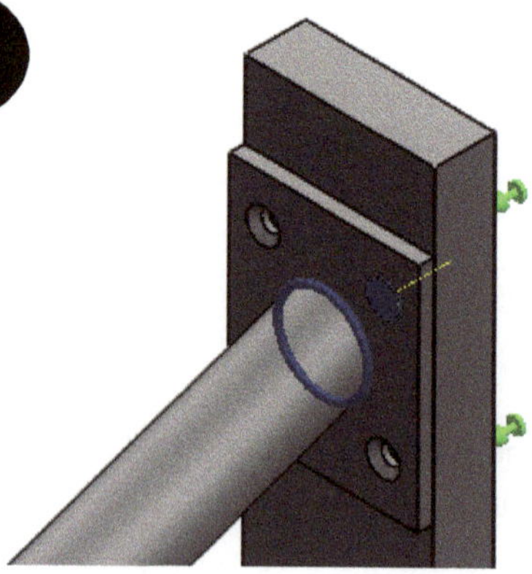

4.118

Section 10: Applying the Load

Now, you need to apply the load.

1. Right-click on the **External Loads** option in the Simulation Study Tree and then click on the **Force** tool in the shortcut menu that appears. The **Force/Torque PropertyManager** appears.

4.119

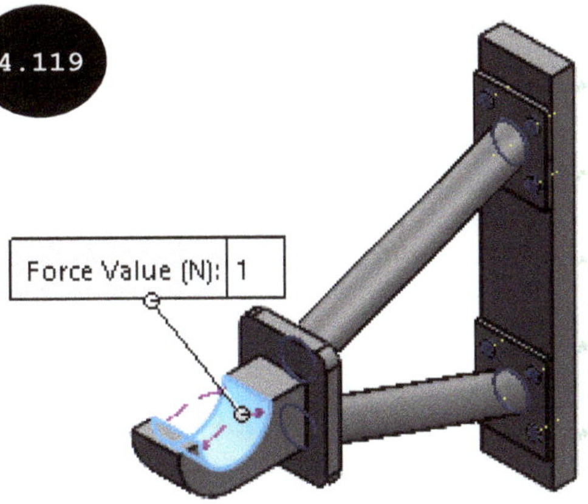

2. Select the inner circular face of the Hook component, see Figure 4.119. The symbols of the load appear on the selected face.

3. Select the **Selected direction** radio button in the **Force/Torque** rollout of the PropertyManager. The **Face, Edge, Plane for Direction** field appears in the rollout.

4. Expand the FeatureManager Design Tree, which is now at the top left corner of the graphics area and then click on the **Top Plane** of the assembly as the reference plane to define the direction of force, see Figure 4.120.

5. Scroll down in the PropertyManager and then click on the **Normal to Plane** button in the **Force** rollout, see Figure 4.121.

6. Enter **600** in the field enabled in front of the **Normal to Plane** button, see Figure 4.121.

4.120

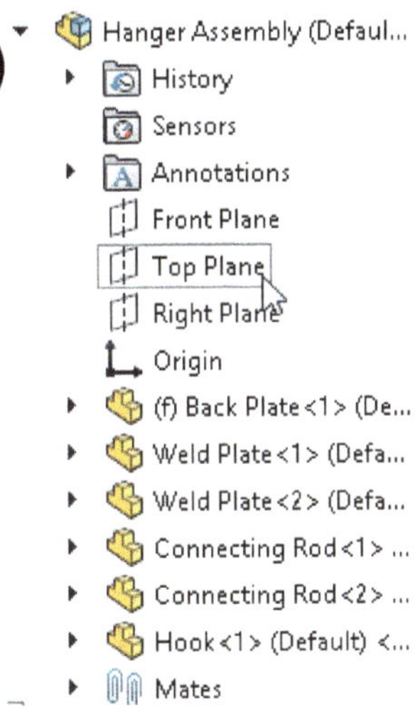

4.121

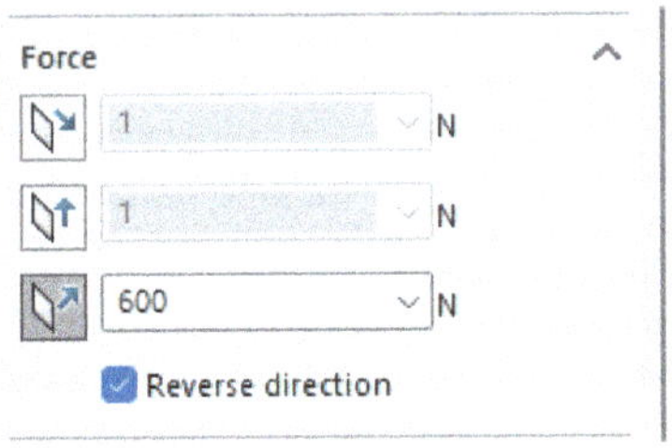

7. Select the **Reverse direction** check box in the PropertyManager to reverse the direction of force downward, see Figure 4.122.

8. Click on the green tick-mark button ✓ in the PropertyManager. The 600 N load is applied on the selected face of the component.

Section 11: Generating the Mesh

Now, you need to generate the curvature-based mesh with default parameters.

1. Right-click on the **Mesh** option in the Simulation Study Tree and then click on the **Create Mesh** tool in the shortcut menu that appears to invoke the **Mesh PropertyManager**.

2. Expand the **Mesh Parameters** rollout of the PropertyManager and then select the **Curvature-based mesh** radio button. Next, accept the other default mesh parameters and then click on the green tick-mark button. The **Mesh Progress** window appears and once the meshing is complete, the meshed model appears, see Figure 4.123.

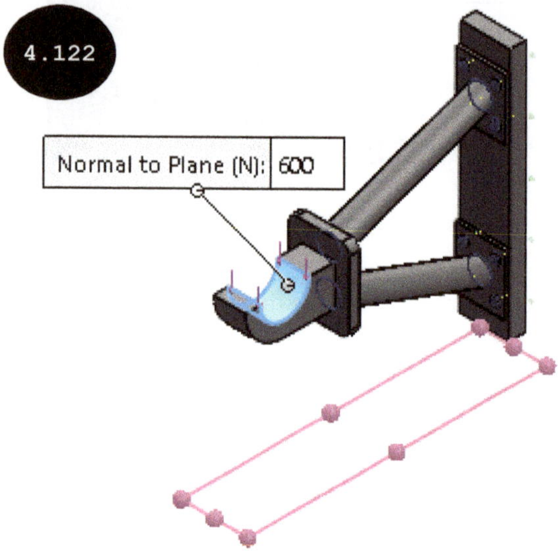

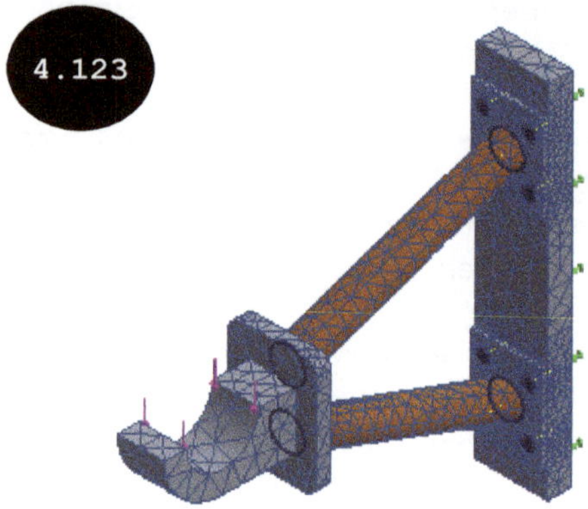

Note: The 3D solid components of the assembly are meshed with solid tetrahedral elements and the surface components (connecting rods) are meshed with triangular shell elements.

Section 12: Running Analysis and Displaying Results

Now, you need to run the analysis.

1. Click on the **Run This Study** tool in the **Simulation CommandManager**. The **Hanger ASM with Weld Study** (*name of the study*) window appears which displays the progress of the analysis.

2. After the process of running the analysis is complete, the **Results** folder is added to the Simulation Study Tree with the stress, displacement, and strain results. By default, the **Stress** result is activated in the **Results** folder. As a result, the stress distribution on the model and the von Mises stress plot appear in the graphics area, see Figure 4.124.

4.124

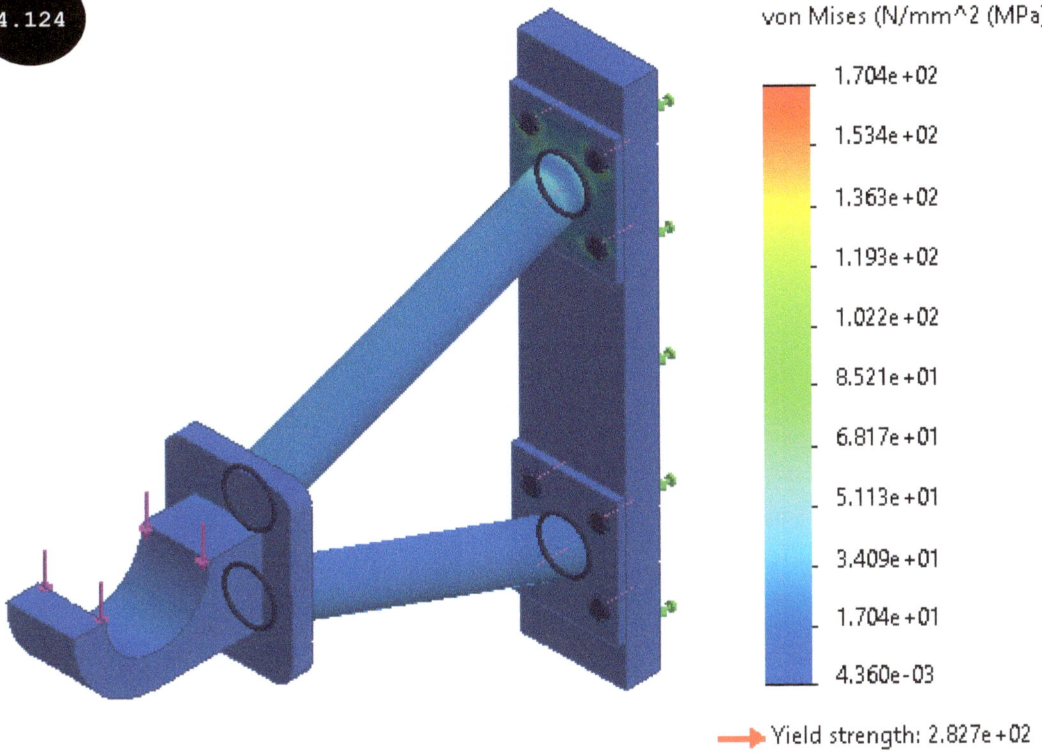

The maximum von Mises stress in the model under the applied load is **1.704e+02** (170.411) N/mm^2 (MPa) which is within the yield stress of the material that is **2.827e+02** (282.685) N/mm^2 (MPa).

3. Annotate the maximum and minimum stress areas of the assembly by editing the stress plot.

4. Double-click on the **Displacement1 (-Res disp-)** option in the **Results** folder to display the displacement distribution on the assembly and the resultant displacement (URES) plot. Similarly, display the strain results by clicking on the **Strain1 (-Equivalent-)** option.

Section 13: Displaying Weld Results

1. Right-click on the **Results** folder in the Simulation Study Tree and then click on the **List Weld Results** tool in the shortcut menu that appears. The **Edge Weld Results PropertyManager** appears, see Figure 4.125.

2. By default, the **Edge Weld Connector-1** option is selected in the **Type** drop-down list of the PropertyManager, see Figure 4.125. As a result, the weld results such as minimum and maximum required weld size, weld throat size, shear forces, and bending moment of the selected weld connector appear in the PropertyManager. Notice that the maximum weld size of this weld connector is **1.5938** mm which is smaller than the specified estimated weld size that is 2 mm. As a result, the selected weld connector can withstand the applied load conditions.

4.125

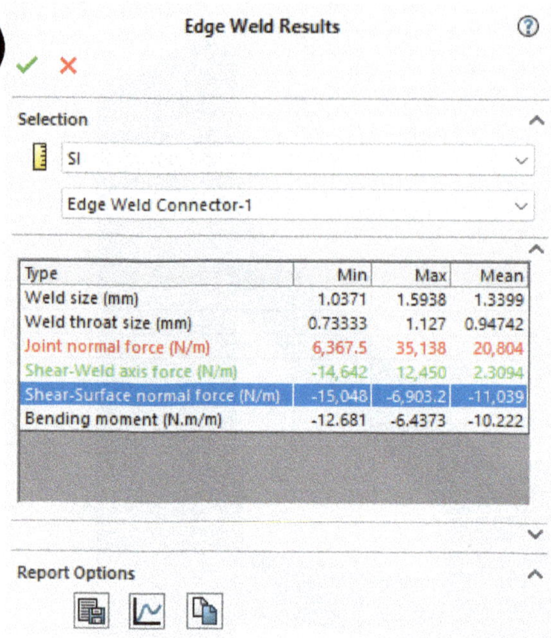

3. Click on the **Plot** button in the **Report Options** rollout of the PropertyManager. The **Edge-weld size plot** window appears, see Figure 4.126. This window displays the required weld size and the weld throat size along the weld seam. After reviewing the weld size plot, close this window.

4.126

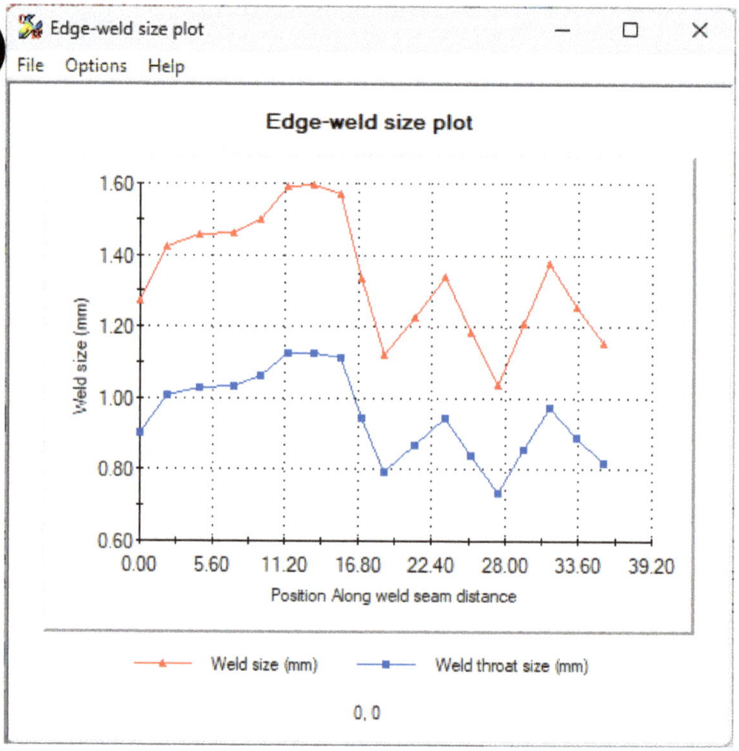

4. Similarly, review the weld results of the remaining weld connectors by selecting the respective weld connector in the **Type** drop-down list of the PropertyManager.

5. After reviewing the weld results, close the PropertyManager by clicking on its green tick-mark button.

Section 14: Saving Results

Now, you need to save the results.

1. Click on the **Save** tool in the **Standard** toolbar. The model and its results are saved in the location > *SOLIDWORKS Simulation > Case Studies > C04 Case Studies > Case Study 3*.

Hands-on Test Drive 1: Static Analysis of a Leaf Spring Assembly

Perform the linear static analysis of a Leaf Spring assembly, (see Figure 4.127) and determine the stress, displacement, strain, and factor of safety under a loading condition.

Project Description

The Leaf Spring assembly is fixed at its bottom leaf and a total of 3000 N load is uniformly distributed along both the ends of the top leaf of the assembly, see Figure 4.128. All leafs of the assembly are made up of **Alloy Steel (SS)** material.

4.127

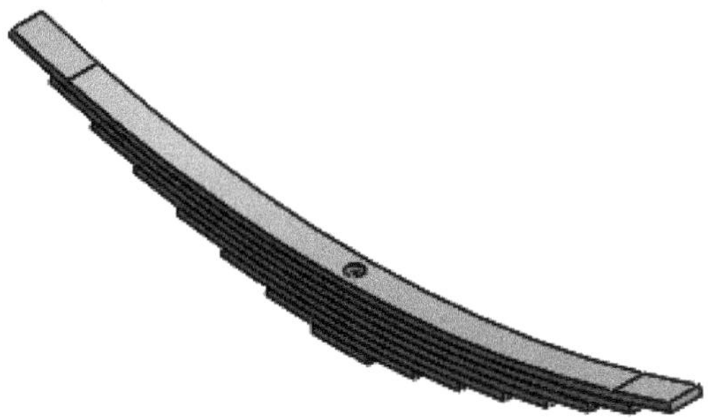

4.128

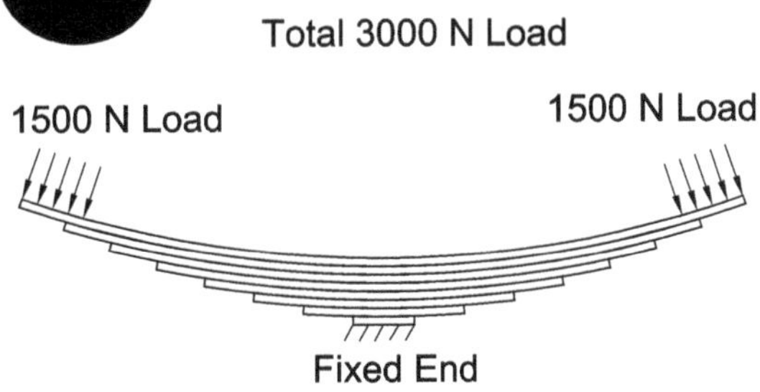

Project Summary

Run a static study of a Leaf Spring assembly shown in Figure 4.127. You need to define the Contact interaction as the component interaction between the components of the assembly with no gap allowance. You need to generate a high-quality curvature-based mesh with default parameters. Specify the unit system to SI (MKS) with displacement in mm and stress in N/mm^2 (MPa) units.

Hint: *In addition to the Fixed Geometry fixture on the bottom face of the lower leaf, you also need to apply the Fixed Geometry fixture on the cylindrical hole faces at the center of all leafs. Besides, you need to restrict the translation movement of all leaf components along the normal direction of their front planar faces.*

Hands-on Test Drive 2: Static Analysis of a Car Jack Assembly

Perform the linear static analysis of a Car Jack Assembly, (see Figure 4.129) and determine the stress, displacement, strain, and factor of safety under a loading condition.

4.129

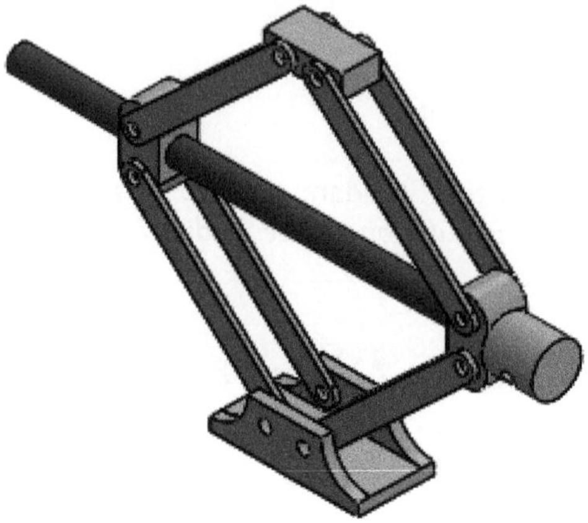

Project Description

The Car Jack Assembly is fixed at its Base Plate and a 900 N axial load is uniformly distributed along the top face of the Top Support component of the assembly, see Figure 4.130. All components of the assembly are made up of **Alloy Steel** material.

4.130

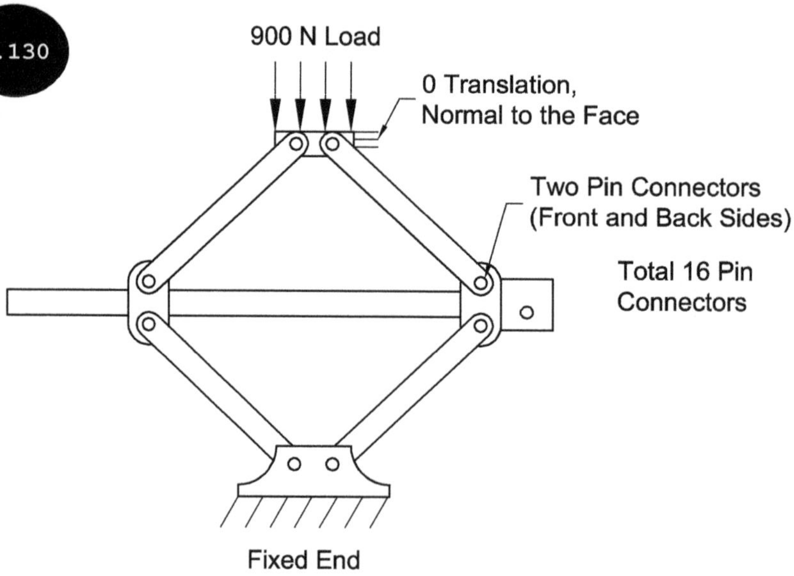

Project Summary

Run a static study on the Car Jack Assembly shown in Figure 4.129. You need to define the Contact interaction as the global component interaction between the components of the assembly. Also, you need to apply total 16 Pin Connectors to allow the rotational movement of all the Link components against the pin. You need to generate a high-quality curvature-based mesh with default mesh parameters. Also, determine the stress, displacement, strain, and factor of safety of the assembly under the applied load. Also, animate the displacement distribution on the model in the true scale. Specify the unit system to SI (MKS) with displacement in mm and stress in N/mm^2 (MPa) units.

Hint: *In addition to the Fixed Geometry fixture on the bottom component, you need to restrict the translation movement of the top component where the load is applied, along the normal direction of its right planar faces, see Figure 4.130.*

Summary

In this chapter, you explored the various interactions and connectors available in SOLIDWORKS Simulation and their role in assembly analysis. You learned how to define interaction conditions and apply connectors to accurately represent real-world behavior in static analysis.

Through case studies, you gained hands-on experience in setting up and analyzing assemblies, understanding how different interaction types affect simulation results. Additionally, you reviewed results for both the entire assembly and individual components, allowing for a deeper evaluation of structural performance.

These concepts provide a strong foundation for performing reliable assembly simulations and optimizing design accuracy.

Questions

Complete the following sentences:

- The ________ interaction is used for preventing interference between components.
- The ________ interaction is used for determining the stresses between the components having interference with each other.
- In SOLIDWORKS Simulation, the interactions are divided into two categories: ________ and ________.
- By default, the ________ component interaction is applied as the global interaction between all the components of the assembly.
- The ________ mesh is used for achieving a smooth mesh transition between the connecting areas of different assembly components.

- You can apply the _________ connector between two components that are connected by a rigid bar.
- The _________ tool is used for displaying forces such as shear, axial, bending, and torque of each connector in the assembly.
- The _________ tool is used for displaying the weld results such as minimum and maximum required weld size, weld throat size, shear forces, and bending moment of the weld connectors.
- The _________ check box of the **Study PropertyManager** is used for converting the bolts (fasteners) of the assembly which are added by using the SOLIDWORKS Toolbox into the bolt connectors, automatically.

CHAPTER

5

Adaptive Mesh Methods

In this chapter, the following topics will be discussed:

- Working with H-Adaptive Mesh
- Working with P-Adaptive Mesh
- Static Analysis of a C-Bracket with Adaptive Meshing
- Static Analysis of a Wrench with Adaptive Meshing

In previous chapters, you learned various meshing techniques for components and assemblies, including standard mesh, curvature-based mesh, and blended curvature-based mesh. You also explored mesh control, which allows refining mesh elements in high-stress regions to improve accuracy.

Beyond manual mesh refinement, adaptive meshing offers an automated approach to optimizing mesh density. It iteratively refines mesh elements in high-stress areas until the desired accuracy is achieved. SOLIDWORKS Simulation provides two adaptive mesh methods:

- H-adaptive meshing
- P-adaptive meshing

The following sections will explore both these methods in detail.

Working with H-Adaptive Mesh

The H-adaptive meshing method automatically refines the mesh in high-stress areas by performing multiple iterations with progressively smaller element sizes until the desired accuracy is reached. To use H-adaptive meshing, you need to define:

- The target accuracy level
- The maximum number of iterations (up to five)

During each iteration, SOLIDWORKS Simulation compares the results against the specified accuracy level and refines the mesh accordingly. The process continues until either the target accuracy is achieved, or the maximum number of iterations is reached.

Figure 5.1 shows a curvature-based mesh without H-adaptive meshing, while Figure 5.2 demonstrates the effect of H-adaptive meshing. Notice that in Figure 5.2, elements are smaller in high-stress areas and larger in low-stress areas, optimizing both accuracy and computational efficiency.

5.1

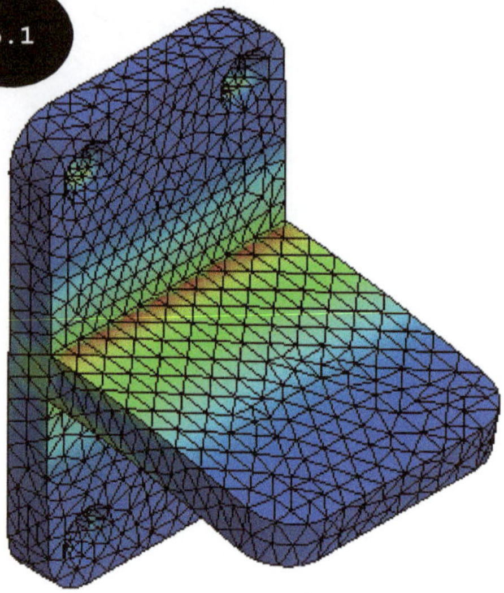

5.2

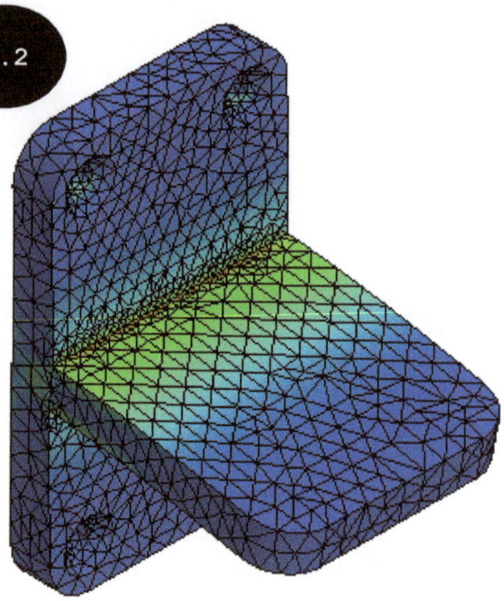

To mesh a model with H-adaptive meshing, right-click on the study name in the Simulation Study Tree. A shortcut menu appears, see Figure 5.3. In this shortcut menu, click on the **Properties** tool. The **Static** dialog box appears. In this dialog box, click on the **Adaptive** tab. Options for specifying an adaptive mesh method and the respective parameters appear in the dialog box, see Figure 5.4.

5.3

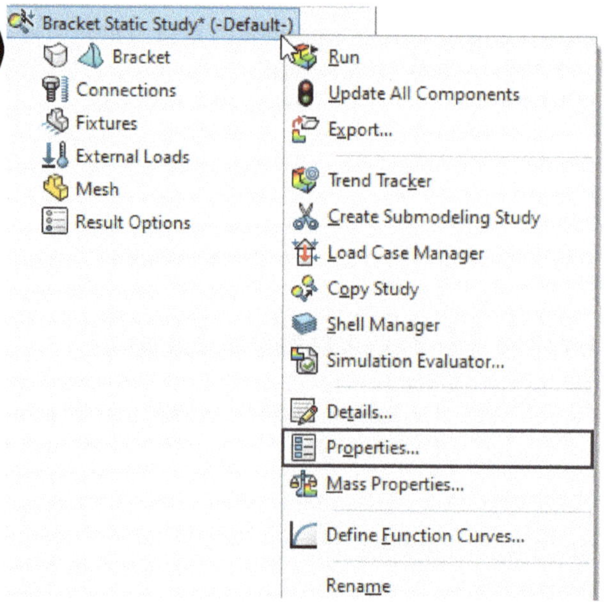

5.4

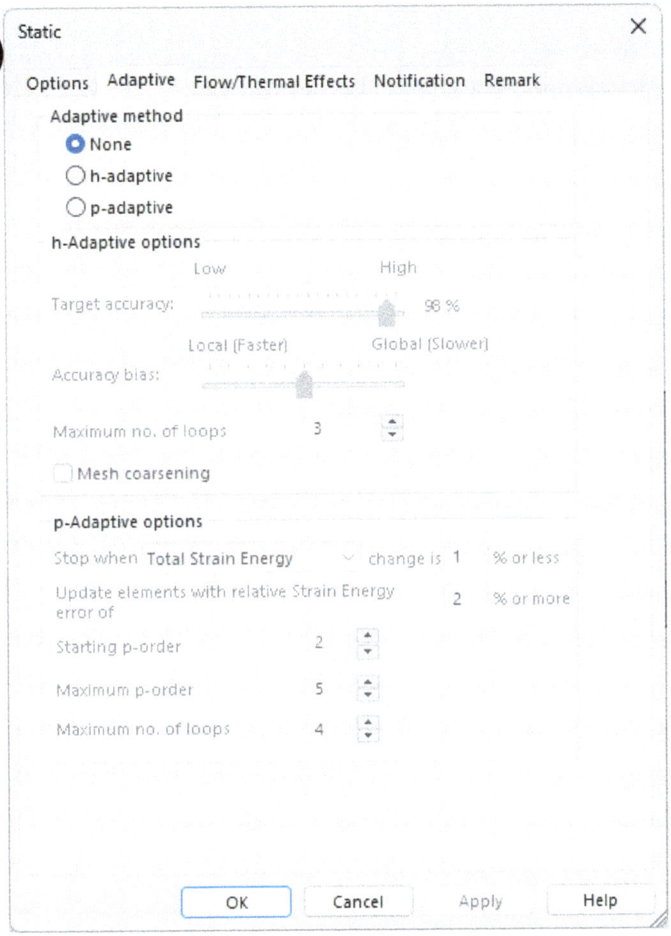

By default, the **None** radio button is selected in the **Adaptive method** area of the dialog box. As a result, none of the adaptive mesh methods are performed on the model. To perform the H-adaptive meshing, select the **h-adaptive** radio button. The options in the **h-Adaptive options** area of the dialog box are enabled to specify the H-adaptive parameters, see Figure 5.5.

5.5

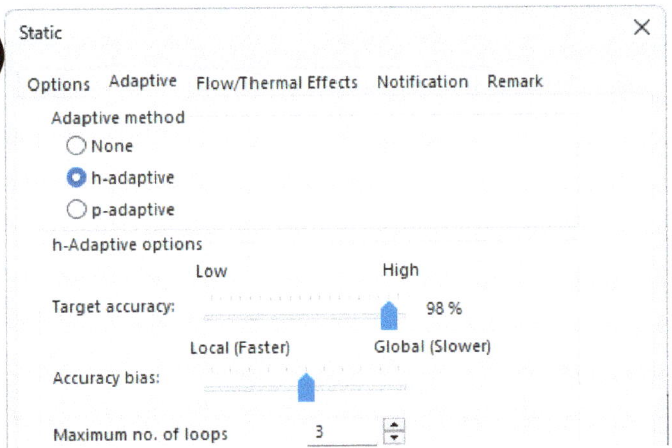

The **Target accuracy** Slider of the **h-Adaptive options** area is used to set the target accuracy to be achieved. Note that the target accuracy defines the change in the strain energy in every iteration. By default, the target accuracy is set to 98%. This means that the difference in the strain energy between two consecutive iterations must be less than 2%. Note that SOLIDWORKS Simulation stops refining the mesh when the difference in the strain energy between two consecutive iterations is achieved less than 2%.

The **Accuracy bias** Slider is used to define whether SOLIDWORKS Simulation achieves accurate stress results in the high-stress areas or accurate global results. If you set the **Accuracy bias** Slider to the left on the **Local (Faster)** side then SOLIDWORKS Simulation refines the mesh with very small elements in the high stress areas to achieve accurate stress results. It is recommended to set the slider in the middle to maintain a proper balance between the high stress concentration areas and the global results of the model.

The **Maximum no. of loops** field is used to set the maximum number of iterations to be performed to achieve the target accuracy. Maximum five iterations can be specified in this field. As discussed, SOLIDWORKS Simulation stops refining the mesh either when the target accuracy is achieved or when the maximum number of iterations are performed.

On selecting the **Mesh coarsening** check box, SOLIDWORKS Simulation generates coarse mesh (larger elements size) in the low-stress areas of the model.

After specifying the H-adaptive meshing parameters, click on the **OK** button in the **Static** dialog box. The H-adaptive meshing is defined for the model. Now, you can run the study by using the **Run This Study** tool in the **Simulation CommandManager**. SOLIDWORKS Simulation performs multiple iterations by refining the mesh in every iteration to achieve the specified target accuracy. When the target accuracy is achieved or the maximum number of specified iterations are performed, the **Results** folder is added to the Simulation Study Tree with different results. Also, the stress distribution on the model appears in the graphics area, by default.

Note: Before running the study with an adaptive method, you need to make the model suitable for the analysis by defining boundary conditions (loads/fixtures), material, and so on.

Working with P-Adaptive Mesh

The P-adaptive meshing method enhances accuracy by adjusting the polynomial order of the elements rather than refining the mesh itself. In areas with high stresses, the polynomial order of the elements is increased automatically during each iteration until the specified target accuracy is met. To use P-adaptive meshing, you need to define:

- The target accuracy level
- The maximum polynomial order (up to fifth-order elements)
- The number of iterations (up to four iterations)

Typically, models are meshed with either first-order elements (draft quality) or second-order elements (high quality). However, P-adaptive meshing allows meshing up to fifth-order elements, significantly improving result accuracy without increasing the number of mesh elements. This approach is particularly useful for capturing stress concentrations while maintaining computational efficiency.

To mesh a model with P-adaptive meshing, right-click on the study name in the Simulation Study Tree and then click on the **Properties** tool in the shortcut menu that appears. The **Static** dialog box appears. In this dialog box, click on the **Adaptive** tab and then select the **p-adaptive** radio button, see Figure 5.6. The options of the **p-Adaptive options** area of the dialog box are enabled to specify the P-adaptive mesh parameters, see Figure 5.6.

5.6

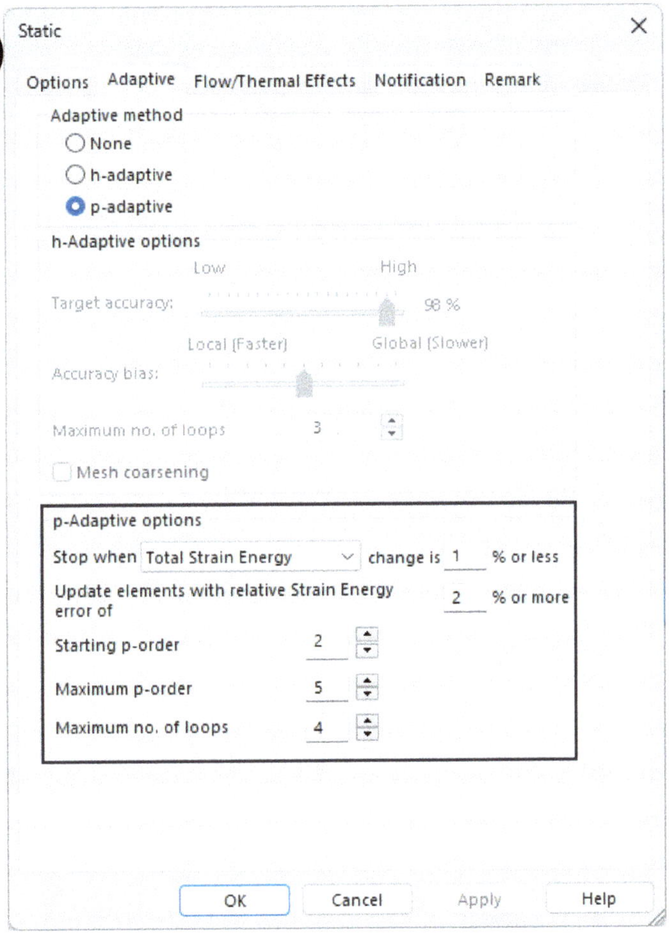

The **Stop when** drop-down list and the **change is** field in the **p-Adaptive options** area of the dialog box are used for specifying the convergence criteria to be achieved. By default, the **Total Strain Energy** option is selected in this drop-down list and **1%** is specified in the **change is** field, see Figure 5.7. As a result, when the change in the total strain energy is 1% or less than 1% between two consecutive iterations, SOLIDWORKS Simulation stops changing the polynomial order of elements and does not perform any further iteration. You can select the convergence criteria as **RMS von Mises Stress**, **Total Strain Energy**, or **RMS Res. Displacement**.

5.7

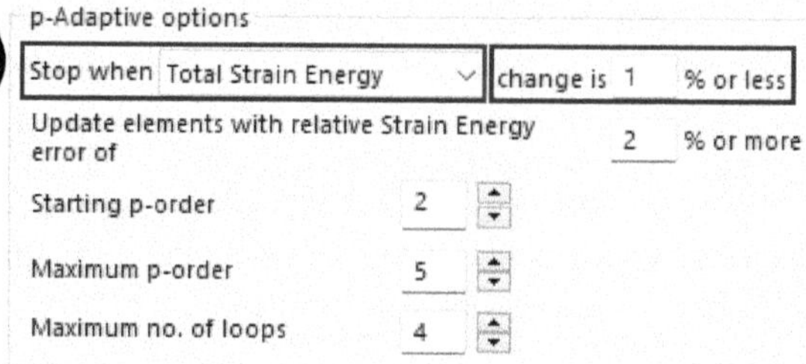

The **Starting p-order** field is used to specify the starting polynomial order for the first iteration. By default, **2** is specified in this field. As a result, second-order elements are used in the first iteration. If the specified convergence criteria are not met in the first iteration then SOLIDWORKS Simulation performs the next iteration with higher polynomial element order and continues with other iterations until the specified convergence criteria is achieved or the maximum number of iterations are performed.

The **Update elements with relative Strain Energy error of** field is used to specify a percentage value to change the order of the polynomial elements having relative strain energy between two iterations equal to or more than the specified percentage value.

The **Maximum p-order** field is used to specify the maximum polynomial element order. You can specify up to fifth-order elements.

The **Maximum no. of loops** field is used to set the maximum number of iterations to be performed to achieve the convergence criteria. Maximum four iterations can be specified in this field. As discussed, SOLIDWORKS Simulation stops changing the polynomial order of elements either when the convergence criteria is achieved or the maximum number of specified iterations are performed.

After specifying the P-adaptive meshing parameters, click on the **OK** button in the **Static** dialog box. The P-adaptive meshing is defined for the model. Now, you can run the study by using the **Run This Study** tool in the **Simulation CommandManager**.

Case Study 1: Static Analysis of a C-Bracket with Adaptive Meshing

In this case study, you will perform three different static studies on a C-Bracket shown in Figure 5.8. You need to perform the first static study without adaptive meshing, second with H-adaptive meshing, and the third with P-adaptive meshing. After performing all the studies, compare their stress results.

5.8

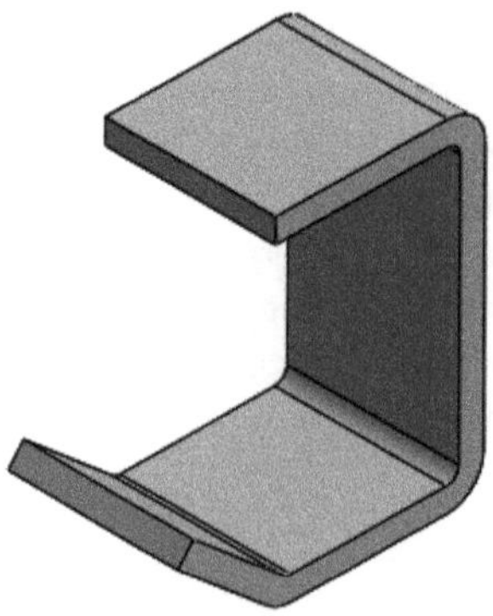

Project Description

The C-Bracket is fixed at its top face and a 900 N load is applied on its bottom horizontal face, see Figure 5.9. The C-Bracket is made up of **Alloy Steel** material.

5.9

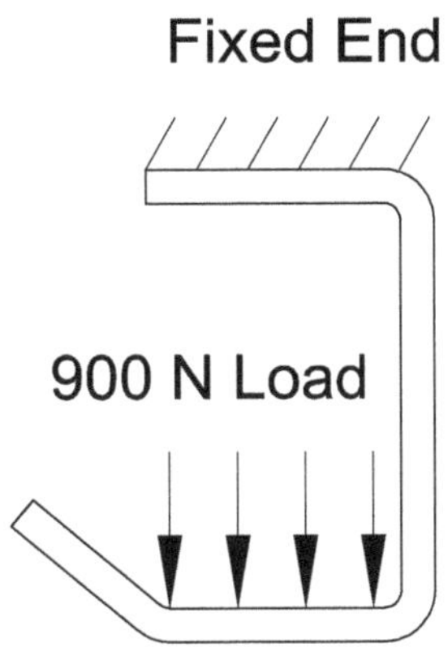

Project Summary

In this case study, you will run three different static studies. In the first static study, you will run the analysis with a default curvature-based mesh. In the second and third static studies, you will run the analysis with H-adaptive meshing and P-adaptive meshing, respectively. After completing all the static studies, you will compare the stress results of all the studies. Specify the unit system to SI (MKS) with displacement in mm and stress in N/mm^2 (MPa) units.

The following sequence summarizes the case study outline:

1. Downloading Files of Chapter 5
2. Opening the C-Bracket
3. Starting the Static Study
4. Assigning the Material
5. Applying the Fixture
6. Applying the Load
7. Generating the Mesh
8. Running Analysis and Displaying Results
9. Creating a New Static Study with H-Adaptive Meshing
10. Creating a New Static Study with P-Adaptive Meshing
11. Comparing Stress Results of all Studies
12. Saving Results

Section 1: Downloading Files of Chapter 5

1. Log on to the CADArtifex website (*cadartifex.com/login/*). If you are a new user, you must first sign up on the CADArtifex website as a **Learner** (*cadartifex.com/register*).

2. After logging, navigate to the textbook titled "**SOLIDWORKS Simulation 2026: A Power Guide for Beginners and Intermediate Users: Colored**" using the **Browse Resources** option available in the left menu to download its resources. Alternatively, you can enter the name of the textbook in the **Search** box to locate it quickly.

3. In the **Online Resources** tab, expand the **Case Studies** rollout and click the **Download** button corresponding to **C05 Case Studies**. In the confirmation window that appears, click the **Confirm** button. The download of the **C05 Case Studies** file will begin. After the download is complete, unzip the file.

4. Save the extracted **C05 Case Studies** folder in the location ***SOLIDWORKS Simulation > Case Studies***.

Section 2: Opening the C-Bracket

1. Start SOLIDWORKS, if not already started.

2. Click on the **Open** button in the **Welcome** dialog box or the **Open** tool in the **Standard** toolbar. The **Open** dialog box appears.

3. Browse to the location > ***SOLIDWORKS Simulation > Case Studies > C05 Case Studies > Case Study 1*** of the local drive of your system. Next, select the **C-Bracket** and then click on the **Open** button in the dialog box. The C-Bracket is opened in SOLIDWORKS.

Section 3: Starting the Static Study

1. Click on the **Simulation** tab in the **CommandManager**. The tools of the **Simulation CommandManager** appear.

Note: If the **Simulation** tab is not added in the CommandManager then you need to add it, as discussed earlier.

2. Click on the **New Study** tool in the **Simulation CommandManager**. The **Study PropertyManager** appears to the left of the graphics area.

3. Ensure that the **Static** button is activated in the **Study PropertyManager**.

4. Enter **Without Adaptive Study** in the **Study name** field of the PropertyManager.

5. Click on the green tick-mark button in the PropertyManager. The **Without Adaptive Study** is added to the Simulation Study Tree, see Figure 5.10.

5.10

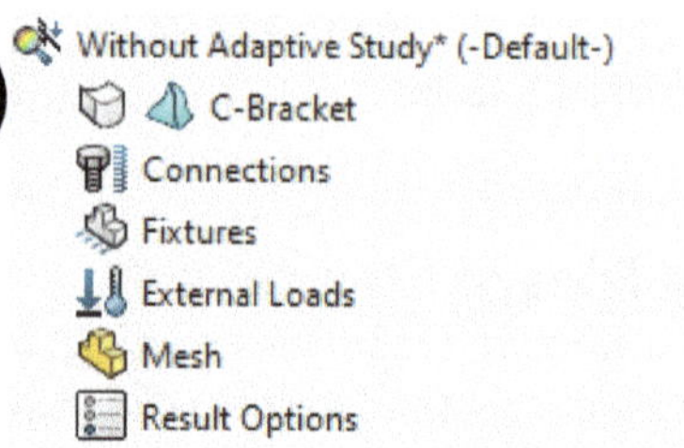

Section 4: Assigning the Material

1. Click on the **Apply Material** tool in the **Simulation CommandManager** to invoke the **Material** dialog box.

2. Select the **Alloy Steel** material in the **Steel** category of the **SOLIDWORKS Materials** library in the dialog box.

3. Click on the **Apply** button and then click on the **Close** button. The Alloy Steel material is assigned to the component.

Section 5: Applying the Fixture

1. Apply the Fixed Geometry fixture on the top planar face of the component by using the **Fixed Geometry** tool, see Figure 5.11.

Section 6: Applying the Load

1. Apply a 900 N uniformly distributed load on the bottom planar face of the component by using the **Force** tool, see Figure 5.12.

5.11

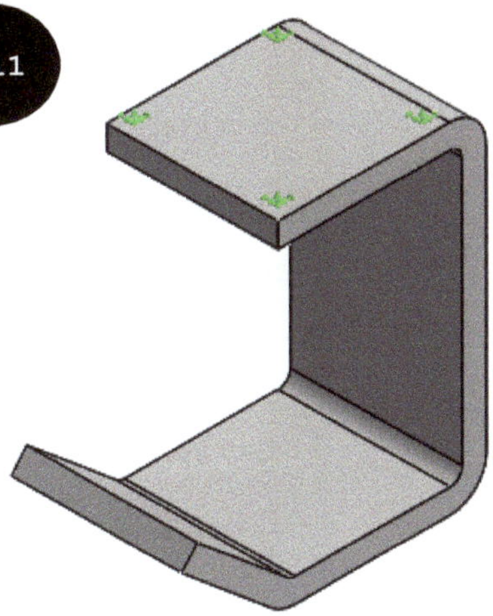

5.12

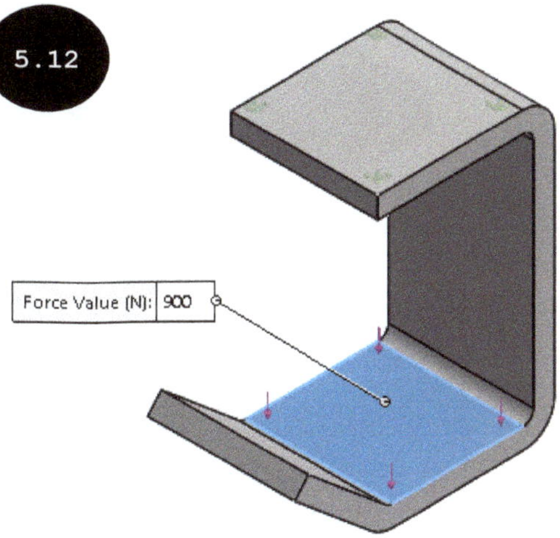

Section 7: Generating the Mesh

Now, you need to generate the curvature-based mesh with default parameters.

1. Right-click on the **Mesh** option in the Simulation Study Tree and then click on the **Create Mesh** tool in the shortcut menu that appears to invoke the **Mesh PropertyManager**.

2. Expand the **Mesh Parameters** rollout of the PropertyManager and then select the **Curvature-based mesh** radio button.

3. Accept the default curvature-based mesh parameters and then click on the green tick-mark button ✓ in the PropertyManager. The **Mesh Progress** window appears which displays the progress of meshing in the model. After the meshing is complete, the meshed model appears, see Figure 5.13.

5.13

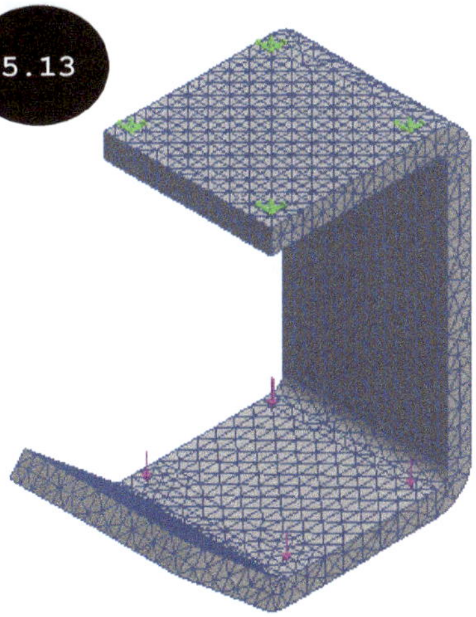

Section 8: Running Analysis and Displaying Results

Now, you need to run the analysis.

1. Click on the **Run This Study** tool in the **Simulation CommandManager**. The **Without Adaptive Study** (*name of the study*) window appears which displays the progress of analysis.

2. After the process of running the analysis is complete, the **Results** folder is added to the Simulation Study Tree with the stress, displacement, and strain results. By default, the **Stress** result is activated in the **Results** folder. As a result, the stress distribution on the model and the von Mises stress plot appear in the graphics area, see Figure 5.14.

5.14

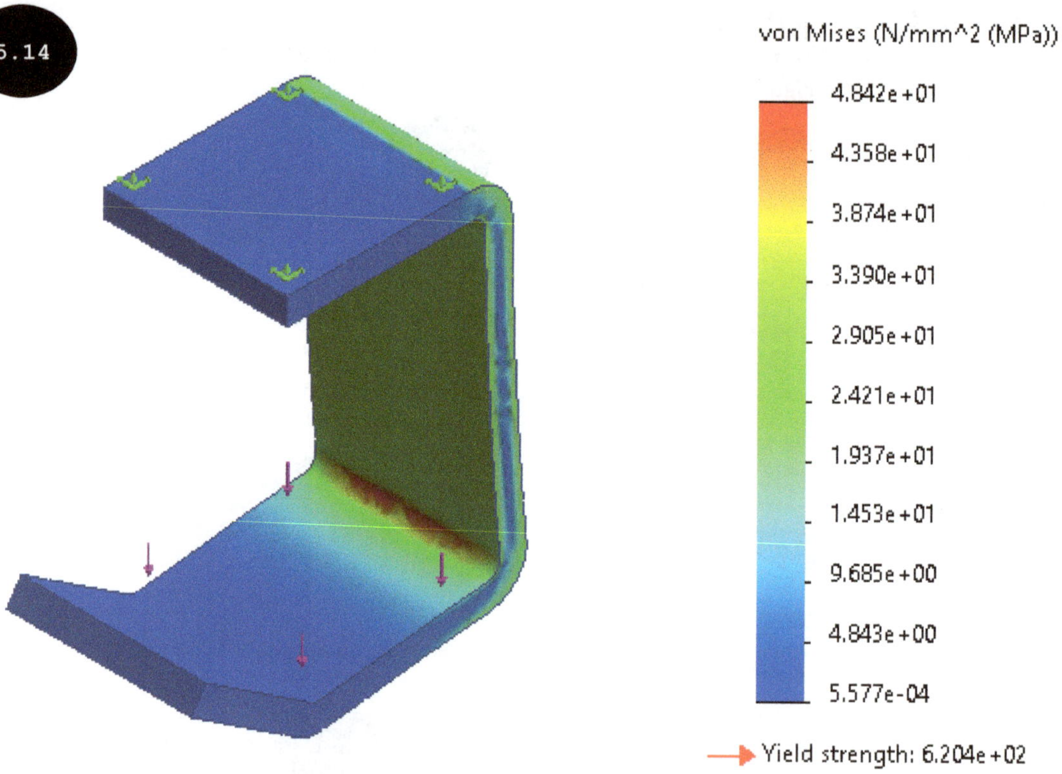

The maximum Von Mises stress in the model under the applied load is **4.842e+01** (48.424) N/mm^2 (MPa) which is significantly within the yield stress of the material that is **6.204e+02** (620.422) N/mm^2 (MPa). You can display the other results of the component as discussed earlier.

Section 9: Creating a New Static Study with H-Adaptive Meshing

Now, you need to create a new study with H-adaptive meshing method and run the analysis. Instead of creating a new study from scratch, you can copy the existing study.

1. Right-click on the **Without Adaptive Study** tab in the lower-left corner of the graphics area and then click on the **Copy Study** tool in the shortcut menu that appears, see Figure 5.15. The **Copy Study PropertyManager** appears to the left of the graphics area.

5.15

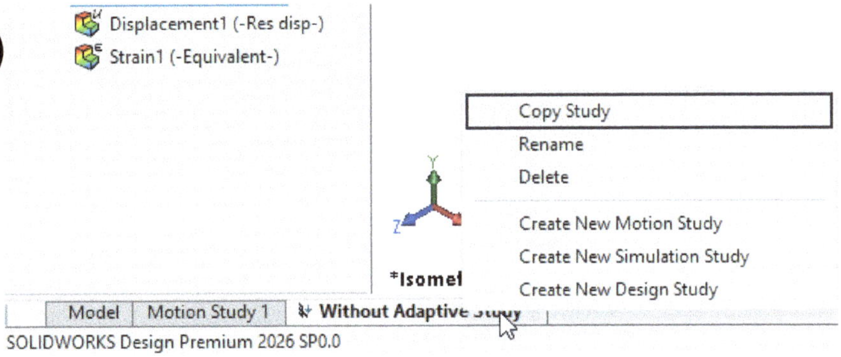

2. Enter **H-adaptive Study** in the **Study name** field of the PropertyManager and then click on its green tick-mark button. A new study with the name **H-adaptive Study** is created in a different tab. Also, the newly created study is activated by default, and appears in the Simulation Study Tree, see Figure 5.16.

   Now, you need to define the H-adaptive parameters for the newly created study.

3. Right-click on the **H-adaptive Study** (name of the study) in the Simulation Study Tree to display a shortcut menu, see Figure 5.17.

5.16

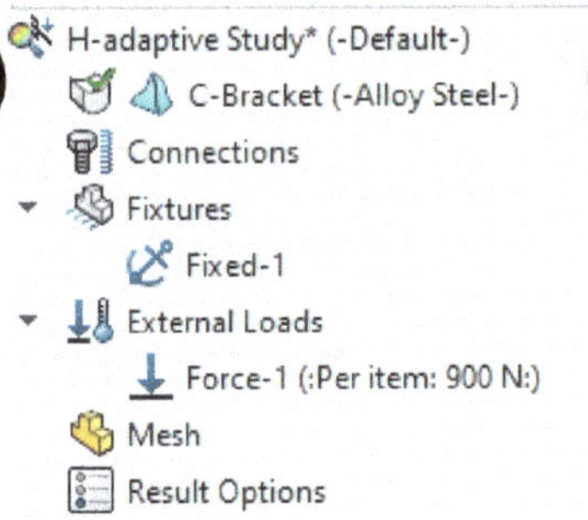

5.17

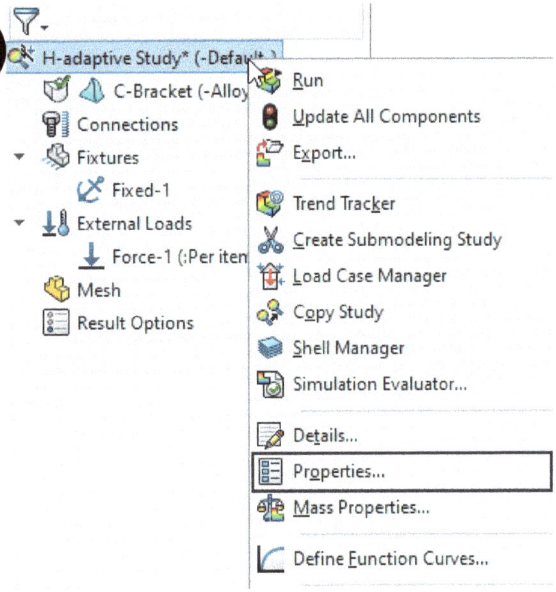

4. Click on the **Properties** tool in the shortcut menu. The **Static** dialog box appears.

5. Click on the **Adaptive** tab in the **Static** dialog box. The options to define the adaptive mesh method and the respective parameters appear in the dialog box.

6. Select the **h-adaptive** radio button to specify the H-adaptive mesh method for analyzing the model. The options in the **h-Adaptive options** area of the dialog box are enabled, see Figure 5.18.

5.18

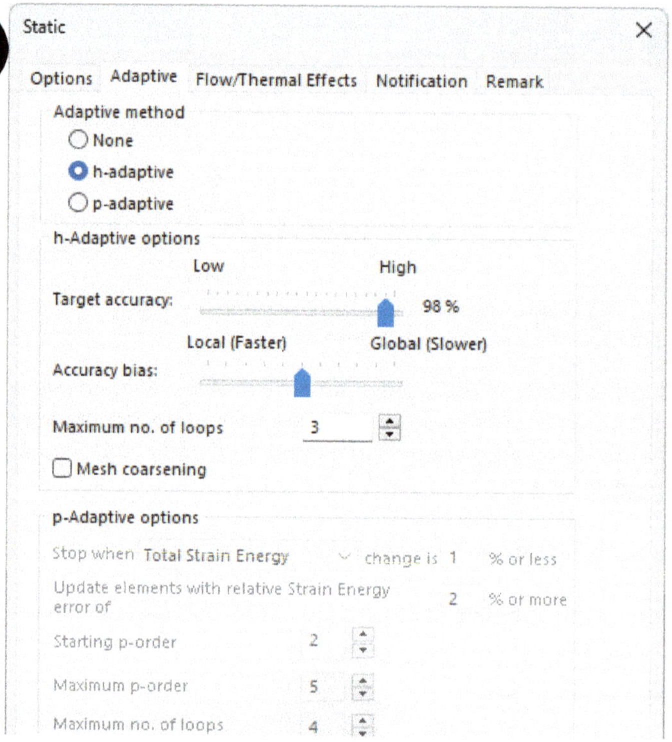

7. Enter **5** in the **Maximum no. of loops** field of the **h-Adaptive options** area in the dialog box as the maximum number of iterations to be performed to achieve the target accuracy.

8. Accept the default specified target accuracy and the accuracy bias in the **h-Adaptive options** area of the dialog box. Next, click on the **OK** button in the dialog box. The H-adaptive meshing is specified for the current study.

   Now, you can run the analysis with H-adaptive meshing. Note that the fixtures, loads, material properties, and so on are the same as in the original study.

9. Click on the **Run This Study** tool in the **Simulation CommandManager**. The **H-adaptive Study** (*name of the study*) window appears which displays the progress of analysis. Note that SOLIDWORKS Simulation performs five iterations with refined mesh element size in every iteration to achieve the specified target accuracy. Once the specified target accuracy is achieved, SOLIDWORKS Simulation stops refining the mesh and the **Simulation** window appears, (see Figure 5.19), informing that the current specified accuracy level has been satisfied.

5.19

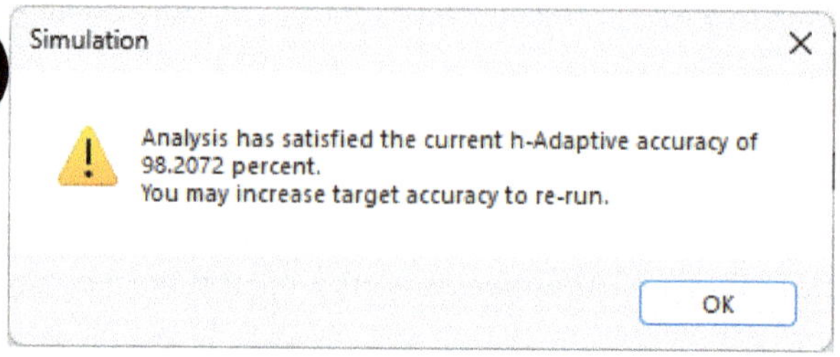

Note: In H-adaptive mesh method, SOLIDWORKS Simulation stops refining the mesh either when the target accuracy is achieved or the maximum number of iterations are performed.

10. Click on the **OK** button in the **Simulation** window. The results get updated in the **Results** folder of the Simulation Study Tree as per the H-adaptive meshing. Also, the updated stress distribution on the model and the von Mises stress plot appear in the graphics area, see Figure 5.20.

5.20

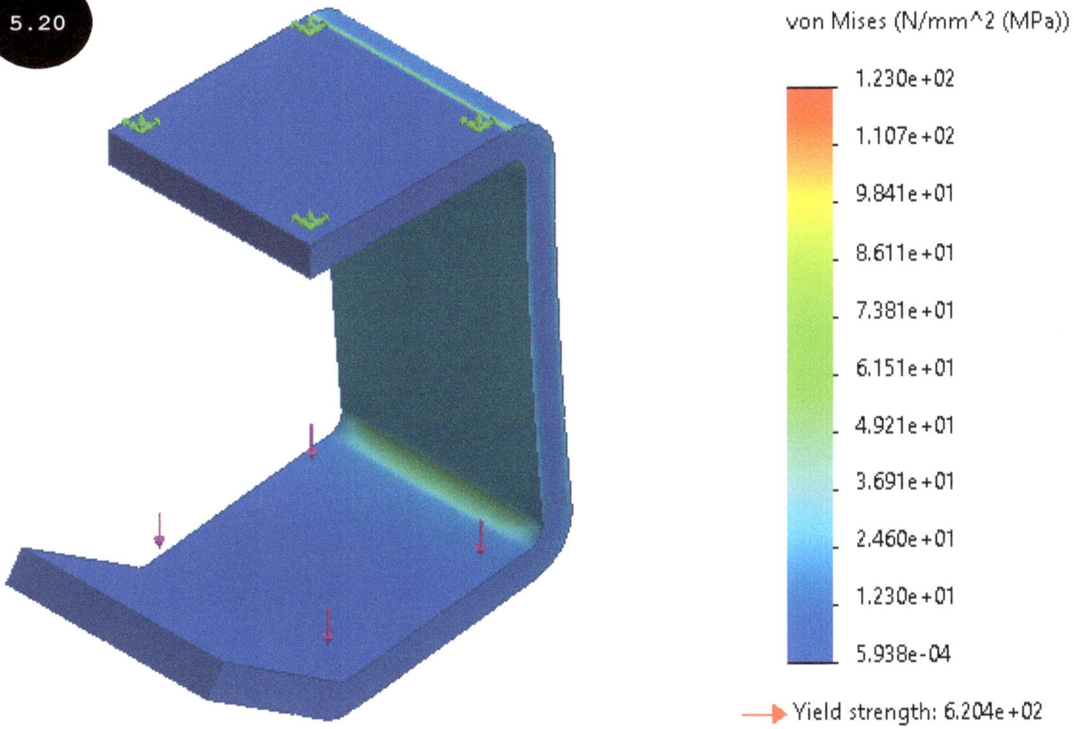

The maximum von Mises stress in the model under the applied load in the H-adaptive mesh method is **1.230e+02** (123.017) N/mm^2 (MPa). You can notice the difference in the results between the studies created with and without H-adaptive method.

Now, you need to display the convergence graph for the H-adaptive mesh method.

11. Right-click on the **Results** folder in the Simulation Study Tree and then click on the **Define Adaptive Convergence Graph** tool in the shortcut menu that appears, see Figure 5.21. The **Convergence Graph PropertyManager** appears, see Figure 5.22.

5.21

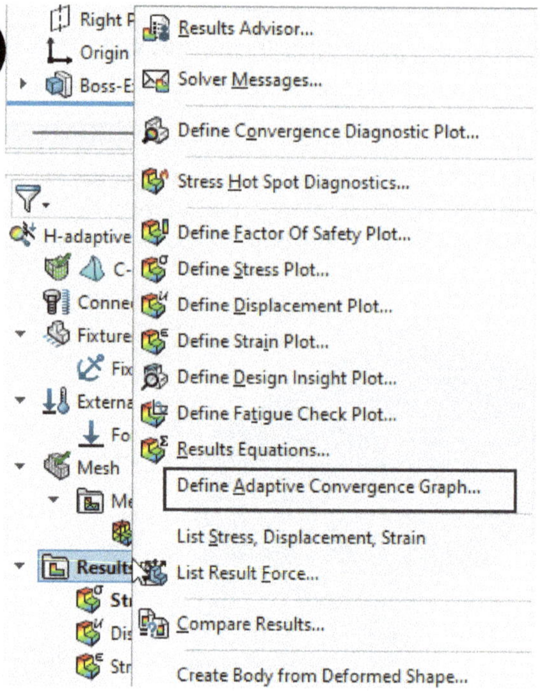

5.22

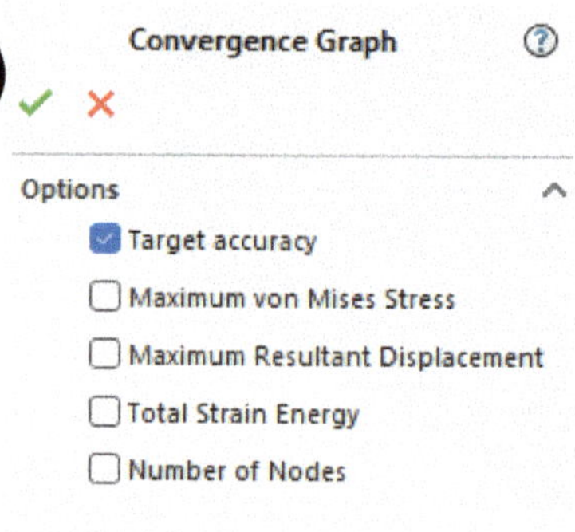

In the **Options** rollout of the PropertyManager, you can select an option to display the respective convergence graph. In this study, you will display the maximum von Mises Stress convergence graph.

12. Select the **Maximum von Mises Stress** check box, clear the **Target accuracy** check box in the PropertyManager and then click on the green tick-mark button. The **Convergence Graph** window appears, see Figure 5.23. It displays the H-adaptive convergence graph for the von Mises Stress against each iteration. Also, the **Graph1** option is added to the **Results** folder of the Simulation Study Tree.

5.23

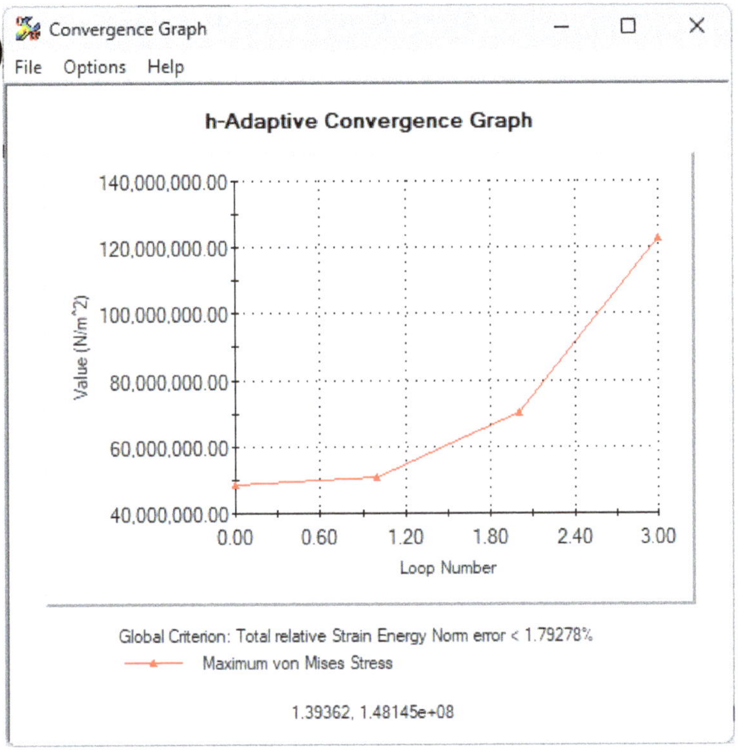

After reviewing the convergence graph, close it. Now, you need to display the meshed model after performing the H-adaptive meshing to view the element size in the high-stress areas.

13. Right-click on the **C-Bracket (-Alloy Steel-)** option (*name of the model*) in the Simulation Study Tree and then click on the **Show Mesh** tool in the shortcut menu that appears, see Figure 5.24. The meshed model appears in the graphics area, see Figure 5.25. Notice that small elements are generated in the high stress areas of the model to achieving the target accuracy.

5.24

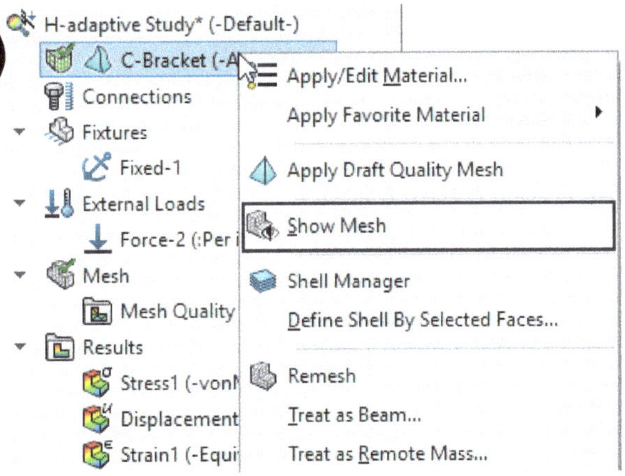

5.25

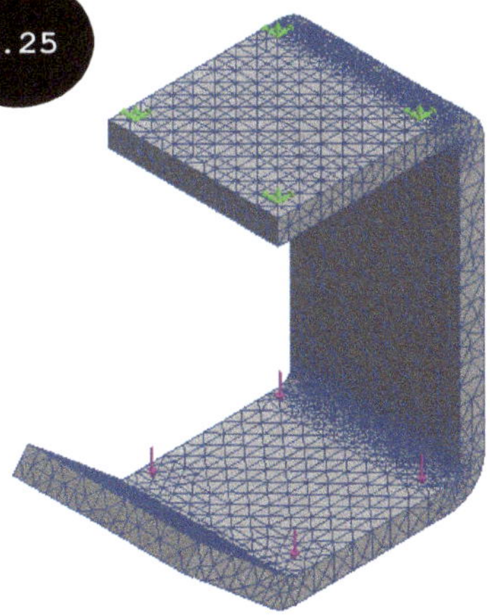

Section 10: Creating a New Static Study with P-Adaptive Meshing

Now, you need to create a new study with P-adaptive meshing method to compare the results with the earlier created studies. Instead of creating a new study from scratch, you can copy the first study created without an adaptive method and specify the P-adaptive parameters.

1. Click on the **Without Adaptive Study** tab in the lower-left corner of the graphics area to activate it.

2. Right-click on the **Without Adaptive Study** tab in the lower-left corner of the graphics area and then click on the **Copy Study** tool in the shortcut menu that appears, see Figure 5.26. The **Copy Study PropertyManager** appears to the left of the graphics area.

5.26

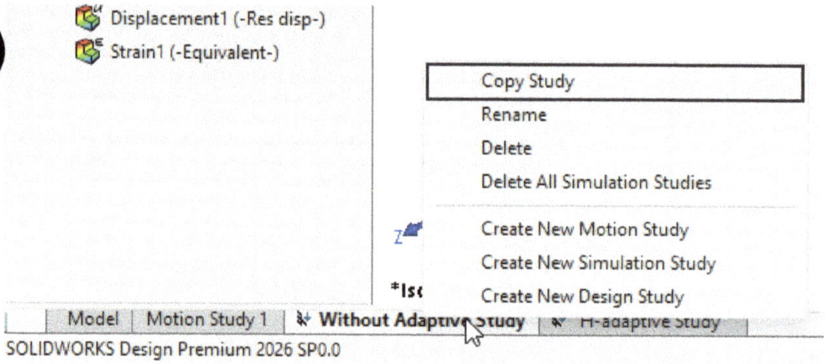

3. Enter **P-adaptive Study** in the **Study name** field of the **Copy Study PropertyManager** and then click on its green tick-mark button. A new study with the name **P-adaptive Study** is created in a different tab. Also, the newly created study is activated by default, and appears in the Simulation Study Tree, see Figure 5.27.

   Now, you need to define the P-adaptive parameters for the newly created study.

4. Right-click on the **P-adaptive Study** (name of the study) in the Simulation Study Tree to display a shortcut menu, see Figure 5.28.

5.27

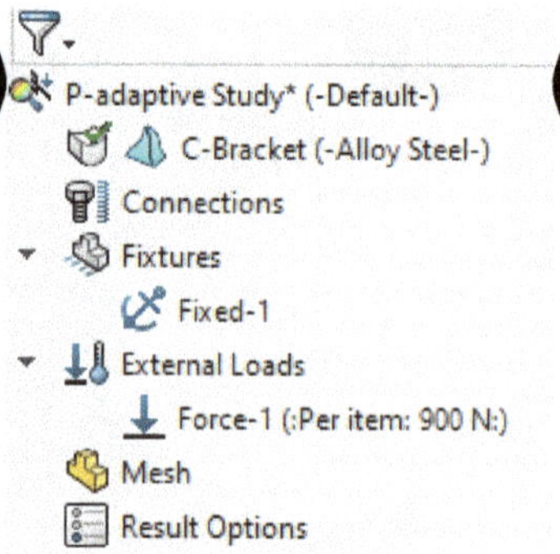

5.28

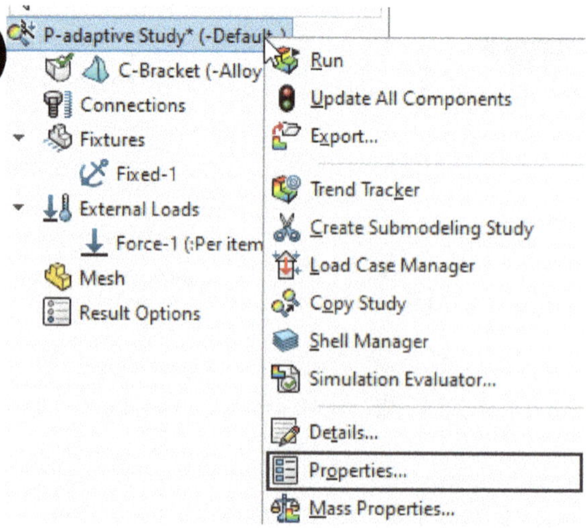

5. Click on the **Properties** tool in the shortcut menu. The **Static** dialog box appears.

6. Click on the **Adaptive** tab in the **Static** dialog box. The options to define the adaptive mesh method and the respective parameters appear in the dialog box.

7. Select the **p-adaptive** radio button in the **Adaptive method** area of the dialog box. The options in the **p-Adaptive options** area of the dialog box are enabled, see Figure 5.29.

5.29

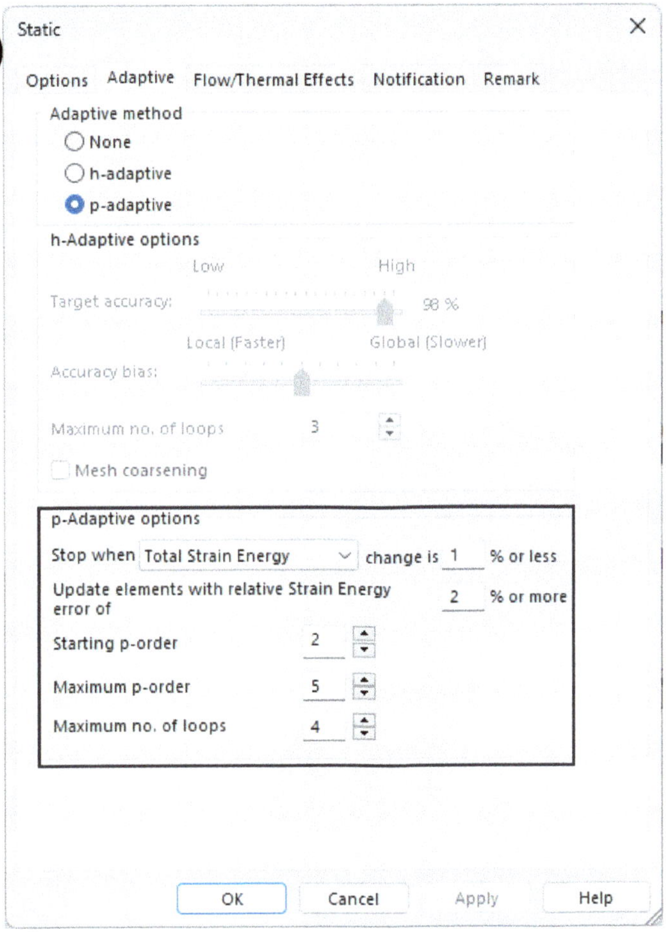

8. Ensure that the **Total Strain Energy** option is selected in the **Stop when** drop-down list and **1%** is selected in the **change is** field of the **p-Adaptive options** area in the dialog box as the convergence criteria to be achieved. On doing so, SOLIDWORKS Simulation stops changing the polynomial order of elements and does not perform any further iteration, when the change in the total strain energy is 1% or less than 1% between two iterations.

9. Ensure that **4** is entered in the **Maximum no. of loops** field of the **p-Adaptive options** area as the total number of iterations to be performed to achieve the specified convergence criteria.

10. Accept the remaining default parameters in the **p-Adaptive options** area. Next, click on the **OK** button in the dialog box. The P-adaptive meshing is specified for the current study.

    Now, you can run the analysis with p-adaptive meshing. Note that the fixtures, loads, material properties, and so on are same as the original study.

11. Click on the **Run This Study** tool in the **Simulation CommandManager**. The **P-adaptive Study** (*name of the study*) window appears which displays the progress of analysis. If the **Simulation** window appears informing that the Jacobian ratio is beyond the limit for an element, click on the **Yes** button to continue.

    Note that SOLIDWORKS Simulation performs four iterations with different polynomial orders of elements in every iteration to achieve the specified convergence criteria. Once the specified convergence criteria is achieved, SOLIDWORKS Simulation stops changing the polynomial order of elements and the results get updated in the **Results** folder of the Simulation Study Tree. Also, the updated stress distribution on the model and the von Mises stress plot appear in the graphics area, see Figure 5.30.

5.30

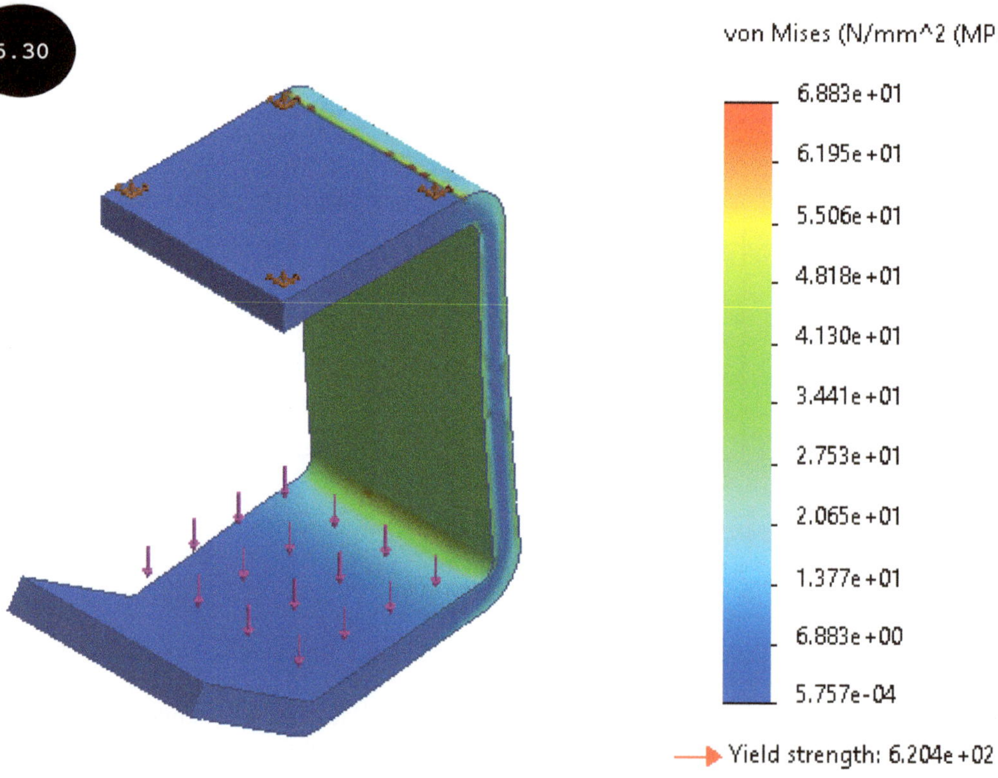

The maximum von Mises stress in the model under the applied load in the P-adaptive mesh method is **6.883e+01** (68.829) N/mm^2 (MPa).

Note that you may observe slight variations in the result values depending on the service pack version of SOLIDWORKS installed on your system. These minor differences occur due to updates and improvements made in different service packs.

Now, you need to display the meshed model after performing the P-adaptive meshing to view the element size in the high stress area of the model.

12. Right-click on the **C-Bracket (-Alloy Steel-)** option (*name of the model*) in the Simulation Study Tree and then click on the **Show Mesh** tool in the shortcut menu that appears, see Figure 5.31. The meshed model appears in the graphics area, see Figure 5.32. Notice that the size of the elements is not changed in the meshed model for achieving the target accuracy, since in the P-adaptive mesh method, only the polynomial order of the elements changes in the high-stress areas.

5.31

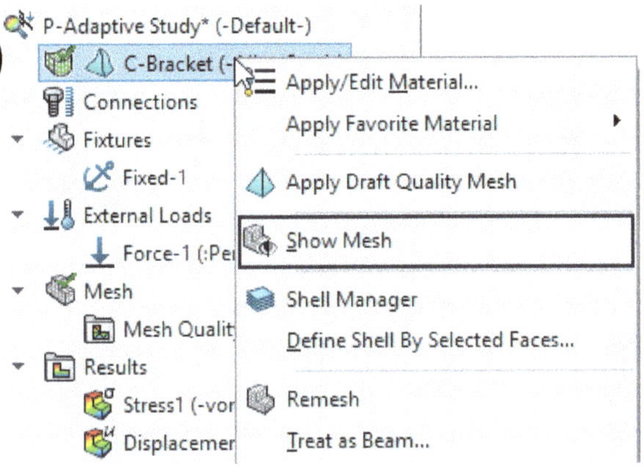

5.32

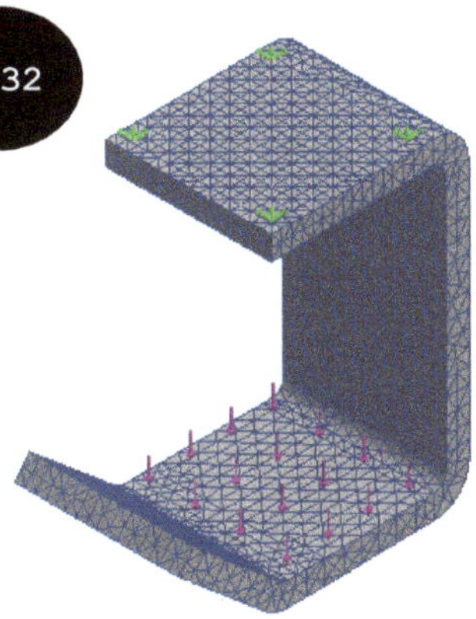

Section 11: Comparing Stress Results of all Studies

After performing the three different static studies (without adaptive method, with H-adaptive method, and with P-adaptive method), you can compare the results. In this case study, you need to compare the stress results of all the three studies.

1. Right-click on the **Results** folder in the Simulation Study Tree of any study and then click on the **Compare Results** tool in the shortcut menu that appears, see Figure 5.33. The **Compare Results PropertyManager** appears, see Figure 5.34.

5.33

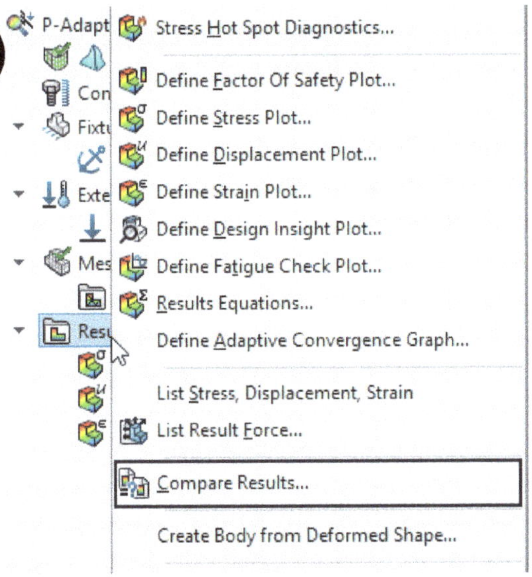

5.34

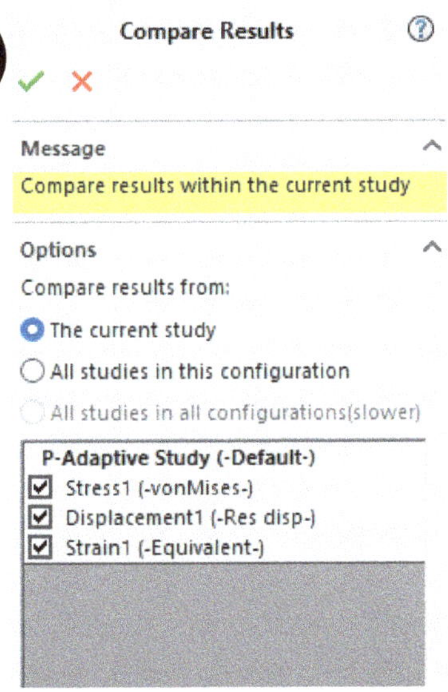

2. Select the **All studies in this configuration** radio button in the **Options** rollout of the PropertyManager. All the performed studies appear in the PropertyManager, see Figure 5.34.

3. Select only the **Stress1 (-vonMises-)** check boxes of all the studies. Next, click on the green tick-mark button in the PropertyManager. The graphics screen of the SOLIDWORKS Simulation gets divided and displays stress results of all the studies, see Figure 5.35.

5.35

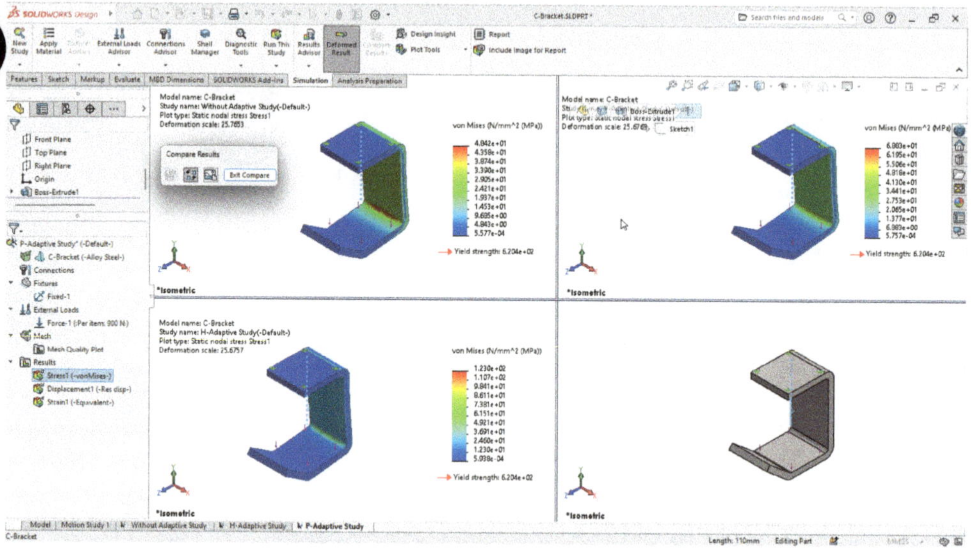

Now, you can compare the stress results of all the studies. The table given below summarizes the results of all the studies.

Study	**Max. Stress [N/mm^2 (MPa)]**
Without Adaptive Study	4.842e+01 (48.424)
With H-Adaptive Study	1.230e+02 (123.017)
With P-Adaptive Study	6.883e+01 (68.829)

4. After comparing the results, click on the **Exit Compare** button in the **Compare Results** window that appears in the graphics area.

Section 12: Saving Results

Now, you need to save the results.

1. Click on the **Save** tool in the **Standard** toolbar. The model and its results are saved in the location > *SOLIDWORKS Simulation > Case Studies > C05 Case Studies > Case Study 1*.

Hands-on Test Drive 1: Static Analysis of a Wrench with Adaptive Meshing

Perform three different static studies, one without adaptive meshing, second with H-adaptive meshing, and third with P-adaptive meshing of a Wrench shown in Figure 5.36 and compare the results of each study.

5.36

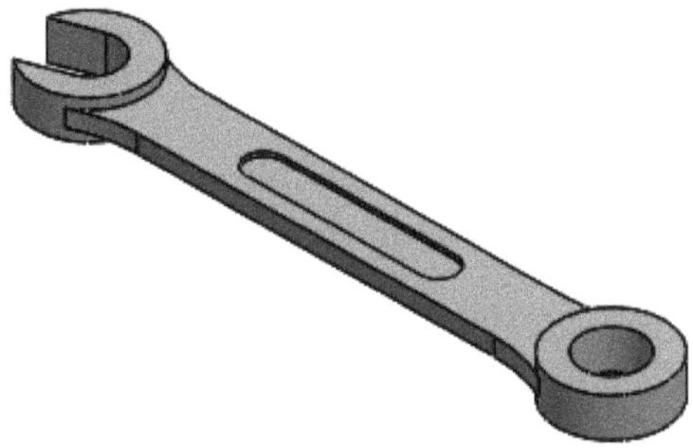

Project Description

The Wrench is fixed at one end due to the tight connection of the nut and a 350 N load is subjected to the other end, which occurs while tightening the nut, see Figure 5.37. The Wrench is made up of **Alloy Steel (SS)** material.

5.37

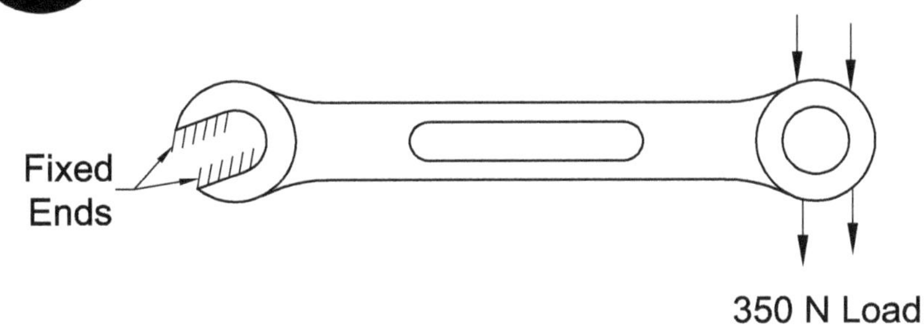

Project Summary

In this case study, you will run three different static studies. In the first static study, you will run the analysis with a default curvature-based mesh. In the second and third static studies, you will run the analysis with H-adaptive meshing and P-adaptive meshing, respectively. After completing all the static studies, you will compare the displacement results of all the studies. Specify the unit system to SI (MKS) with displacement in mm and stress in N/mm^2 (MPa) units.

Summary

In this chapter, you explored the two adaptive meshing methods available in SOLIDWORKS Simulation: H-adaptive and P-adaptive. You learned the key differences between these methods and how to set up and run an analysis using each approach.

Through a case study, you gained practical experience in applying both adaptive meshing techniques, analyzing results, and interpreting an adaptive convergence graph. Additionally, the chapter covered a comparison of results obtained from both methods, highlighting their impact on accuracy and computational efficiency.

These concepts provide a deeper understanding of adaptive meshing, enabling you to refine simulations for improved precision while optimizing performance.

Questions

Complete the following sentences:

- SOLIDWORKS Simulation provides two Adaptive meshing methods: _________ and _________.
- The _________ mesh method is used to refine the mesh automatically in the areas where high stresses are identified and performing multiple iterations with smaller element sizes in every iteration until the specified accuracy level is achieved.
- In the H-adaptive meshing method, the target accuracy defines the change in the _________ energy in every iteration.
- In the H-adaptive meshing method, if the target accuracy is set to 96% then the difference in the strain energy between two iterations should be less than _________ percent.
- You can define maximum _________ number of iterations in the H-adaptive mesh method.
- The _________ mesh method is used to change the polynomial order of elements in every iteration, where the high stresses are identified in the model to achieve the specified accuracy.
- In the P-adaptive mesh method, you can define a maximum _________ number of iterations.
- In the P-adaptive mesh method, you can specify up to _________ order elements.
- The _________ tool is used for defining the adaptive convergence graph of the study.

CHAPTER
6

Buckling Analysis

In this chapter, the following topics will be discussed:

- Introduction to Buckling Analysis
- Buckling Analysis of a Pipe Support
- Buckling Analysis of a Beam
- Buckling Analysis of a Column

In earlier chapters, you explored how to perform static analysis on various components and assemblies. In this chapter, you will focus on buckling analysis, learning how to assess structural stability and predict the critical load at which a structure may fail due to buckling.

Introduction to Buckling Analysis

The buckling analysis is used to calculate the buckling load which is also known as the critical load. It is the load under which a model can start buckling even if the maximum stress developed in the model is within the yield strength of the material. Buckling refers to a larger deformation that may have occurred due to the compressive axial loads acting on the structures such as long slender columns and thin sheet components, see Figure 6.1.

6.1

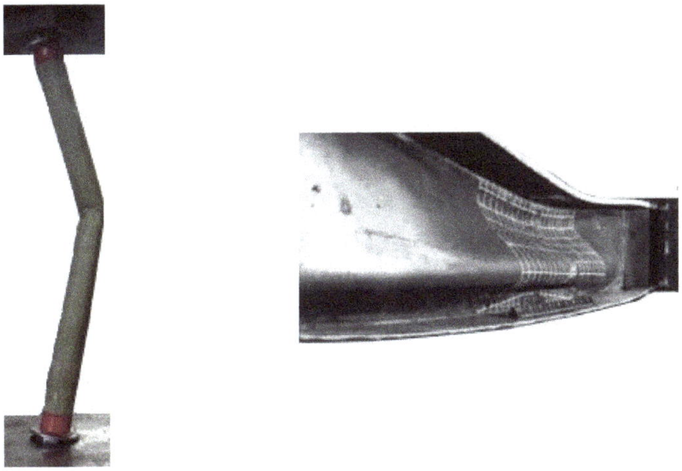

The minimum bucking load or critical load, under which a structure can start bucking is calculated by the following formula:

$$F = \pi^2 EI / (KL)^2$$

Where,
F= Minimum bucking load or Critical load
E = Modulus of elasticity
I = Area Moment of inertia of the cross-section of the structure
K = Structure (column) effective length, which depends on the end conditions
L = Length of the structure

It is clear from the above formula that the buckling load does not depend upon the compressive strength of the material. As a result, the structure can buckle or fail, even if the maximum stress developed in the structure is within the compressive yield strength of the material. Also, on increasing the length of the structure, the force required to buckle the structure gets reduced.

In SOLIDWORKS Simulation, you can perform the buckling analysis of a structure to calculate the minimum buckling load factor and its associated buckling mode shape, when the structure can buckle under the compressive axial loads.

Case Study 1: Buckling Analysis of a Pipe Support

In this case study, you will perform the buckling analysis of a Pipe Support, (see Figure 6.2) and determine its minimum buckling load.

6.2

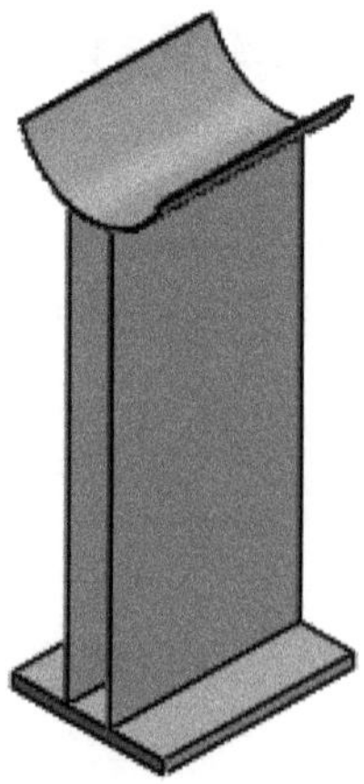

Project Description

The Pipe Support is fixed at its bottom and a 9500 N compressive axial load is subjected on its top face, see Figure 6.3. The Pipe Support is made up of **Alloy Steel** material.

6.3

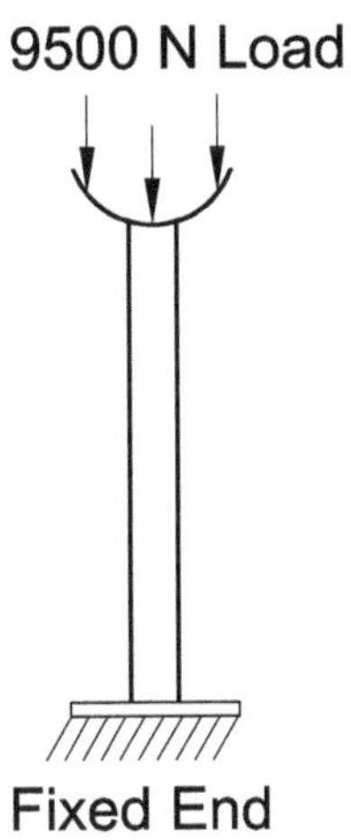

Project Summary

In this case study, you will run the buckling analysis of a Pipe Support and determine its buckling factor of safety under the applied compressive load. Also, you need to calculate the buckling load or critical load based on the buckling factor of safety.

The following sequence summarizes the case study outline:

1. Downloading Files of Chapter 6
2. Opening the Pipe Support
3. Starting the Buckling Study
4. Applying the Material, Fixture, and Load
5. Generating the Mesh
6. Defining the Buckling modes
7. Running the Buckling Analysis
8. Displaying the Buckling Factor of Safety
9. Calculating the Buckling Load or Critical Load
10. Saving Results

Section 1: Downloading Files of Chapter 6

1. Log on to the CADArtifex website (*cadartifex.com/login/*). If you are a new user, you must first sign up on the CADArtifex website as a **Learner** (*cadartifex.com/register*).

2. After logging, navigate to the textbook titled "**SOLIDWORKS Simulation 2026: A Power Guide for Beginners and Intermediate Users: Colored**" using the **Browse Resources** option available in the left menu to download its resources. Alternatively, you can enter the name of the textbook in the **Search** box to locate it quickly.

3. In the **Online Resources** tab, expand the **Case Studies** rollout and click the **Download** button corresponding to **C06 Case Studies**. In the confirmation window that appears, click the **Confirm** button. The download of the **C06 Case Studies** file will begin. After the download is complete, unzip the file.

4. Save the extracted **C06 Case Studies** folder in the location *SOLIDWORKS Simulation > Case Studies*.

Section 2: Opening the Pipe Support

1. Start SOLIDWORKS, if not already started.

2. Click on the **Open** button in the **Welcome** dialog box or the **Open** tool in the **Standard** toolbar. The **Open** dialog box appears.

3. Browse to the location > *SOLIDWORKS Simulation > Case Studies > C06 Case Studies > Case Study 1*. Next, select **Pipe Support** and then click on the **Open** button in the dialog box. The Pipe Support is opened in SOLIDWORKS.

6.4

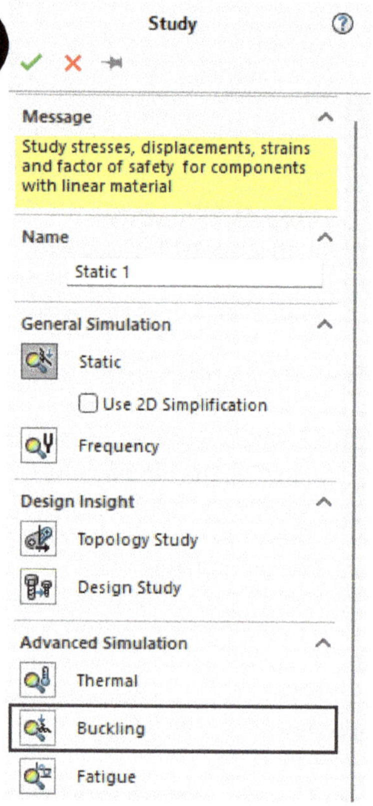

Section 3: Starting the Buckling Study

1. Click on the **Simulation** tab in the **CommandManager**. The tools of the **Simulation CommandManager** appear.

2. Click on the **New Study** tool in the **Simulation CommandManager**. The **Study PropertyManager** appears to the left of the graphics area.

3. Click on the **Buckling** button in the **Advanced Simulation** rollout of the **Study PropertyManager** to perform the buckling analysis, see Figure 6.4.

4. Enter **Pipe Support Buckling Study** in the **Study name** field of the **Name** rollout in the PropertyManager.

5. Click on the green tick-mark button ✓ in the PropertyManager. The **Pipe Support Buckling Study** is added to the Simulation Study Tree.

Section 4: Applying the Material, Fixture, and Load

Now, you need to apply the material, fixture, and load to the model. The procedures to apply the material, fixture, and load in the Buckling analysis are the same as in the static analysis.

1. Invoke the **Material** dialog box by clicking on the **Apply Material** tool in the **Simulation CommandManager** and then apply the **Alloy Steel** material. Next, close the dialog box.

   Now, you need to apply the Fixed Geometry fixture.

2. Right-click on the **Fixtures** option in the Simulation Study Tree and then click on the **Fixed Geometry** tool in the shortcut menu that appears. The **Fixture PropertyManager** appears.

3. Rotate the model such that you can view the bottom face of the Pipe Support model and then select it to apply the Fixed Geometry fixture, see Figure 6.5. Next, click on the green tick-mark button in the PropertyManager.

   Now, you need to apply the compressive axial load on the top face of the model.

4. Right-click on the **External Loads** option in the Simulation Study Tree and then click on the **Force** tool in the shortcut menu that appears. The **Force/Torque PropertyManager** appears.

5. Change the orientation of the model to isometric and then select the top semi-cylindrical face of the Pipe Support model to apply the load, see Figure 6.6.

6.5

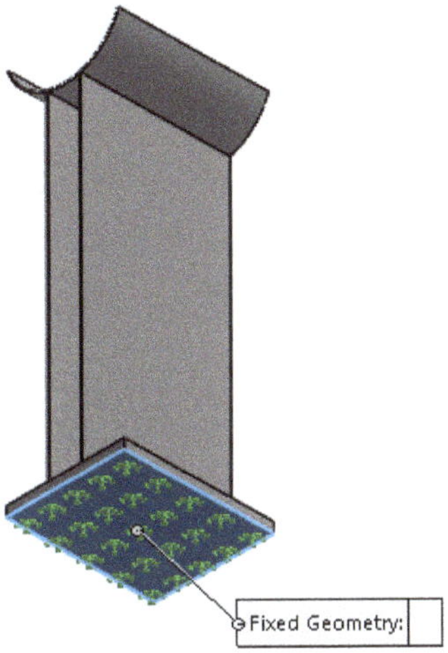

6.6

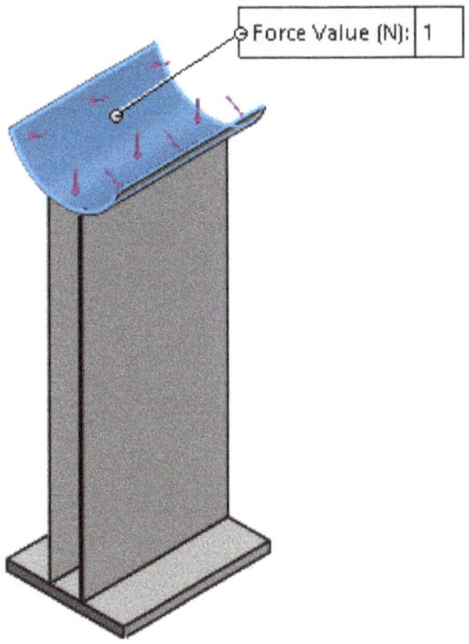

6. Select the **Selected direction** radio button in the PropertyManager. The **Face, Edge, Plane for Direction** field appears.

7. Expand the FeatureManager Design Tree, see Figure 6.7. Next, click on the **Top Plane** as the reference plane to define the direction of force.

8. Click on the **Normal to Plane** button in the **Force** rollout of the PropertyManager and then enter **9500** as the axial load acting on the model, see Figure 6.8.

6.7

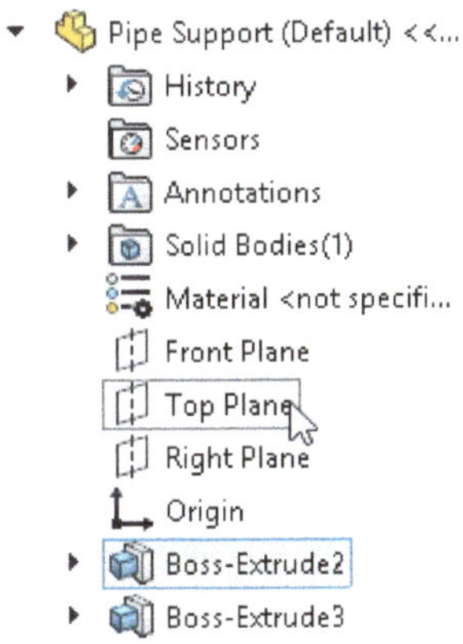

6.8

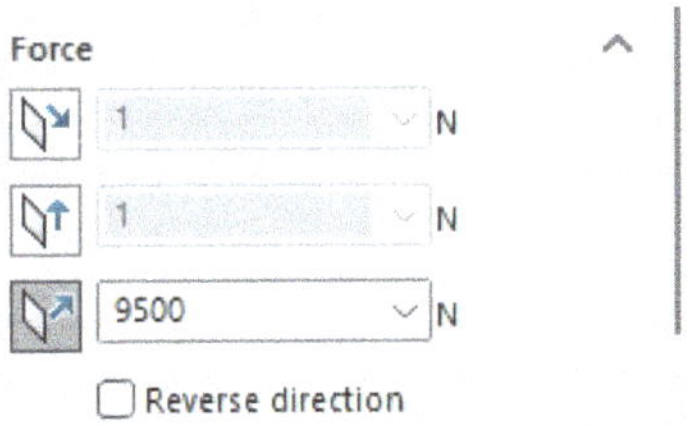

9. Select the **Reverse direction** check box in the **Force** rollout to reverse the direction of force downward, see Figure 6.9.

10. Click on the green tick-mark button in the PropertyManager. The specified compressive axial load is applied to the Pipe Support.

Section 5: Generating the Mesh

1. Generate the curvature-based mesh with the default mesh parameters by using the **Create Mesh** tool. Figure 6.10 shows the meshed model.

6.9

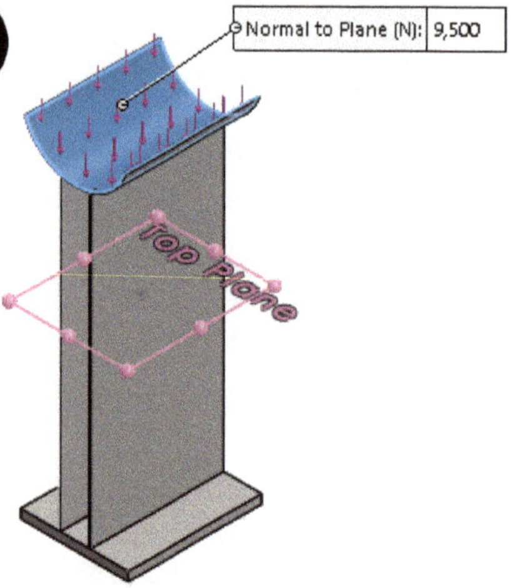

6.10

Section 6: Defining the Buckling modes

Now, you need to define the required number of buckling modes to be calculated by the program. By default, SOLIDWORKS Simulation calculates the first buckling mode of the model.

1. Right-click on the **Pipe Support Buckling Study** (*name of the study*) in the Simulation Study Tree and then click on the **Properties** tool in the shortcut menu that appears, see Figure 6.11. The **Buckling** dialog box appears, see Figure 6.12.

6.11

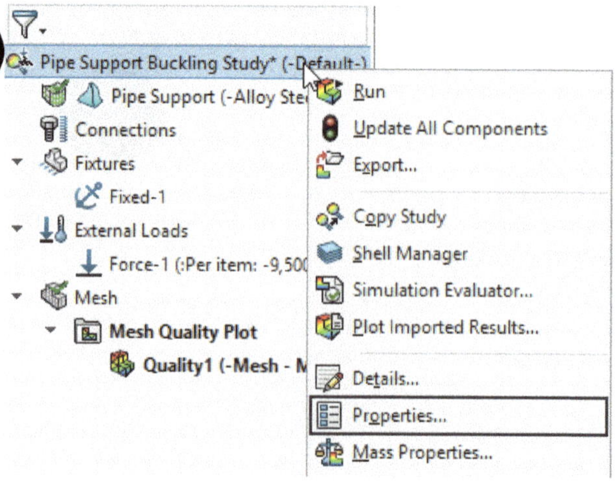

6.12

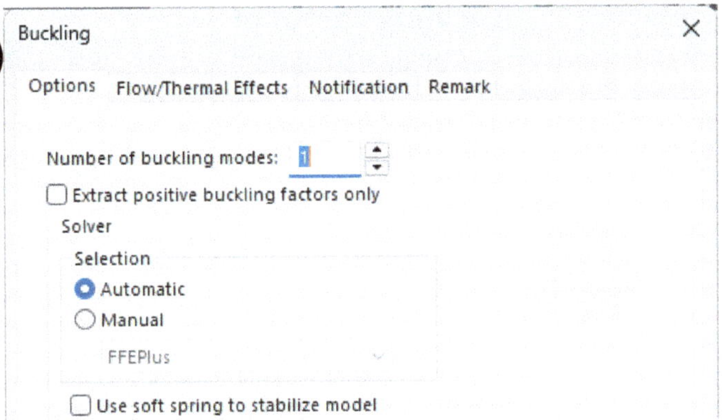

2. Enter **5** in the **Number of buckling modes** field of the **Options** tab in the dialog box to calculate five different buckling safety factors and the associated buckling modes for the Pipe Support.

3. Click the **OK** button in the dialog box. If the **Simulation** window appears, click **No** to overwrite the existing result files. If result files already exist for the study and you want to preserve them, click **Yes** to create a separate copy of the results before updating the study.

Section 7: Running the Buckling Analysis

1. Click on the **Run This Study** tool in the **Simulation CommandManager**. The **Pipe Support Buckling Study** (*name of the study*) window appears which displays the progress of the analysis. After the analysis is completed, the **Results** folder is added to the Simulation Study Tree with the five different mode shapes, see Figure 6.13. By default, the **Amplitude1 (-Res Amp - Mode Shape 1-)** is activated in the **Results** folder. As a result, the first buckling mode shape of the model, which occurs first when the model starts buckling, appears in the graphics area, see Figure 6.14.

6.13

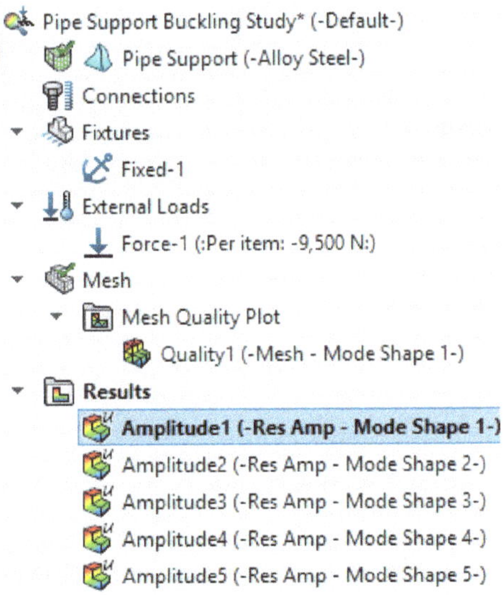

6.14

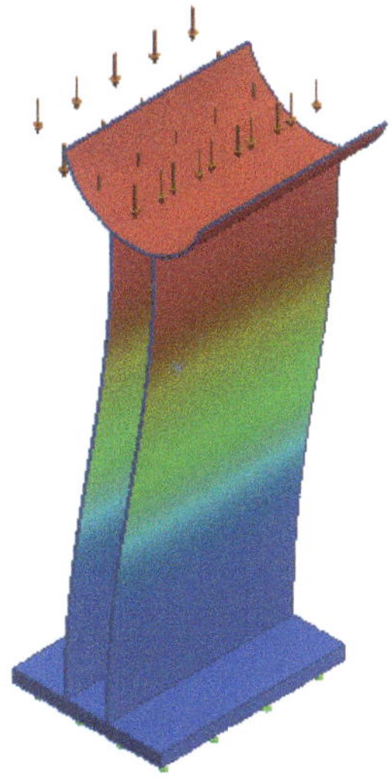

You can also display the remaining buckling mode shapes of the model by double-clicking on the respective option in the **Results** folder of the Simulation Study Tree.

Section 8: Displaying the Buckling Factor of Safety

Now, you need to display the buckling factor of safety of the Pipe Support.

1. Right-click on the **Results** folder in the Simulation Study Tree and then click on the **List Buckling Factor of Safety** tool in the shortcut menu that appears, see Figure 6.15. The **List Modes** dialog box appears, see Figure 6.16.

6.15

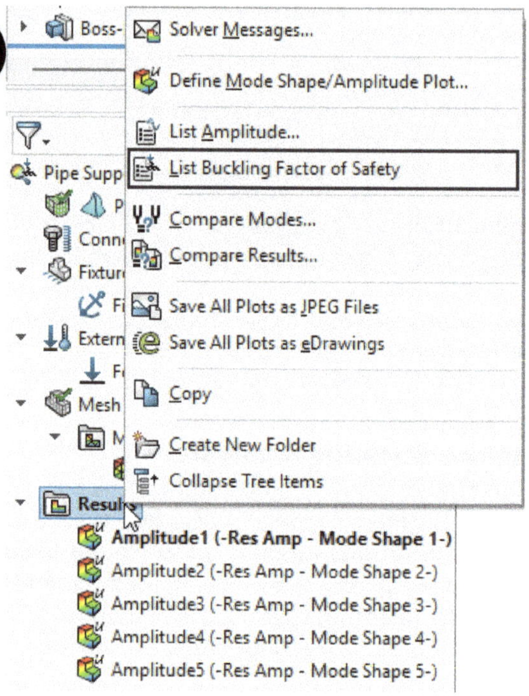

6.16

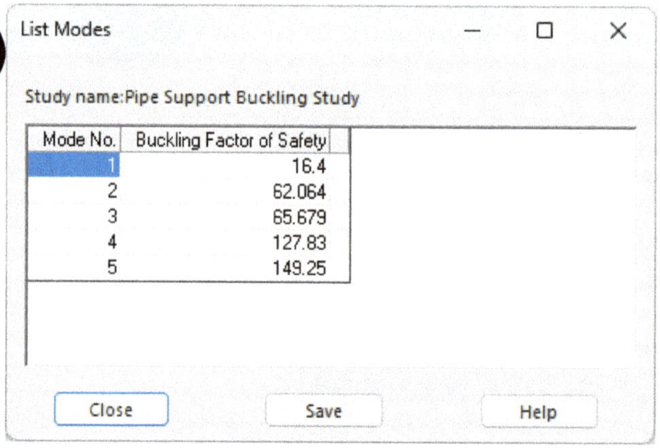

The **List Modes** dialog box displays the specified number of buckling modes and the associated buckling factor of safety of each mode. The first buckling load factor is always smaller than the other buckling load factors and for any given load, it occurs first. Therefore, you can calculate the buckling load or critical load when the model starts buckling by using the first buckling factor of safety.

In this study, the first calculated buckling factor of safety is **16.4**. This means that the design is safe.

Note: The buckling load factor is the ratio of buckling/critical load to the applied load.

Buckling Load Factor = Buckling Load / Applied Load

If the buckling load factor is greater than 1, the design is considered to be safe. If the buckling load factor is equal to 1 then the buckling starts to occur in the design. If the buckling load factor is less than 1, the design is considered to be a failure and buckling begins to occur in the design.

2. Close the **List Modes** dialog box.

Section 9: Calculating the Buckling Load or Critical Load

Now, you need to calculate the buckling load when the Pipe Support starts buckling.

1. Calculate the buckling load by using the following formula.

Buckling Load = Buckling Load Factor X Applied Load
= 16.4 X 9500 N
= 155800 N

The 155800 N load is the calculated buckling load or critical load when the Pipe Support can start buckling.

Section 10: Saving Results

Now, you need to save the model and its results.

1. Click on the **Save** tool in the **Standard** toolbar. The model and its results are saved in the location > ***SOLIDWORKS Simulation* > *Case Studies* > *C06 Case Studies* > *Case Study 1*.**

2. Close the SOLIDWORKS session.

Case Study 2: Buckling Analysis of a Beam

In this case study, you will perform the buckling analysis of a long Beam, see Figure 6.17. Determine the buckling load or critical load when the Beam can start buckling.

Project Description

The Beam is fixed at its bottom and a 14000 N compressive axial load is subjected on its top face, see Figure 6.18. The Beam is made up of **AISI 304** steel material.

6.17

6.18

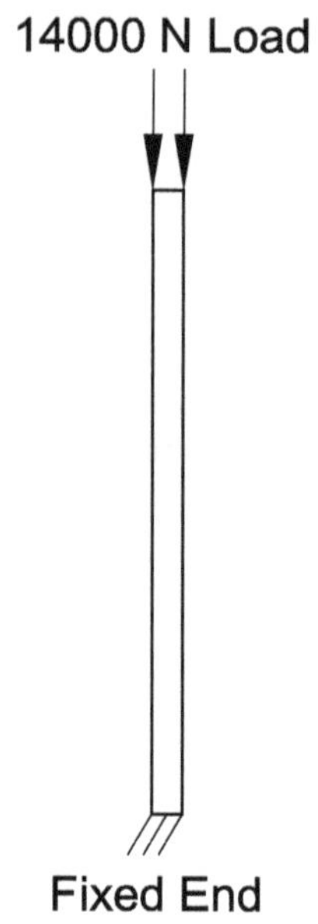

Project Summary

In this case study, you will run the buckling analysis of a beam and determine the buckling factor of safety of the beam under the applied compressive load. Also, you need to calculate the buckling load or critical load based on the buckling factor of safety of the beam.

The following sequence summarizes the case study outline:

1. Starting the Buckling Analysis
2. Applying the Material, Fixture, and Load
3. Generating the Mesh
4. Running the Buckling Analysis
5. Displaying the Buckling Factor of Safety
6. Calculating the Buckling Load or Critical Load
7. Saving Results

Section 1: Starting the Buckling Analysis

1. Start SOLIDWORKS and then open the Beam model from the location > ***SOLIDWORKS Simulation > Case Studies > C06 Case Studies > Case Study 2***.

Note: You need to download the **C06 Case Studies** file by logging on to the CADArtifex website (*cadartifex.com/login*), if it has not already been downloaded.

2. When the Beam model is opened in SOLIDWORKS, click on the **Simulation** tab in the **CommandManager**. The tools of the **Simulation CommandManager** appear.

3. Click on the **New Study** tool in the **Simulation CommandManager**. The **Study PropertyManager** appears to the left of the graphics area.

4. Click on the **Buckling** button in the **Advanced Simulation** rollout of the **Study PropertyManager** to perform the buckling analysis, see Figure 6.19.

5. Enter **Beam Buckling Study** in the **Study name** field of the **Name** rollout in the PropertyManager, see Figure 6.19.

6.19

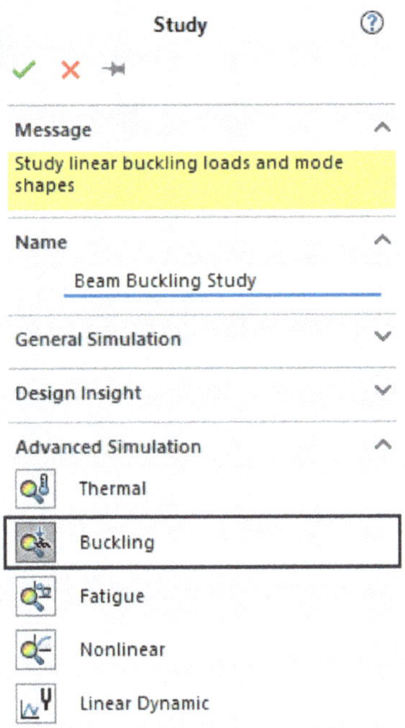

6. Click on the green tick-mark button in the PropertyManager. The **Beam Buckling Study** is added to the Simulation Study Tree, see Figure 6.20. Also, the joints appear on the beam member in the graphics area (see Figure 6.21) as SOLIDWORKS Simulation automatically identifies the geometry as a beam and calculates its joints.

6.20

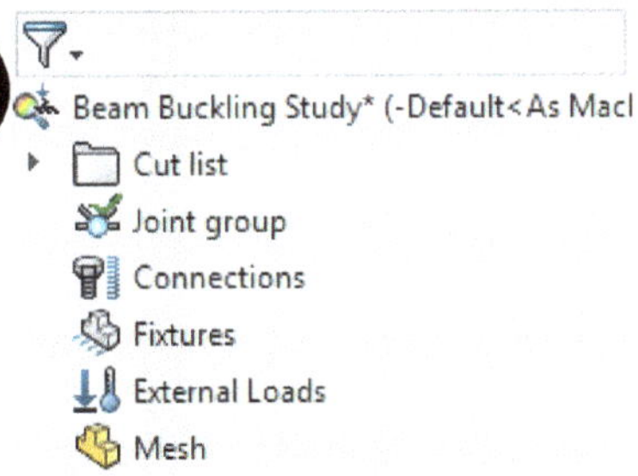

6.21

Section 2: Applying the Material, Fixture, and Load

Now, you need to apply the material, fixture, and load on the beam.

1. Invoke the **Material** dialog box by clicking on the **Apply Material** tool in the **Simulation CommandManager** and then apply the **AISI 304** steel material. Next, close the dialog box.

   Now, you need to apply the Fixed Geometry fixture.

2. Right-click on the **Fixtures** option in the Simulation Study Tree and then click on the **Fixed Geometry** tool in the shortcut menu that appears. The **Fixture PropertyManager** appears.

3. Select the yellow joint that appears at the bottom of the beam in the graphics area, see Figure 6.22. Next, click on the green tick-mark button in the PropertyManager. The Fixed Geometry fixture is applied at the bottom joint of the beam.

6.22

Now, you need to apply the compressive axial load on the top joint of the beam.

4. Right-click on the **External Loads** option in the Simulation Study Tree and then click on the **Force** tool in the shortcut menu that appears. The **Force/Torque PropertyManager** appears, see Figure 6.23.

   By default, the **Vertices, Points** button is activated in the **Selection** rollout of the PropertyManager. As a result, you can select the vertices and points of the beam members to apply the load. On selecting the **Joints** button, you can select a beam joint to apply the load.

5. Click on the **Joints** button in the **Selection** rollout of the PropertyManager to select the beam joint for applying the load.

6. Select the top beam joint. The name of the selected beam joint appears in the field of the **Selection** rollout in the PropertyManager.

7. Click on the **Face, Edge, Plane for Direction** field of the **Selection** rollout in the PropertyManager. Next, expand the FeatureManager Design Tree and then click on the **Top Plane** as the reference plane to define the direction of force, see Figure 6.24.

6.23

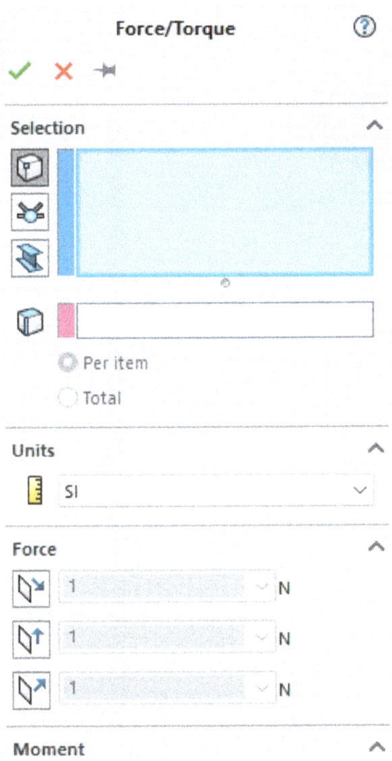

6.24

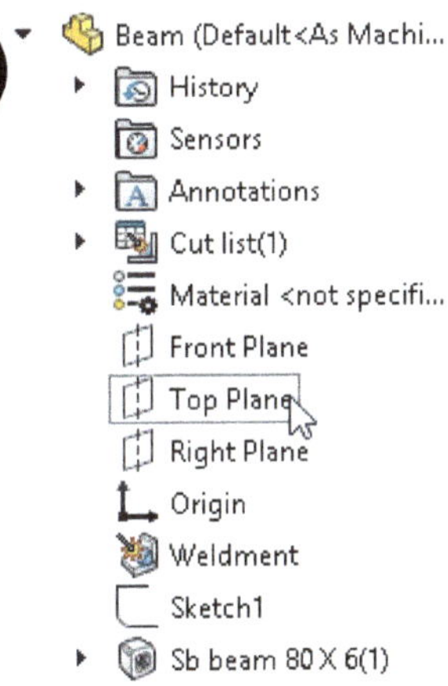

8. Ensure that the **SI** is selected as the unit in the **Unit** drop-down list of the **Units** rollout in the PropertyManager.

9. Click on the **Normal to Plane** button in the **Force** rollout of the PropertyManager and then enter **14000** as the axial load on the beam, see Figure 6.25.

6.25

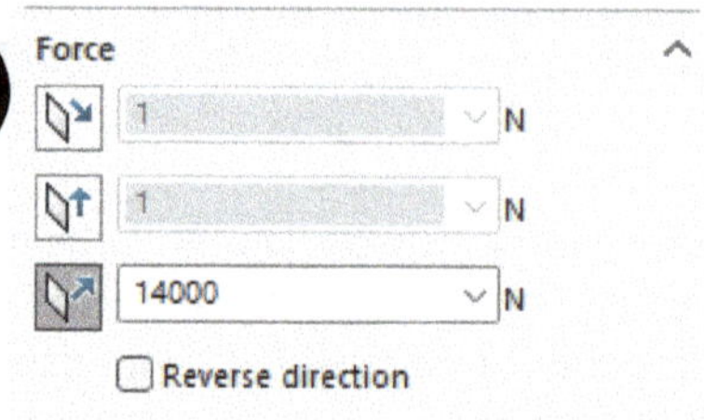

10. Select the **Reverse direction** check box in the **Force** rollout to reverse the direction of force downward, see Figure 6.26.

11. Click on the green tick-mark button in the PropertyManager. The specified compressive axial load is applied to the beam.

Section 3: Generating the Mesh

1. Right-click on the **Mesh** option in the Simulation Study Tree and then click on the **Create Mesh** tool in the shortcut menu that appears. The **Mesh Progress** window appears and the process of meshing the beam starts. After it is complete, the meshed beam with beam elements, which are represented by hollow cylinders, appears in the graphics area, see Figure 6.27.

6.26

6.27

Section 4: Running the Buckling Analysis

1. Click on the **Run This Study** tool in the **Simulation CommandManager**. The **Beam Buckling Study** (*name of the study*) window appears which displays the progress of the analysis. When it is complete, the **Results** folder is added to the Simulation Study Tree with the resultant amplitude of the first mode shape. Also, the first mode shape of the beam appears in the graphics area, see Figure 6.28.

6.28

Section 5: Displaying the Buckling Factor of Safety

Now, you need to display the buckling factor of safety of the beam.

1. Right-click on the **Results** folder in the Simulation Study Tree and then click on the **List Buckling Factor of Safety** tool in the shortcut menu that appears. The **List Modes** dialog box appears, see Figure 6.29.

6.29

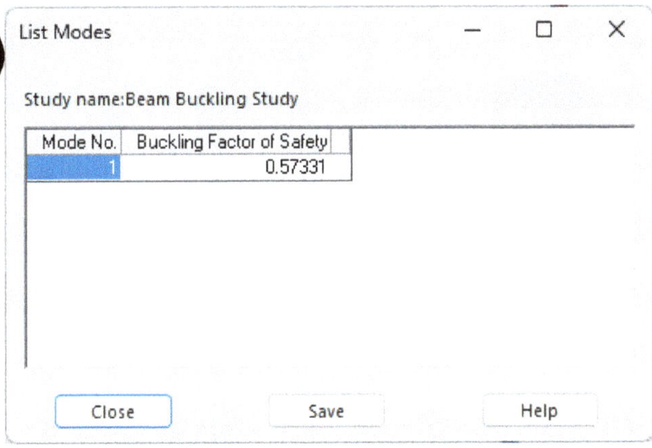

Note: The **List Modes** dialog box displays the number of specified buckling modes and the associated buckling factor of safety of each mode. By default, SOLIDWORKS Simulation calculates the first buckling factor of safety as the first buckling load factor is always smaller and for any given load, it occurs first. However, as discussed in Case Study 1, you can specify multiple buckling modes and the associated buckling factors of safety to be calculated by the program.

The calculated buckling factor of safety is **0.57331**. This means that the design is considered to be a failure and the buckling starts when the applied load is equal to **8026.34 N** [14000 (*applied load*) X 0.57331 (*buckling load factor*)]. Note that you may find a difference in the results due to the service packs installed on your system.

Section 6: Calculating the Buckling Load or Critical Load

Now, you need to calculate the buckling load when the beam can start buckling.

1. Calculate the buckling load by using the following formula:

Buckling Load = Buckling Load Factor X Applied Load
= 0.57331 X 14000
= 8026.34 N

Section 7: Saving the Results

Now, you need to save the results.

1. Click on the **Save** tool in the **Standard** toolbar. The model and its results are saved in the location > *SOLIDWORKS Simulation > Case Studies > C06 Case Studies > Case Study 2*.

2. Close the SOLIDWORKS Simulation session.

Hands-on Test Drive 1: Buckling Analysis of a Column

Perform the buckling analysis of a long hollow column shown in Figure 6.30 and determine the buckling load or critical load when the column can start buckling.

6.30

Project Description

The column is clamped at both its ends (top and bottom). You need to apply the Fixed Geometry fixture at the bottom face of the column to represent its clamped connection with the ground, see Figure 6.31. To represent the clamped connection at the top of the column, you need to restrict the radial and circumferential translations of the column at the top so that the column can only translate along its axial direction due to the applied load, see Figure 6.31. The column is subjected to a 1200 N compressive axial load on its top, see Figure 6.31. The column is made up of Alloy Steel material.

6.31

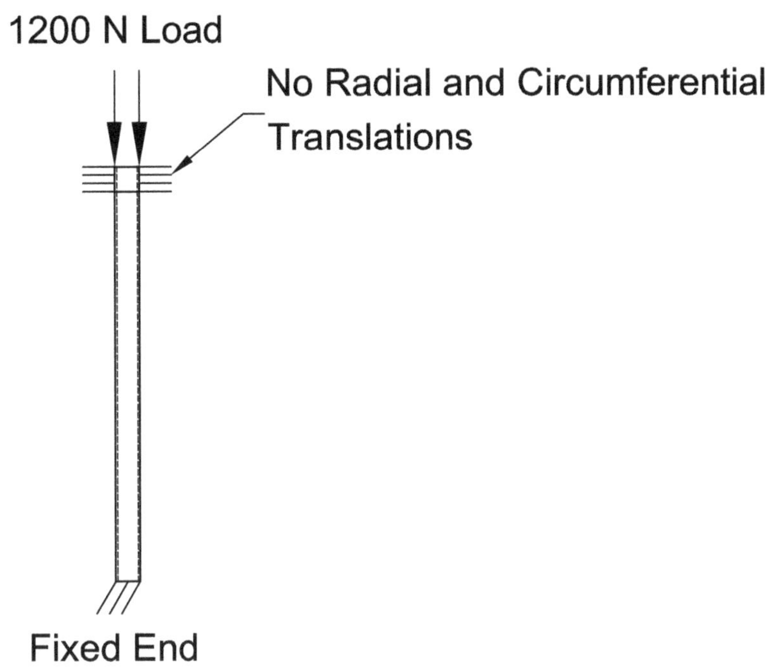

Hint: To restrict the radial and circumferential translations of the column at the top, you can apply the ***On Cylindrical Faces*** *fixture and specify a* **0** *value for the radial and circumferential translations.*

Project Summary
In this case study, you will run the buckling analysis of a column that is clamped at both ends and determine the buckling factor of safety of the beam under the applied compressive load. You also need to calculate the buckling load or critical load based on the minimum buckling factor of safety of the column when it can start buckling.

Summary

This chapter introduced the concept of buckling analysis and its importance in evaluating structural stability. You learned how to perform buckling analysis in SOLIDWORKS Simulation to determine the buckling load factor or critical load, the threshold at which a structure may become unstable. Additionally, the chapter covered techniques for interpreting buckling modes and ensuring that designs can withstand expected loads without failure.

Questions

Complete the following sentences:

- The _________ refers to the larger deformation occurring on a structure due to the compressive axial loads.
- The buckling load is also known as the _________, when the model can start buckling.
- A structure can buckle even if the maximum stress developed in the structure is within the _________ strength of the material.
- The _________ field of the **Buckling** dialog box is used for specifying the number of buckling modes to be calculated by the program.
- The _________ tool is used to display the specified number of buckling modes and the associated buckling factor of safety.
- For any given load, the _________ calculated buckling factor of safety is always smaller than the other buckling load factors.
- The _________ dialog box displays the specified number of buckling modes and the associated buckling factor of safety of each mode.
- The buckling load factor is the ratio of _________ load to the _________ load.
- If the buckling load factor is greater than 1, the design is considered to be _________.
- If the buckling load factor is less than 1, the design is considered to be _________ and buckling occurs in the design due to the applied load.
- On increasing the length of a structure, the force required to buckle it gets _________.
- The buckling load or critical load does not depend upon the _________ strength of the material.
- You can calculate the buckling load or critical load of a structure, when it can start buckling, by using the _________ buckling factor of safety.

CHAPTER
7

Fatigue Analysis

In this chapter, the following topics will be discussed:

- Introduction to Fatigue Analysis
- Fatigue Analysis of a Connecting Rod
- Fatigue Analysis of a Crankshaft

In earlier chapters, you learned about design failure due to stresses exceeding the material's yield strength, known as material failure, as well as failure caused by buckling.

In this chapter, you will explore fatigue failure, which occurs due to repeated loading and unloading or cyclic loads. In real-world applications, most mechanical components experience cyclic loading, which can lead to failure over time, even if the stress levels remain below the yield strength. Understanding fatigue is crucial for predicting the lifespan of a design and ensuring its long-term reliability.

Introduction to Fatigue Analysis

Fatigue analysis is used to calculate the stress at which an object fails due to repeated loading and unloading. Over time, cyclic loading weakens the object, leading to failure even when the applied stress remains within allowable limits. Using fatigue analysis, you can predict the total lifespan of a component and assess the damage caused by cyclic loading.

In SOLIDWORKS Simulation, fatigue analysis can be performed based on the results of linear static analysis, time history linear dynamic analysis, or nonlinear analysis. In this chapter, you will perform fatigue analysis based on linear static analysis to determine the total life of a component and evaluate the effects of cyclic loading.

Case Study 1: Fatigue Analysis of a Connecting Rod

In this case study, you will perform the fatigue analysis of a Connecting Rod (see Figure 7.1) and determine its total life, damage, and load factor due to the cyclic loads of constant amplitudes.

7.1

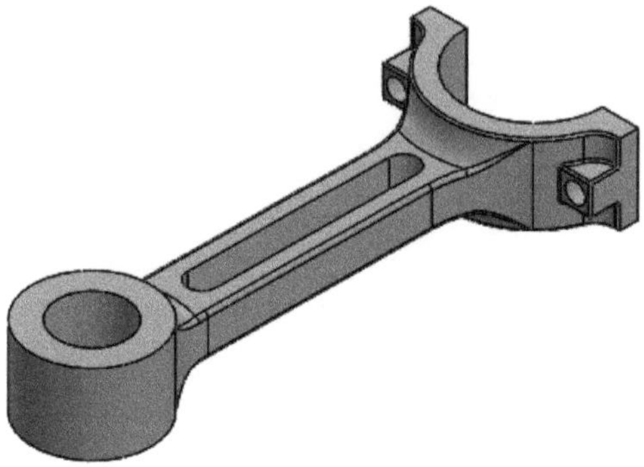

Project Description

The Connecting Rod is fixed at its crank end, see Figure 7.2. Also, an 8000 N compressive load as the combustion force, 3000 N tensile load as the inertial force, and 1800 N lateral load as the momentum force are activated on the pin end of the Connecting Rod, see Figure 7.2. The Connecting Rod is made up of **Alloy Steel (SS)** material.

7.2

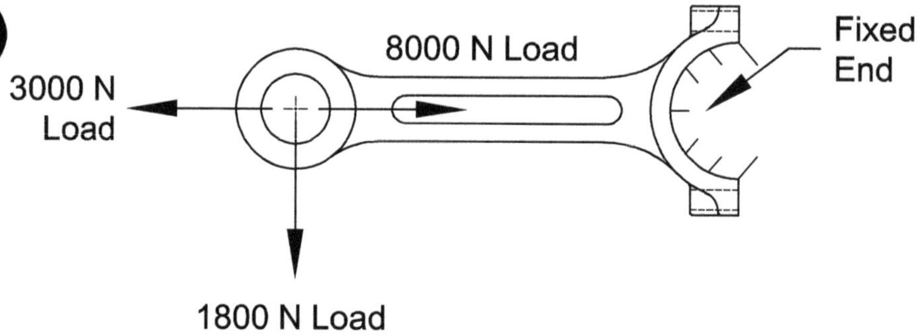

Project Summary

In this case study, you will first perform the static analysis on the Connecting Rod, then based on the results of the static analysis, you need to perform the fatigue analysis to calculate the total life and damage of the product under repeated full reversed loading for 3,00,000 load cycles.

The following sequence summarizes the case study outline:

1. Downloading Files of Chapter 7
2. Opening the Connecting Rod
3. Starting the Static Study
4. Applying the Material, Fixture, and Load
5. Generating the Mesh
6. Running the Static Study and Displaying Results

7. Running the Fatigue Analysis
8. Defining Properties for the Fatigue Analysis
9. Defining the Loading Events for the Fatigue Analysis
10. Defining the Fatigue S-N Curve
11. Running the Fatigue Analysis and Displaying Results
12. Displaying the Load Factor Plot
13. Saving Results

Section 1: Downloading Files of Chapter 7

1. Log on to the CADArtifex website (*cadartifex.com/login/*). If you are a new user, you must first sign up on the CADArtifex website as a **Learner** (*cadartifex.com/register*).

2. After logging, navigate to the textbook titled "**SOLIDWORKS Simulation 2026: A Power Guide for Beginners and Intermediate Users: Colored**" using the **Browse Resources** option available in the left menu to download its resources. Alternatively, you can enter the name of the textbook in the **Search** box to locate it quickly.

3. In the **Online Resources** tab, expand the **Case Studies** rollout and click the **Download** button corresponding to **C07 Case Studies**. In the confirmation window that appears, click the **Confirm** button. The download of the **C07 Case Studies** file will begin. After the download is complete, unzip the file.

4. Save the extracted **C07 Case Studies** folder in the location *SOLIDWORKS Simulation > Case Studies*.

Section 2: Opening the Connecting Rod

1. Start SOLIDWORKS, if not already started.

2. Click on the **Open** button in the **Welcome** dialog box or the **Open** tool in the **Standard** toolbar. The **Open** dialog box appears.

3. Browse to the location > *SOLIDWORKS Simulation > Case Studies > C07 Case Studies > Case Study 1* of the local drive of your system. Next, select the **Connecting Rod** and then click on the **Open** button in the dialog box. The Connecting Rod is opened in SOLIDWORKS.

Section 3: Starting the Static Study

As discussed, first you need to perform the static analysis on the Connecting Rod and then based on the results of the static analysis, you need to perform the fatigue analysis.

1. Click on the **Simulation** tab in the **CommandManager**. The tools of the **Simulation CommandManager** appear.

2. Click on the **New Study** tool in the **Simulation CommandManager**. The **Study PropertyManager** appears to the left of the graphics area.

3. Ensure that the **Static** button is activated in the **Study PropertyManager**.

4. Enter **Connecting Rod Static Study** in the **Study name** field of the **Name** rollout in the PropertyManager.

5. Click on the green tick-mark button in the PropertyManager. The **Connecting Rod Static Study** is added to the Simulation Study Tree.

Section 4: Applying the Material, Fixture, and Load

Now, you need to apply the material, fixture, load to the model.

1. Invoke the **Material** dialog box by clicking on the **Apply Material** tool in the **Simulation CommandManager** and then apply the **Alloy Steel (SS)** material. Next, close the dialog box.

   Now, you need to apply the Fixed Geometry fixture.

2. Right-click on the **Fixtures** option in the Simulation Study Tree and then click on the **Fixed Geometry** tool in the shortcut menu that appears. The **Fixture PropertyManager** appears.

3. Select the semi-circular face of the crank end of the Connecting Rod to apply the Fixed Geometry fixture, see Figure 7.3. Next, click on the green tick-mark button in the PropertyManager.

7.3

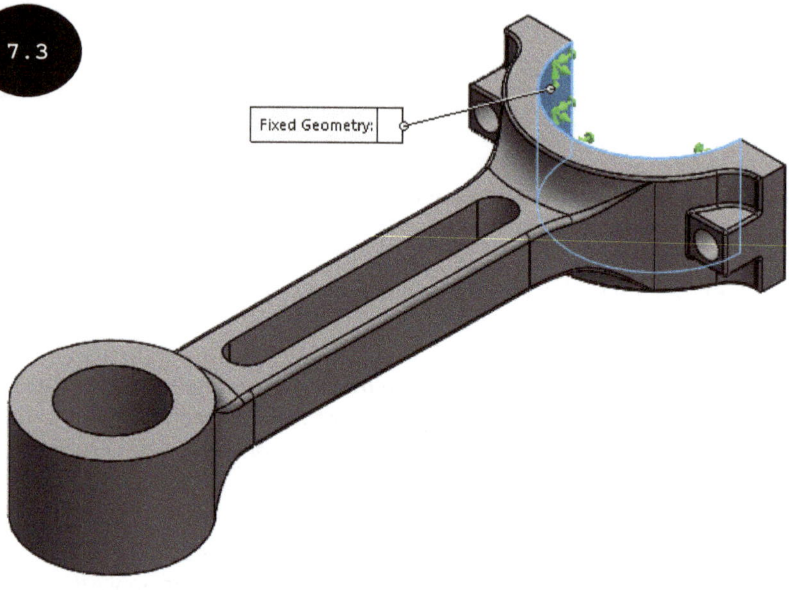

Now, you need to apply the loads on the pin end of the Connecting Rod.

4. Right-click on the **External Loads** option in the Simulation Study Tree and then click on the **Force** tool in the shortcut menu that appears. The **Force/Torque PropertyManager** appears.

5. Select the inner circular face of the pin end of the Connecting Rod to apply the load, see Figure 7.4.

6. Select the **Selected direction** radio button in the PropertyManager. The **Face, Edge, Plane for Direction** field appear in the PropertyManager.

7. Expand the FeatureManager Design Tree, see Figure 7.5. Next, click on the **Front Plane** as the reference plane to define the direction of force.

7.4

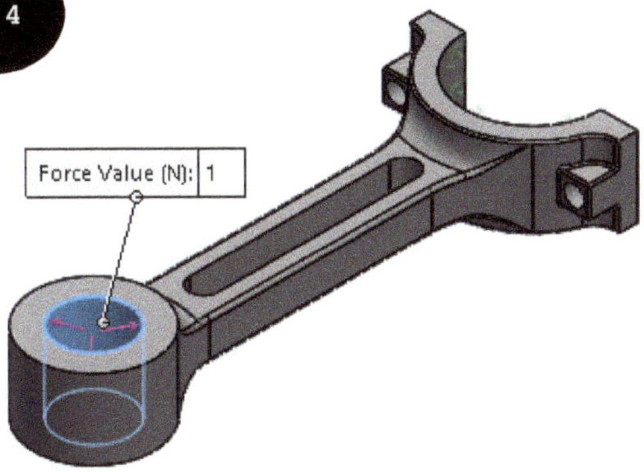

7.5

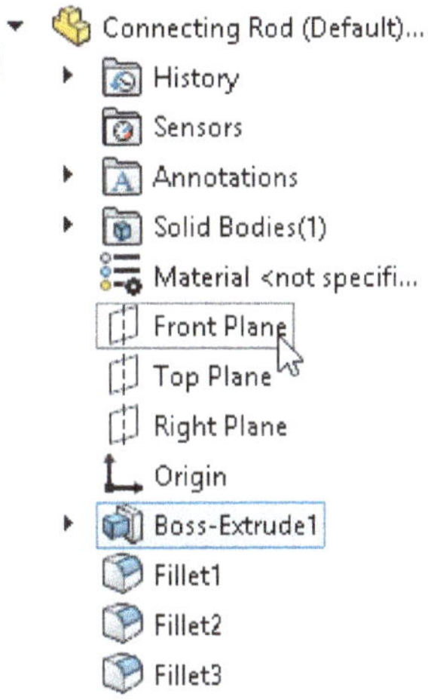

8. Click on the **Normal to Plane** button in the **Force** rollout of the PropertyManager and then enter **8000 N** as the compressive load acting on the Connecting Rod.

9. Select the **Reverse direction** check box in the **Force** rollout to reverse the direction of force toward the crank end of the Connecting Rod, see Figure 7.6.

7.6

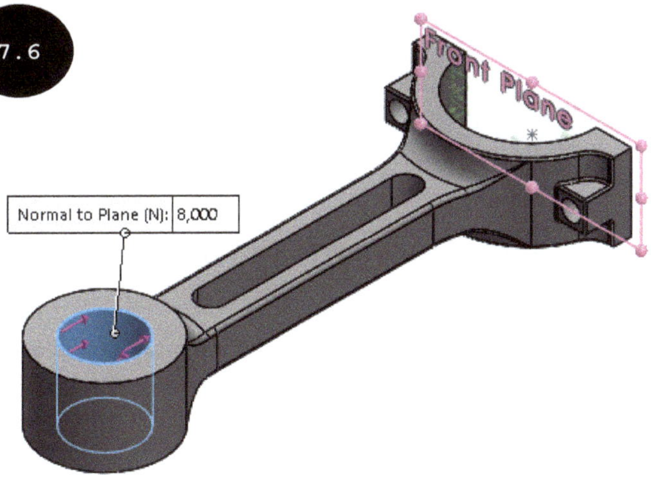

10. Click on the green tick-mark button in the PropertyManager. The specified compressive load is applied to the Connecting Rod.

11. Similarly, apply a tensile load of 3000 N and a lateral load of 1800 N on the pin end of the Connecting Rod, one by one. Figure 7.7 shows the Connecting Rod after applying the compressive, tensile, and lateral loads on its pin end. All the applied loads are listed in the **External Loads** folder in the Simulation Study Tree, see Figure 7.8.

7.7

7.8

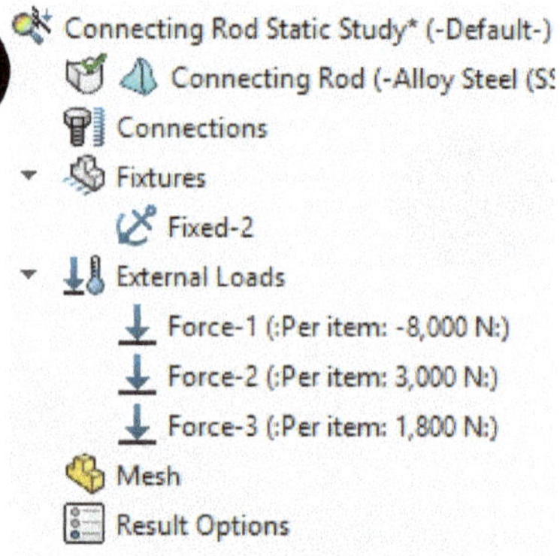

Section 5: Generating the Mesh

1. Generate the curvature-based mesh with default mesh parameters by using the **Create Mesh** tool. Figure 7.9 shows the meshed model.

7.9

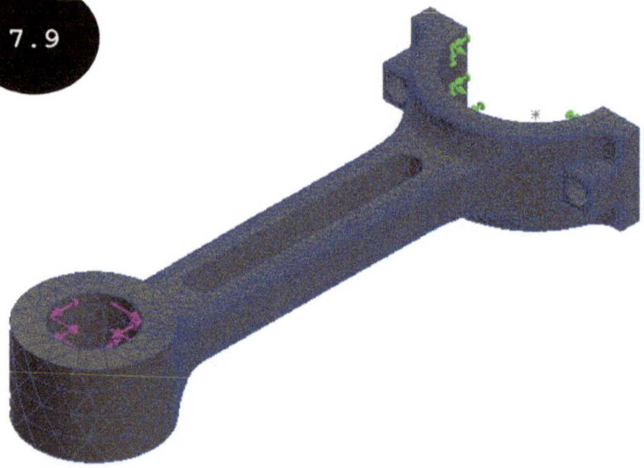

Section 6: Running the Static Study and Displaying Results

Now, you need to run the static study.

1. Click on the **Run This Study** tool in the **Simulation CommandManager**. The **Connecting Rod Static Study** (*name of the study*) window appears which displays the progress of the analysis.

2. After the process of running the analysis is complete, the **Results** folder is added to the Simulation Study Tree with the stress, displacement, and strain results. Also, the stress distribution on the model and the von Mises stress plot appear in the graphics area, see Figure 7.10.

   The maximum von Mises stress in the model under the applied loads is **2.528e+02** (252.752) N/mm^2 (MPa) which is significantly within the yield stress of the material that is **6.204e+02** (620.422) N/mm^2 (MPa). Also, the Factor of Safety of the design is 2.455, which means that the design of the Connecting Rod is safe. You can display the Factor of Safety plot of the model by using the **Define Factor Of Safety Plot** tool which is displayed in the shortcut menu that appears by right-clicking on the **Results** folder of the Simulation Study Tree.

7.10

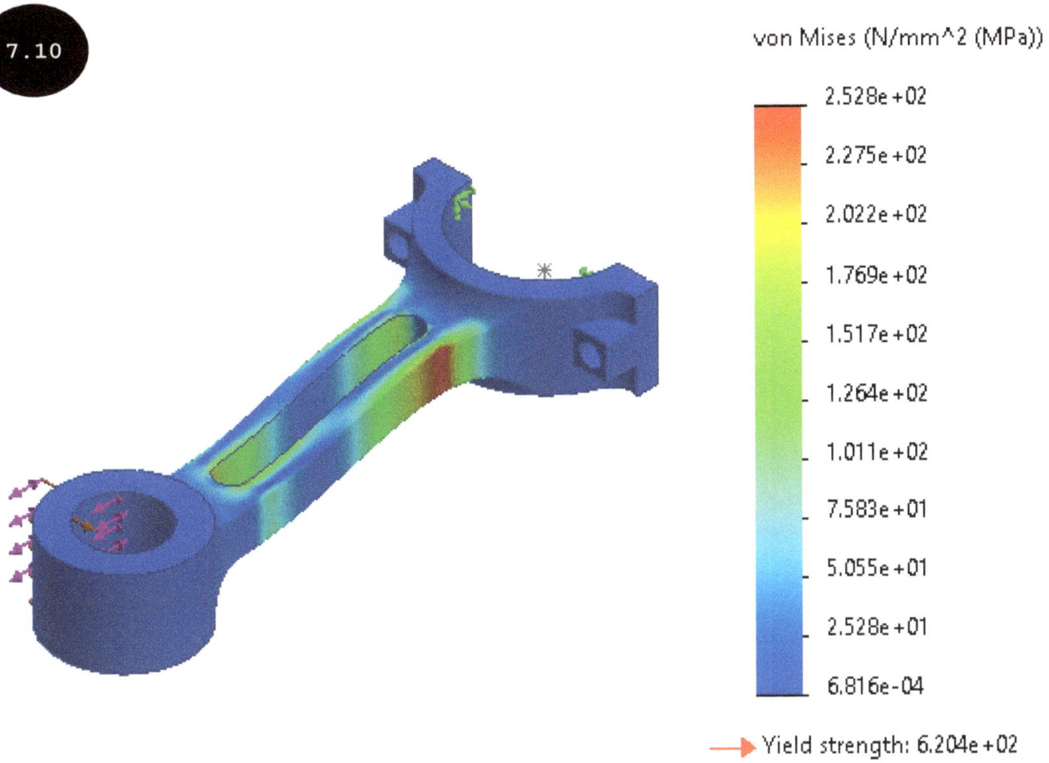

After running the static study of the Connecting Rod, you can perform the fatigue analysis based on the results of the static study to check the life of the design, when it undergoes repeated loading of constant amplitudes.

Section 7: Running the Fatigue Analysis

Now, you need to perform the fatigue analysis on the Connecting Rod, based on the results of the static study.

1. Click on the **New Study** tool in the **Simulation CommandManager**. The **Study PropertyManager** appears.

2. Click on the **Fatigue** button in the **Advanced Simulation** rollout of the PropertyManager, see Figure 7.11.

3. Ensure that the **Constant amplitude events with defined cycles** button is activated in the **Advanced Simulation** rollout of the PropertyManager to perform the fatigue analysis with constant amplitude of cyclic loads, refer to Figure 7.11.

4. Enter **Connecting Rod Fatigue Study** in the **Study name** field of the **Name** rollout in the PropertyManager, see Figure 7.11.

7.11

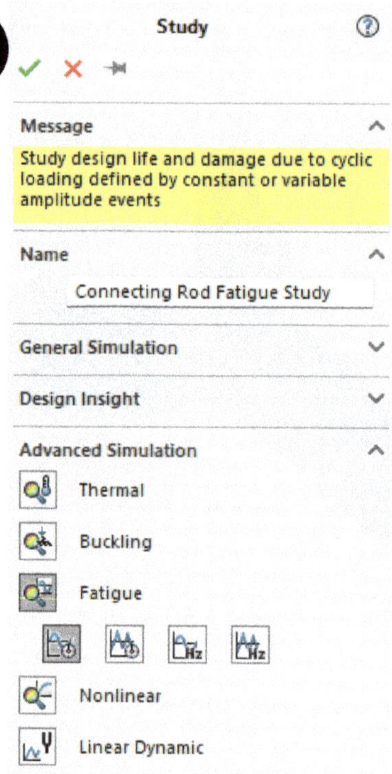

Tip: You can perform the fatigue analysis based on the results of the static study with the constant or variable amplitude of cyclic loads by activating the **Constant amplitude events with defined cycles** or **Variable amplitude history data** buttons respectively, in the **Advanced Simulation** rollout of the **Study PropertyManager**. You can also perform the fatigue analysis based on the linear dynamic harmonic study or linear dynamic random vibration study by activating the **Harmonic-fatigue of sinusoidal loading** or **Random vibration-fatigue of random vibration** buttons respectively, in the **Advanced Simulation** rollout of the PropertyManager.

5. Click on the green tick-mark button in the PropertyManager. A new tab named **Connecting Rod Fatigue Study** is added at the lower left corner of the graphics area and the **Connecting Rod Fatigue Study** is added in the Simulation Study Tree, see Figure 7.12.

7.12

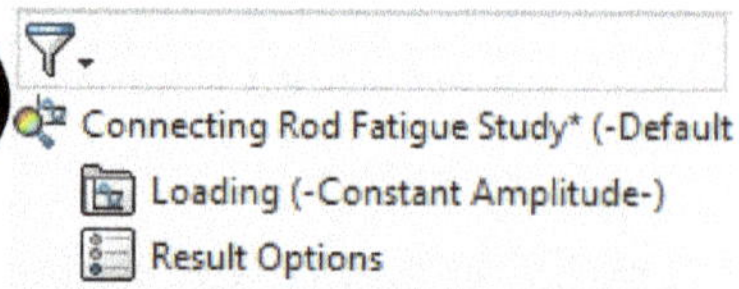

Section 8: Defining Properties for the Fatigue Analysis

Before you start performing the fatigue analysis, you need to define its properties.

1. Right-click on the **Connecting Rod Fatigue Study** (*name of the study*) in the Simulation Study Tree and then click on the **Properties** tool in the shortcut menu that appears, see Figure 7.13. The **Fatigue** dialog box appears, see Figure 7.14.

7.13

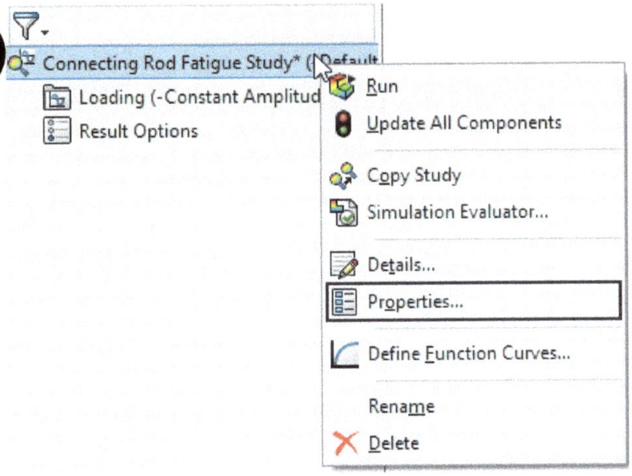

7.14

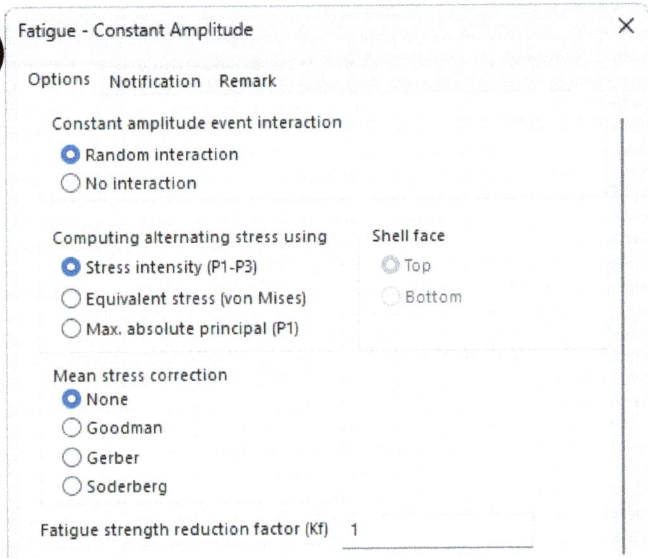

The options in the **Fatigue** dialog box are used to specify the properties of the active fatigue study. By default, the **Random interaction** radio button is selected in the **Constant amplitude event interaction** area of the dialog box. As a result, SOLIDWORKS Simulation considers the random interaction between different events to calculate the alternating stresses. On selecting the **No interaction** radio button, SOLIDWORKS Simulation considers no interaction between the events and all the events occur sequentially. The **Random interaction** radio button is useful when you have specified multiple events for the fatigue analysis especially in the case of performing the fatigue analysis on the ASME Boiler and Pressure vessel. You will learn more about specifying the events later in this case study.

The options in the **Computing alternating stress using** area of the dialog box are used to define the stress type for calculating the alternating stress in the constant cyclic loads. The program extracts the respective data (number of load cycles against the computed alternating stress) from the S-N curve to identify the fatigue failure. You will learn about the S-N curve later in this case study. Figure 7.15 shows a constant amplitude stress diagram for the number of cyclic loads.

7.15

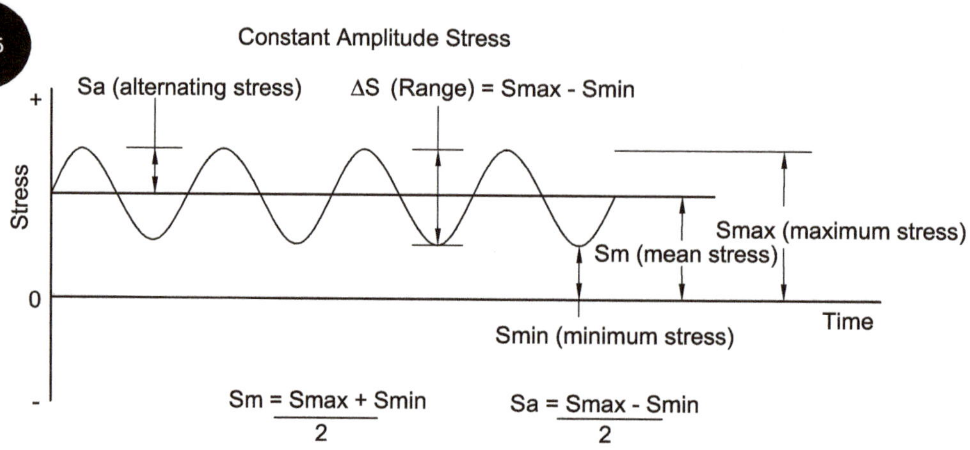

The options in the **Mean stress correction** area are used to define the method for calculating the mean stress correction. SOLIDWORKS Simulation calculates the mean stress along with the alternating stress for each cycle and then it evaluates the mean stress correction using the method specified in this area.

The **Fatigue strength reduction factor (Kf)** field of the dialog box is used to specify the fatigue strength reduction factor. You can specify the fatigue strength reduction factor between the range 0 to 1. SOLIDWORKS Simulation divides the computed alternating stress by the specified fatigue strength reduction factor and then reads the corresponding number of cycles in the S-N curve. If the fatigue strength reduction factor is less than 1 then the number of cycles that can cause failure due to fatigue get reduced.

2. Accept the default specified options in the **Fatigue** dialog box and then click on the **OK** button. The default properties for the fatigue study are specified.

Section 9: Defining the Loading Events for the Fatigue Analysis

After defining the properties for the fatigue analysis, you need to define the loading events.

1. Right-click on the **Loading (-Constant Amplitude-)** option in the Simulation Study Tree and then click on the **Add Event** tool in the shortcut menu that appears, see Figure 7.16. The **Add Event (Constant) PropertyManager** appears, see Figure 7.17.

7.16

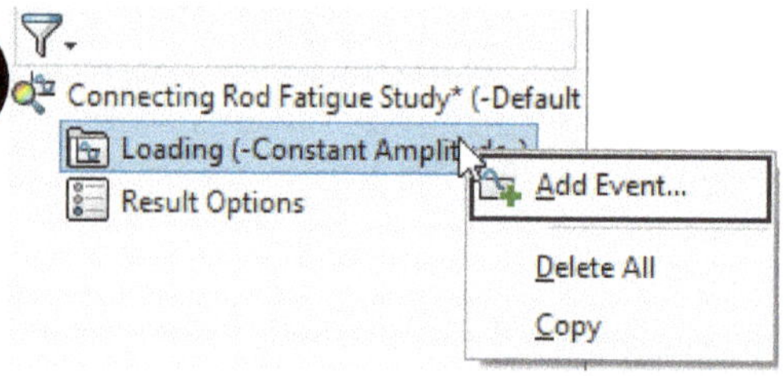

7.17

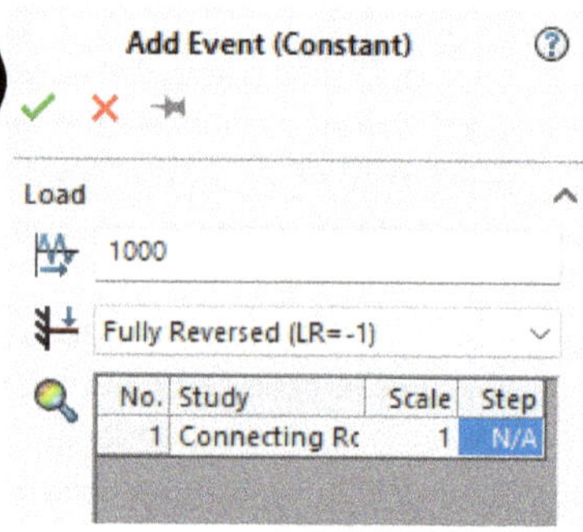

2. Enter **300000** in the **Cycles** field of the PropertyManager as the number of cyclic loads to be carried out on the design.

After specifying the number of cyclic loads, you need to select the type of fatigue loading in the **Loading Type** drop-down list of the PropertyManager. The **Fully Reversed (LR=-1)** option of the **Loading Type** drop-down list is used to specify the fully reverse loading type for the specified number of cyclic loads such that all the applied loads in the study reverse their load magnitudes simultaneously, see Figure 7.18. The **Zero-based (LR=0)** option is used to specify the zero-based loading type for the specified number of cyclic loads such that all the applied loads in the study change their magnitudes from maximum to zero stress values, see Figure 7.19.

7.18

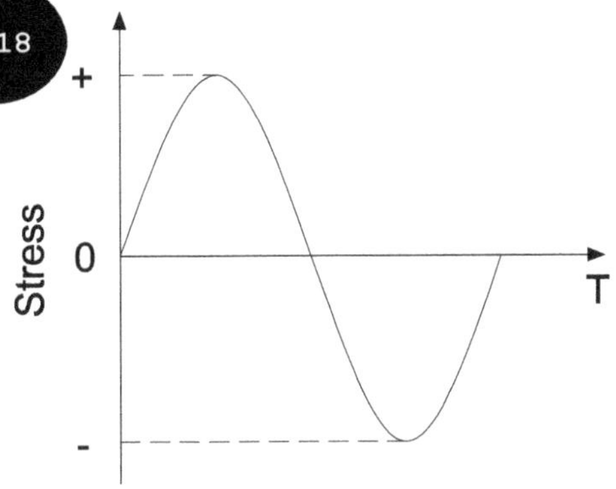

7.19

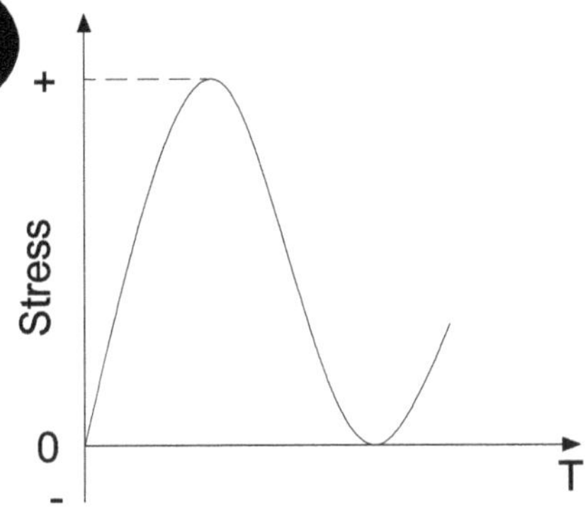

The **Loading Ratio** option is used to specify the loading ratio (R) to define the user-defined loading type such that the applied loads change their magnitudes from maximum to minimum load values, see Figure 7.20. Note that the minimum load value is defined by multiplying the specified loading ratio (R) by the maximum value of the load magnitude (R*Smax = Smin), see Figure 7.20. The **Find Cycle Peaks** option is used to define the loading type based on multiple studies.

7.20

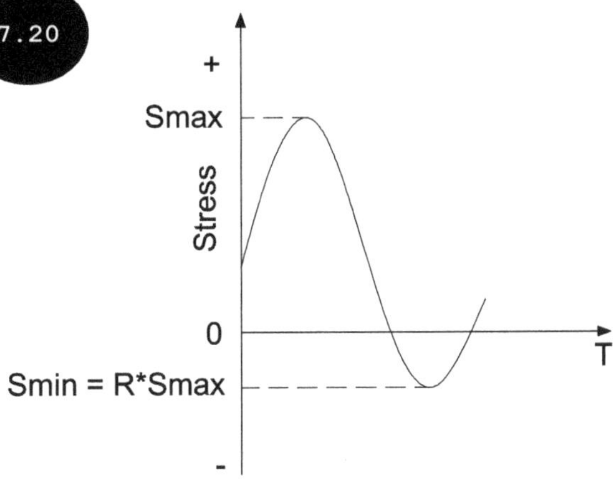

3. Select the **Fully Reversed (LR=-1)** option in the **Loading Type** drop-down list of the PropertyManager, considering the fully reverse loading type for the specified number of cyclic loads.

4. Click on the field of the first row, corresponding to the **Study** column in the **Study Association** table of the PropertyManager. An arrow appears. Next, click on this arrow to invoke a drop-down list, see Figure 7.21. Note that this drop-down list displays the list of all the studies performed earlier on the active design. You have performed a static study of the Connecting Rod earlier. As a result, the same static study is listed in the drop-down list, see Figure 7.21.

7.21

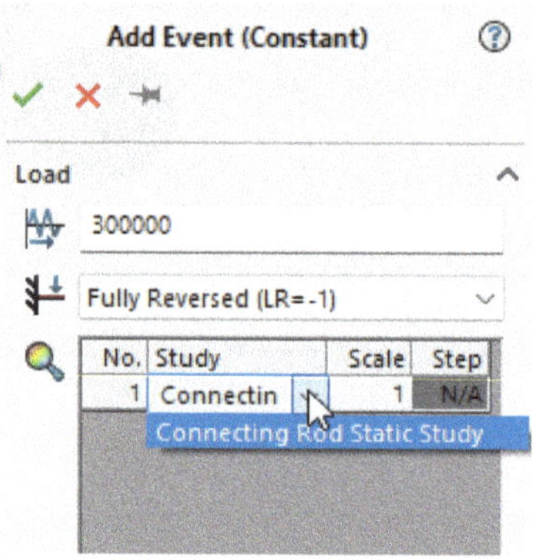

5. Ensure that the **Connecting Rod Static Study** is selected under the **Study** column as the base study to perform the fatigue analysis.

6. Click on the green tick-mark button in the PropertyManager. An event for the **3,00,000** fully reversed cyclic loads is created. Also, it is listed under the **Loading (-Constant Amplitude-)** node of the Simulation Study Tree, see Figure 7.22.

7.22

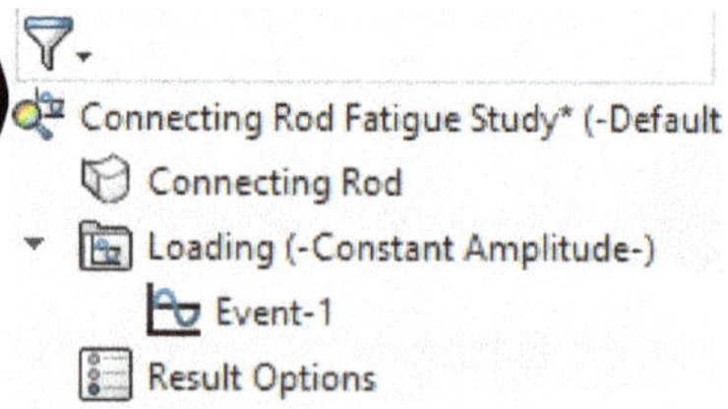

Section 10: Defining the Fatigue S-N Curve

Now, you need to define the S-N Curve (Stress-Life Cycle Curve) data for the material of the model. The S-N Curve determines the fatigue strength at different intervals of cyclic loads, see Figure 7.23. It is only used to perform the fatigue analysis. You can define a new S-N curve by specifying the alternating stress vs number of load cycles values for a material, manually or you can use an existing S-N curve from the material database of SOLIDWORKS Simulation.

Note: As the number of load cycles increases, the fatigue strength of the material decreases. The fatigue occurs in a load cycle where the stress developed due to the applied load is more than its fatigue strength as per the S-N curve.

7.23

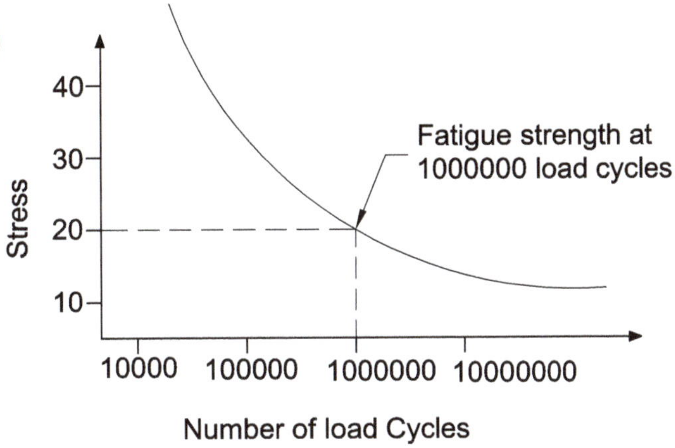

1. Right-click on the **Connecting Rod** (*name of the model*) in the Simulation Study Tree and then click on the **Apply/Edit Fatigue Data** tool in the shortcut menu that appears, see Figure 7.24. The **Material** dialog box appears, see Figure 7.25.

7.24

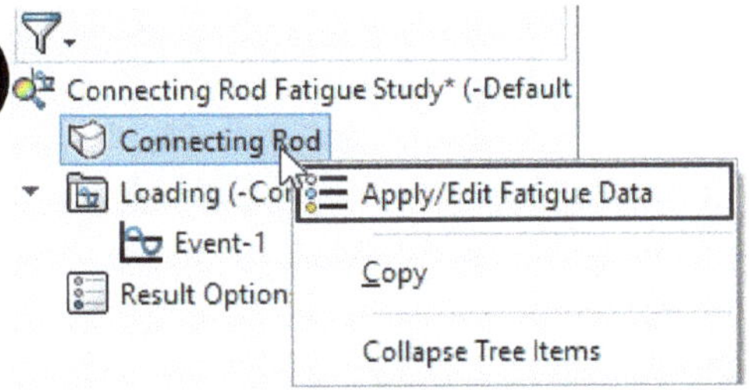

7.25

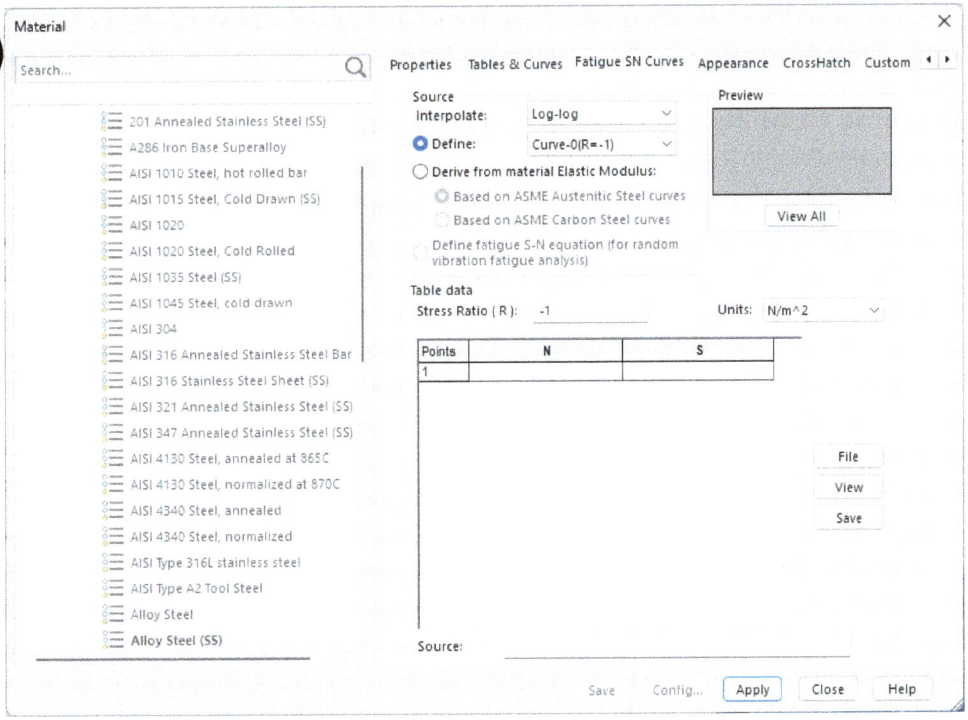

2. Ensure that the **Fatigue SN Curves** tab is activated in the **Material** dialog box, refer to Figure 7.25.

3. Select the **Derive from material Elastic Modulus** radio button in the **Source** area of the dialog box and then ensure that the **Based on ASME Austenitic Steel curves** radio button is selected. The S-N data for various points gets filled in the **Table data** area of the dialog box based on the ASME Austenitic steel.

Tip: You can also enter the S-N curve data in the **N** and **S** columns of the **Table data** area in the dialog box, manually or by importing an existing S-N data file. For doing so, select the **Define** radio button in the **Source** area of the dialog box and then enter the stress ratio/loading ratio in the **Stress Ratio (R)** field of the dialog box. Next, enter the number of load cycles vs alternating stress values in the **N** and **S** columns of the table, respectively. You can also click on the **File** button in the dialog box to invoke the **Function Curves** dialog box.

In this dialog box, you can select an existing material having pre-defined S-N curve data from the left panel of the dialog box. As soon as you select a material, the respective S-N curve data appears on the right panel of the **Function Curves** dialog box. You can edit the S-N curve data of the material as required, by double-clicking the respective fields in the dialog box. You can also import an existing file (*.dat*) having the S-N curve data by clicking on the **File** button of the **Function Curves** dialog box.

After specifying the S-N curve data in the dialog box, click on the **OK** button in the **Function Curves** dialog box. Next, click on the **Apply** button and then the **Close** button in the **Material** dialog box.

4. Click on the **Apply** button and then the **Close** button in the **Material** dialog box. The S-N curve is defined based on the ASME Austenitic Steel material.

Section 11: Running the Fatigue Analysis and Displaying Results

Now, you can run the fatigue analysis.

1. Click on the **Run This Study** tool in the **Simulation CommandManager**. The **Connecting Rod Fatigue Study** (*name of the study*) window appears which displays the progress of fatigue analysis.

2. After the process of running the analysis is complete, the damage and life results of the Connecting Rod are added to the **Results** folder of the Simulation Study Tree. Also, the **Results1 (-Damage-)** result is activated in the **Results** folder. As a result, the damage distribution on the model and the Damage Percentage plot appear in the graphics area, see Figure 7.26.

   The maximum damage percentage of the Connecting Rod is **1.132e+02** (113.21) which means that the specified event for the 300000 load cycles consumes about 113.21% life of the Connecting Rod and the design is considered to be failing. If the damage percentage of a design is more than 100% then the design is considered to be a failure due to fatigue.

7.26

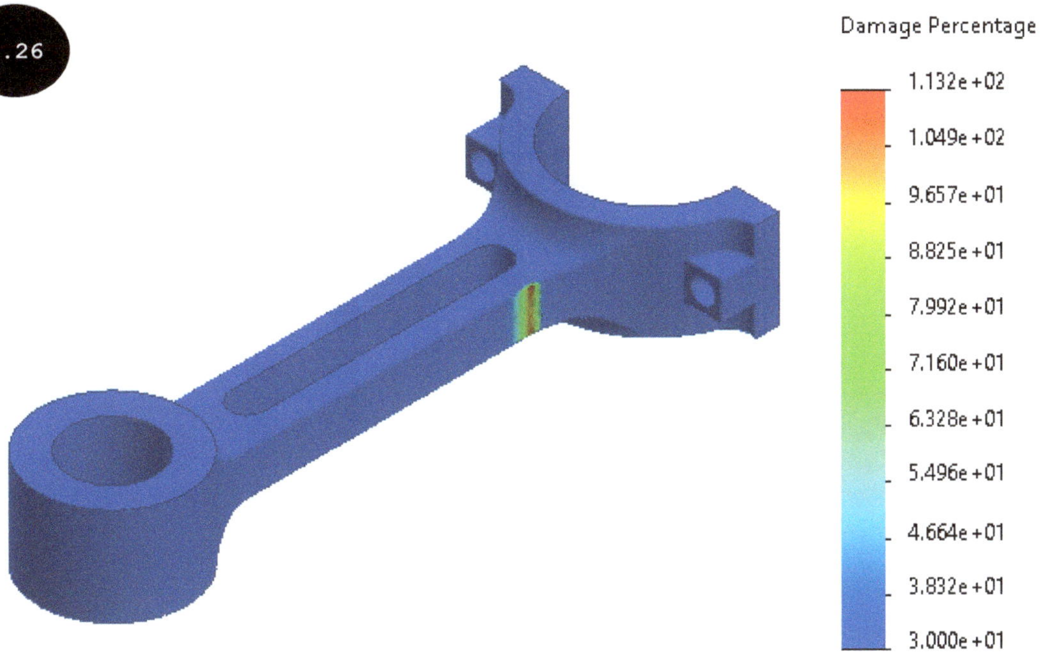

3. Double-click on the **Result2 (-Life-)** result in the **Results** folder of the Simulation Study Tree. The Total Life (cycle) plot appears in the graphics area, see Figure 7.27.

7.27

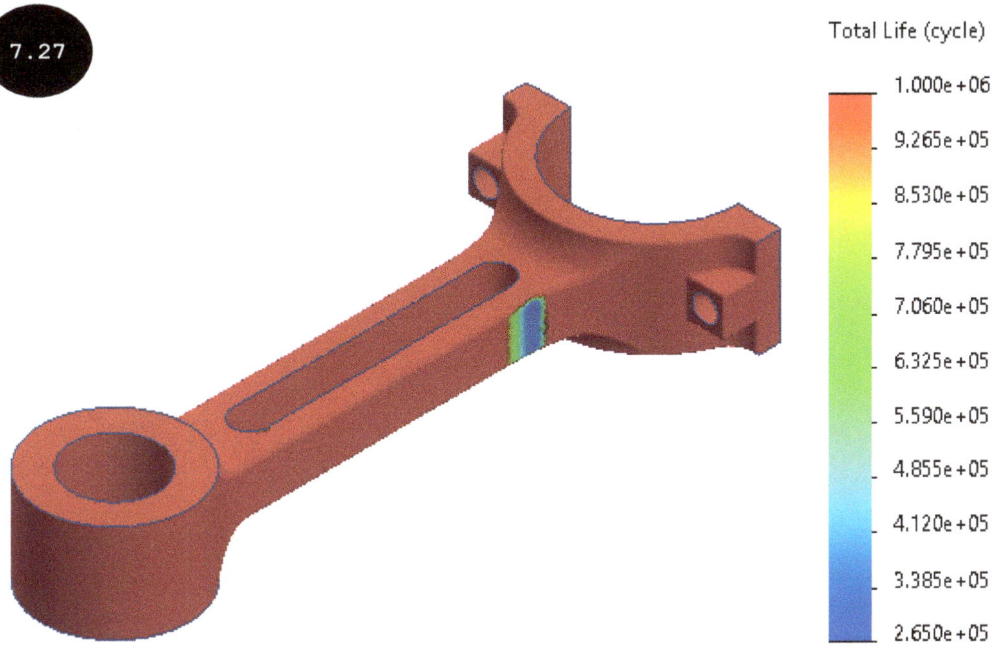

The Total Life (cycle) plot of the Connecting Rod shows that the failure is likely to occur after approximately **2.650e+05** (265000.91) load cycles, see Figure 7.27.

Section 12: Displaying the Load Factor Plot

You can also display the load factor plot of the design to determine the minimum load that the design can withstand for the specified number of load cycles.

1. Right-click on the **Results** folder in the Simulation Study Tree and then click on the **Define Fatigue Plot** tool in the shortcut menu that appears, see Figure 7.28. The **Fatigue Plot PropertyManager** appears, see Figure 7.29.

7.28

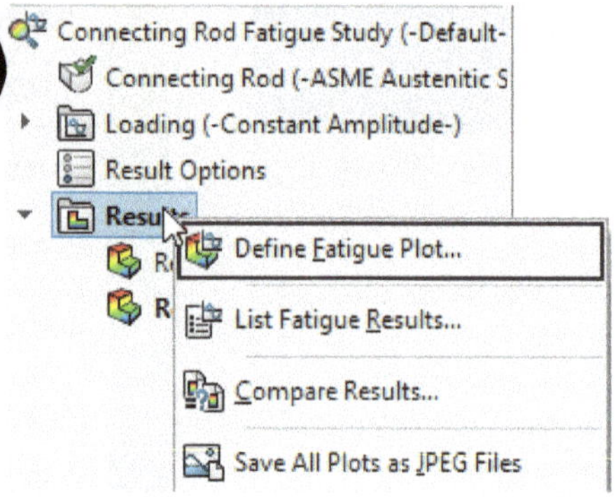

7.29

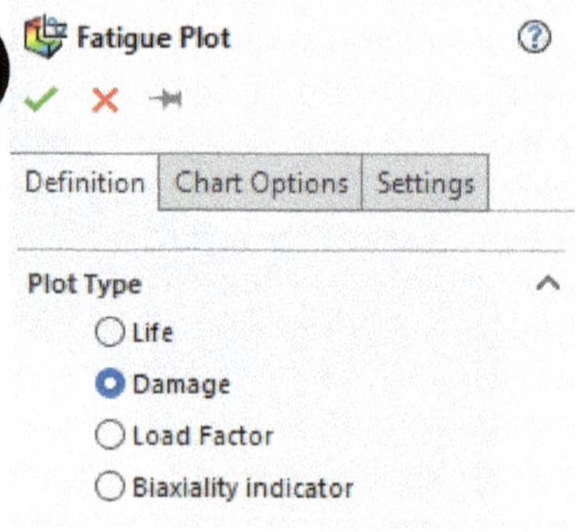

2. Select the **Load Factor** radio button in the **Plot Type** rollout of the PropertyManager.

3. Click on the green tick-mark button in the PropertyManager. The Load factor plot appears, see Figure 7.30.

7.30

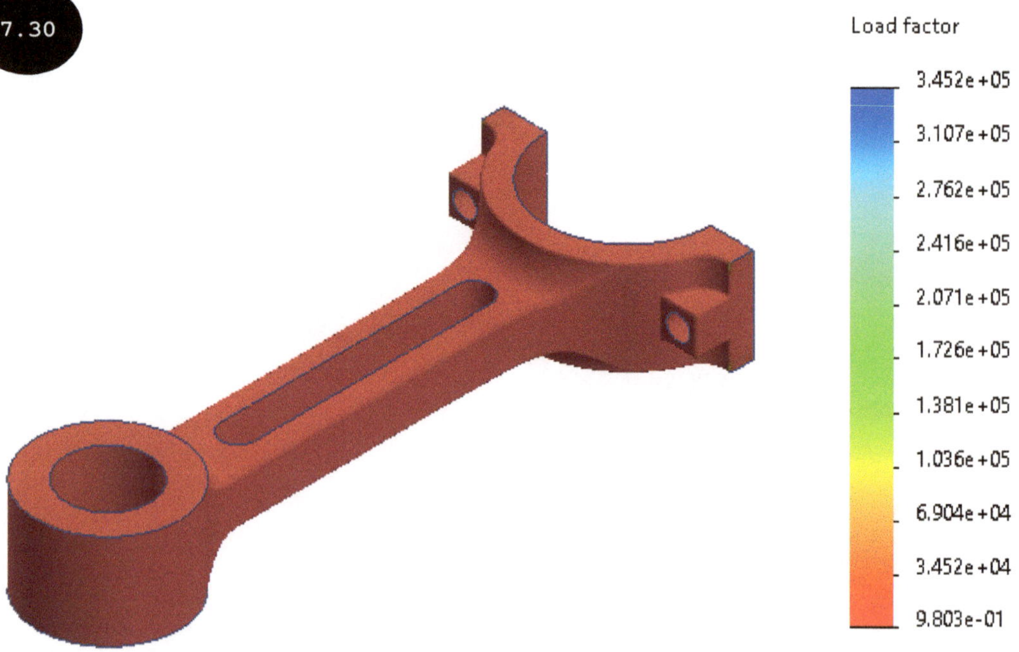

The Load factor plot shows that the minimum load factor of the design is **9.803e-01** (0.980), which indicates the failure of the design. Note that a minimum load factor of less than 1 indicates the failure of the design due to fatigue. The Connecting Rod design fails due to the fatigue at the load which is equal to the current load multiplied by the **9.803e-01** (0.980) load factor, see the formula below:

[*Minimum load when the design can fail = Current load X Minimum Load Factor*]

Section 13: Saving Results

Now, you need to save the model and its results.

1. Click on the **Save** tool in the **Standard** toolbar. The model and its results are saved in the location > ***SOLIDWORKS Simulation*** > ***Case Studies*** > ***C07 Case Studies*** > ***Case Study*** 1.

2. Close the SOLIDWORKS session.

Hands-on Test Drive 1: Fatigue Analysis of a Crankshaft

Perform the fatigue analysis of a Crankshaft shown in Figure 7.31 and its total life, damage, and load factor due to the cyclic loads of constant amplitude.

Project Description

The Crankshaft is fixed at both its ends (see Figure 7.32) and a 5000 N downward load acts on its middle where it connects with the Connecting Rod, see Figure 7.32. The Crankshaft is made up of **Cast Carbon Steel** material.

7.31

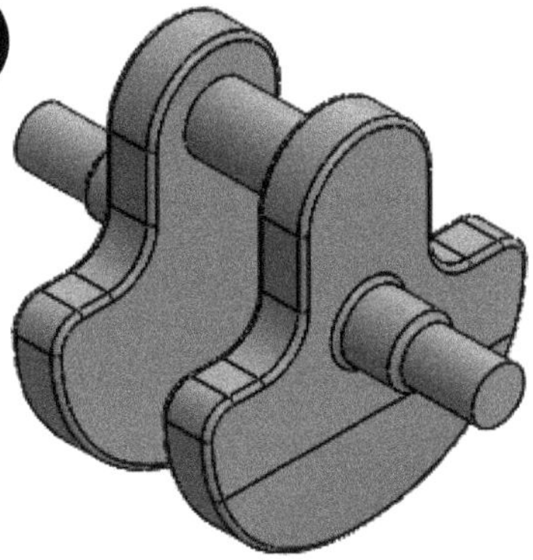

7.32

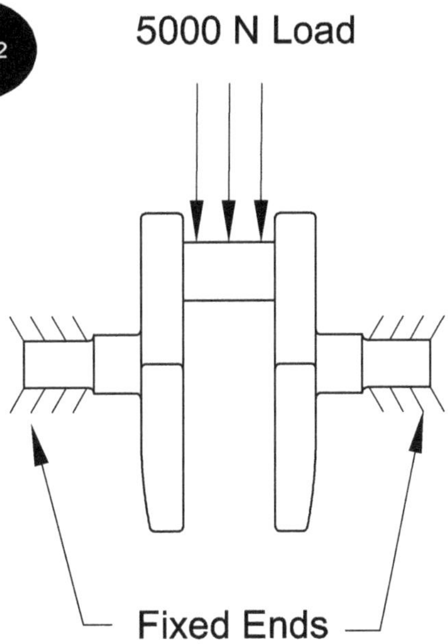

Project Summary

In this case study, you will first perform the static analysis on the Crankshaft and then based on the results of the static analysis, you need to perform the fatigue analysis to calculate the total life, damage, and minimum load factor of the design under the repeated fully reversed loading for 2,00,000 load cycles. You can use the pre-defined S-N curve data of the ASME carbon steel curves.

Summary

This chapter explored the failure of a design due to fatigue when subjected to cyclic loading. You learned how to perform fatigue analysis based on the results of a static study to determine the total life, damage percentage, and load factor of a design. Additionally, the chapter covered different types of cyclic loading and the significance of the S N curve, which defines the fatigue strength of a material over varying cycles of loading.

Questions

Complete the following sentences:

- The phenomena of failure due to repeated loading and unloading on an object is known as _________.
- The _________ button in the **Advanced Simulation** rollout of the **Study PropertyManager** is used for performing the fatigue analysis with a constant amplitude of cyclic loads.
- The _________ option is used to specify the loading type for the specified number of cyclic loads such that all the applied loads in the study reverse their load magnitudes simultaneously.
- The _________ option is used to specify the loading type for the specified number of cyclic loads such that all the applied loads in the study change their magnitudes from the maximum to the zero stress values.
- The _________ determines the fatigue strength at different intervals of cyclic loads.
- As the number of load cycles increases, the _________ of the material decreases.
- The _________ plot indicates the approximate number of load cycles when the failure is likely to occur.
- The _________ plot indicates the minimum load factor when the failure occurs due to the fatigue in the design.
- A design can fail due to the fatigue at a load, which is equal to the current load multiplied by the _________.
- The minimum load factor less than _________, indicates the failure of the design due to fatigue.

CHAPTER

8

Frequency Analysis

In this chapter, the following topics will be discussed:

- Introduction to Frequency Analysis
- Frequency Analysis of a Wine Glass
- Frequency Analysis of a Pulley Assembly
- Frequency Analysis of a Cantilever Beam

In this chapter, you will learn about frequency analysis, which is used to calculate the natural or resonant frequencies of an object. The natural frequency of an object is the energy required to produce vibration, and it depends on factors such as geometry, material properties, and boundary conditions. While real-world objects have an infinite number of natural frequencies, in Finite Element Analysis, they are approximated based on the object's degrees of freedom.

Each natural frequency corresponds to a specific mode shape, representing how the object deforms when vibrating at that frequency. If an external force causes the object to vibrate at a frequency matching one of its natural frequencies, excessive displacement and stress can occur, leading to failure of the object. This phenomenon of failure is known as resonance. For example, a bridge may experience vibrations due to heavy traffic, strong winds, or footfall. If these forces match the bridge's natural frequencies, resonance can cause structural failure.

Introduction to Frequency Analysis

The frequency analysis is used to calculate the natural frequencies of an object and its associated mode shapes. By knowing the natural frequencies of an object, you can ensure that the actual operating frequency of an object will not coincide with any of its natural frequencies to avoid the failure of the object due to resonance.

Case Study 1: Frequency Analysis of a Wine Glass

In this case study, you will perform the frequency analysis of a Wine Glass (see Figure 8.1) and determine its first three natural/resonant frequencies and their associated mode shapes. Also, determine the mass participation in the X, Y, and Z directions.

8.1

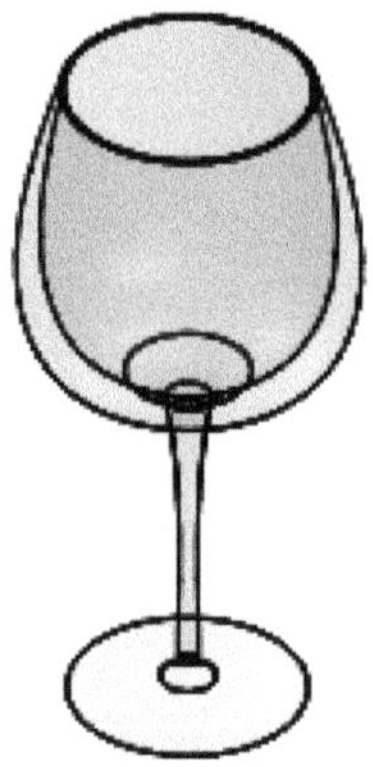

Project Description

Fix the Wine Glass at its bottom to represent its operating conditions, see Figure 8.2. The Wine Glass is made up of **Glass** material.

8.2

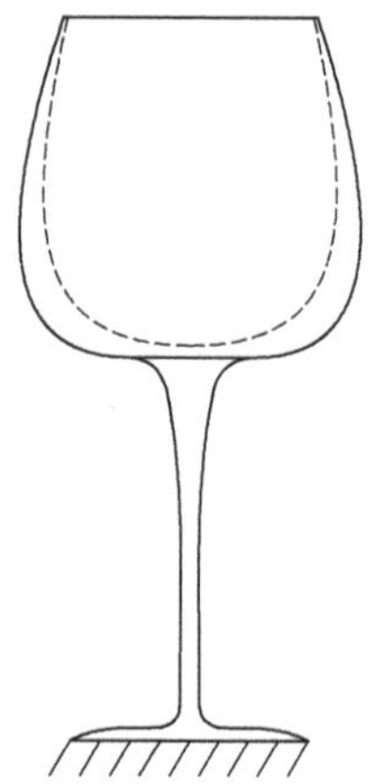

Project Summary

In this case study, you will run the frequency analysis on a Wine Glass without applying any external force.

Note: You can run the frequency analysis with or without applying the fixtures and loads. However, it is recommended to apply the required fixtures to the model to represent its real operating conditions. Although, applying external loads to the model is optional but, if you do so, their effects are considered in the frequency analysis.

The following sequence summarizes the case study outline:

1. Downloading Files of Chapter 8
2. Opening the Wine Glass
3. Starting the Frequency Analysis
4. Defining Properties for the Frequency Analysis
5. Applying the Material and Fixture
6. Generating the Mesh
7. Running the Frequency Analysis
8. Displaying Natural/Resonant Frequencies
9. Viewing Different Mode Shapes
10. Displaying the Mass Participation
11. Saving Results

Section 1: Downloading Files of Chapter 8

1. Log on to the CADArtifex website (*cadartifex.com/login/*).

2. After logging, navigate to the textbook titled "**SOLIDWORKS Simulation 2026: A Power Guide for Beginners and Intermediate Users: Colored**". You can enter the name of the textbook in the **Search** box to locate it quickly.

3. In the **Online Resources** tab, expand the **Case Studies** rollout and click the **Download** button corresponding to **C08 Case Studies**. In the confirmation window that appears, click the **Confirm** button. The download of the **C08 Case Studies** file will begin. After the download is complete, unzip the file.

4. Save the extracted **C08 Case Studies** folder in the location ***SOLIDWORKS Simulation** > **Case Studies***.

Section 2: Opening the Wine Glass

1. Start SOLIDWORKS, if not already started.

2. Click on the **Open** button in the **Welcome** dialog box or the **Open** tool in the **Standard** toolbar. The **Open** dialog box appears.

3. Browse to the location > ***SOLIDWORKS Simulation** > **Case Studies** > **C08 Case Studies** > **Case Study 1*** of the local drive of your system. Next, select the **Wine Glass** and then click on the **Open** button in the dialog box. The Wine Glass is opened in SOLIDWORKS.

Section 3: Starting the Frequency Analysis

1. Click on the **Simulation** tab in the **CommandManager**. The tools of the **Simulation CommandManager** appear.

2. Click on the **New Study** tool in the **Simulation CommandManager**. The **Study PropertyManager** appears to the left of the graphics area.

3. Click on the **Frequency** button in the **General Simulation** rollout of the PropertyManager to perform the frequency analysis, see Figure 8.3.

4. Enter **Wine Glass Frequency Study** in the **Study name** field of the **Name** rollout in the PropertyManager, see Figure 8.3.

5. Click on the green tick-mark button in the PropertyManager. The **Wine Glass Frequency Study** is added to the Simulation Study Tree, see Figure 8.4.

8.3

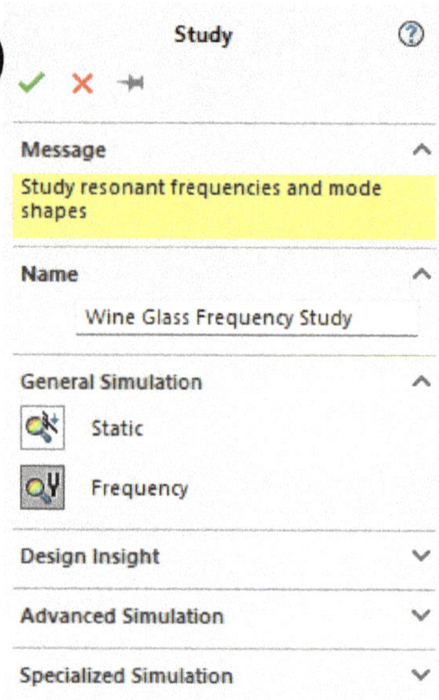

8.4

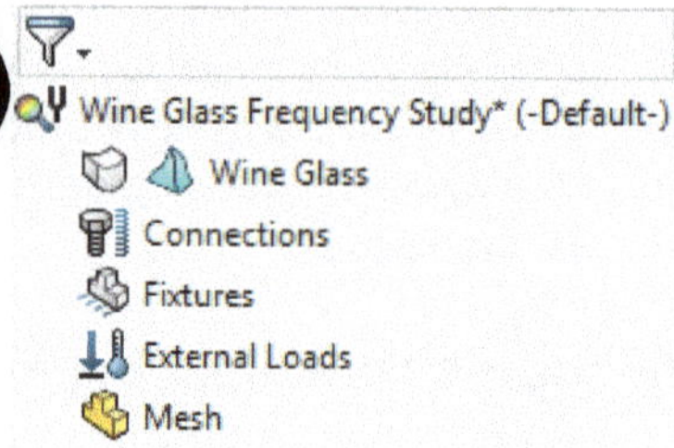

Section 4: Defining Properties for the Frequency Analysis

Before you start performing the frequency analysis, you need to define its properties.

1. Right-click on the **Wine Glass Frequency Study** (*name of the study*) in the Simulation Study Tree and then click on the **Properties** tool in the shortcut menu that appears, see Figure 8.5. The **Frequency** dialog box appears, see Figure 8.6.

8.5

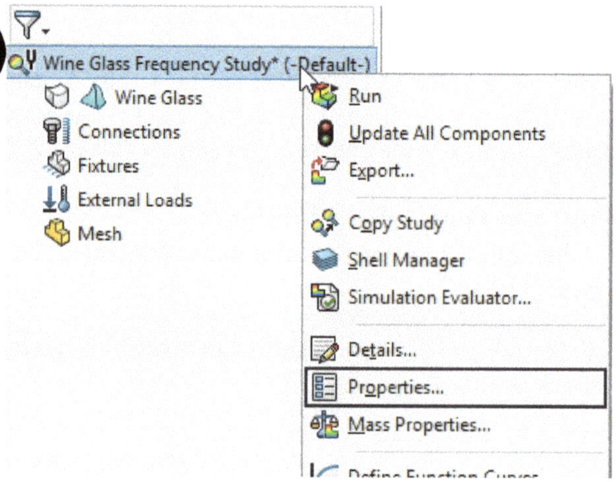

8.6

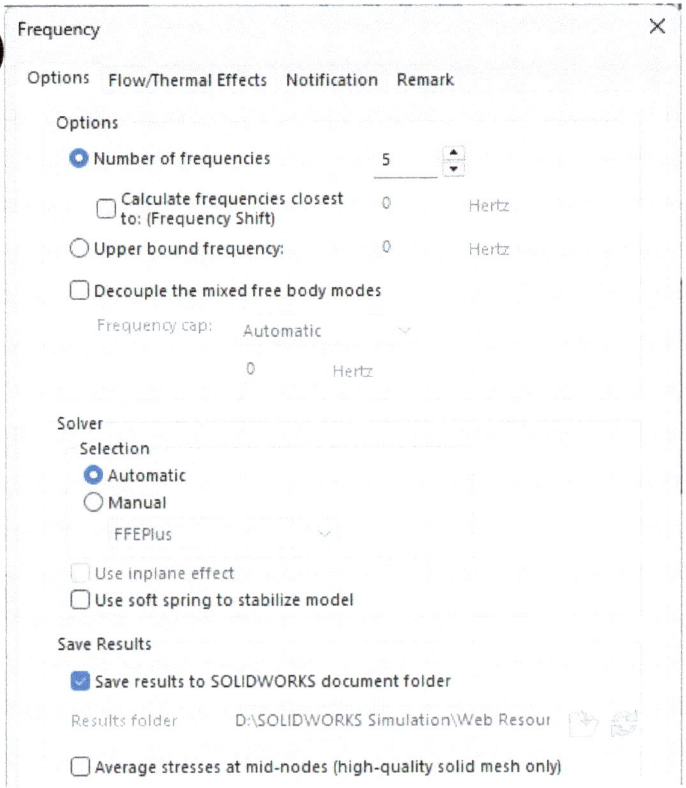

2. Enter **3** in the **Number of frequencies** field of the **Options** area in the dialog box to calculate the first three natural frequencies of the Wine Glass.

Tip: You can also calculate the frequencies closest to the frequency of your interest. To do this, you need to select the **Calculate frequencies closest to: (Frequency Shift)** check box in the **Options** area of the dialog box and then enter the frequency value of your interest. The **Upper bound frequency** radio button is used to specify an upper limit for the frequencies to be calculated. On doing so, the program calculates the frequencies which are below the specified limit.

3. Click on the **OK** button in the dialog box. The first three frequencies to be calculated are defined.

Section 5: Applying the Material and Fixture

Now, you need to apply the material and fixture to the model.

1. Invoke the **Material** dialog box by clicking on the **Apply Material** tool in the **Simulation CommandManager**.

2. Expand the **Other Non-metals** category of the **SOLIDWORKS Materials** library in the **Material** dialog box and then click on the **Glass** material, see Figure 8.7. All the properties of the Glass material appear on the right panel of the dialog box, see Figure 8.7.

8.7

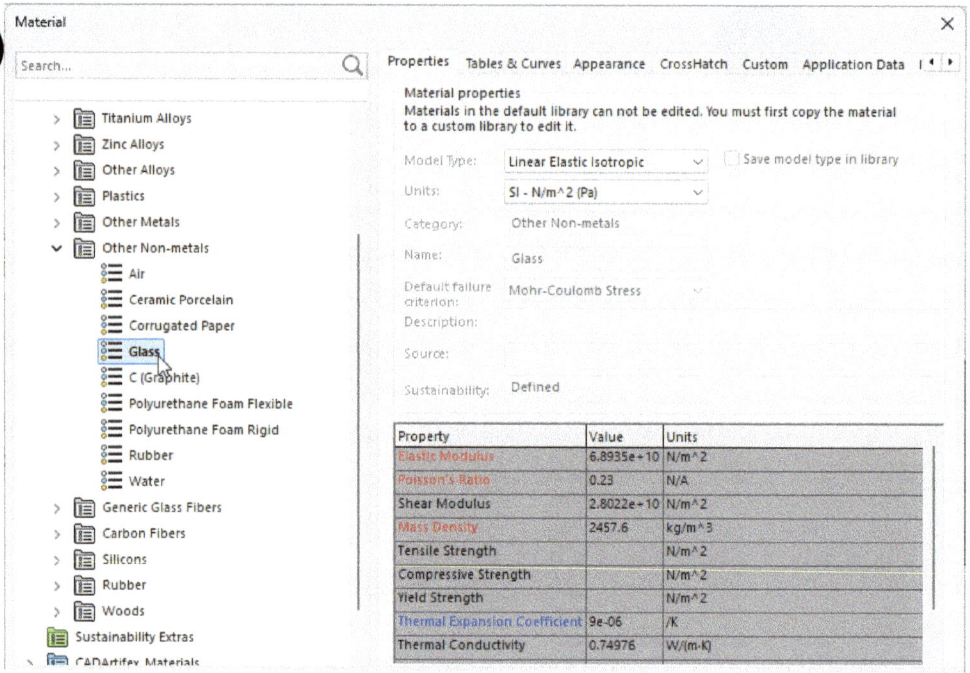

3. Click on the **Apply** button and then click on the **Close** button in the **Material** dialog box. The Glass material is applied to the model and its appearance changes, accordingly in the graphics area.

   Now, you need to apply the Fixed Geometry fixture.

4. Right-click on the **Fixtures** option in the Simulation Study Tree and then click on the **Fixed Geometry** tool in the shortcut menu that appears. The **Fixture PropertyManager** appears.

5. Rotate the model such that you can view its bottom face and then select it to apply the Fixed Geometry fixture, see Figure 8.8.

8.8

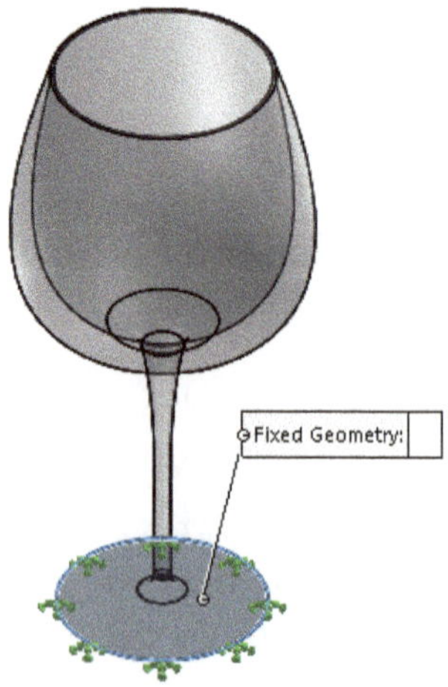

6. Click on the green tick-mark button in the PropertyManager. The Fixed Geometry fixture is applied to the bottom face of the Wine Glass. Now, change the orientation of the model back to isometric.

Section 6: Generating the Mesh

Now, you need to generate the mesh on the model.

8.9

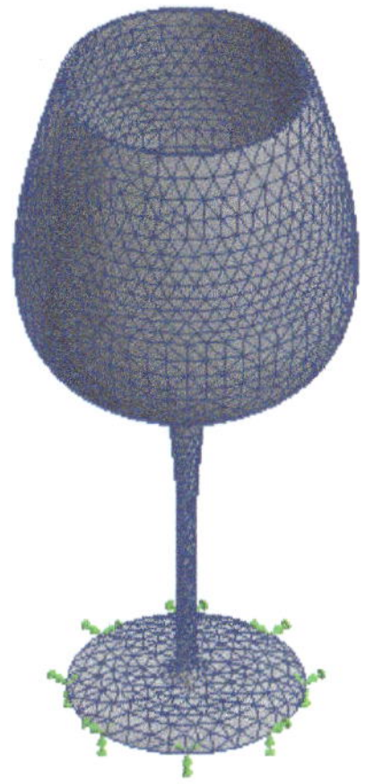

1. Generate the curvature-based mesh with the default mesh parameters by using the **Create Mesh** tool. Figure 8.9 shows the meshed model.

Section 7: Running the Frequency Analysis

Now, you need to run the static study.

1. Click on the **Run This Study** tool in the **Simulation CommandManager**. The **Wine Glass Frequency Study** (*name of the study*) window appears which displays the progress of the analysis. After the process of running the analysis is complete, the **Results** folder is added to the Simulation Study Tree with the amplitude results of a specified number of mode shapes. By default, the first mode shape is activated. As a result, the mode shape and the resultant amplitude plot of the first natural frequency appear in the graphics area, see Figure 8.10.

8.10

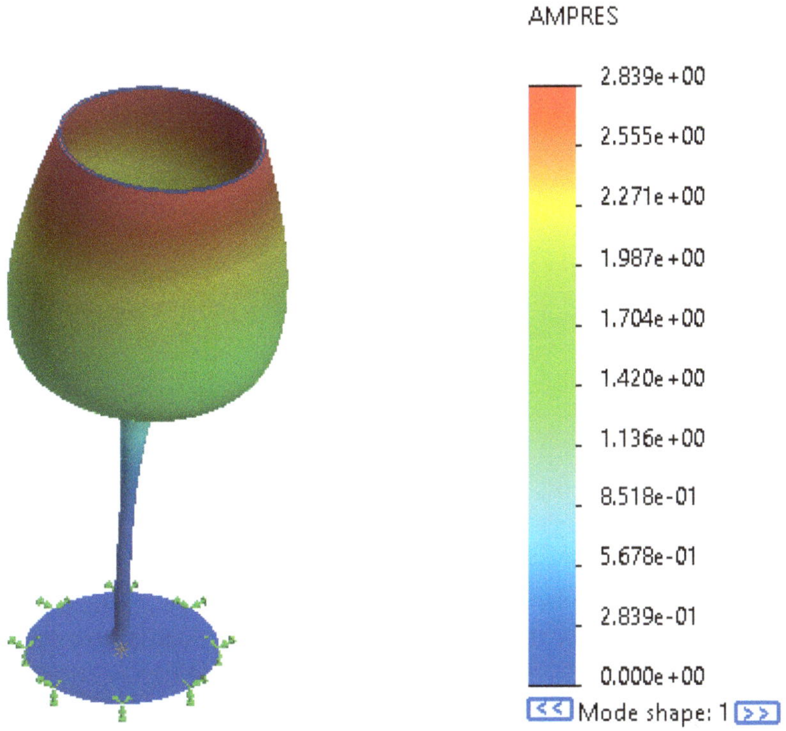

Section 8: Displaying Natural/Resonant Frequencies

Now, you need to display the natural/resonant frequencies of the Wine Glass.

1. Right-click on the **Results** folder in the Simulation Study Tree and then click on the **List Resonant Frequencies** tool in the shortcut menu that appears, see Figure 8.11. The **List Modes** window appears, see Figure 8.12.

8.11

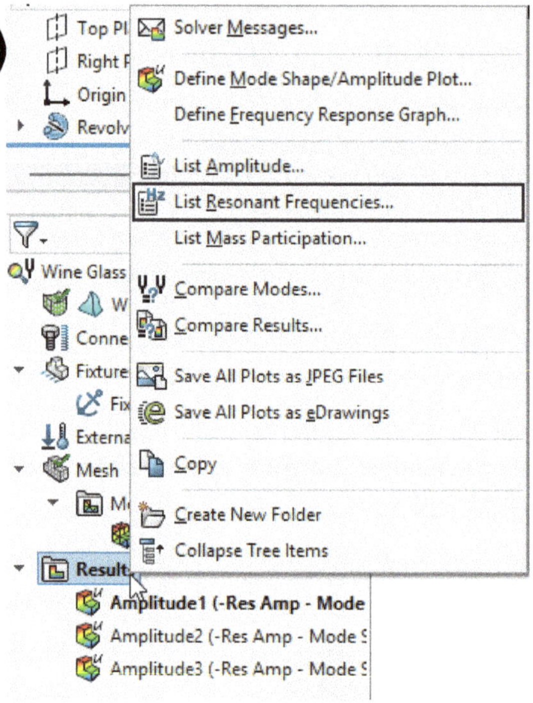

8.12

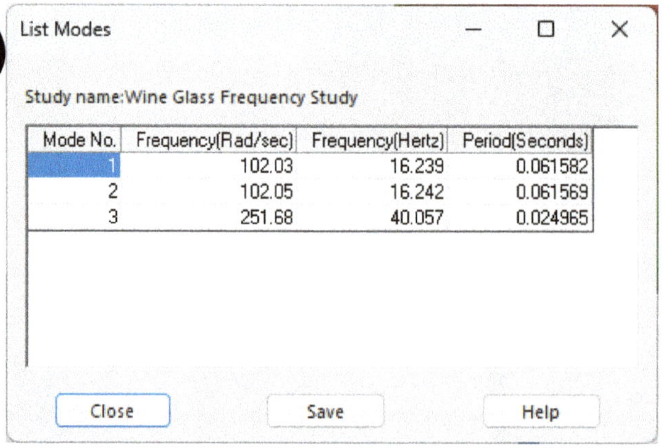

The **List Modes** window displays the list of calculated natural/resonant frequencies of the model associated with the respective mode numbers in Rad/sec and Hertz. Also, it displays the corresponding period in seconds for each natural frequency, refer to Figure 8.12.

2. Review the calculated natural frequency of the Wine Glass for different mode numbers. Mode number 1 has a frequency of 16.239 hertz, mode number 2 has a frequency of 16.242 hertz, and mode number 3 has a frequency of 40.057 hertz. You need to ensure that the Wine Glass does not operate in a frequency that matches any one of its calculated natural frequencies to avoid failure due to resonance.

3. Click on the **Save** button in the **List Modes** window. The **Save As** dialog box appears. In this dialog box, browse to the location where you want to save the calculated results of the natural frequencies. Next, click on the **Save** button in the dialog box. The results file is saved with the *.csv* file extension in the specified location. You can open the *.csv* files in Microsoft Excel.

4. Click on the **Close** button in the **List Modes** window to close it.

Section 9: Viewing Different Mode Shapes

1. By default, the **Amplitude1 (-Res Amp - Mode Shape 1-)** result is activated in the **Results** folder of the Simulation Study Tree. As a result, the mode shape 1 of the Wine Glass appears in the graphics area. To display the mode shapes 2 and 3, double-click on their respective results in the Simulation Study Tree. Figures 8.13 and 8.14 show the mode shapes 2 and 3, respectively.

8.13

8.14

Tip: You can rotate the model to view the mode shapes of the model at different orientations.

Section 10: Displaying the Mass Participation

1. Right-click on the **Results** folder in the Simulation Study Tree and then click on the **List Mass Participation** tool in the shortcut menu that appears, see Figure 8.15. The **Mass Participation** window appears, see Figure 8.16.

8.15

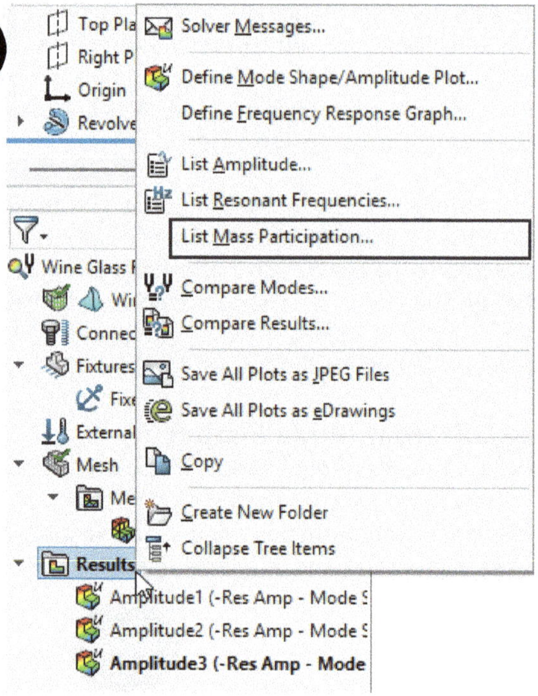

8.16

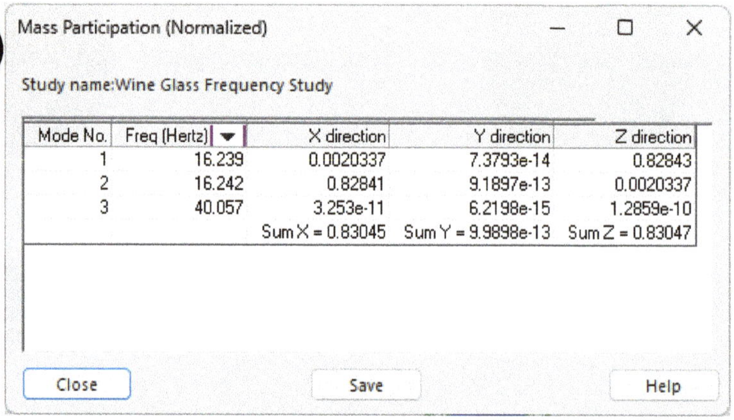

Mode No.	Freq (Hertz)	X direction	Y direction	Z direction
1	16.239	0.0020337	7.3793e-14	0.82843
2	16.242	0.82841	9.1897e-13	0.0020337
3	40.057	3.253e-11	6.2198e-15	1.2859e-10
		Sum X = 0.83045	Sum Y = 9.9898e-13	Sum Z = 0.83047

The **Mass Participation** window displays a list of natural/resonant frequencies and the mass participation in the X, Y, and Z directions for each mode number.

2. Review the mass participation for each mode number in the **Mass Participation** window. For example, the mass participation for mode number 1 is approximately 0.0020337 in the X-direction, 7.3793e-14 in the Y-direction, and 0.82843 in the Z-direction.

Section 11: Saving Results

Now, you need to save the model and its results.

1. Click on the **Save** tool in the **Standard** toolbar. The model and its results are saved in the location > *SOLIDWORKS Simulation > Case Studies > C08 Case Studies > Case Study 1*.

2. Close the SOLIDWORKS session.

Case Study 2: Frequency Analysis of a Pulley Assembly

In this case study, you will perform the frequency analysis of a Pulley Assembly (see Figure 8.17) and determine its first five natural/resonant frequencies and their associated mode shapes.

Project Description

Both the Support components of the Pulley Assembly are fixed at the bottom, see Figure 8.18. All the components of the Pulley Assembly are made up of **Alloy Steel (SS)** material.

8.17

8.18

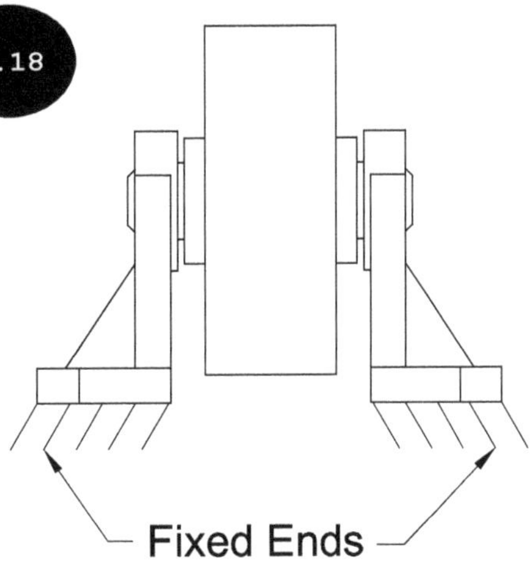

Project Summary

In this case study, you will run the frequency analysis on a Pulley Assembly without applying any external force.

Note: You can run the frequency analysis with or without applying the fixtures and loads. However, it is recommended to apply the required fixtures to the model to represent its real operating conditions. Although, applying external loads to the model is optional but, if you do so, their effects are considered in the frequency analysis.

The following sequence summarizes the case study outline:

1. Starting the Frequency Analysis
2. Defining Properties for the Frequency Analysis
3. Applying Materials and Fixtures
4. Generating the Mesh
5. Running the Frequency Analysis
6. Displaying Natural/Resonant Frequencies
7. Viewing Different Mode Shapes
8. Saving Results

Section 1: Starting the Frequency Analysis

1. Start SOLIDWORKS and then open the Pulley Assembly from the location > *SOLIDWORKS Simulation > Case Studies > C08 Case Studies > Case Study 2*.

Note: You need to download the **C08 Case Studies** file, which contains the files for this chapter, by logging in to the CADArtifex website (*cadartifex.com/login*), if it has not already been downloaded.

2. Click on the **Simulation** tab in the **CommandManager**. The tools of the **Simulation CommandManager** appear.

3. Click on the **New Study** tool in the **Simulation CommandManager**. The **Study PropertyManager** appears on the left of the graphics area.

4. Click on the **Frequency** button in the **General Simulation** rollout of the PropertyManager to perform the frequency analysis, see Figure 8.19.

5. Enter **Pulley Frequency Study** in the **Study name** field of the **Name** rollout in the PropertyManager, see Figure 8.19.

6. Click on the green tick-mark button in the PropertyManager. The **Pulley Frequency Study** is added to the Simulation Study Tree.

8.19

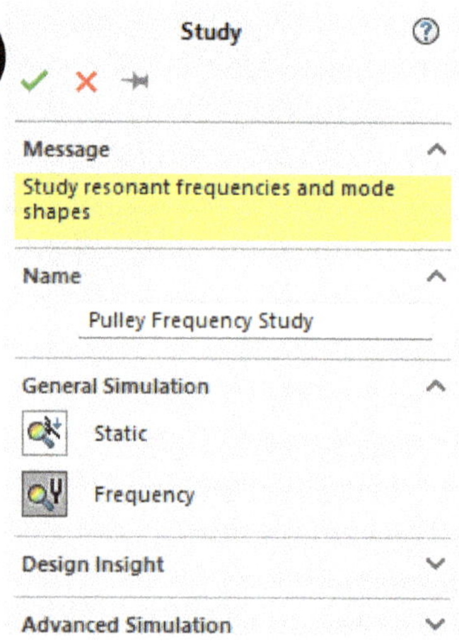

Section 2: Defining Properties for the Frequency Analysis

Before you start performing the frequency analysis, you can define its properties.

1. Right-click on the **Pulley Frequency Study** (*name of the study*) in the Simulation Study Tree and then click on the **Properties** tool in the shortcut menu that appears, see Figure 8.20. The **Frequency** dialog box appears, see Figure 8.21.

8.20

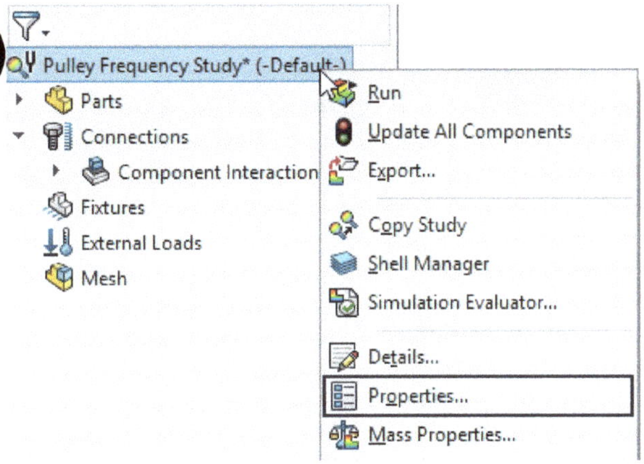

8.21

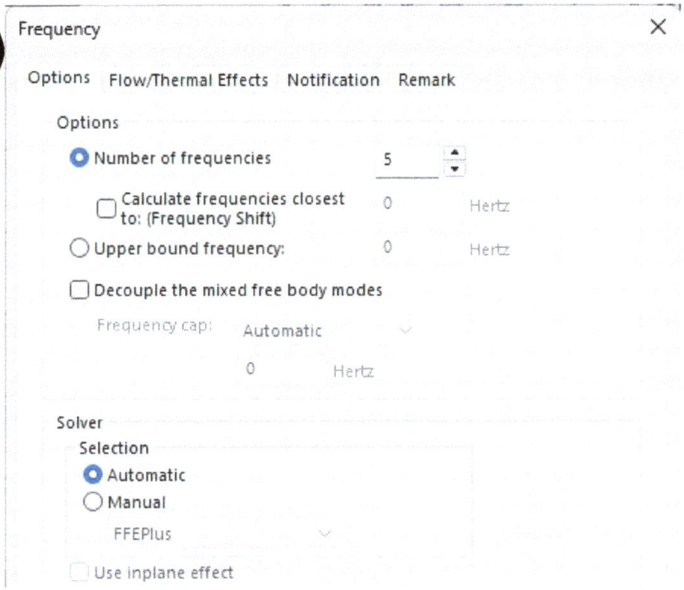

2. Ensure that **5** is entered in the **Number of frequencies** field of the **Options** area in the dialog box to calculate the first five natural frequencies of the Pulley Assembly.

3. Click on the **OK** button in the dialog box.

Section 3: Applying Materials and Fixtures

Now, you need to apply the materials and fixtures to the model.

1. Right-click on the **Parts** folder in the Simulation Study Tree and then click on the **Apply Material to All** tool in the shortcut menu that appears, see Figure 8.22. The **Material** dialog box appears.

8.22

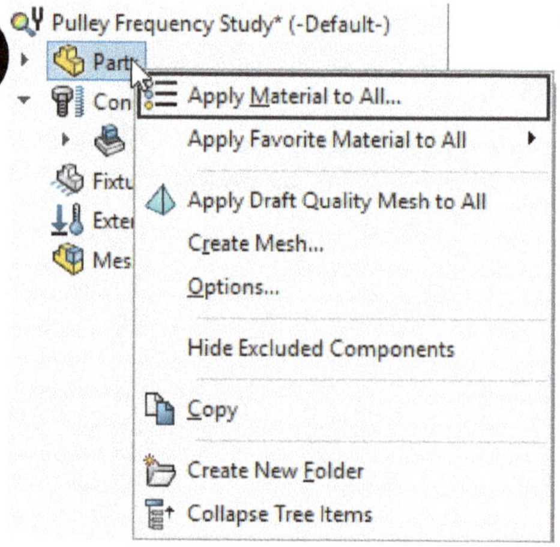

2. Select the **Alloy Steel (SS)** material in the **Steel** category of the **SOLIDWORKS Materials** library in the dialog box.

3. Click on the **Apply** button and then the **Close** button in the **Material** dialog box. The Alloy Steel (SS) material is applied to all the components of the assembly.

   Now, you need to apply the Fixed Geometry fixture.

4. Right-click on the **Fixtures** option in the Simulation Study Tree and then click on the **Fixed Geometry** tool in the shortcut menu that appears. The **Fixture PropertyManager** appears.

5. Rotate the assembly such that you can view its bottom faces. Next, select the bottom faces of both the Support components of the assembly to apply the Fixed Geometry fixture, see Figure 8.23.

8.23

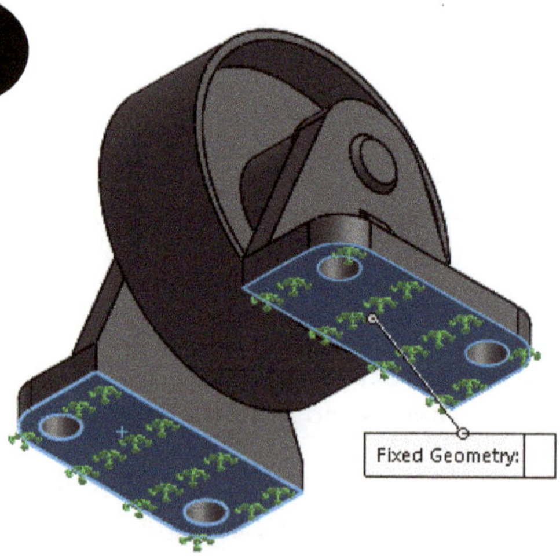

6. Click on the green tick-mark button in the PropertyManager. The Fixed Geometry fixture is applied to the selected faces. Now, change the orientation of the assembly back to isometric.

Section 4: Generating the Mesh

1. Generate the curvature-based mesh with default mesh parameters by using the **Create Mesh** tool. Figure 8.24 shows the meshed assembly.

8.24

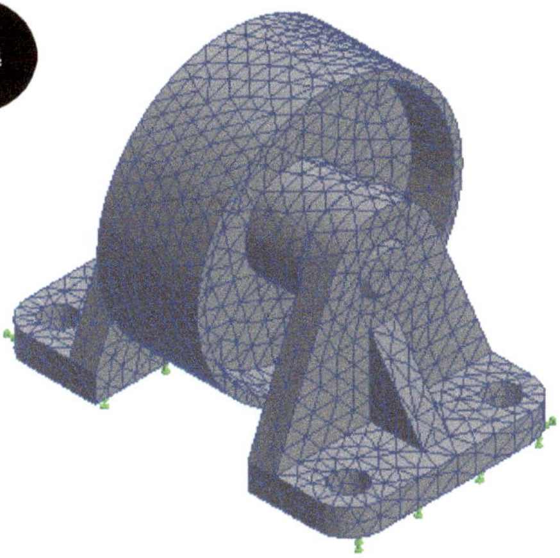

Section 5: Running the Frequency Analysis

1. Click on the **Run This Study** tool in the **Simulation CommandManager**. The **Pulley Frequency Study** (*name of the study*) window appears which displays the progress of the analysis. After the process of running the analysis is complete, the **Results** folder is added to the Simulation Study Tree. By default, the mode shape and the resultant amplitude plot of the first natural frequency appear in the graphics area, see Figure 8.25.

8.25

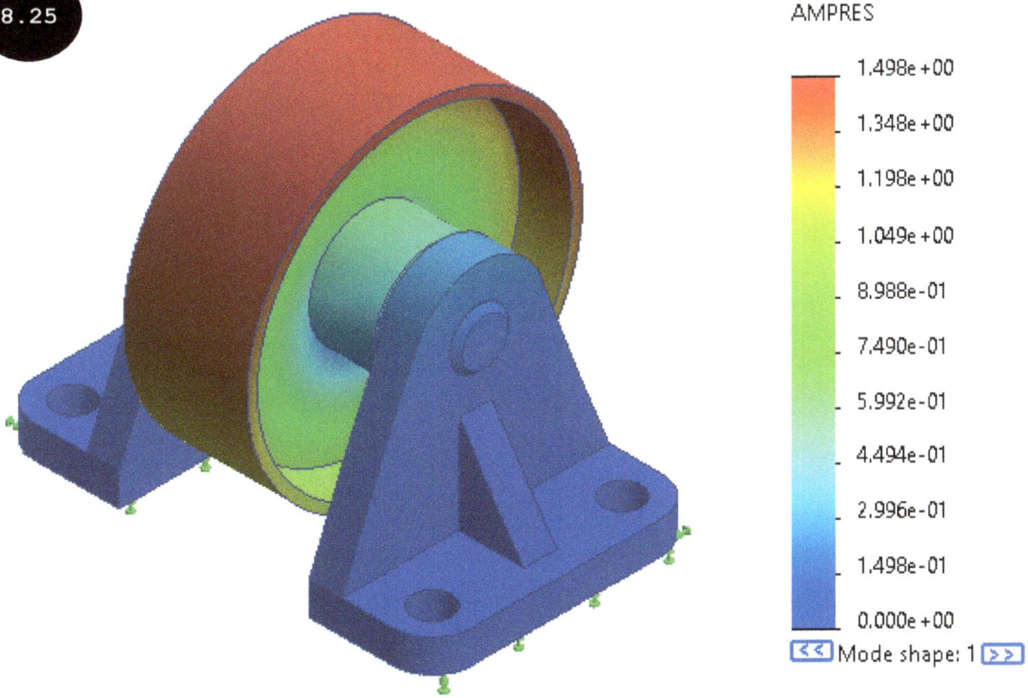

Section 6: Displaying Natural/Resonant Frequencies

Now, you need to display the natural/resonant frequencies of the Pulley Assembly.

1. Right-click on the **Results** folder in the Simulation Study Tree and then click on the **List Resonant Frequencies** tool in the shortcut menu that appears, see Figure 8.26. The **List Modes** window appears, see Figure 8.27.

8.26

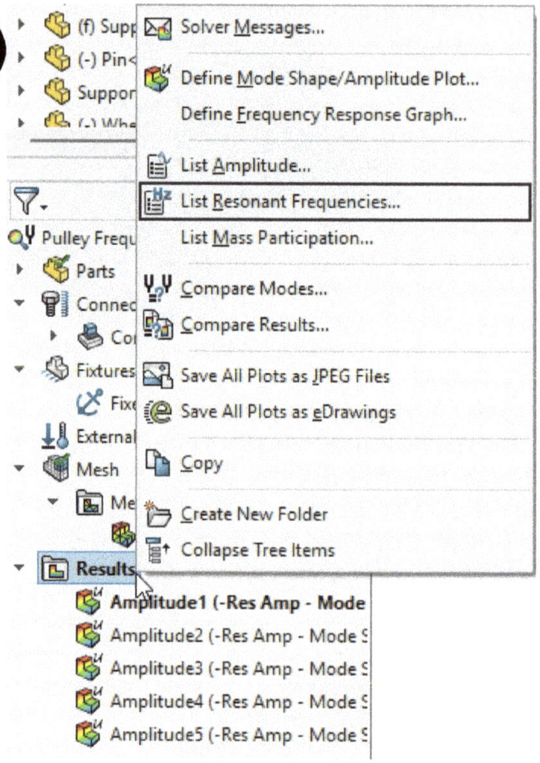

8.27

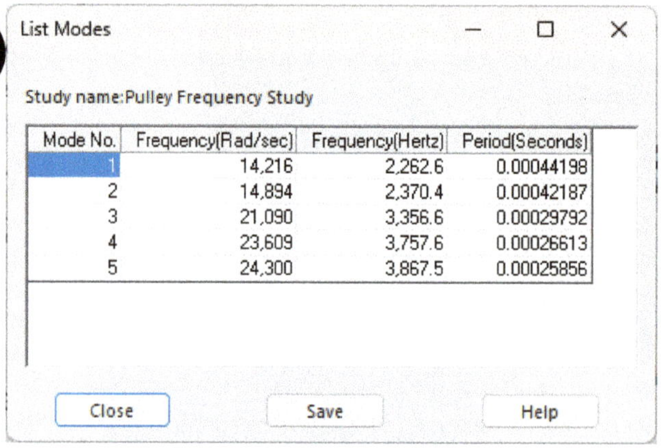
List Modes

Study name:Pulley Frequency Study

Mode No.	Frequency(Rad/sec)	Frequency(Hertz)	Period(Seconds)
1	14,216	2,262.6	0.00044198
2	14,894	2,370.4	0.00042187
3	21,090	3,356.6	0.00029792
4	23,609	3,757.6	0.00026613
5	24,300	3,867.5	0.00025856

Close Save Help

The **List Modes** window displays a list of calculated natural/resonant frequencies in Rad/sec and Hertz for each mode number. Besides, it displays the corresponding period in seconds for each mode number, see Figure 8.27.

2. Review the calculated natural frequency of the Pulley Assembly for each mode number. Mode number 1 has a frequency of approximately 2262.6 hertz and mode number 2 has a frequency of approximately 2370.4 hertz. You need to ensure that the Pulley Assembly does not operate in a frequency that matches with any of its calculated natural frequencies to avoid failure due to resonance. Next, close the **List Modes** window.

Section 7: Viewing Different Mode Shapes

1. By default, the **Amplitude1 (-Res Amp - Mode Shape 1-)** result is activated in the **Results** folder of the Simulation Study Tree. As a result, mode shape 1 of the Pulley Assembly appears in the graphics area, see Figure 8.28. To display the other mode shapes, double-click on the respective results in the Simulation Study Tree. Figure 8.29 shows the mode shape 2 of the assembly.

8.28

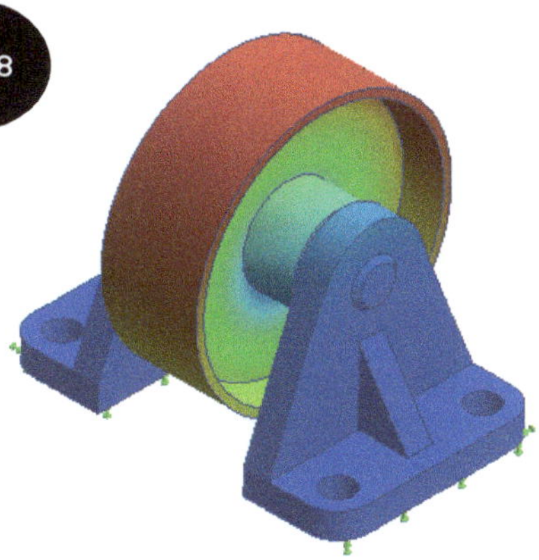

8.29

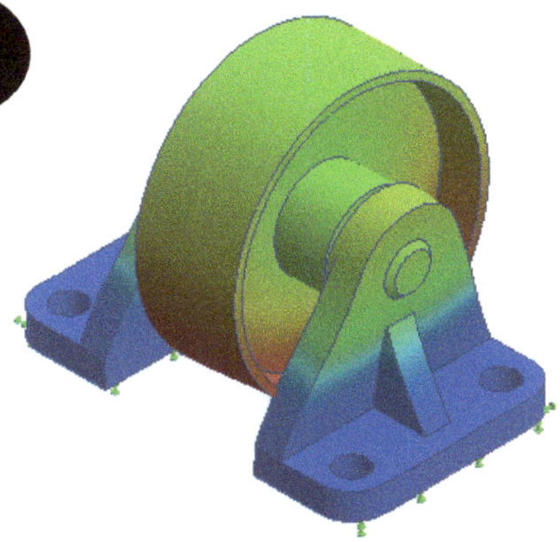

Section 8: Saving Results

1. Click on the **Save** tool in the **Standard** toolbar. The model and its results are saved in the location > *SOLIDWORKS Simulation* > *Case Studies* > *C08 Case Studies* > *Case Study 2*.

2. Close the SOLIDWORKS session.

Hands-on Test Drive 1: Frequency Analysis of a Cantilever Beam

Perform the frequency analysis of a Cantilever Beam, (see Figure 8.30) and determine its first five natural/resonant frequencies and their associated mode shapes.

8.30

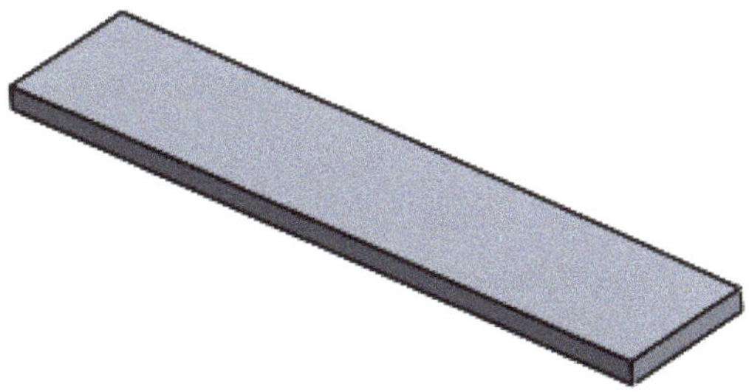

Project Description

The Cantilever Beam is fixed at its left end and a downward load of 900 N is acting on its free end (right), see Figure 8.31. The Cantilever Beam is made up of **AISI 1035 Steel (SS)** material.

8.31

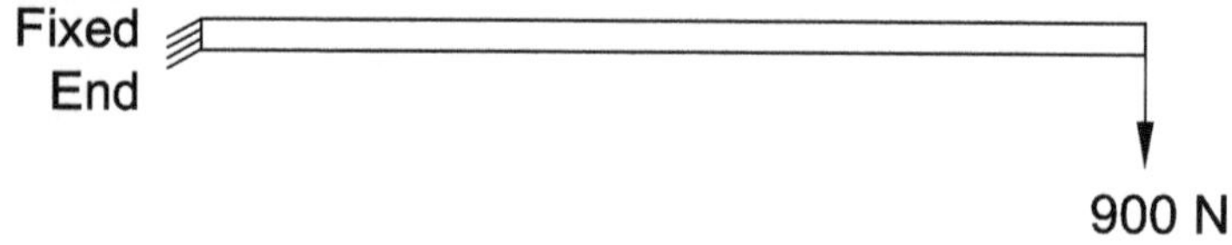

Project Summary

In this case study, you will run the frequency analysis on a Cantilever Beam with 900 N downward load on its right end.

Summary

This chapter introduced the process of performing frequency analysis to determine the natural or resonant frequencies of a structure. You learned how to identify the mode shapes corresponding to each frequency and evaluate mass participation in the X, Y, and Z directions. Understanding these factors helps predict potential resonance issues and ensures structural stability in real-world applications.

Questions

Complete the following sentences:

- The natural frequencies of an object are also known as _________ frequencies.
- Every object has different natural frequencies depending on its _________, _________, and _________.
- Each natural frequency of an object is associated with a shape called _________ shape.
- When an object vibrates due to an external force with a frequency that matches with one of its natural frequencies, the object undergoes large displacements and stresses due to _________.
- The _________ tool is used to invoke the **List Modes** window, which displays a list of calculated natural frequencies.
- The _________ tool is used to invoke the **Mass Participation** window, which displays a list of natural frequencies and mass participation in the X, Y, and Z directions.
- You can save the results of the natural frequencies in an external file having _________ file extension.

CHAPTER

9

Drop Test Analysis

In this chapter, the following topics will be discussed:

- Introduction to Drop Test Analysis
- Drop Test Analysis of a Cylinder
- Drop Test Analysis of a Helmet
- Drop Test Analysis of a Hard Drive

In earlier chapters, you learned about design failures caused by stresses exceeding the yield strength of the material, known as material failure. You also explored failures due to buckling, fatigue, and other factors. In this chapter, you will learn about the failure of a design due to falling on a floor.

In real-world conditions, many products fail due to accidental drops during transportation, installation, repair, or handling. To enhance impact resistance, drop test analysis is conducted by simulating a fall from a specific height or velocity. This analysis helps assess structural integrity and improve product durability.

Introduction to Drop Test Analysis

The drop test analysis is used to analyze the effect of dropping an object (part or assembly) on a rigid or flexible floor. In this analysis, SOLIDWORKS Simulation calculates the impact of a part or an assembly on the floor.

Case Study 1: Drop Test Analysis of a Cylinder

In this case study, you will perform the drop test analysis of a Cylinder (see Figure 9.1) and evaluate its effect of dropping on a rigid floor from a height of 2 feet.

9.1

Project Description

Determine the impact of the Cylinder with the rigid floor when falling from a height of 2 feet at an angle, see Figure 9.2. Note that the 2 feet height is measured from the lowest point of the Cylinder. The Cylinder is made up of **Plain Carbon Steel** material.

9.2

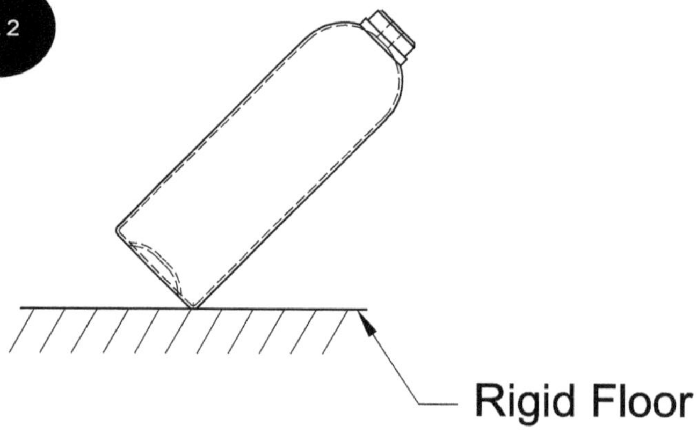

Project Summary

In this case study, you will run the drop test analysis on a Cylinder. In the drop test, you do not need to define any boundary conditions (fixtures and loads).

The following sequence summarizes the case study outline:

1. Downloading Files of Chapter 9
2. Opening the Cylinder
3. Starting the Drop Test Analysis
4. Defining Drop Test Setup
5. Applying the Material

6. Defining Result Options
7. Generating the Mesh
8. Running the Drop Test Study
9. Animating the Stress Result
10. Saving Results

Section 1: Downloading Files of Chapter 9

1. Log on to the CADArtifex website (*cadartifex.com/login/*).

2. After logging, navigate to the textbook titled "**SOLIDWORKS Simulation 2026: A Power Guide for Beginners and Intermediate Users: Colored**". You can enter the name of the textbook in the **Search** box to locate it quickly.

3. In the **Online Resources** tab, expand the **Case Studies** rollout and click the **Download** button corresponding to **C09 Case Studies**. In the confirmation window that appears, click the **Confirm** button. The download of the **C09 Case Studies** file will begin. After the download is complete, unzip the file.

4. Save the extracted **C09 Case Studies** folder in the location ***SOLIDWORKS Simulation > Case Studies***.

Section 2: Opening the Cylinder

1. Start SOLIDWORKS, if not already started.

2. Click on the **Open** button in the **Welcome** dialog box or the **Open** tool in the **Standard** toolbar. The **Open** dialog box appears.

3. Browse to the location > ***SOLIDWORKS Simulation > Case Studies > C09 Case Studies > Case Study 1*** of the local drive of your system. Next, select the **Cylinder** and then click on the **Open** button in the dialog box. The Cylinder model is opened in SOLIDWORKS.

Section 3: Starting the Drop Test Analysis

1. Click on the **Simulation** tab in the **CommandManager**. The tools of the **Simulation CommandManager** appear.

2. Click on the **New Study** tool in the **Simulation CommandManager**. The **Study PropertyManager** appears to the left of the graphics area.

3. Click on the **Drop Test** button in the **Specialized Simulation** rollout of the PropertyManager to perform the drop test analysis.

4. Enter the **Cylinder Drop Test Study** in the **Study name** field of the **Name** rollout in the PropertyManager, see Figure 9.3.

5. Click on the green tick-mark button in the PropertyManager. The **Cylinder Drop Test Study** is added to the Simulation Study Tree, see Figure 9.4.

9.3

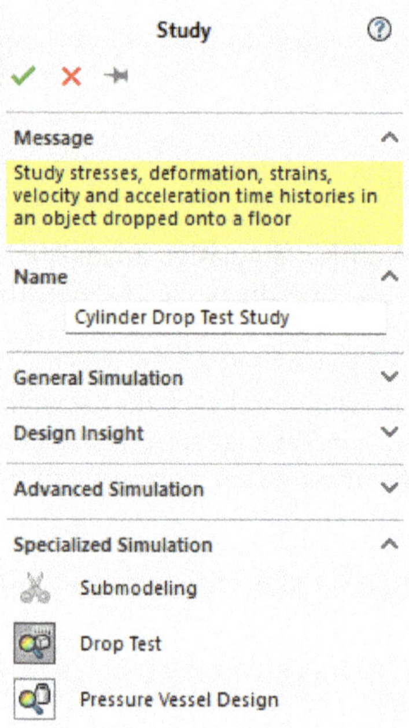

9.4

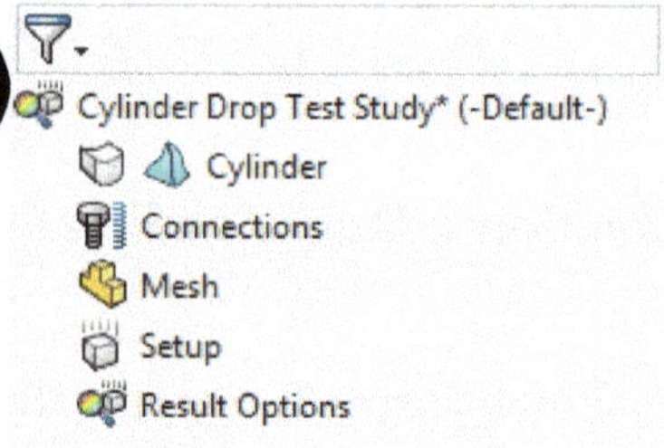

Tip: It is evident from the Simulation Study Tree that the loads and fixtures (restraints) are not required to perform the drop test.

Section 4: Defining Drop Test Setup

Before you start performing the drop test analysis, you need to define the drop test setup.

1. Right-click on the **Setup** option in the Simulation Study Tree and then click on the **Define/Edit** tool in the shortcut menu that appears, see Figure 9.5. The **Drop Test Setup PropertyManager** appears, see Figure 9.6.

9.5

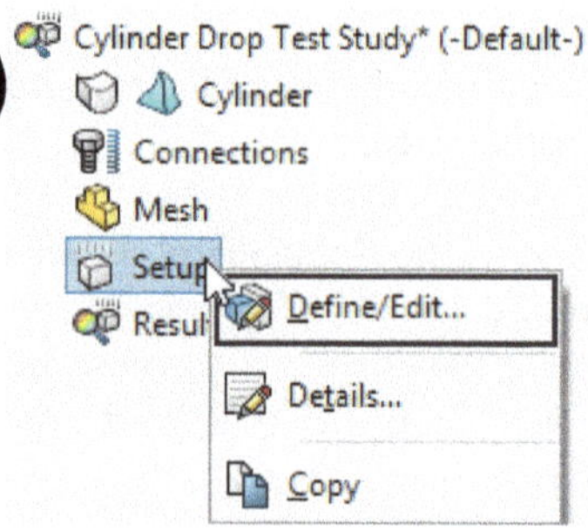

The **Specify** rollout of the PropertyManager is used to specify the type of drop test setup. By default, the **Drop height** radio button is selected in this rollout. As a result, you can specify the drop test setup for an object dropping from a height on a floor. On selecting the **Velocity at impact** radio button, you can specify the drop test setup for an object falling with a velocity on a floor.

9.6

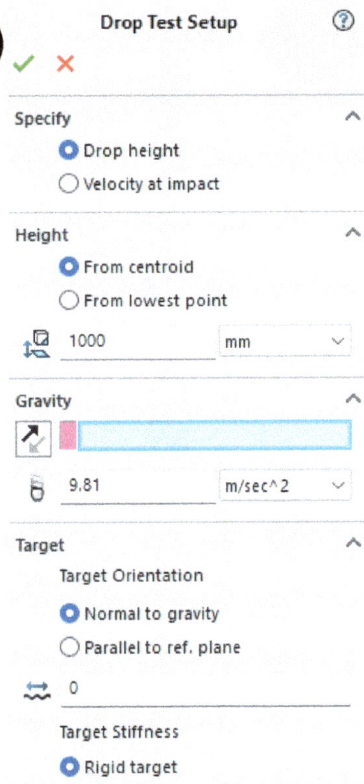

2. Ensure that the **Drop height** radio button is selected in the **Specify** rollout of the PropertyManager, see Figure 9.6.

   The options in the **Height** rollout are used to specify the height from which the object is dropped from rest. On selecting the **From centroid** radio button, the height is measured from the centroid of the object to the floor in the direction of gravity. On selecting the **From lowest point** radio button, the height is measured from the lowest point of the object to the floor.

3. Select the **From lowest point** radio button in the **Height** rollout of the PropertyManager.

4. Select the **ft** (feet) option in the **Unit** drop-down list of the **Height** rollout and then enter **2** in the **Drop Height from Lowest Point** field, see Figure 9.7.

9.7

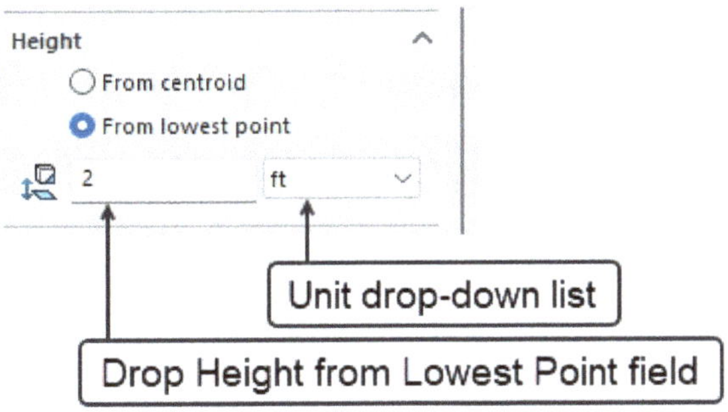

   The **Gravity** rollout is used to define the direction and acceleration value of gravity. You can select a reference plane, an edge, or a planar face to define the direction of gravity. Note that if you select a reference plane or a planar face as the direction of gravity then the gravity will be applied in the direction normal to the selection.

5. Expand the FeatureManager Design Tree, which is now at the top left corner of the graphics area, and then click on **Plane1** to define the direction of gravity, see Figure 9.8. The direction of gravity is defined as normal to the plane selected. Also, an arrow pointing toward the direction of gravity appears in the graphics area, see Figure 9.9.

9.8

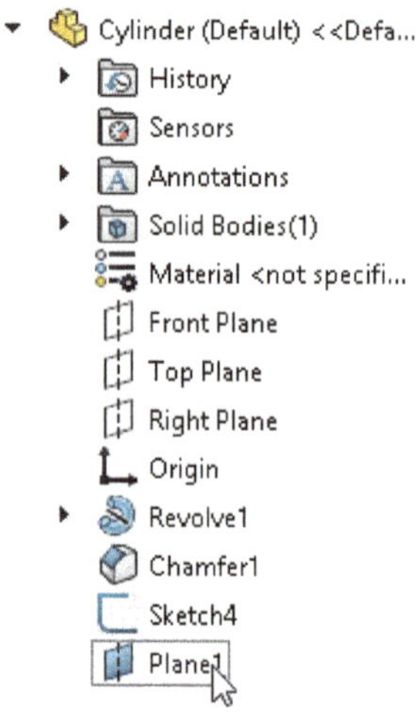

9.9

Note: If needed, you can flip the direction of gravity by clicking on the **Gravity Reference** button in the **Gravity** rollout of the PropertyManager.

The options in the **Target** rollout are used to define the orientation and type of impact (target) plane. By default, the **Normal to gravity** radio button is selected in this rollout. As a result, the impact (target) plane is defined as normal to the direction of gravity. You can also define the impact (target) plane, parallel to a reference plane. To do this, select the **Parallel to ref. plane** radio button. The **Target Orientation Reference** field appears in this rollout. Next, select a reference plane. In doing so, the impact (target) plane is defined parallel to the selected reference plane.

6. Ensure that the **Normal to gravity** radio button is selected in this rollout to define the target plane normal to the direction of gravity.

The **Target Stiffness** area of the **Target** rollout is used to define the type of target plane, see Figure 9.10. By default, the **Rigid target** radio button is selected in this area. As a result, the rigid floor is used as the target. On selecting the **Flexible target** radio button, you can define the flexible target by specifying its properties such as stiffness, mass density, and thickness of the flexible target plane in the respective fields of the **Stiffness and thickness** rollout of the PropertyManager. Note that this rollout appears only when the **Flexible target** radio button is selected.

9.10

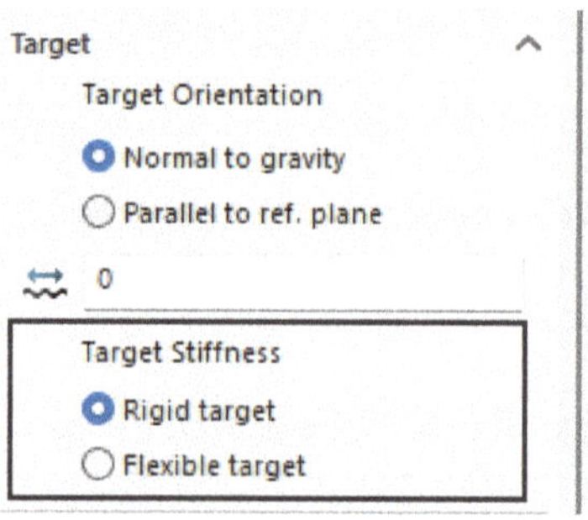

7. Ensure that the **Rigid target** radio button is selected in the **Target Stiffness** area of the **Target** rollout of the PropertyManager.

Tip: You can also set the coefficient of friction between the object and the impact (target) plane by using the **Coefficient of friction** field of the **Target** rollout in the PropertyManager.

8. Click on the green tick-mark button in the PropertyManager. The drop test setup is defined.

Section 5: Applying the Material

Now, you need to apply the material to the model.

1. Invoke the **Material** dialog box by clicking on the **Apply Material** tool in the **Simulation CommandManager**.
2. Apply the **Plain Carbon Steel** material to the Cylinder and then close the **Material** dialog box.

Section 6: Defining Result Options

Now, you need to define the result options such as for how long you want to run the analysis after the impact and the number of result plots to be saved.

1. Right-click on the **Result Options** option in the Simulation Study Tree and then click on the **Define/Edit** tool in the shortcut menu that appears, see Figure 9.11. The **Result Options PropertyManager** appears, see Figure 9.12.

9.11

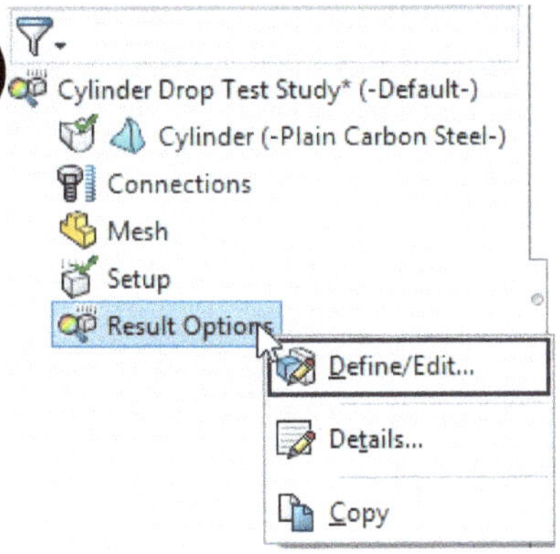

9.12

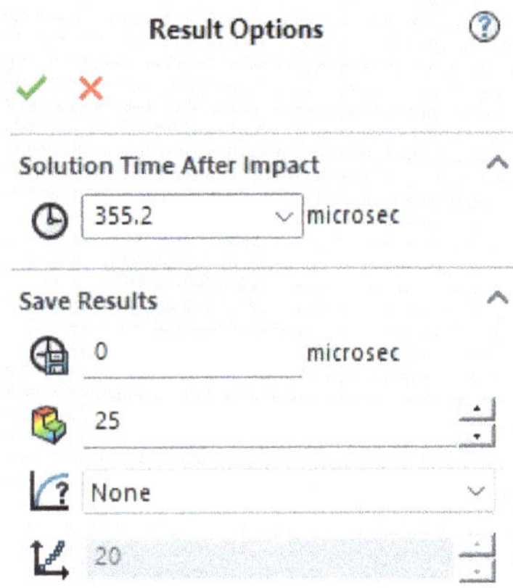

The **Solution Time After Impact** field of the **Result Options PropertyManager** is used to specify how long you want to run the analysis, after the impact. By default, SOLIDWORKS Simulation automatically calculates the appropriate time by using the **3L/Ve** formula. Where **L** is the largest length of the object boundary box size and **Ve** is the square root of the modulus of elasticity.

The **Save Results Starting From** field of the **Save Results** rollout of the PropertyManager is used for specifying the time from when the program will start saving the results. By default, **0** is specified in this field. As a result, the program will start saving the results immediately from the moment of first impact. The **No. of Plots** field is used to specify the number of result plots the program will save.

2. Accept the default specified options in the **Result Options PropertyManager** and then click on the green tick-mark button.

Section 7: Generating the Mesh

1. Generate the curvature-based mesh with the default mesh parameters by using the **Create Mesh** tool. Figure 9.13 shows the meshed model. In this figure, the reference plane is hidden.

9.13

Section 8: Running the Drop Test Study

1. Click on the **Run This Study** tool in the **Simulation CommandManager**. The **Cylinder Drop Test Study** (*name of the study*) window appears which displays the progress of the analysis. During the analysis, if the **Simulation** warning message appears as shown in Figure 9.14, click on the **OK** button to continue with the analysis process.

9.14

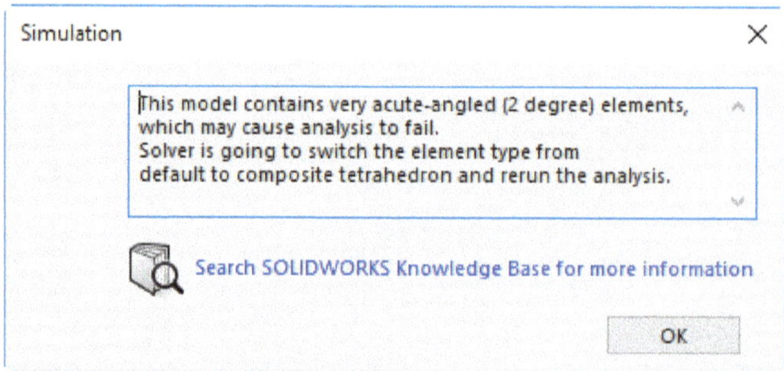

After the process of analysis is completed, the **Results** folder is added to the Simulation Study Tree with the stress, displacement, and strain results. By default, the **Stress** result is activated in the **Results** folder. As a result, the stress distribution on the model after the impact and the von Mises stress plot appear in the graphics area, see Figure 9.15.

Notice that the maximum Von Mises stress in the model at impact is **4.381e+03** (4381.086) N/mm^2 (MPa) which significantly exceeds the yield strength of the material that is **2.206e+02** (220.594) N/mm^2 (MPa). The yield strength of the material is indicated by the red pointer in the von Mises stress plot.

9.15

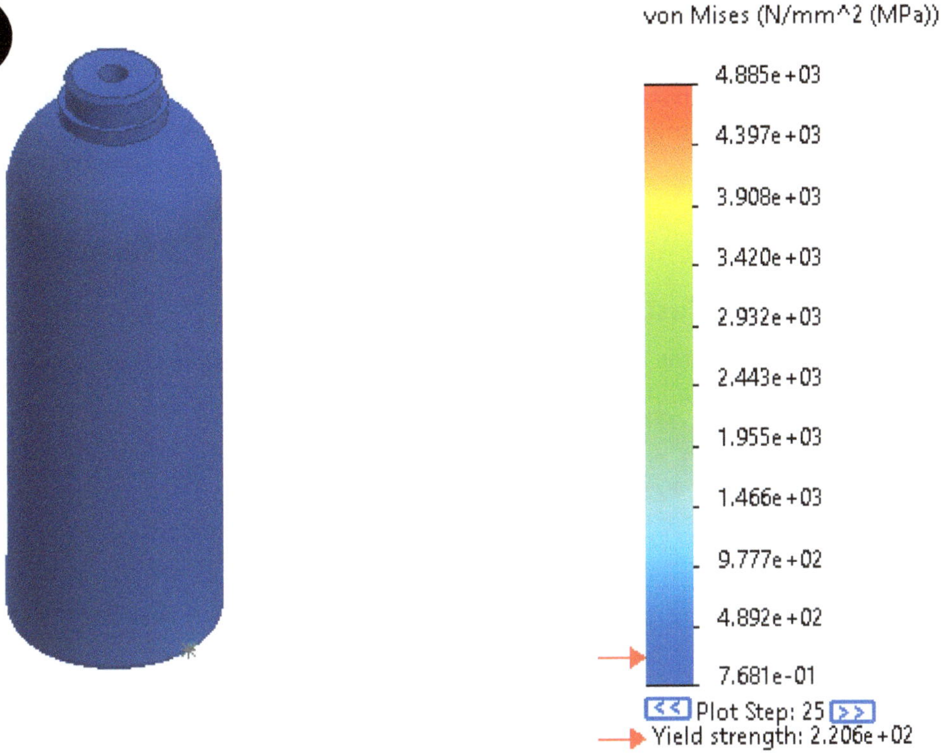

Section 9: Animating the Stress Result

Now, you need to animate the stress result to validate the impact concering time.

1. Right-click on the **Stress1 (-vonMises-)** option in the **Results** folder of the Simulation Study Tree. A shortcut menu appears. In this shortcut menu, click on the **Animate** tool. The **Animation PropertyManager** appears, see Figure 9.16. Also, the animated effect of the object dropping on a rigid floor appears in the graphics area.

9.16

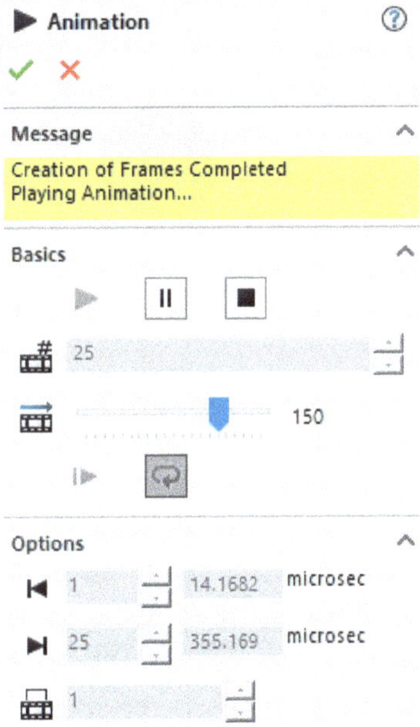

2. Zoom in to the impacted portion of the Cylinder to view its impact with the rigid floor, closely.

3. To save the animation as an AVI file, select the **Save as AVI file** check box in the PropertyManager. Next, specify the path to save the file.

4. After reviewing the animated effects of the deformed shape, click on the green tick-mark button in the PropertyManager to exit the PropertyManager and save the AVI file in the specified location.

Section 10: Saving Results

Now, you need to save the model and its results.

1. Click on the **Save** tool in the **Standard** toolbar. The model and its results are saved in the location *> SOLIDWORKS Simulation > Case Studies > C09 Case Studies > Case Study 1*.

2. Close the SOLIDWORKS session.

Case Study 2: Drop Test Analysis of a Helmet

In this case study, perform the drop test analysis of a Helmet (see Figure 9.17) and evaluate its effect of dropping on a rigid floor from a height of 5 meters.

9.17

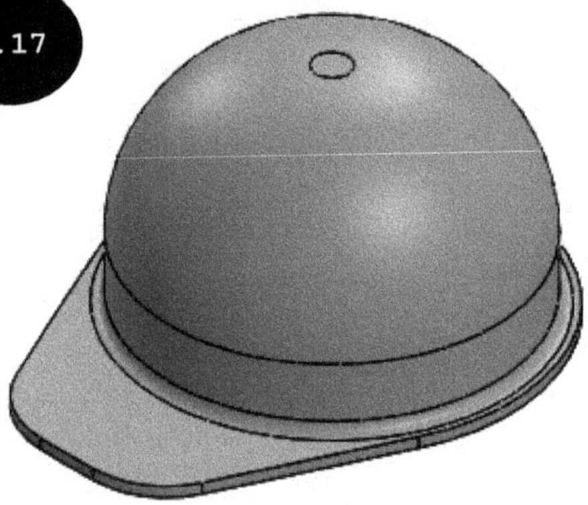

Project Description

Determine the impact of the Helmet on the rigid floor when falling from a height of 5 meters, see Figure 9.18. Note that the 5 meter height is measured from the lowest point of the Helmet. The Helmet is made up of **ABS** material.

9.18

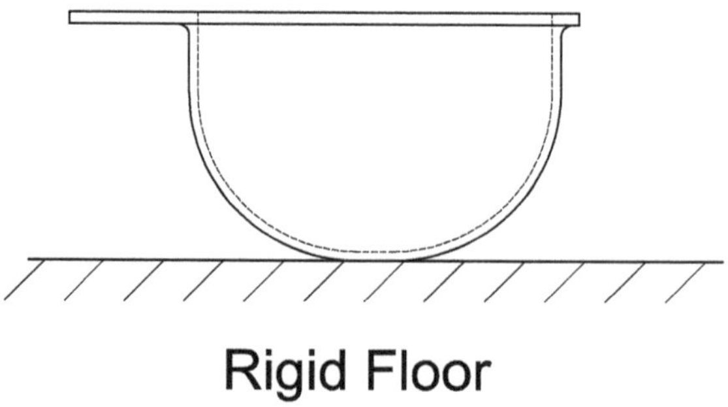

Project Summary

In this case study, you will run the drop test analysis on a Helmet.

The following sequence summarizes the case study outline:

1. Starting the Drop Test Analysis
2. Defining Drop Test Setup
3. Applying the Material
4. Defining Result Options
5. Generating the Mesh
6. Running the Drop Test Study
7. Displaying the Time History Plot
8. Animating the Stress Result
9. Saving Results

Section 1: Starting the Drop Test Analysis

1. Start SOLIDWORKS and then open the Helmet from the location > *SOLIDWORKS Simulation > Case Studies > C09 Case Studies > Case Study 2*.

Note: You need to download the C09 Case Studies file, which contains the files for this chapter, by logging in to the website (*cadartifex.com/login*), if it has not already been downloaded.

2. Click on the **Simulation** tab in the **CommandManager**. The tools of the **Simulation CommandManager** appear.

3. Click on the **New Study** tool in the **Simulation CommandManager**. The **Study PropertyManager** appears to the left of the graphics area.

4. Click on the **Drop Test** button in the **Specialized Simulation** rollout of the PropertyManager.

5. Enter **Helmet Drop Test Study** in the **Study name** field of the **Name** rollout in the PropertyManager.

6. Click on the green tick-mark button in the PropertyManager. The **Helmet Drop Test Study** is added to the Simulation Study Tree, see Figure 9.19.

9.19

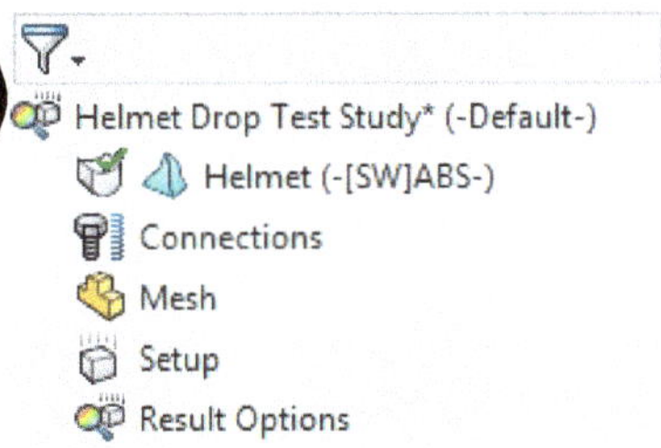

Section 2: Defining Drop Test Setup

Now, you need to define the drop test setup.

1. Right-click on the **Setup** option in the Simulation Study Tree and then click on the **Define/Edit** tool in the shortcut menu that appears, see Figure 9.20. The **Drop Test Setup PropertyManager** appears, see Figure 9.21.

9.20

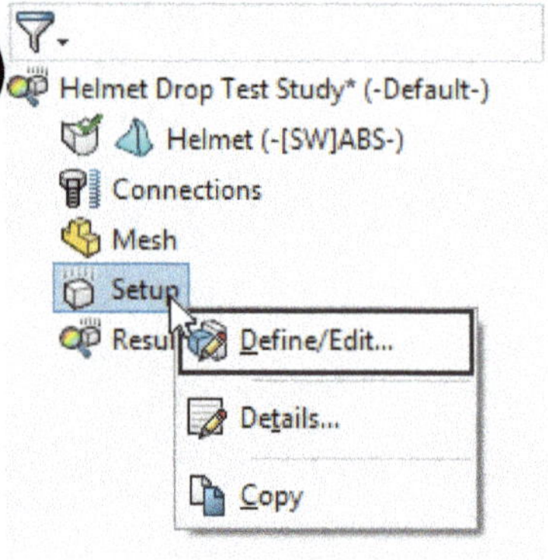

9.21

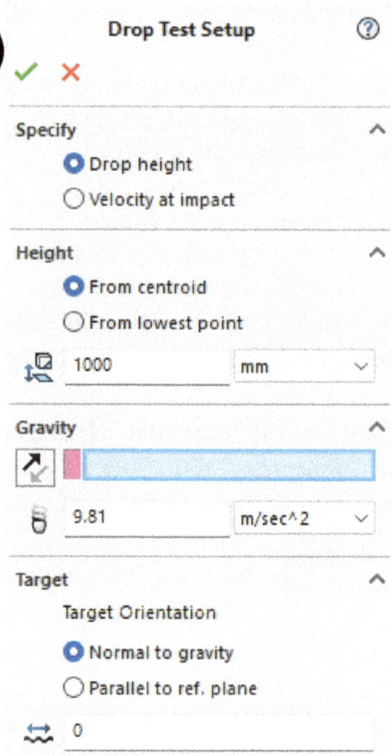

2. Ensure that the **Drop height** radio button is selected in the **Specify** rollout of the PropertyManager.

3. Select the **From lowest point** radio button in the **Height** rollout of the PropertyManager.

4. Select the **m** (meter) option in the **Unit** drop-down list and then enter **5** in the **Drop Height from Lowest Point** field of the **Height** rollout, see Figure 9.22.

9.22

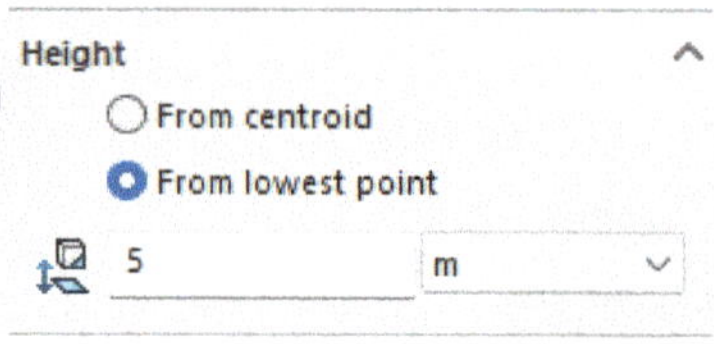

5. Expand the FeatureManager Design Tree, which is now at the top left corner of the graphics area, and then click on **Plane1** to define the direction of gravity, see Figure 9.23. The direction of gravity is defined as normal to the plane selected. Also, an arrow pointing toward the direction of gravity appears in the graphics area, see Figure 9.24.

6. Ensure that the direction of gravity is towards the reference plane selected, see Figure 9.24. If needed, you can flip the direction of gravity by clicking on the **Gravity Reference** button in the **Gravity** rollout of the PropertyManager.

9.23

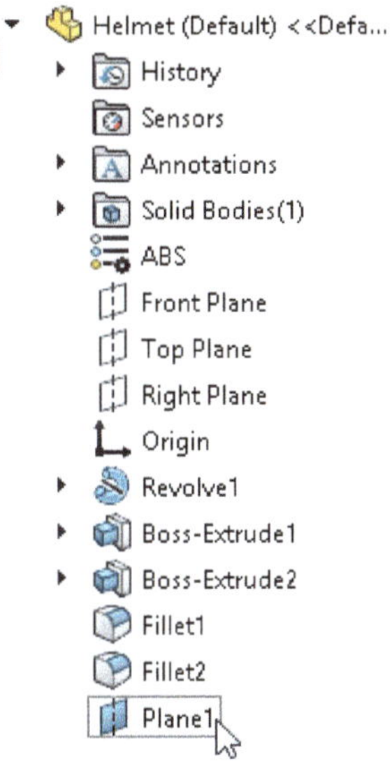

9.24

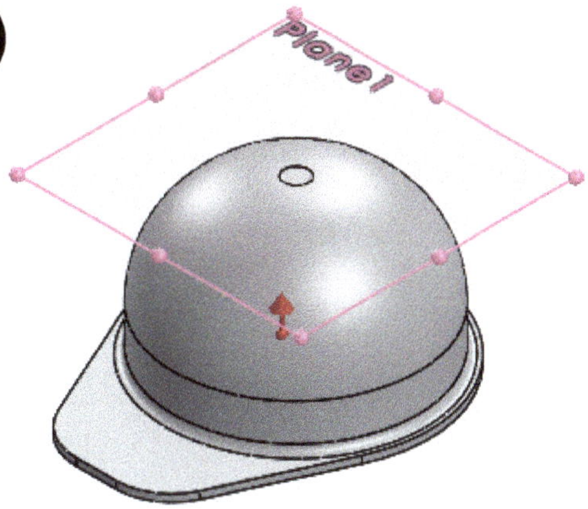

7. Ensure that the **Normal to gravity** radio button is selected in the **Target** rollout of the PropertyManager.

8. Ensure that the **Rigid target** radio button is selected in the **Target Stiffness** area of the **Target** rollout.

9. Click on the green tick-mark button in the PropertyManager. The drop test setup is defined.

Section 3: Applying the Material

Now, you need to apply the material to the model.

1. Invoke the **Material** dialog box by clicking on the **Apply Material** tool in the **Simulation CommandManager**.

2. Apply the **ABS** material to the Helmet and then close the **Material** dialog box.

Section 4: Defining Result Options

Now, you need to define the result options such as, for how long you want to run the analysis after the impact and the number of result plots to be saved.

1. Right-click on the **Result Options** option in the Simulation Study Tree and then click on the **Define/Edit** tool in the shortcut menu that appears. The **Result Options PropertyManager** appears, see Figure 9.25.

9.25

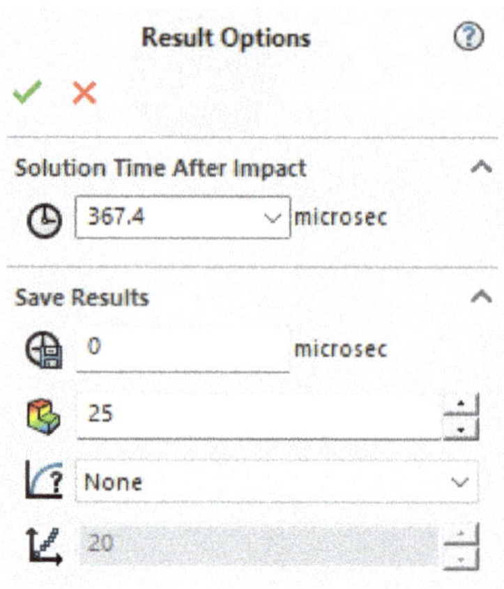

2. Enter **30** in the **No. of Plots** field of the PropertyManager as the number of plots to be saved by the program for all nodes.

3. Click on the green tick-mark button in the PropertyManager.

Section 5: Generating the Mesh

1. Generate the curvature-based mesh with the default mesh parameters by using the **Create Mesh** tool. Figure 9.26 shows the meshed model. In this figure, the reference plane is hidden.

9.26

Section 6: Running the Drop Test Study

1. Click on the **Run This Study** tool in the **Simulation CommandManager**. The **Helmet Drop Test Study** (*name of the study*) window appears which displays the progress of the analysis. After the process of analysis is completed, the **Results** folder is added to the Simulation Study Tree with the stress, displacement, and strain results. By default, the **Stress** result is activated in the **Results** folder. As a result, the stress distribution on the model after the impact and the von Mises stress plot appear in the graphics area, see Figure 9.27.

   Notice that the maximum von Mises stress in the model at impact is **5.200e+01** (52.001) N/mm^2 (MPa).

9.27

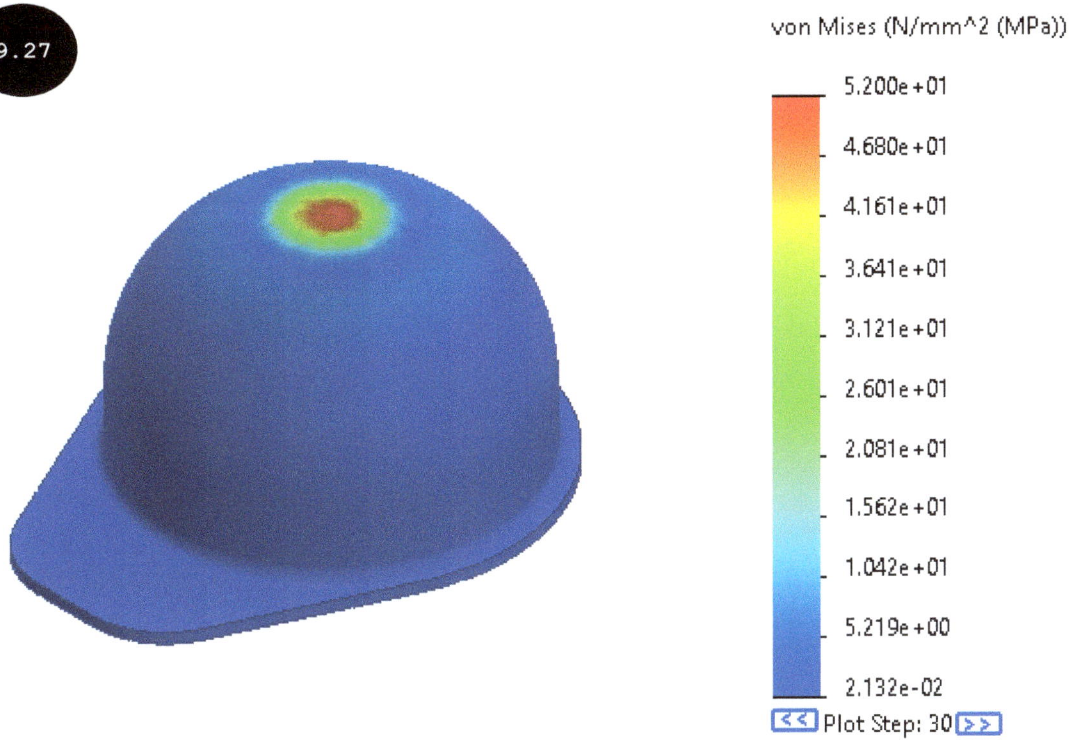

Section 7: Displaying the Time History Plot

1. Right-click on the **Results** folder in the Simulation Study Tree. A shortcut menu appears, see Figure 9.28.

9.28

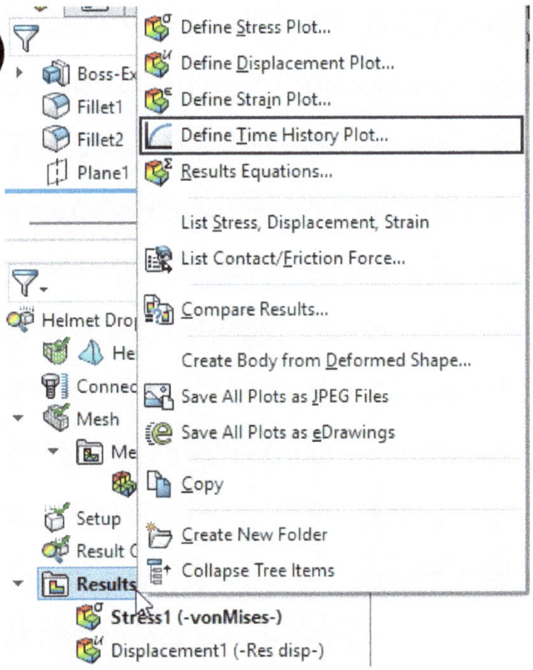

2. Click on the **Define Time History Plot** tool in the shortcut menu. The **Time History Graph PropertyManager** appears, see Figure 9.29.

9.29

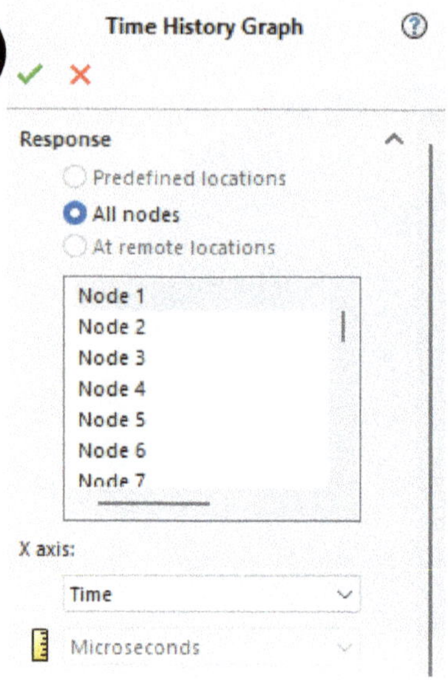

Notice that in the **Response** rollout of the PropertyManager, all the nodes of the model appear in a field. You can select a node or multiple nodes in this field, whose response graph is to be generated. Alternatively, you can click on one or more nodes in the graphics area.

3. Click on a node at the top center (impact area) of the model in the graphics area, see Figure 9.30. The node 9198 at the impact area gets selected. Note that the selected node number of the impact area may differ in your case depending on your selection. Also, the node number 1 is selected, by default.

9.30

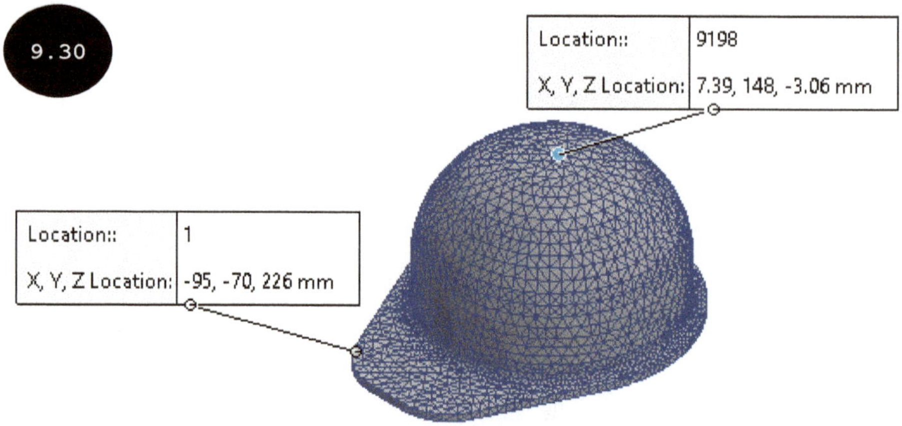

4. Ensure that the **Time** option is selected in the **X axis** drop-down list of the PropertyManager.

5. Ensure that the **Stress** and **VON: von Mises Stress** options are selected in the respective fields of the **Y axis** area in the PropertyManager.

6. Select the **N/mm^2 (MPa)** in the **Units** drop-down list of the **Y-axis** area of the PropertyManager.

7. Click on the green tick-mark button in the PropertyManager. The **Time History Graph** window appears, see Figure 9.31. This window displays the response graphs of the selected nodes (1 and 9198) for the von Mises stress vs solution steps.

9.31

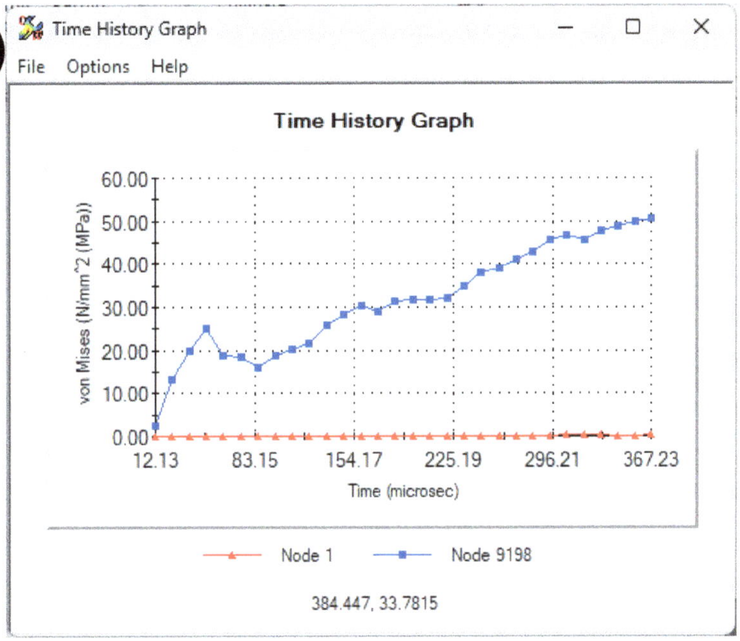

Notice that the maximum von Mises stress on the selected node (9198) is approximately **50** N/mm^2 (MPa), which occurs at time 367.23 microseconds from the impact.

Section 8: Animating the Stress Result

Now, you need to animate the stress result to validate the impact with respect to time.

1. Right-click on the **Stress1 (-vonMises-)** option in the **Results** folder of the Simulation Study Tree. A shortcut menu appears. In this shortcut menu, click on the **Animate** tool. The **Animation PropertyManager** appears. Also, the animated effect of the object dropping on a rigid floor appears in the graphics area. You can zoom in on the high-stress area (impact area) of the object to view its effects closely.

2. After reviewing the animated effects, click on the green tick-mark button in the PropertyManager to exit the PropertyManager.

Section 9: Saving Results

1. Click on the **Save** tool in the **Standard** toolbar. The model and its results are saved in the location > ***SOLIDWORKS Simulation** > **Case Studies** > **C09 Case Studies** > **Case Study 2***. Next, close the SOLIDWORKS session.

Hands-on Test Drive 1: Drop Test Analysis of a Hard Drive

In this case study, perform the drop test analysis of an external Hard Drive (see Figure 9.32) and evaluate its effect of dropping on a rigid floor from a height of 1 meter.

Project Description

Determine the impact of the Hard Drive with the rigid floor when falling from a height of 1-meter, see Figure 9.33. Note that the 1 meter height is measured from the lowest point of the object. The Hard Drive is made up of **PVC Rigid** plastic material.

9.32

9.33

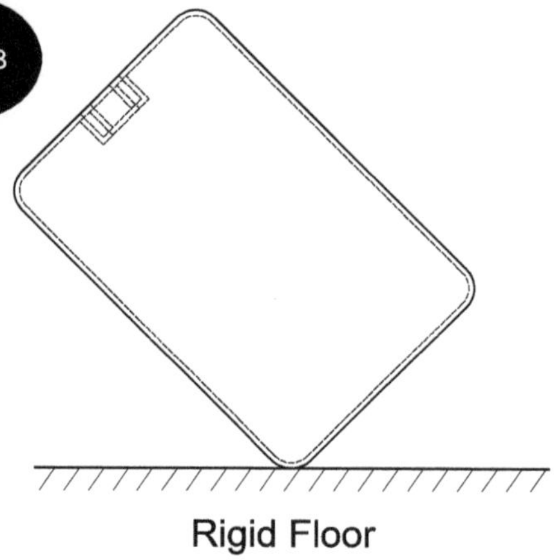

Summary

This chapter introduced the process of performing a drop test analysis to evaluate the impact of a part or assembly when it falls onto a rigid or flexible floor. It covered key aspects of setting up the simulation, analyzing the results, and understanding the effects of impact on structural integrity.

Questions

Complete the following sentences:

- The drop test analysis is used to analyze the effect of dropping an object on a _________ or a _________ floor.
- The _________ radio button of the **Drop Test Setup PropertyManager** is used to measure the drop height from the centroid of the object to the floor in the direction of gravity.
- The _________ radio button of the **Drop Test Setup PropertyManager** is used to define the impact (target) plane, parallel to a reference plane.
- The _________ radio button of the **Drop Test Setup PropertyManager** is used to specify the drop test setup for an object dropping from a height on a floor.
- The _________ radio button of the **Drop Test Setup PropertyManager** is used to specify the drop test setup for an object falling with a specified velocity on a floor.

CHAPTER

10

Non-Linear Static Analysis

In this chapter, the following topics will be discussed:

- Making Assumptions for Non-Linear Static Analysis
- Using Iterative Methods for Non-Linear Analysis
- Using Incremental Methods for Non-Linear Analysis
- Non-Linear Static Analysis of a Shackle
- Non-Linear Static Analysis of a Handrail Clamp Assembly
- Non-Linear Static Analysis of a Cantilever Beam
- Non-linear Static Analysis of a Hook Assembly

In this chapter, you will learn about non-linear static analysis problems. As discussed, in Finite Element Analysis (FEA), certain assumptions are made to define the nature of an engineering problem. Based on these assumptions, the appropriate type of analysis is selected.

This chapter explores key engineering assumptions that determine when a problem requires non-linear static analysis, helping you understand the conditions and factors that make a system behave non-linearly.

Making Assumptions for Non-Linear Static Analysis

Non-Linear static analysis is used to calculate displacement, strain, stress, and reaction forces under the effect of applied load. In mechanical models, the non-linear problems are categorized mainly as material non-linearities, geometric non-linearities, and contact non-linearities. You can consider the non-linear problem and perform the non-linear static analysis if the following assumptions are valid for the engineering problem to be solved.

1. **Geometric Non-linearities:** Displacement is assumed to be very large due to the applied load.
2. **Material Non-linearities:** Material is assumed to exceed its elastic region in the stress-strain curve and behave non-linearly. It implies that the structure is loaded beyond its elastic limits such

that it experiences plastic deformation and does not return to its original configuration even after removing the applied load, see Figure 10.1. Also, the material properties are assumed to change due to the plastic deformation.

10.1

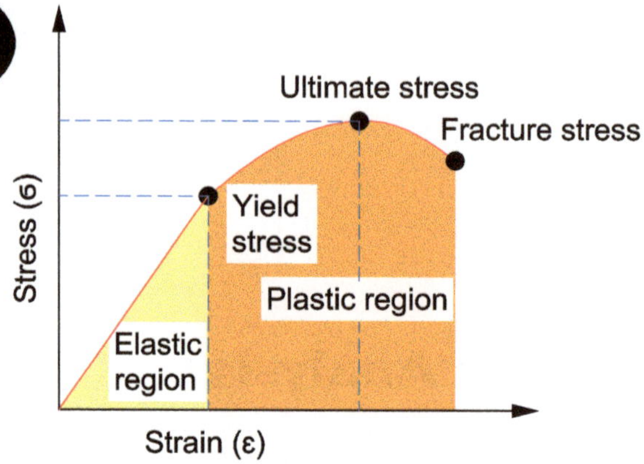

3. **Contact Non-linearities:** In case of contact problems, the boundary conditions are assumed to change due to the motion in the components during the analysis.

Also, in the non-linear problems, the relationship between load and the displacement response is not proportional to each other, see Figure 10.2. As a result, the stiffness is not constant and it changes as the magnitude of the load increases.

10.2

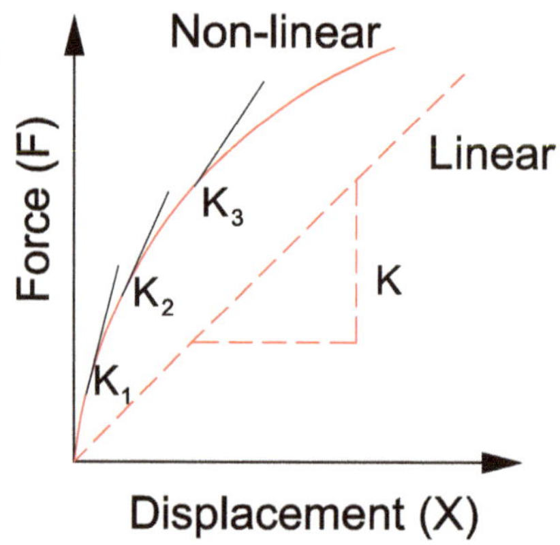

If the above-mentioned assumptions are valid for the problem to be solved, you can perform the non-linear static analysis. In non-linear static analysis, the basic finite element equilibrium equation to be solved is as follows:

$$[F] = [K(X)][X]$$

Where,
F = Applied load
K = System stiffness (*stiffness is not constant and varies as a function of displacement*)
X = Displacement (*large displacement*)

Similar to the linear static analysis, the applied load in the non-linear static analysis is assumed to be constant and does not vary with time. However, the procedure to solve the non-linear static analysis is different than that for the linear static analysis because of the change in the stiffness.

In non-linear static analysis, the load is applied in different incremental steps as the function of pseudo time (not real time), and for every incremental step, the program updates the stiffness to carry out the next incremental step. Also, the program performs multiple iterations to ensure that the equilibrium equation is satisfied in every incremental step. SOLIDWORKS Simulation uses the Newton-Raphson (NR) scheme or the Modified Newton-Raphson (MNR) scheme as the iterative method and the Force, Displacement, or Arc Length technique as the incremental method to converge the final solution. The different iterative and incremental methods are discussed next.

Using Iterative Methods for Non-Linear Analysis

SOLIDWORKS Simulation uses the Newton-Raphson (NR) scheme or the Modified Newton-Raphson (MNR) scheme as the iterative method. Both methods are discussed next.

Newton-Raphson (NR) Scheme

The Newton-Raphson (NR) scheme forms the tangential stiffness matrix to calculate the stiffness at every iteration. In this scheme, the program first calculates the stiffness for the first iteration and then based on the calculated stiffness, it calculates the stiffness for the next iteration, even if the equilibrium equation is not satisfied in the first iteration, see Figure 10.3. It continues performing multiple iterations until the structure reaches the equilibrium state up to the prescribed tolerance in an incremental step.

10.3

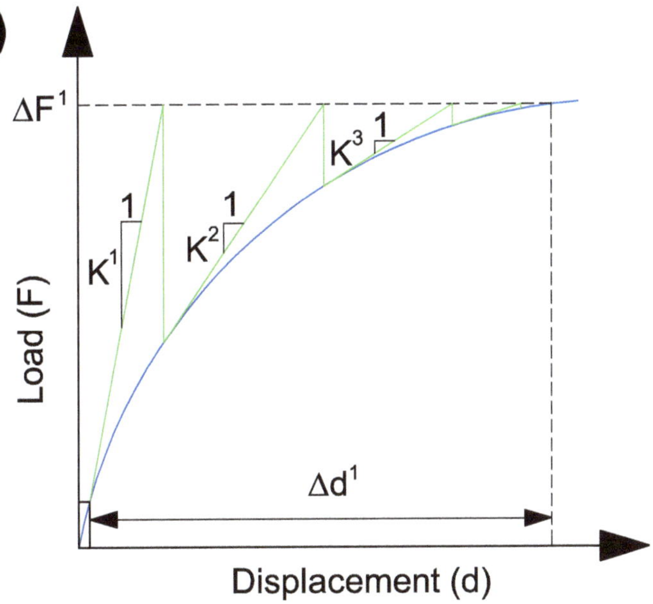

Modified Newton-Raphson (MNR) Scheme

In the Modified Newton-Raphson (MNR) scheme, the stiffness is calculated at the first iteration, and the same is used for the next iterations, see Figure 10.4. It continues performing multiple iterations until the structure reaches an equilibrium state up to the prescribed tolerance in an incremental step.

10.4

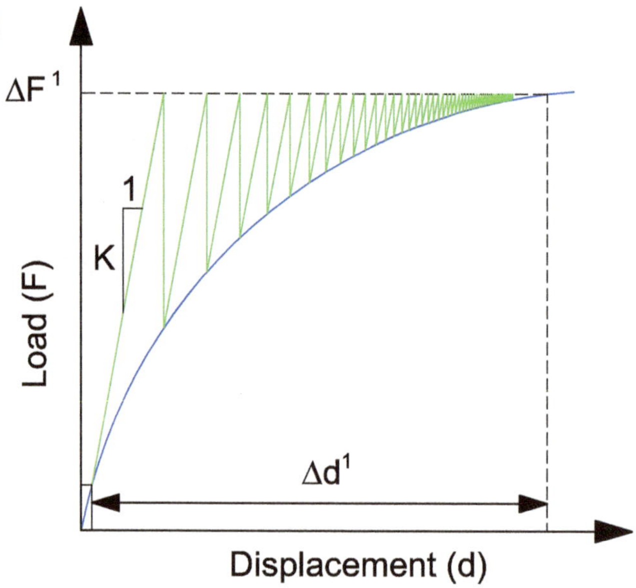

It is clear from the above Figures 10.3 and 10.4 that the Modified Newton-Raphson (MNR) scheme uses more number of iterations than the Newton-Raphson (NR) scheme to converge the solution. However, in the Modified Newton-Raphson (MNR) scheme, every iteration is faster than the Newton-Raphson (NR) scheme, since the stiffness is not calculated in every iteration.

Tip: In some cases where the Newton-Raphson scheme does not converge the solution, the Modified Newton-Raphson scheme may converge it due to more number of iterations.

Using Incremental Methods for Non-Linear Analysis

In addition to defining the iterative methods; Newton-Raphson (NR) or Modified Newton-Raphson (MNR), you also need to define the incremental control method: Force, Displacement, or Arc Length to converge the final solution. The different incremental control methods are discussed next.

Force Incremental Control Method

In the Force control method, the force/load is used as the prescribed variable and increases gradually in different incremental steps to find the equilibrium path, see Figure 10.5. In this figure, the load is applied in different incremental steps and the equilibrium condition is satisfied in every incremental load step by using the Newton-Raphson scheme.

10.5

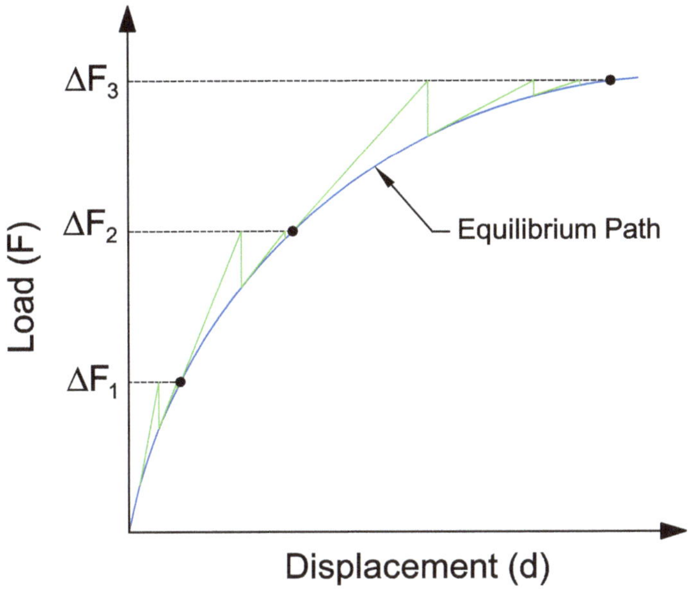

Displacement Incremental Control Method

In the Displacement control method, the displacement is used as the prescribed variable and increases gradually in different incremental steps to find the equilibrium path, see Figure 10.6. In this method, the applied load is not increased directly and is used as a multiplier to calculate the load as the response of the structure.

10.6

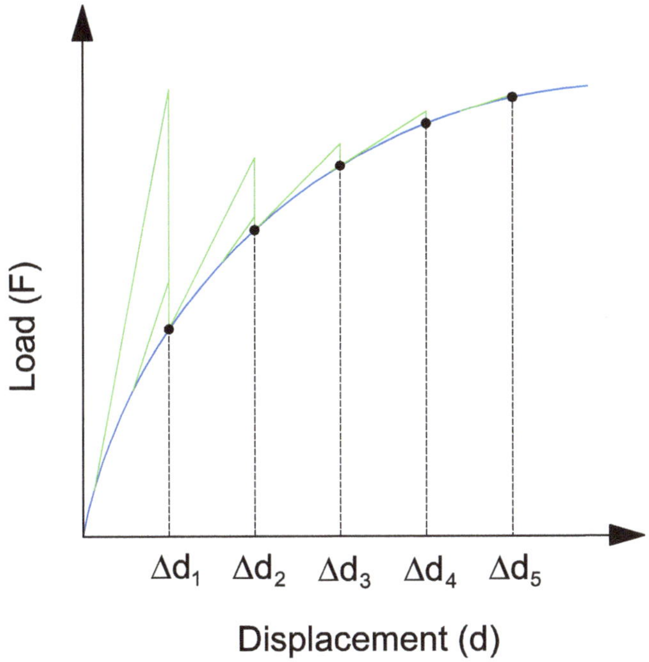

Arc Length Incremental Control Method

The Arc Length incremental control method is a very powerful method to solve non-linear problems when the slope of the equilibrium path undergoes large changes from one equilibrium state to another and the load and displacement control methods fail to converge the equilibrium solution, see Figure 10.7. In the Arc Length control method, the incremental steps are controlled by a combination of both the load and displacement increments of a specified length called arc length. Also, an incremental step is defined by the radius of the arc and a point of intersection between the path and the arc radius, see Figure 10.7.

10.7

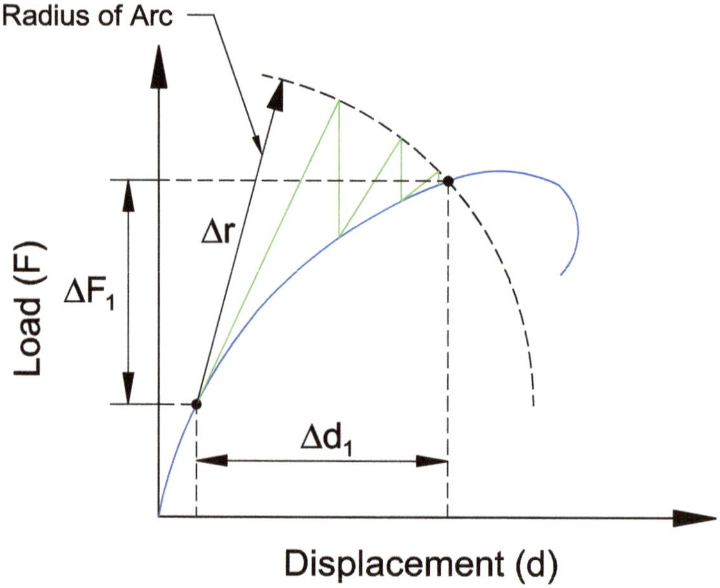

Case Study 1: Non-Linear Static Analysis of a Shackle

In this case study, you will perform the non-linear analysis of a Shackle, see Figure 10.8 and determine the stress under a load.

10.8

Project Description

The Shackle is fixed at its top holes, see Figure 10.9 and a 19000 N downward load is uniformly distributed along the center of the cylindrical face of the model, see Figure 10.9. The Shackle is made up of **AISI 1035 Steel (SS)** material.

10.9

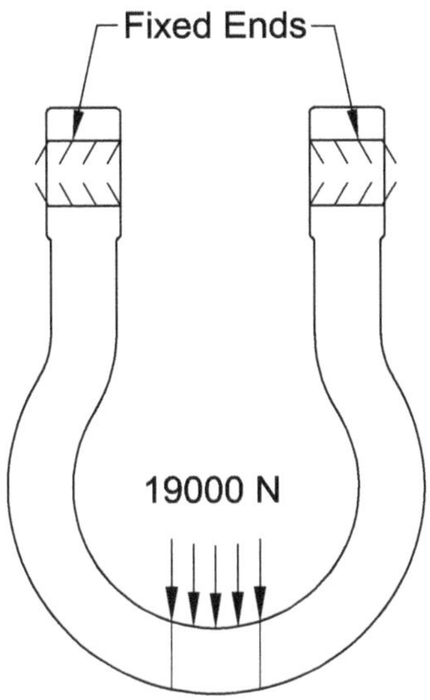

Project Summary

In this case study, you will first run the linear static study and then perform the non-linear static study to compare the difference in the results. In the non-linear static study, you need to use the Force control method and the Newton-Raphson (NR) scheme to converge the final solution. Specify the unit system to SI (MKS) with displacement in mm and stress in N/mm^2 (MPa) units.

The following sequence summarizes the case study outline:

1. Downloading the Files of Chapter 10
2. Opening the Shackle Model
3. Starting the Linear Static Analysis
4. Applying the Fixture, Load, and Material
5. Generating the Mesh
6. Running the Static Analysis
7. Starting the Non-Linear Static Analysis
8. Defining the Properties for the Non-Linear Static Analysis
9. Applying the Fixture, Load, and Material
10. Generating the Mesh
11. Running the Non-linear Static Analysis
12. Generating the Time History Plot in the Non-linear Static Study
13. Saving Results

Section 1: Downloading the Files of Chapter 10

1. Log on to the CADArtifex website (*cadartifex.com/login/*).

2. After logging, navigate to the textbook titled "**SOLIDWORKS Simulation 2026: A Power Guide for Beginners and Intermediate Users: Colored**". You can enter the name of the textbook in the **Search** box to locate it quickly.

3. In the **Online Resources** tab, expand the **Case Studies** rollout and click the **Download** button corresponding to **C10 Case Studies**. In the confirmation window that appears, click the **Confirm** button. The download of the **C10 Case Studies** file will begin. After the download is complete, unzip the file.

4. Save the extracted **C10 Case Studies** folder in the location ***SOLIDWORKS Simulation > Case Studies***.

Section 2: Opening the Shackle Model

1. Start SOLIDWORKS, if not already started.

2. Click on the **Open** button in the **Standard** toolbar. The **Open** dialog box appears.

3. Browse to the location > ***SOLIDWORKS Simulation > Case Studies > C10 Case Studies > Case Study 1*** of the local drive of your system. Next, select the **Shackle** and then click on the **Open** button in the dialog box. The Shackle model opens in SOLIDWORKS.

Section 3: Starting the Linear Static Analysis

As mentioned, first you need to perform the linear static analysis of the Shackle model.

1. Click on the **Simulation** tab in the **CommandManager**. The tools of the **Simulation CommandManager** appear.

2. Click on the **New Study** tool in the **Simulation CommandManager**. The **Study PropertyManager** appears on the left of the graphics area.

3. Ensure that the **Static** button is activated in the **Study PropertyManager** to perform the linear static analysis.

4. Enter **Shackle Static Study** in the **Study name** field of the **Name** rollout in the PropertyManager.

5. Click on the green tick-mark button in the PropertyManager. The **Shackle Static Study** is added to the Simulation Study Tree, see Figure 10.10.

10.10

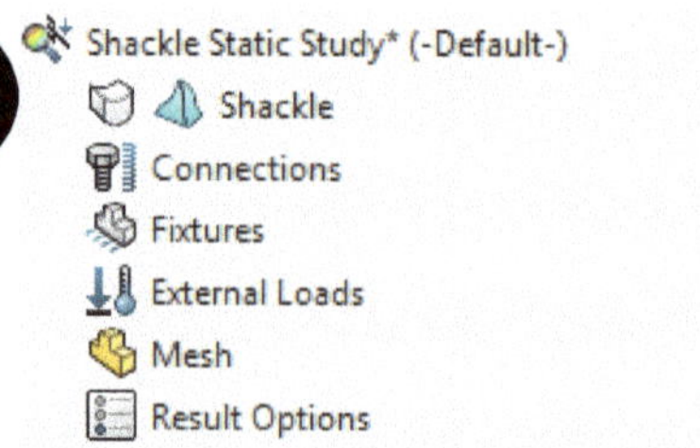

Section 4: Applying the Fixture, Load, and Material

Now, you need to apply the fixture, load, and material to the model.

1. Invoke the **Material** dialog box by clicking on the **Apply Material** tool in the **Simulation CommandManager** and then apply the **AISI 1035 Steel (SS)** material. Next, close the dialog box.

Note: In the **SOLIDWORKS Materials** library, the materials with **(SS)** at their end, represent that the Stress-Strain Curve is defined for that particular material. It defines the behavior of the material in the plastic region and is used when you perform the non-linear analysis.

Now, you need to apply the Fixed Geometry fixture to the holes of the model.

2. Right-click on the **Fixtures** option in the Simulation Study Tree and then click on the **Fixed Geometry** tool in the shortcut menu that appears. The **Fixture PropertyManager** appears.

3. Select the inner circular faces of both the holes of the model to apply the Fixed Geometry fixture, see Figure 10.11.

4. Click on the green tick-mark button in the PropertyManager. The Fixed Geometry fixture is applied.

Now, you need to apply the 19000 N downward load.

5. Right-click on the **External Loads** option in the Simulation Study Tree and then click on the **Force** tool in the shortcut menu that appears. The **Force/Torque PropertyManager** appears.

6. Select the middle split circular face of the model to apply the load, see Figure 10.12.

10.11

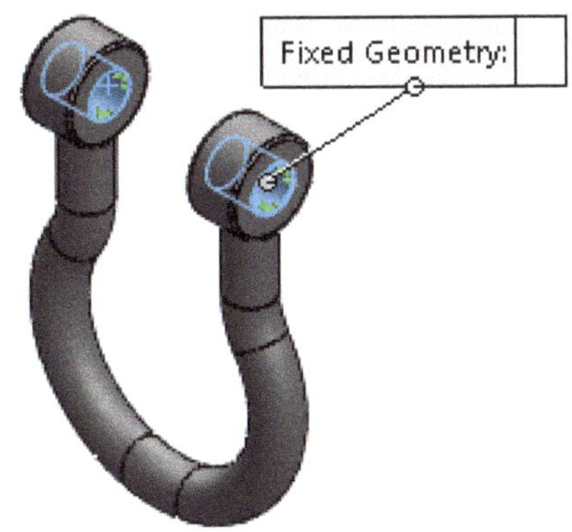

10.12

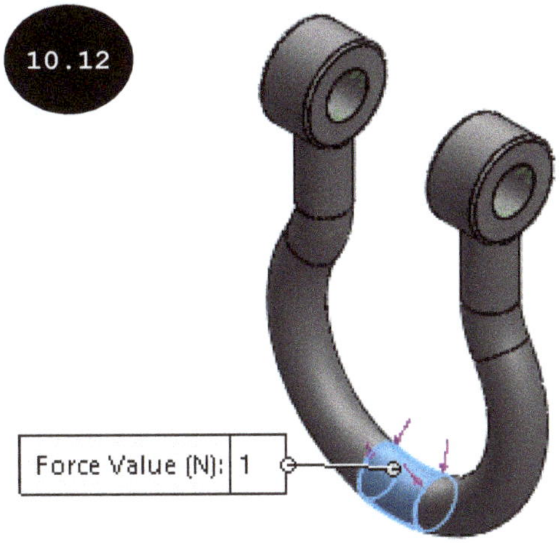

7. Select the **Selected direction** radio button in the PropertyManager and then select the **Top Plane** as the direction reference in the expanded FeatureManager Design Tree. Note that to select the Top Plane as the direction reference, you need to expand the FeatureManager Design Tree which is now available at the top left corner of the screen.

8. Click on the **Normal to Plane** button in the **Force** rollout of the PropertyManager and then enter **19000** as the load value, see Figure 10.13.

9. Select the **Reverse direction** check box in the **Force** rollout of the PropertyManager to reverse the direction of force downward, see Figure 10.14.

10.13

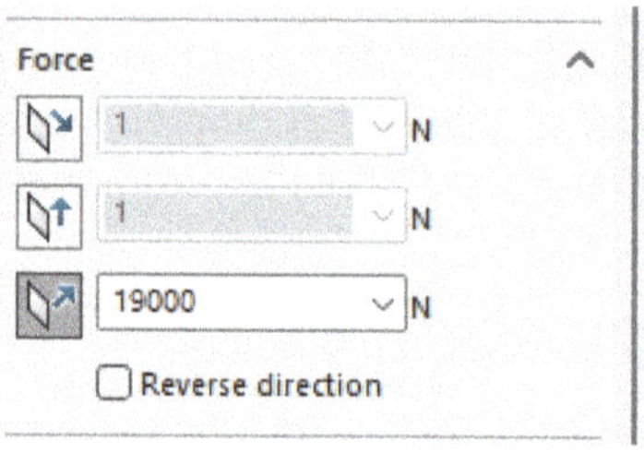

10.14

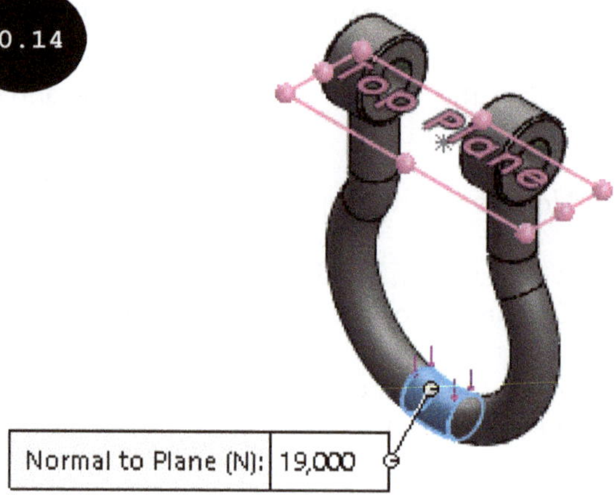

10. Click on the green tick-mark button in the PropertyManager. The 19000 N downward load is applied.

Section 5: Generating the Mesh

1. Generate the curvature-based mesh with the default mesh parameters by using the **Create Mesh** tool. Figure 10.15 shows the meshed model.

10.15

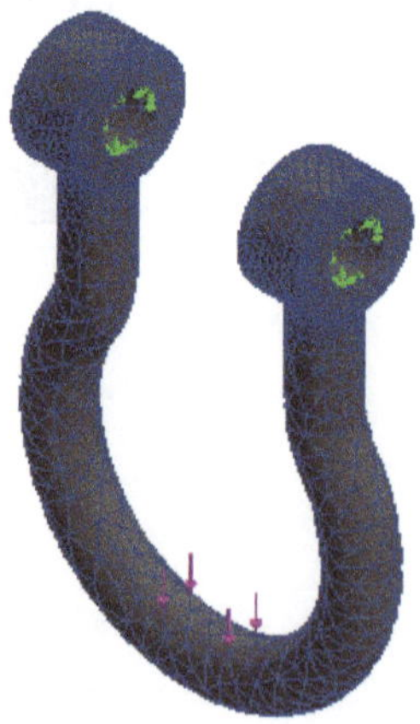

Section 6: Running the Static Analysis

1. Click on the **Run This Study** tool in the **Simulation CommandManager**. The **Shackle Static Study** (*name of the study*) window appears which displays the progress of the analysis. When it is complete, the **Results** folder is added to the Simulation Study Tree with the stress, displacement, and strain results. By default, the **Stress** result is activated. As a result, the stress distribution on the model and the von Mises stress plot appear, see Figure 10.16.

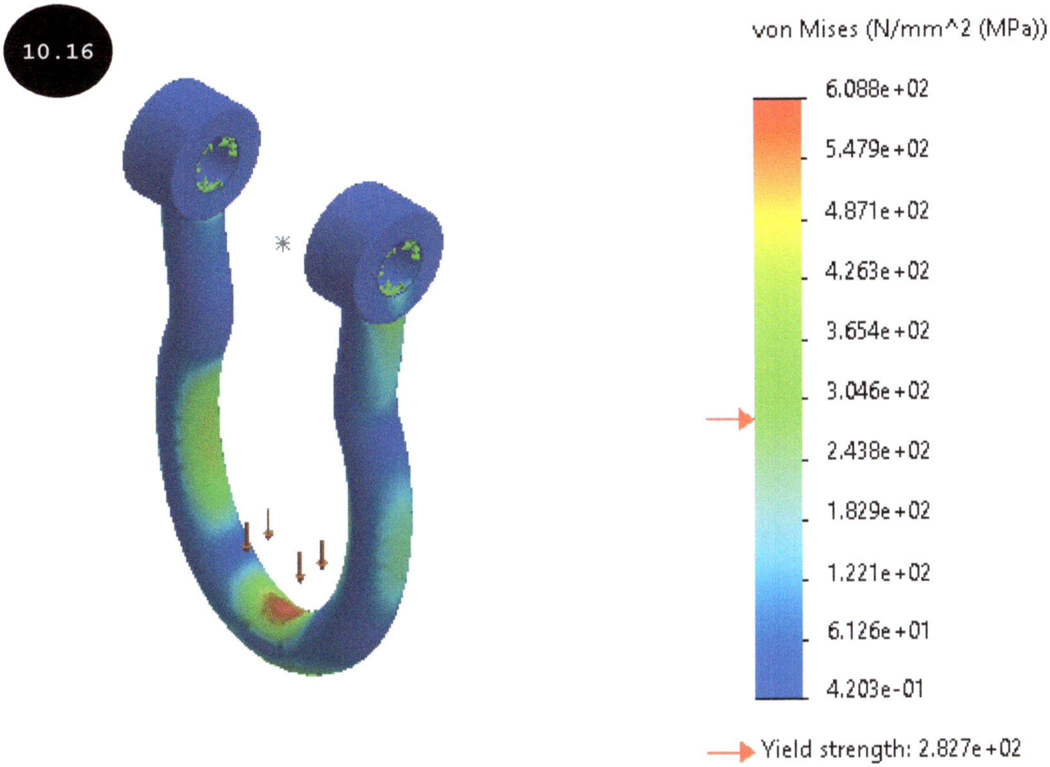

The maximum von Mises stress in the model under the applied load is **6.088e+02** (608.775) N/mm^2 (MPa) which significantly exceeds the yield strength of the material that is **2.827e+02** (282.685) N/mm^2 (MPa). The yield strength of the material is indicated by the red pointer in the von Mises stress plot, refer to Figure 10.16. Note that you may find a slight difference in the result values depending on the service pack installed on your system.

Note that when the maximum von Mises stress of the model exceeds the yield strength of the material, the design is likely to fail under the applied load. Also, after the yield strength, the material experiences plastic deformation and behaves non-linearly (refer to the Stress-Strain curve). Such cases fall under the category of material non-linearities and you can not trust the results of linear static analysis. Therefore, you need to perform non-linear analysis to get the correct results.

Section 7: Starting the Non-Linear Static Analysis

In the linear static analysis results, we have noticed that the maximum von Mises stress in the model exceeds the yield strength of the material, and the material experiences plastic deformation. As a result, you need to perform the non-linear static analysis to get the correct results.

1. Click on the **New Study** tool in the **Simulation CommandManager**. The **Study PropertyManager** appears at the left of the graphics area.

2. Click on the **Nonlinear** button in the **Advanced Simulation** rollout of the PropertyManager, see Figure 10.17.

10.17

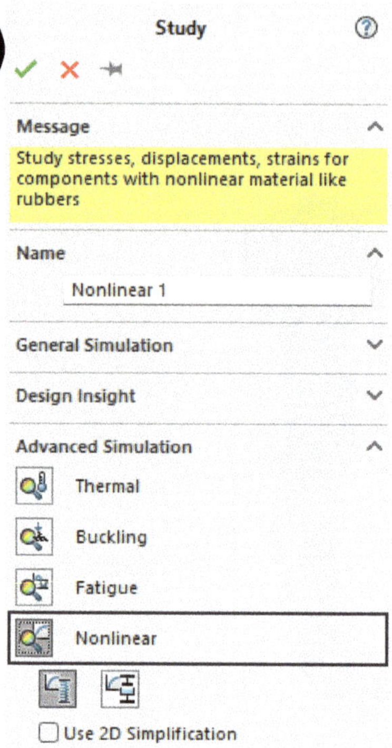

3. Ensure that the **Static** button available below the **Nonlinear** button is activated to perform the non-linear static analysis, see Figure 10.17.

4. Enter **Shackle Nonlinear Study** in the **Study name** field of the **Name** rollout in the PropertyManager.

5. Click on the green tick-mark button in the PropertyManager. A new tab "**Shackle Nonlinear Study**" is added next to the tab of the existing linear static study (**Shackle Static Study**) at the lower left corner of the screen and is activated, by default. As a result, the **Shackle Nonlinear Study** appears in the Simulation Study Tree, see Figure 10.18.

10.18

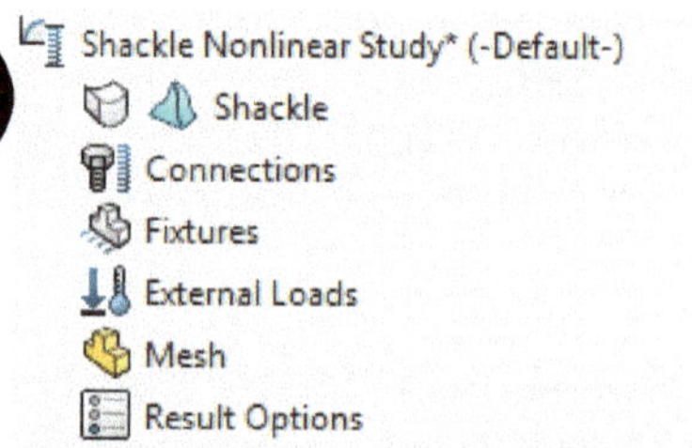

Section 8: Defining the Properties for the Non-Linear Static Analysis

Before you start performing the non-linear static analysis, you need to define its properties to control the solution and the output of the non-linear static study.

1. Right-click on the **Shackle Nonlinear Study** (*name of the study*) in the Simulation Study Tree and then click on the **Properties** tool in the shortcut menu that appears, see Figure 10.19. The **Nonlinear - Static** dialog box appears, see Figure 10.20.

10.19

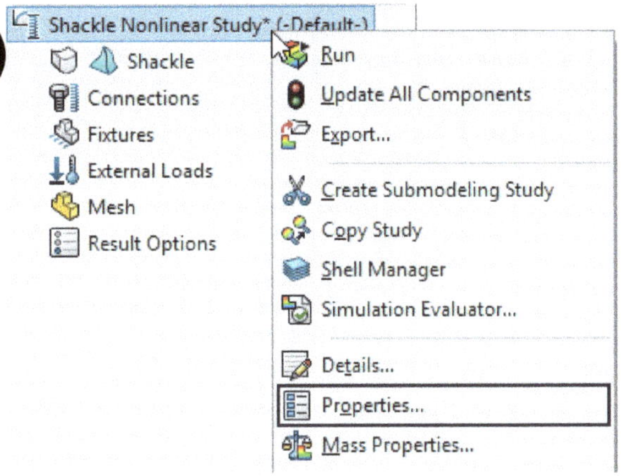
Shackle Nonlinear Study* (-Default-)
Shackle
Connections
Fixtures
External Loads
Mesh
Result Options
Run
Update All Components
Export...
Create Submodeling Study
Copy Study
Shell Manager
Simulation Evaluator...
Details...
Properties...
Mass Properties...

10.20

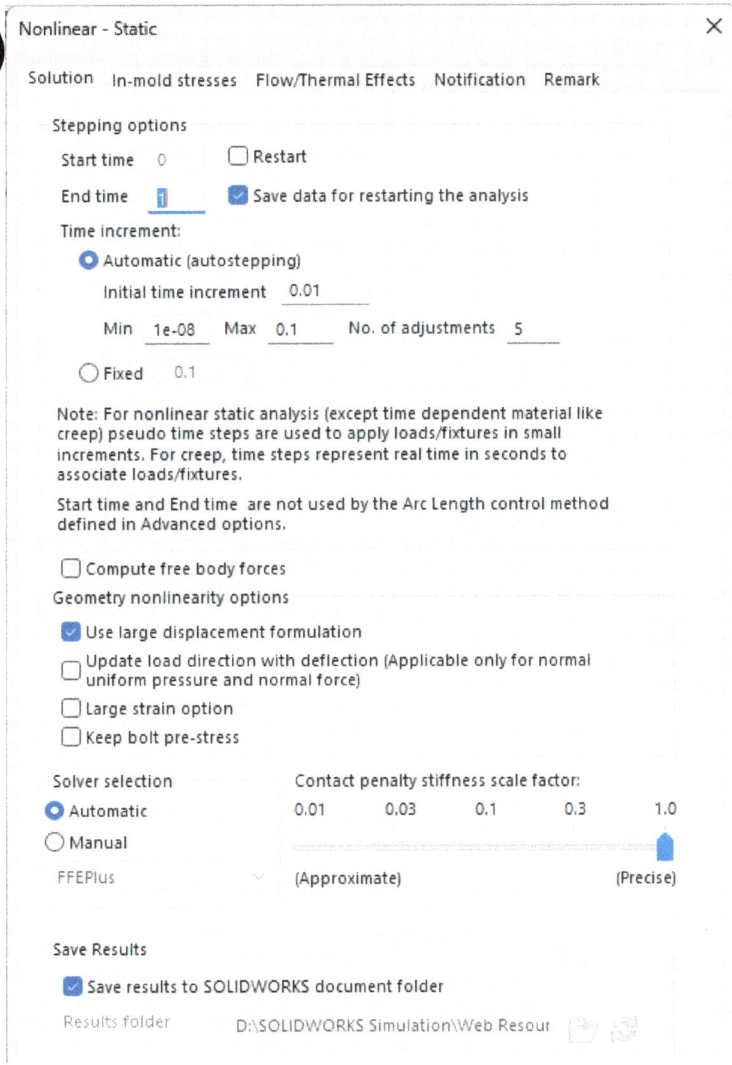
Nonlinear - Static
Solution
In-mold stresses
Flow/Thermal Effects
Notification
Remark
Stepping options
Start time
0
Restart
End time
1
Save data for restarting the analysis
Time increment:
Automatic (autostepping)
Initial time increment
0.01
Min
1e-08
Max
0.1
No. of adjustments
5
Fixed
0.1
Note: For nonlinear static analysis (except time dependent material like creep) pseudo time steps are used to apply loads/fixtures in small increments. For creep, time steps represent real time in seconds to associate loads/fixtures.
Start time and End time are not used by the Arc Length control method defined in Advanced options.
Compute free body forces
Geometry nonlinearity options
Use large displacement formulation
Update load direction with deflection (Applicable only for normal uniform pressure and normal force)
Large strain option
Keep bolt pre-stress
Solver selection
Automatic
Manual
FFEPlus
Contact penalty stiffness scale factor:
0.01
0.03
0.1
0.3
1.0
(Approximate)
(Precise)
Save Results
Save results to SOLIDWORKS document folder
Results folder
D:\SOLIDWORKS Simulation\Web Resour

The **Stepping options** area of the **Nonlinear - Static** dialog box is used to define the start time and end time to control the solution for the non-linear static analysis. Note that it is the pseudo time, not the real-time, and the load is divided into different incremental load steps between the specified period.

You can control the incremental load steps in between the specified period by using the **Automatic (autostepping)** or **Fixed** method. By default, the **Automatic (autostepping)** radio button is activated as the time increment method. As a result, the program automatically determines the incremental load steps based on the converged solutions. You can define a limit for converging a solution by specifying the minimum and maximum time steps in the **Min** and **Max** fields, respectively. Also, you can define the maximum number of iterations to be made, to converge the solution within the specified limit in the **No. of adjustments** field of the dialog box.

On selecting the **Fixed** radio button in the dialog box, you can specify the fixed incremental load steps between the specified period. For example, if the start time is 0 and the end time is 1 then on specifying 0.1 as the fixed incremental load step, the program divides the load into 10 incremental load steps to converge the final solution.

2. Ensure that the start time and end time are set to **0** and **1**, respectively in the **Stepping options** area of the dialog box.

3. Ensure that the **Automatic (autostepping)** radio button is activated in the dialog box as the time increment method to determine the incremental load steps, automatically.

4. Accept the remaining options specified by default in the **Stepping options** area of the dialog box.

   After defining the time period and the time increment method, you need to define the control and iterative methods.

5. Scroll down to the dialog box and then click on the **Advanced Options** button in the **Nonlinear - Static** dialog box. The options to define the control and iterative methods appear in the **Advanced** tab, see Figure 10.21.

10.21

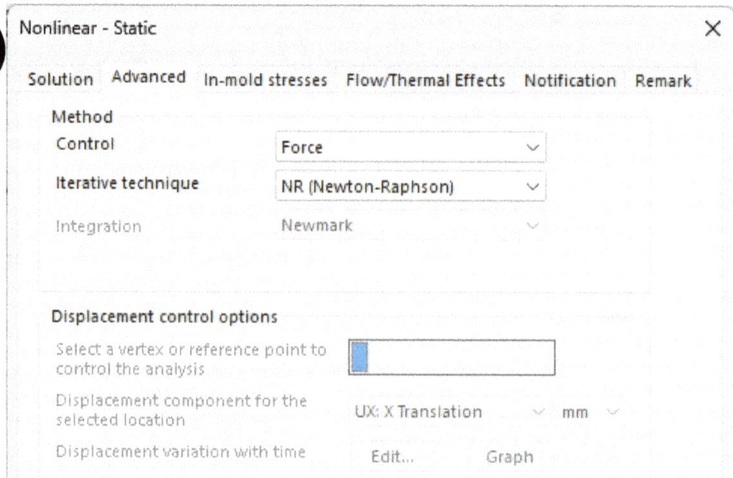

6. Ensure that the **Force** option is selected in the **Control** drop-down list of the **Method** area in the dialog box as the control method, see Figure 10.21.

7. Ensure that the **NR (Newton-Raphson)** option is selected in the **Iterative technique** drop-down list as the iterative method, see Figure 10.21.

8. Accept the values specified by default in the **Step/Tolerance options** area of the dialog box, see Figure 10.22.

10.22

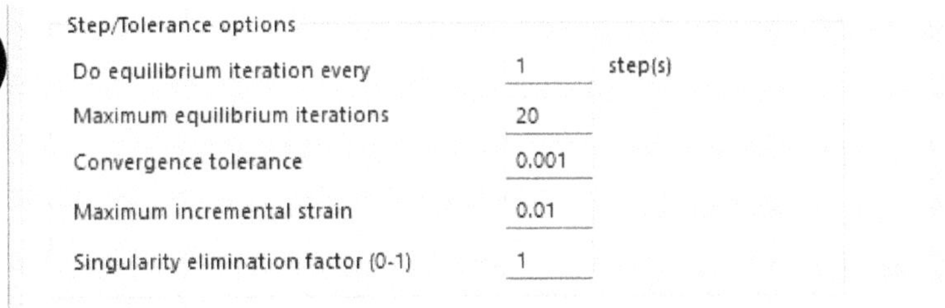

In the **Step/Tolerance options** area, the **Do equilibrium iteration every** field is used to specify the frequency for satisfying the equilibrium equation. The **Maximum equilibrium iterations** field is used to specify the maximum number of equilibrium iterations to be performed. The **Convergence tolerance** field is used to specify the relative displacement tolerance for converging the equilibrium equation. The **Maximum increment strain** field is used to specify the maximum acceptable increment strain for the models having creep or plasticity. The **Singularity elimination factor (0-1)** field is used to specify the singularity elimination factor in the range from 0 to 1 for evaluating the stiffness.

9. Ensure that the **Show intermediate results up to current iteration (when running)** check box is selected in the **Intermediate Results** area of the dialog box to view the intermediate result in the graphics area when the non-linear study is in progress.

10. Click on the **OK** button in the dialog box to accept the changes and close the dialog box.

Section 9: Applying the Fixture, Load, and Material

Now, you need to apply the fixture, load, and material to perform the non-linear static analysis.

1. Invoke the **Material** dialog box by clicking on the **Apply Material** tool in the **Simulation CommandManager** and then select the **AISI 1035 Steel (SS)** material. Do not close the dialog box.

Note: As discussed, a material with **(SS)** at its end, represents that the stress-strain curve is defined for that particular material. The stress-strain curve is used to define the behavior of material in the plastic region.

2. Click on the **Tables & Curves** tab in the **Material** dialog box. The options to define the tables and curves for the selected material appear.

3. Select the **Stress-Strain Curve** option in the **Type** drop-down list of the dialog box, see Figure 10.23. The pre-defined standard values of the stress-strain curve of the selected material appear in the dialog box, see Figure 10.23. Also, the preview of the curve appears in the **Preview** area of the dialog box.

10.23

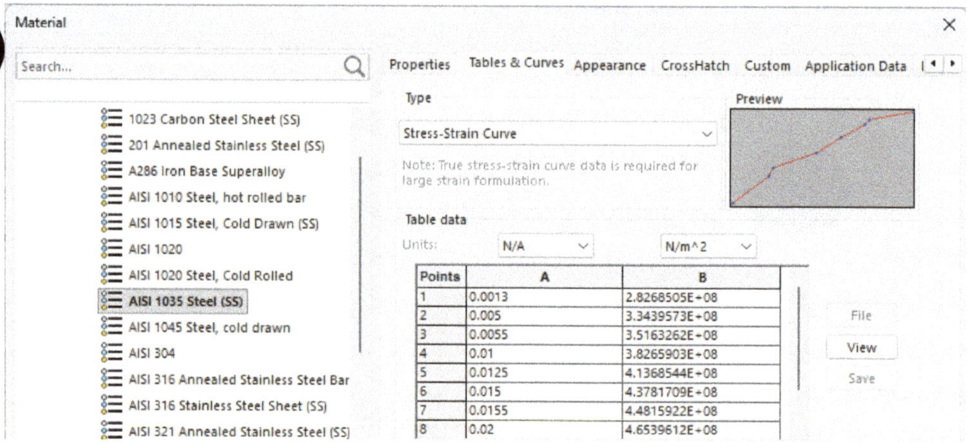

4. Click on the **Apply** button and then the **Close** button in the dialog box to apply the material with pre-defined stress-strain curve.

Note: If the stress-strain curve is not defined for a material then you need to specify it manually to define the behavior of material in the plastic region.

Now, you need to apply the Fixed Geometry fixture and load to the model.

5. Apply the Fixed Geometry fixture to the upper two holes of the model, see Figure 10.24.

10.24

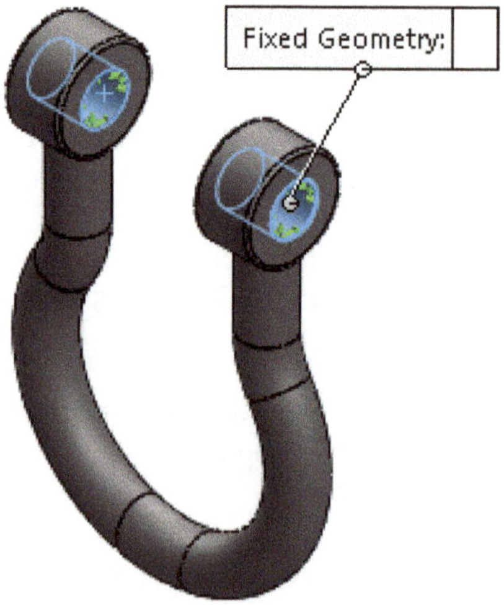

6. Right-click on the **External Loads** option in the Simulation Study Tree and then click on the **Force** tool in the shortcut menu that appears. The **Force/Torque PropertyManager** appears.

7. Select the middle split circular face of the model (refer to Figure 10.25) and then select the **Selected direction** radio button in the PropertyManager. Next, select the **Top Plane** as the direction reference in the FeatureManager Design Tree.

8. Click on the **Normal to Plane** button in the **Force** rollout of the PropertyManager and then enter **19000** as the load value. Next, select the **Reverse direction** check box to reverse the direction of force downward, see Figure 10.25.

9. Select the **Curve** radio button in the **Variation with Time** rollout of the PropertyManager, see Figure 10.26.

10.25

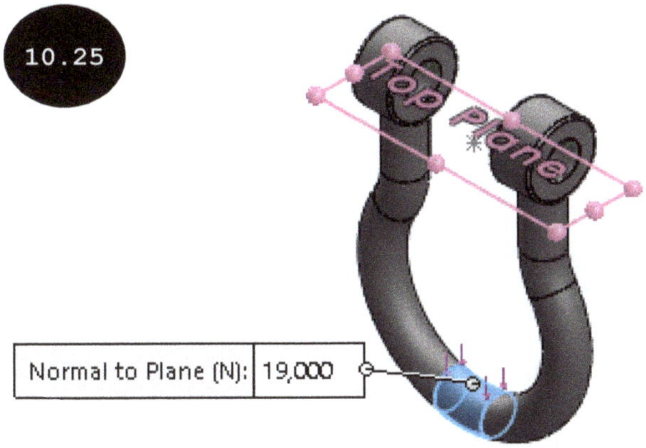

10.26

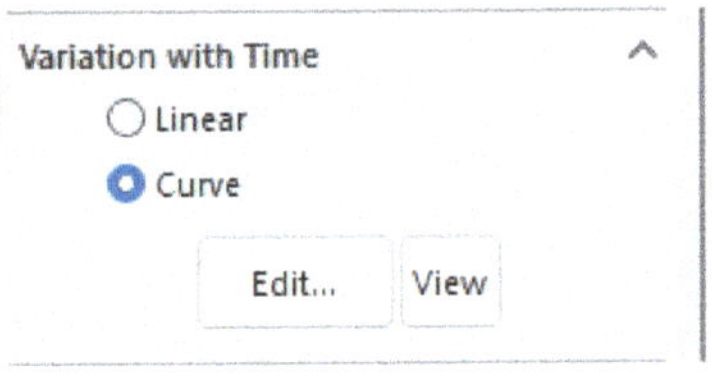

10. Click on the **Edit** button in the **Variation with Time** rollout of the PropertyManager. The **Time curve** dialog box appears, see Figure 10.27. In this dialog box, the X column defines the time and the Y column defines the load multiplier. You can define the variable load concerning the time (pseudo time) by using this dialog box.

10.27

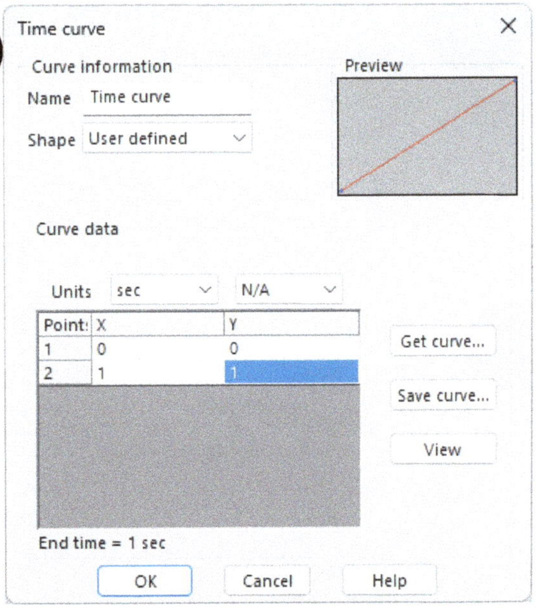

11. Accept the default settings of the **Time curve** dialog box and then click on the **OK** button.

12. Click on the green tick-mark button in the PropertyManager. The 19000 N load is applied.

Section 10: Generating the Mesh

1. Generate a curvature-based mesh with the default mesh parameters by using the **Create Mesh** tool. Figure 10.28 shows the meshed model.

10.28

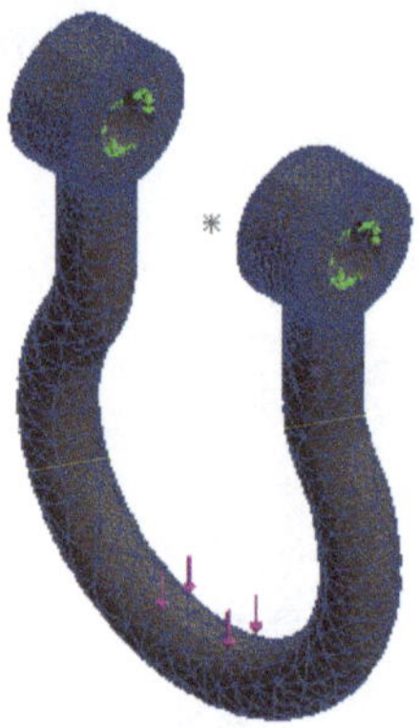

Section 11: Running the Non-linear Static Analysis

1. Click on the **Run This Study** tool in the **Simulation CommandManager**. The **Shackle Nonlinear Study** (*name of the study*) window appears which displays the progress of non-linear static analysis, see Figure 10.29. Also, the **SOLIDWORKS** message window appears which informs that you have chosen to show the intermediate results while running the analysis. For this reason, the analysis will terminate if you switch to another SOLIDWORKS document or close the active model, see Figure 10.30.

10.29

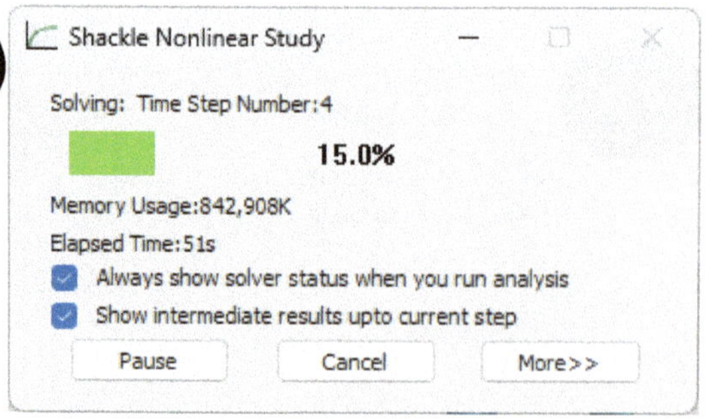

10.30

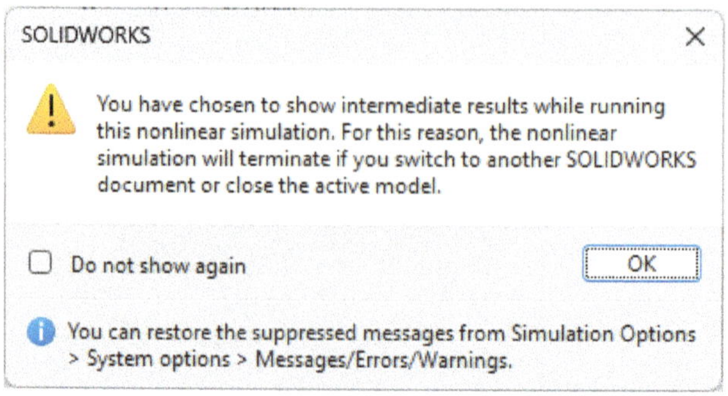

2. Click on the **OK** button in the **SOLIDWORKS** message window. The intermediate results appear in the graphics area when the non-linear static analysis is in progress. When the analysis is complete, the **Results** folder is added to the Simulation Study Tree with the stress, displacement, and strain results. By default, the **Stress** result is activated. As a result, the stress distribution on the model and the von Mises stress plot of the non-linear analysis appear, see Figure 10.31.

10.31

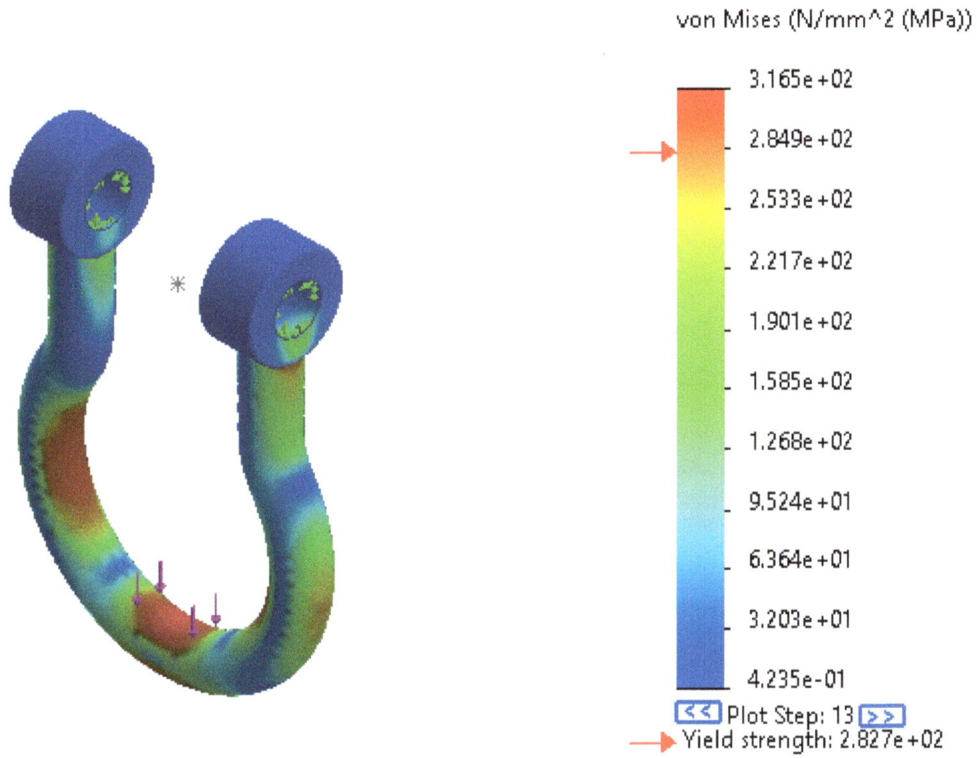

Notice the difference in the results of the linear static analysis and the non-linear static analysis. In the non-linear static analysis, the maximum von Mises stress under the applied load is **3.165e+02** (316.488) N/mm^2 (MPa) (see Figure 10.31) whereas, in the linear static analysis, the maximum Von Mises stress was **6.088e+02** (608.775) N/mm^2 (MPa).

Section 12: Generating the Time History Plot in the Non-linear Static Study

Now, you need to generate the time history graph for the von Mises stress at a node of the high-stress area.

1. Right-click on the **Results** folder in the Simulation Study Tree and then click on the **Define Time History Plot** tool in the shortcut menu that appears, see Figure 10.32. The **Time History Graph PropertyManager** appears, see Figure 10.33.

Notice that in the **Response** rollout of the PropertyManager, all the nodes of the model appear in a selection field. You can select a node or multiple nodes in this selection field, whose response graph is to be generated. Alternatively, you can click on one or more nodes in the model that appear in the graphics area.

10.32

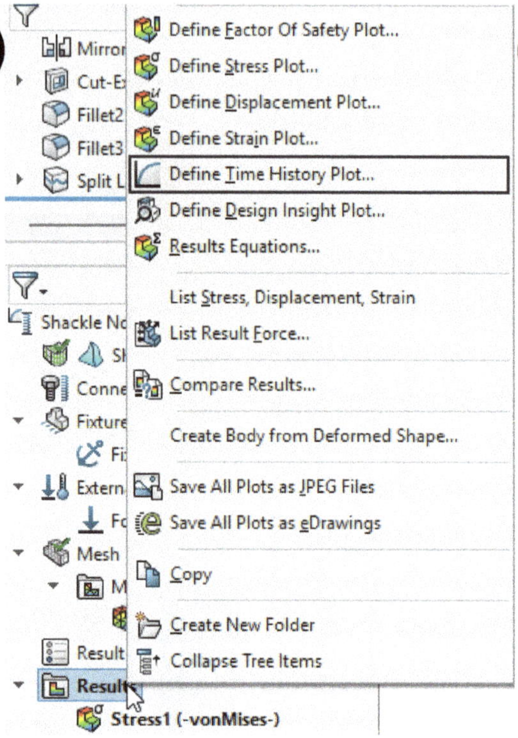

10.33

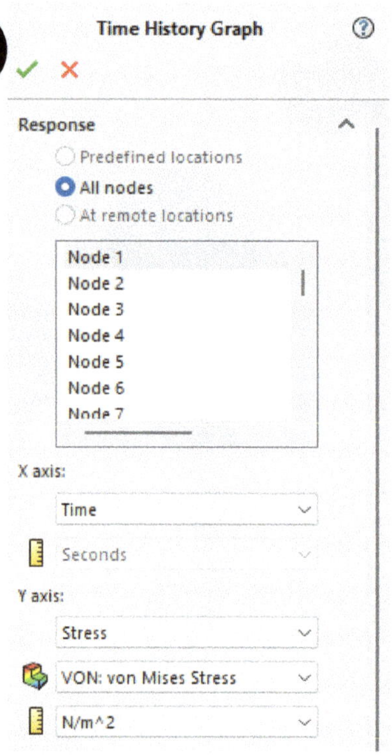

2. Click on a node in the high stress area of the model in the graphics area, see Figure 10.34. The node 1109 of the high stress area gets selected. Note that the selected node number of the high stress area may differ in your case depending on your selection. Also, the node number 1 is selected by default.

10.34

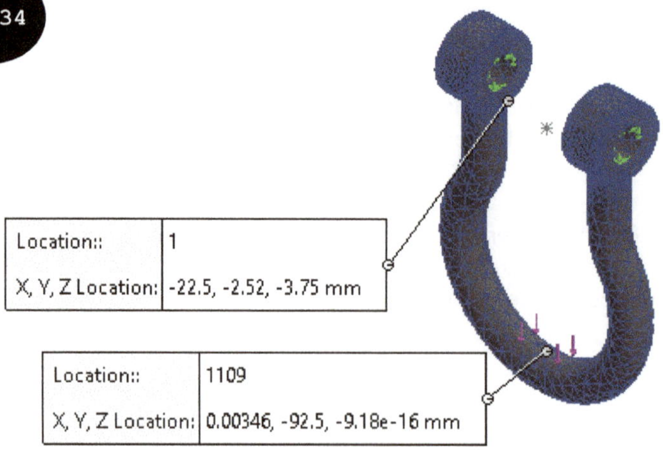

3. Ensure that the **Time** option is selected in the **X axis** drop-down list of the PropertyManager.

4. Ensure that the **Stress** and **VON: von Mises Stress** options are selected in the respective fields of the **Y axis** area in the PropertyManager.

5. Select the **N/mm^2 (MPa)** in the **Units** drop-down list of the **Y-axis** area of the PropertyManager.

6. Click on the green tick-mark button in the PropertyManager. The **Response Graph** window appears, see Figure 10.35. This window displays the response graphs of the selected nodes (1 and 1109) for the von Mises stress vs solution steps.

10.35

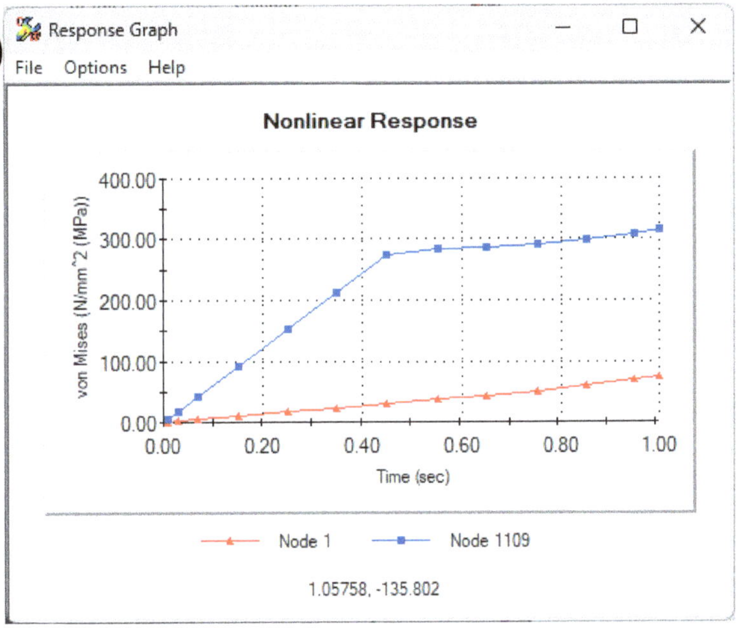

7. After viewing the response graphs, close the **Response Graph** window. The **Response1 (-Time-von Mises-)** result is added to the **Results** folder of the Simulation Study Tree.

Section 13: Saving Results

Now, you need to save the model and its results.

1. Click on the **Save** tool in the **Standard** toolbar. The model and its results are saved in the location > *SOLIDWORKS Simulation* > *Case Studies* > *C10 Case Studies* > *Case Study 1*.

2. Close the SOLIDWORKS session.

Case Study 2: Non-Linear Static Analysis of a Handrail Clamp Assembly

In this case study, you will perform a non-linear analysis of a Handrail Clamp Assembly, see Figure 10.36. The Handrail Clamp part of the assembly is pushed toward the Pipe to clamp it, see Figure 10.37.

10.36

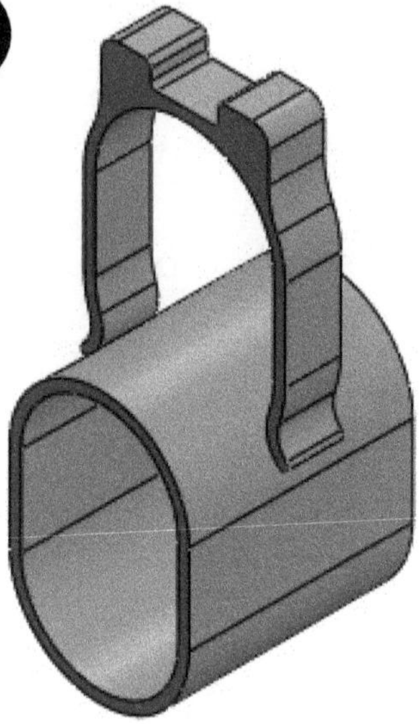

10.37

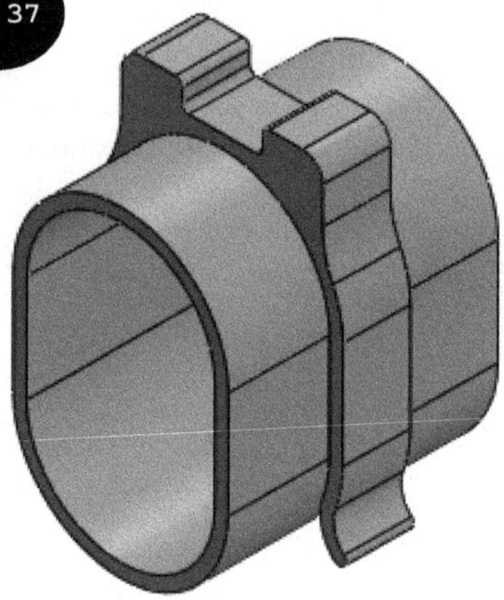

Project Description

The Pipe is fixed at both its ends (see Figure 10.38) and the Handrail Clamp has all degrees of freedom fixed except the translation movement of 34 mm in the downward direction, see Figure 10.38. The Pipe is made up of **AISI 304** steel material and the Handrail Clamp is made up of **ABS** plastic material.

10.38

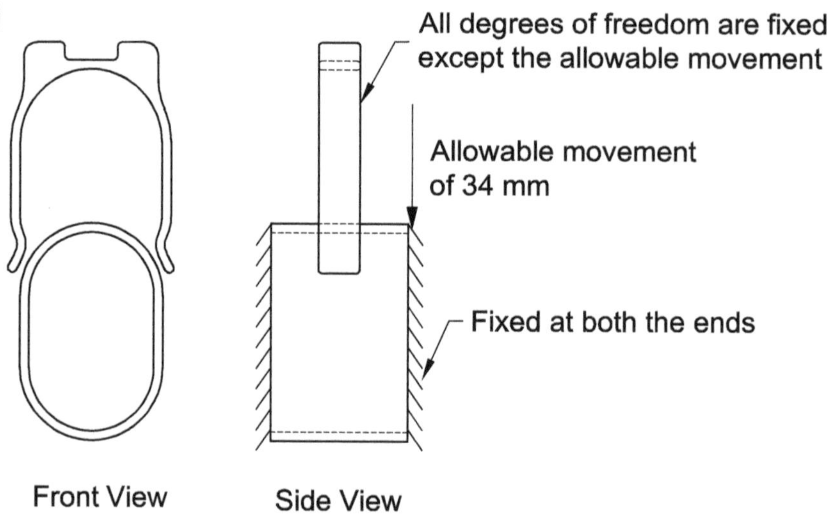

Project Summary

In this case study, you will perform the non-linear static study. You need to use the Force control method and the Newton-Raphson (NR) scheme to converge the solution.

The following sequence summarizes the case study outline:

1. Starting the Non-Linear Static Analysis
2. Defining Properties for the Non-Linear Static Analysis
3. Applying the Fixture, Load, and Material
4. Defining Interactions between the Components
5. Generating the Mesh
6. Running the Non-linear Static Analysis
7. Displaying the von Mises Stress Plot at Different Solution Steps
8. Animating the Stress Distribution on the Model
9. Saving Results

Section 1: Starting the Non-Linear Static Analysis

In this case study, as the Handrail Clamp component will move toward the Pipe and the interaction between the components changes during the analysis, you need to perform the non-linear analysis to solve the problem. This is so because, such cases fall under the category of contact non-linearities.

1. Start SOLIDWORKS and then open the Handrail Clamp Assembly from the location > ***SOLIDWORKS Simulation*** > ***Case Studies*** > ***C10 Case Studies*** > ***Case Study 2***.

Note: You need to download the **C10 Case Studies** file, which contains the files for this chapter, by logging in to the website (***cadartifex.com/login***), if it has not already been downloaded.

2. Click on the **Simulation** tab in the **CommandManager**. The tools of the **Simulation CommandManager** appear.

3. Click on the **New Study** tool in the **Simulation CommandManager**. The **Study PropertyManager** appears on the left of the graphics area.

4. Click on the **Nonlinear** button in the **Advanced Simulation** rollout of the PropertyManager, see Figure 10.39.

5. Ensure that the **Static** button available below the **Nonlinear** button is activated in the **Advanced Simulation** rollout to perform the non-linear static analysis, see Figure 10.39.

6. Enter **Clamp Nonlinear Study** in the **Study name** field of the **Name** rollout in the PropertyManager.

7. Click on the green tick-mark button in the PropertyManager. The **Clamp Nonlinear Study** is added to the Simulation Study Tree, see Figure 10.40.

10.39

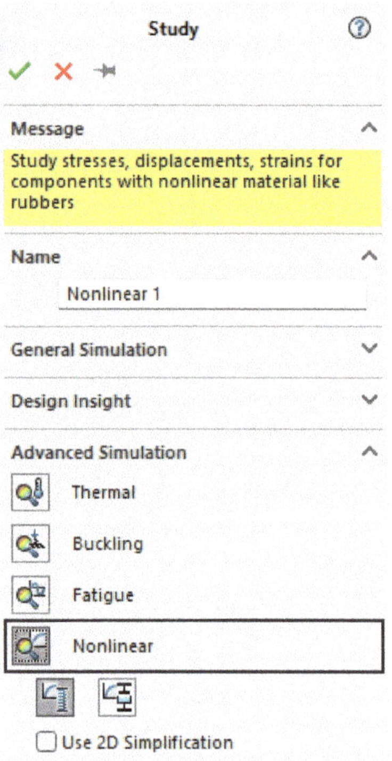

10.40

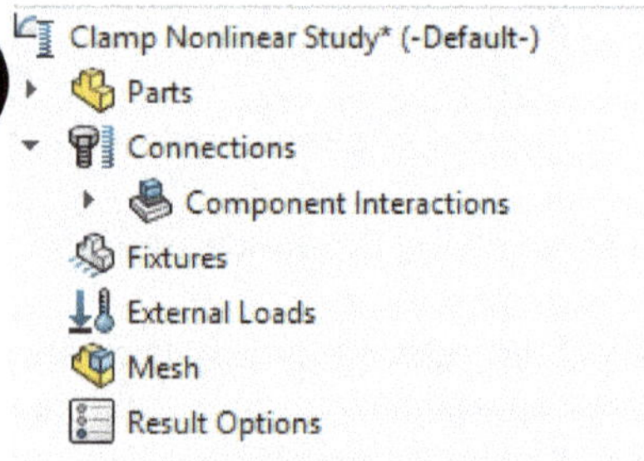

Section 2: Defining Properties for the Non-Linear Static Analysis

Before you start performing the non-linear static analysis, you can define its properties to control the solution and the output of the non-linear static study.

1. Right-click on the **Clamp Nonlinear Study** (*name of the study*) in the Simulation Study Tree and then click on the **Properties** tool in the shortcut menu that appears, see Figure 10.41. The **Nonlinear - Static** dialog box appears, see Figure 10.42.

10.41

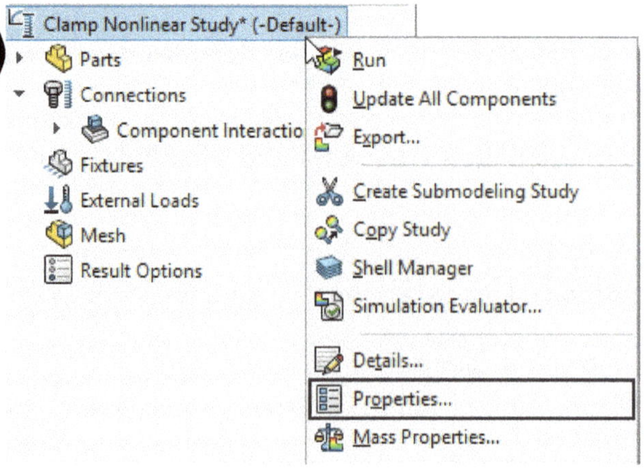

10.42

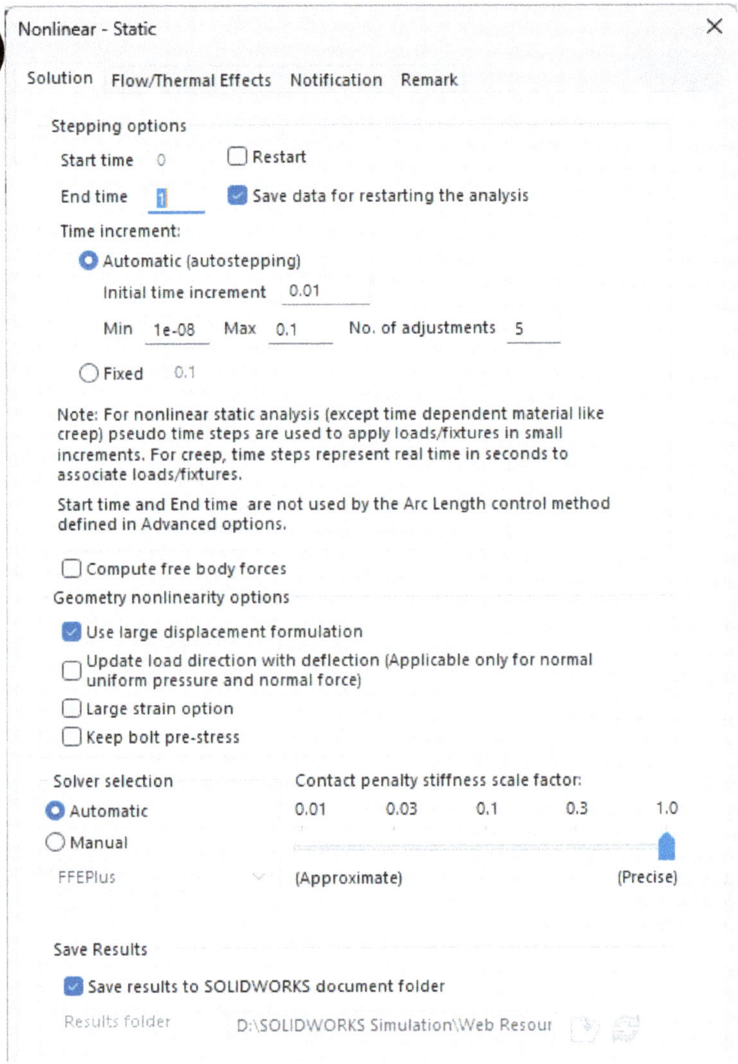

2. Ensure that the start time and end time are set to 0 and 1 respectively in the **Stepping options** area of the dialog box.

3. Ensure that the **Automatic (autostepping)** radio button is activated in the dialog box as the time increment method to determine the incremental load steps, automatically.

4. Accept the remaining default specified options in the **Stepping options** area of the dialog box.

   After defining the period and the time increment method, you need to define the control and iterative methods.

5. Scroll down to the dialog box and then click on the **Advanced Options** button in the **Nonlinear - Static** dialog box. The options for defining the control and iterative methods appear in the dialog box, see Figure 10.43.

10.43

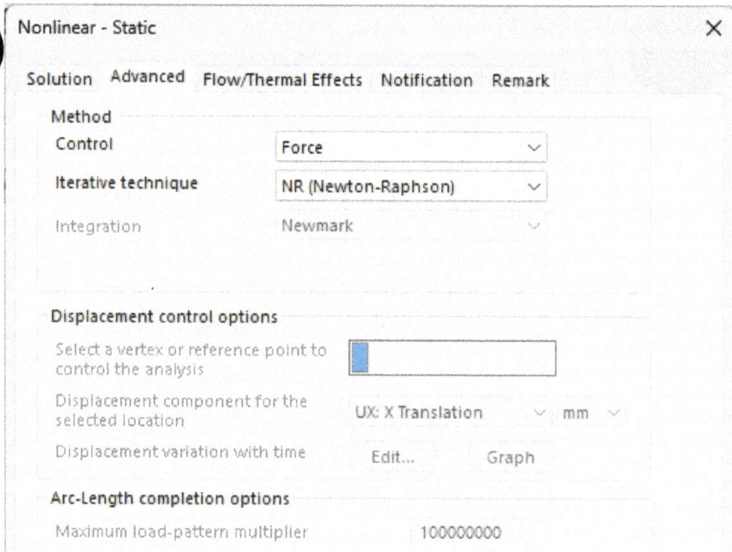

6. Ensure that the **Force** option is selected in the **Control** drop-down list of the **Method** area as the control method.

7. Ensure that the **NR (Newton-Raphson)** option is selected in the **Iterative technique** drop-down list as the iterative method.

8. Accept the values specified by default in the **Step/Tolerance options** area of the dialog box, see Figure 10.44.

10.44

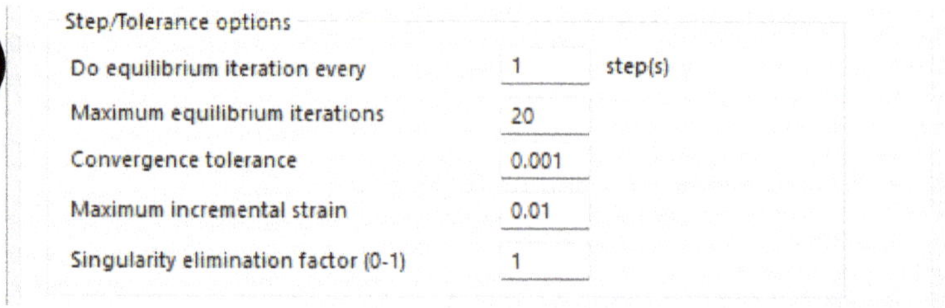

9. Select the **Show intermediate results up to current iteration (when running)** check box in the **Intermediate Results** area of the dialog box to view the intermediate result in the graphics area when the non-linear study is in progress.

10. Click on the **OK** button in the dialog box to accept the changes and close the dialog box.

Section 3: Applying the Fixture, Load, and Material

Now, you need to apply the fixture, load, and material to perform the non-linear static analysis.

1. Expand the **Parts** node in the Simulation Study Tree by clicking on the arrow in front of it to display all components of the assembly, see Figure 10.45.

10.45

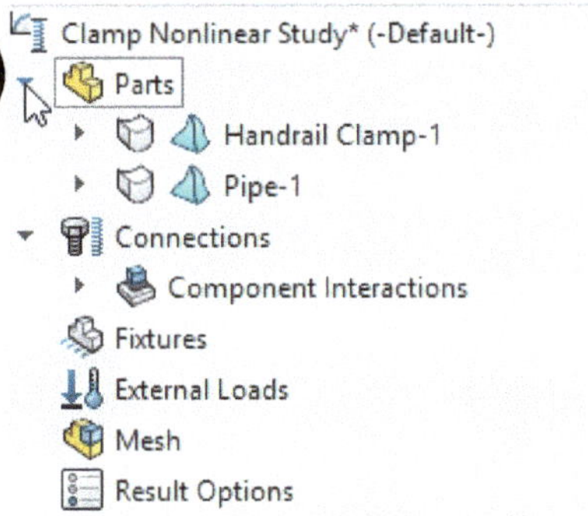

2. Right-click on the **Handrail Clamp** component in the expanded **Parts** node and then click on the **Apply/Edit Material** tool in the shortcut menu that appears, see Figure 10.46. The Material dialog box appears.

10.46

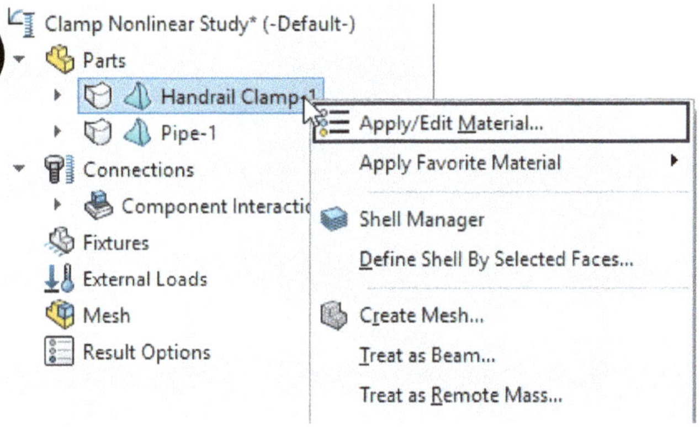

3. Expand the **Plastics** category in the **SOLIDWORKS Materials** library and then click on the **ABS** material. The material properties of the ABS plastic material appear on the right panel of the dialog box.

4. Click on the **Apply** button and then close the dialog box. The ABS plastic material properties are assigned to the Handrail Clamp component and the dialog box gets closed.

5. Similarly, apply the **AISI 304** steel material to the Pipe component.

   Now, you need to apply the required fixtures to fix the Pipe component and allow the Handrail Clamp component to translate 34 mm toward the Pipe component.

6. Right-click on the **Fixtures** option in the Simulation Study Tree and then click on the **Fixed Geometry** tool in the shortcut menu that appears. The **Fixture PropertyManager** appears.

7. Select both ends of the Pipe component to apply the Fixed Geometry fixture, see Figure 10.47.

8. Click on the green tick-mark button in the PropertyManager. The Fixed Geometry fixture is applied to the Pipe component.

9. Right-click on the **Fixtures** option in the Simulation Study Tree and then click on the **Advanced Fixtures** tool in the shortcut menu that appears. The **Fixture PropertyManager** appears with the expanded **Advanced** rollout.

10. Click on the **On Flat Faces** button in the **Advanced** rollout of the PropertyManager, see Figure 10.48.

10.47

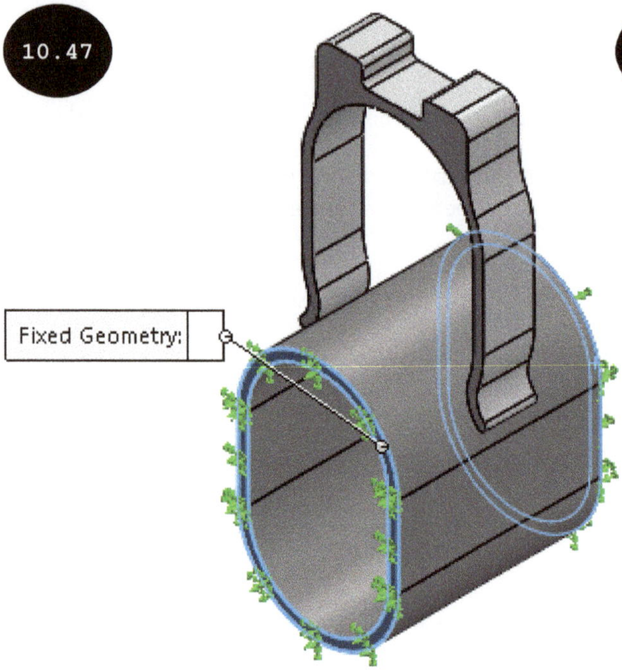

10.48

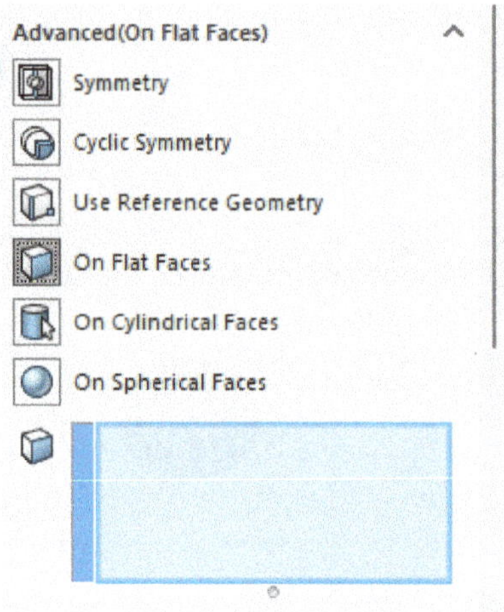

11. Select the top middle face of the Handrail Clamp component to apply the On Flat Face fixture, see Figure 10.49.

10.49

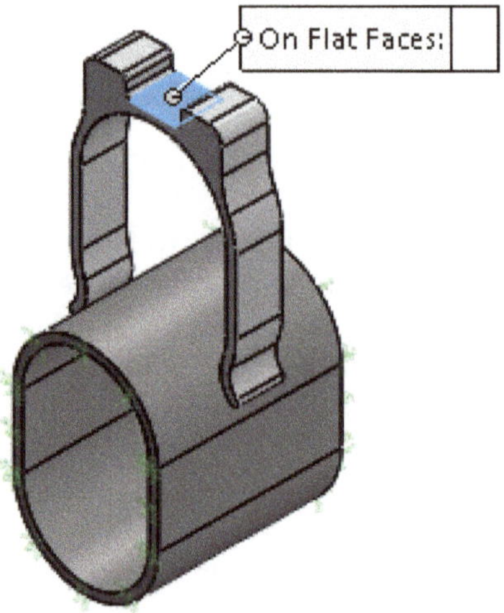

12. Ensure that **mm** is selected as the unit in the **Unit** drop-down list of the **Translations** rollout in the PropertyManager, see Figure 10.50.

13. Click on the **Along Face Dir 1**, **Along Face Dir 2**, and **Normal to Face** buttons to activate the respective fields in the **Translations** rollout of the PropertyManager, see Figure 10.50.

10.50

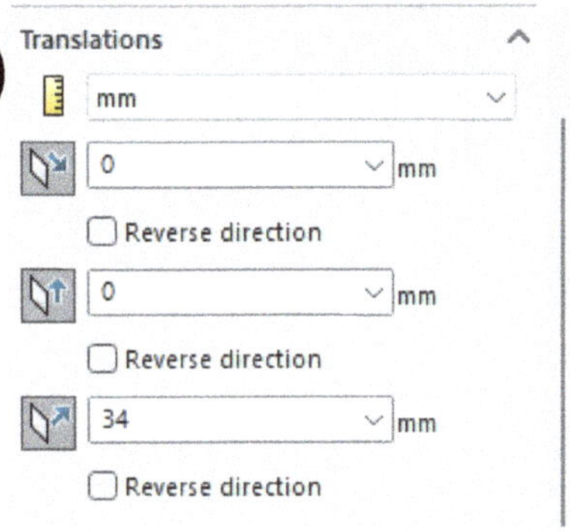

14. Enter **34** in the **Normal to Face** field of the PropertyManager as the translation motion in the direction normal to the face selected, see Figure 10.50.

15. Ensure the 0 (zero) value is entered in the **Along Face Dir 1** and **Along Face Dir 2** fields of the rollout to restrict the translation movements in these directions of the face selected.

16. Ensure that the **Linear** radio button is selected in the **Variation with Time** rollout of the PropertyManager and then click on the **View** button. The **Time curve** dialog box appears, see Figure 10.51.

10.51

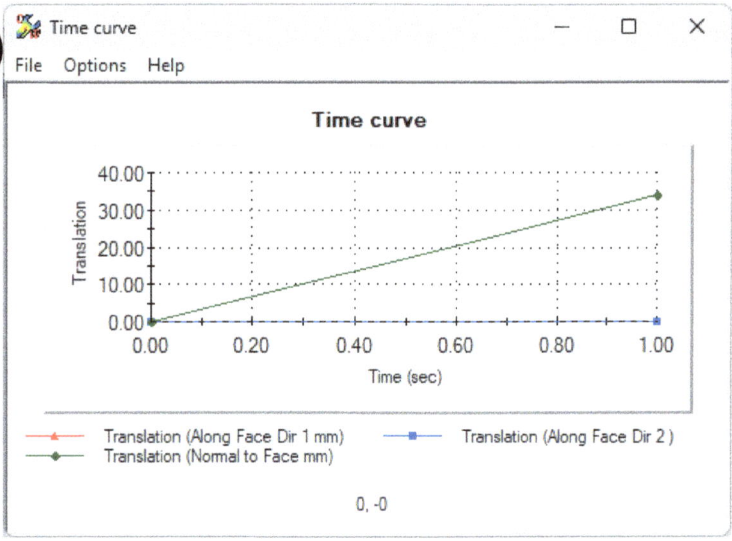

Notice that the program applies the pre-defined translation of 34 mm linearly in different incremental time steps based on the specified time increment method [Automatic (autostepping)]. It starts from zero displacement at the zero time step and then increases up to its full value (34 mm) at the end time step.

17. After viewing the time curve, close the **Time curve** dialog box.

18. Click on the green tick-mark button in the PropertyManager. The On Flat Face fixture is applied to the Handrail Clamp component with the pre-defined translation movement of 34 mm.

Section 4: Defining Interactions between the Components

Now, you need to define the Contact interaction between the interacting faces of the components to override the global interaction conditions.

1. Right-click on the **Connections** node in the Simulation Study Tree and then click on the **Local Interaction** tool in the shortcut menu that appears. The **Local Interactions PropertyManager** appears on the left of the graphics area.

2. Ensure that the **Manually select local interactions** radio button is selected in the **Interaction** rollout.

3. Ensure that the **Contact** option is selected in the drop-down list of the **Type** rollout.

4. Select the outer tangent faces (4 faces) of the Pipe component as the first interaction set, see Figure 10.52. The names of the selected faces appear in the **Faces, Edges, Vertices for Set 1** field of the **Type** rollout in the PropertyManager.

5. Click on the **Faces for Set 2** field in the **Type** rollout and then select the tangent faces (13 faces) of the Handrail Clamp component as the second interaction set that can come in contact with the Pipe component while transaction, see Figure 10.52.

6. Expand the **Advanced** rollout in the PropertyManager and then select the **Node to surface** radio button in the **Contact formulation** area.

7. Click on the green tick-mark button in the PropertyManager. The Contact local interaction is applied.

Section 5: Generating the Mesh

1. Generate the curvature-based mesh with the default mesh parameters by using the **Create Mesh** tool. Figure 10.53 shows the meshed model.

10.52

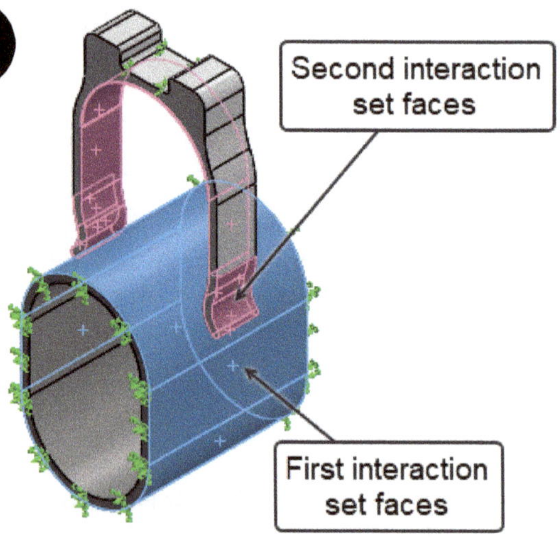

10.53

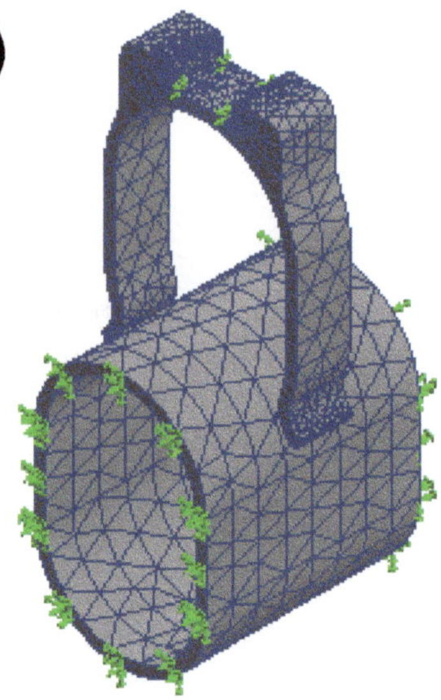

Section 6: Running the Non-linear Static Analysis

1. Click on the **Run This Study** tool in the **Simulation CommandManager**. The **Clamp Nonlinear Study** (*name of the study*) window appears which displays the progress of the non-linear static analysis. Also, the **SOLIDWORKS** message window appears, which informs that you have chosen to show intermediate results while running the analysis. Therefore, the analysis will terminate if you switch to another SOLIDWORKS document or close the active model.

Note: If the **Simulation** message window appears, which informs you that the initial contact between the components is not detected, click on the **No** button in this window to continue with the study.

2. Click on the **OK** button in the **SOLIDWORKS** message window. The intermediate results appear in the graphics area when the non-linear static analysis is in progress. The non-linear static analysis will take considerable time to complete. Once the analysis is complete, the **Results** folder is added to the Simulation Study Tree with the stress, displacement, and strain results. By default, the **Stress** result is activated. As a result, the stress distribution on the model and the von Mises stress plot of the non-linear static analysis appear, see Figure 10.54.

10.54

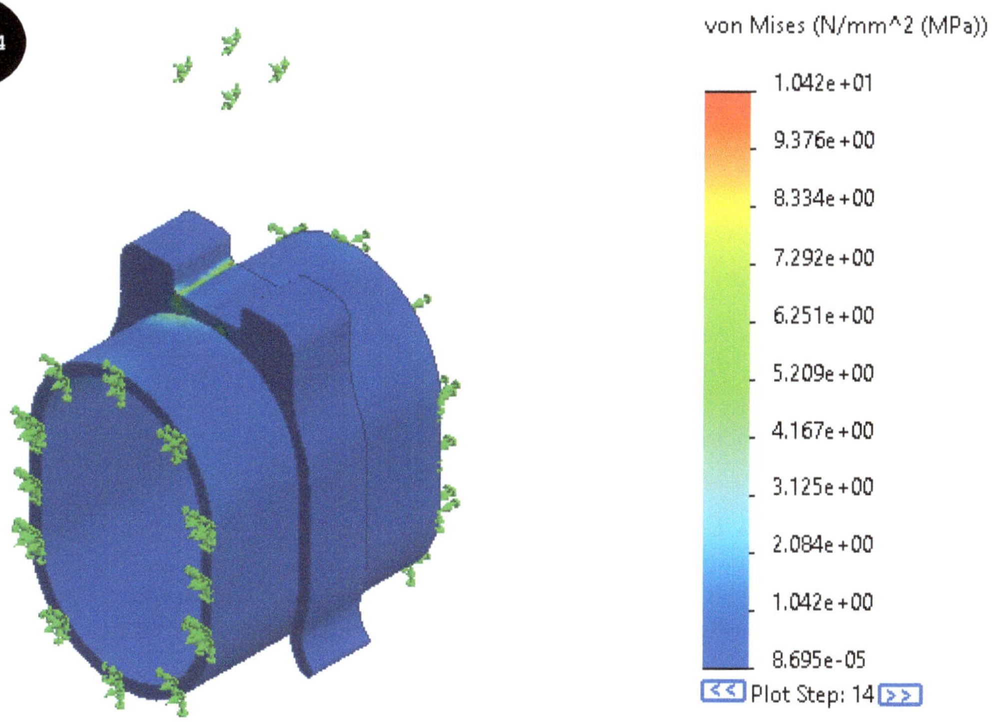

By default, the von Mises stress plot displays the results for the end solution step. The maximum von Mises stress at the end solution step is approximately, **1.042e+01** (10.418) N/mm^2 (MPa), see Figure 10.54. You can display the stress results for different solution steps and the same has been discussed next.

Section 7: Displaying the von Mises Stress Plot at Different Solution Steps

In non-linear static analysis, you can also display the results at different solution steps. By default, the program displays the results for the end solution step.

1. Right-click on the **Results** folder in the Simulation Study Tree and then click on the **Define Stress Plot** tool in the shortcut menu that appears. The **Stress plot PropertyManager** appears, see Figure 10.55.

Tip: To display the displacement plot and the strain plot, you need to click on the **Define Displacement Plot** tool and **Define Strain Plot** tool respectively in the shortcut menu.

2. Ensure that the **Definition** tab is activated in the PropertyManager, see Figure 10.55.

10.55

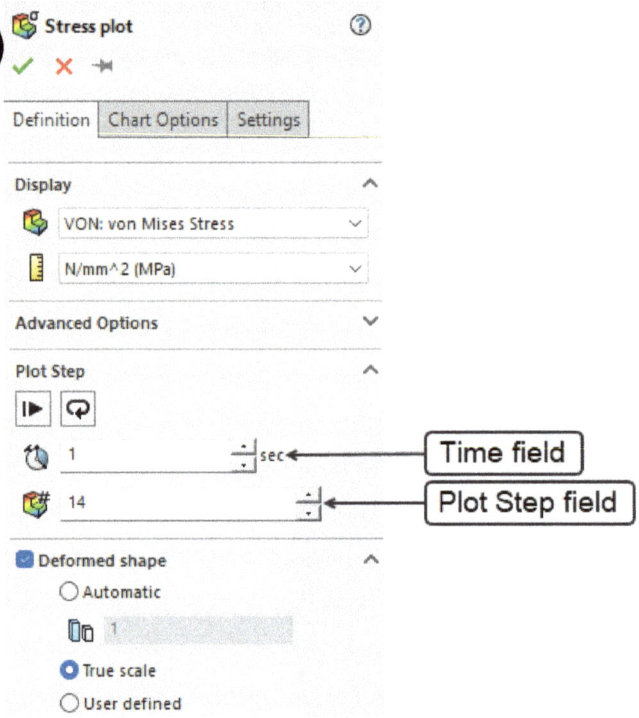

By default, the value 1 is entered in the **Time** field of the PropertyManager, see Figure 10.55. As a result, the von Mises stress plot will display the results for the end solution step, which is 15 in this case study.

3. Enter 7 in the **Plot Step** field of the PropertyManager to display the stress results for the 7th solution step. Next, click anywhere in the graphics area. The time step (0.34 sec) corresponding to the specified solution step (7th) appears in the **Time** field of the PropertyManager.

4. Select the **True scale** radio button in the **Deformed shape** rollout of the PropertyManager to display the deformed shape of the model in true scale.

5. Click on the green tick-mark button in the PropertyManager. The von Mises stress plot for the 7th solution step at 0.34 sec appears in the graphics area, see Figure 10.56. Also, the stress plot (**stress2 (-vonMises-)** of the specified solution step gets added to the **Results** folder in the Simulation Study Tree.

10.56

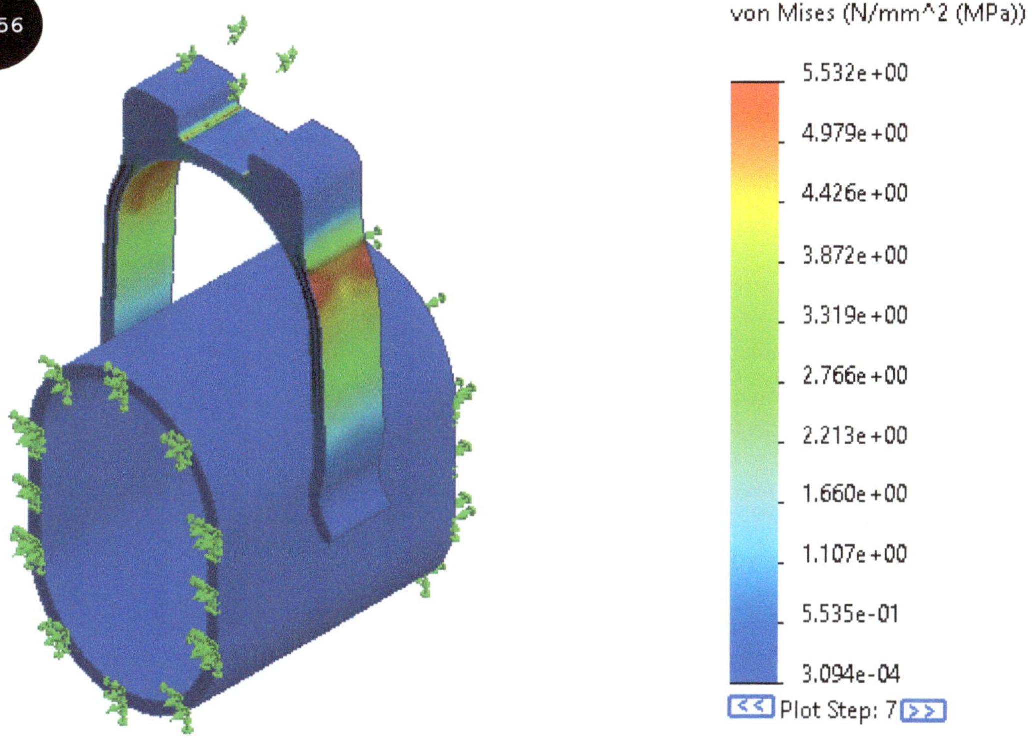

The maximum von Mises stress at the 7th solution step is approximately **5.532e+00** (5.532) N/mm^2 (MPa), see Figure 10.56.

6. Similarly, you can display the von Mises stress plot for different solution steps.

Section 8: Animating the Stress Distribution on the Model

Now, you will animate the stress distribution and review the deformed shape of the model.

1. Double-click on the **Stress1 (-vonMises-)** plot in the Simulation Study Tree to activate it.

2. Right-click on the activated **Stress1 (-vonMises-)** plot in the Simulation Study Tree. A shortcut menu appears. In this shortcut menu, click on the **Animate** tool. The **Animation PropertyManager** appears, see Figure 10.57. Also, the animation starts in the graphics area with the default animation settings. You can change the animation settings by using the PropertyManager.

10.57

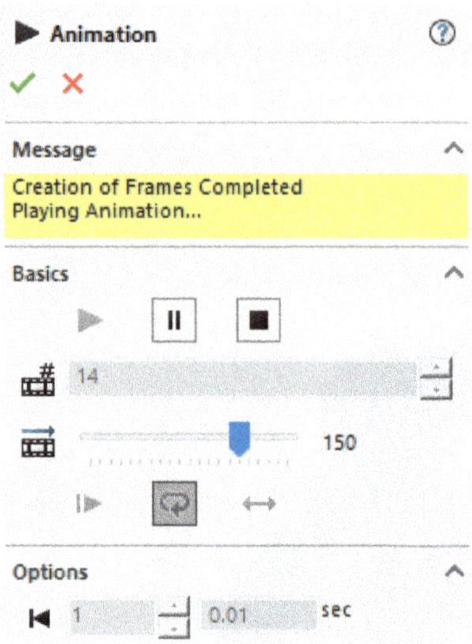

3. To save the animation as an AVI file, select the **Save as AVI file** check box in the PropertyManager. Next, specify the path to save the file.

4. After reviewing the animated effects of the deformed shape, click on the green tick-mark button in the PropertyManager to exit the PropertyManager and save the AVI file in the specified location.

Section 9: Saving Results

1. Click on the **Save** tool in the **Standard** toolbar. The model and its results are saved in the location > *SOLIDWORKS Simulation* > *Case Studies* > *C10 Case Studies* > *Case Study 2*.

2. Close the SOLIDWORKS session.

Case Study 3: Non-Linear Static Analysis of a Cantilever Beam

In this case study, you will perform the non-linear analysis of a Cantilever Beam having a large displacement under the applied load, see Figure 10.58.

10.58

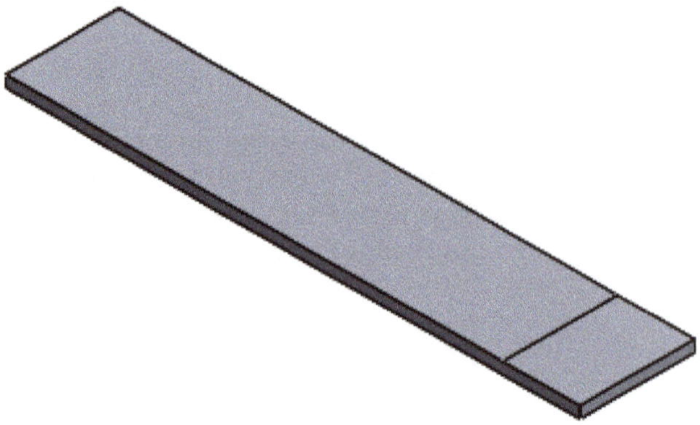

Project Description

The Cantilever Beam is fixed at its one end (see Figure 10.59) and a 180 N downward load acts on the top right small portion of the free end of the Cantilever Beam, see Figure 10.59. Note that the area to apply the load is created by splitting the top face. The Cantilever Beam is made up of **Alloy Steel** material.

10.59

Project Summary

In this case study, you will first run the linear static study to solve the large displacement problem and then perform the non-linear static study to compare the difference in the results. In the non-linear static study, you need to use the Force control method and the Newton-Raphson (NR) scheme to converge the final solution.

The following sequence summarizes the case study outline:

1. Performing the Static Analysis for a Large Displacement Problem
2. Applying the Fixture, Load, and Material
3. Defining Properties for the Linear Static Analysis
4. Generating the Mesh
5. Running the Linear Static Analysis and Displaying Results
6. Performing the Non-Linear Static Analysis and Displaying Results
7. Generating the Response graph of a Node
8. Saving Results

Section 1: Performing the Static Analysis for a Large Displacement Problem

In this case study, you will first perform the linear static analysis to solve the large displacement problem. As discussed, the large displacement problems fall under the category of geometric non-linearities. Therefore to get accurate results, you need to perform the non-linear analysis. However, in SOLIDWORKS Simulation, you can also solve the large displacement problems by performing the linear static analysis, which is discussed next.

1. Start SOLIDWORKS and then open the Cantilever Beam from the location > *SOLIDWORKS Simulation > Case Studies > C10 Case Studies > Case Study 3*.

Note: You need to download the **C10 Case Studies** file, by logging in to the CADArtifex website (*cadartifex.com/login*), if it has not already been downloaded.

2. Click on the **Simulation** tab in the **CommandManager**. The tools of the **Simulation CommandManager** appear.

3. Click on the **New Study** tool in the **Simulation CommandManager**. The **Study PropertyManager** appears on the left of the graphics area.

4. Ensure that the **Static** button is activated in the **Study PropertyManager** to perform the linear static analysis.

5. Enter **Linear Study with Large Disp** in the **Study name** field of the **Name** rollout in the PropertyManager.

6. Click on the green tick-mark button in the PropertyManager. The **Linear Study with Large Disp** is added to the Simulation Study Tree, see Figure 10.60.

10.60

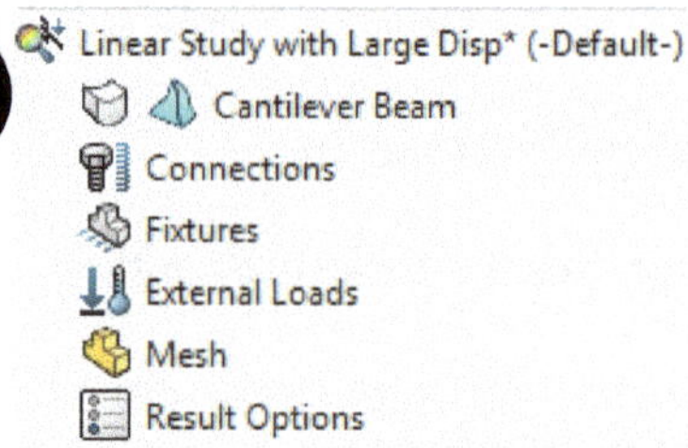

Section 2: Applying the Fixture, Load, and Material

Now, you need to apply the fixture, load, and material to the model.

1. Invoke the **Material** dialog box by clicking on the **Apply Material** tool in the **Simulation CommandManager** and then apply the **Alloy Steel** material. Next, close the dialog box.

   Now, you need to apply the Fixed Geometry fixture to fix one end of the model.

2. Apply the Fixed Geometry fixture on the left end of the Cantilever Beam by using the **Fixed Geometry** tool, see Figure 10.61.

10.61

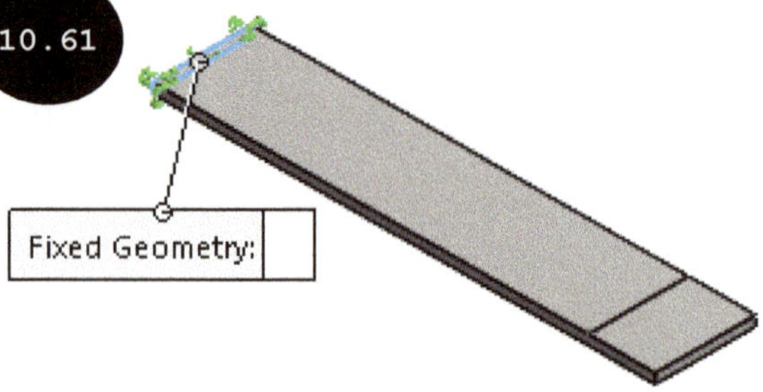

Now, you need to apply the 180 N downward load.

3. Apply the 180 N downward load on the right portion of the top face by using the **Force** tool, see Figure 10.62.

10.62

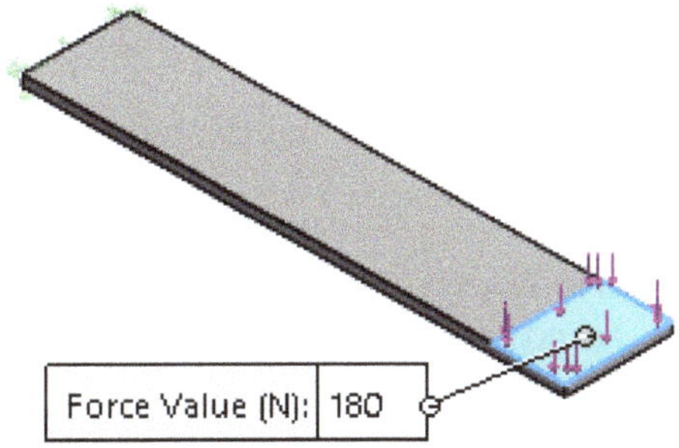

Section 3: Defining Properties for the Linear Static Analysis

Now, you need to define the properties for the linear static analysis.

1. Right-click on the **Linear Study with Large Disp** (*name of the study*) in the Simulation Study Tree and then click on the **Properties** tool in the shortcut menu that appears. The **Static** dialog box appears, see Figure 10.63.

10.63

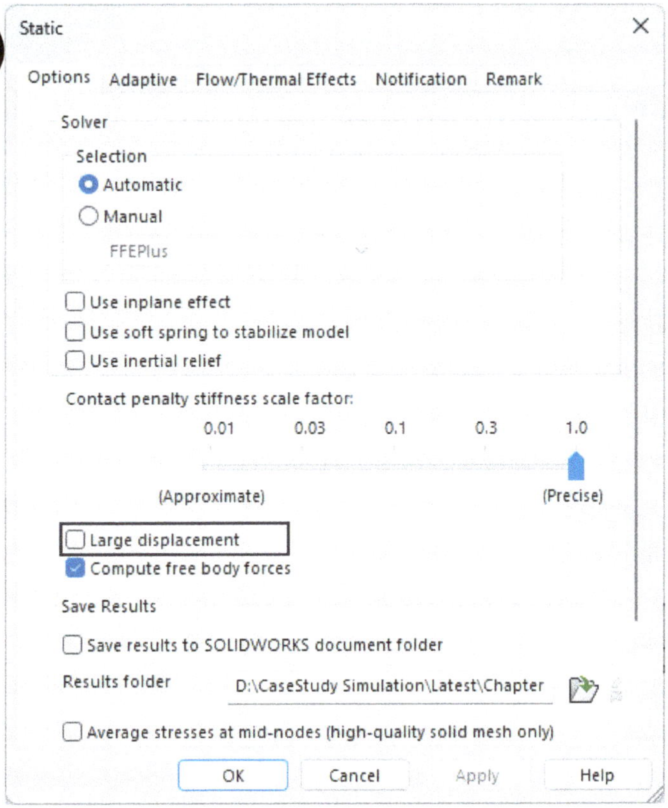

In this dialog box, the **Large displacement** check box is cleared, by default. As a result, the program considers the small displacement in the model due to the applied load and solves the problem. However, if the program identifies the large displacement during the linear static analysis, you will be prompted to choose whether to solve the problem with small displacement or large displacement. If you select the **Large displacement** check box in this dialog box then the program directly performs the non-linear static analysis to solve the problem.

2. Ensure that the **Large displacement** check box cleared in the dialog box and then click on the **OK** button.

Section 4: Generating the Mesh

1. Generate the curvature-based mesh with the default mesh parameters by using the **Create Mesh** tool. Figure 10.64 shows the meshed model.

10.64

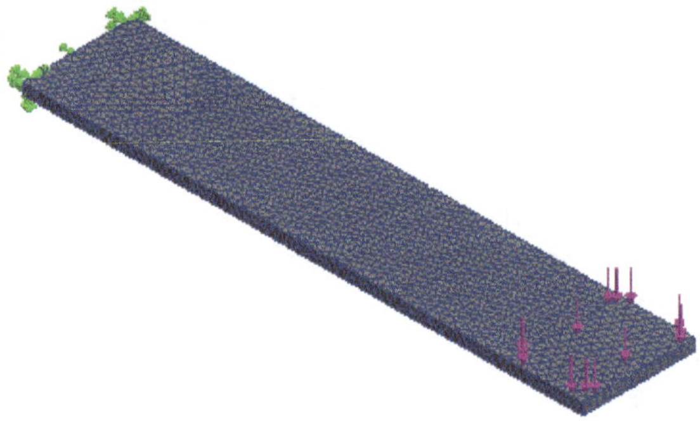

Section 5: Running the Linear Static Analysis and Displaying Results

1. Click on the **Run This Study** tool in the **Simulation CommandManager**. The **Linear Study with Large Disp** (*name of the study*) window appears which displays the progress of linear static analysis. During the analysis, when the large displacement is identified by the program on the model due to the applied load, the **Simulation** message window appears, see Figure 10.65.

   This message window informs you that the excessive displacements were calculated in this model and prompts you to either consider the large displacement option to improve the accuracy of the results or continue with the current settings. If you choose the **Yes** button, the program considers the large displacement option and starts performing the non-linear static analysis. However, if you choose the **No** button then the program continues with the current settings of linear static analysis, which will not give you correct results.

10.65

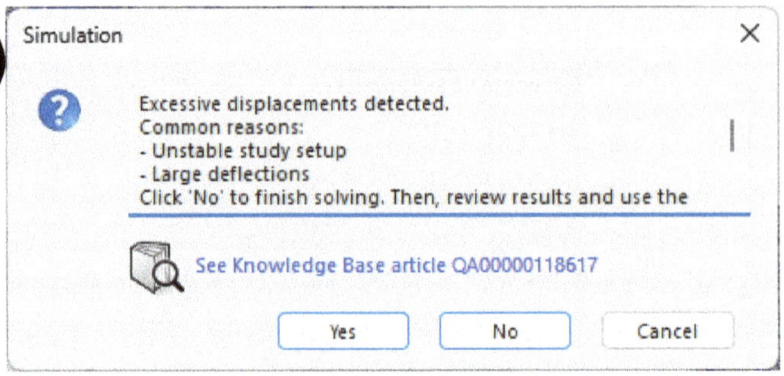

2. Click on the **Yes** button in the **Simulation** message window. The program starts performing the non-linear static analysis by dividing the total load into a small number of incremental steps and calculates the stiffness matrix at every incremental step. When the analysis is completed, the **Results** folder is added to the Simulation Study Tree with the stress, displacement, and strain results. By default, the **Stress** result is activated. As a result, the stress distribution on the model and the von Mises stress plot appear, see Figure 10.66.

   The maximum Von Mises stress in the model under the applied load is **5.616e+02** (561.587) N/mm^2 (MPa) which is within the yield strength of the material that is **6.204e+02** (620.422) N/mm^2 (MPa), refer to Figure 10.66.

3. Double-click on the **Displacement1 (-Res disp-)** result in the Simulation Study Tree. The resultant displacement plot appears in the graphics area, see Figure 10.67.

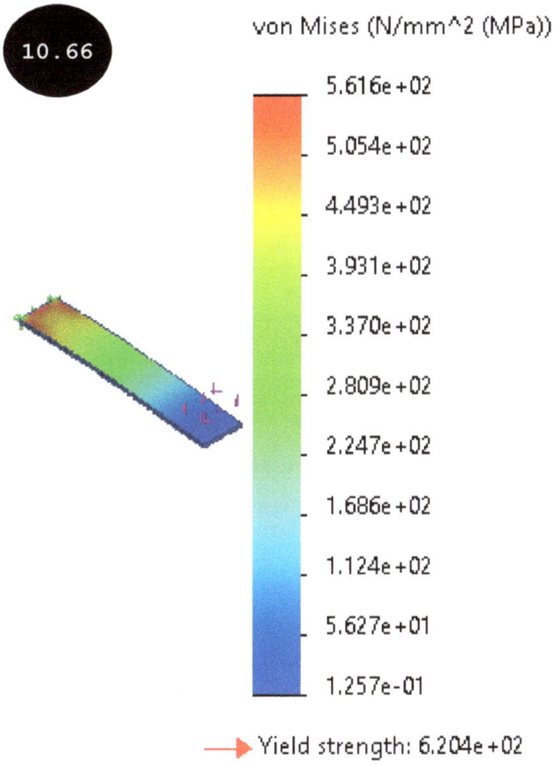

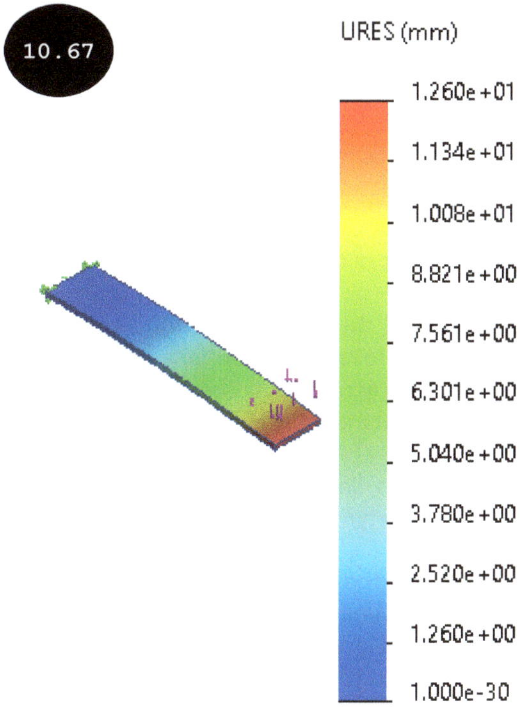

The maximum resultant displacement in the model under the applied load is **1.260e+01** (12.601) mm which is considered a large displacement, see Figure 10.67.

Note: When you perform the linear static analysis with the large displacement option to solve the problems of geometric non-linearities, you cannot view the results at different incremental steps. Also, if the model experiences material or contacts non-linearities as well, the results will not be accurate and you will need to perform the non-linear static analysis to get accurate results.

Section 6: Performing the Non-Linear Static Analysis and Displaying Results

Now, you will perform the non-linear static analysis. You can copy the existing linear static study or create a new study. In this case study, you will copy the existing linear static study and then perform the non-linear static analysis.

1. Right-click on the **Linear Study with Large Disp** tab in the lower-left corner of the screen, see Figure 10.68. A shortcut menu appears.

10.68

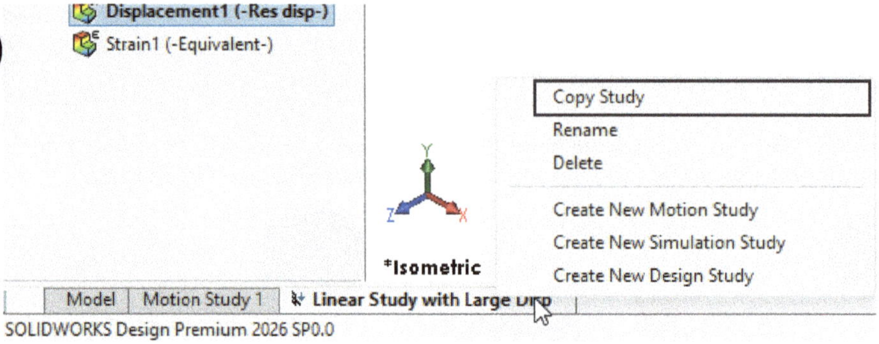

2. Click on the **Copy Study** option in this shortcut menu. The **Copy Study PropertyManager** appears on the left of the graphics area.

3. Click on the **Nonlinear** button in the **Target Study** rollout and then ensure that the **Static** button is activated in the **Options** rollout of the PropertyManager, see Figure 10.69.

4. Enter **Non-linear Study** in the **Study name** field of the PropertyManager, see Figure 10.69.

5. Click on the green tick-mark ✓ button in the PropertyManager. The new non-linear static study is created and a new tab "**Non-linear Study**" is added next to the tab of the existing static study in the lower left corner of the screen.

   Note that the newly created study is activated, by default. You can switch between the studies by clicking on the respective tabs available in the lower left corner of the screen.

   Now, you can define the non-linear properties and run the study. Notice that the material, fixtures, load, and mesh properties are copied from the existing static study.

10.69

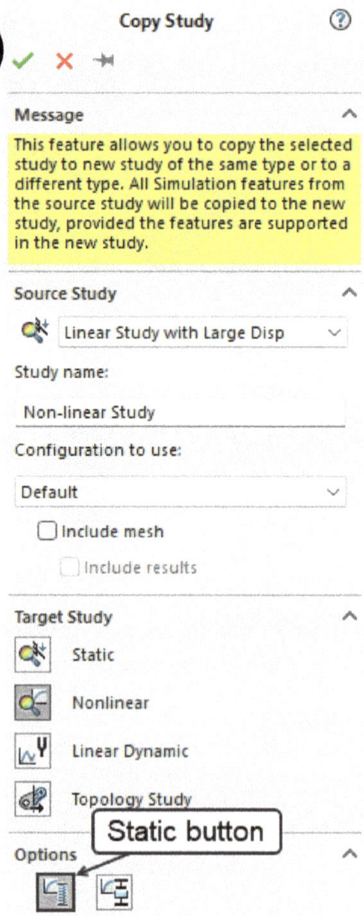

6. Right-click on the **Non-linear Study** (*name of the study*) in the Simulation Study Tree and then click on the **Properties** tool in the shortcut menu that appears. The **Nonlinear - Static** dialog box appears.

7. Ensure that the start time and end time are set to **0** and **1** in the **Stepping options** area of the dialog box.

8. Ensure that the **Automatic (autostepping)** radio button is activated in the dialog box as the time increment method to determine the incremental load steps, automatically.

9. Ensure that the **Automatic** radio button is selected in the **Solver selection** area of the dialog box.

10. Click on the **Advanced Options** button in the **Nonlinear - Static** dialog box. The options to define the control and iterative methods appear in the dialog box.

11. Ensure that the **Force** and **NR (Newton-Raphson)** options are selected in the **Control** and **Iterative technique** drop-down lists of the dialog box, respectively.

12. Select the **Show intermediate results up to current iteration (when running)** check box in the **Intermediate Results** area of the dialog box to view the intermediate result in the graphics area, when the non-linear study is in progress.

13. Accept the remaining default settings and then click on the **OK** button in the dialog box.

    Now, you can run the non-linear static study.

14. Click on the **Run This Study** tool in the **Simulation CommandManager**. The **Non-linear Study** (*name of the study*) window appears which displays the progress of non-linear static analysis. Also, the **SOLIDWORKS** message window appears, which informs that you have chosen to show intermediate results while running the analysis. Therefore, the analysis will terminate if you switch to another SOLIDWORKS document or close the active model.

15. Click on the **OK** button in the **SOLIDWORKS** message window. The intermediate results appear in the graphics area when the non-linear static analysis is in progress. When the analysis is complete, the **Results** folder is added to the Simulation Study Tree with the stress, displacement, and strain results. By default, the **Stress** result is activated. As a result, the stress distribution on the model and the von Mises stress plot of the non-linear analysis appear, see Figure 10.70.

    Notice that in the non-linear static analysis, the maximum von Mises stress is **5.610e+02** (560.955) N/mm^2 (MPa) (see Figure 10.70) which is close to the maximum von Mises stress result of the linear static analysis with the large displacement option [**5.616e+02** (561.587) N/mm^2 (MPa)].

16. Double-click on the **Displacement1 (-Res disp-)** result in the Simulation Study Tree. The resultant displacement plot appears in the graphics area, see Figure 10.71.

10.70

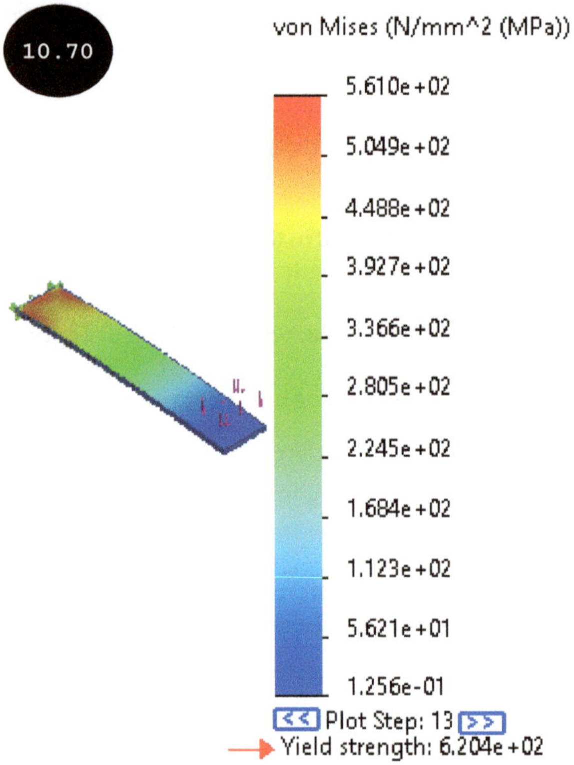

10.71

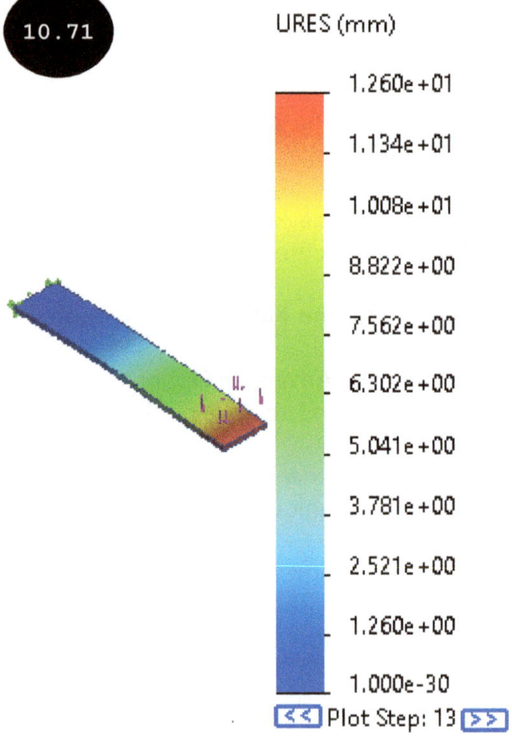

Notice that in the non-linear static analysis, the maximum resultant displacement is **1.260e+01** (12.603) mm (see Figure 10.71) which is close to the maximum resultant displacement result of the linear static analysis with the large displacement option [**1.260e+01** (12.601) mm].

Note: In addition to the large displacement, if the model experiences material or contacts non-linearities as well then the results of the linear static analysis with the large displacement option will not be accurate and you will need to perform the non-linear static analysis to get accurate results. Also, in the linear static analysis, you cannot display the results in different incremental steps.

In non-linear static analysis, you can also display the results at different solution steps. By default, the program displays the results at the end solution step.

17. Right-click on the **Displacement1 (-Res disp-)** result in the **Results** folder of the Simulation Study Tree and then click on the **Edit Definition** tool in the shortcut menu that appears. The **Displacement plot PropertyManager** appears, see Figure 10.72.

    By default, 1 is entered in the **Time** field of the **Plot Step** rollout of the PropertyManager, see Figure 10.72. As a result, the resultant displacement plot displays the results for the end solution step, which is 13th in this case.

18. Enter **5** in the **Plot Step** field of the PropertyManager to display the resultant displacement plot results for the 5th solution step. Next, click anywhere in the graphics area. The time step (0.25 sec) corresponding to the specified solution step (5th) appears in the **Time** field of the PropertyManager.

19. Select the **True scale** radio button in the **Deformed shape** rollout of the PropertyManager to display the deformed shape of the model in true scale.

20. Click on the green tick-mark button in the PropertyManager. The resultant displacement plot for the 5th solution step at 0.25 sec appears in the graphics area, see Figure 10.73.

10.72

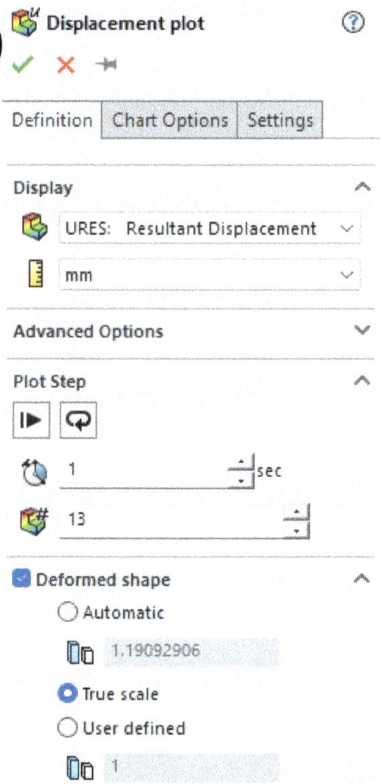

10.73

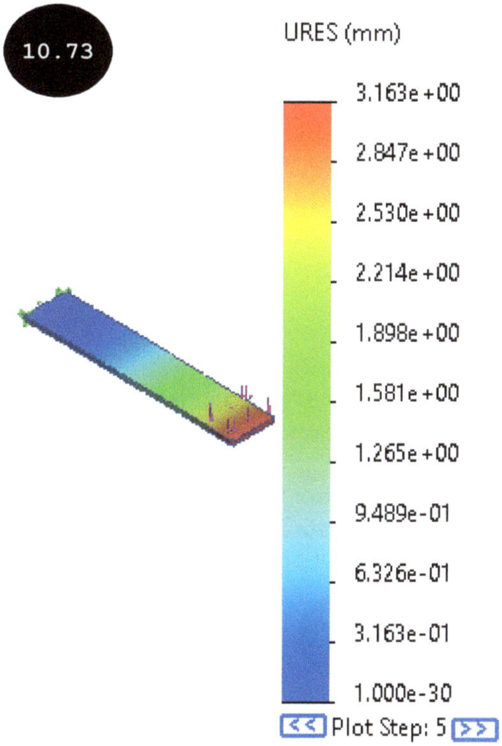

21. Similarly, you can display different results of the non-linear static analysis in different incremental steps.

Section 7: Generating the Response graph of a Node

Now, you need to generate the response graph of a node in the large displacement area.

1. Click on **Plot Tools** in the **Simulation CommandManager**. A flyout appears, see Figure 10.74.

2. Click on the **Probe** tool in this flyout, see Figure 10.74. The **Probe Result PropertyManager** appears, see Figure 10.75.

10.74

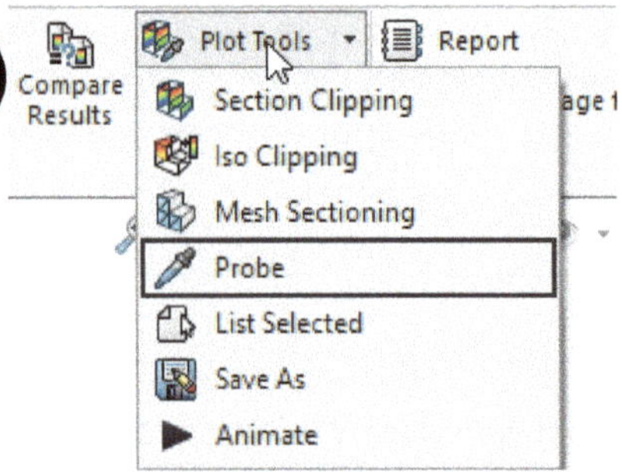

10.75

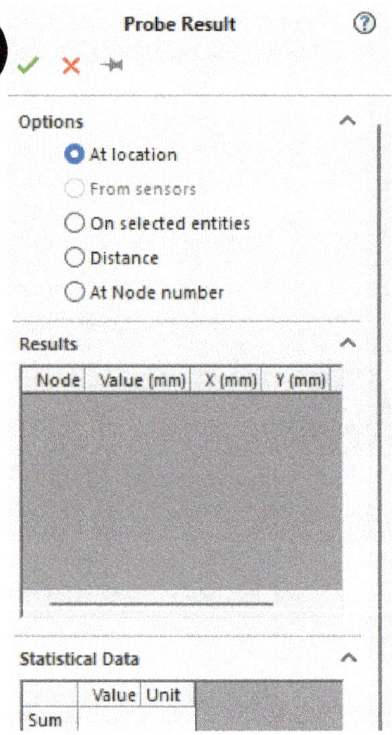

3. Ensure that the **At location** radio button is selected in the **Options** rollout of the PropertyManager to display the results of a node.

4. Move the cursor toward the lower right corner of the model and then click the left mouse button, see Figure 10.76. The node number 7 is selected and the results of the selected node appear in the **Results** rollout of the PropertyManager.

10.76

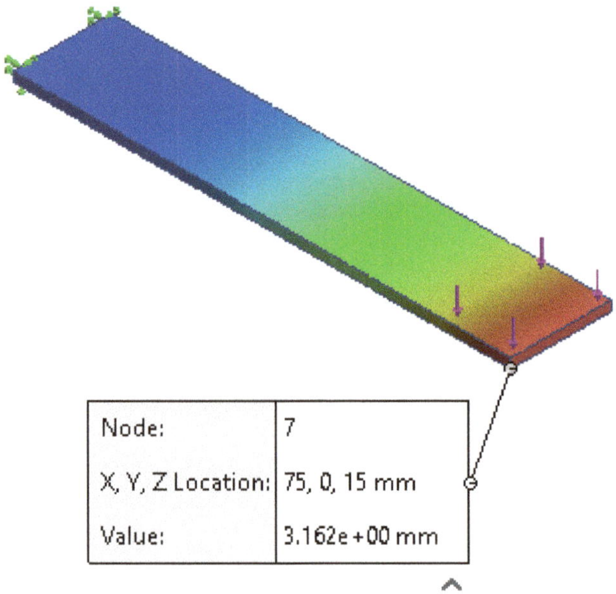

5. Scroll down the PropertyManager and then click on the **Response** button in the **Report Options** rollout of the PropertyManager, see Figure 10.77. The **Response Graph** window appears which displays the response graph of the selected node to the resultant displacement vs time, see Figure 10.78.

10.77

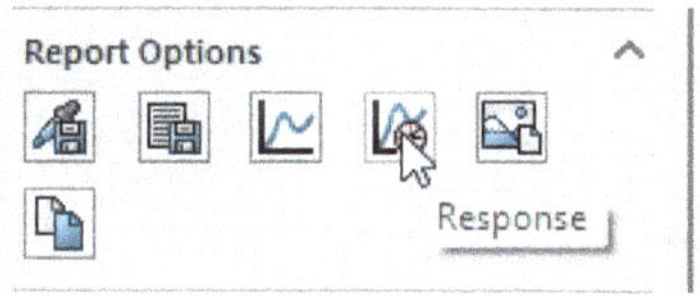

10.78

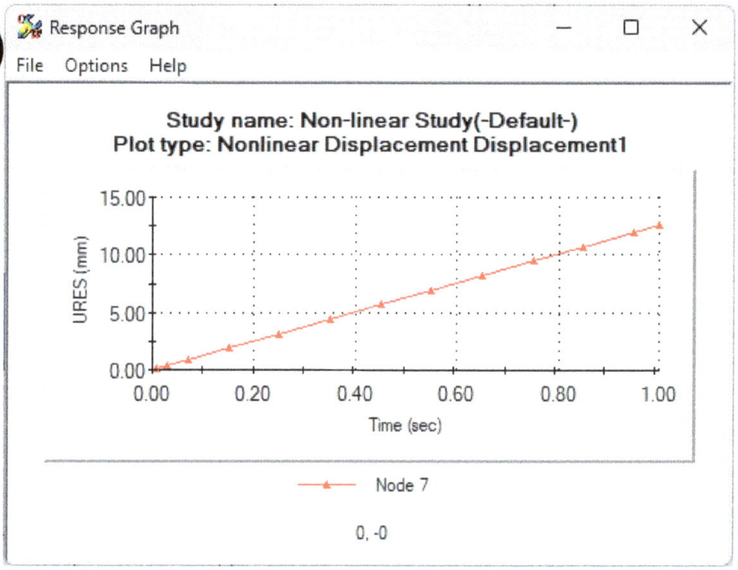

6. After viewing the response graph, close the window and then close the PropertyManager.

Section 8: Saving Results

Now, you need to save the model and its results.

1. Click on the **Save** tool in the **Standard** toolbar. The model and its results are saved in the location > *SOLIDWORKS Simulation > Case Studies > C10 Case Studies > Case Study 3*.

2. Close the SOLIDWORKS session.

Hands-on Test Drive 1: Non-linear Static Analysis of a Hook Assembly

Perform the non-linear analysis of a Hook Assembly, see Figure 10.79. The Hook part of the assembly is pushed toward the other part to snap into it, see Figure 10.80.

10.79

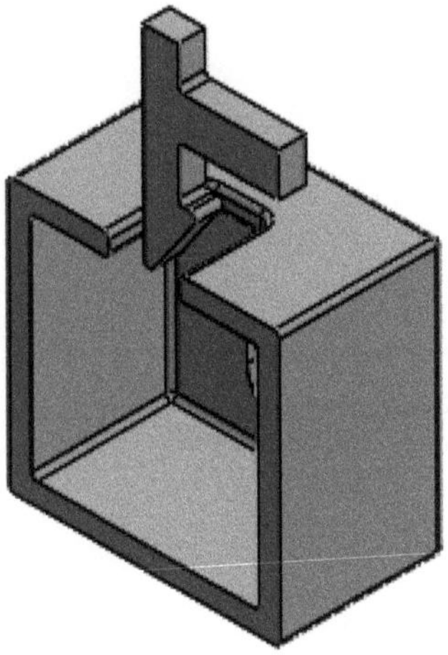

10.80

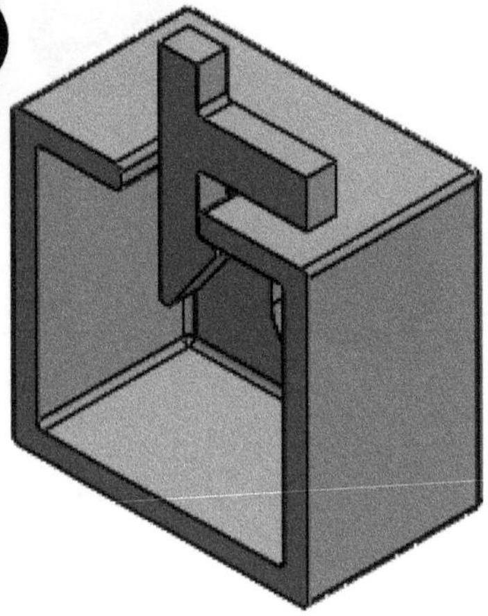

Project Description

The Snap part is fixed at its bottom, see Figure 10.81 and the Hook part has all degrees of freedom fixed except the translation movement of 30 mm downward, see Figure 10.81. Both the parts are made up of **Acrylic (Medium-high impact)** plastic material.

10.81

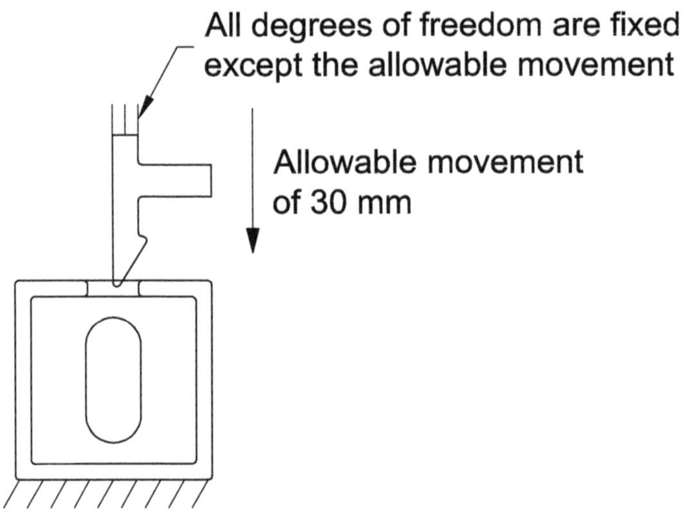

Project Summary

In this case study, perform the non-linear static study by using the Force control method and the Newton-Raphson (NR) scheme to converge the solution.

Summary

This chapter introduced key assumptions for identifying non-linear static analysis problems. It covered different iterative methods, including the Newton-Raphson (NR) and Modified Newton-Raphson (MNR) schemes, as well as incremental methods such as Force, Displacement, and Arc Length, to find equilibrium solutions in non-linear analysis.

Additionally, the chapter explored various types of non-linearities, including material, geometric, and contact non-linearities, along with techniques for conducting non-linear analysis through case studies. It also discussed methods for defining non-linear properties, generating time history plots, displaying results at different solution steps, and creating response graphs of specific nodes to analyze system behavior.

Questions

Complete the following sentences:

- The non-linear problems are categorized mainly as _________, _________, and _________.
- In non-linear problems, the _________ is not constant and it changes as the magnitude of the load increases.
- SOLIDWORKS Simulation uses _________ or _________ as the iterative method to converge the equilibrium equation at every incremental step.
- In the Newton-Raphson (NR) method, the stiffness is calculated at every _________.
- In the Modified Newton-Raphson (NR) method, the stiffness is calculated at the _________ iteration and then the same stiffness is used for the next iterations.
- SOLIDWORKS Simulation uses _________, _________, and _________ as the incremental methods to converge the final solution.
- The _________ non-linearities occur, when the maximum von Mises stress exceeds the yield strength of the material and the material experiences plastic deformation.

- In non-linear static analysis, the load is divided into different incremental steps as the function of _________ time.
- The _________ check box is used to display the intermediate result of the non-linear analysis in the graphics area when the analysis is in progress.
- The _________ curve is used to define the behavior of material in the plastic region.
- The _________ tool is used to generate the time history response graph of the specified nodes or locations.
- In _________ problems, the boundary conditions are assumed to be changed due to the motion in the components during the analysis.
- The _________ check box in the **Static** dialog box allows you to solve the large displacement problems in the linear static analysis.

INDEX

INDEX

Symbols

A

B

C

D

E

M

N

O

P

R

S

Other Publications by CADArtifex

Some of the other Publications by CADArtifex are given below:

AutoCAD Textbooks

AutoCAD 2026: A Power Guide for Beginners and Intermediate Users
AutoCAD 2025: A Power Guide for Beginners and Intermediate Users
AutoCAD 2024: A Power Guide for Beginners and Intermediate Users
and more

AutoCAD For Architectural Design Textbooks

AutoCAD 2023 for Architectural Design: A Power Guide for Beginners and Intermediate Users
AutoCAD 2022 for Architectural Design: A Power Guide for Beginners and Intermediate Users
and more

Autodesk Fusion 360 Textbooks

Autodesk Fusion 360: A Power Guide for Beginners and Intermediate Users (8th Edition)
Autodesk Fusion 360: A Power Guide for Beginners and Intermediate Users (7th Edition)
Autodesk Fusion 360: A Power Guide for Beginners and Intermediate Users (6th Edition)
and more

Autodesk Fusion 360 Surface and T-Spline Textbooks

Autodesk Fusion 360 Surface Design and Sculpting with T-Spline Surfaces (8th Edition)
Autodesk Fusion 360 Surface Design and Sculpting with T-Spline Surfaces (7th Edition)
and more

Autodesk Inventor Textbooks

Autodesk Inventor 2026: A Power Guide for Beginners and Intermediate Users
Autodesk Inventor 2025: A Power Guide for Beginners and Intermediate Users
Autodesk Inventor 2024: A Power Guide for Beginners and Intermediate Users
and more

FreeCAD Textbooks

FreeCAD 1.0: A Power Guide for Beginners and Intermediate Users
FreeCAD 0.21: A Power Guide for Beginners and Intermediate Users
and more

Onshape Textbooks

Onshape 2025: A Power Guide for Beginners and Intermediate Users
and more

PTC Creo Parametric Textbooks

Creo Parametric 12.0: A Power Guide for Beginners and Intermediate Users
Creo Parametric 11.0: A Power Guide for Beginners and Intermediate Users
and more

SOLIDWORKS Textbooks

SOLIDWORKS 2026: A Power Guide for Beginners and Intermediate User
SOLIDWORKS 2025: A Power Guide for Beginners and Intermediate User
SOLIDWORKS 2024: A Power Guide for Beginners and Intermediate User
and more

SOLIDWORKS Sheet Metal and Surface Design Textbooks

SOLIDWORKS Sheet Metal and Surface Design 2026 for Beginners and Intermediate Users
SOLIDWORKS Sheet Metal and Surface Design 2025 for Beginners and Intermediate Users
and more

SOLIDWORKS Simulation Textbooks

SOLIDWORKS Simulation 2026: A Power Guide for Beginners and Intermediate User
SOLIDWORKS Simulation 2025: A Power Guide for Beginners and Intermediate User
SOLIDWORKS Simulation 2024: A Power Guide for Beginners and Intermediate User
and more

Exercises Books

100 AutoCAD Exercises - Learn by Practicing (2 Edition)
Autodesk Inventor Exercises - Learn by Practicing
Autodesk Fusion 360 Exercises Learn by Practicing (2023-24)
SOLIDWORKS Exercises - Learn by Practicing (3 Edition)

Video Courses by CADArtifex

CADArtifex offers a range of video courses designed to support students, educators, and professionals in developing practical CAD skills through structured, project-based learning. Available video courses include:

- SOLIDWORKS Mastery Pack – 11 Courses in 1 | Complete Beginner to Industry Training
- Fusion 360 Mastery Pack: Design, Sculpt & Build Real Projects (6-in-1 Course Combo)
- Learn SOLIDWORKS Sheet Metal: From Concept to Creation
- Complete Fusion 360 All-in-One Course for Beginners (2025)
- Fusion 360 Surface Design & T-Spline Sculpting
- Complete FreeCAD for Beginners – No Experience Needed
- Complete Onshape for Beginners: Project-Based Approach
- Master Autodesk Inventor: From Basics to Advanced
- Mastering AutoCAD 2D & 3D for Beginners

For full course details and access, visit: ***cadartifex.com***

---

www.ingramcontent.com/pod-product-compliance
Ingram Content Group UK Ltd.
Pitfield, Milton Keynes, MK11 3LW, UK
UKHW061546190726
13845UKWH00030B/1038

9 789394 074439